The
Connecticut
Guide

Text and Photographs by

Amy Ziffer

Fulcrum Publishing
Golden, Colorado

To my parents, Helen and Walter.

Copyright © 1998 Amy Ziffer
Interior maps copyright © 1998 Krag Lehmann
Cover image of Mystic Seaport at dusk by Amy Ziffer.
Back cover image of house in autumn hills copyright © 1998 Amy Ziffer.
Back cover image of New Haven skyline copyright © 1998 Jim Brochin.
Interior photographs copyright © 1998 Amy Ziffer unless otherwise noted.
Book design by Deborah Rich

ii

18.95/11.56 11/98

Library of Congress Cataloging-in-Publication Data
Ziffer, Amy.
    The Connecticut guide / Amy Ziffer.
        p.   cm.
    Includes index.
    ISBN 1-55591-343-1
        1. Connecticut—Guidebooks.   I. Title
    F92.3.Z54   1998
    917.4604'43—dc21   98-10474
                                                                        CIP

Printed in the United States of America
0 9 8 7 6 5 4 3 2 1

Fulcrum Publishing
350 Indiana Street, Suite 350
Golden, Colorado 80401-5093
(800) 992-2908 • (303) 277-1623
website: www.fulcrum-books.com
e-mail: fulcrum@fulcrum-books.com

Contents

iii

Southwest Coast   322

Housatonic and Naugatuck River Valleys   394

Acknowledgments

A book this size is never the work of one person. On the professional side, I'd like to thank all the talented people at Fulcrum Publishing, especially editors Carmel Huestis and Daniel Forrest-Bank, for their work on and interest in this project. Thanks also go to the hardworking staff of all of Connecticut's regional tourism districts and chambers of commerce who lent a hand with information or a photograph and to all the individuals at attractions around the state who did the same; to all the dedicated Connecticut Department of Environmental Protection staff with whom I was in contact, but especially field personnel who provided me with invaluable tips about local resources; to Connecticut Photographic for their great developing and printing and for never messing up an order; to state historian Dr. Christopher Collier for his review of the historical information in the introduction to this book; to state archaeologist Dr. Nicholas Bellantoni for his insight into Native American history; to the Tourism Division of the Connecticut Department of Economic Development; and last but definitely not least, to the helpful staff at the Sherman public library for their assistance in procuring research materials from every corner of Connecticut and their lenient overdue fine policy.

On the personal front, thanks to Krag Lehmann for all the nights he ate dinner alone (pizza again!) and didn't complain, for looking after the cats while I was on the road, for general emotional support and for the beautiful maps; to Tiger and Little One, who waited patiently for the mouse toys to be retrieved from under the couch while "Mom" was preoccupied; to friends whose company I cherish but, for a time, could not keep; and to my family, who started this whole thing by taking me traveling.

Chapter/Town Cross-Reference

Because of the format of this book, not every one of Connecticut's 169 towns could be discussed separately. The list below identifies the towns covered in each chapter.

New Haven
East Haven, Hamden, New Haven, North Haven, Orange and West Haven

New London
East Lyme, Groton (except for the West Mystic area), New London and Waterford

New Milford
Bridgewater, New Milford, Roxbury, Sherman and Washington

North Central
Bloomfield, East Granby, East Windsor, Enfield, Granby, South Windsor, Suffield, Windsor and Windsor Locks

Norwalk
Darien, New Canaan, Norwalk, Weston, Westport and Wilton

Norwich and Casino Country
Bozrah, Ledyard, Montville, Norwich and Preston

Old Saybrook/Old Lyme
Chester, Deep River, East Haddam, Essex, Haddam, Lyme, Old Lyme, Old Saybrook and Salem

Storrs
Andover, Bolton, Coventry and Mansfield

Tolland
Ellington, Somers, Stafford, Tolland, Vernon and Willington

Torrington
Barkhamsted, Burlington, Colebrook, Hartland, Harwinton, New Hartford, Torrington and Winchester

Waterbury
Ansonia, Beacon Falls, Bethany, Bristol, Derby, Naugatuck, Plymouth, Prospect, Seymour, Thomaston, Waterbury, Watertown, Wolcott and Woodbridge

Wethersfield
Wethersfield

Woodbury
Bethlehem, Middlebury, Oxford, Southbury and Woodbury

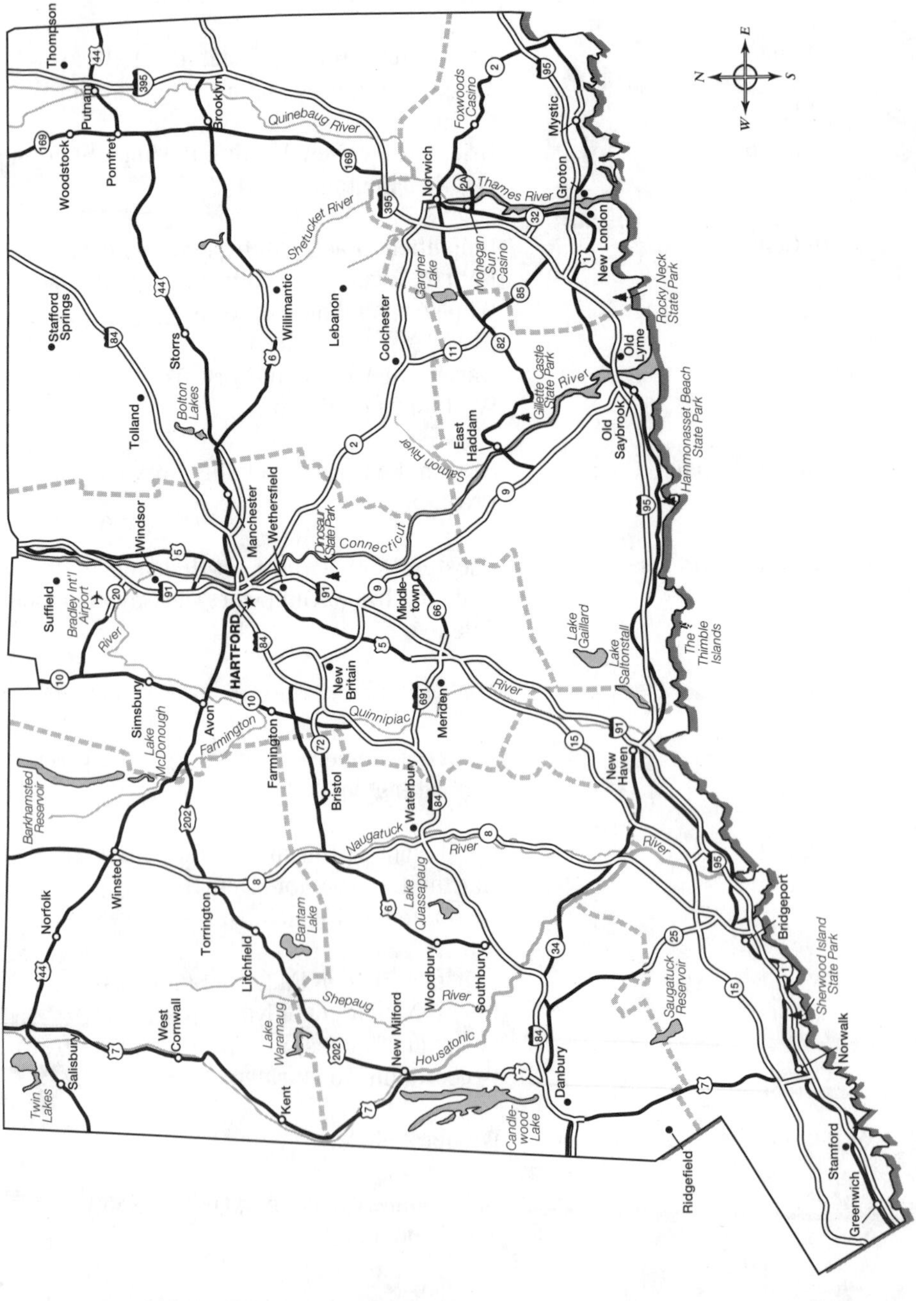

Connecticut

Introduction

Background Information

By whatever name it's known—the Constitution State, the Land of Steady Habits or just "between Boston and New York"—Connecticut is a marvelous place with a long, fascinating history and a recreational richness far beyond what its petite dimensions suggest. You may see an ad for Connecticut tourism that carries the phrase, "You can think of us as a rather small state or a rather large recreation area." Whoever thought that up really hit the mark. Despite being the third-smallest state in the nation, Connecticut has a remarkably diverse landscape ranging from verdant inland mountains to cleansing saltwater beaches, from spectacular city parks to an upland river with a Wild and Scenic federal designation—a wide range of recreational settings all within a few hours' travel time. Perhaps most important of all, Connecticut's natural gifts are fashioned on a human scale—intimate and accessible rather than awe-inspiring and remote. And its four-season climate brings the blessing of almost limitless variety, including the fall foliage show for which all of New England is justly famous.

Connecticut's human history is as rich as its natural legacy. Its official nickname—the Constitution State—reflects its central role in the birth of the United States, and scattered among Connecticut's rolling hills or integrated right into modern urban landscapes you'll find the sites where major events in American history took place. But Native Americans were here for millennia before that and transmitted to Europeans their skills and knowledge of the North American wilderness. Whether you want to better understand their lives or those of 19th-century immigrant factory workers, the past is preserved—and sometimes reenacted—in Connecticut today.

Connecticut's attractions are second to none. For families searching out places where every member can be stimulated, Connecticut has destinations like Mystic Seaport and the Maritime Aquarium. Foxwoods and Mohegan Sun Casinos provide excitement with Las Vegas–style wagering and entertainment. Folks in need of some rest and relaxation will enjoy picturesque and unhurried country villages with a single stoplight (if that). And last but not least, Connecticut's cities are lively and urbane, with the full range of enriching cultural activities and the horizon-broadening influence of institutions like Yale and Wesleyan Universities.

This book is a modest attempt to take a snapshot of Connecticut in the late 1990s so visitors and residents alike can appreciate its uniqueness, for it is the unique qualities of a place that make us want to visit it, know it, care for it and return to it. By taking a comprehensive approach and listing major attractions, outdoor recreation, museums, sightseeing destinations and places to eat and stay overnight, I hope to provide everything you need to plan a great trip.

I am a native daughter of Connecticut, and my enthusiasm and affection for my home state have only grown with the years. I hope that *The Connecticut Guide* helps you discover some small portion of Connecticut's treasures. And if you too are a Connecticuter, perhaps in these pages you'll find surprising places to go and things to see that were always nearby but were just unknown.

******

The Connecticut Guide

Connecticut is a state of just over 5,000 square miles, the most southwesterly of the states collectively called New England. It would fit into Alaska, the largest state in the Union, well over 100 times; of the 50 states, only Rhode Island and Delaware are smaller.

According to the 1990 census, over 3.25 million people call Connecticut home. The southwest corner, comprising lower Fairfield and New Haven Counties, is the most populous area, but people are concentrated all along the coast and up the Central Valley. Connecticut is the fourth most densely populated state in the country, but because of the way the population is distributed, large portions of it feel rural and uncrowded.

Connecticut's most prominent natural features are a 100-mile-long southern coast on Long Island Sound, very old mountain ranges in the northwest that have been weathered to an elevation of under 3,000 feet, a broad valley that roughly bisects the state from north to south and contains the flow of a major river (the Connecticut) for much of its length and a ridged highland occupying the eastern third of the state. The state's visage was shaped extensively by glaciers in the last Ice Age. In fact, the soil forcibly pushed from Connecticut's bedrock by glaciers formed Long Island, a huge glacial moraine.

Water has always been Connecticut's greatest resource. Long Island Sound, a vast inlet of the Atlantic Ocean, is a recreational and commercial asset that has brought the world to Connecticut's doorstep through maritime trade for more than 350 years. In the early years of the Industrial Age, inland rivers drove factory waterwheels and turbines and, as a result, the state's economy. But the Connecticut River, despite being New England's largest, is surprisingly undeveloped, especially south of Middletown; it was saved from overdevelopment by a sandbar at its mouth. So untouched is it by modern standards that the Nature Conservancy calls it one of the 40 Last Great Places in the Western Hemisphere.

Connecticut's economy was once solely agricultural, then largely industrial. In recent years it has suffered the same loss of manufacturing and defense-industry jobs that has negatively impacted so many states. Yet Connecticut remains on average the wealthiest state in the nation, with the highest per capita income. Aerospace and defense manufacturers are still among the state's largest employers, as are insurance companies, hospitals, Yale University and Foxwoods Resort Casino. Household names, such as Duracell and Stanley (the battery and tool makers), are headquartered here, attracted by a well-educated and motivated workforce, easy access to transportation by land, air and sea and proximity to a healthy chunk of the nation's people.

In many coastal towns maritime pursuits still hold sway as in years past. A major naval submarine base is located in Groton, as are the headquarters of Electric Boat, a division of General Dynamics and one of only two submarine manufacturers in the country. The U.S. Coast Guard Academy, where cadets are trained, is situated just across the Thames River in New London, and Norwalk is the home of the largest oystering operation on the Eastern Seaboard.

Connecticut's towns vary dramatically in character. On the coast they range from the dense and prosperous bedroom communities of New York in the southwest (somewhat deprecatingly dubbed the Gold Coast), to summer beach communities such as Old Lyme at the mouth of the Connecticut River, where there are large tracts of salt marsh and the year-round population numbers only a few thousand. Inland, the Central Valley's flat aspect and fertile soil are so equally suited for agriculture and intensive development that five minutes from Bradley International Airport there are fields of shade-grown tobacco. Finally, in the hills of the Northwest and Northeast, many towns look like the traditional New England village that most people picture in their mind's eye: houses clustered around a central green with a church spire rising from the highest point and sinuous stone walls curving across the contours of the land.

Connecticut has eight counties and 169 towns; its capital is Hartford. Garnets, robins and mountain laurels are all honored as official state symbols (for mineral, bird and flower, respectively), but of all the state's symbols, the one with the most colorful history must be the state tree, the white oak. Oaks are magnificent trees long associated with royalty and governmental authority, so it is almost eerie that it was an oak in which Connecticut's charter—the document defining the colony's rights under the British Crown—was hidden during a political crisis in 1687. See p. xiii for more detail on this story.

History

Connecticut's first people, probably Asian in origin, arrived 10,000 to 12,000 years ago. These hardy immigrants found a landscape drastically different from today's: a harsh tundra largely devoid of trees. The glaciers of the last Ice Age, in their retreat 18,000 years ago, had scraped clean Connecticut's countenance. Small pockets of trees—conifers first, then deciduous species—were beginning to spring up. Because ocean levels were considerably lower then, Connecticut's shoreline lay about 100 miles south of where it is today, and Long Island Sound was a freshwater lake, its connection to the ocean not yet formed. The paleo-Indians, as Connecticut's first human inhabitants are called, settled along the rivers and shoreline where wildlife was most abundant.

The early Indians may have seen mastodons wandering the land in that species' last days before extinction; they certainly saw and hunted caribou and reindeer, which haven't roamed these parts for many a year. The Indians' hunter-gatherer lifestyle required their communities consisting of a few families, perhaps 40 to 50 people, to move around to find the most food and fuel.

About 1,000 years ago Connecticut's inhabitants began to cultivate crops. Corn (maize, which had made its way up from Mexico through intertribal trade) and winter squash became staples, because, unlike perishable foods, they provided a relatively reliable source of nutrition during the long winter months. Stable food supplies led to larger populations and more permanent settlements. Villages grew to hold hundreds rather than dozens, and although the Indians still might

have traveled to seasonal food supplies, they returned to their fields each growing season. This is the lifestyle that European traders and explorers encountered in the 1500s, when they first began showing up regularly on North America's shores.

The Indians of 1600

Piecing together the political history of Connecticut's Native Americans just prior to the arrival of white settlers has been difficult for historians, in part due to the lack of a written Indian language and in part due to the widespread destruction of Indian society and the oral history it kept. The history given here is at best an approximation of the facts.

By the early 1600s there were over one dozen distinct indigenous groups living in Connecticut with a total population estimated at 6,000. All of them belonged to the same Algonquian linguistic group. Despite the relatedness of these tribes, however, their relations were not without friction. The Pequots were an aggresive tribe whose importance to the Native American political scene of 1600 almost cannot be overstated. The name Pequot is said to mean "warrior" or "destroyer of people," and apropos of their name the Pequots had many conflicts with other tribes and exacted tribute from some. So, Connecticut's native peoples taken together did not represent a unified nation. Instead, their political life was marked by complex, shifting alliances both within and between tribes.

The Europeans of 1600

The first Europeans to indisputably encounter Connecticut's indigenous peoples were 16th-century entrepreneurs looking for a northwest passage to the Far East or direct trading opportunities with the Indians, rather than a permanent presence on the continent. Adriaen Block, a Dutchman and an agent of the Dutch West Indian Company, is credited with being the first European to sail up the Connecticut River in 1614. The Dutch established a trading post at the site of present-day Hartford in 1633. Mere months later, the English began arriving from Massachusetts and continued to do so in large numbers over the next few years.

Some of the English who came to Connecticut shared the commercial motivation of the Dutch, but many came for compelling religious reasons arising from an unstable political situation in England. The Puritans, who comprised a large percentage of the colonists, specifically intended to establish a Protestant social order of their own liking in the New World and sought to escape what they perceived as a corrupt moral atmosphere in the mother country. They are called Congregationalists in reference to their desire that individual congregations have control over their worship.

Early Indian-European Interaction

Despite the brevity of their visits, the traders of the 1500s were the first of many to impact the Indians in a most unfortunate way: as bringers of disease. In some places Old World afflictions caused dramatic declines in native populations even before permanent European settlements were established. For example, the so-called River Indians of the Hartford area, 1,000 in number, experienced 900 deaths in 1633.

Europeans were variously received by Native Americans. In some places the two groups coexisted as friends, although this equilibrium often lasted only as long as it took for the Indians to feel the impact of English immigration. In other places there were open, early and mutual threats. In yet others, tribes allied themselves with settlers to subdue rival tribes.

The first major conflict between the English and the Indians was the 1637 Pequot War in which that tribe was routed by an alliance of English forces led by John Mason and rival Indians. The Pequot fort near present-day Mystic was attacked at dawn without warning. Those who were not killed in combat burned to death; only a fragment of the tribe survived.

The last major incident of Indian resistance to white encroachment took place in 1675–1676. It was called King Philip's War after the name of the Indian warrior who led the fight, and it ended with his capture and execution. By 1700 the English were clearly in ascendancy, and Native Americans were relegated to

reservations. The Golden Hill Paugussetts at one time had 80 acres in what is now downtown Bridgeport, but settlers seized these and other lands as Indian populations continued their decline.

In a strange twist of fate, however, the Mashantucket Pequot tribe (descendants of survivors of the Pequot War) is now the owner of Foxwoods Casino, a huge gambling complex in Ledyard. Foxwoods is so successful that in only a few years it has become one of the state's top ten employers. In 1996 the Mohegans followed in their footsteps and opened Mohegan Sun Casino in a neighboring town.

One of the legacies left to present generations by Connecticut's original peoples is the state's rich store of Indian place-names. In fact, the name Connecticut is of Indian origin. Often spelled *quinnehtukqut* (a phonetic representation of the word, since the Indians had no written language), the term translates to "beside the long tidal river," a reference to the broad valley down the center of the state that sustained both Indians and Europeans.

The First 150 Years

The first English settlement in Connecticut was at present-day Windsor in 1633. The following year another group arrived in Wethersfield, and in 1636 the Congregational minister and leader Thomas Hooker brought about 100 followers to Hartford. The English were quick to put on paper some code of law to govern daily life in their communities. The Fundamental Orders, adopted by Hartford in 1639, were based on a sermon given by Hooker the previous year. The inhabitants of New Haven, settled in 1638, developed a similar set of laws called the Plantation Covenant. The Fundamental Orders were based upon the idea that government derives its power from the free consent of the governed and are regarded as a precursor to the U.S. Constitution.

Connecticut's first governmental body was a General Court (later called the General Assembly) that served legislative, executive and judicial functions. Government was run by a select group of male landowners. Religious conformity was strictly enforced. For example, the punishment for being a Quaker was death—at least on paper. Usually, less lethal methods were used to ensure the community's godliness.

The Fundamental Orders were an expression of self-governance, but for almost 30 years the Connecticut colonists lived without any explicit recognition from the British Crown. England had gone through political earthquakes during those decades, including the overthrow of a king and a brief and unsuccessful experiment as a republic under Oliver Cromwell. When the monarchy was restored, Connecticut governor John Winthrop, Jr., astutely surmised that the time might be right for the colony to procure some official assurance of its rights. He traveled to England personally and obtained a charter from Charles II, which consolidated the "river towns" around Hartford with New Haven and its subsidiary towns along the coast. New Haven was incorporated reluctantly into the Connecticut Colony, but eventually Hartford and New Haven became cocapitals in which the General Assembly met alternately from 1711 on. The charter also defined Connecticut's boundaries as extending westward to the Pacific Ocean, an absurdity that later gave rise to conflicts over land.

After about 1675 towns in the new and coherent colony were founded with regularity. Not only had the subjugation of the Indians after King Philip's War eliminated much of the danger of moving away from the original settlements, but two generations had been born and grown up. There were population pressures, and the great Puritan experiment was starting to get frayed at the edges. Congregations frequently squabbled and split, leading to the establishment of new parishes and furthering the spread of the population.

Over in England the rule of Charles II gave way to the rule of James II, whose intention was to unite all the New England colonies as the Dominion of New England under one royal governor, Sir Edmund Andros. That meant repealing rights guaranteed in the charter, so Andros was sent to retrieve the document personally. The year was 1687. At a meeting with colonial leaders in Hartford, Andros demanded the charter. But, according to legend, by prearrangement the candles in the room were extinguished and the charter was spirited out the window to a waiting rider and deposited in the hollow of a nearby oak tree. Connecticut submitted to Andros's rule until the deposition of James II in 1689, but never relinquished the charter. Unlike Andros, you can see it. It is displayed prominently at the Museum of Connecticut History in Hartford.

The instability of Connecticut's first half-century expressed itself in unsavory occurrences, such as witchcraft trials, which did not die out until the 1690s. Nonetheless, following the accession of William III to the throne of England in 1689, political life in Connecticut began to calm down. The maturation of the colony was reflected in institutional growth. In 1701 the Collegiate School was founded in Saybrook in order to prepare men for the ministry and political leadership. The school was relocated to New Haven 15 years later and renamed Yale. For many years the General Assembly had met in Hartford at Jeremy Adams's tavern, but between 1717 and 1720 both Hartford and New Haven built state houses. Most authority, however, remained close to home; in a very real sense each town's Congregational minister exerted a stronger influence over people's everyday lives than any governmental body. Congregationalism had held sway over every aspect of life in Connecticut since colonization began. But in the early 1700s the rigid Puritan social order slowly began to give way under the strain of a burgeoning population that could no longer be micromanaged and a shift in the focus of daily life from survival to the acquisition of wealth. In the earliest days of the colony only Congregationalism was permitted and everyone had to pay a tax to support the church. Slowly, other religions became permissible, and the tax, although still universal, could be paid to one's church of choice.

There were growing regional differences too. The roots of western Connecticut's ties to New York and eastern Connecticut's ties to Boston developed early on. Differences in circumstances gave rise to differences in religious and political philosophies. The rift widened as the 1700s advanced, and in the days just prior to the Revolution, Tory sympathy (or, at the least, caution and resignation to British authority) ran high in the west and Patriot fervor in the east. Despite these internal conflicts, rebelliousness was strong enough statewide that the General Assembly issued a Connecticut Declaration of Independence 16 days before the one formulated by the Continental Congress in Philadelphia.

During the war years Connecticut came to be known as the Provision State for its effectiveness in supplying Patriot forces with food, clothing, arms and ammunition. After the war George Washington wrote that victory would not have been possible without the efforts of Connecticut's governor Jonathan Trumbull. Men from every town served as soldiers, and almost 250 privateers (sailors given official sanction to pirate enemy vessels) were active in the waters of Long Island Sound. Native sons such as Ethan Allen and Nathan Hale would become national heroes, but at least one—Benedict Arnold—would become a traitor.

At the Constitutional Convention in Philadelphia in 1787, a Connecticuter, Roger Sherman, was responsible for the "Connecticut Compromise," which made representation in the House proportional to population and representation in the Senate the same for each state, thereby resolving an impasse. Connecticut became the fifth state to ratify the Constitution in January 1788.

From Colony to State

The postrevolutionary years in Connecticut were marked by widespread emigration of Connecticuters to western New York, Pennsylvania and the Ohio territory known as the Western Reserve. Connecticut's claim to these areas dates back to its 1662 charter. Although most of those claims were never asserted, many people were granted land in Ohio as compensation for property destroyed by the British during the Revolutionary War. Others relocated to Vermont or New Hampshire, often holding their first town meeting in a Connecticut tavern prior to departure. This migration was so vast that by the 1830s more than a quarter of all U.S. congressmen were transplanted Connecticut natives.

The War of 1812 was very unpopular in New England, which suffered a depressed economy from trade embargoes. The Hartford Convention of 1814, which took place in the Old State House (then new, having been built in 1795), was a gathering of delegates from across the Northeast who used the occasion to voice all manner of political grievances. The convention was called by Federalists, which may have contributed to the loss of power that party experienced in 1818. The loss resulted in a state constitutional convention and Connecticut's first modern constitution (it was still operating under the 1662 charter), which ended obligatory taxation to support churches and established a government with separate judicial, legislative and executive branches.

The War of 1812 also gave Connecticut industry a start. Trade restrictions focused attention on the need for domestic production of essential goods. Arguably, Connecticut industry really began when two brothers started making tinware in Berlin in the 1740s and selling it door-to-door. They soon advanced to using traveling salesmen, who originated the tradition of the Yankee peddler. Connecticut would become an industrial state rivaling all others. Products historically associated with Connecticut include textiles (northeastern Connecticut), hats (Danbury), brassware (Waterbury), timepieces (Thomaston), silverware (Meriden) and firearms (Hartford and New Haven). These industries have had a tremendous impact on Connecticut's development and character and are documented in places such as the Mattatuck Museum in Waterbury, the Windham Textile and History Museum in Willimantic and the Museum of Connecticut History in Hartford.

Along with industry came the canals and railroads. By 1835 the Farmington Canal snaked its way 86 miles from New Haven to Northampton, Massachusetts, making it the longest ever built in New England. It was New Haven's answer to the economic advantage the Connecticut River gave Hartford. A vast rail system began to crisscross the state, connecting its farthest reaches with Boston, New York, Albany and Springfield.

Slavery was abolished in Connecticut in 1848 after an attempt to educate blacks called the Prudence Crandall affair ended in failure, and the noted *Amistad* legal case (the story was made into a film in 1997) was decided in favor of slaves whose captor's ship ended up off the coast of Connecticut. In the 1850s Connecticut native Harriet Beecher Stowe authored the influential novel *Uncle Tom's Cabin,* which helped gel antislavery sentiment in the North. This was a time of upheaval as the Industrial Revolution eroded agrarian society, helped polarize North and South and began to bring large numbers of non-English people to the state for the first time. As the nation slid into the Civil War, Connecticut's newfound industrial prowess allowed it to take on a role similar to the one it had had in the Revolution. The Provision State refashioned itself into the Munitions State.

To the Present

After the Civil War, Connecticut began to take on the look it has today. In 1875 Hartford became the sole capital and soon thereafter built the spectacular capitol building still in use. Immigrant workers continued to arrive to fill factory jobs, completely transforming the human makeup of the state, erasing more than two centuries of social homogeneity and ushering in a half-century of politics based on cultural, ethnic and religious differences.

The cities grew at an unprecedented rate. At the same time, a representational system in the legislature that gave small towns as much political clout as large cities ensured that state government did little to alleviate urban problems. Two world wars drove Connecticut's industries into high gear, only to be followed by deep downturns during peacetime that, along with the Great Depression, exacerbated urban woes.

Between the wars Connecticut was hit by the worst natural disaster in its recorded history, the 1938 hurricane. Ships were cast up on shore, trees were uprooted by the thousands and the death toll was high. Along the Norwalk shore, the force of the storm cracked the base of Greens Ledge Lighthouse, causing it to lean several degrees and making it necessary subsequently to secure the furniture to the floors. Then in 1955 whole neighborhoods were deluged and left to dig out from under a thick blanket of mud by a monumental flood. The legacy of that wet year is a series of flood-control dams, especially in the Naugatuck River Valley.

The year 1965 was a landmark for Connecticut. A new constitution was finally drafted, belatedly giving the cities population-based representation. The years since have found Connecticut struggling to solve the same modern problems facing Americans everywhere: how to pay for public services (long one of only a handful of states without an income tax, Connecticut finally enacted one in the 1990s), how to manage growth and serve a widely disparate population equitably and how to ensure the wise use and conservation of natural resources.

Geology and Geography

It is fitting that Connecticut as a political entity once stretched to the Pacific Ocean, because as a physical entity in the far-distant past it actually enjoyed continental proportions. Points on the current eastern and western state boundaries originally lay many hundreds or even thousands of miles apart, but were forced together millions of years ago by powerful geologic forces.

If you were to look at a topographic map of Connecticut, you'd see that it can be divided north to south into three sections roughly equal in size, with a fourth narrow section tacked on the southern edge along the coast. The eastern and western thirds are hilly uplands; the central third a fertile valley. The sloping land of the southern edge tapers off into Long Island Sound.

The story of how these divisions arose begins about 500 million years ago when what is now northwestern Connecticut lay on the very edge of the ancient North American continent. An ocean that no longer exists, called the Iapetos, lay to the south and east. Another landmass given the name Avalonia by geologists lay some distance offshore. On the far side of Avalonia lay more ocean and finally ancient Africa. The rest of the world's landmasses lay scattered about the globe. These protocontinents began a 250-million-year march toward cohesion, which they achieved in a collision that formed the supercontinent known as Pangaea and pushed up the Appalachians, which may have been the size of today's Himalayas. At the same time, Avalonia became welded to North America, and the ocean that had lain between them disappeared.

During the next 250 million years, the towering peaks of the Appalachians eroded into a more humble mountain range. The continents were on the move again, but this time in different directions. Pangaea split seams in a number of places before finally settling on what eventually became the Atlantic Ocean. One of these seams formed Connecticut's Central Valley, which filled with sediments still washing off the Appalachians.

If continental movement determined Connecticut's bedrock constituency, the final polish was put on by glaciers and erosion. Glaciation occurred after all the continental acrobatics were finished, while erosion has occurred continuously. Together, these two factors are responsible for the soil that overlays bedrock. The legendary stony soil of the Eastern and Western Uplands—stones here have been called "New England potatoes"—was deposited as the glaciers melted, dropping their whole irregular cargo of sand, silt and boulders wherever the ice relinquished it. Hence, uplands soil is fertile but hard on a plow. Flowing water began carrying the uplands mishmash toward the natural drainage channel of the Central Valley, but water sorts particles by size. Rocks and boulders too heavy to be carried far stayed on the hillsides, whereas fine silts formed layer after layer of arable, stonefree farmland along the Connecticut River. The Central Valley's crops grow in sediments that once lay on Appalachian mountainsides.

Driving across the state on Interstate 84 (I-84) you can see plain evidence of the difference in the underlying rock of the upland regions and the Central Valley. For example, traveling east you'll see that the road cuts in the Waterbury region are gray from metamorphic granite, but a few exits on in Cheshire they have the russet color of sedimentary brownstone. Nowhere is the sharp division between valley and upland more striking than on Rte. 4 at the Burlington/Avon town line, where the Farmington River runs on one side and the hills start to rise up on the other.

Visitor Information

General Information

For more information, contact the **Connecticut Department of Economic Development, Tourism Division,** at **865 Brook St., Rocky Hill, 06067-4355.** Or, call them at **(800) CT-BOUND (282-6863)** or **(860) 258-4355.** Ask for the current *Connecticut Vacation Guide* or, if you are visiting during fall or winter, the *Connecticut Fall/Winter Getaway Guide.* Mention your particular areas of interest, and they will send you any available specialized materials. It's a good idea to make your request at least three weeks in advance of your visit.

In addition, 11 regional tourism offices can provide you with information specific to certain parts of the state. If you find yourself short of information upon your arrival, you can always make a stop at any of the state-run visitors information centers. Check the Services section of each chapter for addresses and telephone numbers of appropriate tourism offices and visitors centers.

If you have a computer and an Internet connection, you can do your legwork online by accessing the following World Wide Web addresses (all except the last preceded by **http://www.): ctstateu.edu/state.html, connecticut.com, state.ct.us/tourism and ctguide.atlantic.com.** America Online users can type in the keyword **Destinations** to get to the AOL travel section, then choose **United States,** then **Connecticut** to get to the appropriate place. (Note: Information such as admission prices and hours are provided for the convenience of readers and were accurate at the time of this writing to the best of the author's knowledge, but they tend to change frequently, so readers must take responsibility for confirming these points. Individual attrac-

xvi

tions, restaurants, hotels and so forth are the ultimate authority for all information pertaining to their activities, facilities and services. Call ahead!)

Tips for Visitors

Drinking and Smoking—The minimum drinking age in Connecticut is 21, and you must be at least 18 in order to buy cigarettes. You will be asked to show a picture ID if you look like you're under 26. Liquor stores close by 8:00 P.M. Mon.–Sat. and are not open at all on Sun., but you can purchase a bottle of wine at a winery on a Sun.

Driving—A friend once said that when she first moved to Connecticut from the Midwest, she wanted to shake out the map like a bedsheet to get the wrinkles out. That anecdote says a lot about driving here. Connecticut is a small state that can be traversed by car in about four hours, but unless you are driving on major highways or interstates, travel will take longer than you might guess based on as-the-crow-flies distances. Back roads are often winding and best driven at speeds no faster than 45 m.p.h. Take these facts into consideration when planning travel times. Besides, it's pretty here—you won't want to rush through it.

Money—Travelers checks should always be in U.S. dollars, since few banks in Connecticut offer currency exchange services. Visa, MasterCard and American Express are widely accepted.

Taxes—No tax is charged on food purchased at grocery stores or clothing under the amount of $50, but there is a 6% tax on all meals eaten out and a 12% tax on overnight accommodations.

Telephones—In 1995 Connecticut graduated to its second area code. New Haven and Fairfield Counties, with the exception of a handful of towns along county borders, kept the old statewide area code of (203). Numbers in all other counties and a few oddball towns

are now preceded by the area code (860). To make a toll call, whether between area codes or within one area code, dial 1 plus the area code and the seven-digit number. For directory assistance within the same area code, dial **411**; for directory assistance outside your area code, dial **1-(203 or 860)-555-1212**. The operator (dial 0) can tell you the area code of any given town. Local calls from public telephones cost $.25.

Time—Connecticut is in the Eastern time zone, one hour later than Chicago (Central time), two hours later than Denver (Mountain time) and three hours later than San Francisco (Pacific time).

Getting There

By Air—Connecticut's **Bradley International Airport** is located in Windsor Locks, an easy 15-minute drive from the outskirts of Hartford. Bradley is big enough to be served by most of the major carriers, yet small enough for easy access, and offers a wide selection of ground transportation options, including rental cars. From Bradley, most parts of the state are no more than a two-hour drive.

Although Bradley is certainly a good choice for air travel to Connecticut, it is not your only choice. **Stewart Airport** in Newburgh, New York, and **Westchester County Airport** in White Plains, New York, are especially suitable if your ultimate destination is in western Connecticut. Stewart is approximately 45 minutes west of the Connecticut/New York state line just off I-84. Westchester County Airport is minutes off I-684. Even Laguardia Airport in Queens, New York, is an option. From there you can ride the Connecticut Limousine shuttle bus service to several Connecticut cities for fares starting around $36. Boston's **Logan Airport** is another possibility for travelers headed to the northeast corner of Connecticut. Finally, commuter airlines serve the **Groton/New London Airport** in Groton, **Sikorsky Memorial Airport** in Stratford and **Tweed–New Haven Airport** in East Haven.

By Train—**Amtrak** offers train service along the Connecticut coast and up the Central Valley from New Haven through Hartford to Springfield, Massachusetts. Call **(800) USA-RAIL (872-7245)** for details. Metro-North provides daily commuter rail service between Manhattan and New Haven on the New Haven Line. Connect in Stamford for service to New Canaan, South Norwalk for service to Danbury and Bridgeport for service to Waterbury. Or, take the Harlem Line for the closest train approach to western Connecticut. Metro-North also offers a number of daytrips to major Connecticut destinations, with transportation and admission covered by one all-inclusive price. Their One-Day Getaways brochure gives full details. Call **Metro-North** at **(800) 638-7646** or **(212) 532-4900** in New York City. (Note: Travelers intending to make train connections in New York City should note that Amtrak operates out of Penn Station, and Metro-North operates out of Grand Central Station. Allow an hour to transfer between the two.) Weekday commuter rail service is extended east of New Haven to New London on **Shore Line East (800-ALL-RIDE** or **255-7433).**

By Car—Connecticut's major interstate highways are I-84 running southwest to northeast, I-91 running down the center of the state, I-95 running along the coast and I-395 running up the eastern edge. I-95 is prone to congestion even outside of rush hours. For reference, Hartford is 130 miles from New York, 115 miles from Albany, 105 miles from Boston, 90 miles from Providence, Rhode Island, and 30 miles from Springfield, Massachusetts.

Rental cars are available at hundreds of locations in and around Connecticut. Check the yellow pages of any phone book for toll-free numbers for the major agencies.

By Bus—**Bonanza Bus Lines (800-556-3815** or **860-456-0440)** operates throughout New England; **Greyhound (800-231-2222)** and **Peter Pan/Trailways (800-343-9999)** offer nationwide service.

By Ferry—Bridgeport and New London are the two Connecticut cities that have ferry service to and from Long Island and several resort islands. See those chapters for details.

Maps—The state tourism office (see p. xvi for address) publishes an excellent free state map. Contact them in advance or pick up a copy at any of the state-run visitors information centers listed in the individual chapters.

For short-range navigating you will want local street maps. Mail-A-Map, Inc., publishes maps of approximately 140 of Connecticut's 169 towns. They are distributed free of charge through chambers of commerce and town clerks' offices, so the best way to get one is by writing to the town clerk in a town you will be visiting.

Discounted and Special State Park/Forest Access

Fortunately, people with physical limitations are being accommodated more and more as time goes on. The state has invested considerable resources in recent years making public lands accessible to all. The **Connecticut Department of Environmental Protection (DEP)** publishes a guide to state parks and forests that specifies the accessibility level of each one's attractions. Write the DEP at **79 Elm St., Hartford, 06106,** or call them at **(860) 424-3200** to explain what you're looking for; they'll send all the current guides that apply.

Senior citizens (age 65 plus) who are Connecticut residents are eligible for the free Charter Oak Pass, which can be presented for free day use of all Connecticut state parks and forests. For more information, contact the DEP. Persons under 65 can still save money by getting a $35 season pass. It is sold by mail from the DEP and at state parks and forests that charge an entry fee.

Weather and How to Dress for It

New England weather is legendary for its unpredictability. As a general rule, the weather gets more extreme the farther from the ocean you go, but all of Connecticut enjoys a temperate climate with four full, glorious seasons.

Local forecasts are best obtained by tuning in the local television or radio news or from a local newspaper. Precipitation in Connecticut is distributed roughly equally through all 12 months of the year. It can rain at any time, summer or winter, so keep an umbrella handy. In spring and fall, it's best to bring along a mix of clothing and dress in layers. On the coast, winds coming off the water can make the temperature seem cooler than it is, making a windbreaker the most useful accessory.

How This Book Is Organized

In order to make the information in this book as useful as possible, it was necessary to divide the state into manageable chunks. Seven regions (sections of this book) are further divided into 26 destinations (chapters of this book). Region lines were drawn primarily along geographic boundaries. Each region is accompanied by a map showing its major roads, rivers and features. Destinations were based on cultural and historical ties and represent areas small enough to be covered in a single short trip. A destination can cover an area as small as one town or as large as a dozen towns, depending on the number and nature of local attractions. The Chapter/Town Cross-Reference beginning on p. vi shows exactly which towns are covered in each chapter.

Chapters begin with an overview and a history of each destination. Reading the overviews is the best way to select a destination if you don't know which part of Connecticut will interest you the most. Next you'll find listings for major attractions; a selection of festivals and events; directions to the destination from Hartford; outdoor activities with individual sections for biking, boating, hiking, swimming and so on; sightseeing and museum-based attractions; suggestions for where to stay and where to eat and, finally, transportation services and sources of additional information that may be helpful. The index will help you navigate your way around the specifics of what you want to see and do in the state.

Festivals and Events

Although you'll find listings for all sorts of events under this category, country fairs deserve special mention. A New England tradition, the country fair is a showcase for all skills domestic and agricultural: the biggest pumpkin, the most perfect pig, the prize-winning jam. A golden August afternoon spent cheering on a drover at an ox-pull or taking turns at midway games is one of the most purely fun and wholesome experiences imaginable. You can get two guides to Connecticut's agricultural fairs. One is a quick chronological listing with a map; the other gives much more detailed information about events at each fair. They are both available from the state tourism office or, for the price of a self-addressed, stamped envelope ($.32 for the brief guide, $.78 for the detailed guide), directly from the **Association of Connecticut Fairs, P.O. Box 753, Somers, 06071.**

Outdoor Activities

Biking

Whatever kind of biking you do, your best starting point is a free brochure called "Connecticut by Bike" published by the **Coalition of Connecticut Bicyclists (CCB)** and *The Ride* magazine. It contains a calendar of major biking events, a list of bike clubs throughout the state and a good list of bicycling publications available through bookstores or directly from the publishers. Call the Coalition at **(860) 527-5200** to request your copy. *The Ride* itself is a good resource. This monthly publication covering all of New England can put you in touch with the local bike shops in the area you'll be visiting and lists organized rides through shops and clubs. Call **(617) 933-1808** for a complimentary copy or drop them an e-mail message at **ridezine@aol.com.**

The Connecticut Bicycle Book is another recommended publication of the CCB. This comprehensive general resource for both road riders and mountain bikers is a massively expanded version of the "Connecticut by Bike" brochure. One highlight is a section with hard-to-find information on equipment and touring for people with physical limitations. It's available for $8.95 from **DEP Publications** at **79 Elm St., Store Level-CU, Hartford, 06106.**

Road riders will want to get their free copy of the Connecticut Bicycle Map from the state tourism office. The map shows suggested routes, loop rides, cross-state routes for long-distance cyclists and, perhaps most importantly, roads that are not recommended for cycling. It also gives the location of commuter parking lots where cyclists out for a short ride can leave their cars. It contains general information too, such as rules of the road, bridge access on major routes, mass transportation and even an address at which to get topographic maps.

There are a few legal points of which road cyclists should be aware. Helmets are required by law for children 12 and under, as are a headlight and front and rear reflectors if you will be riding after dark. Ride on the right side of the road, signal turns and obey all traffic signs.

For clarity, on-road and off-road biking opportunities are usually listed separately in this guide. Unless otherwise noted, access to any site listed is free.

Birding

One of the best ways to get an introduction to Connecticut's bird species is to take part in one of the programs of the **Connecticut Ornithological Association (COA).** Their biggest event of the year is a Fall Field Day, typically held in late September at one of the state's prime birding areas and featuring a dozen or more demonstrations, bird watches, children's programs and lectures. The COA also organizes field trips throughout the year and publishes a listing called "The 10 Best Birding Sites in Connecticut." Contact them at **314 Unquowa Rd., Fairfield, 06430.**

Boating

The *Connecticut Boater's Guide* gives an overview of boating regulations, registration procedures and fees, a list of safety equipment required by law, navigation rules, tide charts and more. The section describing all of Con-

necticut's river, lake and shoreline access points is a good, concise reference for the boater unfamiliar with Connecticut's waterways. The guide is available free of charge in many town halls or directly from the **DEP, Boating Division, P.O. Box 280, Old Lyme, 06371; (860) 434-8638.**

Where appropriate, names and numbers of marinas have been given as a convenience to travelers arriving in Connecticut by boat. However, no attempt is made to provide navigational information, which can be found in specialty publications such as *Embassy's Complete Boating Guide & Chartbook to Long Island Sound,* available from **Embassy Marine Publishing, 142 Ferry Rd., Old Saybrook, 06475; (860) 395-0188.**

Fishing

Freshwater

Anyone age 16 or older wishing to fish in freshwater in Connecticut must have a license, even for catch-and-release. A resident license is $15, a nonresident season license is $25 and a nonresident three-day license is $8. All licenses are sold on a calendar-year basis. They're available in person at town clerks' offices, at selected bait and tackle stores, and at some K-Mart stores. Applications are also available by mail from any town clerk or from the **DEP, Fisheries Division, 79 Elm St., Hartford, 06106; (860) 424-3474.** (Note: The DEP does not actually process applications; the agency only provides the form.) The completed application must be returned to a town clerk's office, and addresses are provided with the document.

When you request your application, also ask for a copy of the free *Connecticut Angler's Guide,* a booklet that will answer virtually any question you might have about fishing in Connecticut. Other guides include *A Guide to Lakes & Ponds of Connecticut,* a detailed handbook to 72 of the best fishing sites in the state, and *Connecticut's Bass Fishing,* an overview of 24 of the state's best bass lakes. The latter two are for sale from **DEP Publications** at the address above; **(860) 424-3555.**

Saltwater

Marine fishing in Connecticut waters for all species except lobster does not require a license. A personal-use lobster license is $50. For more information, contact the **DEP's Licensing and Revenue Division** at the address above; **(860) 424-3105.** Noncommercial shellfish harvesting is regulated by each individual coastal town; contact the local town clerk to obtain a permit, if required.

If you want to try your hand at saltwater fishing but don't own your own boat, you have two options: charter or party boat. In most areas, charters are the only choice. Most charter vessels accommodate ten passengers or less, offering a privacy and intimacy otherwise not found on party boats. Party boat fishing, which is centered in New London, is a predominately social affair. Party boats are large vessels that can accommodate however many people show up on a given day.

Golf

Connecticut has dozens of public golf courses, including a few of exceptional caliber. It was impossible to list them all, so a handful representing the best in quality and/or location were chosen for this book. The best comprehensive guide to the state's courses is the directory *Golf in Connecticut*, which contains course descriptions, information on rules and fees, locator maps and more. It's for sale for $9.95 direct from the publisher at **P.O. Box 1297, Avon, 06001.**

Hiking

Connecticut has lots of great hiking country at elevations that are moderate and manageable for most people. For a guide to state parks and forests or individual park/forest maps, contact the **DEP, Bureau of Outdoor Recreation, State Parks Division, 79 Elm St., Hartford, 06106; (860) 424-3200.** If you are interested in interpretive programs—walks, lectures, movies and such—also request a program schedule. A chart listing facilities at many parks and forests is also printed in the *Connecticut Vacation Guide* available from the state tourism office.

Probably the best known of all the hikes in Connecticut is the Appalachian Trail, which cuts for 53 miles across the northwestern corner of the state. For up-to-date maps, contact **The Appalachian Trail Conference** at **P.O. Box 807, Harpers Ferry, WV 25425; (304) 535-6331.** Maps are also available in boxes along the Trail.

Another wonderful resource is the *Connecticut Walk Book*, a guide to over 500 miles of volunteer-maintained, blue-blazed trails. It's available at some sporting goods retailers or directly from the **Connecticut Forest and Park Association** at **16 Meriden Rd., Rockfall, 06481; (860) 346-2372/8733.** Depending on where you get it, the price falls between $15 and $20. The 18th edition was published in late 1997.

The other source of great hikes in Connecticut is the network of private land trusts. To find out if there is a land trust with public trails in a town you'll be visiting, contact the town clerk in that town or the **Land Trust Service Bureau** at **55 High St., Middletown, 06457; (860) 344-9867.** This affiliate of the Nature Conservancy is an association of all of Connecticut's land trusts. Last but not least, *Country Walks in Connecticut*, a guide to trails on Nature Conservancy land in the state, is available for $8.95 from **DEP Publications, 79 Elm St., Store Level-CU, Hartford, 06106.**

It's a good idea to learn to identify poison ivy and poison oak before touching anything growing by the side of a trail in Connecticut. For anyone unfamiliar with these plants, they exude oils that are extreme skin irritants, and they are very widespread. In particular, poison ivy has three shiny leaflets per stalk, and it grows low to the ground or as a hairy vine up trees. There is an old adage that goes "leaflets three, let it be"—and it's good advice. Poison ivy has the lamentable habit of turning lovely colors in autumn, so don't assume that anything pretty is also safe.

Ticks are also of concern to hikers since they are found in the highest numbers in deep woods, and deer ticks can be carriers of Lyme disease. You can obtain informative pamphlets on this subject from the **American Lyme Disease Foundation, Inc., Mill Pond Offices, 293 Rte. 100, Suite 204, Somers, NY 10589.** By phone, you can reach a recorded message at **(800) 876-5963** or a live operator at **(914) 277-6970.**

Snowmobiling

Snowmobilers should request the handout "Snowmobiling in Connecticut" from the **DEP** at **79 Elm St., Hartford, 06106; (860) 424-3200.** These photocopies of maps are sketchy but adequate. In combination with a good street map, they'll get you to the trail. Note that there are some rules of conduct for snowmobilers listed on the back of each handout.

Seeing and Doing

One caveat with regard to visiting attractions that charge a fee or keep limited hours: hours and prices change with budgets and seasons. Always call first to avoid disappointment, and inquire about tour times. Where tours are available, the last one of the day often occurs an hour or more before closing time.

Antiquing

It's probably safe to say that hardly a week goes by without several antiques shows taking place somewhere in Connecticut. One excellent source of information about upcoming events is *Antiques and the Arts Weekly*, published by *The Newtown Bee*, **P.O. Box 5503, Newtown, 06470; (203) 426-8036.** In mid-December they also publish a calendar of antiques shows and flea markets up and down the East Coast for the coming year. Up in the Northwest, try to pick up a free copy of *The Western Connecticut and Western Massachusetts Antiquer*, which is distributed free through antiques stores.

There are too many large antiques shows held each year to mention them all by name, but a few of the best are the Connecticut Antiques Show, the Nathan Hale Homestead Show and the two annual Farmington Antiques Weekends. See the **Hartford, Storrs** and **Farmington** chapters, respectively, for more information. The foremost antiquing destination

in Connecticut is Woodbury; see the chapter of the same name for details.

Children and Families

Parents trying to combine fun and education should request the booklet entitled "Discovery Guide: Places for Families to Explore Math and Science" from the state tourism office. Many of the regional tourism bureaus also have specialized literature targeting families.

Crafts Centers

Call **(888) CT-CRAFT (282-7238)** to receive a free brochure describing five of Connecticut's biggest crafts centers, where you can see regional work on display or sign up for a workshop to learn a craft yourself. They all have special end-of-year exhibits and sales that are popular with holiday shoppers. In addition, the Connecticut Guild of Craftsmen regularly puts out a calendar of upcoming crafts shows in the state. For a copy, send a self-addressed, stamped envelope to **Crafts in CT, P.O. Box 155, New Britain, 06050.**

Museums and Historic Sites

Far and away the bulk of listings under this category are historic homes run as museums because of their significant architecture or notable former inhabitants. Most are run by local historical societies, but a handful are owned by the **Antiquarian and Landmarks Society.** On request they'll send you a brochure describing all of their properties and a calendar of public programs. Contact them at **394 Main St., Hartford, 06103; (860) 247-8996.**

Connecticut also has an unusual number of excellent art museums, including several located at the site of art colonies. The state played an important role in the development of American Impressionism, which you can track at 11 museums on the Connecticut Impressionist Art Trail. A brochure by that name available from the state tourism office will supply you with all the pertinent information.

Seasonal Favorites

This loosely defined category is the place you'll find listings for activities that are seasonal in nature but don't fit anywhere else, such as visiting a great place to pick pumpkins in Oct. or a maple sugarhouse where you can see sap boiled down in Feb. There are far more of these spots than there is room in this book, however. The state tourism office can provide you with comprehensive guides to apple growers, Christmas tree growers and sugarhouses in Connecticut; many regional tourism districts publish comparable lists for their local area.

Wineries

Wine in New England? Yes, indeed. Connecticut wine is a growing business (no pun intended), and our domestic producers are starting to gain respect. To help with planning your trip to and between Connecticut wineries, request the pamphlet "Connecticut's Wine Trail" from the state tourism office and look for the special wine trail signs on our highways.

Where to Stay

Connecticut has accommodations of all kinds, from charming country inns in colonial-era buildings to conference centers for the largest functions. In this book they are divided into three categories: bed & breakfasts (B&Bs); hotels, motels & inns; and camping. Connecticut also has two youth hostels; see the **Hartford** and **North Central** chapters for details. To help you avoid sticker shock, note that all lodging providers in Connecticut must charge a 12% state room tax in addition to their stated rates. The dollar symbols for each listing indicate the approximate price of one night's stay according to the following guidelines:

$	less than $25
$$	$25 to $50
$$$	$50 to $100
$$$$	$100 and up

A few words of advice are in order with regard to accommodations. At their best, B&Bs provide guests with an atmosphere ranging from homelike to luxurious, allow them to benefit from their host's familiarity with the local area and create a comfortable context for so-

cializing with other guests. Since every B&B, and indeed every room at every B&B, is unique, the more information you get in advance, the more likely that you will not be disappointed upon arrival. If you share your expectations with your hosts, they can select the best room for you. I'd suggest inquiring about any of the following that matter to you: whether smoking, small children and pets are allowed; whether your hosts keep a pet to which you might be allergic; which forms of payment are accepted and what the cancellation policy is and amenities such as air-conditioning, in-room TV and telephone.

Traditional inns are another special category of accommodation that is perhaps more common in New England than in some other parts of the country. Inns usually bridge the size gap between hotels and B&Bs, and many have a restaurant on-site, but the distinction between inns and B&Bs can get pretty fine. Some inns boast that they've been accommodating guests since George Washington's time, but remember that longevity is not in and of itself an assurance of quality.

Camping

Visitors who prefer living close to nature for a while have a choice between commercial and state campgrounds. If you're looking for planned recreation or need a lot of facilities, the former is your best bet. By far the thickest concentration of private campgrounds is in the east-central portion of the state. One good source of information about private campgrounds is the yearly *Connecticut Campgrounds* directory published by the **Connecticut Campground Owners Association (CCOA)**. It contains a chart of member campground's amenities and a locator map. Contact the CCOA at **P.O. Box 27, Hartford, 06141; (860) 521-4704.**

State campgrounds tend to be small and rustic. A picnic table and a grill is about all you'll get in most, with hot showers and flush toilets at some. But because state campgrounds are located on public land that's been preserved precisely because of its natural beauty, they always offer a pretty setting. Although you do not have to have prior reservations, they are recommended. Certain campgrounds fill up fast, especially on weekends and holidays. If you don't have advance reservations, get your permit from the campground office on-site. If you are able to make advance reservations, keep in mind that they are accepted by mail only and must be made at least ten days prior to your arrival date.

The season for state campgrounds extends from the Fri. before the third Sat. in Apr. through Sept. 30. From Oct. 1 through the last day of Dec., camping is permitted at designated campgrounds only, contingent upon site conditions and weather, and the campgrounds selected change from year to year, so inquire about off-season camping beforehand. All state campsites are equipped with drinking water and toilets of some kind, and a few have dump stations for RVs. If you are traveling with a pet you may camp at state forest campgrounds, but not at state park campgrounds. There are other restrictions and rules regarding state campgrounds. For more information, request a camping permit application and the brochure "Camping in Connecticut" from the **DEP, Bureau of Outdoor Recreation, State Parks Division, 79 Elm St., Hartford, 06106; (860) 424-3200.** Mail the completed application to

the campground at which you wish to reserve a site; addresses are in the brochure.

Where to Eat

For each destination you'll find a list of recommended restaurants. They were selected based on personal experience, the experiences of others and established reputations recently confirmed by a reviewer. Unfortunately (or fortunately, depending on how you look at it), there is simply not enough room in this book to list all the good places to eat in Connecticut. Omission of a restaurant does not in any way imply anything negative (especially since new restaurants crop up all the time), so please don't decide against visiting a particular eatery just because it's not listed here. Whenever possible, I've tried to formulate a list covering a variety of cuisines, atmospheres and price ranges. In this category the dollar symbols represent what you can expect to pay for the average dinner entrée or, in the case of breakfast and lunch places, an average meal.

$	under $5
$$	$5 to $10
$$$	$10 to $20
$$$$	$20 and up

The
Connecticut
Guide

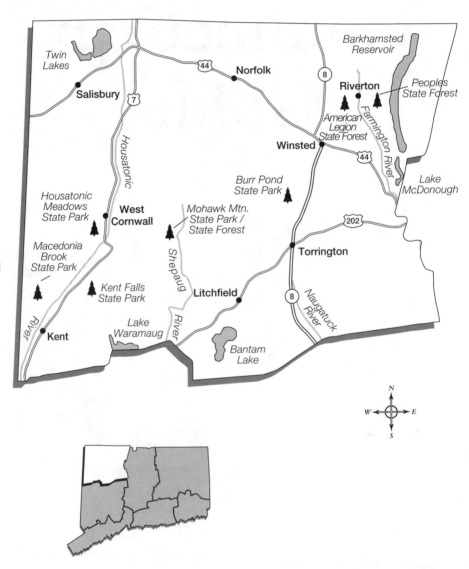

Twin Lakes

Salisbury

44   Norfolk

8

Barkhamsted Reservoir

Riverton

Peoples State Forest

American Legion State Forest

Winsted

44

Lake McDonough

Housatonic

Housatonic Meadows State Park

West Cornwall

Burr Pond State Park

Mohawk Mtn. State Park / State Forest

202

Macedonia Brook State Park

Shepaug River

Torrington

Kent Falls State Park

Litchfield

8   Naugatuck River

River

Kent

Lake Waramaug

Bantam Lake

Farmington River

7

N
W   E
S

Litchfield Hills

Litchfield Hills

3

Far Northwest

The Far Northwest is one of the least developed parts of Connecticut, offering the kind of scenery that can make a simple drive in the country a rewarding way to spend an afternoon. Forested hillsides alternate with valleys dotted with farms and villages, and when these miniature mountains don their multicolored coat in autumn, only nightfall will tear your eyes away from them. A camera is the most essential accessory for travel in the area, especially if you'll be visiting West Cornwall, the site of one of Connecticut's few remaining covered bridges.

The natural beauty of the Far Northwest lends itself to recreational use. The upper Housatonic River contains whitewater stretches for canoeing and rafting in spring, and fly fishers have their own private heaven on a 2-mile stretch of the river in Housatonic Meadows State Park. Mohawk State Forest has prime trails for mountain biking, and in winter Mohawk Mountain Ski Area offers some of the most challenging downhill ski terrain in Connecticut.

If it's hiking you're after, try doing a stretch of the Appalachian Trail, which makes its irregular way across this corner of the state. The highest point in Connecticut is found in the town of Salisbury, where you can climb to 2,380 feet above sea level on the south slope of Mt. Frissell, which actually peaks at a slightly higher elevation in Massachusetts. Bear Mountain, topping out at 2,316 feet, has the honor of being the highest mountain whose summit is within state lines.

Music Mountain in Falls Village and the Ellen Battell Stoeckel estate in Norfolk are the sites of summer chamber music festivals not unlike their more famous counterpart, Tanglewood, in Massachusetts. If you're looking for a different kind of excitement, Lime Rock Park in Lakeville calls itself "the road racing center of the East" and hosts NASCAR races on selected Fri. and Sat. from Apr. through Oct. History buffs will want to visit the Holley House in Salisbury, a unique place to learn about area life and industry in the 1800s with attractions for both adults and children. And you might even consider coming to the Far Northwest to do nothing more than lounge at a fine B&B. Norfolk (locally pronounced as if the "l" were an "r") has a small cluster of luxury establishments, and many more are scattered throughout the region. Up here, the slow pace of life is itself something to enjoy.

History

The forests that cover much of this quiet district might give one the impression that the land has been untouched by either plow or factory, but that is deceptive. This corner of Connecticut didn't escape development, although it did come slowly, rolling over the land like a wave and then quietly passing on by. The population of Cornwall, for example, is about the same now as it was 50 years after the arrival of the first white settlers, and this situation is the rule, not the exception, for towns in the Far Northwest.

The rugged landscape discouraged settlement until the demand for land was so high that colonists had no choice but to farm these rocky slopes, and the first towns were not established until the 1730s, a full century after colonization of the Central Valley around Hartford began. The area was part of the so-called Western Lands that were auctioned off at that time in 80-acre parcels. Settlers came from towns across the developing colony: Norwalk, Stamford and others.

In the decades from roughly 1750 to 1895 this area was an important iron-producing region. A significant deposit of iron ore was discovered in Salisbury at a spot that came to be known as Ore Hill, and blast furnaces to purify the ore sprang up all around. Lakeville was once known by the name Furnace Village in reference to a smelter built there by Ethan Allen and two business partners. The end product of the furnaces was pig iron, so called

because the molten metal was poured into a pattern that resembled piglets suckling at a sow. It has been estimated that in some towns there was hardly a family that did not have some financial interest in iron manufacturing.

During the Revolutionary War many cannons and other projectiles were made locally from ore smelted in Allen's Salisbury Furnace, in which he had by then sold his interest. Other iron products, including axles for railroad cars, were made as late as the Civil War at sites such as the Ames Iron Works in the Salisbury neighborhood still known as Amesville. In part to bring vital iron products to broader markets, the Housatonic Railroad was organized in 1837. It went north into Massachusetts and south to Bridgeport on Long Island Sound. In 1871 it connected with an east-west, Boston-to-Albany route at Canaan.

The iron industry caused a dramatic alteration in the local landscape. Smelting required tremendous amounts of charcoal, which is made by burning wood slowly under controlled conditions. To produce charcoal in the quantities needed, the early settlers deforested acre after acre of countryside, virtually denuding it. Only after pig-iron production had died out (the result of the opening of mines in Pennsylvania, where nearby coalfields fueled smelters more cheaply) did the mountains reclothe themselves in trees. If you're hiking in the area and you see anything resembling a circular trench or depression in the ground about 40 feet in diameter, stop, look down and paw around a bit to see if you can find charcoal bits in the top inch or two of soil. If you find some, chances are you're standing in the middle of what was once a charcoal pit.

Today the stone foundations of iron furnaces (the best-preserved one is in East Canaan) are scattered alongside streams and rivers that provided the hydropower needed to circulate hot air. Heaps of slag, a waste product of iron production that looks like dark, bubbly glass, are usually present at these locations. The Ames Iron Works location, now in the middle of a forest, has been developed into a walking trail with interpretive plaques. The Housatonic Railroad discontinued passenger

5

service decades ago and, after a brief flirtation with scenic excursions, became exclusively a freight carrier. It still operates out of Canaan railroad station, making that structure the oldest depot in use in the country.

With little in the way of industry to support the local population, visitors frequently question what folks here do for a living. Tourism is important, but many people are employees of a number of private primary and preparatory schools, a hospital and small, service-oriented businesses. The passage of intensive industry into the history books is what made the Far Northwest into the restful refuge it is today.

Major Attractions

Lime Rock Park

"What's a raceway doing out here?" is the question that may pop into your mind when you come to Lime Rock, but this village has been a hotbed of racing for well over a century. In the 1800s wealthy residents trained and raced trotters on the current site of the Park, and at one time there were two horse tracks and a bike track in town. Today's Lime Rock Park is an eight-turn road course offering professional and amateur road racing as well as special shows, swap meets and festivals.

There are no grandstands at Lime Rock. Instead, all seating is on the infield and outfield lawns, the outfield rising up to form an amphitheater; bring a blanket to sit on. Highlights of the season include the Dodge Dealers Grand Prix (billed as the largest sports car race in North America) in May, a vintage car festival held on Labor Day weekend, and the Busch Grand National North NASCAR Series in

Skip Barber Racing School participants getting out on the track at Lime Rock Park in Lime Rock.

Oct. The season runs Apr.–Nov. with most start times around 9:00 or 10:00 A.M. Admission prices vary from $10 to $40 per adult; children under 12 are free. An additional $10 will buy you access to the paddock area where you can get close to the cars and drivers. Located on **Rte. 112 about 2 miles west of Rte. 7 in Lime Rock; (800) 722-3577.**

West Cornwall Village and Covered Bridge

West Cornwall is the site of one of only two covered bridges in Connecticut that still carry automobile traffic. The red wooden span traversing the Housatonic River between the village of West Cornwall and the town of Sharon is probably the fourth structure on this site. The original was designed by Ithiel Town in 1841; Town built bridges throughout the state and patented some innovative designs, in addition to designing one of the churches on New Haven green and codesigning another. One night a year, in late May, a Covered Bridge Dance is held in celebration of this landmark. Once you see it you'll know why it is one of the most photographed spots in the state. West Cornwall is also a great place to stop for a meal and do some relaxed shopping. The few stores here are memorable.

West Cornwall is a small town that can't accommodate a lot of automobile traffic. The best way to enjoy it is to park at the canoe launching area a short walk from the main street and then explore on foot. To get to the parking area coming from Rte. 7, turn on Rte. 128, drive across the bridge (stop to look for oncoming traffic before entering—it's one lane wide) and take an immediate right at the end of the guard rail. After about one-tenth of a mile you'll see a dirt road on your right. This leads to the parking area along the river. The river's edge is a great vantage point for taking photographs of the bridge. Then hoof it into town to visit Ian Ingersoll's Shaker furniture store, Cornwall Bridge Pottery, West Cornwall Antique Center, The Wish House (everything from vintage clothing to quirky housewares) and the small assortment of other shops.

Festivals and Events

Salisbury Ski Jump
early Feb.

Four Norwegian brothers by the name of Satre came to Salisbury in the 1920s and established a ski jump in 1926, making it the second-oldest ski jump in the country and the oldest in the East. The Salisbury Ski Jump has since become a training ground for Olympic-caliber combined skiing contenders. It is an official U.S. Ski Association–sanctioned event, with one 55-meter jump and two smaller ones. Practice jumping begins around 11:00 A.M. both mornings of this weekend event; the competition takes place 1:00 P.M.–3:30 P.M. or so. Food is available on-site. Tickets are $6 per person age 13 and over; $1 for children. For directions and more information call **(860) 435-0019.**

Covered Bridge Dance
Sun. of Memorial Day weekend

A few years ago some local folks resurrected the 1940s–1950s custom of a Grange dance at West Cornwall's covered bridge, and it's become a lovely way to enjoy this novel landmark. Rte. 128, the road through the bridge, is closed to traffic, a band plays country swing music and the bridge becomes the dance floor. The time is 5:00 P.M.–midnight, rain or shine. Sandwiches and other inexpensive foods are available. Park in one of the designated lots on Rte. 7 and Rte. 128, and take a shuttle bus to the site. Tickets are $7 adult, $5 youth (or $5 and $4 in advance), free for children under 10. For advance ticket sales and information call **(860) 672-4373.**

Northwest Connecticut Balloon Festival and Craft Fair
last weekend in June (Fri.–Sun.)

One of the Northwest's more colorful events is the annual hot-air balloon fest in Goshen. Come at 6:00 A.M. or 6:00 P.M. to see the bal-

7

Getting There

The towns in the northwestern corner of the state are a one-and-a-half to two-hour drive from Hartford. Rte. 44/202 will take you as far as Canton, at which point the two routes separate. Rte. 44 is the one to take if you're heading for towns in the northern part of this area: Norfolk, Salisbury, Canaan and North Canaan. Rte. 202 takes you through Torrington, where you can pick up Rte. 4 toward Goshen, Cornwall and Sharon. The main north-south road through the area is Rte. 7 paralleling the Housatonic River. There is no service to the area by train or major bus carrier, so you should count on having a car at your disposal.

loons take off, or plan to be on one yourself. Launched rides (those on which you float freely for about an hour) cost about $175 per person. Short tethered rides on which you just go up and come right back down run $8–$10. Although the launches are always weather dependent, mornings are generally more reliable. For the most part the balloons are not visible during the day. To fill the intervening hours there's a large craft fair, music, food, amusement park rides, kite and remote-controlled aircraft demonstrations and a general fair atmosphere. There's plenty of parking on site. Admission: $5 adults, $4 seniors, $3 children 5–12. Hours: Fri., 3:00 P.M.–8:00 P.M.; Sat.–Sun., 5:00 A.M.–8:00 P.M. Held at the **Goshen Fairgrounds** on **Rte. 63 about one-quarter mile south of Goshen town center.** For more information call **(860) 496-5000.**

Music Mountain Summer Music Festival
June–Aug.

On a winding back road in Falls Village is a most surprising find: a concert hall in the woods where, for nearly 70 years, music lovers have been able to hear world-class performances on summer weekends. Music Mountain claims to be the oldest continuous chamber music festival in the United States, but chamber music is not the only offering. Many Sat. evenings are devoted to jazz, folk, blues and baroque music. Gordon Hall seats 335 people, but at performance time the doors are thrown open for the sound to spill out across the adjacent lawn where you can picnic (bring your own food and beverages) while you listen. For ticket prices, a schedule or to order tickets call **(860) 824-7126** or write to **Music Mountain, P.O. Box 738, Lakeville, 06039.** Located on **Music Mountain Rd. roughly midway between Rte. 63 and the Warren Tpke.**

Norfolk Chamber Music Festival
late June–early Aug., sometimes later

The Norfolk Chamber Music Festival began as a series of semiprivate choral concerts organized by heiress Ellen Battell Stoeckel at her Norfolk home in 1906. The concerts are now a Yale Summer School of Music program. The uneuphoniously named Music Shed in which performances take place is an enclosed, 947-seat auditorium set amid beautifully landscaped grounds. There is no lawn seating. A preconcert talk is often given one hour before the performance. Leave some extra time to walk the estate, which is stunning. Performances are given Thu. and Fri. evenings and at varying times on weekends. Individual event tickets run from $9 to $25; subscription pricing is also available. The first Sun. in Aug. is always Family Day, with an afternoon performance and a special price of $12 for adults and $6 for children. The estate is located on **Norfolk's town green at the intersection of Rtes. 44 and 272.** For more information call **(860) 542-3000.**

Canaan Railroad Days
late July

This annual town festival begins the third Thu. in July and runs for 11 days. Its name is a reference to the fact that Canaan has the oldest continuously operating train depot in the country. This low-key event has different activities each day, ranging from dinners to line dancing to magic shows or pony rides. The Housatonic Railroad provides a locomotive for people to tour. An arts and crafts show takes place the last two days, and the blowout event is a fireworks display on the second Sat. of the event, held at **Lawrence Field** on **Rte. 7/44 in the center of town.** Bring a blanket and a picnic to enjoy during the entertainment that precedes the pyrotechnic show. Most events are free, but some involve a nominal fee. For more information call **(860) 824-7580.**

Connecticut Agricultural Fair
last weekend in July (Fri.–Sun.)

The Connecticut Agricultural Fair is one of two country fairs to take place in Goshen. Events range from pig racing to costumed square dancers. There is musical entertainment, agricultural and livestock displays, food and games. Parking is free and adjacent to the fairground. Hours: Fri., noon–9:00 P.M.; Sat., 8:00 A.M.–9:00 P.M.; Sun., 9:00 A.M.–6:00 P.M. Admission: $3 per person on Fri., $4 on Sat. and Sun.; children under 12 free. **Goshen Fairgrounds** (see p. 7) is on **Rte. 63 south of Goshen town center.** For a calendar of events, check local newspapers a week before the fair.

Sharon Arts & Crafts Fair
first Sat. in Aug.

Over 140 exhibitors congregate on picturesque Sharon green on Rte. 41 just north of Rte. 4 for this high-quality juried show featuring the work of regional artisans. Admission is free. Hours: 10:00 A.M.–5:00 P.M. For more information call **(860) 824-1457.**

Goshen Fair
Labor Day weekend (Sat.–Mon.)

The second of the two fairs to be held in Goshen is a great way to spend the last official weekend of summer. Two highlights are horse-related: a daylong draft horse show starting

8

Sat. at 8:00 A.M. and an appearance of the 1st Company Governor's Horse Guard. The Governor's Horse Guard participates in the Sat. morning opening ceremony at 10:00 A.M. and members also parade the grounds Sat. and Sun. An antique tractor pull with over 100 vehicles at noon Mon. is one of the largest in the state. Admission: $5 adults, $4 seniors Sat. only, children under 12 free. On-site parking is free. Hours: Sat.–Mon., 8:00 A.M.–6:00 P.M. **Goshen Fairgrounds, Rte. 63 south of Goshen center.** For more information call **(860) 491-3655.**

Falls Village Historical Festival
weekend after Columbus Day

At this annual festival begun in 1995, you can learn about the events and people that have shaped the Falls Village area. The festival has focused on the Civil War era, although in years to come railroading or other time periods may take center stage. Activities can include a walking tour of the Great Falls, an encampment, vintage cannon firings, lectures and railroading displays. Most take place in the village on Rte. 126. For more information call **(860) 824-7893.**

Outdoor Activities

Biking

Mountain Biking

If you need to rent a bike, give **Housatonic River Outfitters** a call. For $30 a day you get a bike and helmet. They're also starting to experiment with guided trips; call for details. They are located **in the back of the Cornwall Bridge Pottery store on Rte. 128 in West Cornwall; (860) 672-1010.**

Mohawk State Forest

A number of old woods roads and trails crisscross this high plateau area, with access from Rte. 4 east of the Rtes. 4/128/43 intersection. A sign marks the entrance. Just park in the small lot by the side of the road and start riding, or take the road that leads back into the forest until you reach a T intersection. Going to the right takes you to a rickety lookout tower whose view has been blocked by trees. (Several fire towers were built on hilltops in this area over the years, and the ruins of several can still be found.) Going to the left takes you to a large parking lot at some brown maintenance buildings. Trails branch off the road at regular intervals.

River Valley Road

This 3-mile stretch of dirt road from the center of West Cornwall to Music Mountain Rd. runs along the east bank of the Housatonic, crisscrossing the tracks of the old Housatonic Railroad. It is also known by the name River Rd. at its southern end in West Cornwall and Warren Turnpike at the northern end. It can be negotiated by both road bikes and mountain bikes. There are no obstacles or sharp changes in elevation, making this a very pleasant ride for families with children or riders who like to take it easy. Your best bet for the return trip is the way you came. Trying to make a loop back to the beginning will take you over some serious hills and a much longer distance.

Road Biking

The Far Northwest is the most mountainous part of Connecticut. The main roads tend to lie

Birches and wildflowers along the trail in Mohawk State Forest.

in the valleys; back roads traverse the hilly country in between. This leaves the road biker with a tough choice: flat roads that will have to be shared with automobiles or rolling roads with little traffic. Some major roads are busier than others. I'd suggest staying off Rtes. 7, 44 and 41. Rtes. 63 and 43 are relatively quiet and flat (Rte. 43 in particular passes through a valley with a peculiar beauty and a number of little cemeteries and monuments at which to sit and rest or explore), and the elevations on Rte. 4 are not too objectionable. Almost any back road will reward you with pretty country-side—pick an area near where you're staying and go.

Boating

Housatonic River

The Housatonic is one of the loveliest water-ways in Connecticut, but like virtually all the state's rivers, it is dammed at numerous points, artificially regulating the flow of water. Timed releases from these upriver dams make it possible for the principal outfitter in the area—Clarke Outdoors in West Cornwall—to lead scheduled canoe, kayak and raft trips daily from spring through late autumn. The stretch of the river from Falls Village to Cornwall Bridge contains some Class I and II rapids, whereas the section from Ashley Falls, Massachusetts, to Falls Village is flatwater. In Aug. (the driest month) and at other times when the water level is very low, you may only be able to travel the flatwater portion. Clarke can set you up with the proper equipment, instruction, transportation and a guide if you want one. You have your choice of half-day or full-day trips. Call for start times and rates. **Clarke Outdoors** is at **163 Rte. 7, West Cornwall, 06796,** 1 mile south of the covered bridge in West Cornwall and 3 miles north of the Rte. 4/Rte. 7 intersection; **(860) 672-6365.**

North American Whitewater Expeditions leads guided weekend rafting trips on two sections of the river: the Falls Village to Cornwall Bridge stretch mentioned above, and a segment from Bulls Bridge to Gaylordsville

or New Milford. Children must be at least 7 years old to be taken on the former, at least 16 years old on the latter. The lower portion is really only possible to run late Mar.–May. There are Class V rapids at the very start, but they can be avoided easily. Fees include a guide, all equipment, transportation and food. For more information call **(800) 727-4379.**

Twin Lakes

For motorboating in the Northwest, the best option is Lake Washining and Lake Washinee, known together as the Twin Lakes. Individually these bodies of water also go by the names East Twin Lake and West Twin Lake. If you are in a boat small enough to pass under a 6-foot bridge—a canoe or a bass boat, for instance—you can cross from Washining to Washinee and have the latter mostly to yourself. **O'Hara's Landing** offers a private boat ramp where you can launch your own craft for a $5 fee. They also rent everything from paddleboats to pontoon party boats, and they sell tackle and boating and waterskiing equipment. Hourly rentals are also available. The marina's season runs from the third Sat. in Apr. until Nov. (weather permitting). The ramp is open 24 hours a day, so if you're in your own boat you can stay out as late as you want. There is a casual restaurant on the premises open daily in July and Aug. and weekends the rest of the season. Call for hours. Located on Twin Lakes Rd. off Rte. 44 just west of Rte. 126; drive until you see water on your left—you can't miss it. Phone: **(860) 824-7583.**

Other Boat Launches

If the Twin Lakes don't suit you for one reason or another, you can also launch at the town boat ramp at **Wononscopomuc Lake** in Lakeville for a fee. Motors are limited to 12 cubic inches. The ramp is located off Holley St. in Lakeville. For more information call **(860) 435-5185.** There are also free state boating access areas at **Tyler Lake** in Goshen (parking is very limited) and **Mudge Pond** in Sharon. At the latter there is a 7.5 HP, 6 m.p.h. limit, and motors are prohibited at night and near the beach. To get to the former, follow the signs from Rte. 4 west of Goshen. The latter is accessible from Silver Lake Shore Rd. off Rte. 361 north of town.

If you're looking for a quiet body of water for putting in a canoe or car-top boat, try **Mohawk Pond** in Mohawk State Forest (motors prohibited; access via Clark Rd. in Cornwall), **West Side Pond** in Goshen (quite small; access from West Side Rd.), **Dog Pond** in Goshen (access via Town Hill Rd.) or **Wood Creek Pond** in Norfolk (access via Ashpohtag Rd.). Mohawk Pond is probably the prettiest of the lot.

Fishing

Lakes and Ponds
At least half a dozen bodies of water in the Northwest are open for public fishing. **Mohawk Pond** in Mohawk State Forest is stocked with trout. If you plan on fishing from a boat, note that motors are prohibited but access from shore is excellent.

West Side Pond and **Tyler Lake** in Goshen are also stocked with trout and have a good natural population of warm-water species.

Both trout and bass are plentiful in the **East** and **West Twin Lakes** in Salisbury (a fee is charged for launching a boat from the commercial ramp on East Twin Lake) and **Wononscopomuc Lake** in Lakeville (a fee is charged by the town for launching a boat, and there is a motor restriction of 12 cubic inches). At the latter you can also expect to pull in yellow perch, kokanee, chain pickerel and sunfish. Other good spots for those fish are **Dog Pond** in Goshen, **Wood Creek Pond** in Norfolk and **Mudge Pond** in Sharon. For directions to all of these, see the Boating section.

Rivers and Streams
The **Blackberry River** in Norfolk and Canaan is a major trout stream, stocked with adult trout from a point half a mile west of Rte. 272 to Rte. 7. The river is accessible for most of its length along Rte. 44 except where posted.

Another good area trout stream is **Furnace Brook,** which feeds into the Housatonic at Cornwall Bridge.

The **Housatonic River** from the bridge at the junction of Rtes. 112 and 7 in Salisbury to the bridge at the junction of Rtes. 4 and 7 in Cornwall Bridge is one of the state's premier trout management areas. Anglers are limited to catch-and-release, and in Housatonic Meadows State Park only fly fishing is allowed. Consumption of fish from the Housatonic is not advised. Housatonic Meadows Fly Shop is located directly opposite the entrance to Housatonic Meadows Campground.

Outfitters and Guide Services
Housatonic River Outfitters can set you up with a whole fishing package. Prices start at $100 and $150 for half- and whole-day trips, respectively, including equipment, guide services and a substantial lunch. They also sell technical outdoor clothing and light camping gear and rent mountain bikes. They lead trips on the Housatonic, Farmington, Ten Mile and Blackberry Rivers, going after trout and smallmouth bass. Free casting and fishing instruction on request. Trips can be arranged any day of the week. Store hours in high season (Mar. 15–Oct.) are Tue.–Fri., 8:00 A.M.– 5:00 P.M., Sat.–Sun., 7:00 A.M.–7:00 P.M. Off-season hours: Thu., Fri. & Sun., 9:00 A.M.– 5:00 P.M.; Sat., 10:00 A.M.–7:00 P.M. Located **in the back of the Cornwall Bridge Pottery store on Rte. 128 in West Cornwall; (860) 672-1010.**

Housatonic Anglers is a guide service and fishing school with a variety of programs on the Housatonic as well as the Farmington River and Long Island Sound. They are beginning to branch out into rustic lodging since they are located on an old camp on 14 riverside acres. Call them at **(860) 672-4457.**

Hiking

Appalachian Trail
The most famous hiking trail in America, the Appalachian Trail (AT) crosses the towns of Sharon and Salisbury in the utmost northwest corner of the state. The trail intersects several major roads, but these crossings are not as well marked as you might expect. An easier way to find the AT is to take advantage of connecting trails from areas where more ample parking is provided. One of these is the

11

Undermountain trailhead (Bear Mountain/Mt. Riga State Park), and another is Housatonic Meadows State Park, both of which have separate listings below. Maps of the AT are available at map boxes along the route. To get a map in advance, contact the **Appalachian Trail Conference** at **P.O. Box 807, Harpers Ferry, WV 25425; (304) 535-6331.** The AT is also in the *Connecticut Walk Book.*

Bear Mountain/Mt. Riga State Park

Bear Mountain is the second-tallest peak in Connecticut, and because of this distinction it is one of the most heavily hiked areas in the state. The best access is by Undermountain Trail and the AT. You pick up Undermountain Trail about 3.5 miles north of the village of Salisbury on Rte. 41 at a parking lot on the west side of the road marked with a blue oval sign. This lot can overflow on weekends and holidays, so arrive early. Undermountain brings you to the AT, which takes you north to cross the summit of Bear Mountain (2,316 feet). Come prepared if you intend to continue hiking from this point. The north side of Bear Mountain is steep, falling 1,300 feet in half a mile or less, and is recommended only for the experienced hiker. The distance from Rte. 41 to the summit is approximately 3.75 miles.

Berkshire Inn to Inn Hikes

If you want to explore the Northwest's backcountry on foot, but you're not too thrilled with the idea of spending the night in a tent, give Berkshire Inn to Inn Hikes a call and enjoy the best of both wilderness and civilization. They take up to ten people on a Mon.-through-Wed., 37-mile guided hike (a shorter trip is also available), spending days on the trail and evenings comfortably ensconced at inns along the way. The route takes you from Litchfield County up into Massachussetts, with stopovers at the White Hart Inn in Salisbury, Connecticut, Race Brook Lodge in Sheffield, Massachusetts, and The Egremont Inn in South Egremont, Massachusetts. For rates and more information call **(413) 528-6006.**

Dean's Ravine

Along an easily accessible section of the Mohawk Trail in the Housatonic State Forest is a series of small falls culminating in a spectacular cataract where Reed Brook tumbles over a rock ledge. The best time to visit is, of course, during spring runoff or the day after a major rainstorm. At other times the waterfall can be more of a gurgle, but the scenery is always beautiful. The trail switches back because of sharp changes in elevation, so keep an eye out for the blazes to avoid taking a wrong turn. To get to Dean's Ravine, take Rte. 128 going east out of West Cornwall and turn left at the school onto Cream Hill Rd. Go 4–5 miles until you meet up with Music Mountain Rd. At the intersection is a dirt parking lot. A connecting trail perhaps 100 feet in length takes you to the Mohawk Trail. The walk in either direction is great, but take a left to get to the waterfall and, a mile or two along, the AT. You will have to backtrack to return to your car.

Dennis Hill State Park

Dennis Hill is a fairly small state park with a couple of pleasant surprises. Drive through the entrance gates and up a little ways until you come to a small parking lot on the left. On foot, continue up the road until it takes a sharp turn to the right. Ahead of you is a barred path that goes back into the woods about half a mile before forking. From this point on, the trail forms a loop. Take the right fork, which leads fairly quickly through easy terrain to a stone gazebo from which there are good views of the surrounding hills. Continue hiking in a counterclockwise direction to return to the fork. Turn right to return to your car. The whole trail is probably no more than 1.25 miles in length. You can also hike (or drive) the paved road all the way to the top for some really spectacular views from the observation deck at the peak of a huge octagonal picnic pavilion, the shell of a former bungalow built by Dr. Frederick S. Dennis in 1908, a wealthy New York surgeon. The entrance to the park is on Rte. 272 about 2.5 miles south of Rte. 44 in Norfolk.

Falls Village Interpretive Trail and the Great Falls

Falls Village is the site of a pleasant, self-guided, three-quarter-mile hike that gives insight into the relationship between people and the land over the centuries in this corner of the world. This easy riverside walk developed by Northeast Utilities, the local power company, takes you past an overgrown racetrack in an abandoned fairgrounds (now the middle of the forest) and the remains of a failed canal. You pick up the trail at the gravel parking area on Water St. just above the Falls Village Hydroelectric Station.

When you are through with this hike, take Water St. a little farther to the north of the station and cross the bridge to your left. Once over the bridge, look for a path on your right. This is the Ames Historic Trail, which parallels the Housatonic River along a stretch that includes the Great Falls. Because of the short length, easy terrain and educational aspect of both of these hikes, they are especially good for families with small children.

Haystack Mountain State Park

This park has a single paved road that climbs to a cul-de-sac where there is parking for a few cars. Either of two trails at the parking area leads to a 34-foot stone tower at an elevation of 1,716 feet, from the top of which you can see New York state, Massachusetts and, on a very clear day, southern Vermont. The tower was built in the 1920s by the Battell family of Norfolk as a memorial to World War I veterans. The tower is about half a mile from the cul-de-sac, perhaps a 20-minute walk. The entrance to the park is on Rte. 272 a short distance north of the green in Norfolk.

Housatonic Meadows State Park

Drive north on Rte. 7 from Cornwall Bridge about 1 mile, and you'll come to a parking area on the left with a sign letting you know you've found Pine Knob Trail Loop. From this spot you can hike the 1.25-mile loop, the farthest portion of which runs coincident with the AT, or use it as a connector to the AT, which offers a virtually limitless hike in either direction. The meadows in the park's name are to be found on the other side of Rte. 7, and there's no hiking there—just camping and fishing. The trails are mountainous and shaded by stands of hemlock and hardwoods such as maple, oak and hickory.

Mohawk State Forest

See the Biking section for a description of this state forest, which is also suitable for hiking. The forest's name comes from the mountain's supposed use by Tunxis and Paugussett Indians, who lit smoke signal fires atop the peak to alert local tribes when marauding Mohawks were approaching. Today there is a rather unsturdy tower on Mohawk Mountain (1,683 feet), and although the view is blocked by trees, it's still fun to climb up.

Mohawk Trail

The blue-blazed Mohawk Trail follows a route that used to be part of the AT before portions of it were relocated west of Rte. 7 in recent years. If you're a traditionalist, this is the "real" AT from Cornwall Bridge to Falls Village. Hiking it will take you past some interesting areas, including Dudleytown, Cathedral Pines and the Mohawk Mountain Ski Area.

Dudleytown is a New England "ghost town" about which spooky and unverifiable legends abound. Don't select this hike just to see Dudleytown—the climate here ensures that things decay fast, so there are no standing buildings, just some cellar holes out in the middle of the woods—but if you happen to be going past it, it's interesting to know that a large mining community once existed on this spot. Cathedral Pines was an impressive stand of massive pine trees that were laid waste by a freak tornado in 1989. They were virtually destroyed, but the area is still beautiful, even with the devastation plainly evident.

To see these areas, pick up the trail at the southern end. From Baird's, the general store on Rte. 7 in Cornwall Bridge, follow signs for Rte. 4 east. You'll leave Rte. 7 and bear right. Just as the connector road you're on meets Rte. 4 proper, you'll see a sign on the right for Furnace Brook. Park in the dirt lot here and walk back the way you came to Dark Entry Rd., which will be on your left. (The sign may be missing, but it's the only road between the parking area and the store.) Go up Dark Entry Rd. and follow the blue blazes. Don't attempt to park anywhere on Dark Entry Rd.—you will be fined if anyone takes notice. From your starting point it's about 1.5 miles to Dudley-

13

town, 6.5 miles to Cathedral Pines, 7.75 miles to the ski area and 24 miles to where the Mohawk Trail ends at the AT in Falls Village. The Mohawk Trail is mapped in the *Connecticut Walk Book*.

Northeast Audubon Center

This 758-acre National Audubon Society sanctuary has 12 miles of trails through a variety of habitats, including one trail that is wheelchair-accessible. Stretching a third of a mile over nearly flat terrain through forest and field and along a pond's edge, the Lucy Harvey Trail is suitable for young and old. A fee is charged for access to the trails, and although there are plenty of places in the area to hike for free, the Audubon Center offers the advantage of loop trails of varying lengths so you can alter your plans as you go. Depending on the timing of your visit, there may be a naturalist on hand to answer questions about animals and plants you see on your hike. A trail map is posted at the entrance. Grounds hours: dawn–dusk daily. Main building hours: Mon.–Sat., 9:00 A.M.–5:00 P.M.; Sun., 1:00 P.M.–5:00 P.M.; closed on many holidays. Trail access is $3 per adult and $1.50 per child; free to Audubon Society members. **325 Cornwall Bridge Rd.** (Rte. 4) just southwest of Sharon village, **Sharon, 06069; (860) 364-0520.**

Horseback Riding

Rustling Wind Stables

Rustling Wind offers guided trail rides, English or Western saddle, lasting one to two hours through woodland terrain. Children 8 and above can be accommodated on the trail. Pony rides are available for the young ones. Closed on Mon. Reservations required; call for rates. **160 Canaan Mountain Rd., Falls Village, 06031; (860) 824-7634.**

Western Riding Stables

Although this stable is technically over the border in New York state, they offer a riding experience very hard to find in the East, and they're just minutes from Connecticut. In addition to short trail rides, they lead full-day, overnight and moonlight trips that can include meals on the trail, campfires and breaks for pond swimming. They can accommodate both small and large groups, as well as guests with special needs. Co-owner Brian Mulhall stresses that they try to keep the rider-to-wrangler ratio low for everyone's safety and comfort. Western saddles are used unless otherwise requested. Prices start at $30 per person for the introductory trip. Reservations required. Located on **Sawchuk Rd., Millerton, NY; (518) 789-4848.**

Skiing and Snowmobiling

Housatonic State Forest

The snowmobile trails here comprise one of the most extensive networks in the state, with several loop trips of various lengths possible. Access is from West Cornwall Rd., which runs between the villages of West Cornwall and Sharon. The entrance is not marked, but it's not too hard to find. Traveling east (toward West Cornwall), the entrance road is on the left six-tenths of a mile past Eggleston Rd. You come to the parking area almost immediately.

Mohawk Mountain Ski Area

For downhill skiing, this is probably the most challenging ski area in Connecticut. The longest vertical drop is 640 feet, and the longest trail is 1.25 miles in length. There are four double lifts and one triple as well as one surface lift. Twenty percent of the trails are rated green for beginners and 20% are for experts, with the remaining 60% classified as intermediate. About half the runs are lit for night skiing. There is a ski shop and a cafeteria in the main lodge. Mohawk Mountain offers the full gamut of rentals and lesson packages, including a weekend SKIwee program (10:00 A.M.–3:00 P.M.) with full supervision for kids age 5–12. Lift tickets are discounted for women on Ladies' Days (Mon. & Wed.) and gentlemen on Men's Days (Tue. & Thu.). Call for pricing and hours; closed Christmas Day. **46 Great Hollow Rd., Cornwall, 06753; (800) 895-5222** (inside Connecticut and in surrounding states) or **(860) 672-6100.** For a 24-hour taped ski report call **(860) 672-6464.**

Mohawk State Forest

The same roads that make Mohawk State Forest a great mountain biking spot in warm weather (see the Biking section for directions) make it excellent for cross-country skiing in winter. There may be as many as 40 miles of roads and trails here. The area is not groomed, so you'll have to cut your own tracks, and although there are restrooms, don't absolutely count on their being open; take precautions! About 10 miles of those trails are also designated for snow-mobiling. The network contains a few loops but mostly a number of dead-end side trails off a very long central trail. The entrance is on Rte. 4 in Cornwall. Go left at the T intersection and park at the brown maintenance buildings, where you'll see the sign-in log.

Sleigh and Carriage Rides

Loon Meadow Farm

Imagine stepping out the door of your B&B and into a waiting carriage drawn by a beautiful draft horse for a tour of a New England village or the countryside. This rare treat is available at Loon Meadow Farm in Norfolk, a horse and carriage livery that's also a B&B. When there's enough snow on the ground, the sleighs come out. Otherwise, hayrides for up to 16 people are available, followed by mulled cider and a bonfire at the farm. Reservations required; call for rates. **41 Loon Meadow Dr., Norfolk, 06058; (860) 542-6085.**

Western Riding Stables

This stable specializing in trail riding recently began offering carriage rides in an old-fashioned vis-à-vis carriage that can accommodate four people. They also do sleigh rides when conditions allow and hayrides regularly throughout the year. For more information, see the listing under Horseback Riding.

Seeing and Doing

Antiquing

Since 1958 the first Sat. in May and the first Sat. after Labor Day in Sept. (rain or shine)

have been the dates for Antiques in a Cow Pasture, a large gathering of antiques dealers in a field in Salisbury. You'll find a mix of antiques, collectibles and decorative arts. The show draws about 125 exhibitors and 1,500 to 1,800 shoppers. Admission is $4; children under 12 admitted free. Hours are 9:00 A.M.–4:00 P.M. Park free in the field right next door to the show. The field is located on Rte. 44, 1 mile east of the village of Salisbury. For more information call **(860) 435-2034** in the weeks prior to either show date.

Museums and Historic Sites

Beckley Furnace

This iron smelting furnace is one of the best preserved in Connecticut. The iron smelting process was labor-intensive, dirty, dangerous and fascinating. A large complex of buildings once existed on this spot, and the plaque by the smelter shows drawings of how the whole facility might have looked. It also explains the manufacturing process used here from 1847 until 1923, when the furnace was finally shut down. The furnace site, which appears as an "Industrial Monument Historic Preserve" on some maps, is on Lower Rd. in North Canaan close to the Furnace Hill Rd. intersection. There is no sign; you just have to look for a broad driveway sloping down from the south (river) side of Lower Rd. at a sharp angle.

Historical Society Museums

The Norfolk Historical Museum, which has won awards for the excellence of its displays, has two floors of exhibits chronicling Norfolk's past. One permanent exhibit represents a composite of Norfolk country stores through the years. They sometimes display a good collection of Connecticut-made clocks. The museum is housed in the 1840 Norfolk Academy, a former private high school and town hall located on the town green. Admission is free. Hours: Sat.–Sun., 1:00 P.M.–4:00 P.M., Memorial Day–mid-Oct., and by appointment. **13 Village Green, Norfolk, 06058; (860) 542-5761** or **(860) 542-6044.**

15

The **Falls Village-Canaan Historical Society** operates two small local history museums in Falls Village that are worth a quick stop. Their headquarters at 105 Main St. in the town hall contains all sorts of papers and artifacts documenting local history, especially its iron industry. **Beebe Hill School** is a one-room schoolhouse interpreted to the late 1800s, located on the corner of Beebe Hill Rd. and Railroad St. near Rte. 7. The school is open Fri., 1:00 P.M.–4:00 P.M., June–Sept. The museum in town is open during the same hours, but year-round. Admission is by donation. For more information call the town hall at **(860) 824-0707.**

Holley House

This delightful museum chronicles life in the 19th century as seen through the eyes of one Maria Holley Williams. Displays tell the story of the Holley family's various enterprises, including iron smelting and pocketknife manufacturing. Most of the items on display actually belong to the house, having been found in the attic when the property was bequeathed to the town of Salisbury. Holley House is an especially good destination for families because the kids can don Revolutionary War costumes and engage in some serious role playing at the Salisbury Cannon Museum just across the driveway. This children's museum has touchable, pint-sized exhibits. There is also a mowed-grass maze on the other side of Holley House. Admission: $3 adults, $2 seniors, $1 children 5–15. Hours: Sat.–Sun. and holidays, 1:00 P.M.–5:00 P.M., mid-June–late Sept. Located on **Rte. 44 just west of Rte. 41,** **Lakeville, 06039; (860) 435-2878.**

Odds and Ends

Cornwall Bridge Pottery

On Rte. 7 just south of the village of Cornwall Bridge is a low, red barn on the east side of the road with the words "Cornwall Bridge Pottery" written on the side. At the bottom of the dirt driveway is a sign that says "Pottery Exhibit." This is the workshop and home of Todd Piker, a potter who has been creating beautiful and functional ceramics in this exquisite setting for over 20 years. Piker and his apprentices welcome visitors any day of the week, 9:00 A.M.–5:00 P.M. What you'll see when you arrive depends on where they are in the cycle of throwing, glazing and firing pots, so you should call in advance. Piker also keeps a store in the village of West Cornwall where you can see (and buy) his finished works. The workshop is on Rte. 7 about 1 mile south of Rte. 4 or 1 mile north of Rte. 45. The store (also called Cornwall Bridge Pottery) is on **Rte. 128 just east of the covered bridge in West Cornwall; (860) 672-6545.**

Harney & Sons Tea Emporium

While Harney & Sons is not a teahouse, you can still savor tea here by taking part in a tasting. The company imports, blends and packages its own teas and sells about 120 types out of this small shop adjoining their blending and shipping area. They'll brew some for you if you show an interest. Open Mon.–Sat., 10:00 A.M.–5:00 P.M.; closed Sun. **23 Brook St., Lakeville, 06039; (800) 832-8463** or **(860) 435-5050.**

16

Potter Todd Piker at work in his studio; his shop is in West Cornwall.

Hillside Gardens

The owners of this perennial nursery, Fred and Mary Ann McGourty, are nationally known gardening authors who live on the property and have built eye-catching demonstration gardens here over the course of more than 30 years. As a point of interest to gardeners, Norfolk happens to be the coldest town in Connecticut. Hours: 9:00 A.M.–5:00 P.M. daily, May 1–Sept. 15. **515 Litchfield Rd. (Rte. 272), Norfolk, 06058; (860) 542-5345.**

Skip Barber
Racing School/Driving School

If you've ever imagined yourself behind the wheel of a race car, the Skip Barber Racing School is where you can make that dream become reality. It's designed for "the student serious about racing and the nonracer serious about learning." A one-day introduction to racing includes 90 minutes of driving time on Lime Rock's course and an equal amount of classroom instruction. The three-day competition course gets pretty serious, preparing students to apply for racing licenses. The driving school offers one- and two-day classes in street skills for better automobile handling and accident avoidance. For a schedule of dates, write or call the school at **29 Brook St., Lakeville, 06039; (860) 435-1300.**

Performing Arts

Northwest Connecticut recently welcomed a new performing arts venue to its cultural world. **Sharon Stage** is located in the former Sharon Playhouse (ca. 1955), which had fallen on hard times and was closed for several years before its rescue at the hands of a group of Broadway insiders. The interior is a delightful combination of unfinished barn and cushy movie house. The season is summer only, but a single season's schedule might include plays new and old, comedy, cabaret, children's theater, lectures on the arts—even musicals, thanks to a new orchestra pit. Perhaps best of all is the fact that there are performances throughout the week, not just on Fri. and Sat.

nights. **49 Amenia Rd. (Rte. 343, just west of Rte. 41), Sharon, 06069; (860) 364-1500.**

See also the listings for Music Mountain Summer Music Festival and the Norfolk Chamber Music Festival under Festivals and Events.

Scenic Drives

"Touring the Litchfield Hills by Car, Foot, Boat and Bike" is a booklet published by the Litchfield Hills Travel Council to help visitors plan scenic drives and other outings. Pick from among its seven half-day and full-day driving tours throughout the Litchfield Hills. Maps, mileages and detailed itineraries make it possible to just get in the car and go without agonizing over details. Contact the council at **P.O. Box 968, Litchfield, 06759; (860) 567-4506.**

Doing your own planning isn't difficult, however. There are a couple of state-designated scenic drives in the area (Rte. 4 west of Cornwall Bridge, Rte. 41 north and south of Sharon and Rte. 272 from the Massachusetts border to the Goshen town line), but the most beautiful stretch of road is Rt. 7 from Cornwall Bridge to just south of the intersection of Rt. 7 and 112. This is a spot where the Housatonic leaves the valleys underlain by easily eroded marble that it follows for most of its run through the northwestern part of the state and cuts across much harder bedrock. The road becomes narrow and winding with steep, wooded hills rising up on the west side and the river on the east. Take it slow and enjoy the views that are briefly revealed as you come around the curves. You're likely to see lots of folks in waders fly fishing in the river, and occasionally a canoe or a kayak floating by, because this is one of the most popular recreational areas in the state.

Where to Stay

Bed & Breakfasts

In addition to the listings below, you might also try **Fairland B&B** in Sharon ($$$; **860-364-**

0081), the **Earl Grey/Chittenden House** in Salisbury ($$$$; **860-435-1007**) and **Hilltop Haven** in West Cornwall ($$$$; **860-672-6871**).

Angel Hill—$$$$

This 1880 Victorian with four guest rooms is an extraordinary house, beautifully renovated and decorated. All of the rooms are stunning, and a second-floor suite has a bath with a double Jacuzzi. All baths are private, and the beds are mostly queen size. Two rooms have working fireplaces. There are many small touches in all the rooms: robes, VCRs, glasses and wine buckets—enough stuff to make you feel truly pampered. A separate carriage house offering complete privacy and spaciousness is available for rental by the night or the week. Located within walking distance from the center of town and the Norfolk Chamber Music Festival. Payment by cash or check only; young children accommodated in the main house only. **54 Greenwoods Rd. East (Rte. 44), Norfolk, 06058; (860) 542-5920.**

Cathedral Pines Farm—$$$$

You feel as if you have found someplace special when you begin to make your way up the long, sloping driveway leading to Cathedral Pines. Acres of fenced land suggest the presence of farm animals. After a bit of climbing a new 18th-century-style home and the view it enjoys come into sight. The house and surrounding gardens are perched on a hillside overlooking a small valley and the remains of the "cathedral pines" (largely destroyed in a tornado in the late 1980s) from which the B&B takes its name. The house is centered in a light-filled, inviting dining room/kitchen expanse. The sole guest room is comfortably furnished in traditional style with a double bed. Outdoors you'll find a hot tub in an idyllic setting. In the morning a full breakfast awaits you. Perhaps the best reason to stay here is the llamas. Hosts John and Nancy Calhoun raise these exotic creatures and are happy to give guests a chance to stroke and feed them. **10 Valley Rd., Cornwall, 06753; (860) 672-6747.**

Greenwoods Gate—$$$$

Possibly the most luxurious B&B in Norfolk, Greenwoods Gate offers four exquisite suites with dramatically different personalities. The bathrooms, all private, are stocked with every lotion and potion you could imagine, and anyone with an interest in the decorative arts will have a field day looking around the common areas of the house. The morning meal is also something special. Located within walking distance from the center of town. **105 Greenwoods Rd. East (Rte. 44), Norfolk, 06058; (860) 542-5439.**

Under Mountain Inn—$$$$

The uniqueness of Under Mountain Inn lies in its British flavor, which is evident from the Union Jack flying above the front door along with the Stars and Stripes. Host and native Briton Peter Higginson and his American-born wife Marged run the B&B in a sprawling 1700s-era colonial house with a covered front porch and a beautiful backyard view of acres of neighboring farmland. A stay at Under Mountain always includes both breakfast and dinner along with accommodations, in addition to tea and shortbread on the weekend, and rooms are priced accordingly. There is a two-night minimum policy in effect on weekends, but a one-night stay is allowed on weeknights.

All seven of the rooms at Under Mountain are christened with London place-names, which appear on authentic little plaques above the frame of each room's door. On the main floor of the house are common rooms for houseguests as well as the restaurant and a taproom that serves Sam Smith ales. A different selection of British and American dishes is offered each night. Weekend breakfast is British one morning, American the other. There are holiday packages that include such things as horse-drawn sleigh or hayrides, readings of Charles Dickens along with a Dickensian feast or readings of Jane Austen over tea. **482 Undermountain Rd. (Rte. 41), Salisbury, 06068; (860) 435-0242.**

Armstrong B&B—$$$ to $$$$

If you want complete privacy but a neighborhood atmosphere, Armstrong B&B is a great choice. Hosts Cookie and Tom Armstrong have dedicated the second floor of their Victorian home on a side street in Lakeville to guest accommodations. When you make a reservation here, you get the whole floor, which has two bedrooms, one with a queen and one with a double bed. There is a base price for use of one bedroom, and if two couples or a family are traveling together and want to use the second bedroom, there is a surcharge. The private bath has a tub and a shower, and you can enjoy a self-serve Continental breakfast in the eat-in kitchen. A large sitting room provides a cozy place for letter writing or movie watching. Payment by cash or check only. **30 Ethan Allen St., Lakeville, 06039; (860) 435-9964.**

Blackberry River Inn—$$$ to $$$$

The 20 or so rooms at Blackberry River Inn vary in size and level of accommodation, with rates ranging from moderate to quite pricey. The B&B comprises a small Georgian mansion, a separate and rather plain carriage house and a private cottage. The four suites in the mansion are elegant one- and two-room affairs, all with wood-burning fireplaces, king or queen beds and colonial reproduction decor. The cottage consists of one large living room/bedroom with a king bed, a working fireplace and traditional furnishings like those in the main house. The bathroom features a whirlpool tub and a separate shower. Amenities for guests in any of the rooms include an outdoor pool, trails for hiking on 27 acres and access to the Blackberry River for trout fishing. The main house has several beautiful common areas, including some with fireplaces. A morning room makes a sunny setting for your expanded Continental breakfast. Children and pets are accommodated. **536 Greenwoods Rd. West (Rte. 44), Norfolk, 06058; (860) 542-5100.**

Cornerstone B&B—$$$ to $$$$

Two strong points of this B&B are its setting— a sizable, parklike property on a not-too-heavily traveled route through Falls Village—and its central location with easy access to main roads radiating out to all corners of the Far Northwest. Set back a bit on a main road, this white Dutch colonial has a handful of guest rooms and baths that can be combined in a variety of ways. Call owner Gay Rickenbacker to see what's available. A full breakfast is included. Children and pets are accommodated. **159 Belden St. (Rte. 126 a half-mile south of Rte. 44), Falls Village, 06031; (860) 824-0475.**

1890 Colonial—$$$ to $$$$

The interior of this traditionally styled, center-chimney house retains a Victorian spaciousness, although the guest room furnishings and decor are largely modern. Two rooms (one with a queen bed and one with two twins) have private but separate baths, and a suite (twin beds) has an adjoining private bath. A screened porch overlooks a garden and an expansive lawn that resembles a park. Rates include a full breakfast and vary widely depending on the room and the season. **Rte. 41 (at Rhynus Rd.), Sharon, 06069; (860) 364-0436.**

Loon Meadow Farm B&B—$$$ to $$$$

The setting for this B&B is on a quiet Norfolk back road. Owner Beth Denis also operates a horse-and-carriage livery service, so there are several draft horses pastured close to the well-kept 19th-century farmhouse where three guest rooms are located. (Inquire if you are interested in a carriage, sleigh or hayride during your visit.) Each room has a theme: the Carousel Room is decorated with carousel figurines and prints and has a working fireplace, everything in the Rain Forest Room reflects the plants and animals of tropical climates, and the third room is all country. All have queen beds and private baths. A Continental breakfast is served. Small children can be accommodated for parties that rent the entire house. **41 Loon Meadow Dr., Norfolk, 06058; (860) 542-6085.**

Manor House—$$$ to $$$$

Built in what innkeepers Diane and Henry Tremblay call Bavarian Tudor style, Manor House is spectacular both inside and out.

One highlight is a set of Tiffany windows lining the dining room (where you'll be served a full breakfast), living room and library. Since the mid-1980s the house has been a B&B. Each guest room has a unique decor, but in general Victorian lace and wallpaper, area rugs and subtle colors and patterns complement the 1898 interior. When you make your reservation, ask for the details of each room—some have balconies, others have wood-burning fireplaces and others have wonderful bathrooms with a whirlpool or soaking tub. **69 Maple Ave., Norfolk, 06058; (860) 542-5690.**

Skinny Dog Farm—$$$

In just a short time the owners of this relatively new B&B, Andrea Salvadore and Jim Burns, have converted a dilapidated 18th-century center-chimney farmhouse into an engaging home across the street from Lime Rock Raceway. Several common rooms nicely combine elegance with the native rusticity of the house. Upstairs, two guest rooms—one done in bright colors with two twin beds, the other in a subtle pink and white scheme with a king bed—share a bath with a shower. A downstairs guest room in a new addition to the house has a queen bed, an attached private bath with tub and a neutral color scheme. A full breakfast is served. Skinny Dog Farm is the only accommodation within walking distance of Lime Rock Raceway, so if that's your destination you couldn't ask for a more convenient location. **500 Lime Rock Rd. (Rte. 112), Lakeville, 06039; (860) 435-8155.**

Weaver's House—$$ to $$$

The low-key atmosphere at Weaver's House is functional and comfortable, falling somewhere between a small hotel and a youth hostel. Furnishings are somewhat plain, enhanced by handwoven curtains and rugs made by resident hostess Judy Tsukroff, who runs the B&B with her husband Arnold. Evidence of Judy's talent with textiles can be found throughout the house. There are four rooms (one with a working fireplace), which share two bathrooms. An expanded Continental breakfast is included. **58 Greenwoods Rd. West (Rte. 44/272 just north of the green), Norfolk, 06058; (860) 542-5108.**

Hotels, Motels & Inns

In addition to the choices below, also consider **Mountain View Inn (Rte. 272 just south of Rte. 44, Norfolk, 06058; 860-542-6991)** and **Ragamont Inn (8 Main St. [Rte. 44], Salisbury, 06068; 860-435-2372).** At the former, inquire about their package deal including accommodations, breakfast and a four-course dinner daily in the on-site restaurant, wine or champagne and tax. The Ragamont has an excellent restaurant on its main floor.

Interlaken Inn—$$$$

Interlaken is unique in the range of accommodations it offers, including rooms in a modernized Victorian house (the original Interlaken Inn), condominium-like units with kitchens and loft sleeping quarters, standard hotel rooms in the main building and more. A pool, restaurant and lounge, fitness center, tennis courts, chip-and-pitch golf course and private frontage on Lake Wononscopomuc (with canoes), in combination with the number of rooms available, make Interlaken a popular conference and corporate retreat site, but it is appropriate for singles, couples and families too. **74 Interlaken Rd., Lakeville, 06039; (860) 435-9878.**

Iron Masters Motor Inne—$$$ to $$$$

In the motor lodge category, Iron Masters would have to be near the top. Like a motor lodge, all its rooms are on the ground floor and have doors exiting to the parking lot; however, it is set far enough off the road for traffic noise to recede into the distance. The furnishings are above average, there is a pool out back surrounded by a perennial garden, the lobby is a functional sitting area and there is a cute breakfast nook where a complimentary Continental breakfast is served. Prices are also a cut above average for a motor lodge, but this is a good value. **Rte. 44, Lakeville, 06039; (860) 435-9844.**

Wake Robin Inn—$$$ to $$$$

Housed in a century-old building that was once a school for girls, Wake Robin Inn has a distinctly European feel. Old-fashioned and grand, the building's slightly faded elegance is accented with occasional reminders of its institutional beginnings. No two rooms are exactly alike, and all have private baths, telephones and cable TV. Wake Robin Inn offers the advantage of being set back far enough off the road that traffic noise won't disturb your sleep. A Continental breakfast (at a nominal additional charge) is served in the main floor dining room. Pets are allowed and there are some rooms designated for smokers. The owner also has available inexpensive motel units along the driveway leading up to the inn proper, but you'll want to stay in the main house. **Rte. 41/44, Lakeville, 06039; (860) 435-2515.**

The White Hart—$$$ to $$$$

Although The White Hart doesn't deliver the intimacy of a B&B, it certainly offers up the same degree of charm along with the more uniform amenities of a hotel. They have 26 guest rooms and two restaurants in two 19th-century buildings. The White Hart is renowned for its idyllic front porch, on which a tea service is offered on weekend afternoons and drink service toward evening in summer. There are three room categories: singles, doubles and several suites. The rooms are all decorated in similar fashion with Thomasville-style mahogany-finish furniture and lots of chintz. They all have private bathrooms, TVs, telephones and individual heating and air-conditioning controls. Some have decorative fireplaces. **Rte. 41/44 at the top of the green, Salisbury, 06068; (860) 435-0030.**

Hitching Post Country Motel—$$$

This small, family-run motel looks pleasant from the outside and maintains that impression in the clean and recently remodeled rooms. About a dozen units occupy a low, brick building just south of the village of Cornwall Bridge. Rooms come with standard motel furnishings but have a couple of decorative touches that set the Hitching Post a notch above many motels. Inquire about kitchenettes and special rates. **Rte. 7, Cornwall Bridge, 06754; (860) 672-6219.**

Camping

Housatonic Meadows State Park—$

This campground with 95 sites is close to the road but heavily wooded and only a few feet from a beautiful stretch of the Housatonic River, so it is still very desirable. It's a popular retreat for families on summer weekends and fills up fast. Technically speaking, no swimming is allowed in the river. Facilities include hot showers, flush toilets and fire pits. Located on Rte. 7 just north of the village of Cornwall Bridge. Campground office: **(860) 672-6772.**

Lone Oak Campsites—$ and up

Most of the spaces in this huge family campground are given over to RVs, but some secluded tent sites are available, and there are even trailers and a small cabin for rent. Lone Oak is fully developed with every facility and service you could ask for, including cable TV at some sites, entertainment options, a swimming pool, a lounge and a store. It's actually like a small city. They also have special activities for adults and children throughout the year. Call for rates and their activity schedule. **Rte. 44, East Canaan, 06024; (800) 422-2267.**

Where to Eat

In addition to the listings below, this area has its share of inexpensive breakfast and lunch places. **Baird's General Store (Rte. 7 at Rte. 4 in Cornwall Bridge, 06754; 860-672-6578),** located walking distance from Housatonic Meadows State Park, is very convenient for the fishing, hiking and camping crowd, serves basic deli food and keeps early hours. **Cadwell's (421 Rte. 128, West Cornwall, 06796; 860-672-0101)** is a very informal combination bakery, coffee shop and reading room right by the covered bridge that also serves dinner on Thu. and Fri. Farther

21

north, you'll find an assortment of coffees and teas plus light lunch items and an Internet connection at **Riga Mt. Roast (342 Main St., Lakeville, 06039; 860-435-2991)**. Finally, soups and sandwiches are served at the **Whistle Stop Café (81 Main St., Canaan, 06018; 860-824-1163)**, but the real draw is a case of ice creams and a model train circling the store on a track suspended from the ceiling.

Brookside Bistro—$$$

Situated in a renovated old house on the quiet main street of West Cornwall with seating indoors and out, Brookside Bistro has an exceptional dining setting. A rushing stream tumbles right by the bistro before spilling its contents into the Housatonic River just half a block away. The sound is relaxing and nicely shields private conversation from the ears of diners at other tables. *Connecticut* magazine gives the restaurant a three-star rating, lauding both the quality and the quantity of dishes such as coq au vin, brie en croute and homemade desserts. Lunch: noon–2:00 P.M. daily. Dinner: Mon.–Sat., 6:00 P.M.–9:00 P.M.; Sun., 5:30 P.M.–8:00 P.M. **Rte. 128, West Cornwall, 06796; (860) 672-6601.**

The Cannery—$$$

The Cannery is generally recognized as the best restaurant in this remote corner of the state. Through the years it has stayed true to the bistro spirit of sophisticated home-style cooking, with a small but varied menu and a wine list to match. Hours: Wed. & Thu., Sun.–Mon., 5:00 P.M.–9:00 P.M.; Fri.–Sat., 5:00 P.M.–10:00 P.M.; Sun. brunch, 11:00 A.M.–2:00 P.M.; closed Tue. year-round and Wed., Dec.–Apr. **85 Main St., Canaan Village, 06018; (860) 824-7333.**

Keilty's Depot—$$$

Located in Canaan Depot, this casual family restaurant has an open interior with a cathedral ceiling and a pleasant atmosphere. The centerpiece is a long bar stocked with a good selection of both domestic microbrew and imported beers. Overstuffed sandwiches form an integral part of the menu. At dinner this is

supplemented by about a dozen entrées, mostly of the meat-and-potato persuasion. There's also an extensive appetizer menu that makes this a good place for folks looking to relax with a beer and some finger food. Hours: Tue.–Thu., 11:30 A.M.–9:00 P.M. (10:00 P.M. in summer); Fri.–Sat., 11:30 A.M.–10:00 P.M.; Sun., 11:30 A.M.–9:00 P.M. **Canaan Union Station (on Rte. 44 just east of Rte. 7), N. Canaan, 06018; (860) 824-4848.**

Mountain View Inn—$$$

This restaurant on the ground floor of an inn serves dinner only on Fri. and Sat. nights, as well as Sun. during autumn and on some holidays. It has an attractive dining room with west-facing windows and a view down the sloping lawn, as well as a fireplace for ambiance in winter. The menu offers an appealing mix of straightforward American food and dishes that are just enough out of the ordinary to capture your imagination, such as a hot scallop and spinach salad or mushrooms and cheddar cheese en croute. It also offers a good selection of after-dinner drinks. Hours: 5:00 P.M.–9:00 P.M. **Rte. 272 (just south of Rte. 44), Norfolk, 06058; (860) 542-6991.**

The Pub—$$$

The atmosphere of The Pub is very friendly and appealing, with lots of rich wood and exposed brick and seating for both small and large groups. The regular menu has a little bit of everything American. Wed. and Thu. are always theme food nights, with the theme changing every few months. The Pub also does box picnics for the Norfolk Chamber Music Festival. Open Tue.–Thu., 11:30 A.M.–9:00 P.M.; Fri.–Sat., 11:30 A.M.–10:00 P.M.; Sun., 11:00 A.M.–8:00 P.M. **Rte. 44 (just north of the green), Norfolk, 06058; (860) 542-5716.**

Ragamont Inn—$$$

During summer the covered terrace at this 200-year-old inn is *the* place in Salisbury to enjoy an open-air dinner and the quiet pace of the town as it winds down for the night. Chef Rolf Schenkel and his wife Barbara are the proprietors, and given their surname it won't come as much of a surprise that the menu features German and Continental staples such as

Wiener schnitzel, sauerbraten and osso buco. There's plenty of indoor seating. Dress your best. Open May–Oct. only. Hours: Wed. & Thu., 5:30 P.M.–9:00 P.M.; Fri., 5:30 P.M.–10:00 P.M.; Sat., 6:00 P.M.–10:00 P.M.; Sun. brunch, 11:30 A.M.–2:00 P.M. & Sun. dinner 5:00 P.M.–9:00 P.M. Terrace seatings are at 6:00–6:30 P.M. and again at 8:00–8:30 P.M. **8 Main St. (Rte. 44), Salisbury, 06068; (860) 435-2372.**

Tavern at the Inn—$$$

You'll be happy to come upon the Tavern at the Inn if you're traveling Rte. 7 north of Kent around dinnertime because this rather lonely stretch of road hasn't got many places to stop for a good meal or a few drinks. Having just changed hands, the restaurant now features Mediterranean and Provençal specialties. Initial reports are extremely favorable, and the atmosphere is friendly. The bar is open 5:00 P.M.–10:00 P.M., & dinner is served 6:00 P.M.–9:00 P.M., Thu.–Sun. only. **270 Kent Rd. (Rte. 7), Cornwall Bridge, 06754; (860) 672-2825.**

Under Mountain Inn—$$$

The small restaurant is an adjunct to owners Peter and Marged Higginson's B&B. The Higginsons serve dinner to the public on Fri. and Sat. only, seating two tables every half hour from 6:00 P.M. until 8:00 P.M. The menu includes both American selections and traditional English cuisine: roasts, meat pies, bangers and mash (sausage and potatoes) and so forth. The tavern, which is only run as an amenity for houseguests and dinner guests, specializes in Sam Smith ales. Dinner by reservation only. **482 Undermountain Rd. (Rte. 41), Salisbury, 06068; (860) 435-0242.**

West Main Café—$$$

The food at West Main Café is creative, delicious and artfully presented, a mélange of ethnic influences with a Continental grounding. A screened porch makes a cool spot for outdoor dining during warm weather. With the opening of Sharon Stage, the volume will probably pick up on summer weekends, so call ahead on those evenings to ensure a table. Open for lunch Thu.–Sun., 11:30 A.M.–2:30 P.M., & for dinner Tue.–Sat., 5:30 P.M.–10:30 P.M.; Sun., 5:30 P.M.–9:00 P.M. **13 W. Main St., Sharon, 06069; (860) 364-9888.**

The White Hart—$$$

There are a couple of dining options at The White Hart, which is also an inn. For casual and lively, try the Garden Room and Taproom, which feature pub fare as well as more substantial entrées that are American interpretations of classic and ethnic dishes. For a more elegant and dressy experience, try Julie's New American Sea Grill, where you'll find Continental-inspired dishes that promise to be a flavor experience unto themselves. Despite the name, the menu is not limited to seafood. All the dining rooms at The White Hart feature vegetarian options. Tavern and Garden Room hours: breakfast served Mon.–Sat., 7:00 A.M.–10:00 A.M.; lunch served Mon.–Fri., 11:30 A.M.–2:30 P.M. and Sat.–Sun., 11:30 A.M.–midnight; dinner served Sun.–Thu., 5:00 P.M.–9:30 P.M., & Fri.–Sat., 5:00 P.M.–10:30 P.M. Julie's New American Sea Grill hours: dinner served Sun. & Wed.–Thu., 5:30 P.M.–9:00 P.M., and Fri. & Sat., 5:30 P.M.–10:00 P.M.; buffet breakfast served Sun., 8:00 A.M.–10:00 A.M. **Rtes. 44/41 at the top of the green, Salisbury, 06068; (860) 435-0030.**

The Woodland—$$$

The best indicator of The Woodland's quality has got to be the fact that its parking lot is always packed. Its reputation is one of solidly and consistently good food at fair prices, and it's popular with an older crowd. The small menu focuses on baked or sautéed fish and chicken selections, with a nod to seafood, pork and steak. Lunch revolves around salads and sandwiches, as well as omelets, frittata and a pair of full entrées. Lunch hours are Tue.–Fri., 11:30 A.M.–2:30 P.M.; Sat., 11:30 A.M.–2:00 P.M. Dinner is served Tue.–Thu., 5:30 P.M.–9:00 P.M.; Fri.–Sat., 5:30 P.M.–10:00 P.M.; Sun., 5:30 P.M.–8:30 P.M. Closed Mon. and seasonally on other days; it is best to call ahead. **192 Rte. 44/41, Lakeville, 06039; (860) 435-0578.**

Carriages Restaurant—$$ to $$$

Solid American fare is what you'll find at Carriages. With a menu centered on pasta and chicken dishes, as well as sandwiches, pizza and a few other items, most members of the family will probably find something to their liking. Seating is a bit close for comfort, so go on a slow night or dine early. The atmosphere varies from a bright, sunny atrium to dining rooms with a dark, woody, publike feel. Kids and adults will get a kick out of the diorama-like tables in which all sorts of old objects are displayed under glass. Open for lunch 11:30 A.M.–2:30 P.M. daily. Dinner hours: Mon.–Thu., 5:30 P.M.–9:00 P.M.; Fri. & Sat., 5:30 P.M.–10:00 P.M.; Sun., 5:30 P.M.–8:00 P.M. Located on **Rte. 44/41 approximately one-half mile north of town, Lakeville, 06039; (860) 435-8892.**

The Falls Village Roadhouse—$$ to $$$

This restaurant and tavern is a casual place to enjoy American cuisine or relax with a beer at a local watering hole. You'll find reliably good food ranging from burgers to traditional New England fare to southwestern-inspired dishes, with many sandwiches at lunch and a specials board that changes daily. The front porch makes a nice seating area in summer. Lunch hours: Tue.–Sat., noon–3:00 P.M. Dinner hours: Tue.–Thu., 5:00 P.M.–9:00 P.M.; Fri.–Sat., 5:00 P.M.–9:30 or 10:00 P.M.; Sun., 4:00 P.M.–8:00 P.M. A pub menu is available Mon. **33 Railroad St., Falls Village, 06031; (860) 824-1344.**

Chaiwalla Tea Room—$$

Chaiwalla Tea Room came into existence as the result of a trip founder and owner Mary O'Brien made to India more than a decade ago. On that trip she met a chaiwalla—a tea maker—and was drawn to the craft and culture of tea, opening the tearoom in 1988. O'Brien imports teas from around the world, selling them under the Chaiwalla name and, of course, serving them at the tearoom where, if you're lucky and it's slow, you may get the most desirable table: the one in back that overlooks a recirculating waterfall and pond—guaran-

teed to put you in a tranquil frame of mind. There are only about half a dozen tables at Chaiwalla, and the atmosphere is always low-key. To go with your tea, try the "Famous Tomato Pie" and the desserts. Hours: Wed.–Sun., 10:00 A.M.–6:00 P.M.; closed Mar. **One Main St., (Rte. 41/44), Salisbury, 06068; (860) 435-9758.**

Greenwoods Market and Café—$$

If you are attending a Norfolk Chamber Music Festival concert, this is the place to go for boxed suppers (including a vegetarian selection). If you order by 5:00 P.M. on the Thu. preceding the performance, your dinner will be ready for pickup in the foyer of the Music Shed after 5:30 P.M. on concert night. You can also eat in, choosing from an extensive selection of prepared deli salads and hot entrées, soups, sandwiches, baked stuff and ice cream. There are always several vegetarian options. Summer hours: Mon.–Fri., 8:00 A.M.–7:00 P.M.; Sat., 8:00 A.M.–6:00 P.M.; Sun., 8:00 A.M.–3:00 P.M. Winter hours are shorter; call before going. **32 Greenwoods Rd. West, Norfolk, 06058; (860) 542-1551.**

Harvest Bakery—$$

A fairly new establishment, Harvest Bakery has already gained a reputation as the best bakery in these parts and a nice place for a sit-down lunch or dinner. A selection of fresh breads, together with salads, sandwich fillings and assorted yummies available by the pound for take-out would make wonderful picnic fare. At lunch, choose one of the prepared entrées in the display case, and it will be heated for you. The same goes for dinner, which features several specialty pizzas. Or, get stoked up with all-you-can-eat pancakes and French toast at Sun. brunch. Open Mon.–Sat., 9:00 A.M.–7:00 P.M.; Sun., 9:00 A.M.–3:00 P.M.; pizza available 4:00 P.M.–7:00 P.M. **10 Academy St., Salisbury, 06068; (860) 435-1302.**

Services

Local Visitors Information

Litchfield Hills Travel Council, P.O. Box 968, Litchfield, 06759; (860) 567-4506.

Transportation

Bonanza Bus Lines (800-556-3815) connects Cornwall Bridge, Falls Village and Canaan with Danbury and New York to the south and towns in western Massachusetts to the north. Bus service within the region is provided by the **Northwestern Connecticut Transit District.** For fare and schedule information call **(860) 489-2535.**

Kent

Most people come to Kent to do one of two things: browse art galleries or shop. The town's reputation as an art center began in 1923 with the founding of the Kent Art Association by a group of nine transplanted New York artists. The association now has its own gallery in town and mounts four shows annually, but the profusion of other galleries (there are currently eight, nearly all of them located on or just off the two-block-long section of Rte. 7 that forms Kent's main street) means that there is always an abundance of art on view. In the off-season (mid-Oct. to Apr. or May, with the exception of Dec.) most galleries are open weekends or by appointment only; at other times of year their hours are usually extended to include Fri. or other days.

26

The classic New England landmark—a Congregational church, Kent.

Kent is also known for its one-of-a-kind stores, all of them intimate in scale and unique in their wares. Each store has a definite personality. Folkcraft Instruments is notable for its extensive selection of dulcimers, drums and other acoustic instruments, as well as the largest selection you'll find in many miles of folk and traditional music on audiocassette and CD. Another treasure is The House of Books, the kind of place where you can pick a tome off the shelf, pull up a stool and lose yourself for a few hours; no one will bother you. Once you've decided on a purchase, take it over to the Stroble Baking Company and peruse it further while sampling an incredible cookie or pastry. Or, if you need a wake-up call, revitalize yourself with one of the Kent Coffee and Chocolate Company's remarkable brews of the caffeine kind.

Perhaps the best thing about the galleries and shops of Kent is how easily they can be combined with a back-to-nature experience. If you just want to show the kids some pretty scenery, take them 15 minutes up Rte. 7 to Kent Falls State Park, where even in summer there's always a fair bit of water cascading down a steep rock ledge and lots of open space for picnics. For solitude, however, you'll want to visit Macedonia Brook State Park, even closer to town but visited only by people who are serious about hiking. Streamside camping sites and mountain trails make Macedonia Brook a natural choice for an escape from civilization, whether for a few hours or a few days.

History

Kent was one of the original 14 towns into which Connecticut's Western Lands were divided. The first group of settlers, consisting of about ten families from elsewhere in Connecticut, arrived in 1738, and the town was incorporated in Oct. 1739. The original settlement was located about a mile north of the current center of town and was called Flanders; it is still easy to locate. A prominent historical marker giving a capsule history of Kent is located there on the east side of Rt. 7 where that

road converges with Cobble Rd. and Studio Hill Rd. This spot is also the location of Seven Hearths, a colonial-era home that currently serves as a museum.

There were Indians living in Kent when the settlers arrived. The Scatacook tribe was a small group that lived along the west bank of the Housatonic River in an area they called Schaghticoke. Today it is the site of one of Connecticut's five Indian reservations.

Throughout the Litchfield Hills iron production was a core industry from about 1750 on, and Kent was a center of this activity. The hulking ruins of Kent Furnace, just one of several that operated in the immediate area, can be seen on the grounds of the Sloane-Stanley Museum just north of the town center. Tobacco farming was also important to the economy of the region, although farmers took their chances having the crop fall prey to hail, insects and diseases by growing it in the open air, unlike the farmers of Tobacco Valley (the Connecticut River Valley), who now grow theirs under tents.

The arrival of the railroad in 1840 did two things. It put a stop to the oxcarts that daily passed through the covered bridge on the Poughkeepsie Turnpike (now Bulls Bridge Rd.) carrying loads of pig iron to the west, and it gave rise to the current center of town, which sprang up around the station, relegating Flanders to a picturesque spot on the road north. The closure of the last iron furnace in 1895 marked the end of Kent's industrial era. The town declined in population and fortune until its discovery by New York artists in the 1920s. Since then it has become one of the last outposts for weekenders up from the city, an exurb with a provincial town at its heart.

Major Attractions

Art Galleries

The type of art you'll see displayed in Kent depends on the gallery at which you see it. Art is a matter of personal taste, but some of my favorites are the Bachelier-Cardonsky Gallery (above The House of Books) and The Caboose, with the Paris-New York-Kent Gallery and Rose Gallery close behind. Luckily, you can see all the galleries in Kent in a day, with plenty of time for lunch and possibly some shopping. A map of all the galleries in town, complete with addresses and phone numbers, is available by mail. Send a self-addressed, stamped envelope to **Kent Chamber of Commerce, P.O. Box 124, Kent, 06757,** or call them at **(860) 927-1463.** You may also be able to get a copy from one of the galleries during their regular hours. The **Kent Art Association** (KAA) gallery is open to the public only when a show is hanging between May and

Morning sunlight filters through the mist at Bull's Bridge, Kent.

Oct. Shows generally run six weeks with two-week breaks in between. Hours then are Thu.–Sun., 1:00 P.M.–4:00 P.M. For information on the next KAA show call **(860) 927-3989.**

Bulls Bridge

This covered bridge is one of only two in Connecticut that are still open to vehicular traffic. Going south from Kent on Rte. 7, proceed to the light at Bulls Bridge Rd. and turn right. You'll come to the bridge almost immediately. Cross over and park in the turnoff provided on the other side, then come back to inspect the bridge on foot. It was recently rebuilt, so it is once again in excellent condition. Below yawns a gorge, and just upstream there is a dam and a tumble of pitted rocks over which water cascades all year round. Although the swirling water is most impressive during spring runoff, Aug. is perhaps the best time to visit. With the water level at its lowest, dramatic rock formations are exposed. A few feet farther down the road you'll find access to the Appalachian Trail on both sides of the street.

Kent Falls and Macedonia Brook State Parks

When Kent has satiated your desire for culture and your credit cards are exhausted, head for the undemanding territory of two of Connecticut's loveliest state parks: Kent Falls and Macedonia Brook. Kent Falls is a beautiful spot that can be easily explored in an hour but can also occupy you for an entire afternoon. Water cascades down a 200-foot drop in a series of small falls and pools. You can make your way to the top of Kent Falls via trails on either side. I recommend going up by the trail on the south side. Although it is the steeper of the two, rock stairs make it possible even for those in unsuitable shoes to make the climb, and there are numerous worthwhile overlooks right at water's edge. At the top you can cross the stream that feeds the falls and circle back to the parking lot via a trail on the other side. The park is a popular site for family picnics, so expect a crowd on summer weekends. It's located on Rt. 7, 10–15 minutes north of Kent town center by car. A parking fee of $5 per car is charged on weekends and holidays, Apr.–Dec. Open 8:00 A.M.–dusk; **(860) 927-3238.**

Macedonia Brook is an exceptionally beautiful park occupying 2,300 acres a short distance west of Kent off Rt. 341. Thirteen miles of blazed trails in good condition make for fantastic hiking, the highest attainable elevation being about 1,350 feet. The summit of Cobble Mountain affords views of the Taconic and Catskill Mountains in New York state. Macedonia Brook itself runs through the center of the park from north to south, forming some deep gorges and falls. A broad, grass-covered Conservation Corps road has a gentle incline that makes a great cross-country ski run in winter, as does the main park road. Free; open 8:00 A.M.–dusk. Located on **Macedonia Brook Rd. off Rte. 341 in Kent; (860) 927-3238.**

Sloane-Stanley Museum and Kent Furnace

Eric Sloane was a noted American landscape painter of the 20th century. During his life, he grew fascinated with the skills and lives of the early settlers and acquired quite a collection of mostly handmade tools and implements. He donated this collection to the state, and they are now housed in a museum donated by

Stanley Works, the famous tool manufacturer headquartered in New Britain. Fittingly, the museum is at the site of the Kent Furnace ruins. This remnant of Kent's iron industry is testament to the ingenuity the early settlers showed in fashioning the tools they required out of raw materials. On display in a separate area are several of Sloane's canvases and a mock-up of Sloane's studio housed in a cabin he built himself according to plans found in an early settler's diary. Admission: $3 adults, $1.50 seniors and children. Open Wed.–Sun., 10:00 A.M.–4:00 P.M., mid-May–Oct. Located on **Rt. 7 about a mile north of the center of town, Kent, 06757; (860) 927-3849** or **(860) 566-3005.**

Festivals and Events

EAWRC Championship Regatta
early to mid-May

The Eastern Association Women's Rowing Colleges league championship is the largest women's rowing regatta in the country, with participation from Ivy League and other schools. The top three contenders at this event go on to the NCAA finals. The date alternates between the second and the third weekend of the month, but the location is always the same: Lake Waramaug. The best view is from the finish line of the 1,950-meter course in Lake Waramaug State Park, where spectators set up lawn chairs or blankets, picnic and just hang out. Sat. is practice time, whereas Sun. morning (8:00 A.M.–11:00 A.M.) is devoted to heats and Sun. afternoon (1:00 P.M.–4:30 P.M.) to competition. For more information call **(860) 868-7207.**

Connecticut Antique Machinery Association Fall Festival
usually the last weekend in Sept.

This highly specialized event draws about 10,000 antique machinery buffs each year.

They come to see working farm equipment and demonstrations by craftspeople who keep the stuff running, gas and steam power exhibits, a tractor barn, full-scale railroad cars and the Association's museum, Cream Hill School, which is said to have been the first agricultural school in the nation. The Gothic building dating from 1845 was moved here from its original location in West Cornwall and now contains exhibits relating

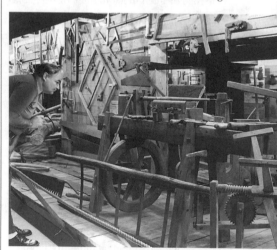

Examining a tool display at the Sloane-Stanley Museum, Kent. Photo courtesy Litchfield Hills Travel Council.

to agricultural education. The festival also features vendors selling antique machinery parts. Admission is charged. Hours: Sat.–Sun., 10:00 A.M.–4:00 P.M. Held at the Connecticut Antique Machinery Association's headquarters on **Rte. 7, 1 mile north of the center of Kent.** Look for the CAMA sandwich board out front. For more information call **(860) 868-0283.**

Outdoor Activities

Biking

Two of the best rides in Kent are along the west bank of the Housatonic River. River Rd., a quiet, dead-end dirt path, is the perfect place for a quiet nature appreciation ride rather than heart-pumping climbs and downhills. There is abundant wildlife in summer and ever-changing views of the river in winter when the trees are bare. For directions and more information see the listing under Birding.

The counterpart of River Rd. south of Rte. 341 is Schaghticoke Rd. This takes you behind a private school and past the small Schaghticoke Indian Reservation (please do not disturb the inhabitants). At the southern end of the road turn left to get to Bulls Bridge, cross Rte. 7 (there is an interesting antique store at this corner, usually open only on weekends) and continue to South Kent Rd. Turn left, ride to Rte. 341 and turn left again to return to the center of town.

Both of these rides are most suitable for mountain bikes, but because most of the Schaghticoke Rd. route is on paved roads, you could manage it on a touring bike. If you are driving into the area with your bike, park in the IGA supermarket lot just off Rte. 7 right in town. The market is a good place to stock up on beverages and food for the ride.

Birding

The northerly, riverside habitat of the upper Housatonic, bordered with tall, dense stands of evergreens, suits golden-winged and cerulean warblers that nest here in summer and migrate in spring and fall. Quite a few duck species—migrant, mallard, black, common merganser, hooded merganser, wood, blue- and green-winged teal—are also found here in Apr. and May, resting and feeding. To catch a glimpse of them, head to River Rd. You reach it via Skiff Mountain Rd. off Rte. 341 opposite Kent School. A mile or so down you come to a fork at a sign saying "Appalachian National Scenic Trail." The right fork—the one that continues riverside—is River Rd., and it's dirt from here on out. You can bike, hike or drive about 4 miles to a gate and parking area where the road ends. Drive slowly; the Appalachian Trail (AT) coincides with this road for about half its length, so there's a high probability of encountering hikers. The AT continues beyond the gate, but no cars, bikes or horses are allowed past that point. There is also a pullout labeled "Hiker Parking" at the point where the white-blazed AT meets the road.

Boating

The best place to get out on the water in Kent is **Lake Waramaug.** At 680 acres, the lake is quite large, but its serpentine shape keeps large portions of the shore hidden from view, so there's always a new vista around the next bend. Motors are allowed here, but there's only a car-top launch. Put in at the state park at the northwest corner of the lake. You are allowed to pull off to the side of the road along the picnic area or near the beach for as long as it takes to unload. Then park in the lot. See the listing under Swimming for more information, or call **(860) 868-2592.**

If you want something even smaller and more secluded, there is a car-top launch at **South Spectacle Lake** in Kent. There are signs at a pullout on Rte. 341 east of town. It's a short walk through the woods from the parking area to the lake.

Fishing

The **Housatonic River,** one of Connecticut's major trout streams, is stocked with browns, brooks and rainbows. You can access the western bank from points along River Rd. (see the

Birding section for directions) and at Bulls Bridge, where trails lead to spots above and below a small dam. For trout also try **Macedonia Brook** in the park of the same name described under Major Attractions.

The other option is **Lake Waramaug,** Kent's biggest and best body of water, shared with the towns of Washington and Warren. It's home to smallmouth bass, yellow perch, calico bass, bullheads, lake trout and rainbow trout. Leave your car in the state park lot (see the Boating section for more information) and fish from the picnic area along the shore or from your boat.

Hiking

See also the listings for Kent Falls and Macedonia Brook State Parks under Major Attractions.

Appalachian Trail
Nearly everyone has heard of the AT, that continuous footpath from Georgia to Maine, and although there is nothing that makes the AT qualitatively different from any other good hiking trail in Connecticut, it is fun to walk even a short part of it and imagine how far you could go if you wanted to. Easy access to the AT can be had from the parking area just west of Bulls Bridge on Bulls Bridge Rd. Another good access point is on River Rd. (described under Birding). Along this stretch of trail you'll see the remains of what look like old homesteads, and climbing up (rather than along the road) from the hiker parking pullout will bring you to some rocky outcroppings high above the river known as St. John's Ledges.

Iron Mountain Reservation
A nice loop trail through the woods that isn't too long or too mountainous, Iron Mountain Reservation can be negotiated by nearly everyone in reasonable health, but be aware that there is some climbing. The "iron" in its name is a reference to the mining and smelting industries that once fueled the region's economy. Iron Mountain Reservation is on Treasure Hill Rd. just south of Flat Rock Rd.

Swimming

One of the prettiest developed swimming areas in the state of Connecticut is at **Lake Waramaug State Park** on Lake Waramaug Rd. A shaded picnic area is adjacent to the beach, and the parking area and concession stand are just across the road. There may or may not be lifeguards, depending on availability that particular summer. Paddleboats are available for rental to visitors who would like to get out on the water rather than in it. The weekend and holiday parking fee Memorial Day–Labor Day is $5 for cars with Connecticut plates, $8 for out-of-state vehicles. Weekday and out-of-season parking is free. Hours: 8:00 A.M.–dusk. For more information call the park office at **(860) 868-2592.**

Seeing and Doing

Antiquing

Antique stores are scattered up and down Rte. 7 all the way from Brookfield (half an hour to the south) to the northern boundary of Kent, including a few right in Kent town center. Occasionally one of the stores will fund the publication of a map showing the location of several shops in and around town. Stop at Pauline's Place on the main strip or at any other antique shop that catches your eye and inquire. Many stores also carry *The Western Connecticut and Western Massachusetts Antiquer,* a free newspaper guide to antiques and where they can be found in this region.

Museums

Cream Hill School
This 19th-century agricultural boarding school housed in a Gothic building is now a museum on the grounds of the Connecticut Antique Machinery Association (CAMA). There are antique tractors and full-scale railroad cars on display in addition to exhibits on agricultural education. Hours: Sat.–Sun., 10:00 A.M.–4:00

P.M., Memorial Day–Labor Day. Admission is by donation. CAMA is located on Rte. 7, 1 mile north of the center of Kent. For more information, see the listing for the Association's Fall Festival under Festivals and Events or call **(860) 868-0283.**

Seven Hearths

This 1751–1754 era home is on the National Register of Historic Places. A tour of it provides a look at how some of the early settlers lived. Built by John Beebe, Jr., to house both his family and his general store, it represents three years of work by him, his father and brothers. On display are period furnishings and iron implements. Note the width of the wooden planks, floorboards and sheathing found throughout the house, testament to the size of the trees the settlers found here. Most of the paintings on the walls are the work of noted painter George Laurence Nelson, who resided here from 1919 until his death in 1978. Seven Hearths is also the headquarters for the Kent Historical Society. Donation requested; tours happen whenever people show up rather than on a strict schedule. Open Sat.–Sun., 2:00 P.M.–4:30 P.M., May–mid-Oct. & by appointment. **4 Studio Hill Rd., Kent, 06757; (860) 927-3419.**

Scenic Drives

Virtually any back road in Kent and Warren will provide you with scenic views, but if you want the certainty of a planned route request "Touring the Litchfield Hills by Car, Foot, Boat and Bike" from the **Litchfield Hills Travel Council, P.O. Box 968, Litchfield, 06759; (860) 567-4506.** This booklet gives maps, mileages and detailed itineraries for 19 half-day and full-day outings in the area, 7 of them driving tours. These tours are a great way to familiarize yourself with a wide area and pick out spots to explore more fully on a subsequent day.

Rte. 7 from Bulls Bridge to Kent Falls State Park is a state-designated scenic drive. In addition, I recommend the circle of roads around Lake Waramaug. If you just try to keep the water in view, you can't go wrong, and you can make a detour up to Hopkins Vineyard for a

wine tasting and a great view out over the lake. At lunch, try Hopkins Inn, The Boulders Inn, Doc's or Oliva. (For more on these restaurants and Hopkins Vineyard, see the **New Milford** chapter.)

The streets in South Kent, an area roughly bordered by Rte. 341, South Kent Rd., Bulls Bridge Rd., Camps Flat Rd. and Treasure Hill Rd., cut through forest as well as rolling farmland. There is a stunning view on Treasure Hill Rd. going south as you start to descend into New Milford. There really are no attractions or restaurants to stop at in this area, although on Treasure Hill you could get out for a hike at Iron Mountain Reservation. One final recommendation is the ride up and over Skiff Mountain on the road of the same name. If the views make you want to get out of your car for a while, the trails of Macedonia Brook State Park are nearby.

Shopping

The main drag of Kent has enough shops to keep you busy for a day, and they offer a wonderful selection of merchandise. If you are a die-hard shopper, you'll find even more stores in a cluster of buildings near Kent Green just north of the railroad tracks. On Sat. in summer a small farmer's market is held in the parking lot here.

If you want to shop in a truly quaint atmosphere, make a foray a few miles into neighboring New York state and visit **Webatuck Craft Village,** located in the tiny town of Wingdale. To get there, take Rte. 55 west from the center of Gaylordsville in New Milford about 5 miles and follow the signs. At Webatuck a cluster of refurbished houses and barns house an assortment of craftspeople including a potter and a glassblower, as well as Hunt Country Furniture, a traditional furnishings maker. A river runs through the "village," and a grassy bank makes a great spot for an impromptu picnic, although food is available streamside at The Buttonwood Café. The quality of merchandise is high, and if you arrive at the right time you might even be able to see some of it being made.

Where to Stay

Bed & Breakfasts

Chaucer House—$$$

The hosts of Chaucer House, Alan and Brenda Hodgson, hail from Canterbury, England, and named their B&B after the 14th-century poet Geoffrey Chaucer, who authored the classic *Canterbury Tales*. Despite the name, the decor of Chaucer House is thoroughly American. The Hodgson's 1940s-era colonial is set back from the road and surrounded by a spacious lawn. All four guest rooms have queen beds and private baths. Some baths actually adjoin the rooms for which they are reserved, and others are just a few steps down the central hall. The Hodgsons serve a full breakfast in the dining room and will prepare your preference from among a wide range of choices. **88 N. Main Street (Rte. 7, walking distance from Kent town center), Kent, 06757; (860) 927-4858.**

Constitution Oak Farm—$$$

A former dairy farm that has been in host Debbie Devaux's family since 1912, the Constitution Oak Farm is reasonably priced and very quiet. The guest quarters are completely private and located in the original part of the house, which dates from the late 1700s. The most desirable room is the former front parlor, which overlooks a small herb garden and has a private bath. Another room on the first floor also has a private bath; the two rudimentary upstairs rooms, outfitted with multiple (mostly twin) beds, share a bath. All the bedrooms share a small library, a larger sitting room and a dining room with a refrigerator where pastries and coffee are served in the morning. Cereals and other foods are available self-serve from a stocked pantry. **36 Beardsley Rd., Kent, 06757; (860) 354-6495.**

The Country Goose—$$$

Hosts Phyllis and George Dietrich have been welcoming guests for more than a decade to their 1740s center-hall colonial that sits estatelike on a gentle hill rising up from the road. Three main bedrooms on the second floor, each with a different theme, have double beds and are decorated with beautiful linens, quilts and gorgeous furniture. A fourth room, intended for couples traveling with a child, is furnished with a daybed and writing desk. There are two shared bathrooms. A Continental breakfast served in the dining room (originally the kitchen, it contains a working fireplace with beehive oven) features freshly baked treats. There is also a gazebo out back for enjoying the sunset and views of the mountains to the west. Closed Mar. 1–Apr. 10. **211 Kent-Cornwall Rd. (Rte. 7), Kent, 06757; (860) 927-4746.**

Gibbs House—$$$

Hosts Morette and Brian Orth operate their establishment in a picture-perfect 1790 colonial farmhouse that has been in Morette's family for some years. Two of their three rooms share a bath; the third, located on the top floor, has not only a private bath with step-up tub but a sitting room and small kitchen too. All rooms have a TV and a coffeemaker. A Continental breakfast is left by your door in the morning. **87 North Main St. (Rte. 7, walking distance from the center of town), Kent, 06757; (860) 927-1754.**

Mavis' Bed & Breakfast—$$$

The 1860 Greek Revival home of Don and Mavis Scholl is as quirky an example of this architectural style as you could hope to find. Three main rooms are reserved for guests, but only two are ever in use at the same time so as to allow each to have a private bath. A small studio room can sometimes be combined with one of the main rooms to accommodate parties of three. In addition, a "cottage" attached to the house but having a separate entrance has a private bath as well as cable TV and a telephone, and it is handicapped-accessible. Guests have the run of virtually the entire house, with both the living room and the den (with fireplace) serving as common areas. An expanded Continental breakfast is served in the dining room. **230 Kent-Cornwall Rd. (Rte. 7, about 2.5 miles north of town), Kent, 06757; (800) 600-4334 or (860) 927-4334.**

33

Hotels, Motels & Inns

Fife 'n Drum—$$$

The Fife 'n Drum is a pleasant surprise in the family-run motel genre. The furnishings are a couple notches above your standard-issue motel modular units. Each of the eight rooms has a bath with tub, and bed sizes range from twin all the way up to king. One room on the ground floor is handicapped-accessible. A 10% discount is given to customers paying by cash or traveler's check. The gift shop and restaurant on the premises don't generate enough noise to be a liability, and the whole complex is located at the top of Kent's shopping district. **53 N. Main St. (Rte. 7), Kent, 06757; (860) 927-3509.**

Resorts

Club Getaway—$$$$

This summer camp-style, self-described "sports resort" on 300 acres offers Fri.–Sun. package deals at an all-inclusive price (excluding beer, cocktails and sundries). Weekdays are reserved for children's camps, so Club Getaway is closed to the public Mon.–Thu. It provides accommodations in rustic cabins that sleep two or four (twin beds only), all meals and an array of recreational options. The camp has a private lake with a sandy beach and lifeguards, canoes and other watercraft, tennis and volleyball courts, hiking trails, artificial rock-climbing walls, all the equipment you might need for most of these activities, sports instruction available at no extra charge—even lectures on health and fitness. Certain weekends feature daytime and evening activities. It serves a buffet breakfast and lunch and a sit-down dinner. Call for rates and information about shuttle bus service from New York City. Located on **South Kent Rd. about one-quarter mile south of Rte. 341, Kent, 06757; (800) 643-8292** or **(860) 927-3664.**

Camping

Lake Waramaug State Park—$

This small state park consists of a 78-site campground and a beach. The sites are all grassy and shaded (although not especially private), with picnic tables and fire pits or grills, and the proximity of the beach makes it a great choice for visitors looking for a lake experience. There are showers, flush toilets and a dump station. Use of the beach is included in your camping fee. Located on West Shore Rd. at the northwest corner of the lake. Campground office: **(860) 868-0220.** Park office: **(860) 868-2592.**

Macedonia Brook State Park—$

There are 80 sites in Macedonia Brook State Park, but you'd hardly know it because they are so spread out. This is a more primitive campground than Lake Waramaug, with only pit toilets and water pumps—no showers. Some sites are wooded and private and some more open. See the listing under Major Attractions for more on what Macedonia Brook has to offer. Located on Macedonia Brook Rd. off Rte. 341 in Kent. Campground office: **(860) 927-4100.** Park office: **(860) 927-3238.**

Where to Eat

Bulls Bridge Inn—$$$

Located in a building that's been the site of some sort of business continuously since the early 1800s, Bulls Bridge Inn is a quiet establishment that serves only dinner and Sun. brunch. The atmosphere can best be described as tavernlike. The meat-and-potato cuisine is classic American, but there is also a salad bar featuring a selection of fresh breads and an assortment of salad fixings. A bar area with a fireplace kept roaring during winter is a warm denlike place to have a nightcap. Hours: Mon.–Thu., 5:00 P.M.–9:30 P.M.; Fri.–Sat., 5:00 P.M.–10:00 P.M.; Sun., noon–9:00 P.M. **333 Kent Rd. (Rte. 7 at Bulls Bridge Rd.), Kent, 06757; (860) 927-1617.**

Fife 'n Drum—$$$

At the top of Main Street in Kent is the Fife 'n Drum, a cozy restaurant that is best appreciated in winter when the staff keep a roaring fire going all day long. The barnlike interior, replete with weathered wood planking and

Eric Sloane prints on the walls, is not authentically old, but it is convincing, and skylights keep the atmosphere airy. The menu has creative treatments of classic American fare, most of it based on meat, fish or poultry. There are always daily specials worth trying, and two or three vegetarian items, mostly Mexican in flavor, are regular offerings. The dessert menu, like the main menu, features classics with a twist. Fife 'n Drum has won numerous *Wine Spectator* awards for its wine list. Open for lunch Mon. & Wed.–Sat., 11:30 A.M.–3:00 P.M. Dinner hours: Mon., Wed. & Thu., 5:30 P.M.–9:30 P.M.; Fri., 5:30 P.M.–10:00 P.M.; Sat., 5:30 P.M.–10:30 P.M.; Sun., 11:30 A.M.–9:00 P.M. with brunch served until 3:00 P.M. **53 N. Main St. (Rte. 7), Kent, 06757; (860) 927-3509.**

Michael's Restaurant on the Green— $$ to $$$

Michael's is a casual restaurant with a comprehensive Italian menu featuring many veal, chicken and fish dishes in addition to pasta, pizza, grinders and small portions for children. Although it's a small place with only about a dozen tables, strategically placed mirrors make it look more spacious, and the ambiance is pleasant. It can be smoky because of an adjacent pub where entertainment is offered on Fri. & Sat. nights, as well as on some Sun. & Mon. Hours: Sun.–Thu., 11:00 A.M.–10:00 P.M.; Fri.–Sat., 11:00 A.M.–11:00 P.M. Located in the main commercial plaza in Kent. From the intersection of Rtes. 7 and 341, go north on Rte. 7 (Main St.) past the railroad tracks. Look for the restaurant's sign on the right. Pay attention to the one-way entrance and exit lanes. **(860) 927-3774/3114.**

The Villager Restaurant—$ to $$

This busy breakfast-and-lunch establishment has a fairly expansive menu. The prices are low and the milkshakes are so large they're difficult to finish. In summer you can eat al fresco on the front patio. Hours: Mon.–Fri., 6:00 A.M.–4:00 P.M.; Sat., 7:00 A.M.–3:00 P.M.; Sun., 8:00 A.M.–2:00 P.M. **28 N. Main St. (Rte. 7), Kent, 06757; (860) 927-3945.**

Stosh's—$

Right where the railroad tracks cross Rte. 7 in Kent is the old train depot, which is now home to Stosh's, Kent's homegrown ice cream maker. The storefront is seasonal, opening Apr. 1 and closing by early Nov. It serves fast food in addition to frozen treats and is busy on summer weekends. Open 11:00 A.M.–10:00 P.M. daily during the summer months, closing at 6:00 P.M. early and late in the season; **(860) 927-4495.**

Services

Local Visitors Information

Litchfield Hills Travel Council, P.O. Box 968, Litchfield, 06759; (860) 567-4506.

Transportation

Bonanza Bus Lines (800-556-3815) connects Kent with Danbury and New York to the south and towns in western Massachusetts to the north. Bus service within the northwestern Connecticut region is provided by the **Northwestern Connecticut Transit District.** For fare and schedule information call **(860) 489-2535.**

Litchfield

Litchfield is often named as the quintessential 18th-century Connecticut town. Its hilltop green, beautifully maintained 1829 Congregational church and historic homes are a textbook example of the early settlers' way of ordering both the land and society. In 1959 Litchfield became the first Connecticut borough to be designated a state historic district. The town strives to retain its colonial flavor even while offering the modern amenities that urbane visitors expect and appreciate.

A visit to Litchfield must start at the town green. Expansive, cool and lovely in summer, the green is the site of occasional entertainment and a tranquil buffer between the bustling shops and restaurants that line its east side and the historic homes that parade up its west side. The tiny white kiosk right on the green is a visitors information booth where you can find out about the day's special events.

Two of Connecticut's finer historical museums are found in Litchfield: the Litchfield Historical Society Museum and the Tapping Reeve House and Law School, both in the center of town. The former gives a broad overview of Litchfield life through the centuries and showcases fine art and crafts. The latter is the site of the first law school in the nation, established by Tapping Reeve in 1782.

On a summer weekend, Litchfield is one of the most enjoyable shopping destinations in the state. Work your way from store to store along the green, and don't miss Cobble Court, a cobble-paved courtyard that you enter through a narrow alley. The Wilderness Shop, about a half-block below the green, is one of western Connecticut's biggest outdoor outfitters. More choices can be found along Rte. 202 west of town all the way to Bantam. When hunger strikes, you pretty much can't go wrong with any of the restaurants and delis in town, and at Barnidge & McEnroe, a bookstore/gift shop, you can even get a great cup of coffee and browse the best-seller list at the same time.

Attractions outside the town center include the Lourdes in Litchfield Shrine, a winery, a beach on the largest natural lake (Bantam Lake) in the state and miles of trails for hiking, biking and cross-country skiing at White Memorial Foundation, a massive preserve. So whether you prefer museums, shopping and dining or the natural beauty of the outdoors, Litchfield is a prime destination.

History

In 1720, when families from Hartford, Windsor, Wethersfield and Farmington arrived in the area and began constructing homes, Litchfield became the first town in the Northwest to be settled. During its first decade of existence it was a frontier community, and the settlers fortified some houses for protection against Indian attack. As the Western Lands further to the northwest were auctioned off and settled, many of the roads to them were built through Litchfield, so the town rose to a position of prominence and was designated the county seat in 1751.

During the Revolutionary War, Litchfield was staunchly Patriot in sympathy. One almost humorous tale from that period recounts how a lead statue of George III, taken from Bowling Green in New York, was secreted here and then melted down to make ammunition. Another Revolutionary War escapade, the taking of Fort Ticonderoga on Lake Champlain, was led by Col. Ethan Allen, who was born in Litchfield on January 10, 1738.

Immediately following the war, two important institutions were founded in Litchfield. The first was the Tapping Reeve Law School, the first in the fledgling nation to develop an organized and comprehensive law curriculum. Shortly thereafter Sarah Pierce founded a finishing school, which later came to be known as the Litchfield Female Academy and the Litchfield Female Seminary. It was regarded as the foremost school for young women in the state. Many Litchfield households drew income from boarding students of these two schools, and the presence of so many young

people in town gave rise to a vibrant local cultural life.

One student of Miss Pierce's School was Harriet Beecher Stowe, who later went on to write *Uncle Tom's Cabin*, one of the most influential American novels of the 19th century, in which she expressed the strong abolitionist sympathies that she had grown up with as the daughter of Lyman Beecher, minister of the Litchfield Congregational Church from 1810 to 1826.

The schools and an active local manufacturing scene made Litchfield the fourth-largest town in the state in 1820. But despite the presence of many mills, iron furnaces, a hatting industry, clock-making shops and other enterprises, Litchfield never developed the large-scale manufacturing that some other communities did. The railroad bypassed it, and the center of town remained untouched by factories. After a period of decline in the mid-1800s, interest in Litchfield was revived by the Colonial Revival movement. The local historical society was organized in 1856 and has been active in preservation ever since. A fire in 1886 and a repeat of that disaster only two years later wiped out most of the early commercial buildings on the green, but most of the homes on North and South Sts. (Rte. 63) survived, and there are still many pre-1800 structures to enjoy strolling past. The Litchfield of today is prosperous, picturesque and among the most worthwhile tourist destinations in the state.

Major Attractions

Litchfield Historical Society Museum

The museum's holdings document the history of northwestern Connecticut with a focus on the period 1780–1840—a "Golden Age" for Litchfield the town and the area as a whole, during which development moved at a swift pace. The museum is notable not only for the quantity and condition of the artifacts, which include fine furniture, paintings and period clothing, but also for the effectiveness of the displays and the background information that helps to put it all in context. Admission: $3. Open Apr.–mid-Nov. Hours: Tue.–Sat., 11:00 A.M.–5:00 P.M.; Sun., 1:00 P.M.–5:00 P.M. At the **corner of Rte. 63 and West St. on the green, Litchfield, 06759; (860) 567-4501.**

Lourdes in Litchfield Shrine

Modeled at least conceptually after the famous Grotto of Our Lady of Lourdes in France, Lourdes in Litchfield is a Roman Catholic shrine built in the 1950s by the Montfort Missionaries in order to make "the message of Lourdes come alive in New England." The shrine is actually several shrines—areas devoted to prayer and meditation—the main one built into a natural rock formation. There is also a steep, quarter-mile pathway lined with sculptures illustrating the Stations of the Cross. Even if you don't wish to engage in religious reflection, the shrine is a nice place for a short walk. Services are held on the grounds daily except Mon., early May–mid-Oct., but the grounds are open year-round during daylight hours. Call for a schedule of services. Located on **Rte. 118 less than a mile east of the center of Litchfield; (860) 567-8434.**

Tapping Reeve House and Law School

Although the premise of this museum might seem a little dry, in fact it is one of the more interesting historical sites in Connecticut. Established informally in 1782, this was the first law school in the United States. Reeve, the founder, lectured in his front parlor until after two years the size of the classes became unwieldy, and he had to build a schoolhouse to accommodate the burgeoning student body.

The first law school in the country was established at the Tapping Reeve House (now a museum), Litchfield.

Many of the men who graduated from Tapping Reeve, such as Vice Presidents Aaron Burr and John C. Calhoun, became principal figures in American political life. The exhibits tell the story of the everyday lives of the students and their accomplishments after graduation, explore social life in post-revolutionary Litchfield and explain Reeve's life and his impact on legal education in America. Admission charged. Hours: Tue.–Sat., 11:00 A.M.–5:00 P.M.; Sun., 1:00 P.M.–5:00 P.M., mid-May–mid-Oct. Located on **Rte. 63 South, Litchfield, 06759; (860) 567-4501.**

Topsmead State Forest

In contrast to the majority of Connecticut's state forests, which give the impression of wilderness, Topsmead is a former estate/working farm. The centerpiece is a Tudor-style house that is surrounded by broad swaths of lawn and garden in addition to acres of unspoiled woodland. Topsmead is an ideal place to hike, picnic or cross-country ski. The house is even open for tours on selected weekends. More information about each of these activities can be found below. To get to Topsmead from the center of Litchfield, take Rte. 118 east out of town to East Litchfield Rd. on your right. Turn and go to your first right, which will be Buell Rd. Turn again and go to the park entrance a short distance down on your right. The parking lot is up the driveway about two-tenths of a mile. Maps are usually available at a kiosk. Hours: 8:00 A.M.–dusk daily, year-round. For more information call **(860) 567-5694.**

White Flower Farm

White Flower Farm is a perennial nursery and specialty gardening retailer with a nationwide reputation. People visit not only to buy plants but also to view the demonstration garden beds, which are in bloom from late May into Oct. and showcase the plants White Flower Farm sells. The gift shop is stocked with books, decorative pots and gardening paraphernalia. Die-hard gardeners will love it. Hours: Mon.–Fri., 10:00 A.M.–5:00 P.M.; Sat. &

38

Sun. & holidays, 9:00 A.M.–5:30 P.M., mid-Apr.–mid-Dec. Located on **Rte. 63 (3.3 miles south of the town green), Litchfield, 06759; (860) 567-8789.**

White Memorial Foundation and Conservation Center

In the late 1800s the White family of New York, having made a fortune in beaver hats and wishing to escape urban unrest following the Civil War, built a spectacular mansion, known as Whitehall, west of Litchfield. In later years they accumulated thousands of acres of land in northwest Connecticut and then preserved it for public use along with an endowment to provide funds for maintenance. Thus was born the White Memorial Foundation, one of Connecticut's most revered natural areas, as well as many of the state parks and forests in this corner of the state.

White Memorial is used year-round for hiking, cross-country skiing, horseback riding, biking, birding, picnics, summer camps and more. There is a natural history museum on the grounds. Museum admission: $2 adults, $1 children 6–12; access to the grounds is free. Grounds hours: dawn–dusk daily. Museum/gift shop hours: Mon.–Sat., 9:00 A.M.–5:00 P.M., Sun., noon–4:00 P.M. Located on **Rte. 202 (approximately 2.5 miles west of the town green), Litchfield, 06759; (860) 567-0857.**

Festivals and Events

Borough Days is a new festival celebrating Litchfield held around the first Sun. in Sept. Call the **Litchfield Hills Travel Council (860-567-4506)** for details. Another event that's a favorite with locals is the **Morris Bluegrass Festival,** where amateur and professional musicians play all day for an appreciative crowd. It's held the second Sun. in Aug., noon–dusk, in Memorial Park at the intersection of Rtes. 61 and 109 in Morris. Call **(860) 567-4278** for details.

Getting There

Litchfield is located approximately 35 miles west of Hartford, but leave at least one hour for the trip since the majority of it is on two-lane highways. Take I-84 west out of Hartford. In Farmington take the Rte. 4 off-ramp and continue west through Unionville (at which point development falls off and things start to look very rural) and Burlington. In Harwinton pick up Rte. 118, which runs directly to the top of the Litchfield green.

A Taste of the Litchfield Hills
mid-June

This annual, two-day gustatory fest on the grounds of Haight Vineyard is an opportunity to sample some of the best food and drink the Litchfield Hills have to offer. Upward of a dozen of the area's finest restaurants have selections from their menus on hand for the tasting. There is entertainment and a small business expo. Tables and seating are provided. Admission is $5 for adults and kids over 12, and all food and beverage purchases are additional. For dates, times and directions, call **(800) 577-9463** (in Connecticut) or **(800) 567-4045** (out-of-state). Haight Vineyard is at **29 Chestnut Hill Rd. in Litchfield.**

Litchfield Jazz Fest
third weekend in Aug.

A new effort in 1996 on the part of Litchfield's local performing arts society, the Litchfield Jazz Fest promises to grow and prosper through the years. In its first year it drew 3,500 to listen to two days of traditional and progressive jazz music by eight performers, including headliner J. J. Johnson, Ahmad Jamal and the Diana Krall trio. The concerts take place on the grounds of the White Memorial Foundation, a 4,000-acre preserve just outside the village of Litchfield, running from around midday to dinnertime. About 1,200

39

seats are arranged under a large tent, but there's also lots of open space for blankets and lawn chairs. Attendees are invited to bring picnic food, beer and wine, but no hard liquor or pets. There's parking available adjacent to the concert site, and shuttle bus service to other lots. Daily ticket prices run $17 for lawn seating, $35 and up for tent seating; children under 6 admitted free. For a schedule or to order tickets call **Litchfield Performing Arts** at **(860) 567-4162.**

Holiday House Tour
mid-Dec.

This annual event draws about 1,500 people to Litchfield and surrounding towns to see the area's stateliest homes dressed to the nines for the holidays. You can tour the houses on a Sat. from 10:00 A.M. to 4:00 P.M. (ticket prices: $20 in advance, $25 on day of tour), or attend the $50 preview party, tour and auction the night before as part of a privileged group of only 200 visitors. Boutiques featuring the work of local artists are held either at the individual tour stops or at a separate location, and at each home area musicians enhance the atmosphere with performances of traditional seasonal music. For more information call **Litchfield Performing Arts** at **(860) 567-4162.**

Outdoor Activities

Biking

For gentle off-road rides, **White Memorial Foundation** (described under Major Attractions) is a good destination. Biking is allowed on wooded roads but not on hiking trails. Obtain a map at the gift shop during open hours or check the one posted just outside.

As far as touring goes, Litchfield is fairly hilly, so be prepared for some climbing wherever you go. The northwest part of town in the vicinity of Milton Rd. heading toward Goshen and Cornwall is especially pretty.

Birding

Bird species that tend to nest in or frequent open fields, such as bobolinks and meadowlarks, are drawn to the open terrain of **Topsmead State Forest,** described under Major Attractions. A good place to view them is around Jefferson Hill Rd., an abandoned town road that forms the principal northwest/southeast path through Topsmead. These species are mostly migratory, with the largest numbers present in early summer.

Boating

At 916 acres, **Bantam Lake** is Connecticut's largest natural lake and one of its loveliest, thanks to White Memorial Foundation, which owns nearly half the shoreline and protects it from development. No motors are allowed from 11:00 P.M. to 5:00 A.M., and waterskiing tow boats are prohibited within 150 feet of the shore. Follow the signs to the public boat launch on East Shore Rd. off Rte. 109 in the town of Morris.

Fishing

In **Bantam Lake** in Morris you can expect to find northern pike and smallmouth bass, as well as largemouth bass, white perch, yellow perch, sunfish and brown bullhead. You can launch a boat here or fish from anywhere outside the swimming area at Sandy Beach on East Shore Rd. off Rte. 109 in Morris.

Northfield Pond is another destination for largemouth bass. The pond is at the intersection of Knife Shop and Newton Rds. in the Northfield township of Litchfield. It's lovely but very small, so you're pretty much limited to fishing from shore.

Hiking

With 35 miles of trails, many of them across gentle terrain, **White Memorial Foundation** is a gem of a spot for hiking and jogging. Aside from the Foundation's own trails, you can also pick up the 8.5-mile-long southern portion of the blue-blazed Mattatuck Trail here. **Topsmead State Forest** is similar but on a smaller scale, and it also has a seven-tenths-mile nature trail through deep woods. Both of these hiking areas are described under Major Attractions.

Horseback Riding

Lee's Riding Stable offers walk/trot trail rides on a dedicated equestrian trail through fields and woods in Topsmead State Forest as well as indoor rink riding for rainy days. Tack and helmets are included in the rate ($22 per person per hour). Children must be age 5 or above to go on the trail. Pony rides are available for tots. Call ahead for directions and reservations. **57 E. Litchfield Rd., Litchfield, 06759; (860) 567-0785.**

Skiing

Cross-Country

There are no commercial cross-country ski areas in this region, so you have to come with your own equipment or rent. One excellent place to rent skis and snowshoes is the **Wilderness Shop** in Litchfield, which is just a short distance from the two unofficial ski areas listed below. The Wilderness Shop is located on **Rte. 202 near the foot of Litchfield green.** Call them at **(860) 567-5905** for hours and rates.

Topsmead State Forest

The Bernard H. Stairs Trail here is designated for cross-country ski use and blazed with a blue-and-white mark, but in fact all of the trails and open fields at Topsmead are appropriate for skiing when there is sufficient snow cover, so you could ski here all day before you'd see the same scenery twice. The trails are not groomed; cut your own tracks. Access is free. For directions, see the listing under Major Attractions.

White Memorial Foundation

All 35 miles of trails and acres of open land here are available for cross-country skiing when conditions allow. Trails are ungroomed, but admission is free. There are outhouses along the trails, and the museum is open daily. Inquire there about weekend programs or walks, which can be a nice way to break up a day of skiing. Museum hours in winter are Mon.–Fri., 8:30 A.M.–4:30 P.M.; Sat., 9:00 A.M.–4:30 P.M.; Sun., noon–4:00 P.M. The grounds are always open dawn–dusk. For more information, see the listing under Major Attractions.

Swimming

Part of White Memorial Foundation's Bantam Lake shoreline is devoted to **Sandy Beach,** which offers changing rooms, rest rooms, a water slide for kids and the security of a lifeguard. It's open Memorial Day–Labor Day, weekends only until late June but daily thereafter. Hours are 9:00 A.M.–7:00 P.M. There is a public boat launch at nearby Morris Town Beach, although that beach is not open to the public. Admission: $5 per car; $1 for hikers and bikers. Sandy Beach is a few miles down East Shore Rd. off Rte. 109 in Morris.

Seeing and Doing

Antiquing

Antique stores are scattered along Rte. 202 all the way from New Preston east to Litchfield. Traveling this road and stopping at any store that looks interesting would make a great day trip for anyone searching for vintage New England furniture and artifacts. One of my personal favorites is **The Old Carriage Shop,** a multidealer store located in a 19th-century carriage and sleigh factory in the center of Bantam. Over 20 dealers have stalls here, prices are great and it's fascinating walking from area to area to see the different dealer specialties. Hours: Wed.-Sun., 11:00 A.M.–5:00 P.M. **920 Bantam Rd. (Rte. 202), Bantam, 06750; (860) 567-3234.**

Art Galleries

Although Litchfield is not a major destination for art, there are a few galleries in and around town. Call the **New Arts Gallery (931**

Bantam Rd. [Rte. 202], Bantam, 06750; 860-567-4851) and **Bantam Fine Arts (352 Bantam Lake Rd. [Rte. 209], Bantam, 06750; 860-567-3337)** for current hours.

Museums and Historic Sites

For information on the area's major museums, see the listings under Major Attractions. The historical society of the small town of Morris also keeps a museum **(12 South St., Morris; 860-567-1102)** documenting the history and people of that community. It's open Sat. in summer, 1:00 P.M.–4:30 P.M. In Litchfield, be sure to visit or at least take a look at the **Litchfield Congregational Church,** said to be the most photographed church in Connecticut. From 1810 to 1826 the congregation was led by Lyman Beecher, father of abolitionist author Harriet Beecher Stowe and abolitionist minister Henry Ward Beecher. The elder Beecher's six sermons on intemperance, widely read and published in his time, were preached in Litchfield. A marker on the green with a bas-relief of Beecher and his wife Roxanna marks the spot of the meeting house where those sermons took place.

The interior of the present meeting house is noted for its old-fashioned high pulpit, but of even more interest is the fact that it is both the third and the fifth church to serve its congregation. How can it be both? It was built in 1829 and used for 50 years before the parishioners decided that because it was in need of major renovations, and because Gothic Revival churches were then all the rage, they would build a new church rather than refurbish the old one. So they moved the entire building off-site using oxen and built a new church that remained in use for the next 50 years. By then the Gothic church too was in need of repairs, but three townswomen made generous contributions toward restoration of the old church to the green and asked for matching gifts. The congregation complied. Little more than the shell of the original building remained after half a century of neglect, but the interior was meticulously re-created under the guidance of

Richard Henry Dana (architect of nearby Topsmead) and rededicated 100 years after the first service was given there. Visitors are invited to join the congregation for services Sun. mornings at 10:30 A.M. (9:30 in July & Aug.). You can also view the interior of the church whenever the front or side doors are open, generally from 9:00 A.M. to 5:00 P.M. weekdays. Weekend hours are catch as catch can. Located at the **corner of Rtes. 202 and 118 at the top of the green in Litchfield.**

Nightlife

To the extent that there is a nightlife in this corner of the world, it's to be found at restaurants and lounges that have live entertainment on weekends. A unique alternative is **Bantam Cinema (Rte. 209 south of Rte. 202, Bantam, 06750; 860-567-0006),** Connecticut's oldest continuously operating movie theater. Originally a mainstream theater, it went independent in 1990. They offer the best of the first-run movies as well as art flicks and foreign films you may not otherwise see on the marquee at the megaplex. They show only one movie at a time for only one or two weeks at a stretch and have occasional guest appearances by celebrities who give talks about film. There are evening performances nightly (two on Fri. and Sat. unless a film is over two hours long), as well as discounted Sun. and Wed. matinees.

Performing Arts

Litchfield owes its active cultural scene at least in part to **Litchfield Performing Arts,** a small organization dedicated to "service to the community through the arts." Their annual Command Performance Series consists of four to nine performances throughout the year. One month it might be a chamber music concert, the next time choral works, dance or a brass ensemble. The series draws the sort of world-class artists that you might also see at Lincoln Center, but in Litchfield you have the rare opportunity to enjoy their work in the intimate atmosphere of the historic Congregational church on the town green. For a current schedule and ticket prices call **(860) 567-4162.**

Scenic Drives

The **Litchfield Hills Travel Council (P.O. Box 968, Litchfield, 06759; 860-567-4506)** publishes a brochure of recommended driving tours that make a good starting point for trip planning. The Milton township of Litchfield, in the northwest part of town, is especially picturesque. Start off on Milton or Brush Hill Rds. heading toward Seeley Rd., which turns into College St. when you cross the town line into Cornwall. This puts you in the neighborhood of Mohawk State Forest, tens of miles of very quiet back roads and tiny communities defined by little more than a general store and an intersection.

The Northfield township of Litchfield is also very pretty, and Bantam Lake is exquisite, especially when its waters reflect the colors of autumn leaves. If you're not in the mood to plot your own course, here's a loop that will fill a few hours if you stop to enjoy the things you'll pass, but I do not recommend taking it unless you have a map. Starting at the green in Litchfield, go east on Rte. 118. If you'd like to visit the Haight Vineyard wine-tasting room, take a short detour down Chestnut Hill Rd. and then return to the main road. From Rte. 118, take a right on East Litchfield Rd. and another right on Buell Rd. This will take you past the entrance to Topsmead State Forest (described under Major Attractions). Go left on Marsh Rd. and take it a couple of miles to Campville Rd. on the right. Then turn right on Fenn Rd. and left on Newton Rd. Newton Rd. meets Knife Shop Rd. at tiny little Northfield Pond, which makes another nice stop to watch waterfowl and enjoy the sound of water trickling over a small dam. Getting back in your car, take a right on Knife Shop Rd. and cross over Rte. 254 onto Main St. Stay straight onto Goodwin Hill Rd., and then make a left on Moosehorn Rd., which ends at Rte. 109. Turn right, drive several miles to Rte. 209 and make another right. You'll be at the southern tip of Bantam Lake, which will come into view almost immediately. The drive up the western shore on a sunny fall day is breathtaking. Rte. 209 takes you into Bantam at Rte. 202. You'll find shops and restaurants in either direction, but you'll have to turn right eventually to return to the green in Litchfield.

Shopping

The green in Litchfield is lined with stores, and don't miss Cobble Court at the end of a narrow alley off West St. **Troy Brook Visions (860-567-2310),** a fine furniture maker, is housed there in an old blacksmith's shop. The **John Steele Bookshop (860-567-0748)** sells antiquarian and used books and is conveniently located on South St. immediately opposite a coffeehouse. One of the largest sporting goods retailers in northwest Connecticut, the **Wilderness Shop (860-567-5905),** is just a half-block below the green. More choices can be found at Litchfield Commons, a small cluster of shops about a half-mile south of the green on the east side of Rte. 202, and in the township of Bantam. Along Rte. 202 you'll find **Gilyard's (860-567-9885),** a clothing retailer specializing in functional sportswear, several great antique shops and much more.

Susan Wakeen Doll Co. (425 Bantam Rd. [Rte. 202], Litchfield, 06759; 860-567-0007), a maker of fine collectible and play dolls, is worth special mention. The company's showroom, with its coral pink trim and awnings, looks like a one-story wedding cake and is hard to miss even though it is set back from the road. Founder Susan Wakeen is the most-awarded baby doll designer in the country and has also received awards in many other categories of doll design. At the showroom you can see this year's crop of her elaborately dressed, limited edition collectible dolls, which are designed, made and assembled on-site. Open Mon.–Sat., 9:00 A.M.–5:00 P.M.; Sun., 10:00 A.M.–4:00 P.M.

Tours

At the information booth on the Litchfield green, you should be able to get a copy of a two-page, typewritten document describing historic sites in Litchfield. These are principally older homes that are all located within two blocks of the green. Only a handful of the buildings listed, such as the Historical Society Museum and the Tapping Reeve House, are open to the public, but it's a good excuse for getting out for a walk to see what Litchfield is most famous for: its well-preserved examples of colonial architecture and its classic New England green.

All too infrequent, but worthwhile, are tours of the Edith Morton Chase home at Topsmead State Forest. Chase was a brass company president's daughter. The house, completed in 1925, is built in English Tudor style. A wide range of high-quality materials, finely crafted, were used in the construction of the house, and the furnishings are English antiques. The house is surrounded by several small gardens that are enjoyable to walk through. Tours take place on the second and fourth full weekends of each month, June–Oct., between noon and 5:00 P.M. (except for the last Sun. of the year, when the house closes an hour early). For directions to Topsmead, see the listing under Major Attractions.

Wineries

Litchfield's only winery, **Haight Vineyard,** grows its own chardonnay, riesling and other grapes on hilltop fields east of town. Haight operates a tasting room at this location and a second one across the state in Mystic. **29 Chestnut Hill Rd., Litchfield, 06759; (860) 567-4045** (in Connecticut) or **(800) 577-9463** (out-of-state).

Where to Stay

Bed & Breakfasts

College Hill Farm—$$$ to $$$$
Set in the rural Milton section of Litchfield, this rustic, early-19th-century farmhouse on 20 acres is far from any source of noise or bustle, yet still convenient to the shopping of Litchfield and the rivers and mountains of the Northwest. Rooms have double and/or twin beds and share bathrooms. Three of the rooms have fireplaces for ambiance only. You'll enjoy a view of pasture, horses and gardens from your window, and you can get up from the breakfast table and walk right onto the Mattatuck Trail, which crosses owner Roberta Tyson's property. Closed mid-Nov.–May. **128 College St., Litchfield, 06759; (860) 672-6762.**

Tir'na nO'g Farm—$$$ to $$$$
Host Catherine Weeks's mid-18th-century house has been in her family for nearly four decades; she opened the B&B in 1996. Two attractive double rooms share a bath and a sitting room, or for a higher rate (subject to availability) you can have the guest quarters to yourself. Continental breakfast and midafternoon tea are included. Additionally, the only commercial heliport in Litchfield County is next door, so visitors who can make their own chopper arrangements can fly directly to the B&B; inquire about tie-down accommodation. **261 Newton Rd., Northfield, 06778; (860) 283-9612.**

Abel Darling—$$$
Abel Darling is the only place to stay in Litchfield that is within walking distance of the green. This small B&B, the first to open in Litchfield, is inviting and comfortable, and the rates are very reasonable. The setting is a 1782 colonial decorated with a charming mix of country and Victorian furnishings. Two rooms that share a bath are large and bright with exposed ceiling beams and hardwood floors. The third and smallest room has a private, detached bath. A Continental breakfast is included. **102 West St. (Rte. 202), Litchfield, 06759; (860) 567-0384.**

Country B&B—$$$
A recent endeavor on the part of hosts John and Dorothy Anderson, Country B&B has the ingredients for a very relaxing stay. You'll be the only guest in this private home on 11 acres backed up against state forest land. There is a private entrance via a wooden deck where breakfast is served in good weather. The room has a double bed and an unusual Japanese soaking tub. A Continental breakfast is included. Guests are also free to use the

Anderson's heated in-ground pool in season. **74 Marsh Rd., Litchfield, 06759; (860) 567-4056.**

Hotels, Motels & Inns

The Litchfield Inn—$$$ to $$$$

This modern hotel has a Georgian manor house façade that makes it appear as if you are a guest on a large historic estate. In fact, The Litchfield Inn was built in the early 1980s. The high ceilings and formal furnishings of its public areas make this a frequent setting for weddings. Standard rooms are spacious and traditionally decorated; all have two queen beds. For something a little different, try one of their eight tastefully decorated theme rooms, whose names—Sherlock Holmes, American West, Presidential Quarter—reflect these motifs. These theme rooms are priced considerably higher, but they also have VCRs and refrigerators; some have king beds. One standard room and one theme room have extrawide doors to accommodate wheelchairs, and an elevator allows access to any room on the second floor. There are also a couple of dining options on-site. Located on **Rte. 202 (1.5 miles west of the town green), Litchfield, 06759; (800) 499-3444 or (860) 567-4503.**

Toll Gate Hill Inn & Restaurant—$$$ to $$$$

This inn and restaurant complex comprises two historic and one new building. The Samuel Bull Tavern is a colonial (ca. 1745) structure, the age of the schoolhouse is indeterminate and the Samuel Bull House was built around 1990. Twenty guest rooms are spread out between the trio, with four of the five suites (large rooms with a distinct sitting area) in the new building. The suites all have a wood-burning fireplace and a sofa bed. In the tavern building, which also houses the restaurant, all the rooms have a double bed, and some have a fireplace. The rooms are furnished with reproduction colonial pieces that match the flavor of the older buildings. All rooms have a private bath, TV and telephone. A Continental breakfast is included, served either in the restaurant

or, for a tray charge, in your room. The corporate rates (without breakfast) available Sun.–Thu. represent a significant savings. **Rte. 202 and Tollgate Rd., Litchfield 06759; (860) 567-4545.**

Camping

White Memorial Foundation—$

WMF offers 65 camping sites with drinking water and pit toilets. Most of the sites are at Point Folly, a peninsula jutting into Bantam Lake, one of Connecticut's nicest recreational lakes. It is worth pointing out that motorboats are allowed on Bantam Lake, and you will almost undoubtedly hear them if you camp near the shore during a weekend. A smaller number of sites are located at Windmill Hill, a wooded area away from the shore. From your campsite you'll be able to explore all 4,000 acres of WMF.

The camping season runs early May–Columbus Day at Point Folly and Memorial Day–Labor Day at Windmill Hill. Reservations can be made by mail until Memorial Day and also in person thereafter—never by phone. To request an application and brochure, write to **WMF** at **P.O. Box 368, Litchfield, 06759.** To get to the campground store where you check in, take North Shore Rd. off Rte. 202 just west of the main entrance to WMF about 2.5 miles west of Litchfield town green. For more information, see the listing under Major Attractions.

Where to Eat

In case none of the options below quite fit, a couple of other choices are **Deer Island Gate (Rte. 209, Morris, 06763; 860-567-4622),** known for German specialties and seafood and their enclosed porch overlooking Bantam Lake; **DiFranco's (19 West St., Litchfield, 06759; 860-567-8872),** a casual, family-style pizzeria restaurant; **La Cupola (637 Bantam Rd. [Rte. 202], Bantam, 06759; 860-567-3326),** serving Northern Italian cuisine in a stunning granite house (ca. 1850);

and **Spinell's Litchfield Food Company (West St. on the green, Litchfield, 06759; 860-567-3113),** a bakery and gourmet deli where you can eat in or take out.

Toll Gate Hill Inn & Restaurant—$$$ to $$$$

The restaurant part of this inn complex is housed in an old tavern with all the atmosphere that would suggest. It's been called romantic, and the food is acclaimed. There are small dining areas on two floors with a third-story loft where live piano music is offered some Sat., as well as a terrace for warm weather. The seasonal American menu is on the small side but supplemented by daily specials, with a fairly even balance of fish, seafood, meat and fowl. In addition to lunch and brunch, they serve a fixed-price ($15) champagne brunch. The wine list is extensive. Reservations recommended. Lunch/brunch hours: noon–3:00 P.M. daily. Dinner served 5:30 P.M.– 9:30 P.M. (10:30 on Fri. & Sat.). In winter (Jan.–May approximately) the restaurant is closed all day Tue. & for lunch on Wed. Located on **Rte. 202 and Tollgate Rd., Litchfield; (860) 567-4545.**

Bantam Inn—$$$

If you're heading to the Bantam Cinema and you want a restaurant extremely convenient to the theater, try the Bantam Inn. They offer an American menu with an especially good selection of fish and meat entrées. In addition, there are daily specials and a children's menu. Lunch hours: Tue.–Fri., 11:30 A.M.–2:30 P.M. Dinner hours: Tue.–Thu., 5:00 P.M.–9:00 P.M.; Fri.–Sat., 5:00 P.M.–10:00 P.M.; Sun., noon–8:00 P.M. **810 Bantam Rd. (Rte. 202), Bantam, 06750; (860) 567-1770.**

Grappa—$$$

Grappa's wood-fired oven pizza has been getting rave reviews from food critics. The menu extends to full-blown entrées such as gnocchi, pastas, seafood and chicken. There is a full bar and a wide variety of seating options, including a canopied terrace during warm-weather months. Grappa is a family-oriented restaurant with low prices and food choices that can

be shared easily. Open for dinner only Tue.– Thu. & Sun., 5:00 P.M.–9:00 P.M.; Fri.–Sat. until 10:00 P.M. **Litchfield Commons, Rte. 202, 06759; (860) 567-1616.**

La Tienda Café—$$$

For over 15 years La Tienda has been one of the few places in the area to get good food with some bite to it. Most menu items come in a vegetarian version, and along with the customary spiced beef and chicken fillings for fajitas, burritos and the like, you can also get Andouille sausage. It recently began offering an all-you-can-eat buffet for $11.95 on Tue. & Wed. nights, and there is occasionally entertainment on Fri. & holidays. Hours: Mon.– Wed., 4:00 P.M.–9:00 P.M., Thu. & Sun., noon–9:00 P.M., Fri.–Sat., noon–10:00 P.M.; bar open later. Located at **Federal Square, Rte. 202, Litchfield, 06759; (860) 567-8778.**

The Litchfield Inn—$$$

The house restaurant of The Litchfield Inn is actually two restaurants. The informal Bistro East steak house serves lunch and dinner, has an adjacent bar and features live, low-key entertainment most Fri. and Sat., whereas the Joseph Harris dining room is appropriate for more formal occasions. The steak house is publike, woody and rather dimly lit with the exception of a small atrium where a few tables lie in bright little alcoves directly beneath skylights. The formal dining room (dinner only) is lit in the late afternoon and evening by a long line of windows and features a large fireplace whose soft light would make for a pleasing ambiance on a winter's eve. A recent change of chefs has been for the better, and the dining room now offers an American menu of grilled meats, fish and poultry. The pub has an excellent selection of beers. Kitchen hours (the pub is open later): lunch, 11:30 A.M.–3:00 P.M.; dinner, 5:30 P.M.–9:30 P.M.; Sun. brunch, 11:30 A.M.–2:30 P.M. Located on **Rte. 202 (1.5 miles west of the town green), Litchfield, 06759; (800) 499-3444** or **(860) 567-4503.**

West Street Grill—$$$

Both the atmosphere and the menu at Litchfield's trendy eatery are *au courant*. The decor is gleaming, warm and vibrant. The dinner menu is adventurous and quite small, presumably to allow the kitchen to focus on a more flavorful preparation of each dish. Luncheon options are more expansive: a number of pasta dishes, sandwiches, salads and soups. Prices seem reasonable in some cases and inflated in others, but West Street Grill has earned three stars from *The New York Times* and four stars from *Connecticut* magazine and *The Hartford Courant*, so you may well find it worth the chunkier tab. Lunch hours: Mon.–Fri., 11:30 A.M.–3:00 P.M.; Sat.–Sun., 11:30 A.M.–4:00 P.M. Dinner hours: Sun.–Thu., 5:30 P.M.–9:00 P.M.; Fri.–Sat., 5:30 P.M.–10:00 P.M. **43 West St. (on the green), Litchfield, 06759; (860) 567-3885.**

Aspen Garden—$$ to $$$

Aspen Garden is a casual restaurant where you're practically guaranteed to find something to satisfy every member of the family. It offers a little bit of everything—Greek, Italian, American—and the largest outdoor seating area of any restaurant in town. Hours: Sun.–Thu., 11:00 A.M.–9:00 P.M. (until 10:00 P.M. for pizza and grinders); Fri.–Sat., 11:00 A.M.–10:00 P.M. for all menu items. **51 West St. (on the green), Litchfield, 06759; (860) 567-9477.**

The Village Restaurant—$$ to $$$

Litchfield's "hometown" restaurant offers good food in a casual but attractive atmosphere. Seating is divided between comfortable, high-backed booths on one side and tables on the other. At lunch the pot pie of the day is a staple of the menu. You'll also find many sandwiches, each one just a little beyond the ordinary, plus pastas and meat-and-potato entrées. Sun. brunch is a fixed-price ($13.95), à la carte affair featuring hearty pancakes, omelets, sausages and such, served with coffee and mimosas. No beer or wine is served. Lunch hours: Mon.–Sat., 11:30 A.M.–3:30 P.M.; Sun. brunch, 11:30 A.M.–3:00 P.M. Dinner is served Sun.–Thu., 5:00 P.M.–9:00 P.M.; Fri.–Sat., 5:00 P.M.–10:00 P.M. **25 West St. (on the green), Litchfield, 06759; (860) 567-8307.**

Hattie's Family Restaurant—$$

A straightforward diner that serves breakfast and lunch seven days a week, Hattie's is a bright and comfortable place to spread out the morning paper while you wait for your eggs to arrive. Hours: Mon.–Sat., 6:00 A.M.–2:00 P.M.; Sun., 7:00 A.M.–noon. Located on **Rte. 202 (halfway between Bantam and Litchfield), Litchfield, 06759; (860) 567-3335.**

Coffeehouses, Sweets & Treats

Mocha Lissa Café—$$

Conveniently located right across from a great antique shop, this tiny eatery serves soup, sandwiches, desserts, ice cream and other frozen treats and coffees of all kinds in a little old house with country decor. Hours seem to be somewhat at the discretion of the proprietor, but are posted as Wed.–Sun., noon–6:00 P.M. Located on **Bantam Rd. (Rte. 202), Bantam, 06750; (860) 567-1559.**

The County Seat—$

A serious coffee bar whose threshold you should cross only if you're not on a diet, The County Seat is the kind of place where you know you've found your destiny—and your destiny is dessert. From pastries to ice cream, it's all irresistible. You could kill an entire afternoon here curled up in a voluminous couch, playing chess or making a dent in a used book from John Steele Bookshop across the road, and working your way slowly through the coffee list. **3 West St., Litchfield, 06759; (860) 567-8069.**

The Dutch Epicure—$

Almost every day a few customers come into The Dutch Epicure and strike up a conversation in Dutch or German with the store's owners, a European couple who have kept this little bit of the Continent in Litchfield for 30 years. It's the best-smelling shop in Connecticut. There are display cases filled with wonderful pastries, tarts and goodies, substantial breads, prepared foods and shelves of imported European foods and candies. You might

47

even find a pair of wooden clogs that fit. Hours: Wed.–Sat., 9:00 A.M.–5:00 P.M.; Sun., 9:00 A.M.–2:00 P.M. **491 Bantam Rd. (Rte. 202), Litchfield, 06759; (860) 567-5586.**

Services

Local Visitors Information

Litchfield Hills Travel Council, P.O. Box 968, Litchfield 06759; (860) 567-4506.

Visitors Information Center, Litchfield village green. Open 10:00 A.M.–4:30 P.M. daily, mid-June–Sept., and on weekends in early June and early Oct.

Transportation

Regional bus service throughout this corner of the state is provided by the **Northwestern Connecticut Transit District** at **(860) 489-2535.**

Torrington

For sheer ruggedness and remoteness, no other part of Connecticut quite equals this one. There are two large communities here—Torrington and Winsted—but north and east of them is a district of unyielding mountains that have resisted any kind of intensive development. It was in North Colebrook that the last stand of virgin forest in Connecticut stood before being logged in 1912, and recently the federal government designated the portion of the Farmington River from Goodwin Dam in Hartland downstream 14 miles to the New Hartford/Canton town line as a Wild and Scenic river, the only river in Connecticut and one of only four in New England to be so designated.

Fishing, canoeing, kayaking and tubing are all popular activities on the river, where one gorge whose rapids are for experts only goes by the rather ominous name Satan's Kingdom. The hiking terrain is also superb. In fact, about half of the dry land in the towns of Hartland and Barkhamsted is state forest cut with trails. Nearby Ski Sundown, a downhill ski area in New Hartford, puts steep slopes to perfect use during the winter months.

The tremendous natural beauty of the area is also easily enjoyed behind the wheel of a car on a long, slow drive. One possible destination is the tiny town of Riverton, where Connecticut's famed Hitchcock chairs were once made 150 years ago and a revived Hitchcock Chair Co. does business once again. If your interest in antique furnishings runs deep, don't miss the Hitchcock Museum, where one display shows how to tell a real Hitchcock chair from a copy. To cap off your day, whether spent in pursuit of a 5-pound bass or a new living room set, Torrington and Winsted are just big enough to offer some real choices for dining and entertainment as well as museums of their own.

History

Torrington and most of the towns around it were part of Connecticut's Western Lands that

were settled between 1730 and 1760. The rocky mountainsides were never really suitable for any sort of agriculture except dairy farming. The abundance of trees, however, did encourage timber harvesting and charcoal production early on. Beginning in the early 1800s the river valleys became manufacturing centers. Winsted, on the Mad River, was the site of iron forges, a scythe factory, tanneries and the Gilbert clock factory where timepieces were made from 1807 until well into the 20th century. In Torrington the Naugatuck River powered mills that made woolens, brass, mantle clocks, needles, ice skates and bicycles. Gail Borden, whose name is still on cans of evaporated and condensed milk sold in grocery stores, developed those products locally. A historical society museum adjacent to the Hotchkiss-Fyler House in Torrington documents the industries that contributed to the growth of the area.

In the early 20th century the local landscape began to take on the aspect it has today. Many mills closed, arresting or at least slowing urban development in the Mad and Naugatuck River Valleys. The American Legion and Peoples State Forests were established in 1927 and 1933. In order to guarantee a water supply for the growing Hartford metropolitan area, dams were constructed on both branches of the Farmington River in the 1930s, giving rise to the Barkhamsted, Colebrook, Goodwin and McDonough Reservoirs. Yet, even with these massive public works projects, this part of Connecticut remains among the least altered by human activity and the most suitable for a dose of therapeutic solitude.

Major Attractions

Riverton

The little town of Riverton is literally one block long, and its fortune has been inexorably tied up with something most of us don't give a second thought to: chairs. In the mid-1800s Lambert Hitchcock established a chair factory in a small town on the Farmington River. The chairs were such a hit that the town soon came to be known as Hitchcocksville. The typical Hitchcock chair was elaborately decorated with complex stenciling that required a high degree of skill to execute, and the chairs were prized for their beauty. Nonetheless, the business eventually failed and Hitchcock's factory on the banks of the Farmington River's west branch closed.

Almost a century later another entrepreneur of sorts, John Tarrant Kenney, saw the ruined factory while on a fishing trip in the area. Learning its story, he decided to reestablish the chair-making industry in Hitchcocks-

ville (by then renamed Riverton) in the original building. You can get the whole story at the Hitchcock Museum, housed in an old Episcopal church in Riverton. Today Hitchcock chairs are manufactured just down the road in New Hartford and assembled in Riverton, but not in the original factory on Rte. 20, which is now the Hitchcock Showroom **(860-379-4826).** If you're a furniture maker or in the market for some new pieces for your home (it's not just chairs any more), you'll find a day in Riverton pleasantly spent.

Festivals and Events

Laurel Festival
third weekend in June (Fri.–Sun.)

Connecticut's state flower, the mountain laurel (Kalmia latifolia), is honored in this three-day festival in Winchester. Many of the events, such as the Sat. night ball and Sun. afternoon parade, provide judging opportunities for contenders for the title of Laurel Queen. The local history museum has an open house, and there are suggested driving routes through the town to view mountain laurel in bloom. Schedules are distributed free through local stores. For more information call **(860) 379-9389.**

Hartland Folk Fest
late July

For about a decade this one-day annual folk festival in Hartland has continuous music from late morning until 9:00 P.M., as well as crafts and vendors for amusement. It's held at Berg Field on Rte. 20 in East Hartland. Ticket prices run $15 for adults in advance or $22 the day of the show; $5 for children age 6–12. Reduced price tickets are available for the over-65 crowd, day of show only. Call **(800) 843-8425** near the show date for more information.

Harwinton Fair
first full weekend in Oct.

Harwinton's fair is a real pleasure to attend, both for the events and for the bucolic setting

50

this small town provides. Come early, though, because they don't keep going after dark. Highlights include horse shows both mornings at 9:00 A.M. and the "Early Americana" exhibit, a building dedicated to demonstrations of traditional crafts such as weaving, wood carving and spinning. These plus all the usual livestock barns, contests, rides and food add up to a great family-oriented day. Admission: $5 adults, children 12 and under free. Hours: Sat.–Sun., 8:00 A.M.–dusk. Harwinton Fairground is on **Locust Rd. (follow signs from Rte. 4) in Harwinton.** For more information call **(860) 485-9066.**

Outdoor Activities

Biking

Mountain Biking

Nepaug State Forest

Mountain biking is permitted but restricted at this state forest described more fully under Hiking. Tipping Rock Trail, Shelter Four Trail and Overlook Trail are closed to mountain bikes. The yellow-blazed, multiple-use trail is the one you want. The best access point is off Rte. 202 immediately west of the Farmington River in Canton. Heading west on Rte. 202, take the first right you can and then bear left. You can bike the gravel road into the forest. For more information call the park office at **(860) 379-2469.**

Peoples State Forest

Mountain bikers may ride on Greenwoods Rd. and the snowmobile trail only. For directions, see the listing under Hiking. For more information call the park office at **(860) 379-2469.**

Road Biking

There are two things to remember about road riding in this area. First, the land from Torrington north to the Massachusetts line gets hillier and hillier as you climb into the Berkshire Mountains. Second, there are relatively few back roads here because there isn't

Getting There

Torrington is about an hour's drive due west of Hartford. Although the distance doesn't look great on a map, it does take a while to drive because you have to travel on small secondary highways. Take Rte. 44 west out of Hartford and stay on it. It merges with Rte. 202 in Avon and the two go straight to Torrington.

the population density to require them, so you really must spend a good bit of your time on main roads. The good news is that with the exception of Torrington, Winsted and Rte. 202 in general, even the main roads don't carry much traffic. The main roads also tend to follow the path of least resistance (i.e., the valleys).

One ride that deserves specific mention is the loop around Barkhamsted Reservoir. This is a long, demanding haul (perhaps 25 miles) with few opportunities for refreshment or rest rooms along the way, but if that doesn't intimidate you, it's a great ride. Don't expect to see the water, though. The view is completely blocked by trees and the road is actually quite a distance from the reservoir, but the forest scenery is very rewarding.

A good starting point is the convenience store/gas station at the intersection of Rtes. 318 and 181 in Pleasant Valley, where they won't begrudge you a parking space if you stock up on supplies there before your ride. You climb up as you head north on either side of the reservoir. To make a clockwise loop, head east on Rte. 318/181. Where they split a short way up the road, take Rte. 181. It merges into Rte. 20 after several miles, and this road takes you around the top of the reservoir. Turn on Rte. 179 when you come to it to start the downhill part of your ride. Take Rte. 219 when it curves off to your right, and turn right again on Rte. 318. This takes you over a dam and back into Pleasant Valley.

A second, much less demanding ride is a long, narrow, flat loop up one side of the west branch of the Farmington River and down the other. From the same starting point take Rte.

318/181 east again, but immediately after crossing the river, turn left onto East River Rd. Peoples State Forest rises up sharply to the east and slopes down to the river on the west. About 4 miles of riding will bring you into Riverton, where there are several diversions (see the listing under Major Attractions), a general store and a couple places to eat. West River Rd. effectively retraces your steps, but on the other side of the river, and brings you back out to Rte. 318 where you started.

Boating

In addition to these listings, visitors looking for a quiet spot for paddling or rowing should see the entries for Lake Winchester and Park Pond under Fishing.

Burr Pond State Park

This small and shallow but very picturesque lake is really most appropriate for canoes and small sailboats, although motors are allowed. The launch is on Burr Mountain Rd. just west of the park's main entrance, and parking is free. There is canoe and paddleboat rental in summer near the swimming area, but a fee is charged to park. For directions, see the listing under Swimming.

Colebrook River Lake

A reservoir above an Army Corps of Engineers dam, Colebrook River Lake is very deep and ideal for motorboating. There is a 20 m.p.h. speed limit, and water contact sports are not allowed. A concrete ramp is open dawn–dusk daily, year-round, at no charge. If water levels are very high the ramp may be closed, so call before going. The boat launch area is located on Rte. 8 about 5 miles north of Winsted and 200 yards south of Beech Hill Rd. For more information call **(860) 379-8234.**

Farmington River

For canoeing, there's nothing like a river, and in this area that means the upper Farmington. Releases from dams keep the river passable year-round, although you'll find nothing more challenging than Class II rapids, even in spring. The **Farmington River Watershed Association (FRWA)** publishes a map and

guide to all canoe access points on the river. You can get it for $5 by writing to the FRWA at **749 Hopmeadow St., Simsbury, 06070.** For the current water flow rate on the river call them at **(860) 658-4442.**

One good put-in spot is at the Riverton Fairgrounds on Rte. 20 across from the Hitchcock furniture store, although the parking lot can be crowded if there's an event going on. You can then take out at the area known as Church Pool (keep an eye out for anglers) where Rte. 318 crosses the river in Pleasant Valley. A downriver alternative is to take out at the Satan's Kingdom access area. Only experienced boaters should attempt anything below this point, where you'll encounter Class III rapids. The take-out point is on the west side of the river about 200 yards upriver of the Rte. 44 bridge. If you choose to run the Satan's Kingdom portion, take out either where the tubers do on the north side of the river near the junction of Rtes. 44 and 179 or way down in Collinsville on the east side of the river one-quarter mile north of the Rte. 179 bridge. Below this there's an impassable dam.

Highland Lake

This tall, narrow body of water on the outskirts of Winsted covers 444 acres. A fee is charged for launching a boat from the paved ramp in summer. To get to it from Winsted, go west on Rte. 263 (Boyd St.), then bear left on Lake St. At the end of the road turn right and follow the signs.

Fishing

You can learn more about Connecticut's fish hatcheries and fish-stocking programs with a visit to **Burlington Trout Hatchery** on Belden Rd. south of Rte. 4 in Burlington; **(860) 673-2340.** This is an older facility where you can get up close instead of viewing the operation through windows. Much of it is outside, so dress appropriately. Tours are given for groups of six or more with advance notice. Hours are 8:00 A.M.–4:30 P.M. daily, year-round.

Farmington River West Branch

This major trout stream is the most heavily stocked in the state. The Farmington River

Trout Management Area is the section from about 1 mile north of the Rte. 318 bridge south to the Rte. 219 bridge. In this area anglers are limited to catch-and-release (see the *Connecticut Angler's Guide* for regulations). The best access point is the parking lot in Pleasant Valley on the south side of Rte. 318 east of the river and directly opposite East River Rd. This spot is known as Church Pool. A handicapped ramp and platform built by the Metropolitan District Commission make fishing possible for those with impaired mobility.

For more suggestions pick up "A Guide to Fishing the Farmington River," a thick booklet put out by the Farmington River Angler's Association. You can find it at the Riverton General Store on Rte. 20 in the middle of town. A bargain at $10, it's the bible for fishing the Farmington. The general store is open from 6:00 A.M. to 8:00 P.M. daily, and it stocks fishing supplies.

Lakes and Ponds

Largemouth bass are plentiful in warm, shallow **Burr Pond**. Fishing is possible both from anywhere along the shore except the swimming area or from a small boat. This is also a popular spot for ice fishing in winter for perch and pickerel. For directions and more information, see the listing under Swimming.

An Army Corps of Engineers dam formed **Colebrook River Lake**, a deep reservoir with excellent fishing for trout, pike and both largemouth and smallmouth bass. In spring, fish from the boat launch area. In summer when the water level drops, old Rte. 8 is exposed and you can walk up the western perimeter of the reservoir to fish wherever a spot suits you. The boat launch area is located on Rte. 8 about 5 miles north of Winsted and 200 yards south of Beech Hill Rd. For more information call **(860) 379-8234**.

There's a good chance of reeling in some large trout at **Highland Lake**, a heavily stocked Trophy Trout lake where conditions are considered near ideal for that fish. Largemouth bass are also plentiful. You can fish from the boat launch area on West St. in Winchester, especially from the peninsula to one side, or from a boat. Highland Lake sees heavy

traffic, and a parking fee may be charged here in summer.

Like Highland Lake, **West Hill Pond** is a busy Trophy Trout lake. Access the boat launch at the northern end from Perkins Rd. off West Hill Rd. off Rte. 44 in Barkhamsted. There is minimal shoreline access, but a paved boat ramp for launching your own boat and boat rental from Pond Livery at the southern end of the lake. The livery is on West Hill Rd. in New Hartford, a different road from the one of the same name that leads to the boat launch. In summer there's a 7.5 HP limit and a 15 m.p.h. speed limit in effect.

Tree-lined, alpine **Lake McDonough** is one of the prettiest bodies of water in Connecticut. You can launch a boat from East Beach (10 m.p.h. speed limit; see the listing under Swimming for details) to fish for the brown, brook and rainbow trout with which it's stocked or the smallmouth bass that are naturally plentiful. The fee for parking and launching a boat is currently $8. Or, fish for free from shore by using one of a number of pullouts along Rte. 219 to park. There's also a free handicapped-access area with a ramp and a fishing pad on the same stretch of road, located about 2 miles south of East Beach. For more information call the **Metropolitan District Commission** at **(860) 379-0938**.

Shallow, warm and good for perch and sunfish, **Lake Winchester** offers more shore fishing access than many others. The water is deepest above the dam at the southern end, and from here you can walk north along either shore. The lake is rather quiet and suitable for canoes and other small craft. The boat launch is on West Rd. off Rte. 263 in Winchester.

Shore fishing for largemouth bass at shallow **Park Pond** is limited to the boat launch area on Blue St. in Winchester, but the low level of motorboat traffic makes it very suitable for a canoe, dinghy or small motorboat.

Handicapped Access

Metropolitan District Braille Trail

The Metropolitan District Commission, a water utility, has built a self-guided nature trail with guide ropes, wheelchair ramps and Braille signage on the west shore of Lake McDonough. Along the quarter-mile paved path are 30 stations where natural landmarks are identified and described. Hours: 8:00 A.M.–sunset, Apr.–Oct. The entrance is on Goose Green Rd. in Barkhamsted. For more information call **(860) 379-0938** or **(860) 379-0916**.

Hiking

John Muir Trail/Burr Pond State Park
The John Muir Trail is a blue-blazed trail of moderate length that connects developed Burr Pond State Park with undeveloped Sunnybrook State Park and Paugnut State Forest. Leave your car in the parking area at Sunnybrook State Park on Newfield Rd. about 3 miles north of Rte. 4 in Torrington. The trail starts on the east side of the road, climbing toward Walnut Mountain (elevation 1,390 feet), the summit of which is accessed via a side trail. The main trail continues roughly north for about 4 miles to connect with the loop trail around Burr Pond.

Nepaug State Forest/Tunxis Trail
This trail is actually a massive system of 19 interconnected trails in three sections that starts all the way down in Southington, halfway to Long Island Sound, and continues up into Massachusetts. They take you through mountainous woodland and to the summits of some 1,200-foot hills that afford good views. Pick up the Tunxis Trail from Rte. 44 north of Nepaug State Forest, Rte. 202 south of Nepaug State Forest, Rte. 219 between Rtes. 318 and 179, or Rte. 20 near the top of Barkhamsted Reservoir (east side). The first of those road crossings is in Satan's Kingdom State Recreation Area, where there is easy parking. If you hike south of Rte. 44 in Nepaug State Forest, it's possible to make loop trips on Shelter Four and Tipping Rock Trails. North of Rte. 44 there is just one trail, and you must either backtrack or drop off a vehicle in advance for the return trip.

Peoples State Forest
This forest got its name as a tribute to the ordinary citizens who contributed funds to acquire its nearly 3,000 acres in 1923. Perhaps the best-known spot in Peoples is Barkham-sted Lighthouse, which was never a lighthouse at all, and today is nothing more than a ruined foundation. One way to the lighthouse site is via Jessie Girard Trail, which starts on East River Rd. at a well-marked parking area. The trail climbs steeply. If after reaching the lighthouse you're prepared for more climbing, hike the 299 stone steps laid by the Civilian Conservation Corps (CCC). At the top you'll reconnect with the Jessie Girard Trail and be treated to a rewarding view.

Another great starting point in Peoples is the Stone Museum, located a short distance up Greenwoods Rd. off East River Rd. This 1930s structure is ruggedly beautiful and characteristic of CCC buildings of this period. It houses nature exhibits including taxidermy, pelts and bark samples, a historic diorama depicting the Barkhamsted Lighthouse, stories about the area and more. Special programs on Native Americans, the river and its fauna and other topics take place here throughout the summer. The museum is open Sun. in June, July & Aug. from 12:30 P.M. to 4:30 P.M., and Sat. in July & Aug. from 10:00 A.M. to 4:30 P.M. For a schedule of programs call **(860) 379-6118**.

Sessions Woods Wildlife Management Area
This wildlife management area has two trails for a total of just over 4 miles through woodland. Educational displays offer examples of resource management that you can practice on your own property, such as landscaping to attract and sustain wildlife. The main loop trail has a wide, even surface and goes past wetlands with detours to an observation tower and a waterfall. It meets a section of the blue-blazed Tunxis Trail on which you can hike for many miles. Bikes are allowed, but only on trails with a gravel surface. Grounds hours: dawn–dusk daily, year-round. Located on **Rte. 69 halfway between Rtes. 4 and 6 in Burlington; (860) 675-8130**.

In the Air

Tek Flight out of Winsted offers hang gliding instruction beginning at $85 per five-hour day as well as a "hang gliding experience" in which

54

you get to ride in a glider attached to a cable. The latter has a four-person minimum at $100 per person and is for folks not interested in becoming qualified pilots, because they focus on having fun, not inculcating good habits. Call **(860) 379-1668** for details.

River Tubing

As an alternative to canoeing, give river tubing a try. You ride down 2.5 miles of the Far-mington River over three sets of rapids and stretches of calm water. The start point is the **Farmington River Tubing** concession at Satan's Kingdom State Recreation Area. The ride takes from one and a half to three hours depending on the flow of the river. Signs tell you where to exit. Rates are $10 per person including tube, required life jacket and trans-portation back to the start point. To be allowed to tube, everyone in your party must know how to swim and must be at least 10 years old and a minimum of 4 feet 5 inches tall. Memorial Day–mid-June and Labor Day–end of Sept., the concession is open weekends only. Mid-June–Labor Day, it's open daily. Hours: 10:00 A.M.–5:00 P.M. Located on **Rte. 44 in Satan's Kingdom State Recreation Area on the New Hartford/Canton line; (860) 693-6465** dur-ing the open season or **(941) 695-3299** dur-ing off-season.

Skiing

Cross-Country

Maple Corner Farm Ski Touring Center just over the state line in Massachusetts is a ski touring center with a twist. They operate a sugarhouse on the property, so if you go on a weekend during sugaring season (Mar. and early Apr.) you can get a pancake breakfast with newly made maple syrup for a few extra dollars. They have 12 miles of groomed and 6 miles of ungroomed cross-country trails through 500 acres of pasture and hemlock for-est. Plan on spending about $17 per adult or $10 per child per weekend day for trail access, skis, boots and poles. Lessons are available, and there's a snack bar. To get to the ski area

from Connecticut, take Rte. 189 north from Granby over the state line to Granville center. Go west on Rte. 57 for 4.1 miles and turn right on North Ln. From that point, follow signs 6 miles to the ski area located at **794 Beech Hill Rd., Granville, MA 01034; (413) 357-6697.**

Downhill

Although it has the full range of trails from easy to difficult, **Ski Sundown (126 Ratlum Rd., New Hartford, 06057)** is an especially good ski area for beginners who are just on the verge of graduating to intermediate trails: 53% of the trails are classified as easy, 27% as intermediate and 20% as expert. With a maximum vertical drop of 625 feet, you've got as much elevation here as you'll find anywhere in Connecticut. There's a total of 15 trails, 14 of which are lit for night skiing. Three triples and one double lift get you to the top, and they have full snowmaking ability. Skiing is in three sessions; inquire for times and prices. Re-freshment is available in the lodge, which was just expanded to three times its original size. Ski Sundown also has a ski shop carrying soft goods, rental equipment and an extensive ar-ray of ski instruction options. Hours: Sun.–Thu., 9:00 A.M.–10:00 P.M.; Fri. & Sat., 9:00 A.M.–11:00 P.M. To get to the ski area, follow Rte. 219 north out of New Hartford about 2 miles and look for signs. Call **(860) 379-7669** for a recorded message with directions, hours and conditions or **(860) 379-9851** to reach an operator.

Snowmobiling

At **Peoples State Forest** there's a trail desig-nated for snowmobile use whenever there's 6 inches of snow cover. A straight section of trail leads to an extensive cluster of loops that could keep you busy most of the day. Park at Mathies Grove off East River Rd. in Bark-hamsted.

Swimming

Burr Pond State Park

Burr Pond is a pretty mountaintop swimming area with a sandy beach, canoe and paddleboat rental, a great picnic grove, fishing from shore or canoe and a boat launch. Lifeguards are generally on duty 10:00 A.M.–6:00 P.M. on weekends in May and daily June–Labor Day. Park hours: 8:00 A.M.–sunset. A parking fee of $5 for in-state vehicles and $8 for out-of-state vehicles is charged on weekends. Those rates go down to $4 and $5, respectively, on weekdays. Located on Burr Mountain Rd. 1 mile or so west of Winsted Rd. in Torrington. For more information call **(860) 482-1817.**

Lake McDonough

West Beach, Brown's Beach (also known as East Beach) and Goose Green Beach are three bathing and picnicking areas on Lake McDonough maintained by the Metropolitan District Commission (MDC), a water utility. The mountainous setting is exceptional. Brown's Beach is open daily from the third Sat. in Apr. until Labor Day. West Beach and Goose Green Beach are open Sat., Sun. & holidays. Hours: weekdays, 10:00 A.M.–8:00 P.M.; weekends, 8:00 A.M.–8:00 P.M. Lifeguards are on duty after 10:00 A.M. during summer only. Rowboat and paddleboat rentals are also available at Brown's Beach. There is a $4 per car parking fee, but seniors over 62 can apply for a Golden Eagle pass that gives free access to MDC properties. Call **(860) 278-7850, ext. 3209** for more on this program. Brown's Beach is off Rte. 219 just south of Rte. 318. West Beach is on Rte. 318 just west of Saville Dam, which holds back Barkhamsted Reservoir. Goose Green Beach is on Goose Green Rd. off Rte. 318 west of the dam. For more information call **(860) 379-3036.**

Seeing and Doing

Museums

In addition to the listings below, two smaller museums in the area are worthwhile. The **Colebrook Historical Society Museum (Rte. 183 in the center of Colebrook, 06021; 860-738-3142)** has excellent exhibits on local history and people, and the **Solomon Rockwell House (225 Prospect St. at Lake St., Winsted, 06098; 860-379-8433),** dubbed "Solomon's Temple" for its grand, almost southern appearance, is a Greek Revival house full of displays documenting Winsted and industries that thrived along the Mad River. Call for hours and season.

Hitchcock Museum

This museum is devoted to the life and work of Lambert Hitchcock, founder of the first incarnation of the Hitchcock Chair Co. Many of his mid-19th-century chairs are on display; they come from the private collection of John Tarrant Kenney, the man who restarted the Hitchcock Chair Co. in the 1950s. The old Episcopal church in which the museum is housed was actually built with substantial funding from Lambert Hitchcock. The bell in the belfry still works, and children are occasionally invited to ring it. The beautiful organ inside—one of the oldest in Connecticut—still works and sounds impressive. Admission is by donation. Hours: Thu.–Sun., noon–4:00 P.M., Apr.–Dec. Located on **Riverton Rd. half a block from Rte. 20 in Riverton; (860) 738-4950.**

Beautifully restored interiors such as this are part of the tour of the Hotchkiss-Fyler House, Torrington.

Hotchkiss-Fyler House

A largely undiscovered treasure, the Hotchkiss-Fyler House is a grand but not overly large Victorian house with wonderful examples of stenciling, murals, rich woodwork and intricate chandeliers. This 16-room mansion was built in 1900 as the home of Orsamus Fyler, one of Torrington's leading businessmen. The house is furnished with original Fyler family possessions. There are several collections on display, including art glass, porcelain and Fabergé spoons. A small museum adjacent to the house is used for changing exhibits on Torrington history. Admission: adults $2, children under 12 free. Hours: Mon.–Fri., 9:00 A.M.–4:00 P.M., & Sat., 10:00 A.M.–3:00 P.M., May–Oct. & from the second week of Dec. through the end of the month; closed major holidays. Guided tours begin as needed but start no later than 45 minutes before closing. **192 Main St., Torrington, 06790; (860) 482-8260.**

Performing Arts

A 1,700-seat movie house built in the 1930s, closed in 1981, then reopened in 1983, the Warner Theatre is currently the biggest stage in the area for musicals, concerts (mostly country and acoustic artists) and comedy. The season for musicals, performed by the non-Equity Warner Stage Company, runs Feb.–Nov. Every year near Christmas the Nutmeg Ballet stages a production of *The Nutcracker*. The affiliated 150-seat Studio Theatre across the street is the venue for dinner theater and a summer Dramafest.

The Warner, named for the studio that built it, was a so-called "preview theater," a venue where the big movie studios of the 1930s and 1940s gauged audience reaction to their new flicks before releasing them in major markets. It struggled to stay open after movie studios stopped managing theaters in the 1960s, and it is here today only because concerned citizens got involved. Half-hour tours are available by appointment Mon.–Fri. during box office hours, but you must schedule two weeks in advance. Box office hours: Mon.–Wed. &

Fri., 10:00 A.M.–5:00 P.M.; Thu., 10:00 A.M.–8:00 P.M.; Sat., 10:00 A.M.–2:00 P.M. **68 Main St., Torrington, 06790; (860) 489-7180.**

Scenic Drives

In the arc north of Torrington you hit the mother lode of scenic drives in the state. Rte. 202, where it hugs the southern perimeter of Nepaug State Forest between Bakersville and Rte. 179, is a state-designated scenic road. You may not encounter another car the whole way around Barkhamsted Reservoir on Rtes. 181, 20 and 179 but don't expect to see the reservoir—there is no overlook and vegetation blocks the view five months out of the year. My favorite drive in all of Connecticut is a brief couple of twisting miles of Rte. 219 along the eastern shore of Lake McDonough where occasional glimpses of the lake are tantalizing.

East and West River Rds. from Pleasant Valley to Riverton traverse the American Legion and Peoples State Forests, and from East River Rd. you can take a short detour up Greenwoods Rd. to the Stone Museum, worthwhile both for the beauty of its stone and wood construction and for its nature exhibits.

Finally, Hogsback and Colebrook Dams on West Branch Reservoir are spectacular edifices that are worth the effort to find. You may have to ask directions in Riverton or Colebrook because few maps show these dams or the roads leading to them. Still, there is an easy way to Hogsback Dam from the center of Riverton. Go north on Rte. 20 out of town, take your first left on Hogsback Rd., and go a couple of miles until you see what looks to be a prominent driveway on your left. This road crosses the apex of Hogsback Dam, where you'll find a large parking and viewing area. On drizzly mornings the mountains exhale mist, and Colebrook Dam, visible upriver, is monumental even at a distance.

Seasonal Favorites

Hogan's Cider Mill (Rte. 4 at Johnnycake Mtn. Rd., Burlington, 06013; 860-675-7320) is a picturesque farm market where they press cider late Sept.–Oct. and have a great selection of pumpkins in fall, plus a gift shop, pies, specialty foods and seasonal produce. Hours: 10:00 A.M.–5:00 P.M. daily, Christmas–Easter; 10:00 A.M.–6:00 P.M. daily the rest of the year.

In Feb. and Mar. head to family-run **LaMothe's Sugar House** to see the process of boiling down maple sap to make syrup, sugar and candies. The shop is open year-round. Hours: Mon.–Thu., noon–7:00 P.M.; Fri.–Sun., noon–5:00 P.M. Located behind the LaMothe family home at **89 Stone Rd., Burlington, 06013; (860) 675-5043.** Follow signs from Rte. 69.

Where to Stay

Bed & Breakfasts

B&B By the Lake—$$$
B&B By the Lake consists of four second-floor bedrooms arranged loft-style above a large, open living room in the cottage-style home of Gayle Holt and Anastasio Rossi, located right on West Hill Lake. The furnishings are very homey, and beds run the gamut from twin to queen. As a guest of the house, you have access to the community beach a short walk away as well as the small household dock at the foot of the driveway. A Continental breakfast with homemade baked goods is included. Open May–Oct. only. **19 Dillon Beach Rd., Barkhamsted, 06098; (860) 738-0230.**

Good for You B&B—$$$
This modern, ranch-style log house with two comfortable guest rooms, well off the main drag, is situated perfectly for guests who like long walks on quiet back roads. One room has a queen and the other a king bed. They share a bath with a tub and shower. Although theirs is not a historic home, hosts Normand and Melissa Bellerose have made sure it has its share of interesting points, including an Indonesian temple door that frames the entrance to the living room. They offer a substantial discount for single occupancy, which makes this B&B a

real bargain for solo travelers. Call for directions; their street isn't on most maps. **259 Mill St., Riverton, 06065; (800) 354-1005.**

The Rose & Thistle B&B—$$$
The surroundings at The Rose & Thistle are among the most magnificent of any B&B in the state. Set amid nine remote acres of mixed woodland practically a stone's throw from five state forests, this English Tudor-style house has two ground-floor rooms, one of which is outfitted with extrawide doors and wheelchair accessibility. Both rooms have private baths with tub and shower and branch off a great room with a massive stone fireplace. There is a deck, a garden, a pond for skating in winter and a grassy area for lawn games in summer. Call for directions—the road isn't on any map. Payment by cash or check only. The house is in Barkhamsted, but if you send mail, address it to **24 Woodland Acres, Collinsville, 06022; (860) 379-4744.**

Hotels, Motels & Inns

In the hotel and inn category, there are only a few options in this part of the world. The **Old Riverton Inn (Rte. 20 at East River Rd., Riverton, 06065; 800-EST-1796 or 860-379-8678)** has a gracious service-oriented staff, adequate accommodations, an excellent breakfast and a location convenient to the Hitchcock Showroom. If your activities will be taking you to downtown Torrington, consider the **Yankee Pedlar Inn (93 Main St., Torrington, 06790; 800-777-1891 or 860-489-9226).** Dating from 1891 it has an older look and feel amplified by stenciled Hitchcock furniture and bathrooms with old-fashioned fixtures. Both of these inns have a restaurant on the premises and prices in the $$$ to $$$$ range.

On the budget side you can't beat the local **Super 8 Motel (492 E. Main St., Torrington, 06790; 800-800-8000 or 860-496-0811).** It's clean, convenient, dependable and inexpensive ($$ to $$$), which is why it always fills up on summer weekends. Make a reservation at least a couple of weeks in advance.

Camping

Austin Hawes Camp Area/American Legion State Forest—$

On summer weekends you don't have a prayer of getting into this campground without advance reservations. Its 30 sites among pine trees are very popular because they are more than twice the size of most state campsites, allowing for as much privacy as you can expect to find at a public campground. Facilities include flush toilets, showers and a dump station. The campground is on the west side of West River Rd. in the town of Barkhamsted about 2 miles north of Pleasant Valley. Campground office: **(860) 379-0922.** Forest headquarters: **(860) 379-2469.**

Taylor Brook Campground/Burr Pond State Park—$

Although the campground is not actually in Burr Pond State Park, day use of all the park's facilities (usually $5 per car) is included in the camping fee. All 39 sites are nestled in deep woods on flat ground, and the campground is well off any main road, so you can really get away from it all here. Facilities include hot showers (some of them handicapped-accessible), flush toilets, phones and a dump station. Located on Mountain Rd. (not Burr Mountain Rd.) one-tenth of a mile west of Peck Rd. near the Winchester/Torrington town line. Campground office: **(860) 379-0172.** Park office: **(860) 482-1817.**

Where to Eat

Hilltop Inn—$$$

Hilltop Inn specializes in prime rib and rack of lamb at reasonable prices. Located in an old house with lots of history still evident in the decor, the restaurant has a leaded glass entryway, fireplaces (unfortunately not used) and old-fashioned radiators, which add to the casual, vaguely Victorian ambiance. Seating is at large round tables in one open dining room. A pub is located in the rear. Lunch hours: Tue.–Sat., 11:30 A.M.–2:30 P.M. Sun. brunch: noon–8:00 P.M. Dinner hours: Tue.–Sat., 5:00 P.M.–9:30 P.M. Located at **the intersection of Rtes. 183 and 202, Torrington, 06790; (860) 482-3326.**

Jessie's—$$$

Jessie's serves Italian food that occupies the middle ground between upscale and home-style, specializing in pastas and veal dishes with a children's menu to encourage family dining. It's located in a lovely old Victorian house that's been divvied up into several dining areas, some designated for smokers, some for nonsmokers and one for both. There's also a covered, glassed-in porch for year-round use as well as a brick patio for summer dining. A lounge upstairs has billiard tables and stays open later than the restaurant. Hours: Sun.–Mon. & Wed.–Thu., 4:00 P.M.–9:00 P.M.; Fri.–Sat. until 10:00 P.M. **142 Main St., Winsted, 06098; (860) 379-0109.**

Old Riverton Inn—$$$

The dining room of the Old Riverton Inn has a pleasant and authentic colonial atmosphere, with wideboard flooring and an exposed beam ceiling. There's one large main dining area that takes on the look and sound of a family reunion on a busy night. The food is American—seafood, steak, prime rib—and good. The inn's baked, stuffed pork chops are the closest thing to a specialty of the house. Old Riverton Inn is virtually the only dinner place in town, but thankfully it doesn't seem to be complacent. Reservations recommended. Lunch hours: Wed.–Sat., noon–2:30 P.M. Dinner hours: Wed.–Fri., 5:00 P.M.–8:30 P.M.; Sat., 5:00 P.M.–9:00 P.M.; Sun., noon–7:30 P.M. Located at **Rte. 20 at East River Rd., Riverton, 06065; (800) 378-1796** or **(860) 379-8678.**

Tributary—$$$

The winner of *Connecticut* magazine's readers' choice award for best seafood in Litchfield County for six years running is a comfortable, smoke-free place for either lunch or dinner. Seafood is indeed a specialty, but the menu includes many other American cuisine choices, a selection of lighter fare at lesser prices than full entrées and a small salad bar. The comfortable, somewhat dark interior has a rich, parlorlike atmosphere. A separate

59

lounge with a bar and some wooden booths has more of a pub feel. A solo pianist performs Fri. & Sat. nights after 6:00 P.M. Reservations recommended. Hours: Tue.–Thu. & Sun., 11:00 A.M.–8:30 P.M.; Fri.–Sat., until 9:30 P.M. **19 Rowley St. (in the small shopping center), Winsted, 06098; (860) 379-7679.**

Venetian Restaurant—$$$

The Venetian is a Torrington institution with a long-standing reputation for serving its very dedicated clientele. The kitchen is known for its homemade pastas and delicate sauces. Both salad dressings and sauces are available for purchase. Murals of Venetian scenes adorn the walls. Cream-colored leatherette booths make for fairly private seating in the front dining room, and a second room at the rear can accommodate larger parties at tables. Reservations recommended. Hours: Mon. & Wed.–Sat., noon–2:30 P.M. for lunch and 5:00 P.M.–10:00 P.M. for dinner; Sun., noon–9:00 P.M. **52 E. Main St., Torrington, 06790; (860) 489-8592.**

Yankee Pedlar Inn—$$$

Entering this restaurant through the subterranean Food and Grog pub makes you feel as if you're descending into a ship's hold. The menu features steaks, ribs, roasted chicken and broiled seafood. The lunch menu is sandwiches, soups, salads and burgers. If you like your pubs on the dark, old-fashioned side, you'll be comfortable here. A breakfast buffet is served 6:30 A.M.–10:00 A.M. on weekdays & 7:00 A.M.–11:00 A.M. on weekends. Lunch is served from 11:00 A.M. to 2:30 P.M. daily; dinner hours are 4:00 P.M.–9:00 P.M., Sun.–Thu., & 4:00 P.M.–10:00 P.M. on Fri. & Sat. **93 Main St., Torrington, 06790; (860) 489-9226.**

Cassille's—$$ to $$$

Cassille's is the perfect place to stop for lunch or dinner during or after a foliage drive through Burlington, which lies at the striking boundary of the northwest uplands and the Central Valley. The fare is Italian done well and family-style, with a wide selection of familiar entrées, pizzas and hot grinders. The portions are large, and not as compensation for quality. There are also always a couple of New England–type dinner specials, such as roast pork or corned beef, and the eggplant parmigiana is a personal favorite. Prices are reasonable. Although the restaurant is usually bustling, the service is fast, which keeps the crowd moving. Hours: Sun.–Wed., 11:00 A.M.–8:30 P.M.; Thu.–Sat., 11:00 A.M.–9:30 P.M. **232 Rte. 4, Burlington, 06013; (860) 673-4337.**

Catnip Mouse Tearoom—$$

Set in a charming old house on the main road of Riverton, this is the sort of place where you think of getting luncheon rather than lunch. It serves light fare such as sandwiches, quiche, soups and desserts and schedules teas periodically. Serving lunch(eon) only Tue.–Sat., 11:30 A.M.–2:00 P.M. **Rte. 20, Riverton, 06065; (860) 379-3745.**

Café de Olla—$ to $$$

A vibrant decor and the most colorful facade in town make this place pretty easy to find. Inside you'll find piñatas, sombreros and ristras all about. The eats are inexpensive if you order off the à la carte menu, but there are also full dinners that go for a bit more. The salsa is so good you might be tempted to eat it without chips. A wildly painted bar area with tiny café tables and chairs would be a neat place to hang out with friends. Lunch hours: Mon. & Thu.–Sat., 11:30 A.M.–3:00 P.M. Dinner hours: Mon., Wed., & Thu., 5:00 P.M.–9:00 P.M.; Fri.–Sat., 5:00 P.M.–10:00 P.M.; Sun., 3:00 P.M.–9:00 P.M. **578 Main St., Winsted, 06098; (860) 379-6552.**

McGrane's Restaurant—$ to $$$

An unabashedly family restaurant, McGrane's is an exercise in chrome, formica and leatherette. It serves everything from oatmeal to omelets, liver and onions to surf 'n' turf, and breakfast is available all day. Hours: Mon.–Fri., 5:00 A.M.–8:00 P.M.; Sat., 6:00 A.M.–9:00-ish; Sun., 7:00 A.M.–3:00 P.M. **19 Rowley St. (in the small shopping center), Winsted, 06098; (860) 379-0730.**

Skee's—$ to $$

This legendary diner is a must-visit for any diner aficionado. The interior details make it look like a converted train car, but I'm told it's a vintage diner, built for that purpose. The food is typical diner fare along with a smattering of Lebanese dishes ever since 1996 when the present chef and his Lebanese wife took over operations. The whole place can't hold more than maybe 15 people, so come here when you're feeling sociable. Hours: Tue.–Wed., 5:00 A.M.–3:00 P.M.; Thu.–Sat., 5:00 A.M.–8:00 P.M.; Sun., 6:00 A.M.–2:00 P.M. Located at the **intersection of Rte. 4 and Main St., Torrington, 06790; (860) 482-6819.**

Services

Local Visitors Information

Litchfield Hills Travel Council, P.O. Box 968, Litchfield, 06759; (860) 567-4506.

Transportation

Local bus service is provided by the **Northwestern Connecticut Transit District.** Call **(860) 489-2535** for schedule and fare information.

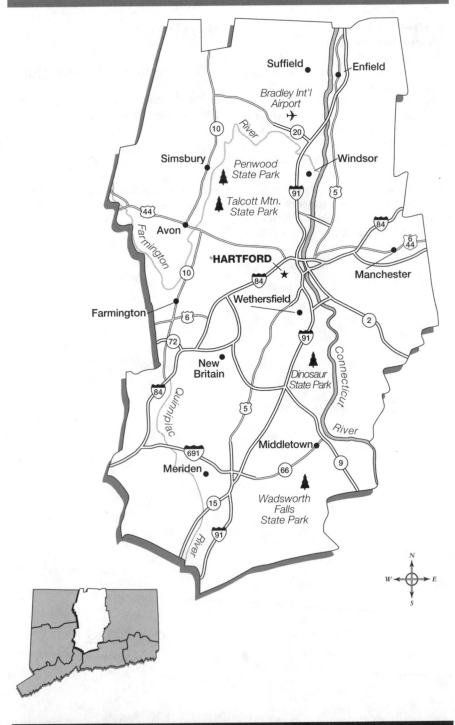

Central Valley

Central Valley

63

Farmington

The Farmington River runs through a small north-south valley contained entirely within the much larger Central Valley. Defined by the Metacomet Ridge to the east, where Heublein Tower atop Talcott Mountain catches the first rays of the sun each day, and the first folds of the Western Uplands on the opposite side, the valley is exceptionally pretty. Its low-lying areas have the rich soil found throughout the Central Valley, which made Farmington the first inland town to be settled west of the Connecticut River and one in which agriculture is still practiced.

The river itself is among the area's main attractions. As one of the most heavily stocked trout streams in the state, it draws many anglers throughout its length. Within the valley the river is almost exclusively flatwater, offering many opportunities for easy guided and self-guided canoe tours, but whitewater stretches also occur on both of the valley's mountainous edges.

There are several ways to enjoy a view of the valley, but the most spectacular is unquestionably from the Heublein Tower, which can be reached only on foot. Once up there, you can follow the crest of the Metacomet Ridge along the Metacomet Trail. If your taste or ability runs toward something a bit less strenuous, try a dawn or dusk hot-air balloon ride. Farmington is the ballooning capital of the state.

Although the valley's loveliness never inspired an Impressionist art colony the way Greenwich and Old Lyme did, the Hill-Stead Museum in Farmington is one of the foremost places in the state to see Impressionist art. Other major museums include Massacoh Plantation, documenting several centuries of Simsbury history, and the Stanley-Whitman House, a historic home noted for its post-medieval architecture.

The area is famous for the Antiques Weekends held at the Farmington Polo Grounds twice a year. As the biggest antiques events in the state, they pull in hundreds of exhibitors, and for year-round browsing there are a number of major multidealer stores in the valley. Sports and outdoor recreation are also big draws. The largest ice skating rink complex in Connecticut is located in Simsbury, biking and jogging are possible on the greenway being created from the former towpath of the Farmington Canal and Stratton Brook State Park offers pond swimming in an exceptionally beautiful environment. The valley is also a perfect starting point for excursions to other parts of the state. **Unique Auto Tours (P.O. Box 879, Canton, 06019; 860-693-0007)** can help you design a self-guided valley-based vacation itinerary that includes use of one of their vintage Rolls-Royces or Cadillacs.

With all of these things to do and see in the Farmington River Valley, it's easy to think of it just in terms of discrete attractions. Yet somehow the best thing about the area is quite indefinable. The valley always manages to be more than the sum of its parts, perhaps because of a unique beauty that simply has to be experienced to be understood.

History

The town of Farmington, first called Tunxis for the Indians who inhabited it, was colonized possibly as early as 1640 by families from Hartford. For about 15 years the two groups coexisted peaceably, with the Tunxis living on one side of the Farmington River and the settlers on the other, but the 1657 murder of a pregnant white woman by a Tunxis Indian compelled the tribe to take collective responsibility for the murderer, who had fled, and they were resettled farther west.

About the same time, families from Windsor began to move into Simsbury, which was at first called Massacoh Plantation after native Massacoh (pronounced Muh-SAH-ko) Indians. The razing of Simsbury in March 1676 was a major event in the brief colonist-Indian conflict known as King Philip's War. The year before, when the war had broken out, the concern for Simsbury was great enough that the

General Court ordered the settlers back to Windsor. So, when Wampanoag Indians burned about 40 buildings there was no loss of life, but just the loss in property made Simsbury the Connecticut town hardest hit during the war.

After about 1700 the Farmington Valley towns were no longer on the frontier, and things settled down. In 1705 copper was discovered in a part of Simsbury that is now East Granby. Samuel Higley mined the copper and in the 1730s minted from it coins that were among the first made in the colonies. Samples can be seen at the Massacoh Plantation museum in Simsbury.

The original town of Farmington was much larger than it is today, containing parts or all of at least a half-dozen other towns that would eventually be incorporated from it. In part because of its sheer acreage, by the time of the Revolutionary War it was the largest town in Hartford County, having surpassed even the county's namesake. Small industries were beginning to develop here and there, such as tinware, in what would become Berlin and Southington. The Farmington River was too slow moving through much of the valley to provide sufficient water power for mills (the Unionville part of Farmington is one exception), but where it spilled out of the Litchfield Hills in Canton and where it broke through the Metacomet Ridge at Tariffville on the edge of Simsbury the situation was different. The first American carpet factory was established at Tariffville in 1825. The following year Samuel Collins founded the Collins Axe Company in Canton, which would eventually become the biggest edge-tool manufacturer in the world. To house his workers, he built a factory town that came to be known as Collinsville. Both of these factory complexes still stand, having been converted to other uses, and in Canton the town celebrates an annual Samuel Collins Day.

One factor crucial to the success of Farmington Valley industry and agriculture from 1828 on was the construction of the Farmington Canal, which ran from New Haven to Northampton, Massachusetts. It brought a period of explosive growth to the valley be-

cause it finally gave all the Central Valley towns separated from the Connecticut River by the Metacomet Ridge a direct connection to a major port. The canal was short-lived, supplanted by a railroad in 1848. But it had given the area a 20-year head start in developing an industrial base and finding distribution for its products. Today the canal path is being converted into a greenway, some of which is already open for recreation.

Around 1840 Connecticut found gripping drama in the proceedings of a celebrated court case: that of the *Amistad* slaves (see p. xv). After their acquittal, the town of Farmington offered to care for the former captives while money was raised for their return to Africa. Housing was built, education provided and attempts were made to Christianize them. The whole episode seems to have awakened in Farmington an abolitionist fervor that manifested itself in bustling Underground Railroad activity for the next couple of decades. Farmington has been called the Grand Central Station of that figurative railroad in Connecticut.

Also in the 1840s a Farmington landmark came into existence when Miss Sarah Porter opened a celebrated preparatory school for young women. Theodate Pope, architect of the Hill-Stead House (now a museum in town) and Avon Old Farms, another private school nearby, was educated here. The institution is still in existence today and is still known by its prim, old-fashioned name: Miss Porter's School. In fact, many of the beautiful old houses lining Main St. in Farmington are school dormitories.

Today the Farmington Valley towns are highly desirable bedroom communities of Hartford, and quite a few acres of land are still devoted to agriculture. The largest pick-your-own farming operation in Connecticut is in Avon, and it doesn't take much looking to find tobacco barns in Simsbury still in use. Although the main roads through the valley are busy, sometimes even congested, as a whole the area has a verdant, romantic landscape that makes it a real pleasure to visit.

Major Attractions

Hill-Stead Museum

If you love art, architecture or great landscapes, a visit to the Hill-Stead Museum should be number one on your list of things to do in the Farmington area. Hill-Stead was the home of Alfred Atmore and Ada Brooks Pope, whose fortune was made in malleable iron. Originally from Cleveland, Ohio, the Popes sent their daughter Theodate to Farmington's noted Miss Porter's School. Theodate liked Connecticut so much she didn't want to leave even after graduation, so her parents moved to Farmington to be near her. Theodate was a talented architect who designed her parent's Colonial Revival house to be both pragmatic and elegant, incorporating such forward-thinking features as a bathroom for every bedroom and walk-in closets. She had her own house within view of Hill-Stead, whose name is a contraction of "homestead on a hill."

The Pope's collection of French Impressionist paintings by Degas, Monet, Manet, Cassatt and others make Hill-Stead a designated stop on the Connecticut Impressionist art trail. Outside, a sunken garden designed by acclaimed landscape gardener Beatrix Farrand and extensive grounds invite exploration. Stop by in Sept. for the one-day Hill-Stead Festival, with pony rides, arts and crafts and other activities. Admission: $6 adults, $5 students and seniors, $3 children 6–12. Hour-long tours given Tue.–Sun. every half hour from 11:00 A.M. to 3:00 P.M. (Nov.–Apr.) or 10:00 A.M.–4:00 P.M. (May–Oct.). The grounds are open for strolling during daylight hours. **35 Mountain Rd., Farmington, 06032; (860) 677-9064.**

Massacoh Plantation

Taking its name from the original name of Simsbury, Massacoh Plantation's uniqueness

Hill-Stead in Farmington is both an art museum and a historic home.

as a museum stems from the breadth of its properties and exhibits. Nine buildings here from different periods tell different stories about the area, its people and their industries. Two highlights are an exact replica of a 1670 meeting house and the 18th-century Captain Elisha Phelps House. All the other buildings take about an hour and a half to tour, so leave plenty of time for your visit and arrive as early as possible. The museum also presents occasional coffeehouse lectures with exceptional speakers exploring various facets of Connecticut history; request a schedule. Admission: $5 adults, $4 seniors, $2.50 children under 18. Hours: 1:00 P.M.–4:00 P.M. daily, May–Oct. Tours leave as needed, with the last one starting at 2:30. **800 Hopmeadow St. (Rte. 10), Simsbury, 06070; (860) 658-2500.**

Talcott Mountain State Park/Heublein Tower

The tower at the top of Talcott Mountain, a traprock ridge, is a Farmington Valley landmark, rising 165 feet above the ridge's 1,000-foot elevation. From its observation deck you have one of the most commanding views of countryside anywhere in Connecticut. On a clear day you can see into New Hampshire and to Long Island Sound. Closer at hand you can survey the Farmington River snaking below and several towns spread out in front of you. The tower was built by hotelier and restauranteur Gilbert F. Heublein as a summer home in 1914. Rooms of the house, which is attached to the tower, are being refurbished, refurnished and opened to the public on a regular basis.

When you visit, pack a picnic lunch to enjoy at one of the tables scattered around the tower, but also carry a spare bag to pack out your trash because garbage cans are not provided. If you care to hike more after reaching the tower, you can take the Metacomet Trail, which follows the Central Valley's spine of traprock ridges (collectively known as the Metacomet Ridge) north and south. You could hike up here for a couple of days without retracing your steps.

Getting There

Farmington is located about 15 minutes southwest of Hartford by car. Pick up I-84 westbound to exit 39 and take Rte. 4 west to the center of Farmington; then take Rte. 10 north to reach Avon and Simsbury. You can also take Rte. 44 directly from Hartford to Avon.

Tour hours are Thu.–Sun., 10:00 A.M.–5:00 P.M., mid-Apr.–Aug., as well as 10:00 A.M.–5:00 P.M. daily, Labor Day weekend–Oct. Park hours are 8:00 A.M.–sunset daily, year-round. To get to the tower, take the park entrance road off Rte. 185 near the Simsbury/Bloomfield town line. This ends a short way up at a turnaround/helipad where the trail starts. Park along the road and put on your walking shoes. On your way up the mountain don't be surprised if you encounter hang gliders getting ready to jump—Talcott Mountain is a favorite launch site. For more information between Apr. and Nov. call **(860) 677-0662.** At other times try **(860) 566-2305** or **(860) 424-1158.**

Festivals and Events

Early American Hearth Tours
winter

This ten-week series of Sat. events combining history, entertainment and food is a wonderfully social way to enjoy the area's rich resource of museums. You might even get to visit a museum that would not normally be open at this time of year. Each event typically includes a tour of or a special presentation at one of the area's historic properties, such as the Hill-Stead Museum or Massacoh Plantation, plus anything from a tea party to a full hearth-cooked meal that you help prepare from authentic colonial recipes. Program prices vary widely. For a schedule of the current season's tours call the **Farmington Valley Visitors Association at (800) 493-5266 or (860) 651-6950.**

67

Winter Carnival
first full weekend in Feb. (Fri.–Sun.)

Every year Simsbury's civic organizations sponsor a celebration of winter featuring horse-drawn sleigh rides, exhibition figure skating, a snow sculpture contest, cross-country skiing, family games, ice skating and apple pie judging. Most activities are free; some involve a small charge. Hours: Fri., 4:15 P.M.–9:30 P.M.; Sat., 8:00 A.M.–9:30 P.M.; Sun., noon–4:30 P.M. Held at the **Simsbury Farms** recreation complex on **Old Farms Rd. in W. Simsbury, 06092; (860) 658-6246.**

Farmington Polo Grounds Crafts Fairs
four times a year

The largest outdoor craft shows in Connecticut are held here on Mother's Day weekend (mid-May), Father's Day weekend (mid-June), a mid-July weekend and Columbus Day weekend (early Oct.). Admission: $5 adults, free to children 12 and under. Hours for all shows: Sat., 10:00 A.M.–6:00 P.M.; Sun., 10:00 A.M.–5:00 P.M. To get to the event from I-84 exit 39, take Rte. 4 west 2 miles to Town Farm Rd. in Farmington. Turn right and follow the signs. For more information call **(860) 871-7914.**

Riversplash
first Sat. in June

The Farmington River Watershed Association (FRWA) sponsors this free, one-day festival designed to encourage people to experience the Farmington River watershed firsthand. The event has two aspects: a central location on the river where there are food vendors, children's games, pontoon boat rides, canoe rentals and the like for the better part of the day; and a series of activities throughout the watershed, an area incorporating 10–15 towns. Because it's a celebration of the watershed and not just the river, activities can include mountain bike rides and hikes in addition to tours of dams, fish ladders and fish hatcheries. The central location is at Drake Hill Bridge in Simsbury. Park on Iron Horse Blvd. or in the lots directly off it behind the town's business district. Hours at the central location are 11:00 A.M.–4:00 P.M., but activities elsewhere can take place earlier and later. For more information call the **FRWA** at **(860) 658-4442.**

Farmington Antiques Weekend
second full weekend in June and Labor Day weekend

Twice each year the biggest antique markets in Connecticut take place at the Farmington Polo Grounds. Each show more than 600 exhibitors. The merchandise is exclusively antiques or vintage collectibles—no flea market stuff. If you want first crack at the goods, purchase an "Early Buyer" ticket for $20, which entitles you to admission on Sat. from 7:00 A.M. to 10:00 A.M. General admission ($5) begins at 10:00 A.M. and goes until 5:00 P.M. Your ticket is good for both days, and parking is free and right on the field. The Polo Grounds are on **Town Farm Rd. in Farmington.** For more information call **(508) 839-9735** or, during show weeks only, **(860) 677-7862.**

Farmington Horse Show & Chili Festival
last weekend in June (Fri.–Tue.)

This benefit for the University of Connecticut Health Center starts off with the Horsin' Around Dance on a Fri. night with dancing to a DJ, a buffet, a cash bar and a silent auction. Sat. 10:00 A.M.–4:00 P.M. is the Farmington Valley District chili cook-off, a competitive event sanctioned by the International Chili Society and accompanied by tastings, live music, horse show warm-ups and entertainment for the general public. The Class A horse show begins Sun. with the Budweiser Classic, 10:00 A.M.–5:00 P.M. Hunter and jumper events continue through Tue. Admission is charged for all events, which take place at the **Farmington Polo Grounds on Town Farm Rd. in Farmington.** For more information call **(860) 677-8427.**

Septemberfest
weekend after Labor Day (Fri.–Sun.)

Simsbury's community festival is a favorite among locals and draws lots of people from outside the area. With participation from many local restaurants, Septemberfest is partly a "Taste of …" type of event. There are also family games, hayrides, tethered balloon rides, entertainment and a business expo. Admission and parking are free. Septemberfest takes place off **Iron Horse Blvd. in Simsbury.** For more information call **(860) 651-7307.**

Samuel Collins Day
third Sat. in Sept.

This hometown festival is a reference to an important figure from Canton's past—the founder of the Collinsville Axe Co. that operated here from 1826 to 1956 and became the largest edge-tool maker in the world. The factory buildings still stand alongside the Farmington River, housing one of the biggest antiques stores in the state. During the festival there are things going on all over town, but the main event is a fair at the Canton Volunteer Fire Department field on Canton Spring Rd. You'll find a made-in-Canton booth featuring local products, arts and crafts, an invitational birdhouse silent auction, a stage with ongoing live entertainment, a children's game area and booths where you can sample food from local restaurants at low cost. Free walking, biking, artist studio and museum tours go on all day. Free shuttle buses run between the main site and Collinsville. Admission is free. The festival takes place rain or shine, 10:00 A.M.–5:00 P.M. (but you can get a pancake breakfast as early as 7:00). For more information call **(860) 693-7841.**

Simsbury Antiques Show
early Nov.

This selective show is a benefit for Massacoh Plantation, a local history museum. There are usually 80-plus dealers displaying furniture and collectibles. Hours: Sat., 10:00 A.M.–5:00 P.M.; Sun., 11:00 A.M.–4:00 P.M. Admission: $4. The location is the Henry James Jr. High School at **155 Firetown Rd. in Simsbury.** For more information call **(860) 658-2500.**

Opening Night
Sat. before or after Thanksgiving

Simsbury's Opening Night is similar to the First Night events that take place on New Year's Eve throughout Connecticut, but with a pre-Christmas theme. A four-block area of the town's main road, Hopmeadow St., is closed to auto traffic and becomes a big pedestrian mall. About 30 performing arts events, including music, theater, choral works and puppetry, go on throughout the evening. In addition, there are strolling clowns, jugglers and other entertainers on Hopmeadow and an outdoor tree lighting ceremony with Santa Claus, accompanied by caroling. Admission is by purchase of a button available in advance for $5 or, on the night of the event, for $7. Hours: 4:00 P.M.–10:00 P.M. For more information call **(860) 658-3255.**

Three Centuries by Candlelight
early Dec.

This holiday tour program takes place at Massacoh Plantation, where nine museum properties span 300 years of local history. Led through Massacoh by guides with lanterns, you'll be put through your paces in an old schoolhouse, have a Victorian Christmas encounter and see portrayals of early life in Simsbury. The tour takes one and a half hours. Tickets: $9 adults, $6 children. The event currently takes place on three successive nights. Tours leave every half hour, beginning at 6:30 P.M. on a Fri. & 5:30 P.M. on Sat. & Sun. The last tour leaves at 8:00 P.M. each night. Reservations required. **800 Hopmeadow St. (Rte. 10), Simsbury, 06070; (860) 658-2500.**

Outdoor Activities

Simsbury Farms Recreation Center is a large, town-owned sports complex with an

Central Valley

activity for every member of the family. It's simply the best place around for any recreational pursuit that requires facilities. In addition to what's listed under Golf, you'll find an outdoor pool, basketball and volleyball courts, a fitness trail, playing fields and a playground. Use of the picnic tables and playground is free. Fees vary with the activity; call for rates and specify if you are a nonresident. Grounds hours: dawn–dusk except for special activities. Located on **Old Farms Rd., W. Simsbury, 06092; (860) 658-3836.**

Biking

Mountain Biking

Stratton Brook State Park/Town Forest Bike Path

Because of the easy parking, Stratton Brook is the best access point for a bike path that passes through the park but also continues beyond its boundaries. The path surface in the park is finely crushed rock that is safe for road bikes. Other portions of the path are paved; some are on the rough side. Within the park the path is multiple-use and only suitable for low-key biking. Be prepared to share it with people in wheelchairs, pushing strollers or just strolling. To the west of the park the path continues to Stratton Brook Rd. For the next mile or two, it coincides with Town Forest Rd. before cutting away from the road again (a sign marks the spot) just beyond Town Forest Park and finally ending at W. Mountain Rd. just south of Rocklyn Ct. From Memorial Day to Labor Day you will have to pay a parking fee of $4 for cars with Connecticut plates and $5 for cars with out-of-state plates on weekdays, $5 and $8, respectively, on weekends. Alternatively you could leave your car in the Town Forest Park lot on Town Forest Rd. Hours: 8:00 A.M.–sunset. The park entrance is on Rte. 309 in Simsbury. For more information call **(860) 658-5593.**

Winding Trails Recreation Area

You can avoid the sticky issue of finding public land where mountain biking is allowed by coming to this private recreation area and paying

a small fee to ride on 12.5 miles of wooded trails that are used for cross-country skiing in winter. The setting is quite nice, and maps are provided that indicate the relative difficulty of each trail. They don't rent bikes or give lessons, however, so you must have all your own gear. Trail access is $5 adults, $3.50 children 15 and under. Between May 1 and Oct. 31, they're open daily 10:00 A.M.–7:00 P.M. **50 Winding Trails Dr., Farmington, 06032; (860) 678-9582.**

Rentals/Lessons

Best known for its guided canoe tours, **Huck Finn Adventures** also rents mountain bikes. From the rental site (call for directions) you can ride directly to a state forest with trails as well as a quiet neighborhood with pretty and paved but hilly back roads. The owner also gives about four classes a year covering introductory mountain biking techniques. **P.O. Box 137, Collinsville, 06022; (860) 693-0385.**

Road Biking

The **Farmington Canal Trail** is part of what will eventually be a greenway from New Haven to Springfield, Massachusetts. Portions of the trail were being completed and put into service as this was being written, so the situation might be different when you visit. By combining a portion of this trail with some of the area's quieter back roads, you can have a pleasant ride from the heart of Avon to the center of Simsbury. Pick up the trail in Avon in back of the school on Rte. 10 just north of Rte. 44. You may have to muck around a bit to find the trailhead. The trail currently ends at or near Deer Park Rd. a couple of miles to the north, where you should turn right and keep straight onto Rte. 185. After crossing the Farmington River, turn left onto East Weatogue Rd. At Riverside St. turn left and cross the Farmington River again on the bridge at Drake Hill Rd. Iron St. on the right will take you behind the commercial district of Simsbury to shops, restaurants, historic museums and lodgings. Iron St. ends at Rte. 10 about 2 miles north, and your best route back is the way you came. For information on the current status of the Farmington Canal Trail call the **Farmington Canal Rail-to-Trail Association** at **(203) 785-1482.**

Boating

Farmington River

The Farmington River in this area has two distinct characters. Portions are very slow moving and make good flatwater canoeing. However, the area known as Tariffville Gorge is quite treacherous because of elevation changes and blown-out dams and should only be negotiated on kayaks or rafts by experienced paddlers. If you're looking for a tranquil experience, make sure you stay on the right portion of the river! For information about tubing on the Farmington River, see the **Torrington** chapter.

The **Farmington River Watershed Association (FRWA)** publishes a map and guide to all canoe access points on the river as well as "An Interpretive Guide to the Farmington River," which covers its cultural history, geology and recreational resources. For ordering information, write to the FRWA at **749 Hopmeadow St., Simsbury, 06070.** For the current water flow rate on the river, call them at **(860) 658-4442.** They also offer organized canoe rides on the river four times a year, July–late Sept., and they can provide equipment.

If you plan to do some flatwater canoeing on your own, try putting in below Tariffville Gorge at Spoonville Bridge where Rte. 187 crosses the river on the Bloomfield/East Granby town line. You can take out above Rainbow Dam at the Rainbow Reservoir state boat launch on the north side of the river. There will be a charge for parking on summer weekends at the Rainbow Reservoir end. The launch is located off Merriman Rd. off Rainbow Rd. in Windsor.

Upriver of Tariffville Gorge, there are a couple of good options. Put in at the Pinchot Sycamore where Rte. 185 crosses the Farmington River in Simsbury and float north to the take-out spot at Curtiss Park. To park your car at Curtiss Park in advance, look for the gated road leading into the park on the northwest side of Rte. 315. There are also picnic tables and portable toilets here. This trip will take about two hours. For an even longer float, there's a good but nameless put-in spot in Farmington. From Rte. 10 head west on Rte. 4. As soon as you cross the river, turn left onto a dirt road leading to a large dirt parking lot. The ride to the Pinchot Sycamore will take about three and a half hours.

Now for the whitewater portion. Curtiss Park (described above) and Tariffville Park in Simsbury are two good put-in spots. Tariffville is the start of a Class III whitewater section. You soon hit a blown-out dam with a drop of 8–15 feet that is boatable on kayaks and rafts only and manageable under commonsense conditions. Take out at Spoonville Bridge, described above, or continue 5 miles downriver to the Rainbow Reservoir boat ramp, also described above. Tariffville Park is at the end of Main St. in Tariffville. Follow the small arrow sign on the right to the park entrance. Take the dirt road leading past the picnic pavilion. A good launch spot can be found at the turnaround at the very end of this road. The gates at both Curtiss and Tariffville are locked one hour after sunset, so plan your trip to be back before dark.

Rentals and Tours

Collinsville Canoe & Kayak

This outfitter both rents and sells canoes and sea kayaks. They're located right on the Farmington River in Collinsville, so you can put in right behind the store or take a canoe you're thinking of buying for a test paddle. Rentals range in price (subject to change) from $8 per day to $45 for a weekend, including life jackets, paddles and spray skirts for kayaks. They also rent all sorts of miscellaneous items, such as wet suits, and offer a full complement of group and individual lessons and guided trips. Rental canoes are for flatwater use only. Call for hours; they can vary widely but are usually 10:00 A.M.–5:00 P.M. daily; closed some Tue. **41 Bridge St. (Rte. 179 in the heart of Collinsville), 06022; (860) 693-6977.**

Huck Finn Adventures

You can rent canoes from John Kulick by the hour or day (he also provides a shuttle service

71

back to your starting point), but his real specialty is guided tours. He offers two basic options. The first is flatwater canoeing on a shallow section of the Farmington River in canoes that can seat up to four. As you pass landmarks like the Pinchot Sycamore and King Philip's Cave, he narrates the trip, giving historical background. Evening rides are available too. He also offers whitewater instruction in canoes and inflatable kayaks. Huck Finn operates spring through fall. Call for pricing and transportation details. **P.O. Box 137, Collinsville, 06022; (860) 693-0385.**

Fishing

Batterson Park Pond
In the middle of a municipal park on the Farmington/New Britain town line, a minute or two from I-84 exit 37, Batterson Park Pond gives the unusual combination of a fairly quiet fishing spot and easy access. Only rowboats more than 10 feet in length and equipped with oars, oarlocks and bailing can are allowed on the water. There's a public launch area on Alexander Rd. on the south side of the pond. Expect to pull in largemouth bass and panfish.

Farmington River
Although trout aren't the only fish you can catch here, the Farmington is more heavily stocked with browns, brooks and rainbows than any other river in Connecticut, attracting lots of anglers. Along Rte. 179 from Collinsville down to Unionville, there are numerous pullouts right by the river for direct access. One is located just north of the Rte. 4/179 intersection. Just a few yards south there's also a dirt road leading to a riverside parking lot. Or, heading southeast on Rte. 4, just before the railroad overpass in the River Glen section of Farmington, take a right into a small park with ball fields and paths that lead to the river. Farther down Rte. 4 there's a large access area just before the road crosses the river near the center of Farmington.

The river is slow moving by this point, and you're at the very bottom of the trout fishing area. Downstream from this point you're more

likely to catch rock bass, largemouth and smallmouth bass and white and yellow perch. If you'd like to go for any of those fish, you'll find another spot where you can get down to the river easily on the north side of Old Farms Rd. in Avon, and where Rte. 185 crosses the river at the Pinchot Sycamore in Simsbury there's more access. The river is still slow moving here with a shifting, sandy bottom. Your chances are best fishing from a boat at spots where brush dips into the water. Not too much further on, the river picks up speed as it heads for Tariffville Gorge.

To get outfitted for fly fishing on the Farmington, head to **Quiet Sports (100 Main St., Collinsville; 860-693-2214).** They sell equipment and offer instruction in fly fishing, fly casting and fly tieing. Inquire about their guided outings on the Farmington and Housatonic Rivers. Hours: Mon.–Wed. & Fri., 10:00 A.M.–6:00 P.M.; Thu., 10:00 A.M.–9:00 P.M.; Sat., 10:00 A.M.–5:00 P.M.

Golf

Simsbury Farms
Rated one of Connecticut's ten best municipal golf courses by *Connecticut* magazine, Simsbury Farms **(Old Farms Rd., W. Simsbury; 860-658-6246)** is noted for its mix of tough and easy holes that alternately challenge and give you a shot at a decent score. Fees are currently $22 weekdays, $26 weekends for 18 holes. Tee times are taken two days before your play date, beginning at 7:00 A.M. for residents and 10:00 A.M. for non-residents. A pro shop, snack bar, club and cart rental, group and private lessons and practice areas for driving, putting and chipping are all available. Season: Apr.–Nov. The course is part of a huge town recreation complex, so you'll also find showers, lockers, tennis courts and many other facilities at your disposal.

Hiking

For more information on hiking at **Talcott Mountain State Park,** see the listing under Major Attractions. Nearby **Penwood State**

Park is described in the **North Central** chapter, and a listing for **Roaring Brook Nature Center** can be found under Nature Centers.

Great Pond State Forest
This smallish tract of land contains several trails through impressive stands of pine and hemlock circling a marshy pond. The terrain is mostly flat and suitable for hikers of all abilities. The pond is home to a great deal of wildlife, such as beaver, kingfishers and herons. The mature pines, relics of a period beginning in the 1930s when Great Pond was a tree farm, create a cathedral-like setting for a unique outdoor chapel. Another holdover from tree farm days is a rhododendron grove, which you should visit in spring. Pinicking is permitted here at benches scattered throughout the forest, but you won't want to try lugging a cooler in, and you will have to pack out any waste. Hours: 8:00 A.M.–sunset daily, year-round. Located on **Great Pond Rd. in Simsbury.** Park office: **(860) 242-1158.**

Metacomet Trail
With a few small breaks, the blue-blazed Metacomet Trail runs for 51 miles, from Meriden to the Massachusetts state line. For the most part it follows the crest of the Metacomet Ridge, the only substantive break in the flat plain of the Central Valley, passing through Talcott Mountain State Park (described under Major Attractions) and by the tower there. Both the ridge and trail are named for Metacom, an Indian chief also known as King Philip, whose warriors burned Simsbury in 1676. Because of its elevation, the trail has numerous lookout points with views of the valley landscape below. The easiest place to access it locally is either at Talcott Mountain or in Penwood State Park across the street.

Stratton Brook State Park
The hiking trails at this park in Simsbury are not extensive (there's just one loop), but biking, swimming and picnicking are all allowed here, which makes it a nice destination for family groups whose different members have different interests. This is one of the most handicapped-accessible parks in Connecticut,

offering wheelchair ramps to the edge of a swimming pond, picnicking and a long, flat trail through the woods that can be negotiated by wheelchairs. For details, see the listings under Biking and Swimming.

Ice Skating

International Skating Center of Connecticut
Although it's known as a training facility for a number of famous athletes, the ISCC is also a fantastic recreational resource for the local community, especially since it's open year-round. It's got dual rinks, frequent public skating hours (call for a schedule), rental of both figure skates and hockey skates, lesson availability, occasional sticks-and-pucks times, a café and a pro shop. Admission to public skating sessions is $3 for Simsbury residents with picture ID, $6 for all others. Rental skates are $2.50. And if you haven't come across any of the Central Valley's famous tobacco barns yet, make sure to take a look at the ones near the entrance. **1375 Hopmeadow St., Simsbury, 06070; (860) 651-5400.**

Simsbury Farms
Weather permitting, there are Fri.–Sun. afternoon outdoor skating sessions at this town recreational complex. Admission is in the $5 range. Located on **Old Farms Rd., W. Simsbury, 06092.** For more information call **(860) 658-3836.**

In the Air

The Farmington area is the hub of hot-air ballooning in Connecticut. It started about 25 years ago when a local high school teacher got into it, and the sport caught on. Balloon pilots fly in the early morning (dawn) and late afternoon (about an hour before dusk) when conditions are most conducive to the activity. As tough as you might find it to get up at 4:00 A.M. for a balloon flight, mornings are best. Your trip will be highly weather-dependent. When you book a balloon flight, expect a call from the pilot immediately prior to the flight letting you know whether it's a go or not. As for how

73

to dress, layers are best. It can be cool at dawn but warmer by the time you've been in the balloon for an hour, so don't overdo it. There is no wind chill because you are traveling with the wind, and it's only a couple of degrees colder up there.

Pilots fly at elevations that vary according to conditions and customer preferences, but you can expect to spend most of your time about 500 feet above the ground. Reservations are always required for balloon flights, and you'll find that prices are quite consistent from operator to operator—usually around $175 per person. Your rapport with the pilot when you speak to him or her is as good a reason as any to go with one operator over another.

Airventures

Airventures is probably the largest balloon tour company in the state, operating out of several locations in central Connecticut. It has baskets that can accommodate from 2 to 20 passengers as well as a handicapped-accessible balloon that can accommodate up to four patrons in wheelchairs and four nonhandicapped passengers. It flies daily, year-round, weather permitting. Discovery flights group you with other parties, but charter flights are private. It designs custom charters and weeklong or two-weeklong excursions to balloon festivals where you can live and learn ballooning for a package price, including accommodations, food and transportation. If you need transportation from Bradley International Airport, train stations or local hotels, it can accommodate. **15 Hedgehog Ln., West Simsbury, 06092; (860) 651-4441** (in Connecticut) or **(800) 535-2473** (out-of-state).

KAT Balloons

Katherine and William Wadsworth can take up to four passengers on flights in and around the Farmington River Valley year-round, weather permitting. If you've ever wanted to learn how to pilot a balloon yourself, inquire about lessons, because they also offer instruction. Transportation from Farmington hotels can be provided. **40 Meadow Lane, Farmington, 06032; (860) 678-7921.**

Windriders

Extremely personable pilot Mike Bellea flies year-round, weather permitting, and can carry up to four passengers. **314 South Rd., Farmington, 06032; (860) 677-0647.**

Skiing

Cross-Country

Hill-Stead Museum

The parklike grounds here make excellent ungroomed terrain if you have all your own equipment. For directions, see the listing under Major Attractions.

Stratton Brook State Park/Town Forest Bike Path

A multiple-use path at this park for biking and hiking during the summer makes a perfect course for cross-country skiers in winter as long as enough snow has penetrated the hemlocks that shade it. The roads through the park also make good ungroomed terrain. Only the outermost part of the entrance road is kept plowed in winter, so you'll have to park just inside the ticket booth (there's no charge to enter in winter) and ski from there. Hours: 8:00 A.M.–sunset. Located on **Rte. 309 in Simsbury; (860) 658-5593.**

Winding Trails Recreation Area

If you need rentals and/or want groomed, blazed trails, this is the place. They have 12.5 miles of them, plus a lodge with minimal facilities but a big fireplace. Group and private lessons are available. If you're an experienced skier and up for a nighttime outing, inquire about their guided Moonlight Tours. Make sure to pick up a copy of the map, which shows the difficulty level of each trail and includes suggested routes for skiers of various abilities. Admission: $8 adults, $5 children. Hours: 9:00 A.M.–4:30 P.M. daily. Season: as conditions permit. **50 Winding Trails Dr., Farmington, 06032; (860) 678-9582.**

Swimming

The pair of ponds at **Stratton Brook State Park** are both artificial, but they look so pretty you wouldn't know it. They're shaded by exceptionally tall stands of pine and complemented by picnic tables, bathhouses and a delightful covered bridge. One of the ponds has a sandy beach with platforms and ramps for wheelchair access. A parking fee is charged in summer. Hours: 8:00 A.M.–sunset. Located on **Rte. 309 in Simsbury; (860) 658-5593.**

Seeing and Doing

Antiquing

The biggest concentration of antiques stores in the Farmington River Valley is in Collinsville, but other worthwhile stores are scattered throughout the region. The "Farmington Valley Visitors Guide" available from the **Farmington Valley Visitors Association (800-493-5266 or 860-651-6950)** lists many individual dealers in addition to those described below. Also see the Festivals and Events section for major antiques shows.

Antiques on the Farmington

The picturesque setting of this multidealer shop is irresistible. It's housed in an old red barn literally located on the bank of the Farmington River, next to a fabulous minigolf course and ice cream shop. Hours: 10:00 A.M.–5:00 P.M. (4:30 P.M. in winter) daily. **218 River Rd. (at Rte. 4), Unionville, 06085; (860) 673-9205.**

The Collinsville Antiques Company

The single biggest antiques store in the area has 15,000 square feet of display space on two floors filled with antiques of all kinds. It's located in an old red brick axe mill on the Farmington River. The sheer size of it is a little overwhelming, but this could be a one-stop shopper's dream. Once you're here, poke around town a bit. There are more shops across the street. Hours: Wed.–Mon., 10:00 A.M.–5:00 P.M.; closed Tue. Located on **Maple St. near Rte. 179, Collinsville, 06022; (860) 693-1011.**

Simsbury Antiques

This great store right in the commercial heart of Simsbury has about two dozen dealers

(soon to be expanding to over 60) with a large selection of good-quality furniture and decorative items for the home displayed in an artful way. Hours: 10:00 A.M.–6:00 P.M., closing at 8:00 P.M. on Thu. & 5:00 P.M. on Sun. **744 Hopmeadow St. (Rte. 10), Simsbury, 06070; (860) 651-4474.**

Crafts Centers

Farmington Crafts Common

About 200 craftspeople exhibit their work in this nice center a few minutes distant from the congested center of Farmington. You'll find everything from jewelry to unfinished furniture, plus Irish imports, a gourmet food shop, a Christmas room, a café and more. Hours: Tue.–Sat., 10:00 A.M.–5:30 P.M. (Thu. until 7:00 P.M.); Sun., 11:00 A.M.–5:00 P.M. **248 Main St., Farmington, 06032; (860) 674-9295.**

Farmington Valley Arts Center

What makes the Farmington Valley Arts Center special is the occasional opportunity to see artists at work in their studios. A gallery/shop in this converted safety-fuse factory exhibits the work of artists-in-residence as well as others from around the state and country. The center's annual Holiday Exhibit & Sale begins in early Nov., during which the gallery keeps expanded hours and has even more items on display than usual.

You never know whether you'll find any of the studios open for browsing on any given day, but it's worth taking a chance if you're in the area, and the gallery keeps regular hours. The center is trying to get an annual weekend-long open house off the ground. The first one was held in 1996 during the second weekend in Dec.; call for details. The center is a little hard to find because of a lack of signs. From Rte. 44 (the main road through Avon), take Ensign Dr., which passes between two stone walls that say Avon Town Office and Avon Park North on either side. Circle around to Arts Center Ln. and take a left. Park in a designated spot, and the center is right in front of you. Normal gallery hours: Wed.–Sat., 11:00 A.M.–5:00 P.M.; Sun., noon–4:00 P.M. Expanded Holiday Exhibit hours: Mon.–Sat., 10:00 A.M.–5:00 P.M. (Thu. until 8:00 P.M.); Sun, noon–5:00 P.M.

25 Arts Center Ln., Avon, 06001; (860) 678-1867.

Equestrian Events

1st Company Governor's Horse Guard

The oldest continuous cavalry unit in the United States began in 1778 as an escort for the governor during the Revolutionary War and as a military unit for the protection of Hartford, where they were then stationed. They are a state militia unit attached to the National Guard and can be called out to active duty at any time. Every Thu. beginning at 7:30 P.M., year-round, you can view a formation, tour their facilities and then watch horseback maneuvers performed outdoors in a lit field at no charge. The whole event lasts about two hours. In addition to the regularly scheduled drills, there are occasional special events on the grounds and horse shows in June and Oct. Enter the grounds from Arch Rd. in Avon. For more information call **(860) 673-3525.**

Museums and Historic Sites

Canton Historical Museum

One of the largest historical society museums in the state is located in a building that was originally part of the Collins Axe Co., the one-time largest edge-tool maker in the world. The museum boasts "one of the largest collections of Victoriana under one roof in the nation," containing costumes, jewelry, glassware, furniture, dolls, toys and more. Other highlights include a working-scale model railroad running around a set of Collinsville as it looked in the late 1800s, a display of tools that were made at the axe factory and sold internationally between 1826 and 1956, farm and domestic implements plus the contents of an early local general store as well as a barber ship, blacksmith shop and post office. Guided tour lasts one to one and a half hours. Admission: $3 adults, $2 seniors, $1 children 6–15. The museum is open Apr.–Nov., Wed.–Sun., 1:00 P.M.–4:00 P.M. (8:00 P.M. on Thu.). The remainder of the year it's open weekends only.

11 Front St., Collinsville, 06022; (860) 693-2793.

Day-Lewis Museum of Indian Artifacts

A major archaeological dig on a Native American trading site yielded the collection at this museum owned by Yale University and exhibited in a 1750 house. The collection includes spear points, arrowheads, knives and other tools representing 10,000 years of Native American occupation. Admission: $2 adults, $1 students. Hours: Wed., 2:00 P.M.–4:00 P.M., Mar.–Nov., and by appointment. **158 Main St., Farmington, 06032; (860) 678-1645.**

Living Museum of Avon/Pine Grove Schoolhouse

These are two one-room museums maintained by the Avon Historical Society. The small but very accessible collection of artifacts at the **Living Museum (8 E. Main St., Avon [but enter from Rte. 10])** makes a good introduction to area life 150–200 years ago, with a focus on the Farmington Canal. **Pine Grove Schoolhouse (W. Avon Rd. [Rte. 167] near Harris Rd., Avon)** served eight grades of children simultaneously in one room from 1865 until 1949 and still boasts its original post–Civil War desks and ca. 1925 textbooks. They have seasonal events for children such as a party with a spelling bee and games in early June, and scarecrows and apple bobbing in fall. Admission to both museums is free. Hours: Sun., 2:00 P.M.–4:00 P.M., May–Oct. For more information on either call **(860) 678-7621.**

Mende *Amistad* Sites

For nine months Farmington was the home of a group of Africans who were saved from slavery in the celebrated 1840s court case that was the basis for Steven Spielberg's 1997 film *Amistad.* They lived in the area while funds were raised to pay their passage back to Africa. A fuller account of their story is given in the **New Haven** chapter. Farmington sites integral to the story are described in the "Connecticut Freedom Trail" brochure available at most visitors information centers or by calling **(860) 572-5338. The Farmington Historical**

Society, at **(860) 678-1645,** also gives one-hour walking or driving tours of these sites. The fee is $2 per person with a $20 minimum; call a week or two in advance.

Stanley-Whitman House
A beautiful example of colonial architecture, this center-chimney saltbox house (ca. 1720) has an overhang with exceptional decorative pendant drops and hand-split clapboarding. An addition at the back has been converted into a visitors center with a gift shop and some historical displays. The sparse furnishings and dark interior of the main house give an accurate idea of domestic atmospheres in the 1600s and early 1700s. There is also an active schedule of public programming and an annual Corn Roast in late Sept., at which costumed interpreters give demonstrations of 18th-century domestic skills. Admission: $5 adults, $4 seniors, $2 children 6–12. Summer (May–Oct.) hours: Wed.–Sun., noon–4:00 P.M. Winter (Nov.–Apr.) hours: Sun., noon–4:00 P.M. **37 High St., Farmington, 06032; (860) 677-9222.**

Nature Centers

Located amid pretty scenery at the edge of the Western Uplands, **Roaring Brook Nature Center** offers a trail system for hiking and an interpretive building with exhibits for kids. Injured screech owls, bald eagles and other spectacular birds are cared for here and can be viewed. Pets are not permitted on the trails. Guided walks ($2 per person, generally 90 minutes long) are sometimes offered on Fri. evenings, Sat. mornings and Sun. afternoons in summer. They also organize special programs, such as outings to watch the hawk migration in fall. Admission: $2 adults, $1 seniors and children under 12. Nature Center hours: Tue.–Sat., 10:00 A.M.–5:00 P.M.; Sun., 1:00 P.M.–5:00 P.M. Also open Mon. in July/Aug. Grounds hours: dawn–dusk daily, year-round. **70 Gracey Rd., Canton, 06019; (860) 693-0263.**

Nightlife

The Borders chain of music/bookstores has become so popular that it may not need an introduction, but for those who haven't experienced one yet, expect a library of music and books with a café, performances by musical guests, book signings, poetry readings and all sorts of other programs that make the stores mini–performing arts centers. You'll find this **Borders** on the same stretch of road as Westfarms Mall. **1600 South East Rd. (New Britain Rd. or Rte. 71), Farmington, 06032; (860) 674-8110/1758.**

If you're a fan of Irish music, stop in at **Four Green Fields,** a pub/restaurant, Thu.–Sat. around 8:30 P.M. for live entertainment featuring songs from the Emerald Isle. They serve a pub menu featuring Dublin coddle (a sausage stew), fish 'n' chips, beef stew and other traditional Irish fare. **136 Simsbury Rd. (Rte. 10) in the Riverdale Farms Shopping Center, Avon, 06001; (860) 677-1549.**

Performing Arts

Every summer a beautiful and intimate venue in Simsbury is the site of the Centennial Theater Festival as visiting music and dance artists perform and an in-house theater company produces several Equity shows. There are 36–40 performances over a short season running mid-June–early Aug., meaning there's something going on almost daily. (They are dark every Mon.) Since many theater companies take the summer off, this schedule fills the gap in summer programming elsewhere. The venue, which seats 400, is opulent in the style of an old European opera house, and it's handicapped-accessible. Tickets are $12–$30, and parking is free. The theater is located on the campus of the private preparatory Westminster School, and picnicking on the lovely grounds before shows is encouraged. Bring a blanket or lawn chair and make an evening of it. **995 Hopmeadow St. (one block north of Iron Horse Blvd.), Simsbury, 06070; (860) 651-7295.**

Scenic Drives

The **Farmington Valley Visitors Association** at **(800) 493-5266** can provide you with a Scenic Drive brochure covering two routes in

Simsbury: the village of Tariffville and the district known as Terry's Plain. The Tariffville trip covers the architecture of a 19th-century mill village, and the Terry's Plain route cuts through a residential area with some notable examples of colonial architecture. Another short but nice drive in the valley is Nod Rd. in Avon, with stops at the Pickin' Patch to stock up on produce or the Pinchot Sycamore for a picnic.

Because you're in a valley, some of the most spectacular scenery can be found on the roads that lead up and over the highlands on either side. Try a drive on Rte. 185 up the Metacomet Ridge, with a detour into Talcott Mountain State Park for a hike or Penwood State Park in Bloomfield for a slow drive down a heavily wooded lane with a wonderful picnic area and nice east-facing vistas at the end. Coming back down Rte. 185, the view is the best you'll find short of hiking up to Heublein Tower. Or take Rte. 4 west of Farmington until the countryside gets mountainous. At this point the road and the Farmington River hug the very abrupt edge of the Western Uplands. A drive up Rte. 4 into Burlington is exhilarating. Or, go farther to Rtes. 202 or 44, which take you past lovely reservoirs and mountains.

Seasonal Favorites

Avon Cider Mill
Like most cider mills, this one sells not only cider but also produce, plants, honeys and jams, baked goods and more treats, so although cider is only made in autumn, the mill is worth a stop any time they're open from spring through Christmas. They make cider most mornings when apples are in season. If you want to see the process, come before 11:00 A.M., and call ahead to confirm. Hours: 9:00 A.M.–5:00 P.M. daily. **57 Waterville Rd. (Rte. 10 just south of Rte. 44), Avon, 06001; (860) 677-0343.**

Flamig Farm
In Oct. hayrides out to the pumpkin patch at Flamig Farm take place continuously from noon to 4:00 P.M. on weekends. The cost is $2.50 for kids 12 and under and $5 for adults.

They also offer pony rides ($2) during those same hours mid-Apr.–Thanksgiving and a petting zoo ($2 per person) 9:00 A.M.–6:00 P.M. daily in warm weather. At any time of year you can arrange for a private ride in a hay wagon, carriage or sleigh (conditions permitting) with prices starting around $100. **7 Shingle Mill Rd. (off W. Mountain Rd.), W. Simsbury, 06092; (860) 658-5070.**

The Pickin' Patch
The Pickin' Patch boasts the largest assortment of pick-your-own fruits and vegetables in Connecticut, grown on one of the oldest family farms in the state. In addition to the usual berries, apples and pumpkins, it also offers sweet peas, beans, squash, cole crops, corn, tomatoes, peppers and more. The season starts with asparagus in Apr. and ends with Christmas trees in Dec. It also sells vegetable seedlings in early spring. When pumpkin time comes around, hayrides run to the fields all day long. **Woodford Farm, 276 Nod Rd. (1.5 miles north of Rte. 44), Avon, 06001; (860) 677-9552.**

Tours

For information on Early American Hearth Tours, see the listing under Festivals and Events. Tours of the Mende *Amistad* sites are described under Museums and Historic Sites.

Heritage Trails Sightseeing Bus Tours
The same gentleman who gives daily tours of Hartford also offers one-hour bus tours of Farmington followed by dinner at an area inn. The bus departs Hartford hotels at 5:30 P.M. and Farmington hotels at 6:00 P.M. There's a 7:15 P.M. seating for dinner, and the evening ends around 9:15 P.M. The cost is $30 per person, inclusive of meal. The tour narrator is Ernest Shaw, the author of several books about local history. Nights in Oct. he also gives Ancient Graveyard Tours, in which you visit two Farmington cemeteries, and he offers tours on audiocassette for purchase; inquire for details. Payment is by cash or traveler's check only. Reservations are required but can be made on short notice by calling **(860) 677-8867.**

Where to Stay

Bed & Breakfasts

Merrywood B&B—$$$$

This B&B has an intriguing location amid woodland on the shoulder of the Metacomet Ridge. As soon as you leave the main road, you feel like you're entering another world. A long driveway winds through a pine grove to the elegant formal entrance of a picture-perfect house on 5 acres. Hosts Mike and Gerlinde Marti have filled their home with artifacts gathered on world travels. They have three guest rooms, one of them a true two-room suite, another with a Jacuzzi and steam bath. They're all impeccably furnished, each one with a private bath, air conditioning, telephone, TV and VCR. A full breakfast is included, and they also offer packages including a candlelit dinner for two and discounted admission to some area attractions. **100 Hartford Rd. (Rte. 185), Simsbury, 06070; (860) 651-1785.**

Barney House—$$$

This University of Connecticut–owned conference center also functions as a B&B when rooms are available. It is appropriate for guests who don't mind the possibility of a function going on downstairs. The house itself is quite grand, and the grounds are formal and well maintained. Furnishings are comfortable but not luxurious. There are half a dozen spacious guest rooms, most with twin or double beds, all with private bath, TV and telephone. There's a beautiful veranda for lounging and a library for browsing, in addition to an outdoor swimming pool and tennis court and access to other health facilities at a nearby fitness center. A Continental breakfast is included in the rate. **11 Mountain Spring Rd., Farmington, 06032; (860) 674-2796.**

Hotels, Motels & Inns

Avon Old Farms Hotel—$$$$

A lovely red brick exterior, brick walkways and a truly impressive three-level lobby with a curving staircase and sparkling chandelier make this hotel popular for functions. There are standard, deluxe and luxury rooms here in addition to minisuites. The more expensive rooms are preferable both in terms of location (they're farther removed from the road) and decor and are really quite reasonably priced. Inquire about their package deals. At the **junction of Rtes. 10 and 44, Avon, 06001; (800) 836-4000** or **(860) 677-1651.**

The Farmington Inn—$$$$

The Farmington Inn offers very nice accommodations for not much more than you'd pay for a mediocre room elsewhere. A mood of low-key elegance is set in the appealing lobby, where paintings by local artists are displayed, and this carries through to the rooms, which are outfitted with traditional, oversized furnishings. All the rooms have one queen or king or two double beds, and some suites are available. There's a small café on-site where a complimentary Continental breakfast is served. The hotel is very centrally located near the main intersection of Farmington. **827 Farmington Ave., Farmington, 06032; (800) 648-9804** or **(860) 677-2821.**

Simsbury 1820 House—$$$$

This gambrel-roofed colonial with a veranda and porte cochere was built in 1820 (hence its name) and is set back, estatelike, from the main road of Simsbury. A large sloping lawn buffers it from the busy street below, but it remains only a short walk from the village's shops, restaurants and Massacoh Plantation museum. Guest rooms are located in both the main house and the carriage house. Many, but not all, of the rooms in the main house have a classic decor done in conservative colors, featuring plushly upholstered wing chairs, heavy floral drapes and four-poster beds. Some rooms are much more plain, so inquire if the furnishings are important to you. All rooms have a private bath (modern and in great condition), telephone, TV and individual climate control. The carriage house is quite different and more hotel-like in feel; call for details. They offer many package deals worth inquiring about, and there's a very good restaurant on-site. **731 Hopmeadow St., Simsbury, 06070; (800) 879-1820** or **(860) 658-7658.**

The Simsbury Inn—$$$$

This modern hotel with a manor house exterior is really somewhat of a self-contained resort. It has about 100 attractive rooms decorated with furnishings that make subtle French country references. Standard rooms have one king or two double beds, and you can request brass or four-poster bedsteads. It also offers one- and two-bedroom suites with separate sitting areas and sofa beds. All the rooms have extras like refrigerators and hair dryers. The health facilities are extensive, including an indoor heated pool, exercise room, Jacuzzi, saunas and tennis court. There's an excellent restaurant on-site, an elegant lounge and a café where a Continental breakfast (included in the rate) is served. Also offered are valet service, room service and free shuttle service to Bradley International Airport and Union Station in Hartford. **397 Hopmeadow St., Simsbury, 06089; (800) 634-2719 or (860) 651-5700.**

Centennial Inn—$$$ to $$$$

Centennial Inn is an exceptional bargain, especially for couples traveling together and families who need more room than conventional hotel rooms afford. This all-suites facility has one- and two-bedroom units that feature a fully equipped kitchen/dining area, queen or king bed, television and VCR, full bathrooms and central heating and air-conditioning. There are five different layouts, most with a fireplace, some with sofa beds. Second-floor units have cathedral ceilings and skylights. An outdoor pool, a whirlpool and an exercise facility round out the amenities. Although the setting is bucolic, the complex is on a main road and only a few minutes from the center of town. A Continental breakfast is included. **5 Spring Ln., Farmington, 06032; (800) 852-2052 or (860) 677-4647.**

Ironhorse Inn—$$$ to $$$$

Ironhorse Inn is a value hotel offering some real conveniences and good condition for the price. Rooms have kitchenettes (but are not stocked) with a two-burner stove or a microwave. Queen beds are standard. Some rooms have small balconies. If you want to use yours,

request a room facing the rear to minimize traffic noise from the road. **969 Hopmeadow St. (Rte. 10), Simsbury, 06070; (800) 245-9938 or (860) 658-2216.**

Marriott—$$$ to $$$$

This attractive, large hotel is just a jog off the interstate, yet it enjoys a quiet location behind a woodsy business park. Standard rooms are really just as nice as concierge rooms, but the latter do have nicer work facilities for business travelers. It also has several different kinds of suites. Extras include an on-site restaurant, coffee shop, lounge, exercise facilities, indoor and outdoor pools, tennis courts, a game room and jogging trails. The pricing schemes are rather complicated, with many possible packages, including late Sun. checkout for weekend guests and discounted meals at the in-house restaurant; call for details. This hotel is very business traveler–oriented, so take advantage of lower weekend rates to enjoy a really nice place at a great price. **15 Farm Springs Rd., Farmington, 06032; (800) 229-9290 or (860) 678-1000.**

Where to Eat

The Farmington River Valley is another part of Connecticut where the number of worthwhile restaurants exceeds the space available to describe them. Those listed in detail below are among the best, but here are a few additional suggestions.

If you're looking for a place to get excellent prepared foods or breads for a picnic, try **Ann Howard Cookery (Brick Walk Ln., Farmington; 860-678-9486)**. **One-Way Fare Restaurant (4 Railroad St., Simsbury; 860-658-4477)** is a quick and inexpensive place to grab lunch in Simsbury. It's housed in a former railroad depot, so it's rather dark and woody on the inside, but there's also a small deck for outdoor dining in good weather. If you like that, check out **Checkers (774 Hopmeadow St. at the corner of Wilcox, Simsbury; 860-651-9886)** in the evening, where they've got a selection of 50–60 beers and pub food from bangers and mash on up. Craving Indian food? **Uptown India (250 Albany Tpke. [Rte. 44], Canton; 860-693-0080)** is one of the few Indian restaurants in the state outside a major city.

Italian food in all its forms is as popular here as elsewhere in Connecticut. **Ristorante Italia (Rte. 10 in the Riverdale Farms shopping center, Avon; 860-677-7721)** offers mostly Southern Italian cooking and a nice, dressy atmosphere just right for a night out. Four-star Northern Italian dining is ahead for you at **Piccolo Arancio (819 Farmington Ave., Farmington; 860-674-1224),** a sister restaurant to Peppercorn's Grill in Hartford.

The Farmington River Valley also has a strong showing of excellent hotel dining rooms. They are as reliable for breakfast and lunch as for dinner and should not be overlooked. **Seasons** at **Avon Old Farms Hotel (junction of Rtes. 10 and 44, Avon; 860-677-6352)** serves regional American food with fixed-price options at every meal, always complemented by à la carte offerings. Over at the **Simsbury Inn (397 Hopmeadow St., Simsbury; 860-651-5700), Evergreens Restaurant** has an elegant yet rustic atmosphere, and the equally appealing **Twig Lounge** is adjacent. They serve American cuisine and are known for their $19.95 ($9.95 for children) Sun. brunch, a feast of uncommon dishes.

Apricots—$$$$

One of the most popular restaurants in the area, Apricots offers the combination of a small, semiformal upstairs dining room and a casual, lively downstairs tavern. It serves creative American cuisine from a menu that changes seasonally. You can always expect some unique flavors, such as the grilled sardines, lobster-fennel sausage and pepita-crusted salmon from a recent summer menu. The bar has its own pub fare. Lunch here can rival dinner for size, but there are a few sandwiches and salads if you want something lighter. It also has a riverside terrace for dining in good weather. Lunch and Sun. brunch hours: 11:30 A.M.–2:30 P.M. daily. Dinner hours: Mon.–Sat., 6:00 P.M.–10:00 P.M.; Sun., 5:30

P.M.–9:00 P.M. **1593 Farmington Ave. (Rte. 4), Farmington, 06032; (860) 673-5405.**

Avon Old Farms Inn—$$$$

Although this restaurant's name is similar to that of the Avon Old Farms Hotel across the street, and it's easy to be confused when sitting at the intersection trying to figure out which is which, Avon Old Farms Inn is exclusively a restaurant, despite the "inn" designation. It's an institution in Farmington that goes back years, but its menu was recently revitalized by a new chef. Its famous Sun. champagne brunch ($15.95) is quite extensive. Come with an appetite and make it your main meal of the day. Hours: Mon.–Sat., 11:30 A.M.–3:00 P.M. for lunch & 5:30 P.M.–9:30 P.M. for dinner; Sun., 10:00 A.M.–2:30 P.M. for brunch & 5:30 P.M.–8:30 P.M. for dinner. **One Nod Rd. (at the eastern junction of Rtes. 10 and 44), Avon, 06001; (860) 677-2818.**

Simsbury 1820 House—$$$$

81

Located in a historic house, now an inn, on Simsbury's main street (see the Where to Stay section for details), this restaurant serves a small menu of American and Continental staples such as rack of lamb, a daily risotto, tenderloin steak, Caesar salad, baked brie and crab cakes. The subterranean dining rooms are cool in summer and warmed by a fireplace in winter. There is also some outdoor seating in good weather. Hours: lunch served Mon.–Fri., 11:00 A.M.–2:30 P.M.; dinner served daily 5:30 P.M.–9:00 P.M. The restaurant can be closed for functions, so it is wise to call for reservations. **731 Hopmeadow St., Simsbury, 06070; (800) 879-1820 or (860) 658-7658.**

Cafe Allègre—$$$ to $$$$

This Continental restaurant is housed in a most unusual building that looks like a little alpine ski chalet set just off the highway. The menu changes weekly and is based on country French and Italian dishes. You're welcome to bring any alcoholic beverage you'd like to have with your meal, and they generously do not charge a corkage fee. It has only nine tables (supplemented by some seasonal outdoor seating), so the dining room is very intimate and reservations are required. Lunch/brunch is served Tue.–Fri. & Sun., 11:30 A.M.–2:00 P.M. During the week (Tue.–Thu.) & on Sun., dinner is available from 6:00 P.M. until 8:30 or 9:00 P.M., but on Fri. & Sat. there are two seatings only at 6:00 P.M. & 9:00 P.M. Located in **Gateway Office Park** at **50 Albany Tpke. (Rte. 44), Canton, 06019; (860) 693-1009.** If you're a cigar fan, top off dinner at Cafe Allègre with a visit to **Aperitif (860-693-9373);** open Mon.–Sat., noon–8:00 P.M. & Sun. until 5:00), a cigar store located in another part of the office park.

Chart House—$$$ to $$$$

Chart House restaurants are a chain of unique restaurants serving American cuisine in historic properties. This Chart House is situated in a former tavern with multiple fireplaces and wideboard floors. The moderately sized menu features steaks, prime rib, seafood and pasta. Hours: Mon.–Thu., 5:00 P.M.–9:00 P.M.; Fri.–Sat., 5:00 P.M.–10:00 P.M.; Sun., 5:00 P.M.–10:00 P.M. **4 Hartford Rd. (Rte. 185 at Rte. 10), Simsbury, 06089; (860) 658-1118.**

The Grist Mill—$$$ to $$$$

Still fairly new yet growing in reputation, The Grist Mill is indeed located in a restored mill along the Farmington River. It's a small place with low ceilings, close-set tables and good views of the water. The menu features broad-based northern Mediterranean cuisine. It's noted for its delicious desserts, and its location is very convenient to the Farmington museums. Hours: lunch/brunch served daily, noon–2:00 P.M.; dinner served nightly 5:30 P.M.–9:00 P.M. (Sun. from 5:00). **40 Mill Ln., Farmington, 06032; (860) 676-8855.**

Dakota—$$$

With a name evocative of the Old West and a Native American decorative theme, Dakota stands out a bit from the crowd. The menu features a wide range of steaks, seafood, prime rib, salmon and a salad bar with organic produce. Desserts also tend toward food that even the kids would devour, such as ice cream and mud pie. Sun. brunch is a large buffet ($15.95 for adults, $6.95 for kids) definitely designed to satiate big appetites. Hours: Mon.–Thu.,

5:00 P.M.–10:00 P.M.; Fri. until 11:00 P.M.; Sat., 4:00 P.M.–11:00 P.M.; Sun. brunch, 10:00 A.M.–2:00 P.M.; Sun. dinner, 4:00 P.M.–9:00 P.M. **225 W. Main St., Avon, 06001; (860) 677-4311.**

Métro Bis—$$$

For a taste of the Old World in a most surprising location, head to Métro Bis, filled with a wonderful assortment of Parisian subway (Métro) fixtures, oil paintings and chandeliers. Breakfast, served on weekends, consists mostly of omelettes. Lunch is sandwiches and soups with a few Mediterranean entrées, all accompanied by baguettes or croissants and quite reasonably priced. Dinner features classic French dishes such as pâté, escargots and crêpes in addition to many savory Mediterranean and Continental entrées. Breakfast/lunch hours: Tue.–Fri., 11:00 A.M.–2:00 P.M.; Sat.–Sun., 9:00 A.M.–2:00 P.M. Dinner served Tue.–Thu., 5:30 P.M.–9:00 P.M.; Fri.–Sat., 5:30 P.M.–10:00 P.M.; Sun., 5:00 P.M.–8:00 P.M. **928 Hopmeadow St. (in the Simsburytown Shops mall), Simsbury, 06070; (860) 651-1908.**

Murasaki—$$$

This Japanese restaurant is a pleasant surprise to come across on a side street of Simsbury. The menu will be familiar to anyone accustomed to Japanese food: great fresh fish and seafood, teriyakis, tempura, one-pot meals and so forth. A private tatami room is available for a small charge. Hours: lunch served Tue.–Fri., 11:45 A.M.–2:00 P.M.; dinner served Tue.–Sun., 5:00 P.M.–9:30 P.M. (Fri.–Sat. until 10:00). **10 Wilcox St., Simsbury, 06070; (860) 651-7929.**

Village Green—$$$

Located in the Farmington Marriott and definitely a cut above many hotel restaurants, Village Green serves American cuisine with a broad menu selection to suit virtually anyone in the family. For the value-conscious they have early-bird specials and dinner buffets Thu.–Sat. There are always a few vegetarian options and a salad bar. The menu helpfully suggests which selection from the restaurant's microbrewery beer and wine list might go best with each dish. Breakfast served Mon.–Fri., 6:30 A.M.–11:00 A.M.; Sat.–Sun., 7:00 A.M.–

noon, with a buffet on Sun. continuing until 2:00 P.M. Lunch hours: 11:00 A.M.–2:00 P.M. daily. Dinner served nightly 5:00 P.M.–10:00 P.M. **15 Farm Springs Rd., Farmington, 06032; (860) 678-1000.**

La Baguette—$$ to $$$

Only the name suggests what you'll find at La Baguette, because it looks for all the world like a very busy and popular diner. But instead of blue plate specials it serves surprising, hearty and savory French-American dishes, in addition to salads, sandwiches, prime rib and some wonderful baked goods. This is a great place to get a fairly sophisticated meal without having to dress up. You could come here in your shorts after spending the day swimming at nearby Stratton Brook State Park and not be out of place, and there's enough on the menu that kids find appetizing to make this a great family restaurant. **135 West St. (Rte. 167), Simsbury, 06070; (860) 651-1113.**

Lily's-of-the-Valley/Lily's—$$ to $$$

The fun and vibrant interior of Lily's-of-the-Valley looks like someone bought the entire holdings of an antiques and curios shop and deposited it here with minimal sorting, yet somehow it escapes looking tacky. As for the menu, a guest register by the door is filled with the comments of patrons past, and "comfort food" is a phrase that occurs with some frequency. The kitchen's "famous" cream of tomato soup really is a soup lover's dream. Dinner goes upscale a bit, but is still fundamentally hearty and simple. At both meals there are always a few meatless items. Phone in advance to have your name put on the list and thereby minimize the wait for a table. Open for lunch/brunch daily 11:30 A.M.–2:30 P.M. (3:00 on Sun.) & for dinner Tue.–Sun., 5:00 P.M.–close. An attenuated menu is served in the bar between lunch and dinner, so something is available continuously. **142 Hopmeadow St. (Rte. 10), Simsbury, 06089; (860) 651-3676.**

Lily's-of-the-Valley has a sister restaurant, Lily's, in nearby Canton that is also worth seeking out. The menu is even more down-home and dineresque, and this is *the place* to come for breakfast. Hours: Tue.–Fri., 8:00 A.M.–2:30 P.M., changing over from breakfast to lunch at 11:30; Sat., 8:00 A.M.–11:30 A.M. for breakfast & noon–2:30 P.M. for lunch; Sun., 8:00 A.M.–2:00 P.M. with continuous breakfast. It's also open for dinner Tue.-Sat. beginning at 5:00 P.M. **160 Albany Tpke. (Rte. 202/Rte. 44), Canton, 06019; (860) 693-3700.**

Max-a-Mia—$$ to $$$

Second in the Max "chain" of three local and popular restaurants, Max-a-Mia serves Northern Italian cuisine, including pastas, gnocchi, a daily risotto, pizzas and lasagna in addition to roast chicken, pork and veal dishes. The kitchen is also happy to accommodate special requests. It does serve continuously once it opens for lunch, but between 2:30 P.M. and 5:00 P.M. it's pizzas and salads only. Seating is in one large, modern dining room with banquettes along the walls and tables in the middle. There's little separation from the bar, so it can get loud. On weekends reservations are taken only for groups of six or more. Hours: Mon.–Thu., 11:30 A.M.–10:00 P.M.; Fri.–Sat., 11:30 A.M.–11:00 P.M.; Sun. dinner served 4:00 P.M.–9:00 P.M. **70 E. Main St. (Rte. 44), Avon, 06001; (860) 677-6299.**

Saybrook Fish House—$$ to $$$

True to its name, the focus here is fish and seafood. It's part of a small chain, and this one is in the unlikely location of decidedly landlocked Canton. (The one in Old Saybrook on the shore wins *Connecticut* magazine's readers' poll award for best seafood in the state year after year.) This is a family-oriented restaurant, casual and comfortable. Hours: Mon.–Thu., 11:30 A.M.–9:00 P.M.; Fri., 11:30 A.M.–10:00 P.M.; Sat., noon–10:30 P.M.; Sun., noon–9:00 P.M. The dining room makes the change from lunch to dinner at 4:00–4:30 P.M., but the lunch menu is always available in the lounge, so this is also a good place for light eaters. Located at the **intersection of Rtes. 44, 202 and 179, Canton; (860) 693-0034.**

Bagels Plus Deli—$

Craving a bagel before a day tubing on the Farmington? The ones here are genuinely

83

good, and the store is open early enough for outdoor types. Hours: Mon.–Fri., 6:00 A.M.–4:00 P.M.; Sat., 7:00 A.M.–2:00 P.M.; Sun., 7:00 A.M.–1:00 P.M. **220 Albany Tpke. (Rte. 44 in the Canton Village Plaza), Canton, 06019; (860) 693-8905.**

Coffeehouses, Sweets & Treats

Gertrude & Alice's—$

A combination coffee bar/bookstore, Gertrude & Alice's is very convenient if you're antiquing in Collinsville and need a light pick-me-up. In addition to beverages, they serve bagels, baked goods and sandwiches. Hours: Wed.–Thu., 10:00 A.M.–9:00 P.M.; Fri.–Sat., 10:00 A.M.–11:00 P.M.; Sun., 10:00 A.M.–4:00 P.M. **2 Front St., Collinsville, 06019; (860) 693-3816.**

Munson's Chocolates—$

This Connecticut chocolate maker has several stores, but this one is in a unique 12-sided building that looks like a circus tent. They sell everything from chocolate and hard candies to tins, bags, cards, baskets and so on. Hours: Mon.–Fri., 10:00 A.M.–9:00 P.M.; Sat., 10:00 A.M.–8:00 P.M.; Sun., 10:00 A.M.–6:00 P.M. Lo-cated at the **corner of Rtes. 44/202 and 167, Avon, 06001; (860) 658-7605.**

Services

Local Visitors Information

Farmington Valley Visitors Association, P.O. Box 1015, Simsbury, 06070; (800) 493-5266 or **(860) 651-6950.**

Greater Hartford Convention and Visitors Bureau, 234 Murphy Rd., Hartford, 06114; (800) 793-4480 or **(860) 244-8181.**

Transportation

Farmington is served by two bus lines that both have toll-free numbers for schedule and fare information. You can can reach **Bonanza Bus Lines** at **(800) 556-3815** and **Peter Pan/Trailways** at **(800) 343-9999.** Regional bus service between towns in the Farmington Valley and Hartford areas is provided by the **Greater Hartford Transit District** at **(860) 247-5329** and **CT Transit** at **(860) 525-9181.**

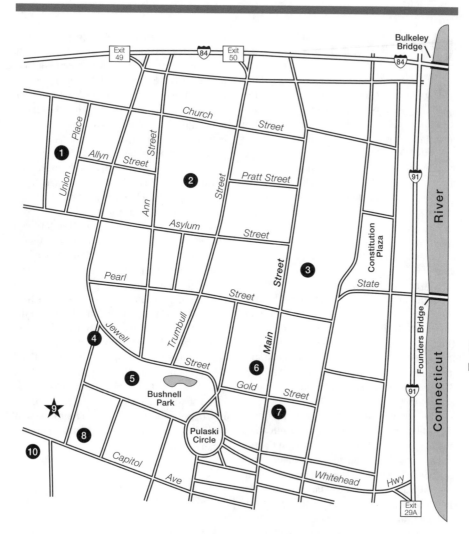

85

HARTFORD

- 1 - Union Train Station
- 2 - Civic Center
- 3 - Old State House
- 4 - Soldiers & Sailors Memorial Arch
- 5 - Bushnell Park Carousel
- 6 - Ancient Burying Ground / Center Church
- 7 - Wadsworth Atheneum
- 8 - The Bushnell
- ★ 9 - State Capitol
- 10 - Museum of Connecticut History

Hartford

In describing Hartford, I must fall back on the words of the city's most famous resident and a well-traveled man, Mark Twain: "Of all the beautiful towns that it has been my fortune to see, this is the chief. ... You won't know what beauty is if you have not been here." Things have changed a lot since Twain's time, but Hartford is still an ideal capital city: manageable in size, yet large enough to offer everything cities are supposed to have—a stimulating cultural life, fine dining, beautiful parks, monumental public architecture and much more.

Nowhere can history buffs get a more complete picture of Connecticut's past than in Hartford. It has a stunning Capitol building and the historic Charles Bulfinch–designed Old State House, both of which are open for tours, and it's the repository of all the state's important governmental documents of the last 350 years at institutions like the Museum of Connecticut History.

The green heart of the city is Bushnell Park, an exquisitely clean and well-maintained public space that lies adjacent to the Capitol and serves as an extension of its immaculate grounds. In addition to being an informal arboretum, the park is the site of numerous events, most notably the new Mark Twain Days festival, celebrating the life and times of the city's adopted son. Those traveling with children must take them for a ride on the Bushnell Park Carousel, a turn-of-the-century gem that revolves to the music of a vintage pump organ all summer long. Among the landmark monuments in the park are Corning Fountain, an unusual memorial celebrating the American Indian, and the Soldiers and Sailors Memorial Arch, honoring Hartford's Civil War casualties in the Battle of Antietam.

Hartford lies on the Connecticut River, which has for the past 15 years been undergoing a revitalization that has earned it a designation as one of the country's most improved urban rivers. Riverside parks continue to be built and linked together to form what will eventually be a continuous greenway several miles long on both banks with boat launches, pathways for strolling and biking and piers for fishing. The Connecticut River itself has been substantially cleaned up and supports healthy populations of fish. There's a major rowing regatta on the river every year; canoeing is also popular, and a riverboat makes daily sightseeing trips in summer. Riverfront Recapture, one of the forces responsible for this turnabout, has also instituted an annual Fourth of July celebration called Riverfest.

There is so much to see in Hartford you should come expecting to stay a while. Among the must-do's: the Wadsworth Atheneum, the oldest public art museum in the country; Elizabeth Park's municipal rose garden, the first in the United States and an amazing site in June when 14,000 bushes burst into bloom; and the Mark Twain and Harriet Beecher Stowe houses, chronicling the lives of two of the city's most influential residents. All in all, the Hartford area might be the best surprise of any destination in Connecticut for visitors who come not knowing what to expect. For centuries travelers to Hartford have regretted only having to leave, and with luck you will have the same experience.

History

The first Europeans to set up shop in Connecticut were Dutch traders who, in 1633, established a trading post at Hartford (known by the Indian name Suckiaug, meaning "black earth"), calling it the House of Good Hope. The Dutch remained in the area for the next 20 years but in the end were simply crowded out.

The English community at Hartford, originally called Newtown, was settled in 1636 when the Reverend Thomas Hooker moved his entire congregation of about 100 people to the site from Newtown (to become Cambridge), Massachusetts. It was the third English settlement in Connecticut, after Windsor and Wethersfield. In 1638 Hooker preached the famous sermons that became the basis for Connecticut's government.

Hartford, equidistant from Windsor and Wethersfield, was the seat of authority from the start. It was from Hartford that Connecticut governor John Winthrop, Jr., departed in 1661 on his successful quest for a charter from Charles II that would guarantee the colony some rights, and it was to Hartford that Sir Edmund Andros came in Oct. 1687 to rescind the charter and take control of Connecticut government under a new, more authoritarian king, James II. In a now legendary incident, the charter was spirited away from under the nose of Andros and hidden in the hollow of an oak tree on the Hartford property of one Samuel Wyllys. The so-called Charter Oak in which the document was secreted stood near the corner of present-day Charter Oak Pl. and Charter Oak Ave. It is estimated that the tree was more than 1,000 years old when it fell in 1856, the victim of a violent storm. Inside, there was indeed a huge cavity, easily large enough to have concealed the charter. Amazingly, the tree was immortalized on canvas a mere ten years before its demise by landscape painter and Hartford native Frederic Edwin Church, who was a pupil of Thomas Cole, the founder of the strongly romantic Hudson River School of painting.

During the Revolutionary War, Hartford was a hotbed of activity. Washington, La-Fayette, Rochambeau and many other principal figures of the war passed through and met in Hartford on several occasions. The Council of Safety, a committee that essentially ran the war effort, did their work from both Hartford and Lebanon.

In the early 1800s the Old State House was the site of the landmark Prudence Crandall and *Amistad* court cases (see the **Far Northeast** and **New Haven** chapters, respectively). The first public art museum in the United States, the Wadsworth Atheneum, was founded here in 1842. Hartford alternated with New Haven as the state's capital city until 1875.

The Hartford area is notable for several manufacturing and technological "firsts," beginning with the Hartford Woolen Company in 1788, the first in the country to be devoted to

the production of woolen cloth. The first bicycles were also made here by the Pope Manufacturing Co., established in 1877. The Hartford Electric Light Co. was the first utility to transmit high-voltage alternating current over long distances, and Hartford was the first city to be fully lighted by electricity. A few industries, however, came to dominate the city, sometimes both economically and physically.

When Samuel Colt made the first functional revolver, he built a city within a city on land reclaimed from the Connecticut River in order to mass-produce it. Colt's Patent Fire-Arms Manufacturing Co., a.k.a. the Colt Armory, turned out "the gun that won the West" by the tens of thousands. His onion dome-topped factory still stands, now filled with a variety of businesses and artists studios, and can be seen easily from I-91. It is the second on the site. The first burned during the Civil War, allegedly at the hands of Southern arsonists.

Hartford has long been known as the insurance capital of the country. In a recent survey it was found that three of the top ten nongovernmental employers in the state were insurance companies headquartered in Hartford. It all began with a policy issued by the Hartford Fire Insurance Co., dated 1794. Aetna Insurance, Connecticut Mutual, The Travelers, Phoenix Mutual and many other insurers were founded here as the industry snowballed, developing life, accident and other types of insurance as circumstances demanded them. By the 1930s there were 44 insurers based in the city, writing up to 20% of the national total of some types of policies. For many years the Travelers Tower was the tallest building in New England and is still the second tallest in the city.

The gothic Capitol in Hartford and a monument to a Connecticut hero.

Major Attractions

The Capitol

Hartford is the capital of Connecticut, the seat of state government, so it's a great place to see government in action (or inaction, as the case may be). The State Capitol building is a sterling example of civic architecture, situated at the top of a small hill overlooking the rolling lawns of Bushnell Park. Built in 1878 in High Victorian Gothic style, its exterior is so ornate—with leaders of Connecticut government enshrined on pedestals like saints and a few empty pedestals for heroes to come—it could almost be mistaken for a church. The stenciled interior is no less spectacular.

Luckily for visitors, the Capitol was renovated between 1979 and 1989 and currently is in the best condition since it was built. If you have time to do nothing else in Hartford, take the free Capitol tour led by members of the League of Women Voters. It takes a little more than an hour and covers both the Capitol itself and the new Legislative Office Building nearby.

Connecticut has a bicameral legislature. When the legislature is in session, you can view the proceedings in the Senate and Assembly chambers. If you're lucky, on your tour you'll be able to sit in the "wishing chair" in the Senate chamber. Constructed of wood from the famed Charter Oak, it is known by this name because it is said that the lieutenant governor, presiding over the Senate, sits in it and wishes to become governor.

Don't miss the Hall of Flags, where some fascinating historical artifacts from Connecticut's past are displayed. Self-guided tour literature of both buildings as well as a booklet explaining the Capitol's statuary are also available. Parking is at a premium in the Capitol area. You might try the Legislative Office Building garage off Capitol Ave. west of the Capitol building. Tours take place Mon.–Fri. on the quarter hour from 9:15 A.M. to 1:15 P.M., and also at 2:15 P.M. in July and Aug., as well as Sat. on the quarter hour from 10:15 A.M. to 2:15 P.M., Apr.–Oct. For more information, contact **Capitol Information and Tours, State Capitol, 210 Capitol Ave., Hartford, 06106; (860) 240-0222.**

Nook Farm: The Mark Twain and Harriet Beecher Stowe Houses

Connecticut's principal airport, Bradley International, is located about 20 minutes north of Hartford in Windsor Locks. Several options for ground transportation are available right at the airport. I-84 and I-91 meet in Hartford, making the city easily accessible by car from any direction.

In the late 1800s the Nook Farm neighborhood of Hartford was home to some of the city's most creative, forward-thinking residents, among them author Harriet Beecher Stowe and her abolitionist/suffragist family, novelist Mark Twain and actor/playwright William Gillette before he built his castle on the Connecticut River. It was by all indications a lively community in which a great deal of entertaining and debate went on. Nook Farm's unique atmosphere, depending as it did upon impermanent personalities, was short-lived. By 1896 Stowe was dead, and Twain was facing financial troubles and personal tragedy. Years later both houses faced the possibility of demolition, and it is little short of a miracle that they are here today.

The Stowe and Twain houses are completely separate, although they are next to one another. A tour of either one is a complete experience in itself, but visiting both yields an experience greater than the sum of its parts. In Dec. Nook Farm sports extensive holiday displays and hosts First Night festivities.

Harriet Beecher Stowe House

A visit to the "cottage" on Forest St. is an exploration of the life and times of the noted author of *Uncle Tom's Cabin,* one of the most influential American novels of the 19th century. Stowe came from a family of abolitionists, and the antislavery sentiments expressed in the book arose from deep convictions. Although this work guaranteed her fame, Stowe wrote over 30 others in addition to countless magazine articles. She was a tireless advocate of the application of science to housekeeping, the occupation that monopolized the time of women everywhere, and wrote prolifically on the subject. Hour-long guided tours begin in

the visitors center behind the house, where there is also an excellent gift shop. Admission: $6.50 adults, $6 seniors, $2.75 children 6–16. Hours: Tue.–Sat., 9:30 A.M.–4:00 P.M.; Sun., noon–4:00 P.M.; also open Mon. June 1–Columbus Day & in Dec.; closed major holidays. **73 Forest St., Hartford, 06105; (860) 525-9317.**

Mark Twain House

Few people know that Mark Twain spent 20 years of his life in Hartford and wrote all of his principal works there. Fewer still know that he was quite well off, thanks to a wife from a wealthy family. In fact, much of the interior design work in his home was done by Louis Comfort Tiffany of Tiffany lamp fame. His house, which was built to his specifications in High Victorian Gothic style, was considered a monstrosity by his neighbors. After coming close to demolition in the 1920s, it was saved by some farsighted preservationists and has been restored with period pieces, some authentic to the Twain household but many simply authentic to the time. The tour guides are knowledgeable and enthusiastic, and the gift shop is an excellent place to stock up on Twain books and Victoriana. Be sure to ask your tour leader about the theories concerning the origin of the name Mark Twain. Admission: $7.50 adults, discounts for seniors and children. Hours: Mon. & Wed.–Sat., 9:30 A.M.–5:00 P.M.; Sun., noon–5:00 P.M.; also open Tue. between Memorial Day & Columbus Day, & in Dec.; last tour leaves by 4:00 P.M. **351 Farmington Ave. (at Woodland St.), Hartford, 06105; (860) 493-6411.**

89

The Wadsworth Atheneum, Hartford, was the first public art museum in the United States.

Wadsworth Atheneum

90

The Wadsworth Atheneum is the nation's oldest public art museum and one of Hartford's gems. Named after founder Daniel Wadsworth, a politician and early industrialist, this landmark institution is housed in a complex of five buildings with a Gothic masterpiece at its heart. One of the architects was Ithiel Town, who is also responsible for two of the churches on New Haven's green and the original covered bridge at West Cornwall.

The museum houses permanent and changing exhibits that explore industry and society as well as art. Highlights include the American furniture and decorative arts collection of noted Colonial Revivalist Wallace Nutting and the largest collection of Hudson River School landscape paintings in the country.

In conjunction with particular exhibits, there may be concerts, lectures, walking tours, screenings, theatrical performances, children's programs and family-oriented, hands-on activities. The Atheneum is also the home of the Auerbach Art Library, the largest in the state; call for hours. The museum is completely wheelchair-accessible and has TDD devices available for the hearing impaired. Museum general admission: $6 adults, $4 seniors, $3 children 6–17; admission can be

higher for special exhibitions and programs. Admission for individuals is free all day Thu. and before noon on Sat.; restrictions apply. Hours: Tue.–Sun., 11:00 A.M.–5:00 P.M.; open until 8:00 P.M. the first Thu. of each month; closed Mon. & major holidays. Call for group rates and museum shop and café hours. **600 Main St., Hartford, 06103; (860) 278-2670.** Museum café: **(860) 728-5989.**

Festivals and Events

In addition to the events listed below, there are plans to start up a Hartford Lighter Than Air Balloon Festival on Father's Day weekend every year. The event would be modeled after the Windham Lighter Than Air Balloon Festival covered in the **Far Northeast** chapter. For more information call the **Lighter Than Air Fund** at **(860) 456-7666.** The new **Red Hot Blues and Chili Cookoff** in East Hartford also promises to become a well-attended annual event. Look for an early Aug. date; call **(800) 446-9255** for more information on this fundraiser. Also in East Hartford, the **Podunk Bluegrass Music Festival** is a new event currently planned for the last Fri. and Sat. in late July. Camping in the rough is available by prior reservation. Call **(860) 282-7577** for details on activities, hours and cost.

First Thursdays
first Thu. of every month

One day per month you may find special activities, extended hours or discounted or free admission at museums, theaters, public buildings and other sites citywide. For example, there are often screenings and musical entertainment at the Wadsworth Atheneum, which stays open that night until 8:00 P.M., or a local company might offer a free concert in its lobby. A schedule of First Thursday activities appears in the *Hartford Advocate* (a free news and arts weekly) published the day before the event. You can also pick up a schedule at the **Arts & Entertainment district office** at **225 Trumbull St. in Hartford** up to a week in advance. For more information call their office at **(860) 525-8629**.

Taste of Hartford
mid-June (Thu.–Sun.)

The largest food festival in New England features 40 restaurants, all from the greater Hartford area, serving up their best in small portions so you can graze your way through it all. The event is held in Constitution Plaza near Market and State Sts. east of the Old State House. Hours: Thu., 11:00 A.M.–9:00 P.M.; Fri.–Sat., 11:00 A.M.–10:00 P.M.; Sun., 11:00 A.M.–8:00 P.M. For more information, contact the **Hartford Downtown Council** at **(860) 728-3089**.

Riverfest
early July

This Fourth of July celebration held the Sat. closest to the holiday features the largest display of fireworks in southern New England. Activities take place all day long on both sides of the Connecticut River in the Hartford area. There are four stages, two on either side of the river, for musical performances and children's entertainment. Other activities are designed to draw attention to a pedestrian plaza and 8-mile walkway under development that will connect downtown Hartford with the waterfront and sites up and down both sides of the river. Riverfest is a free event. Shuttle buses run between the festival sites and parking garages on both sides of the river. For more information or a schedule, contact **Riverfront Recapture** at (860) 293-0131.

Mark Twain Days
third weekend in Aug. (Fri.–Sun.)

This kooky festival is a new and hugely successful celebration with activities inspired by one of the city's most famous residents. Multiple sites host such goings-on as a frog jumping contest on the grounds of the Old State House, a joust (yes, a joust) in Bushnell Park and riverboat rides on the *Becky Thatcher*

Jousting in Hartford's Bushnell Park is a highlight of Mark Twain Days.

from Charter Oak Landing. This is truly a citywide celebration with participation by many of Hartford's galleries, museums, public buildings and parks, but beautiful Bushnell Park is the activities headquarters, with a Civil War encampment and concerts by major artists. Ride the Bushnell Park carousel or play a game of baseball by 19th-century rules. To top it off, tour the Mark Twain House and get to know better the man who gave rise to all this zaniness. Free programs are available on-site. Free shuttles run continuously between all the sites, and most events are free. For more information call **(860) 247-0998**.

Kid'rific
weekend following Labor Day

Child-oriented activities and attractions characterize this outdoor street festival where you'll find a petting zoo, hayrides, pony rides, art and music workshops, face painting, storytelling and more. Several blocks of Main St. are closed to auto traffic and turned into a pedestrian mall to accommodate the crowds. Admission is just $1 with no additional charge for most activities. Hours: 11:00 A.M.–5:00 P.M. both days. For more information call **(860) 728-3089**.

Hooker Day Parade
early Oct.

Named for Hartford's first civic leader, the Reverend Thomas Hooker, the Hooker Day Parade is the brainchild of a group of Hartford residents who wanted to have an annual fun event for the downtown area. Anyone can march in the parade, and the wackier the costume the better. The 2-mile route winds through the downtown and ends at the site of a festival on Arch St. For more information call **(860) 523-9510.**

Haunted Happenings
every night in Oct.

Haunted Happenings is New England's largest indoor Halloween event. A guide (or maybe a ghoul!) leads small groups through 40,000 square feet of sets, computer-controlled devices and sound and lighting effects that put them in the middle of the action. The tour takes half an hour and is appropriate for ages 8 and up. Admission: $10 adults, $6 children. Arrive as early as possible to avoid a long wait. Hours: Mon.–Fri., 6:00 A.M.–9:00 P.M.; Sat.–Sun., 2:00 P.M.–9:00 P.M. At the former G. Fox department store building at **960 Main St., Hartford; (860) 527-0478.**

Festival of Lights
day after Thanksgiving through Jan. 6

The city's official kickoff of the holiday season begins with an evening of special events in Constitution Plaza the day after Thanksgiving. Caroling starts around 5:30 P.M. in preparation for the 6:00 P.M. arrival of Santa by helicopter, who descends 22 floors in a neon sleigh to turn a magic key that transforms the plaza into a holiday landscape blazing with 200,000 lights. Through Jan. 6 the lights are on nightly 4:00 P.M.–midnight. Constitution Plaza is in **downtown Hartford near the intersection of Market and State Sts.** For more information call **(860) 728-3089.**

Winter Wonderland
day after Thanksgiving through Dec.

You could practically find your way to Winter Wonderland by following the trail of people walking around downtown Hartford on Dec. nights with bits of artificial snow clinging to their hair. They've been playing in the former G. Fox department store, which is transformed every winter into the country's largest indoor Christmas attraction. Six-plus floors of the store are filled with model train layouts, Santas from around the world, a life-sized Dickensian village with shopkeepers in costume, miniature dollhouses and collectibles, a forest of ornately decorated 12-foot-high Christmas trees, a 15-room Santa's Workshop display and a racetrack that kids 6 and under can ride on. Leave at least two hours to see it all. Concession food is available. Admission: $8 adults, $5 children 5–12. Hours before Christmas are Thu.–Fri., 4:00 A.M.–9:00 P.M.; Sat.–Sun., noon–9:00 P.M. If Christmas Eve falls on a day when they're open, closing time is 6:00 P.M. After Christmas, it's open daily noon–6:00 P.M. through Dec. 31. **960 Main St. in Hartford; (860) 527-0478.**

First Night
Dec. 31

Several years ago towns throughout Connecticut took to planning safe and fun family-oriented New Year's Eve celebrations as an alternative to unruly, impromptu festivities. First Night celebrations differ from town to town, but Hartford certainly does it biggest and arguably best. Activities run the gamut from open houses at historic sites, art exhibits, comedy, children's entertainment and secular music of all sorts to inspirational music and candlelight church services. Activities begin around 2:00 P.M. and continue until midnight, when the city greets the new year with a fireworks display. Admission is by a button that can be purchased in advance for about $5 for adults and $1 for children under 12. (Note: During the last week before Dec. 31 the adult price goes up a couple of dollars.) For a schedule of events or information on where to purchase the buttons call the **Hartford Downtown Council** at **(860) 728-3089** during business hours, call their 24-hour event hotline at **(860) 522-6400** or stop at the Civic Center Visitors Information Desk.

Outdoor Activities

Biking

Mountain Biking

To the west of Hartford is a huge tract of land containing several **Metropolitan District Commission (MDC)** reservoirs that supply the area with water. The surrounding land is open for public recreation and may be the best place to mountain bike in the state. It is crisscrossed with paved roads that you'll need to share with walkers and joggers and less frequented trails through hilly woodland. Bikes are allowed on all the roads and on trails marked for bike access; respect any signs restricting use on some trails. Picnic tables are available at several spots, and portable toilets are located at the main parking area. Access is free. Hours: dawn–dusk daily, year-round. A topographic map of the area is available for $2.35 by mail from **MDC, Attn: Mapping, P.O. Box 800, Hartford, 06142,** or call **(860) 278-7850, ext. 3209.** Or request the free pocket-size map, which you can also pick up in person at the administration building on-site during normal business hours. Maps are also posted at the site. Enter the southern portion of the property via Hawley Rd. off Farmington Ave. (Rte. 4) in West Hartford right at the Farmington town line. The entrance to the northern portion of the property is on Albany Ave. (Rte. 44) in West Hartford. Rte. 44 divides the MDC area in two, but you can access both halves from either parking lot via one trail that crosses over. If you want to get away from the crowds, head for the northern section.

Road Biking

The only place that is truly safe to bike in this densely populated area is off-road. One good location is the series of linear parks being constructed along the riverfront in Hartford, East Hartford and surrounding towns. For more information see the listing under Hiking and Strolling. Currently there is bicycle access to two bridges across the Connecticut River. To get on Charter Oak Bridge (Rte. 15), follow signs from Reserve Rd. on the Hartford side or Riverside Dr. on the East Hartford side. To get on Bulkeley Bridge (I-84), follow signs from Market St./State St. on the Hartford side and East River Rd. in East Hartford. On both of these bridges you will ride in a separate lane rather than with traffic.

Boating

As part of its overall effort to improve public access to and appreciation of the Connecticut River, **Riverfront Recapture** has initiated a popular community rowing program in Hartford. Members of the general public can occasionally participate in one-day courses or arrange private or group lessons. You can get more information at **(860) 293-0131.**

Boat Launches

Riverside Park and Charter Oak Landing are two Hartford town parks that are integral links in the chain of recreational spaces up and down the Connecticut River waterfront. Both have boat launches that can accommodate powerboats and car-top boats. A launch fee is charged in summer. In East Hartford on the opposite side of the river, there's a recently improved launch in Great River Park. The fee for nonresidents to launch a boat here is $15. Riverside Park is located on Leibert Rd. off Jennings Rd. near I-91 exit 33, Charter Oak Landing is located on Reserve Rd. near I-91 exit 27 and Great River Park is located on East River Dr. For more information call **Riverfront Recapture** at **(860) 293-0131.**

Canoeing

John Kulick, the proprietor of Huck Finn Adventures, a canoe rental and tour service, has come up with a new and unique guided outing that is the equal of the adventures of Huck Finn himself: a canoe trip underneath the city of Hartford. The Park River, which ran roughly

Central Valley

where Jewell St. does now along the northern border of Bushnell Park, was taken underground years ago because of its habit of flooding the city. He leads you on a 2-mile course through massive tunnels lit only by the headlamps you wear. You'll beach the canoes in a large cavern to look at an underground spillway and eventually exit outdoors at the Connecticut River. The whole trip is about two hours long. Call for pricing and transportation details. **P.O. Box 137, Collinsville, 06022; (860) 693-0385.**

Cruises

See the city from a fresh perspective by taking a riverboat cruise up and down the Connecticut River on the *Lady Fenwick*. The boat departs from Charter Oak Landing for hour-long lunchtime cruises ($6) at noon & 1:00 P.M., two-and-a-half-hour trips ($10) at 2:30 P.M., hour-and-a-half cocktail cruises ($7) at 5:30 P.M. & Thu. & Fri. evening theme outings with Cajun food and music ($14.50) at 7:30 P.M. There's also a full-day, 50-mile fall foliage cruise to Old Saybrook ($25) on Columbus Day. Cruises run daily, Memorial Day–Labor Day, then weekends only Labor Day–mid-Oct. with Jambalaya cruises continuing through late Sept., but call for a complete schedule. Fares are half-price for children 3–11; discounts are given to seniors. Free parking is available at Charter Oak Landing on Reserve Rd. in Hartford. For more information, contact **Deep River Navigation Company** at **(860) 526-4954.**

Fishing

Connecticut River

In early spring, the Connecticut River is full of American shad, blueback herring, alewives (as well as striped bass that follow them to feed) and white perch. Later in the year you'll find smallmouth and largemouth bass that are best caught from a boat, as well as white catfish and channel catfish that are easily caught from shore. In protected coves and bays there is also calico bass. Riverside Park, Charter Oak Landing and Great River Park all offer shore

access and boat launches for anglers, and parking is free. See the Boat Launches section for directions.

Tournaments

Riverfront Recapture, a nonprofit agency working on revitalizing the riverfront in the Hartford area, has a hand in running a number of fishing events. In conjunction with National Free Fishing Week in early June, they hold a Bass and Catfish Tournament. There is no fee to enter, but there are cash prizes. They also hold weekly bass and catfish tournaments at Charter Oak Landing in Hartford on Wed. nights late May–mid-Sept. There is a charge to enter the weekly events, and you compete for the pot. For more information call **(860) 293-0131.**

Hiking and Strolling

Metropolitan District Commission Reservoirs

The Connecticut Audubon Society sponsors two-hour, naturalist-led hikes at this spectacular recreation area. They take place on selected Sat. and Sun., Apr.–Oct., starting at the main parking area in the southern portion of the MDC property. The hikes are free, and no reservations are needed. Alternatively, you can take a hike of your own choosing at any time the grounds are open. For directions and more information on the MDC site, see the listing under Biking. For more information about the hike series call the **Connecticut Audubon Society** at (860) 633-8402.

The Riverfront

Virtually all riverfront land in Hartford and East Hartford is being linked into one linear park with pathways for walking and biking and facilities for concerts and other events. The project represents 15 years of work toward making the Connecticut River accessible to urban residents after a long period of neglect. Most of the project is already complete. The East Hartford section of the park and Charter Oak Landing are already connected via the Charter Oak Bridge walkway. The pathways here are flat, easy and accessible from the heart of the city. Access them from Riverside Park on Leibert Rd. off Jennings Rd. in Hartford, Charter Oak Landing on Reserve Rd. in Hartford and Great River Park on East River Dr. in East Hartford. For more information call **Riverfront Recapture** at **(860) 293-0131.**

Ice Skating

Elizabeth Park

When conditions permit, you can skate outdoors on a small pond in this stunning horticultural park, but bring your own skates. Lighting adjacent to the pond provides enough illumination for skating after dark. There's signage at the pond indicating when the ice is safe, or you can check on it in advance by calling **(860) 543-8888.** Enter on Asylum Ave. between Prospect Ave. and Steele Rd. in West Hartford and drive to the Pond House, which is sometimes used as a warming hut.

Veterans Memorial Ice Rink

This year-round rink offers an extensive but complicated schedule of public skating hours, so call for specifics. Fall through spring it's open daily, but in summer hours are limited. Admission for nonresidents is in the $5–$7 range and skate rentals are available for a few dollars. **56 Buena Vista Rd., West Hartford, 06107; (860) 521-1573.**

Seeing and Doing

The most current and comprehensive guide to upcoming events, concerts, art shows, etc., in this area is the *Hartford Advocate,* a free periodical available at newsstands, convenience stores and many attractions. Also check *The Hartford Courant* for listings.

Antiquing

If you're in downtown Hartford and have a special interest in antique and estate jewelry, stop at **The Unique Antique (860-522-9094)** in the Civic Center Mall. It's open six days a week at 10:00 A.M., closing Mon.–Fri. at 7:30 P.M. &

Sat. at 6:00 P.M. If you want to make plans around an antiquing event, however, it's got to be the yearly **Connecticut Antiques Show** at the Connecticut State Armory every Oct. This is a show of museum-quality pieces held to benefit the Antiquarian and Landmarks Society. It's kicked off with an opening night preview party on Fri. with ticket prices of $50. General admission on the weekend is $8 (parking included). Hours are 11:00 A.M.–8:00 P.M. on Sat. & 11:00 A.M.–5:00 P.M. on Sun. There are always a few special presentations or symposia held in conjunction with the event. The armory is located at Capitol Ave. and Broad St. in Hartford. For more information call the **Antiquarian and Landmarks Society** at **(860) 247-8996.**

Art Galleries

For information on the **Wadsworth Atheneum,** see the listing under Major Attractions.

Hartford Steam Boiler Inspection and Insurance Co.

An important collection of paintings by Impressionist, Hudson River School, Barbizon and Tonalist artists is displayed in this insurance company's corporate offices. Among the works is the 1846 painting of Hartford's Charter Oak by Frederic Edwin Church. There is a free one-hour tour of the collection by appointment only. Call as far in advance as possible and have alternate dates in mind. **One State St. (enter on Columbus Blvd.), Hartford, 06102.** For more information call **(860) 722-5175.**

Joseloff Gallery

This excellent gallery on Hartford University's main campus mounts approximately five shows a year of faculty and student work of a very high caliber, as well as contemporary work from artists around the world. The gallery itself is quite beautiful and is located right next to the equally worthwhile Museum of American Political Life. They have short down times between shows; call before going. Admission is

95

free. During the school year (Sept.–May) hours are Tue.–Fri., 11:00 A.M.–4:00 P.M.; Sat.–Sun., noon–4:00 P.M.; call for summer hours. When you enter the campus, register at the information booth and get directions.

If you're looking for a nice lunch before or after your visit to the gallery and you want the convenience of something on campus, try the **1877 Club.** They serve an inexpensive, all-you-can-eat lunchtime buffet that beats anything else around, and they're just a few steps away. Their hours are Tue.–Fri., 11:30 A.M.–1:30 P.M. Call **(860) 768-4876** one day in advance to make a reservation, which is the only way you can be assured of getting a table. The museum and restaurant are located in the Harry Jack Gray Center. The campus entrance is at **200 Bloomfield Ave., West Hartford, 06117; (860) 768-4089.**

The Pumphouse Gallery

With the most unusual setting of any art gallery I know, the Pumphouse is really worth going out of your way for. This lovely little Tudor structure in Bushnell Park was built by the Army Corps of Engineers in the 1940s. It is a functioning pumphouse that helps keep the downtown from flooding when the Connecticut River backs up into the Park River, which runs below Hartford's streets. Part of the pumphouse is used as a gallery featuring the work of Connecticut artists. Shows are juried for quality and change about every six weeks. Admission is free. Hours: Tue.–Sat., 11:00 A.M.–2:00 P.M. Located at the **southeast corner of Bushnell Park near Pulaski Circle in central Hartford; (860) 722-6536.**

Children and Families

Parents should request the free "KidStuff" brochure from the **Greater Hartford Tourism District** at **(800) 793-4480.** This pamphlet describes dozens of activities in and around Hartford that kids will enjoy. Also search out CT Kids, a newspaper insert calendar of events published ten times a year and distributed in *The Hartford Courant* or in single-copy form at places frequented by parents in West Hartford and towns in the Farmington Valley. If you have

the flexibility to plan your trip around an event, come to Hartford for Mark Twain Days, an exceptional weekend full of family-oriented activities described under Festivals and Events. See the Nature Centers section for a description of Westmoor Park, a demonstration farm where kids can both learn something and have a blast.

Bushnell Park Carousel

If you have kids, you can't leave Hartford without visiting the carousel in Bushnell Park. Built in 1914 and installed here in 1974, this grand, old-fashioned ride revolves to music pumped out of an authentic Wurlitzer organ. Hours are Tue.–Sun., 11:00 A.M.–5:00 P.M., late May–mid-Sept., & weekends only during the same hours the rest of the year. Rides cost only \$.50. In summer there may be a crowd, but the carousel holds a lot, so the line moves pretty fast. It's covered against inclement weather but can be closed when conditions are truly prohibitive. Call **(860) 246-7739** for general information and **(860) 249-2201** for information on weather closings.

Hartford Children's Theatre

This local performing arts group specializes in producing shows for young audiences. Past efforts have ranged from the lighthearted *The Wizard of Oz* to the dramatic *The Witch of Blackbird Pond*. They mount four shows per Oct.–June season, with each one running about two weeks. Performances take place Fri. evenings and Sat. and Sun. afternoons at different venues around the Hartford area. Tickets are very reasonable. For a schedule call **(860) 249-7970** or write to them at **P.O. Box 2547, Hartford, 06146.**

Lutz Children's Museum

This small facility has live animals and two rooms with changing educational exhibits appropriate for kids from preschool to middle elementary age. There's one new exhibit every six months. Picnic tables are available during the summer months, and families are invited to hike an easy trail system on Oak Grove St. just off Autumn St. about 2 miles away. Admission to the museum is $3 adults, $2.50 children 1–17. Hours: Tue.–Wed., 2:00 P.M.–

5:00 P.M.; Thu.–Fri., 9:30 A.M.–5:00 P.M.; Sat.–Sun., noon–5:00 P.M. The trails are open dawn–dusk daily at no charge. **247 S. Main St., Manchester, 06040; (860) 643-0949** for a recorded message; **(860) 649-2838** for further questions.

Science Center of Connecticut
Designed for elementary school-age kids, the Science Center of Connecticut is one of the largest hands-on childen's museums in the state. When you approach the door you're greeted by a sculpture of a sperm whale (the state animal and the museum's mascot) large enough to walk around in. The wildlife connection is continued inside, where you'll find numerous animals that were injured and are unable to live in the wild, and exotic creatures that were confiscated by the authorities after being kept or transported illegally. Programs in which kids may touch the animals are given daily in conjunction with feedings.

Other highlights include a large hall devoted to traveling exhibits that change four times a year, the new Gengras planetarium giving astronomy programs and evening laser light shows, an area called the Kids Factory with games for kids 7 years and under and benches for worn-out parents and a computer lab where you can sign on to the Internet (with help from guides on weekends). There are several admission options, but the planetarium and exhibits combination costs $7 for adults, $6 for children and seniors. Hours: Tue., Wed. & Fri., 10:00 A.M.–4:00 P.M.; Thu., 10:00 A.M.–8:00 P.M.; Sat., 10:00 A.M.–5:00 P.M.; Sun., noon–5:00 P.M.; closed Mon. (except holidays), Thanksgiving, Christmas & Easter. **950 Trout Brook Dr., West Hartford, 06119; (860) 231-2824.**

Gardens and Arboreta

Elizabeth Park Rose Gardens
The first municipal rose garden in the United States is also one of the largest. Fourteen thousand bushes representing 900 types of America's favorite flower are planted here. Come in June to see the roses at their peak, although many rebloom throughout the summer. In addition to the roses, there's a rock garden, perennial and annual gardens, the largest collection of ornamental trees in the greater Hartford area and greenhouses filled with conservatory plants open Mon.–Fri., 7:30 A.M.–3:00 P.M., year-round. The park is the site of a spring flower show and many special programs.

Paved park roads and a small network of paths are pleasant for walking and low-speed biking. Concessions and handicapped-accessible rest rooms are located in the Pond House. Close by is a picnic grove with tables and grills available on a first-come, first-served basis; pack out your trash. Park hours are dawn–dusk daily, year-round. Enter the park from Asylum Ave. between Prospect Ave. and Steele Rd. in West Hartford. For more information, request a schedule from **Friends of Elizabeth Park** at **(860) 242-0017.**

Historic Sites

The single best concise piece of literature on Hartford is a brochure entitled "Hartford Dreamers and Doers: Legacies of a Victorian City," which conveys a wealth of historic information while describing 24 historically significant sites around the city and giving inspired insight into Hartford's soul. The brochure is available from the visitors information centers listed in the Services section of this chapter.

Ancient Burial Ground
This cemetery was the first "final" resting place of several of Connecticut's first European settlers. Thomas Hooker, the prominent Puritan minister, who is widely regarded as the father of Connecticut, was interred here in 1647. A map at the entrance on Gold St. helps you locate markers by the name of the interred. The cemetery gates are in theory open from dawn–dusk, but they often remain open longer, and the church itself (which has Tiffany windows) can be viewed Wed. & Fri., 11:00 A.M.–2:00 P.M., Apr. to the second week in Dec. Located behind Center Church at the **intersection of Main and Gold Sts. in Hartford; (860) 249-5631.**

Central Valley

Museums

There are more than two dozen museums of various types in the Hartford area, ranging from small historic homes to monumental institutions. For information on the **Harriet Beecher Stowe House, Mark Twain House** and **Wadsworth Atheneum,** see the listings under Major Attractions. For information on the Lutz Children's Museum, see the listing under Children and Families.

Butler-McCook Homestead

Nearly all of the private homes that once lined Main St. in downtown Hartford have given way to modern offices and shops. Perhaps the sole survivor is this white clapboard 1782 property owned by the Antiquarian and Landmarks Society. It was occupied by the same family for almost 200 years, so their accumulated possessions of two centuries were preserved intact. Photographs dating from 1910 allowed the society to set the house up to accurately depict that period. In the back there is what is believed to be the oldest domestic garden in Hartford (ca. 1865). Admission: $4 adults, $1 children. Hours: Tue., Thu. & Sun., noon–4:00 P.M., mid-May–mid-Oct. **396 Main St., Hartford, 06103; (860) 247-8996.**

Connecticut Historical Society Museum

The Connecticut Historical Society offers two things for the general public: a museum with permanent and changing exhibits, and an extensive series of imaginative programs throughout the year. Permanent displays include the Barber collection of 18th- and 19th-century furniture and three galleries of Connecticut landscapes. A recent calendar included events as varied as a presentation on 18th-century American cookery, a lecture on the industrial history of the Connecticut River Valley, a celebration of Election Day and a walk along the route of the Farmington Canal. Call for a schedule of exhibits and special events. Admission: $3 adults, free to children under 18, free for all the first Sun. of each month. Hours: Tue.–Sun., noon–4:45 P.M.; closed Mon., Sat. Memorial Day–Labor Day &

major holidays. **One Elizabeth St., Hartford, 06105; (860) 236-5621.**

Museum of American Political Life

The focus of this museum located on the campus of Hartford University is presidential politics and how it has shaped and been shaped by the lives of ordinary citizens. History buffs will love the timeline of presidential elections, which attempts to assign relative importance to historical events. There are also displays on suffrage, the perennial issue of reform, the media and more. Admission is free. Hours: Tue.–Fri., 11:00 A.M.–4:00 P.M. The university is at **200 Bloomfield Ave., West Hartford, 06117; (860) 768-4090.** Register at the information booth near the entrance and get directions.

Museum of Connecticut History

All the original important documents of the state—the 17th-century charter (the one at the center of the Charter Oak legend) and Fundamental Orders, the constitutions of 1818 and 1965—are on display here. Other exhibits are concerned with Connecticut industry (the Colt Firearms collection is in permanent residence) and political life. Admission is free. Hours: Mon.–Fri., 9:30 A.M.–4:00 P.M. **231 Capitol Ave. (across from the Capitol building), Hartford, 06103; (860) 566-3056.**

Noah Webster House

It's easy to find the Noah Webster House. Just look for the sign by the side of the road cleverly written with diacritical marks, as if it were a dictionary entry. Noah Webster is *the* Webster, credited with having compiled the first dictionary of American English in the early 1800s. Begin your visit by watching a short video on Webster's life and viewing an original copy of the 1828 printing of his dictionary in two volumes. A costumed interpreter leads you through the simple house in which Webster was born, telling anecdotes about Webster and explaining the design and function of many of the implements and artifacts on display. Admission: $5 adults, $4 seniors, $1 children 6–12. Hours (Sept.–June): Thu.–Tue., 1:00 P.M.–4:00 P.M. Hours (July/Aug.): Mon., Tue., Thu. & Fri., 10:00 A.M.–4:00 P.M.; Sat.–Sun.,

1:00 P.M.–4:00 P.M. **227 South Main St., West Hartford, 06107; (860) 521-5362.**

Old State House

The red brick façade of the Old State House provides a wonderful counterpoint to the modern skyscrapers that populate downtown Hartford. It was closed for several years of refurbishment and reopened with a big celebration in 1996, so it's currently in wonderful shape. The Old State House was the second building to house Connecticut's state government, from the destruction of the first in a fire in the late 1700s until the opening of the current Capitol building in the late 1800s. It is the oldest extant statehouse in the country, and was designed by noted American architect Charles Bulfinch, who also designed one in Boston. The 1818 constitution was framed here, and it was the site of the *Amistad* and Prudence Crandall trials (see the **New Haven** and **Far Northeast** chapters, respectively). On view are exhibits relating to Connecticut's history and culture. Admission is free. Hours: Mon.–Fri., 10:00 A.M.–4:00 P.M.; Sat., 11:00 A.M.–4:00 P.M.; closed Sun. **800 Main St., Hartford, 06103; (860) 522-6766.**

Other Museums

If you can find it open, the **Connecticut Sports Museum and Hall of Fame (860-724-4918)** is located on the upper level of the Civic Center Mall in downtown Hartford. Currently the hours are Mon., Wed. & Fri., 10:30 A.M.–2:30 P.M., & by appointment.

The **Cheney Homestead** is a local history museum documenting the brothers who founded the silk industry for which Manchester was once known. Admission: $1 adults, free to children under 16. Hours: Thu. & Sun., 1:00 P.M.–5:00 P.M., & by appointment, year-round; closed major holidays. **106 Hartford Rd., Manchester, 06040; (860) 643-5588.**

The Connecticut Firemen's Historical Society has a fitting site for its **Fire Museum:** a firehouse (ca. 1900) that helps bring to life their collection of fire-fighting equipment and other artifacts. Admission by donation. Hours: Fri.–Sat., 10:00 A.M.–5:00 P.M.; Sun., noon–5:00 P.M., mid-Apr.–mid-Nov. **230 Pine St., Manchester, 06040; (860) 875-5003.**

For an inside look at police life and training, take a self-guided tour of the **Hartford Police Museum,** where photographs, retired equipment, an old jail cell, uniforms and memorabilia tell the story of Hartford's law enforcers. Hours: Mon.–Fri., 9:00 A.M.–4:30 P.M. **101 Pearl St., Hartford, 06103; (860) 722-6152.**

The **Huguenot House** is a restored 1761 gambrel-roofed home built by a saddle maker. A guided tour focuses on the house, its pre-1800 furnishings and the families that inhabited it; you also get a ghost story for good measure. A one-room schoolhouse (ca. 1820) and a blacksmith shop on the premises are open for self-guided tours. Admission is by donation. Hours: Thu., Sun. & holidays, 1:00 P.M.–4:00 P.M., Memorial Day–Sept., & by appointment. **307 Burnside Ave. (Rte. 44), East Hartford, 06118; (860) 568-6178/5032.** This is also the site of a Civil War Reenactment and Living History event held in late Aug. There are fife and drum performances, interpreters in period clothes, skirmishes and an encampment; call the museum for details.

By appointment only you can tour the **Isham-Terry House (211 High St., Hartford; 860-247-8996),** one of the few 19th-century Italianate houses in Hartford to have escaped conversion to apartments or offices. Nothing in the house has been changed since the 1920s, so it gives an accurate insight into the lifestyle of an upper-middle-class family in the city.

The **Old Manchester Museum** is a comprehensive museum of that town's history, with exhibits on local industries, a country store, military artifacts and ladies' gowns. Admission: $1 adults, free to children under 16. Hours: Mon., 9:00 A.M.–noon; Sun., 1:00 P.M.–4:00 P.M. **126 Cedar St., Manchester, 06040; (860) 647-9983.**

The **Sarah Whitman Hooker Homestead** is interesting for its architecture (it's a 1720 saltbox converted to Federal style in 1805), its furnishings (all pre-1830), the family that occupied it for nearly 200 years and the Tories who were confined here on an honor system during the Revolutionary War. Admission: $3. Hours: Mon. & Wed., 1:30 P.M.–3:30 P.M. year-round except holidays & in bad weather; arrive by 2:30 to get the full one-hour tour. **1237 New Britain Ave., West Hartford, 06110; (860) 523-5887** or **(800) 475-1233.**

Finally, students of health sciences might find special appeal in the **Historical Museum of Medicine and Dentistry,** where you can learn how far medicine has progressed in the last 200 years. Admission is free. Hours are Mon.–Fri., 10:00 A.M.–4:00 P.M. Located in the Hartford Medical Society Bldg., **230 Scarborough St., Hartford, 06105; (860) 236-5613.**

Nature Centers

Westmoor Park is a combination community environmental education center and town park. The two main attractions are a barnyard where you may see animals being fed or groomed and 3 miles of hiking trails (a half-mile of them handicapped-accessible). On Farm Day (second Sat. in May) you can see animal demonstrations and enjoy hayrides, music, games and more. The Pumpkin Festival (second Sat. in Oct.) includes all that plus marshmallow roasting, pumpkin decorating and such. Other special events are offered as well and take place noon–4:00 P.M. Regular hours are 9:00 A.M.–4:00 P.M. daily, year-round. **119 Flagg Rd., West Hartford, 06117; (860) 232-1134.**

Nightlife

Hartford has a very active nightlife, although pickings get pretty slim on Mon. Most of the clubs are in the heart of the downtown: west of Main St., east of Union Pl., north of Pulaski Circle and south of Church St. You don't have to go any further than the train station, where **Union St. Café** (open Thu.–Sat.; **860-525-5191**) keeps a decent list of beers on tap and has dancing, a video wall and pool tables. **Bar With No Name (Corner of Asylum and Trumbull Sts.; 860-522-4646)** is a loud, dark and crowded club with dancing to live bands and DJs. "Barbeque and blues" is the

motto at **Black-eyed Sally's (350 Asylum St.; 860-278-7427),** a personality-laden club/restaurant. It's one giant homage to musical greats, with a down-home rusticity that suits the Cajun food and live blues music Thu.–Sat. On nonmusic nights, come for the food alone. For casual drinks with friends, you can't beat the atmosphere on the top floor of **The Brickyard (113 Allyn St.; 860-249-2112).** It's one big room with high ceilings, brick walls, pool tables, hockey and basketball shooting cages and a large bar. It's very casual and comfortable, and you'll always find sports on the screen. They're open Tue.–Sat., 4:00 P.M.–close and for some Civic Center events. There's also a dance club down below; call for details. On the sports theme, **Coach's (187 Allyn St.; 860-522-6224)** is a neat bar and restaurant where the building itself incorporates elements borrowed from sports, such as the boards from a hockey rink used as a seating divider. They serve lunch and dinner, and they're open seven days a week; call for hours. **Hartford Brewery (35 Pearl St.; 860-246-2337),** only five years old yet the senior citizen of the brewpub scene in Connecticut, is an unpretentious place for beer lovers. Of the several dozen they make, you'll find about a half-dozen on tap at any one time. Mon.–Sat. before 8:00 P.M. you can purchase a 2-liter plastic bottle to take home. They also have pub games, a humidor filled with cigars, a lunch menu that's heavily sandwich-oriented and a dinner menu of full-fledged meals. **Pauli's Jazz & Blues Café (88 Pratt St.; 860-522-7623)** is a coffeehouse by day, club by night. They serve pizza, sandwiches, a long menu of desserts, coffees and coffee cocktails. They have live music Thu.–Sat. starting around 9:30 P.M. Pauli's is connected to low-key **Lord Jim's Pub,** which has pretty much the English pub atmosphere you'd expect from the name. **The Russian Lady (191 Ann St.; 860-525-3003)** is a dance club with mosh pits fronted by a great English-style pub. That's a sampling of what you can find, but by all means just take a walk around town on any given night and you'll find more. And to prove that there is a nightlife in the area outside downtown Hartford, **Borders Books and Music (59 Pavilions Dr.,**

Manchester, 06040; 860-649-1433) is the site of regular concerts, lectures, poetry readings and storytelling.

Performing Arts

Hartford has its share of great performance venues. Theater, dance and recitals by students and guest artists are offered on two stages at the **Austin Arts Center at Trinity College (300 Summit St., Hartford, 06106; 860-297-2199)** during the school year. The nearby Cinestudio shows a broad mix of art flicks, classics and first-run movies, usually at bargain prices. You can reach the **Cinestudio hotline** at **(860) 297-2463.**

Nearly 70 years old, the **Bushnell (corner of Trinity and Capitol Aves., Hartford; 860-246-6807)** is the grand dame of city venues. You might recognize it as the site of the 1996 Hartford presidential debate. This is where you'll see performances by the **Hartford Ballet, Hartford Symphony** or **Connecticut Opera.** They also have a Broadway musical and drama series, a Bank of Boston–sponsored series of popular music and dance performances and a host of other events. Free parking is available in government lots up and down Capitol Ave., and there are also pay lots nearby. See the Tours section for details on getting a backstage look at the Bushnell, which has a noted Art Deco interior.

You can also contact the **Connecticut Opera** directly at **(860) 527-0713.** Ditto for the **Hartford Ballet (860-525-9396)** and the **Hartford Symphony Orchestra (860-244-2999).** By special arrangement the **Museum Café** at the Wadsworth Atheneum is sometimes open for dinner on evenings when the symphony performs. Call **(860) 728-5989** for reservations.

The in-house company at **Hartford Stage (50 Church St. opposite Christ Church Cathedral, Hartford; 860-527-5151)** presents old and new theatrical works in a season running Oct. through June. They offer both evening and matinee performances, and their schedule is not limited to weekends; call for a program.

Contemporary works for the stage by American playwrights is the specialty of **Theater-Works (233 Pearl St., Hartford; 860-527-7838),** a regional professional company. They mount productions year-round, giving evening performances Wed.–Sat. at 8:00 P.M. and matinees on Sun. at 2:30 P.M. Ticket prices are in the $17–$21 range.

The **Meadows Music Theatre (61 Savitt Way, Hartford, 06120)** is a new venue that features mostly big-name popular music artists and large-scale dance productions. It's a unique place with a conventional covered auditorium; the back wall can be opened in summer to a large lawn, where you can spread a blanket or set up a folding chair to enjoy the performance in the open air. Free parking is available at lots on Weston St.; look for signs. Call **(860) 548-7370** for directions or event information; dial **ProTix** at **(860) 422-0000** for tickets.

Real Art Ways (56 Arbor St., Hartford, 06106; 860-232-1006) presents new art in all media in its own gallery, sponsors public art around town and recently opened a cinema showing a mix of mainstream and less commercial films. Plans are to complement the existing facilities with a stage and a café down the line. The gallery is open Wed.–Fri., noon–5:00 P.M., & nightly 6:30 P.M.–9:30 P.M. There can be downtime between shows, so call before going. Films are shown nightly.

Two towns east of Hartford but only a short drive away, you'll find historic **Cheney Hall (177 Hartford Rd., Manchester, 06040; 860-645-6743),** home to the Little Theatre of Manchester and the site of folk, jazz and poetry performances and family entertainment. This beautiful 1867 structure with an impressive profile is said to be the oldest operating theater building in Connecticut. It was recently renovated and is in great shape.

Shopping

The **Civic Center Mall** has a small selection of shops and is literally in the center of downtown Hartford between Asylum, Trumbull, Ann and Church Sts. There's a parking garage on

101

Church St. directly connected to the mall. Hours are Mon.–Fri., 10:00 A.M.–7:30 P.M.; Sat., 10:00 A.M.–6:00 P.M.; call **(860) 275-6100** for information.

The open-sided, barnlike buildings on Main St. opposite the Old State House house contain what's known as **Main St. Market,** a seasonal shopping spot where you can get unusual foods to go, ethnic crafts, produce in season and more. Next to the Old State House is the small **Pavilion at State House Square,** where there are good, fast and cheap breakfast and lunch counters on the second level. The shops serve local office workers primarily, so hours are limited to weekdays 10:00 A.M.–6:00 P.M., but the restaurants open at 7:00 A.M.

Hartford's equivalent of the big wholesale food and flower markets in New York and Los Angeles is the Department of Agriculture's **Connecticut Regional Farmers' Market.** It's open to the public 365 days a year, 5:00 A.M.–10:00 A.M., but the variety and amount of goods are heavily dependent on the season, and Sat. are most active. The market is located on Reserve Rd. in Hartford. For more information call **(860) 527-5047.**

If you like flea markets, don't pass up the opportunity to visit a big one in the famous Colt Building every weekend, Sat.–Sun., 9:00 A.M.–4:00 P.M. Parking and admission are free. Enter from Huy Shope Ave.

In West Hartford, Farmington Ave. in the vicinity of Main St. has high-end stores that cater to West Hartford's largely upscale residents. The neighborhood is full of boutiques, coffeehouses and restaurants.

East of the Connecticut River, head to the **Buckland Hills Retail Area,** a series of open-air and enclosed malls off I-84 exits 62 and 63 in Manchester. The centerpiece is known as Pavillions at Buckland Hills. For more information call **(860) 644-1450.**

Sports

Hartford Wolf Pack/
Hartford Civic Center

When Hartford's NHL Whalers moved on, the city became home to the AHL **Wolf Pack,** a farm team for the New York Rangers. They play 40 home games, Oct.–Apr., at the Hartford Civic Center, with ticket prices around $12–17. For more information call **(860) 246-7825** or order tickets direct from **Ticketmaster** at **(860) 525-4500.** For information on other Civic Center sports events such as basketball and figure skating, call **(860) 727-8010.** The facility is bordered by Asylum, Trumbull, Ann and Church Sts. in downtown Hartford. Plentiful parking is available in lots and garages and in metered spaces close by.

Riverfront Rowing Regatta

College teams compete in this 2,000-meter race on the Connecticut River every Sept., and lots of spectators are always on hand to cheer on their favorites. The date changes from year to year, so call **Riverfront Recapture** at **(860) 293-0131** for more information.

Tours

Take one of the organized tours listed below or design your own using the "Hartford Dreamers and Doers" brochure described in the Historic Sites section of this chapter. For riverboat excursions, see the listing under Cruises. For guided canoe trips, see the listing under Boating. Information on touring the Capitol is given under Major Attractions.

Backstage at the Bushnell

The Bushnell, designed by the same architectural firm responsible for Radio City Music Hall in New York City, has been Hartford's premier performing arts venue for almost 70 years. Built by Dotha Bushnell Hillyer as a memorial to her father, the popular theologian Reverend Horace Bushnell, its interior has been recognized as a significant example of the Art Deco style, although you'd never guess it from the outside. The Bushnell has hosted many stage and musical greats who have left their signatures in the Autograph Room, just one of the sights you'll see when you tour it. Some others are the largest hand-painted ceiling mural in the country, a 5,000-pipe organ that is still used on occasion and behind-the-scenes areas such as the projection booth.

Free, guided, 45-minute tours are offered Wed. & Thu., 11:00 A.M.–3:00 P.M., year-round. Reservations required. **166 Capitol Ave., Hartford, 06106; (860) 987-6000.**

Governor's Residence

The beautiful 1909 Georgian Revival home has been the official governor's residence since 1945 and has benefited tremendously from recent restoration efforts. Open to the public for free hour-long tours Tue. & Wed. at 10:00 A.M. by appointment only. **990 Prospect Ave., Hartford, 06105; (860) 566-4840.**

Hartford Guides
Historic Walking Tour

One of Hartford's goodwill ambassadors leads a two-hour downtown walking tour on weekdays at 1:00 P.M., spring–fall. The cost is $5 per person, and the tour starts at the **Hartford Police Museum** at **101 Pearl St.** Weekend tours for groups are also available by advance reservation. For more information call **(860) 522-0855.**

Heritage Trails
Sightseeing Bus Tours

Daily two-hour narrated bus tours of the city are given by Ernest Shaw, the author of several books about local history. He gives a comprehensive overview of Hartford's history, architecture, important sites and people. There are departures every two hours from 9:00 A.M. to 5:00 P.M. year-round. Cost: $15. He offers pickup service at major hotels in the Hartford area. Audiocassette tours can also be purchased; inquire for prices. Reservations are required but can be made on short notice. Payment by cash or traveler's check only. For more information call **(860) 677-8867.**

Soldiers and Sailors Memorial Arch/ Bushnell Park

Two beautiful, interconnected, vaguely Romanesque brownstone towers stand silent guard at the Trinity St. entrance to Hartford's Bushnell Park. These form the Soldiers and Sailors Memorial Arch, dedicated on Sept. 17, 1886, the 24th anniversary of the Civil War battle at Antietam, to commemorate the Hartfordians who were killed and wounded on that day. For Connecticut troops, Antietam was the most bloody battle of the entire war. The towers feature one of the largest continuous terra-cotta friezes in existence. The north side depicts the battle, and the south side shows returning vets being welcomed home. A circular staircase inside the eastern tower takes you up 96 steps to an observation deck at the top affording excellent views of the Capitol area. The arch can be toured Thu., noon–1:00 P.M., May–Oct. It's free (donations accepted) and no reservations are required. For more information on self-guided tours of the arch or Bushnell Park call the **Bushnell Park Foundation** at **(860) 232-6710.** Groups of ten or more can arrange for special tours of the arch by calling two weeks in advance.

Travelers Tower

View Hartford from one of the highest points in the city on the observation deck of the tower at Travelers Property Casualty Co. The open-air deck is open to the public Mon.–Fri., 10:00 A.M.– 3:00 P.M., from mid-May to mid-Oct. To visit the deck you must be able to negotiate 72 steps up a spiral staircase after a 24-floor elevator ride. The tour is free and starts every half hour. Reservations are preferred, even for individuals. Simply call **(860) 277-4208** and leave a message on the machine saying which day you'll be coming. **One Tower Square, corner of Main and Gold Sts., Hartford, 06183.**

Where to Stay

Hotels, Motels & Inns

It's a weekend traveler's market in Hartford, where hotels do most of their business Mon.–Thu. and drop their rates to try to fill rooms on Fri. and Sat. Barring a big special event, that means you can pick and choose. Give even the more expensive hotels a call to see if they have something in your price range on those days. For more suggestions, contact the **Greater Hartford Tourism District** at **(860) 244-8181** (in Connecticut) or **(800) 793-4480** (out-of-state).

Central Valley

Clarion Suites Inn—$$$ to $$$$

Although you don't gain a whole lot in terms of price by staying outside downtown Hartford, this hotel is a good choice if you want or need to. It appears to be patterned after another all-suites chain of hotels but adapted for a more budget-minded traveler. It has one- and two-bedroom units, some with fireplace and pull-out sofa. A fully equipped kitchenette and breakfast nook, king beds (two twins in the second bedroom) and TV with VCR are all standard. A buffet breakfast comes with the room. Facilities include a coin-op laundry, a swimming pool, a whirlpool spa, a sports court and a small exercise room, and it offers weekday valet dry cleaning and a free grocery shopping service. **191 Spencer St., Manchester, 06040; (800) 992-4004 or (860) 643-5811.**

The Goodwin Hotel—$$$ to $$$$

The Goodwin Hotel is one of Hartford's landmark older buildings. It offers such elegant touches as a doorman to greet you and bell-hops to carry your bags. It is the hotel of choice for business travelers entertaining clients in the beautiful lounge and award-winning restaurant. Accommodations range from standard rooms to many different types of suites, some on two levels and some with skylights. The decor is neutral, and furnishings are virtually identical throughout the hotel. For the fitness-oriented, there's an on-site exercise facility with weight training and cardiovascular equipment. **One Haynes St., Hartford, 06103; (800) 922-5006 or (860) 246-7500.**

Hastings Hotel—$$$ to $$$$

The hotel where President Clinton stayed during the 1996 presidential debate is a large conference center located about 1 mile from the center of downtown. It underwent renovation in 1996–1997, so everything looks quite new and modern. It has standard rooms as well as executive suites with completely private sleeping and living areas and smaller studio suites. Suites include a fully equipped kitchen. There are three different restaurants on-site, and at least one is open for every meal. Room service and complimentary park-

ing are available as well as an exercise facility. **85 Sigourney St., Hartford, 06105; (800) 777-7803 or (860) 727-4200.**

Holiday Inn—$$$ to $$$$

Only slightly removed from the downtown, the Holiday Inn is separated from the business district by I-84. Standard rooms offer conventional business class accommodations, and attractive suites with an open floor plan are furnished with some reproduction 18th-century pieces. Guests on the executive floor can avail themselves of a private lounge where complimentary afternoon hors d'oeuvres, beverages and a Continental breakfast are served. Rooms on that floor have two phone lines, a coffee maker, turn-down service and other perks. There's also an exercise facility, an outdoor pool, parking in a covered, attended garage, free shuttle service to downtown, on-site dining and a low-cost shuttle to the airport. **50 Morgan St., Hartford, 06120; (860) 549-2400.**

Sheraton—$$$ to $$$$

If you are staying in town for a Civic Center event, the Sheraton offers the most convenient location, since it is directly connected to that venue via a skywalk. It offers attractive business-class accommodations, and rooms on the club level have even nicer furnishings and come with Continental breakfast for one, bathrobe, in-room coffee and a private lounge for afternoon hors d'oeuvres. It has casual dining at two facilities, an exercise room, an indoor pool, on-site parking and a low-cost shuttle to the airport. **315 Trumbull St., Hartford, 06103; (800) 325-3535 or (860) 728-5151.**

Other

Hartford Youth Hostel—$ to $$

Also called the Mark Twain Youth Hostel, this is one of only two American Youth Hostel facilities in Connecticut. The Hartford Hostel is housed in an old Victorian on a side street in a good neighborhood on Hartford's west side. There are separate men's and women's dormitories as well as pricier private rooms for couples. Linens are available, or bring your own for a discount. Guests have full kitchen privileges and can take part in a wide range of free and low-cost organized activities. Local buses that stop about half a block away provide easy transportation from the train station. The hostel is about 2 miles from the heart of downtown. **131 Tremont St., Hartford, 06105; (860) 523-7255.**

Where to Eat

The Hartford area offers a lot of exceptional dining possibilities, and not just in the downtown. You can be in any neighboring town in about ten minutes by car, so traveling a bit farther afield to reach something that sounds especially interesting is definitely worth it. The downtown does offer the advantage of being on the small side and very walkable if you want to have dinner and then see an event at Hartford Stage, the Civic Center or the Bushnell. Whether you come by train, car, bus or taxi, once you're downtown there's little reason to get back in a vehicle until it's time to leave. Contrary to its name, **No Fish Today (80 Pratt St., Hartford; 860-244-2100)** always has fish and lots of it. The atmosphere is very casual and pubby. **Chuck's Steakhouse (860-241-9100),** whose fare is self-explanatory, has a prime location right in the Civic Center. Many downtown restaurants have limited hours on weekends, especially at lunch, but Chuck's serves lunch and dinner practically every day of the year, closing only for the biggest holidays, and it's a good choice for families. **City Steam Brewpub (942 Main St., Hartford; 860-525-1600)** is a brand-new microbrewery/restaurant located in an 1870s structure featuring vintage wood- and ironwork and a multilevel dining area.

South Hartford has traditionally been the city's Little Italy—and still is, although other cuisines are horning in on the business. **Chalé Ipanema (342 Franklin St.; 860-296-2120)** serves Brazilian chow. Although other Indian restaurants have more fashionable locations, the Indian food at **Kashmir (481 Wethersfield Ave.; 860-296-9685)** is what counts.

Truc (735 Wethersfield Ave.; 860-296-2818) is probably the most respected of the Vietnamese restaurants around, and down the street **Costa del Sol (901 Wethersfield Ave.; 860-296-1714)** serves Spanish food. If it's Italian you want, however, **Corvo (494 Franklin Ave.; 860-296-5800)** is near the top of the heap.

Farmington Ave. in West Hartford has its own cluster of eateries. **Ann Howard Cookery (981 Farmington Ave.; 860-233-5561)** has an outpost here selling great baked goods and upscale deli fare. You know the food at a restaurant whose owners are named Inge and Helmut is authentically German, and that's what you'll find at **Edelweiss (980 Farmington Ave.; 860-236-3096).** Indian, Thai and Japanese choices are all within a block of these. Food with a general Mediterranean flair is the specialty at **Tapas (1150 New Britain Ave., West Hartford; 860-521-4609).** In the same vein, **Restaurant Bricco (78 LaSalle Rd., West Hartford; 860-233-0220)** is a popular and lively place for wood-oven pizza and grilled items.

Finally, in the diner category, **Oasis (267 Farmington Ave., Hartford; 860-241-8200)** is renowned for its 1940s look, and **Hal's Aquarius Restaurant & Lounge (2790 Main St., Hartford; 860-247-0435)** is a local favorite.

Carbone's—$$$ to $$$$

Carbone's, which has been honored by *Connecticut* magazine readers for having the best Italian food in Connecticut, has been run by the same family for 60 years. It specializes in veal, fish and pasta, offering tableside service for some dishes. There are about a half-dozen dining rooms, each with a different decorative theme, ranging from very casual to moderately formal. Reservations are recommended on weekends. Lunch is served Mon.–Fri., 11:30 A.M.–2:00 P.M.; dinner is served Mon.–Sat., 5:00 P.M.–9:30 P.M.; closed on major holidays. **588 Franklin Ave., Hartford, 06114; (860) 296-9646.**

Cavey's—$$$ to $$$$

Cavey's is actually two restaurants in one, with separate dining rooms, kitchens and staffs.

One half specializes in Northern Italian and the other in French with Asian influences. The former is fairly casual and can accommodate large groups, whereas the latter is more formal, intimate and a bit pricier. The name is derived from that of the owners (Cavagnaro), who have been running the restaurant for more than 50 years. Reservations recommended. Lunch is served in the Italian restaurant only Mon.–Sat., 11:30 A.M.–2:30 P.M., except during July & Aug. when the whole restaurant is closed at midday. Dinner is served at both restaurants Mon.–Thu., 5:30 P.M.–9:30 P.M., & Fri.–Sat. until 10:00. **45 E. Center St., Manchester, 06040; (860) 643-2751.**

Civic Café—$$$ to $$$$

Possibly the most flamboyant of any restaurant in downtown Hartford, the Civic Café has a decor that has been called "Star Trek Art Deco" with visible ductwork and lighting diffusers that hang above the main, two-story dining room. You have your choice of seating at booths, tables and banquettes, some of which are spaced a bit on the tight side. A second-story loft with a few more tables makes an interesting perch from which to watch the busy scene below or get a close-up view of the wall mural of a stylized Hartford downtown. The sleek bar is one of the most beautiful in town. There's a little bit of everything here from vegetarian to steak, all of it delightfully spiced and dressed up. Many of the dishes show an international inspiration and your taste buds may get a workout. Casual dress is okay, but dressy is better. Reservations recommended. Open for lunch Mon.–Fri., 11:00 A.M.–2:30 P.M.; open for dinner Mon.–Sat., 5:00 P.M.–10:00 P.M. (a light fare menu is served until 11:00 P.M. every day except Mon.); Sun., 4:00 P.M.–10:00 P.M. **150 Trumbull St., Hartford, 06103; (860) 493-7412.**

Max Downtown—$$$ to $$$$

Max Downtown is one of three excellent restaurants with similar names and the same owner. Max Downtown anchors CityPlace, a high-rise office complex that is the tallest building in Connecticut. The main dining room is appealing, with high ceilings and deeply upholstered booths and tables, but I actually prefer the tavern, where cozy booths give you plenty of luxurious space to stretch out. The cuisine is adventurous, featuring lots of Asian and Continental influences, sometimes simultaneously in one dish. There's a cigar bar off the main dining room, and the restaurant occasionally hosts special evenings with package pricing ($75) for a four-course dinner, wine, cognac, coffee and cigars. A tavern menu is available from opening until closing each day. Reservations are essential on weekends and strongly suggested at other times. Hours: lunch served Mon.–Fri., 11:30 A.M.–2:30 P.M.; dinner served Mon.–Thu., 5:00 P.M.–10:30 P.M.; Fri.–Sat. until 11:30 P.M.; Sun., 4:00 P.M.–9:30 P.M. **185 Asylum St. (across from the Civic Center), Hartford, 06103; (860) 522-2530.**

Peppercorn's Grill—$$$ to $$$$

One of the most recommended restaurants in Hartford, located a little outside the downtown area, Peppercorn's Grill does truly creative Northern Italian food featuring wonderful seasonal ingredients and occasional, novel flavor combinations. Highlights of the menu include risottos, housemade pastas, elaborate appetizers that are worth considering as a meal if ordered in combination and a small number of "simply grilled" meats, fish and chicken. It offers a large selection of wines by the glass, as well as a good selection of domestic and imported beers. Peppercorn's is especially convenient to the Wadsworth Atheneum and makes an exceptional weekday choice for lunch if you are visiting that museum. Hours: lunch served Mon.–Fri., 11:30 A.M.–2:30 P.M. Dinner served Mon.–Wed., 5:00 P.M.–10:00 P.M.; Thu. until 11:00 P.M. & Fri. & Sat. until midnight; also open some Sun. when there are events at the Bushnell. **357 Main St. (at Capitol), Hartford, 06106; (860) 547-1714.**

Pierpont's—$$$ to $$$$

The restaurant in the Goodwin Hotel has been voted best hotel restaurant in the state for several years running by readers of *Connecticut* magazine. It's designed to resemble the inside of a yacht, so it's quite posh. Yachting is also referenced in the name of the lounge across the way, called the America's Cup. The food is Continental with some international influences, complemented by a large wine list. It has light choices at lunch and a wide range of à la carte and buffet choices for breakfast. Although a bit pricey, Sun. brunch ($19.95) is extensive. Breakfast served Mon.–Fri., 6:30 A.M.–10:30 A.M., & Sat., 7:00 A.M.–10:30 A.M. Sun. brunch: 10:00 A.M.–2:00 A.M. Lunch served Mon.–Fri., 11:30 A.M.–2:00 P.M. Dinner hours: Mon.–Sat., 5:30 P.M.–10:00 P.M. **One Haynes St., Hartford, 06103; (860) 522-4935.**

The Savannah—$$$ to $$$$

The Savannah serves food that is mostly regional American, but there are influences as varied as southwestern, Asian and Indian. It's especially gratifying to see distinctively American foods, such as pumpkin, collard greens and black-eyed peas, used creatively for a change. There's one dining room with walls of exposed brick and seating at banquettes and tables, plus a bar at the rear that enjoys pleasant natural lighting. Hours: Mon.–Thu., 5:30 P.M.–9:00 P.M.; Fri. & Sat. until 10:00 P.M. **391 Main St. (enter from Capitol Ave.), Hartford, 06106; (860) 278-2020.**

Hot Tomato's—$$$

Hot Tomato's is noted for its accommodating staff and affordable, delicious Italian food. The "Hot" in the name is presumably a reference to menu items starred as being "authentic, very hot and spicy." The menu is broken down into seafood, chicken and veal sections, plus a hodgepodge of other dishes. Located at the train station with a glass-sided dining room overlooking Asylum St. Lunch hours are Mon.–Fri., 11:30 A.M.–3:00 P.M. Dinner served Mon.–Wed. & Sun., 4:30 P.M.–9:30 P.M.; Thu.–Sat., 4:30 P.M.–10:30 P.M. **One Union Pl., Hartford, 06103; (860) 249-5100.**

Butterfly—$$ to $$$

Voted best Chinese restaurant in the state for several years running, the Butterfly offers a few things you don't normally find at Chinese restaurants: a pianist performing nightly 6:00 P.M.–8:00 P.M., a happy hour, karaoke on weekends and a champagne brunch on Sun. It serves continuously, 11:30 A.M.–10:00 P.M. Sun.–Thu. & until 11:00 P.M. Fri. & Sat. **831**

Farmington Ave., West Hartford, 06119; (860) 236-2816.

Skywalk Restaurant—$$ to $$$

A great place to eat in Hartford, especially if you have kids, is in this restaurant located right in the Civic Center skywalk across Trumbull St. It serves deli sandwiches, burgers, pasta, chicken and fish. On nights when there is an event at the Civic Center, it has a special dinner menu that also features prime rib. Enter through the Civic Center or from Pratt St., where you'll find an escalator. Hours vary depending on events at the Civic Center, but it is always open at least the following times: Mon.–Fri. beginning at 6:00 A.M. for breakfast from the deli; Mon.–Fri., 11:30 A.M.–2:00 P.M. for lunch; Thu.–Sat., 5:00 P.M.–8:00 P.M. for dinner; & on Sat. 11:30 A.M.–8:00 P.M. for lunch & dinner. For more information call **(860) 522-7623.**

Timothy's—$$ to $$$

Catering to the student body of nearby Trinity College, this casual restaurant is also a coffeehouse that stays open late on weekends for coffee and dessert. It's an especially good dinner destination if you're spending the evening at an Austin Arts Center performance, but don't expect anything upscale. The menu consists of meal salads, Tex-Mex items with some creative, unusual twists, straightforward meat and potato dishes, international cuisine and lots of vegetarian choices. Hours: Mon.–Thu., 7:00 A.M.–8:00 P.M.; Fri.–Sat. 9:00 A.M.–11:00 P.M. (kitchen closes at 9:00); Sun., 9:00 A.M.–8:00 P.M. **243 Zion St., Hartford, 06106; (860) 728-9822.**

Vito's by the Park—$ to $$$

On a sinuous strip of road bordering Bushnell Park, this new outpost of a Wethersfield eatery has a full-service dining room and a quick take-out pizza parlor side by side. *The* place to come in downtown Hartford for pizza, their slices are so large that they stretch the meaning of the word. There's also a full menu of very good Italian food. Although it gets three dollar signs for the dinner entrées, its slices make cheap lunch eats and lunch is a major reason to come here. Lunch hours are Mon.–Fri.,

11:30 A.M.–3:00 P.M., & dinner is served nightly from 5:00 P.M. **26 Trumbull St., Hartford, 06103; (860) 244-2200.**

Congress Rotisserie—$ to $$

For a quick bite at lunch there's no better place than Congress Rotisserie, which is indeed known for its rotisserie chicken plates that are very reasonably priced. You'll also find about ten meal salads, a good-sized list of deli sandwiches, minisandwiches for small appetites and good soups. The restaurant is basically a take-out place for the working crowds downtown, but there is a small, self-service loft dining room that's bright and pleasant. Hours: Mon.–Fri., 7:30 A.M.–5:00 P.M. **208 Trumbull St., Hartford, 06103; (860) 525-5141.**

Coffeehouses, Sweets & Treats

If you're looking for either a place with enough atmosphere to sit and enjoy a daytime cup of coffee or that steamy downtown joint where everybody hangs after hours, **Zuzu's (103 Pratt St. across from the Civic Center, Hartford; 860-244-8233)** is it. On Fri. and Sat. nights you may need to grease yourself up before coming in order to be able to slither between the other bodies. Hours: Mon.–Thu., 7:00 A.M.–1:00 A.M.; Fri.–Sat., 7:00 A.M.–3:00 A.M.; Sun., 10:00 A.M.–midnight. Also see the listing for **Pauli's Jazz & Blues Café** under Nightlife, or just cast your eyes down Trumbull St., where there's a Starbucks and some other possibilities.

Services

Local Visitors Information

Arts & Entertainment District, 225 Trumbull St., Hartford, 06123; (860) 525-8629. They publish a great detailed map showing the location of roughly 100 restaurants and attractions in the 20-block downtown area. Hours: Mon.–Fri., 8:30 A.M.–5:00 P.M.

Greater Hartford Tourism District, 234 Murphy Rd., Hartford, 06114; (800) 793-4480 (outside Connecticut) or **(860) 244-8181.** Request their *Hartford and Southern New England Guide* for the current year and the "Adventures and Escapes in Greater Hartford" brochure (an exceptional calendar of events) for the season during which you'll be visiting.

Hartford Downtown Council, 250 Constitution Plaza, Hartford, 06103; (860) 728-3089; Event Hotline: **(860) 522-6400.**

SNET Access is an automated current events hotline sponsored by Southern New England Telephone. Dial **(860) 725-5050** and then punch in the code **1310** to access current information on theater, music and other activities in the greater Hartford area.

State Welcome Center, Bradley International Airport, Windsor Locks; (860) 627-3590 or **3940** or **3051.** There are two centers, one in Terminal A and one in Terminal B. When possible, they're both staffed 9:00 A.M.–9:00 P.M. daily, year-round.

Visitors Information Desk, Hartford Civic Center, bordered by Church, Trumbull, Asylum and Ann Sts., downtown Hartford; (860) 275-6456. Hours: Mon.–Sat., 10:00 A.M.–7:30 P.M.; Sun., noon–5:00 P.M.

Visitors Information Desk, Old State House, 800 Main St., Hartford; (860) 522-6766. Hours: Mon.–Fri., 10:00 A.M.–4:00 P.M.; Sat., 11:00 A.M.–4:00 P.M.; closed Sun.

Visitors Information Desk, State Capitol (Capitol Ave., Hartford; (860) 240-0222. Hours: Mon.–Fri., 9:00 A.M.–3:00 P.M., year-round; also Sat. (Apr.–Oct. only), 10:15 A.M.–3:15 P.M.

Hartford Guides

Hartford Guides are general hospitality providers who try to make sure that visitors to Hartford have the best experience possible. They answer questions, give directions and give assistance to those who need help getting around. They'll escort you to your car, the bus or the train station from downtown spots. They can summon the police or other emergency personnel and even open car doors if you've locked yourself out. They also lead informative walking tours of the city (see the Tours section for more information). A uniform makes them easy to identify. They wear khaki pants, white shirts with red lettering on the back, and red baseball caps. All their services except the tours are free, thanks to funding from numerous public and private entities and the city of Hartford. Hours (subject to change): Mon.–Tue., 10:00 A.M.–9:00 P.M., Wed.–Sat., 10:00 A.M.–11:00 P.M. On Sun. they have a guide on duty at the Civic Center information booth noon–5:00 P.M., but no guides on the street. Their office is at the Hartford Police Museum, **101 Pearl St., Hartford, 06103.** For general inquiries call **(860) 522-0855.** To summon a guide call **(860) 293-8105.**

Transportation

Although not in Hartford or in the area covered by this chapter, the main airport serving Hartford is Connecticut's largest, **Bradley International** in Windsor Locks about 20 minutes north of the capital. Simply go to the ground transportation area in the airport to arrange for whatever service you need.

The greater Hartford area is served by three interstate bus lines with toll-free numbers for schedule and fare information: **Bonanza Bus Lines** at **(800) 556-3815, Peter Pan/Trailways** at **(800) 343-9999** and **Greyhound** at **(800) 231-2222.** Regional bus service between towns in the Hartford area is provided by the **Greater Hartford Transit District** at **(860) 247-5329** and **CT Transit** at **(860) 525-9181.**

Hartford's Union Station has daily **Amtrak** train service to Springfield, Massachusetts, and to Washington, D.C., through New Haven, New York and Philadelphia. For details call **(800) 872-7245.**

Middletown

Stretching from Wallingford, near New Haven, to Glastonbury, a suburb of Hartford on the opposite side of the Connecticut River, the broad area covered by this chapter roughly corresponds to the lower half of Connecticut's Central Valley. Middletown lies near the center of this heartland region but actually got its name from its situation halfway between Old Saybrook and Windsor, two of the state's first settlements. A university town on the Connecticut River, Middletown has the type of traditional, broad main street lined with shops, churches and restaurants that will remind visitors of small cities all across the United States.

The city enjoys the civilizing influence that institutions of higher learning can exert. Wesleyan University, founded 1831, is called one of the "Little Three" with Amherst and Williams. It is the oldest college founded by the Methodist Episcopal Church, although today it is a nonsectarian institution with a strong liberal arts mission. A host of art galleries and performing arts venues are located on the campus mere blocks away from downtown Middletown. The school's presence guarantees the area a full schedule of cultural and after-hours activities.

Although most of the lower Central Valley is suburban, agriculture still has a strong foothold. The best evidence of that is the huge country fair—the largest in Connecticut—held in Durham every year. On a year-round basis you can enjoy the harvest festival atmosphere of the renowned Lyman Orchards farm store in Middlefield.

The lower Central Valley is a geologically fascinating region where traprock ridges, volcanic in origin, rising from a flat valley floor make it the rock-climbing center of the state. Conversely, this is also where the flattest town in the state (Plainville) is located and where the Connecticut River unexpectedly departs the Central Valley and traverses the much harder bedrock of the Eastern Uplands for the rest of its trip to Long Island Sound—a fact for which geologists don't have an explanation.

You can see the transition firsthand by taking a sightseeing riverboat ride from Harborpark in Middletown. Another way to enjoy the river, especially if you need to cross it, is to take a brief ride on the Rocky Hill-Glastonbury ferry, the oldest continuously operating ferry in the United States. Just be sure to avoid rush hour, because it carries only three cars at a time!

Geology is also responsible for Dinosaur State Park. The soft sediments from which the valley's sandstone formed were suitable for capturing the footprints of the world's largest creatures, and in 1966 a huge cache of Jurassic-era tracks were discovered in Rocky Hill. Kids in their dinosaur fascination phase will clamor to visit the spot, where they can come away with a plaster cast of a dinosaur footprint made from a real track.

You can makes tracks of your own in Cheshire and Hamden, where a 6-mile portion of the Farmington Canal Towpath (ca. 1820s) has been converted into a unique linear park, the first stretch of what hopefully will be an 80-mile greenway stretching from New Haven to Northampton, Massachusetts. The path is flat, smooth and tree-lined—ideal for strolling, jogging, leisurely biking and roller blading. Other ways to enjoy the outdoors include a couple of notable golf courses and (rather unexpectedly) two downhill ski areas, one situated on a traprock ridge, the other on the "Western Wall" of the valley—the edge where the Western Uplands begin.

History

Settlement of the lower Central Valley occurred first along the Connecticut River, with communities such as Glastonbury, Middletown and Cromwell having settlers as early as 1640–1650. Towns at the southern tip of the valley were established by families from Wallingford, which in turn was an early outgrowth of New Haven. Much of the landlocked acreage of the valley was originally part of the ancient town of Farmington, which was on the frontier until after 1676, the conclusion of King Philip's War and the subsidence of the

Indian threat. As late as 1721 Plainville supposedly had only one settler.

One of the first industries to develop in the region was quarrying. It took little time for the sandstone of Portland to be noted as a beautiful building material. The first permanent settler of that town was a stonecutter, and as early as 1665 the residents placed the first restrictions on the removal of their valuable resource. Portland stone was sent all around the country, but most of it ended up in the façades of New York City's famed brownstone apartment buildings.

When the flood of 1692 changed the course of the Connecticut River and left Wethersfield without a deep-water port, most of that town's waterfront activity was transferred to Rocky Hill. Shipbuilding became a major industry in all the towns bordering the river, which fed the nascent U.S. Navy with battleships during the Revolutionary War.

Metalworking would become the most dominant industry in the valley. By the 1740s tinware (perhaps the first made in the colonies) was being fashioned in Berlin and Southington. Nearby New Britain was an early smithing center, and hardware manufacture was an outgrowth of the smithy's skill. Although not the first to make hardware, the Stanley family became preeminent. Frederick T. Stanley began doing business in the 1840s and sold his products from a buggy, founding the company known today as Stanley Works (its tools are probably its best-known products) in 1852. Early in its history this company made the sleigh bells that announced the arrival of the traveling peddler selling its other wares. Stanley Works is still headquartered in New Britain.

In 1845 the first cutlery company in Connecticut was established in Meriden, where pewter and Brittania (an alloy of tin, antimony and copper) had been made well before 1800. Meriden would eventually output half of all the silverware produced in the United States. A merger of several companies over the course of 60 years eventually gave rise to the International Silver Company, one of the most enduring names in the industry.

In the early 1800s the Metacomet Ridge was still a major barrier to trade. That ended

with the opening of the first stage of the Farmington Canal in 1828. Modeled after the Erie Canal but not destined to partake of the same success, it passed through Cheshire, Southington and Plainville, providing an important shipping channel south to New Haven. The canal was closed in 1848 but replaced by an even more efficient mover of goods: the railroad. Today the Plainville Historic Center offers visitors a thorough introduction to the history of the canal.

Fittingly, this geologically fascinating area includes the birthplace of Connecticut's first state geologist. Berlin was the hometown of James Gates Percival (1795–1856), who began

Dilophosaurus may have made the ancient tracks on display at Dinosaur State Park. Photo by Thomas Giroir/Dinosaur State Park.

the first geological survey of Connecticut in 1835, traveling around the state by horse-drawn wagon and on foot. The project was supposed to take a year, but he spent six before the legislature forced him to publish a 495-page "hasty outline" of his findings, which just goes to show that even 160 years ago people were discovering that there's a lot more packed into this small state than seems possible.

In the 20th century many Central Valley manufacturing jobs disappeared. Not only did inexpensive imports provide competition, but new materials began to supplant the old. Although silverware is pretty much a thing of the past in terms of local manufacturing, New Britain is still "Hardware City" (a phrase that appears even in the name of the local baseball team). As with other parts of Connecticut where one or two dominant manufacturing pursuits gave way to dozens of more diversified businesses, most of the Central Valley's towns ceased to be associated with one product. The area remains vital, though, as expanding suburbs have made much of it solidly residential.

Major Attractions

Dinosaur State Park

Looking for a neat souvenir of your trip to Connecticut? You won't top what you can bring home from Dinosaur State Park: a dinosaur footprint. The largest known dinosaur track site in North America was discovered here in 1966 by an alert bulldozer operator excavating a construction site. Five hundred of the 200-million-year-old in situ tracks are on view inside a geodesic dome. They are believed to be the tracks of Dilophosaurus, the largest carnivorous dinosaur on the planet in the early Jurassic. Bring along 10 pounds of plaster of Paris and one-fourth cup of cooking oil for each cast, plus a 5-gallon plastic bucket, cloth rags and paper towels (the museum can provide you with a list of places in the area at which to purchase these materials), and you'll go home with a life-sized cast of dino's ancient tootsies. (Note: The casting area is open May–Oct. only, and you must begin making your cast by 3:30.) It takes 40 minutes to an hour for casts to dry, and it's best to come on a dry day since it's done outside.

The casting area is only a small part of the park's attractions, however. There's also an early Jurassic diorama, exhibits on geology, wildlife gardens, a trail system where guided walks are given on weekends at 2:00 P.M. in summer, a picnic area and more, and recent improvements make this one of the most accessible parks in the state. Call for a schedule of interpretive programs and films. Admission to the exhibits is $2 adults, $1 children 6–17; admission to the grounds and casting area is free. The exhibit center is open Tue.–Sun., 9:00 A.M.–4:30 P.M.; the grounds are open daily during the same hours. Located on **West St., 1 mile east of I-91 exit 23, Rocky Hill, 06067.** Call **(860) 529-8423** for a recorded information line or **(860) 529-5816** to reach the park office.

New Britain Museum of American Art

This excellent art museum is at the heart of cultural life in the lower Central Valley. Their exhibits of American art from 1740 to the present, including works by Childe Hassam, John Singer Sargent, Georgia O'Keeffe and Thomas Hart Benton, are only part of what they have to offer. On Wed. evenings, mid-July–late Aug., 5:00 P.M.–7:30 P.M., their Café on the Park program is in full swing. For about $10 you can enjoy a buffet dinner on the terrace of the museum overlooking Walnut Hill Park (designed by Frederick Law Olmsted), plus live music and admission to the museum. First Fridays, held on the first Fri. of each month Oct.–May (except Jan.) from 5:30 P.M. to 8:00 P.M., are similar. The cost for an evening of jazz music, good munchies including wine and beer and an art activity is only $7 ($5 for members). In addition, gallery talks are given most Sun. at 2:00 P.M.

Although it enjoys an unusual setting in a small mansion on a residential side street, the museum is accessible to the physically challenged. Inquire about guided tours (by appointment, at additional charge) and arrangements for the visually impaired. Admission: $3 adults, $2 seniors and students 12–18. Admission is free on Sat. 10:00 A.M.–noon. Hours: Tue.–Fri., 1:00 P.M.–5:00 P.M.; Sat., 10:00 A.M.–5:00 P.M.; Sun., noon–5:00 P.M. **56 Lexington St., New Britain, 06052; (860) 229-0257.**

Festivals and Events

Berlin Crafts Festivals
early June and mid-Aug.

This pair of three-day events takes place at Berlin Fairground on Beckley Rd. in Berlin, where 200–250 juried crafters set up booths indoors and outdoors. Admission: $5, seniors $4, children 14 and under free. Hours: Fri.–Sun., noon–7:00 P.M. For the current year's dates call **(860) 693-6335.**

Main Street, U.S.A.
mid-June

This major street festival celebrates the diverse ethnic makeup for which New Britain is known. Games, rides, civic booths and lots of food are on hand to fill the day. It's always held on a Sat.; call for the current year's date. The location is **downtown New Britain near the**

Getting There

Middletown is only 20 minutes south of Hartford by car. The fastest route is I-91 south to Rte. 9 south into Middletown.

intersection of Main and S. Main Sts. Admission is free. Hours: 9:00 A.M.–5:00 P.M. For more information call **(860) 229-1665.**

The "Great" Connecticut River Raft Race
late July/early Aug.

This unusual event is a lighthearted yet competitive race of homemade, self-propelled rafts down a stretch of the Connecticut River on either the last Sat. in July or the first Sat. in Aug., rain or shine. The best viewing is near the starting line, and a good spot for spectators is Harborpark on Harbor Dr. in Middletown, where there's a nice grassy sward on which to set up a blanket or lawn chair. Bring binoculars. Rafters begin heading for the starting line as early as 7:00 A.M., and the cannon goes off around 10:00. The *Aunt Polly,* a riverboat, may run a sightseeing excursion during the race. The finish is at Dart Island in the middle of the river, which is accessible by boat only. Folks who can transport themselves to the island on their own boats are welcome to join in the party following the race. For

113

A sample of the works on display at the New Britain Museum of American Art: Thomas Hart Benton's Arts of the West.

Go aloft at the Plainville Hot Air Balloon Festival. Photo courtesy Connecticut Department of Environmental Protection.

more information call the **Connecticut River Valley and Shoreline Visitors Council** at **(800) 486-3346** or **(860) 347-0028.**

Plainville Hot Air Balloon Festival
late Aug.

This celebration of hot-air ballooning begins with a Fri. evening Night Glow, in which the balloons are illuminated from the inside, and fireworks. It continues with balloon launches Sat. at 6:00 A.M. and 6:00 P.M., while the hours in between are filled with a crafts fair, car show and entertainment. A balloon launch on Sun. at 6:00 A.M. closes the festival. All launches take place weather permitting, and be aware that the balloons are only aloft at designated launch times. Admission all three days is free; pay as you go for rides, food, etc. Hours: Fri., 4:00 P.M.–11:00 P.M.; Sat., 6:00 A.M.–8:00 P.M.; Sun., 6:00 A.M.–9:00 A.M. For more information call **(860) 747-0283.**

Connecticut River Powwow
weekend before Labor Day

This intertribal powwow (from an Algonquian word meaning "gathering of the people") is a celebration of Native American culture with a strong educational aspect. It draws participants from as far away as Canada and South America. Highlights include competitive dancing, native foods, singing, crafts, kids' games, storytelling and programs with live birds of prey and timber wolves. There are also demonstrations of skills such as basket weaving, skinning and flint knapping (the making of stone points). Admission: $7 adults, $5 seniors and children 6–12. Hours: Sat.–Sun., 11:00 A.M.–7:00 P.M. This powwow used to be held at the Farmington Polo Grounds in Farmington but was recently moved to the Durham Fairgrounds. To confirm the location and the date of the event for the current year call **(860) 684-6984.**

Durham Fair
last full weekend in Sept.

As the largest country fair in Connecticut, more and bigger is the order of the day in Durham. In addition to all the customary country fair activities—livestock, horse shows, a midway, entertainment and food—they also have a llama competition, a special Connecticut Department of Agriculture display of all the state's agricultural endeavors, crafts and antiques for sale and a farm museum open only during the fair with more than 4,000 farm tools and machines on exhibit. Don't miss the Battle of the Barns, in which all the exhibitors in each barn team up to compete in an absurd Olympics. You get things like the dairy barn vs. the swine barn in a test of pie eating or hay bale moving, and the winning barn gets a pizza party and a banner as a trophy. There's free parking with shuttle buses from remote lots. Admission: $6 adults, children under 12 free. Hours: Fri.–Sat., 9:00 A.M.–11:00 P.M.; Sun., 9:00 A.M.–7:00 P.M. The Durham Fairgrounds are **off Rte. 17 near Rte. 68 in Durham; (860) 349-9495.**

Berlin Fair
first weekend in Oct.

Timed to coincide with the start of the fall foliage and one of the last fairs on the calendar in Connecticut, Berlin Fair is truly a send-off to the agricultural year. Its 50th anniversary is in 1998, so look for lots of special events. One perk for families in any year is free admission for kids under 16 Fri. until 6:00 P.M. Berlin is one of only a few fairs in the state to have a rodeo, which takes place at noon on Sun. with roping, tying and barrel-racing events. Another special feature is a portion of the midway dedicated to kiddie rides and games for entertaining really small children. Plus, don't miss the animal barns, the harvest exhibits and all the usual contests of strength and skill. Admission: $5 adults, $3 seniors and children. On-site parking is free. Hours: Fri., noon–10:00 P.M.; Sat., 9:00 A.M.–10:00 P.M.; Sun., 10:00 A.M.–7:00 P.M. Berlin Fairground is **on Beckley Rd. in Berlin.**

Apple Harvest Festival
first two weekends in Oct.

Surrounded by apple orchards, Southington is known as the Little Apple, so it's only fitting that the town should celebrate this crop. It takes place over two weekends: Sat. & Sun. of the first one, Thu.–Sun. of the second one, ending the day before Columbus Day. Activities include a carnival, apple picking, a baby contest, a parade, a craft fair and a silly bed race in which civic groups decorate beds, put them on wheels and race through the streets. Everything takes place in downtown Southington at the town green, which is on Rte. 10 near Columbus Ave. Follow signs to the designated parking lots and take the free shuttle buses provided. Admission is free, and you pay as you go for rides, food, etc. Hours are 6:00 P.M.–9:00 P.M. on Thu. & Fri., 11:00 A.M.–9:00 P.M. both Sat., 11:00 A.M.–7:00 P.M. the first Sun. & noon–5:00 P.M. on closing day. For more information, including a schedule, call the **Southington Chamber of Commerce** at **(860) 628-8036.**

Head of the Connecticut Regatta
Sun. of Columbus Day weekend

The largest single-day regatta in the Northeast is a typical "head" race: 3 miles long and a timed event with staggered departures from the starting line, so you don't really know who's won until everyone in a race has finished. The participants cover all ages and all abilities. The 600 or so entrants take off all day long from 9:00 A.M. to 5:00 P.M., starting in Cromwell and finishing 1 mile below Middletown's Harborpark on Harbor Dr., which is where spectators gather. There's no charge to watch. For more information call **(860) 346-1042** or the **Middletown Chamber of Commerce** at **(860) 347-6924.**

Seasons of Celebration: A Victorian Holiday
first Sat. in Dec.

For Wallingford's annual Christmas fete, actors dressed in Victorian clothing sing and entertain on the street, tea is served at a historic home, ice carvers compete to create the most beautiful temporal sculptures, free rides are given in carriages and hay wagons and Santa and Mrs. Claus greet children and distribute small gifts. The day ends with caroling on the green. Most of the activities take place in the downtown along North and South Main Sts. and Center St. Hours: 11:00 A.M.–6:00 P.M. For more information call **(203) 284-1807.**

Outdoor Activities

Biking

Both mountain bikes and road bikes will be able to negotiate the **Farmington Canal Trail,** a paved linear park that will eventually trace the 80-mile route of the former Farmington Canal from New Haven to Northampton, Massachusetts. Six contiguous miles of this greenway are finished and open in Cheshire and Hamden. One section known as Lock 12 Park, just south of N. Brooksvale Rd. in Cheshire, contains a restored lock original to the canal and a small museum. You'll be sharing the "road" with many joggers and roller bladers, so only slow speeds are appropriate. This is an especially great place to bring young

115

kids, since there is no automobile traffic to worry about and the terrain is absolutely flat. The park is open from dawn until dusk daily. Parking is available in lots on Cornwall Ave., N. Brooksvale Rd. and Mt. Sanford Rd. in Cheshire; look for the bike trail signs. For more information call **(203) 785-1482.**

Another great ride for fit cyclists on any type of bike is **Hubbard Park.** A paved road (open Apr.–Oct., 10:00 A.M.–5:00 P.M.) ambles past a calm reservoir overhung by traprock ridges and then climbs 1.75 miles, sometimes rather steeply, to the top of East Peak, one of the Hanging Hills of Meriden. Your reward for making the journey is a stunning view from the top of Castle Craig, a stone tower at the summit about 1,000 feet above sea level. The park entrance is on W. Main St. in Meriden. For more information, see the listing under Hiking.

If you'll be riding on surface streets and need to cross the Connecticut River, you can take the Arrigoni Bridge (Rte. 66) between Middletown and Portland. Walk your bike over using the sidewalk; do not ride in the main traffic lanes. Your other alternative is the seasonal Rocky Hill-Glastonbury ferry at Rte. 160.

Boating

Most of the lakes and ponds in this central part of the state are on the small side and in heavy demand, yet well worth seeking out. There are public boat launches at **Crystal Lake** on Livingston Rd. in Middletown (35 acres; motors prohibited); **Dooley Pond** on Rte. 17 in Middletown (28 acres; 8 m.p.h. speed limit); **Beseck Lake** on Rte. 147 in Middlefield (120 acres; 8 m.p.h. speed limit except on summer days); **Black Pond** off Rte. 66 in Middlefield (76 acres; no internal combustion engines); **Silver Lake** on Norton Ln. in Berlin (151 acres; 8 m.p.h. speed limit except on summer days) and **North Farms Reservoir** on Rte. 68 in Wallingford (62 acres; 8 m.p.h. speed limit). Beseck Lake and Silver Lake are appropriate for waterskiing; Crystal Lake is the best for canoeing.

The other boating option is the **Connecticut River.** There are no state boat launches along this stretch of the river, but marinas will allow you to launch for a fee. **Seaboard Marina (860-657-3232;** VHF 68) in South Glastonbury offers the greatest number of facilities, services and transient berths in the area and is open year-round. In Portland you'll find **Yankee Boat Yard (860-342-4735;** VHF 60) with transient slips and moorings and a full range of boater needs, as well as **Petzold's (860-342-1196)** and **Portland Boat Works (860-342-1085).** If you're looking for a meal riverside, you can dock at **America's Cup (860-347-9999)** in Middletown's Harborpark for free while you eat. For navigational details, charts and complete lists of marine facilities throughout this area, your best source of information is *Embassy's Complete Boating Guide & Chartbook to Long Island Sound,* which also covers the Connecticut River up to Hartford. Contact the publisher at **142 Ferry Rd., Old Saybrook, 06475; (860) 395-0188.**

Fishing

Bass, sunfish, catfish and other warm-water species are all found in the small, shallow ponds of the lower Central Valley. If you'll be fishing from a canoe or rowboat, try **Crystal Lake** on Livingston Rd. in Middletown, where motors are prohibited. There's also a small pier by the boat ramp. **Dooley Pond** on Rte. 17 is state-owned, so there is both a boat launch and good access to the relatively undeveloped shore. You'll probably want to fish from a boat at **Beseck Lake** off Rte. 147 in Middlefield, the largest and perhaps busiest body of water in the area, where there is little in the way of shore access. Also in Middlefield, **Black Pond** off Rte. 66 has no shoreline development and a nice atmosphere despite the highway passing close by, but is heavily fished because it's so visible and accessible. Internal combustion engines are forbidden. Finally, **Silver Lake** on Norton Ln. in Berlin has good shoreline access to the northwest bank along a railroad right-of-way and is the subject of ongoing improvement efforts.

For trout, head to **Roaring Brook** in Glastonbury or the **Coginchaug River** in Middletown, both of which are stocked. Access the former where it crosses Coldbrook Rd. in the Hopewell section of town. You can just park and fish in this rural area. There's also a ramp for wheelchair access at Angus Park on Fisher Hill Rd. off Rte. 83. (For more information on this call **Glastonbury Parks and Recreation** at **860-652-7679.**) The best place to access the Coginchaug River is at Wadsworth Falls State Park. If you enter through the gate on Rte. 157, you'll have to pay a parking fee in summer, but you have free and equally good access from the pullout on Cherry Hill Rd. One pond that's stocked with trout and gets little pressure due to its somewhat remote location is **Miller Pond** in the state park of the same name off Haddam Quarter Rd. in Durham. The shore is undeveloped and open for fishing, or you can carry in a car-top boat.

For shore access to the **Connecticut River,** where you can catch northern pike, bass, white perch and channel catfish, among other species, try Harborpark on Harbor Dr. right in downtown Middletown, the portion of Rte. 17A in the Gildersleeve section of Portland where the road runs right alongside the river or Wangunk Meadows Wildlife Management Area at the end of Tryon St. in South Glastonbury.

Golf

Some of the best golfing in Connecticut is concentrated in the lower Central Valley. All three of the courses described below were rated among the ten best in the state by *Connecticut* magazine recently.

Hunter Golf Club

This 18-hole, 6,243-yard municipal course offers all rentals, practice areas for driving, putting and chipping, a golf pro, showers, lockers, a pro shop, a restaurant and a bar. It's first-come, first-served Mon.–Fri. Weekend tee times are assigned by a lottery system; you must come into the shop before Wed. noon to fill out a card. Leftover weekend times can be reserved by phone. The course is closed to the public for league play Tue.–Thu., 3:30 P.M.–5:30 P.M. Season: Apr.–Nov. **685 Westfield Rd., Meriden, 06450; (203) 634-3366.**

Lyman Orchards Golf Club

Lyman Orchards' two 18-hole courses have been lauded by *Golf Digest.* The Player Course, named for designer Gary Player, was called "the Connecticut course most worth a visit" for its challenging nature, although the editors cautioned that you probably will feel too abused at the end to want to play there all the time. Lyman Orchards is praised as a good all-around course for players of all abilities. Other features include putting greens, a driving range, a clubhouse restaurant, rentals and instruction. Season: late Mar.–Nov. Located on **Rte. 157, Middlefield, 06455.** Call **(860) 349-8055** for 24-hour automated tee times.

Timberlin Golf Club

With a yardage of 6,342, this 18-hole municipal course enjoys an especially beautiful setting in the shadow of some small mountains. Call two days in advance beginning at 7:00 A.M. for tee times. It offers all rentals; a golf pro; a pro shop; practice areas for chipping, driving and putting; showers and lockers; a restaurant; a bar and tennis courts. Season: mid-Mar.–mid-Dec. Located on **Rte. 364, Kensington (part of Berlin), 06037; (860) 828-3228.**

Hiking

For more information on the **Farmington Canal Trail,** a paved, flat, 6-mile trail very suitable for walking and jogging, see the listing under Biking. It provides an exceptional opportunity for the physically challenged to access the outdoors, and designated handicapped parking spots are available in the lots on N. Brooksvale Rd. in Cheshire and Todd St. in Hamden. There's also hiking at **Wadsworth Falls State Park,** described under Swimming. Nature trails and a swamp boardwalk are part of **Dinosaur State Park,** described under Major Attractions. Finally, the facilities described under Nature Centers have easy trail networks suitable for families with small children.

Cheshire Land Trust/Roaring Brook

The Environment Commission of Cheshire and the Cheshire Land Trust together recently published a comprehensive guide to all the trails in that town. It is one of the top guides of its kind in Connecticut. In addition to hiking opportunities, the book suggests a canoe trip and half a dozen on-road bike rides. The background information on flora, fauna and geology will enhance any trip you take with this book as a guide. You can obtain a copy by mail for $9.95 from **The Environmental Commission of Cheshire, 84 S. Main St., Cheshire, 06410; (203) 271-6670**, or stop by on weekdays to purchase it.

One selection from the book is Roaring Brook, a Cheshire stream that flows over a traprock ridge, dropping 80 feet to form the second-highest waterfall in Connecticut. An orange-blazed trail leads to an overlook with a view of the falls, then makes a small loop before heading back. At the furthest point of the loop, the trail connects with the blue-blazed Quinnipiac Trail, on which you can hike south all the way to New Haven and north to Rte. 68 in Prospect. The start point is at a small paved parking area on Roaring Brook Rd. three-tenths of a mile west of Mountain Rd. in Cheshire.

Hubbard Park

Meriden's vast city park is both a convenient and a challenging place to hike. The park contains East Peak and West Peak, the so-called Hanging Hills of Meriden. These south-facing reddish cliffs are among the most spectacular of the Central Valley's traprock ridges. At the apex of East Peak is Castle Craig, a crenellated stone tower from which you can survey the land for miles to the south from an elevation of 1,002 feet. The Metacomet Trail, one of Connecticut's network of blue-blazed trails, crosses the peaks, and you can continue on it for several miles to the northeast. The roads surrounding Mirror Lake at the base of the peaks are good for jogging, and in early spring Hubbard Park is awash in blooming daffodils. You'll find trail maps posted in the park, which is located on **W. Main St. just a few minutes from downtown Meriden; (203) 630-4259.**

Mattabesett Trail

Another of Connecticut's blue-blazed trails, the Mattabesett can be accessed at several spots. One is the corner of Rtes. 68 and 157 in Durham. There's a small dirt parking lot there. Look for the blue blazes directly opposite Rte. 68 from the lot. Another good place is on Rte. 66 in western Middlefield, near Black Pond and the Meriden town line. At the point where the road goes from two lanes to four lanes, you'll spot a dirt parking lot on the north side of the road. Again, cross the road and look for the blue blazes. This section of trail may be among the prettiest stretches of the Mattabesett, crossing 800-foot ledges with good views of Black Pond below. The Mattabesett is mapped and described in full in the *Connecticut Walk Book.*

Ragged Mountain Preserve

A 6-mile loop on New Britain Water Department land takes you to the summit of Ragged Mountain (761 feet) and an overlook in three directions. For a time the loop coincides with the blue-blazed Metacomet Trail, which continues many miles north and south of the preserve. Follow the trail blazed blue with a red dot to make the loop. The entrance is on West Ln. in Berlin about half a mile west of Rte. 71A.

Shenipsit Trail

The Shenipsit is one of the longest blue-blazed trails in Connecticut, covering 33 miles in several sections. A particularly nice section with good views from high ledges can be picked up off Hill St., a dead-end road off Rte. 94 in Glastonbury. Park and hike north into the woods. The trail is mapped and described in detail in the *Connecticut Walk Book.*

Ice Skating

Several towns in the area maintain ponds for skating when conditions permit. Perhaps the most spectacular setting is Hubbard Park on W. Main St. in Meriden, where there is an incredible view across **Mirror Lake** to a unique geological formation, the hanging hills of Meriden from the skate house/warming hut. Wallingford also maintains a pond at **Doolittle Park** on S. Elm St. Both ponds are lit at night. There is no charge, and you must bring skates. Skate only if the ice is posted as safe. For more information call the **Parks and Recreation**

Departments of Wallingford at **(203) 294-2120** and **Meriden** at **(203) 630-4259.**

In the Air

Berkshire Balloons (P.O. Box 706, Southington, 06489; 203-250-8441) gives morning and evening hot-air balloon flights daily through Cheshire, Southington and the lower Farmington River Valley. Call for pricing and details.

Skiing

Two of Connecticut's smaller ski areas—with vertical drops around 500 feet—are found in the lower Central Valley. With slopes that are very manageable for the beginner and intermediate skier, both offer many instruction options, night skiing, snowmaking, ski and snowboard rentals, lodges, ski shops and dedicated snowboard areas. Mount Southington **(396 Mt. Vernon Rd., Southington; 800-982-6828 [in Connecticut]** or **860-628-0954)** has a dozen downhill trails, two chair lifts and four surface lifts. It offers the SkiWee children's supervised instruction program for kids 4–12. Inquire about their learn-to-race program and timed racecourses. **Powder Ridge (Powder Hill Rd., Middlefield; 800-622-3321 [in Connecticut], 800-243-3377 [from the tri-state area and Rhode Island]** or **860-349-3454)** has 14 downhill slopes and four lifts, including one quad. It has a Time Ticket system that allows you to purchase four or eight hours of daytime skiing and show up whenever you want rather than at the start of a session, and on Fri. & Sat. they stay open until 1:00 A.M.

Sleigh and Carriage Rides

At **Wimler Farm (601 Guilford Rd. [Rte. 77], Durham; 860-349-3190)**, you can take hour-and-a-half horse-drawn hayrides in summer and sleigh rides in winter on private wooded roads. They charge $2.50 per person with a $25 minimum. **DeMaria Family Farm (1164 Edgewood Rd., Berlin; 860-828-6724)** offers one-hour tractor-drawn hayrides and sleigh rides through fields and woods on the farm, and they have a private recreation area for rent. The cost is $5 per person, $50 minimum. Reservations are required at both locations.

Swimming

The main feature of **Wadsworth Falls State Park** is an artificial swimming pond filled with water diverted from the Coginchaug River. It has a pretty wooded setting, sandy beach, lifeguards and bathhouses. There's also a shaded picnic grove and easy trails for hiking, and there are trout in the river. The falls themselves are located at the opposite end of the park off Cherry Hill Rd. The charge for parking in the main lot by the pond on weekdays is $4 for Connecticut vehicles and $5 for out-of-state vehicles. The weekend charges are $5 and $8, respectively. Hours: 8:00 A.M.–sunset daily, year-round. Located on **Wadsworth St. (Rte. 157) in Middletown.** Park office: **(860) 663-2030.**

Seeing and Doing

Art Galleries

Two exhibit spaces are part of the **Center for the Arts** on the Wesleyan campus. The **Davison Art Center,** located in the historic 1840s house, is where the renowned print and photographic holdings of the university's collection are generally displayed. The work of students, faculty and contemporary artists can be found at the **Zilkha Gallery.** Hours: Tue.–Fri., noon–4:00 P.M.; Sat.–Sun., 2:00 P.M.–5:00 P.M.; closed in summer and during school holidays. The galleries are on the **Wesleyan campus off High St. between Wyllys and Washington Sts. in Middletown; (860) 685-2695.**

Central Connecticut State University's **Samuel T. Chen Art Gallery** is run much like a private gallery, featuring the work of invited artists in all styles and media. It is closed in summer, during school holidays and briefly

119

between shows, so call before going. Hours: Tue., Wed. & Fri., 1:00 P.M.–4:00 P.M.; Thu., 1:00 P.M.–7:00 P.M. Located in **Maloney Hall on the campus at 1615 Stanley St. in New Britain; (860) 832-2633.**

Children and Families

Most kids will be enthralled by the things to see and do at Dinosaur State Park, described under Major Attractions. Very young children might enjoy the petting zoo and pony rides at **Amy's Udder Joy (27 North Rd., Cromwell; 860-635-3924),** a very rustic barnyard attraction. Two other attractions with a farmyard or natural science leaning are the nature centers listed under that category below. The **New Britain Youth Museum (30 High St., New Britain; 860-225-3020)** has educational and play-oriented exhibits for young children, many of them participatory, as well as an outdoor play area for preschoolers. **Hidden Valley Miniature Golf (2060 West St., Southington; 860-621-1630)** is one of the most elaborate and attractive courses around, with gazebos, covered bridges and a waterwheel, plus batting cages, a playground, a snack bar and a small picnic grove. Call for hours and rates. The Copernican Space Science Center described under Observatories has special shows for children at the times listed. Children might also really enjoy the tour at Lock 12 Park, described under Museums, since children are the tour guides. Last but not least, **Oddfellows Playhouse (128 Washington St., Middletown; 860-347-6143)** is a unique youth theater where the actors and even the technicians are usually kids age 6–20. It does two shows in fall, one or two in winter and two in spring. Productions run one or two weekends with performances Thu.–Sun. at 8:00 P.M. Tickets are very reasonable at $6–$8. It also puts on a circus in early Aug. at Palmer Field off Rte. 66 in Middletown.

Crafts Centers

Wesleyan Potters is a "school and cooperative" that began when a group of local residents wanted to learn pottery making back in 1948. Now it offers classes in weaving and pottery, jewelry and basket making, and the shop sells the juried work of students as well as faculty and outside artists. You may be able to tour the studios if classes are not in session when you visit. During the annual holiday sale (starting the Sat. after Thanksgiving and running for two weeks), the shop's inventory expands dramatically. Hours during holiday show: Sat.–Wed., 10:00 A.M.–6:00 P.M.; Thu.–Fri., 10:00 A.M.–9:00 P.M. Regular hours: Tue.–Sat., 11:00 A.M.–5:00 P.M. **350 S. Main St. (Rte. 17), Middletown, 06457; (860) 344-0039 or (860) 347-5925.**

Museums and Historic Sites

Most of the towns in this area have one or more historic homes maintained by a local historical society. They often have period furnishings and tools plus exhibits examining local industries, families and lifestyles. For information on the **Berlin Historical Society Museum** at **Main and Peck Sts.,** call **(860) 828-1891.** Call **(203) 272-5819** for details on the Cheshire Historical Society's **Hitchcock-Phillips House** (ca. 1785) on the town green at **Rte. 10 and Church St.** Exhibits at the **Museum on the Green (1944 Main St. at Hubbard St.)** in Glastonbury's 1840 Old Town Hall chronicle 350 years of local history, industry and notable residents. The 1808 **Kellogg-Eddy House** at **679 Willard Ave.** and the **Enoch Kelsey House** at **1702 Main St.** are opened to the public by the **Newington Historical Society** at **(860) 666-7118.** The latter is noted for its trompe l'oeil and other murals. The emphasis at Southington's **Barnes Museum (85 N. Main St.; 860-628-5426)** is the Victorian era.

One of Wallingford's local history museums is the 1759 Dutch colonial **Samuel Parsons House** at **180 S. Main St.; (203) 294-1996.** Among the displays are locally made silver and pewter. Two other important properties in town are works in progress and may be completed by the time you read this. The

Nehemiah Royce House at **538 N. Main St.** is the oldest home in town. Although it was built around 1672, plans are to develop it to emphasize the Colonial Revival phase of its history. The **American Silver Museum** of Wallingford, recently relocated from the nearby town of Meriden, will document the important silver industry of central Connecticut. For information on the latter two museums call the **Wallingford Historic Preservation Trust** at **(203) 265-4025.**

Other topic-based museums include the **Submarine Library Museum (440 Washington St., Middletown; 860-346-0388)**, containing all sorts of documentation, models and other artifacts pertaining to submarines and the **New Britain Industrial Museum (185 Main St., New Britain; 860-832-8654)**, whose collection comprises hardware, appliances, saddlery, industrial machines, wire products and other products made in the area from the 1800s to the present.

Note that the Barnes Museum, the Museum on the Green and the New Britain Industrial Museum are open weekdays only, whereas most of the other museums are open weekends only, and many of the smaller museums are seasonal.

General Mansfield House

The Middlesex County Historical Society is housed in this 1810 home of a Civil War general who died at Antietam. There are displays on the Civil War, decorative arts (furniture, needlework, painting and more) from the 18th and 19th centuries and changing exhibits. Admission: $2 adults, $1 children under 12. Hours: Sun., 2:00 P.M.–4:30 P.M.; Mon., 1:00 P.M.–4:00 P.M., & by appointment; usually closed holiday weekends. **151 Main St., Middletown, 06457; (860) 346-0746.**

Lock 12 Historical Park

This section of the Farmington Canal Trail contains a restored lock and a small museum in which costumed children guide visitors through displays including tools, lock keys and a Plexiglas model of the canal. The 20-minute tours are given Sun., 1:00 P.M.–4:00 P.M., Apr.–June & Sept.–Nov. The park is on the trail just south of the parking lot on N. Brooksvale Rd. in

Cheshire. For more information call **Cheshire Parks and Recreation** at **(203) 272-2743.**

Plainville Historic Center

One of the larger town historical society museums in the state is perhaps best known for its Farmington Canal room containing a diorama of Plainville as it was in 1830 when activity on the canal was in full swing. Other highlights include several room vignettes with period furniture and fixtures, a nature room with some impressive stuffed bird specimens and Indian artifacts and a large collection of farm implements. **29 Pierce St., Plainville, 06062; (860) 747-6577.**

Solomon Goffe House

This living history museum keeps very limited hours, but it makes an exceptional effort when open. The oldest part of Meriden's oldest house was built in 1711 and contains period paneling and floorboards. Nearly every Sun. you'll find costumed interpreters giving demonstrations of how cooking, spinning, weaving and other everyday chores were done in the 18th century. Special annual events include a tea party in June, an ice cream social in July and candlelight evening tours in Dec. Admission: $2 adults, free for children under 12. Open the first Sun. of each month, 1:30 P.M.–4:30 P.M. **677 North Colony Rd., Meriden, 06451; (203) 634-9088.**

Welles-Shipman Ward House

The Historical Society of Glastonbury maintains this mid-18th-century house noted for its exceptional paneling and woodwork and furnishings (ca. 1755–1840). Household implements, farm tools and old vehicles are displayed in its outbuildings, and there's a dooryard garden. There are special activities on most Sun. that they're open—a weaver working on an antique loom, open-hearth cooking or kids' days—plus an annual benefit antiques show the first Sat. in Aug. on the town green. Admission: $2 adults, free to children under 12. Hours: Sun., 2:00 P.M.–4:00 P.M. in May, June, Sept. & Oct.; Wed., 2:00 P.M.–4:00 P.M. in July; closed Aug. **972 Main St. (Rte. 17), S. Glastonbury, 06073; (860) 633-6890.**

Nature Centers

Connecticut Audubon Center at Glastonbury

Sometimes referred to by the name Holland Brook, this small nature center has a Discovery Room with a Connecticut River diorama and exhibits of small mammals, reptiles and taxidermy; a feeding station for birds; a nature store and 2 miles of easy trails through a park alongside the Connecticut River. Admission: $1 for nonmembers. Nature center hours: Tue.–Fri., 1:00 P.M.–5:00 P.M.; Sat., 10:00 A.M.–5:00 P.M.; Sun., 1:00 P.M.–4:00 P.M. **1361 Main St., Glastonbury, 06033; (860) 633-8402.**

The Hungerford Center

Technically called the New Britain Youth Museum at Hungerford Park, this 80-acre, wooded, former equestrian park is the largest nature center in the area. There's an exhibit building with mounted birds, exotic animals and other displays; a barnyard with farm animals; a network of broad hiking trails; picnic facilities; wildlife gardens and special events such as maple sugaring in March. Admission: $2 adults, $1.50 seniors, $1 children 2–17. Nature center hours: Tue.–Fri., 1:00 P.M.–5:00 P.M.; Sat., 10:00 A.M.–5:00 P.M. When local schools are out (late June–Aug.) or on break it opens at 11:00 A.M. on weekdays. The grounds are open for hiking and picnicking dawn–dusk daily, year-round. **191 Farmington Ave., Kensington, 06037; (860) 827-9064.**

Nightlife

Some of the most stimulating evening entertainment around can be found at the New Britain Museum of American Art, whose First Fridays and Café on the Park programs are described under Major Attractions. Equally animated but even more eclectic is **The Buttonwood Tree (605 Main St., Middletown; 860-347-4957)**, a bookstore-cum-performance venue where you never know what's going to happen next. You could be treated to a dramatic recitation of Milton's *Paradise Lost* one night and the sounds of a jazz quartet the next.

Poetry has a special home here—The Buttonwood Tree regularly hosts poetry slams, in which ordinary Joes and Janes recite their own work and are judged by representatives from the audience. You might also encounter storytelling, performance art, lectures, dance or comedy. Just a few doors down from the Buttonwood is **Eli Cannon's (695 Main St., Middletown; 860-347-3547),** a friendly, casual beer-lover's pub with about two dozen selections on tap and about 100 bottled brews, including several made in Connecticut. Glastonbury's answer to Eli Cannon's is **The Alewife Grille and Brewery (2935 Main St.; 860-659-8686),** where they brew their own and you can order 6-ounce samplers.

Although it doesn't fit the conventional definition of nightlife, the planetarium shows and stargazing at the Copernican Space Science Center described in the next section are nighttime activities. For live rock 'n' roll, blues, heavy metal, comedy and more, visit **The Sting (667 W. Main St., New Britain; 860-225-2154),** Connecticut's largest nightclub. Call for a schedule of upcoming acts.

Observatories & Planetariums

Planetarium shows are given at **Central Connecticut State University's Copernican Space Science Center** every Fri. & Sat. night (except state holidays) at 8:30 P.M., followed by stargazing through their telescope. Special children's planetarium shows are given Fri. at 7:00 P.M. & Sat. at 1:30 P.M. Admission: $3.50 adults, $2.50 children. **1615 Stanley St., New Britain, 06050; (860) 832-3399** or **(860) 832-2950.**

Wesleyan University's Van Vleck Observatory is frequently open to the public on Wed. nights, weather permitting, during the school year. The observatory is located at the highest point on the Wesleyan campus. Park on High St. or any street ringing the campus and look for the building with the white domes. Check on upcoming dates and times by calling their public information line at **(860) 685-3140.**

Performing Arts

Oakdale Theater (95 S. Turnpike Rd., Wallingford; 203-265-1501) used to be a small, open-air, theater-in-the-round venue that people loved for its intimate atmosphere and hated for its uncomfortable seats. In the mid-1990s it was completely redesigned as an enclosed theater offering plush comfort and a high level of technical sophistication. The programming consists of touring musicals Oct.–Mar., with concerts by major pop, country and rock artists nearly every night in summer.

One of the state's largest community theater groups is the **Repertory Theatre of New Britain (23 Norden St., New Britain; 860-223-3147).** They present dramas and musicals with wide appeal Sept.–May in a wheelchair-accessible, 261-seat auditorium. Tickets are $12–$15 with discounts for children, seniors and students. Productions run three weekends each. Call for more information.

Hole in the Wall Theater (10 Harvard St., New Britain; 860-229-3049) operates on the premise that everyone who wants to be able to see theater should be able to. So, although it has a $10 suggested donation, it will allow patrons to pay whatever they can afford. It presents dramas, comedies and musicals approximately 30 weekends per year. Performances are given Fri. & Sat. at 8:00 P.M. (8:30 P.M. for musicals).

Several university and private school arts centers also contribute to the cultural life of the area, but note that the majority of the programming is scheduled during the school year, Sept.–May. The **Paul Mellon Center for the Arts (333 Christian St., Wallingford; 203-697-2398/2423)** on the campus of Choate Rosemary Hall features a visiting artists series of dance, theater and music, including an annual *Nutcracker* in Dec. The center is also the home of the **Wallingford Symphony Orchestra** and the site of regular student shows and offers a summer music program in some years. The WSO can be contacted directly at **(203) 265-1427.** In addition to its regular winter season of classical performances, it gives several free pops concerts on the lawn in front of the center in summer, including a Fourth of July spectacular.

The **Wesleyan University Center for the Arts,** also listed under Art Galleries, offers a film series with over 50 screenings per semester, professional and student theater, music, dance and an abridged summer arts program including noontime concerts on Tue. The Arts Center buildings are all off High St. between Wyllys and Washington Sts. in Middletown. For more information call **(860) 685-2695** or **(860) 685-3355.**

Much cultural programming also takes place at **Central Connecticut State University** at **1615 Stanley St. in New Britain,** but there is no central number to call for information. Instead, check local papers for special events or call the **Art Dept.** at **(860) 832-2620,** the **Theater Dept.** at **(860) 832-3150** and the **Music Dept.** at **(860) 832-2900.** The university box office is **(860) 832-3164.** One regular guest at the university's Welte Hall is the **New Britain Symphony Orchestra (860-826-6344),** conducted by Jerome Laszloffy. Occasional classical concerts, often with a guest artist, are given Sun. afternoons at 3:00 P.M.

Scenic Drives

Probably the single most scenic and unusual drive in the area is the road climbing to the top of East Peak in Meriden's Hubbard Park. East Peak is one of the so-called Hanging Hills of Meriden, cliffs that jut up abruptly out of relatively flat surroundings. On the drive up you'll see exposed walls of the reddish-brown volcanic traprock that forms the cliffs, and at the top you'll find a stone tower and terrific views to the south. In spots you can get close enough to see the characteristic columnar formation of the rock and piles of talus at the base of cliffs where the weathering action of rain and the seasons has made the rock shatter, fall to the ground and collect in heaps. The road is open Apr.–Oct., 10:00 A.M.–5:00 P.M. From W. Main St. turn into the park at Reservoir Rd. and follow the signs to the peak.

Exceptional areas to visit if you have a map and you're prepared to wander include southeast Wallingford around McKenzie Reservoir, where you'll find rolling farmland and meadows surprisingly close to one of the state's densest population centers; South Glastonbury, with a stop at the Rocky Hill-Glastonbury ferry landing, as well as eastern Glastonbury and northeast Portland where there are numerous blocks of Meshomasic State Forest and Berlin around Timberlin Golf Course. These all have winding lanes, quaint houses and attractive scenery that's pleasant to meander through at a slow pace.

Seasonal Favorites

There are probably two dozen area farms where you can enjoy a leisurely couple of hours picking your own berries, pumpkins or other fruit, get freshly pressed cider and shop in a farm store. The tourism districts listed below under Services can provide you with a list, but one of the biggest and best is **Lyman Orchards.** It's been in the same family for eight generations and over 250 years. From June to Oct. they offer strawberries, blueberries, raspberries, peaches, pears, apples, pumpkins and, if the weather cooperates, tomatoes. You even get pretty views from their 1,100 ridge-top acres. About 1 mile away you'll find their delightful farm store, where they have produce, cheeses, a deli serving sandwiches to eat in or out, candies, a bakery and a cider bar where, for a quarter, you can sample to your heart's content. Ducks and geese congregate at a pond (to the delight of all the children who visit), and they sell cracked corn for feeding the birds. Hours: 9:00 A.M.–7:00 P.M. daily, year-round. The store is on Rte. 157 just north of South St. in Middlefield. Some of the fields are opposite the store; others are on Powder Hill Rd. Call **(860) 349-1566** for recorded pick-your-own information and **(860) 349-1793** to reach the store.

Sports

Canon Greater Hartford Open
This nationally televised PGA Tour golf tournament is a major spectator event. It's hosted by the **Tournament Players Club** at River Highlands. It's always a six-day (Tue.–Sun.)

summer event, but the dates change yearly. The course is on **Golf Club Rd. off Rte. 99 in Cromwell.** For ticket prices and schedule call **(860) 246-4446.**

Connecticut Wolves
The Wolves are Connecticut's women's amateur soccer and men's Division II professional soccer teams. The latter is a developmental team for the New England Revolution out of Massachusetts. The men play in Veteran's Statium, Willow Brook Park, S. Main St. in New Britain. The women play at different locations around Connecticut. The season runs Apr.–Sept. Tickets are $10; call **(860) 223-0710** for a game schedule.

Hardware City Rock Cats
New Britain's Eastern League AA baseball team, a Minnesota Twins affiliate, plays at the new 6,100-seat New Britain Stadium. (The "Hardware City" part of the name refers to New Britain's manufacturing heritage.) The team plays 71 home games Apr.–Sept. Weeknight games are at 7:00 P.M. (a little earlier in Apr.), & Sun. games are at 2:00 P.M. Ticket prices range from $2 for children to $6 for reserved adult seats; general admission is $5. **Willow Brook Park, S. Main St., New Britain, 06050; (860) 224-8383.**

Tours

Riverboat Cruises
Fall foliage tours down the Connecticut River to Gillette Castle depart Middletown on Oct. weekends. The name of the riverboat, the *Aunt Polly,* is a reference to both Mark Twain and William Gillette. She was Tom Sawyer's aunt, and Gillette had a steamboat by the same name. Fare: $16 adults, half-price for children 3–11, discounts for seniors. Free parking. Departures are Sat. & Sun. at noon, returning at 4:00 P.M. The dock is at Harborpark on Harbor Dr. in Middletown. For more information call **Deep River Navigation CO.** at **(860) 526-4954.**

Walking Tours
You can take a self-guided tour of Middletown using the 16-page brochure "Trees of Middletown" as a guide. It leads you on a route

perhaps 2 miles in length, down a portion of Main St., briefly along the Connecticut River and across the Wesleyan University campus, introducing you not only to dozens of tree species but also botany and the architecture and history of Middletown. The booklet is available from the Connecticut River Valley and Shoreline Visitors Council (see the Services section for address and hours).

"Your Guide to the Historic Sites of Central Connecticut," available from the Central Connecticut Tourism District (see the Services section for address and hours), is a brochure you can use to formulate walking and driving tours in a five-town region covering Berlin, Cheshire, New Britain, Plainville and Southington.

Where to Stay

Bed & Breakfasts

B&Bs in this area are noteworthy for moderate rates, often below those of hotels. The detailed listings below represent some personal favorites. Other establishments with simple, casual accommodations that will go easy on your budget include **Captain Josiah Cowles Place (184 Marion Ave., Southington; 860-276-0227),** a modernized farmhouse having one guest room with a queen bed; **Chaffee's B&B (28 Reussner Rd., Southington; 860-628-2750),** having a delightful hostess and one guest room with twin beds in a modern ranch house and **Udderly Woolly Acres (581 Thompson St., Glastonbury; 860-633-4503),** a working organic farm with country roads for walking right outside the door and a small suite of rooms with twin beds.

Butternut Farm—$$$
This unique B&B is like a small farm in the suburbs. The centerpiece is a 1720 farmhouse with lots of original details and 18th-century antique furnishings that combine to create an authentic colonial atmosphere. A barn out back is home to goats, fowl and other small animals that children will especially enjoy.

There are several rooms in the main house and one apartment adjacent to the barn, all with private baths. A full breakfast is included. **1654 Main St., Glastonbury, 06033; (860) 633-7197.**

The Croft—$$$
The Croft offers guests a choice of two guest rooms in a colonial house on a large lot in a residential neighborhood. Located on a quiet side street in Portland, it's still only a few minutes by car from downtown Middletown. The rooms have a casual, country feel, and the prices are very reasonable. The Tansy Suite has a pineapple theme (the traditional symbol of hospitality), a queen bed, a delightful private breakfast nook, a small refrigerator and a private bath. The Bergamot Suite is a little more utilitarian in decor but has two bedrooms to accommodate from one to four people. These share a sitting area, kitchen and bath. Inquire about breakfast. **7 Penny Corner Rd., Portland, 06480; (860) 342-1856.**

High Meadow—$$$
A beautiful country setting and appealing colonial character are high points of High Meadow, the most convenient B&B to Choate Rosemary Hall. This center-chimney farmhouse (ca. 1742) has original wood paneling and wideboard floors throughout. There are two guest rooms in the main house with private baths and a shared sitting room; the one with a king or two twin beds also has a working wood-burning fireplace. A third overnight option is a private cottage overlooking a pond on the property. Built with architectural salvage, it has a cathedral ceiling, lots of windows and a Murphy bed, plus it's handicapped-accessible. A full breakfast is included. **1290 Whirlwind Hill Rd., Wallingford, 06492; (203) 269-2351.**

Rowson House—$$ to $$$
The only B&B located right in Middletown, Rowson House (named after the proprietors) is within walking distance of both Wesleyan University and the city's rich assortment of Main St. restaurants. From the outside, Rowson House looks much like the other neatly kept homes in its urban residential

125

neighborhood. Inside, however, beautiful woodwork is evident, especially in the living room. Of the three rooms, Lady Louise and Blue Heaven are the two largest, each with queen beds and antique furnishings. The Paisley Twin is the smallest room but can accommodate three people because one of its two twin beds is a trundle. An exceptional full breakfast is included. **53 Prospect St., Middletown, 06457; (860) 346-8479.**

Hotels, Motels & Inns

The listings below describe a selection of hotels in the middle to upper price ranges. Other options in the midprice category include **Holiday Inn Express (120 Laning St., Southington; 860-276-0736)** located next door to Brannigan's Restaurant, famed for its ribs; **Holiday Inn (4 Sebethe Dr., Cromwell; 800-HOLIDAY or 860-635-1001); Howard Johnson (400 New Britain Ave., Plainville; 800-1-GO-HOJO or 860-747-6876)** and **Ramada Inn (65 Columbus Blvd., New Britain; 800-2-RAMADA or 860-224-9161),** the only major hotel in downtown New Britain.

In the budget category, the **Susse Chalet (20 Waterchase Dr., Rocky Hill; 800-5-CHALET or 860-563-7877)** is acceptable and has an especially good senior citizen rate. Even less expensive accommodations are clustered along Rte. 5/15, which is called the Wilbur Cross Highway in Berlin and the Berlin Tpke. in Newington, and on Queen St. (Rte. 10) in Southington. For further suggestions, contact any of the tourism districts listed under Services.

Residence Inn—$$$$

This all-suites hotel has one- and two-bedroom units, some with fireplace, all with fully equipped kitchens and queen beds. The two-bedroom suites come with two baths, so two couples could share and stay overnight very cheaply. They're also excellent for families, allowing kids to have a real bedroom instead of a cot. There's a social area by the lobby where complimentary hors d'oeuvres are served Mon.–Thu. and an expanded Continental breakfast daily. Other features include an out-door pool and spa, a sport court, an exercise room, a laundry room, valet dry cleaning, a free grocery shopping service and limited shuttle service. The inn can accommodate pets for a nonrefundable $200 fee. **390 Bee St., Meriden, 06450; (800) 331-3131 or (203) 634-7770.**

Marriott—$$$ to $$$$

This business traveler–oriented hotel offers weekenders special "Two for Breakfast" packages at very reasonable rates; inquire for details. Standard rooms have two double or one king bed, plus in-room hair dryer, iron and ironing board. A concierge level offers guests extra amenities and services. There's a restaurant on-site, an indoor pool and an exercise room. **100 Capital Blvd., Rocky Hill, 06067; (800) 228-9290 or (860) 257-6000.**

Radisson—$$$ to $$$$

As a hotel that caters primarily to business travelers, the Radisson offers traditionally furnished rooms with coffeemakers, irons and ironing boards, turn-down service and a low-cost shuttle to Bradley International Airport. On weekends leisure travelers can enjoy all the same amenities at lower prices. The hotel has a restaurant, indoor pool, whirlpool, sauna and exercise facility. Located right off I-91 exit 21. **100 Berlin Rd. [Rte. 372], Cromwell, 06416; (800) 333-3333 or (860) 635-2000.**

Ramada Plaza—$$$ to $$$$

One of the most luxurious hotels in the Connecticut heartland has a business traveler focus, but with low weekend rates leisure travelers can stay here for little more than some less well appointed hotels. It offers standard rooms, suites and some rooms with butler pantries designed for extended stays. Rounding out the facilities are a nice restaurant with a good salad bar, a lounge, an indoor pool and a fitness center. **275 Research Parkway, Meriden, 06450; (800) 272-6232 or (203) 238-2380.**

Courtyard by Marriott—$$$

If your timing is right, rates can be quite low at this nice hotel right off I-91 exit 15. The rooms, most with king beds, encircle an enclosed central courtyard with an indoor pool. It also has a whirlpool, an exercise room, a restaurant and lounge, a coin-operated laundry and valet dry cleaning. **600 Northrop Rd., Wallingford, 06492; (800) 321-2211** or **(203) 284-9400.**

Hampton Inn—$$$

One of the best values you'll find in the area in the moderate price category has little in the way of extra facilities (gym, pool, etc.) but nice rooms and an elaborate Continental breakfast included. There's no extra charge for a third person or kids under 18. **10 Bee St., Meriden, 06450; (800) 426-7866** or **(203) 235-5154.**

Riverdale Motel—$$$

If you're traveling east of the Connecticut River, the Riverdale is a good choice for low-cost but clean, safe overnight accommodations. It's located on a pleasant grassy hillside above the Connecticut River with picnic tables that are nice for an outdoor breakfast. It also has a coin-operated laundry. Request a room in the new building, which is more modern and set back from the road. Wheelchair-accessible rooms are available. **Rte. 66, Portland, 06480; (860) 342-3498.**

Susse Chalet—$$$

Among the nicest of this chain in Connecticut, the Susse Chalet in Wallingford was recently renovated and represents a good value. It has an outdoor pool and a coin-operated laundry, and a light breakfast is set out in the morning. Kids under 18 stay free in your room. The location right by I-91 exit 15 is very convenient. **100 Chalet Dr., Wallingford, 06492; (203) 265-4703.**

Where to Eat

The Connecticut heartland is no less diverse than other parts of the state, and that applies to food as well. Several of the restaurants listed below specialize in food that can be a bit challenging to some palates. Other options include **Cracovia (60 Broad St., New Brit-** **ain; 860-223-4443),** serving New Britain's large Polish population. It's in a slightly scruffy part of town, but it's supposed to be the real thing when it comes to Polish food, serving up homemade pierogis, blintzes, kielbasa, stuffed cabbage and the like daily from 8:00 A.M. For Japanese food, visit the sushi bar at **Mikado (3 Columbus Pl., Middletown; 860-346-6655).** Located in a former rathskeller, it's an especially cool and pleasant retreat on a hot day. Thai food in a casual, storefront setting is available at **Thai Gardens (300 Plaza Middlesex [Main St. near College St.], Middletown; 860-346-3322).** It serves all the popular dishes such as Pad Thai and coconut chicken soup plus a good selection of vegetarian offerings.

If casual American food is more to your liking, you also have plenty of choices. **Cornerstones (corner of Washington and Main Sts., Middletown; 860-344-0222)** is a friendly, publike place with a central Middletown location. To the west, try **J. Timothy's (143 New Britain Ave., Plainville; 860-747-6813),** a landmark building that was Cooke's Tavern for ages and ages. It has a large pub, numerous dining rooms and live entertainment on weekends. **Main St. Bar & Restaurant (39 N. Main St., Wallingford; 203-265-7100)** has a casual English pub air and is convenient to Oakdale Theater. The state's favorite place for steak (at least according to *Connecticut* magazine's annual poll) is **Ruth's Chris Steak House (2513 Berlin Tpke., Newington; 860-666-2202).** At **The Victorian House (226 Maple Ave., Cheshire; 203-272-5743)** you can enjoy the setting of a real "painted lady." And if you find yourself driving on I-84 in this neck of the woods and hungry at an odd hour, pull off exit 21 and stop for a bite at **Cromwell Diner (135 Berlin Rd., Cromwell; 860-635-7112).** It's open 24 hours a day, every day, and they offer a larger-than-average menu (even for a diner) in very comfortable surroundings. All of these restaurants are appropriate for family dining. Finally, if you're heading out for a picnic, **Eleanor Rigby's Delicatessen (360 Main St., Middletown; 860-343-1730)** is a good place

127

to get sandwiches, deli salads and green salads to go.

Main & Hopewell—$$$ to $$$$

Well-balanced preparations that hit the middle ground between subtle and flavorful are the hallmarks of this American/Continental restaurant. Its three small dining rooms are housed in an attractive older structure that lies on the cusp of urban Hartford and the city's pastoral surroundings. It serves a Sun. jazz brunch, and live jazz is offered Thu.–Sat. evenings in the downstairs bar, where a pub menu is available. Lunch hours: Mon.–Fri., 11:30 A.M.–2:00 P.M. Dinner hours: Mon.–Thu., 5:00 P.M.–9:00 P.M.; Fri.–Sat. until 10:00 P.M. Located at the **corner of Main St. and Hopewell Rd., South Glastonbury, 06073; (860) 633-8698.**

Ambassador of India—$$$

Indian restaurants tend to have large menus, but the selection at Ambassador of India goes beyond even that impressive standard, with goat and lamb dishes to challenge the Western palate in addition to more frequently seen choices. At the same time there are some concessions to the Western world (or perhaps adaptations would be a better word), such as a wine list with suggested food pairings and some non-Indian desserts. But for the paintings on the walls, the decor might be that of a Continental restaurant. Hours: Tue.–Sun., 5:00 P.M.–10:00 P.M. **2333 Main St., Glastonbury, 06033; (860) 659-2529.**

America's Cup—$$$

What could be a better casual setting for seafood than a converted yacht club overlooking the Connecticut River? There's indoor seating on three levels, plus several decks and a large bar. Live music is sometimes offered, both inside and out. It also serves steak and pasta. Lunch/Sun. brunch hours: 11:30 A.M.–2:30 P.M. daily. Dinner served Sun.–Thu., 4:30 P.M.–9:00 P.M., & Sun., 4:30 P.M.–10:00 P.M. **80 Harbor Dr., Middletown, 06457; (860) 347-9999.**

Café Angelique—$$$

Unpretentious from the outside, Café Angelique is much more stylish (although a bit dark) inside, where you'll find a Mediterranean color scheme and seating at small tables. The bistro fare is an exceptional bargain at lunch, when many entrées go for only $5 or $6. Plus, vegetarians get choices at both lunch and dinner. Open Tue.–Sat., 11:30 A.M.–3:00 P.M. for lunch & 5:30 P.M.–9:00 P.M. (10:00 on Fri.–Sat.) for dinner. **30 Berlin Rd. (Rte. 372), Cromwell, 06416; (860) 632-8982.**

Cornwall Grille & Pub—$$$

The understated elegance of a 200-year-old house is the perfect setting for classic American dishes such as prime rib and steamed lobster. In marked contrast to the dining rooms, which are bright and stylish, the basement bar is cool and dark, but a dartboard and a couple of small tables keep it strangely cozy. Hours: lunch served Mon.–Fri., 11:30 A.M.–2:30 P.M.; dinner served Thu.–Sat., 5:00 P.M.–10:00 P.M., & Sun.–Wed., 5:00 P.M.–9:00 P.M. Pub menu available beginning at 4:00 P.M. **200 S. Main St., Cheshire, 06410; (203) 272-1600.**

Max Amore—$$$

The newest of the Max "chain" (along with Max Downtown in Hartford and Max-a-Mia in Avon) specializes in Northern Italian food. The menu is broken down into pizzas ("stone pies"), sandwiches (at lunch), pastas and grilled items. Upscale yet casual, it has a beautiful bar for hanging out. Hours: Mon.–Thu., 11:30 A.M.–10:00 P.M.; Fri.–Sat., 11:30 A.M.–11:00 P.M.; Sun., 5:00 P.M.–9:00 P.M. **140 Glastonbury Blvd. (in The Shops at Somerset Square), Glastonbury, 06033; (860) 659-2819.**

Michael's Trattoria—$$$

Located in an innocuous little storefront with only a few tables, this cute restaurant serves a mix of classic Italian dishes. It's one of the in-demand places for dinner before shows at Oakdale, so reservations are strongly suggested. Hours: Mon., 4:30 P.M.–9:30 P.M.; Tue.–Thu., 11:45 A.M.–9:30 P.M.; Fri., 11:45 A.M.–10:30 P.M.; Sat., 4:30 P.M.–10:30 P.M. **344 Center St., Wallingford, 06492; (203) 269-5303.**

Nardi's Old Mill—$$$

Housed in an actual old mill building with wooden sheathing and exposed beams, Nardi's is rich in atmosphere, which serves to enhance the excellence of the Northern Italian and American food. Sit in one of the high-backed booths covered with the carved initials of patrons from decades ago, or at a table overlooking a little pond and ornamental water-wheel. Lunch hours: Tue.–Fri., 11:30 A.M.–4:00 P.M. Dinner hours: Tue.–Sat., 5:00 P.M.–10:00 P.M.; Sun., 3:00 P.M.–8:00 P.M. **493 South End Rd., Southington, 06479; (860) 620-0300.**

Saybrook Fish House—$$$

One of a small chain of Connecticut restaurants that specializes in fish and seafood, Saybrook Fish House is casual and family-oriented. It also serves pasta, meat and poultry to satisfy other tastes, and its location is very convenient to Dinosaur State Park. The dining room is closed 2:30 P.M.–4:30 P.M., but a light pub menu is still available. Hours: Mon.–Fri., 11:30 A.M.–9:30 P.M.; Sat., noon–10:30 P.M.; Sun., noon–8:00 P.M. **2165 Silas Deane Hwy., Rocky Hill, 06067; (860) 721-9188.**

The Watch Factory—$$$

This self-described "Austrian country kitchen" serves Germanic specialties such as Wiener schnitzel as well as Continental/American dishes that tend toward the classic and un-complicated. It's located in The Watch Factory Shoppes, an old brick factory complex that's been converted into retail space. Lunch hours: Tue.–Sat., 11:30 A.M.–2:00 P.M. Dinner served Tue.–Sat., 5:00 P.M.–9:00 P.M. **122 Elm St., Cheshire, 06410; (203) 271-1717.**

Yankee Silversmith—$$$

A local institution, the Yankee Silversmith has a couple of gimmicks that make it a fun and memorable place to eat out. One is its novel Victorian parlor car cum dining room, where you can have lunch or light fare. (The full dinner menu is served in a tavern dining room.) The other is a bake shop where you can buy its breads and trademark popovers to take along. It has a large menu of American food ranging from classic pot roast and turkey dinner to seafood, pasta and meal salads, plus children's portions. And on Sun., this is the spot for brunch. Lunch/brunch hours: Tue.–Sat., 11:30 A.M.–4:00 P.M.; Sun., 11:00 A.M.–2:00 P.M. Dinner served Tue.–Sun. from 4:00 P.M. in the parlor

car & from 5:00 P.M. (4:00 on Sun.) in the tavern. **1033 N. Colony Rd. (Rte. 5 at Merritt Pkwy. exit 66), Wallingford, 06492; (203) 269-5444.**

It's Only Natural—$$ to $$$

Also known by the acronym ION, this vegetarian restaurant operates side-by-side with a natural foods grocery and New Age bookstore/gift shop. The atmosphere is as homey as the food: watercolors, plants, lacy curtains and suitably eclectic music on the sound system set the right mood. Dinner starts with a basket of fresh homemade breads displayed on a table and cut before your eyes. The menu draws from a variety of ethnic cuisines, but most dishes rely extensively on grains, tofu, tempeh and tahini, and are only moderately spiced. Several soups are available daily. Most or all of the offerings are vegan. A high point of the menu is the wide variety of "alternative" beverages: veggie juices, macro tea, herbal tea and substitute coffee (in addition to the real thing). Several dressings and spreads are also available for purchase by the pound. Lunch and Sun. brunch hours: 11:30 A.M.–3:00 P.M. daily. Dinner hours: Tue.–Sat., 5:00 P.M.–9:00 P.M. **686 Main St., Middletown, 06457; (860) 346-9210.**

Taj of India—$$ to $$$

For Indian food on the west side of the Connecticut River or just another vegetarian option right in Middletown, Taj of India is the place. The interior is neutral and understated with Indian art on the walls, suitable for a casual meal or a pre-theater feast. Hours: 11:00 A.M.–10:00 P.M. daily. **170 Main St., Middletown, 06457; (860) 346-2050.**

Tuscany Grill—$$ to $$$

One of the more visually stylish restaurants in Middletown, Tuscany Grill serves Italian food at prices pleasantly lower than what you'd expect from a spot that looks so trendy. The menu includes brick-oven pizza and classics like veal marsala, shrimp Fra Diavolo and many pastas. It also has a larger-than-average selection of wines, mostly Italian and California vintages, by the glass and the bottle. Warm yellow and terra-cotta tones create a suitably

129

Mediterranean ambiance inside, where a loft overlooks a two-story space above a large bar. The sidewalk café is a lively spot on a summer evening. Live music is offered some nights. Hours: Mon.–Thu., 11:30 A.M.–10:00 P.M.; Fri.–Sat., 11:30 A.M.–11:00 P.M.; Sun., noon–10:00 P.M. **600 Plaza Middlesex (off Main St. near College St.), Middletown, 06457; (860) 346-7096.**

O'Rourke's Diner—$$

O'Rourke's is the sort of place you might walk right by if someone didn't tell you about it. It inhabits a blast-from-the-past, 1945-vintage, stainless steel diner that's comfortable, homey and fun. Its breakfast menu is five pages long, all of it available all day (and half the night if you count the hours it's open before sunrise). Also check out its daily specials and the unusual omelets it offers for weekend brunch. Hours: Mon.–Fri., 4:30 A.M.–3:00 P.M.; Sat.–Sun., 4:30 A.M.–1:00 P.M. **728 Main St., Middletown, 06457; (860) 346-6101.**

Coffeehouses, Sweets & Treats

Blue Bottle Bakery & Café (330 Main St., Cheshire; 203-699-1337) is a good stopping place when you want something quick, easy and not too expensive, sans the chain restaurant atmosphere, plus it's open early (6:00 A.M. daily) and as late as 11:00 P.M. on summer weekends. In addition to soup and sandwiches, you'll find great moist muffins, pastries, breads and Manhattan bagels. Another early bird in this category (open weekdays at 7:00 A.M., weekends at 8:00) is **Klekolo Coffeehouse (181 Court St., Middletown; 860-343-9444).** In addition to the more common espressos, cappuccinos and lattés, it serves incredible, award-winning specialty coffee drinks that approach cocktails in their complexity. This is a Wesleyan student hangout with modern art on the walls and a selection of well-thumbed reading materials on hand for perusal. For a real literary choice, visit **Atticus Café (45 Broad St., Middletown; 860-347-1194),** both coffeehouse and bookstore. And for a full-service restaurant with an exceptional number of specialty coffees to enjoy

after your meal, try **Café Angelique (30 Berlin Rd., Cromwell; 860-632-8982),** also listed in the restaurant section.

Services

Local Visitors Information

Central Connecticut Tourism District, One Grove St., Suite 310, New Britain, 06053; (860) 225-3901. Hours: Mon.–Fri., 9:00 A.M.–5:00 P.M.

Connecticut River Valley and Shoreline Visitors Council, 393 Main St., Middletown, 06457; (800) 486-3346 or (860) 347-0028. Hours: Mon.–Fri., 8:00 A.M.–4:00 P.M.

Greater Hartford Tourism District, 234 Murphy Rd., Hartford, 06114; (800) 793-4480 or (860) 244-8181.

State Welcome Centers

These free rest areas all have shaded picnic tables and grills, rest rooms and vending machines open 24 hours a day as well as visitor information. One is located off I-84 eastbound between exits 28 and 29 in Southington; call **(860) 621-3939.** From Memorial Day to Columbus Day, visitors information is available 8:00 A.M.–6:00 P.M. daily. Hours from Columbus Day to Dec. 31 are Thu.–Sun., 9:00 A.M.–4:00 P.M. Two other centers where visitor information is available 24 hours a day from self-serve racks are located off I-91 southbound between exits 15 and 14 in Wallingford **(203-265-5803)** and off I-91 northbound between exits 19 and 20 in Middletown **(860-238-6010).**

Transportation

Rocky Hill-Glastonbury Ferry

The oldest continuously operating ferry in the nation crosses the Connecticut River between Rocky Hill and Glastonbury, and it's a hoot to ride. The bargelike flatboat is towed across the river by a tug, taking only three cars per trip. The fare is $2.25/car (or motorcycle) and driver plus $.75 for each additional passenger; $.75 for bikes and pedestrians. Season: May–Oct. Hours: Mon.–Fri., 7:00 A.M.–6:45 P.M.; Sat.–Sun., 10:30 A.M.–5:00 P.M. There is no set schedule; the ferry departs whenever someone is waiting. To get to the Rocky Hill terminal, follow signs from Silas Deane Hwy. (Rte. 99) and Glastonbury Rd. (Rte. 160). In Glastonbury the terminal is at the end of Ferry Ln. (Rte. 160). For more information call **(860) 443-3856.**

Interstate bus service to Middletown and Meriden is provided by **Peter Pan/Trailways** at **(800) 343-9999** and **Greyhound** at **(800)** 231-2222. The **Middletown Transit District** at **(860) 346-0212** has routes connecting many towns in the Central Valley. For regional bus service between Cheshire and the Naugatuck Valley region, call the **Greater Waterbury Transit District** at **(203) 757-0535.** The **Northeast Transportation Company** provides service between Meriden and Wallingford; call **(203) 753-2538** for details. The New Britain/Bristol area is covered by **Dattoo** at **(860) 229-4878** and **New Britain Transportation** at **(860) 828-0511.** Finally, bus service north toward and beyond Hartford is provided by the **Greater Hartford Transit District** at **(860) 247-5329** and **CT Transit** at **(860) 525-9181.**

North Central

The North Central area is roughly the uppermost part of the Connecticut River Valley. Despite their proximity to Hartford, Springfield, Massachusetts, and the airport, towns here are almost entirely suburban and rural. They contain some of the richest farmland in Connecticut, the result of sediment deposited by an ancient glacial lake. In fact, the area is historically the state's Tobacco Valley. Leaves for binding and wrapping cigars have been grown here since about 1800, and other types of tobacco were grown as far back as 1640. The tobacco fields start about five minutes outside the airport grounds, and Windsor is the site of the fascinating museum documenting the history of the enterprise.

Windsor is even more notable for being the site of the first English settlement in Connecticut, and therefore the state's oldest town. The early colonists found this fertile plain an extremely attractive place to settle. The Windsor Historical Society maintains a museum complex in a lovely historic district that also contains the meetinghouse of the first church society in Connecticut and the oldest marked gravestone (that of Reverend Ephraim Huit) in the state, dated 1644.

Other attractions of a historic nature include Old Newgate Prison, a unique site where you can descend into the tunnels of an old copper mine cum jail; museums that document the life, architecture and industry of the area, such as the Hatheway House and King House and the New England Air Museum, whose displays trace the development of human flight from the days of ballooning onward.

With both the Connecticut River and the lower stretch of the Farmington River cutting through the area, opportunities for fishing and boating abound. The spring shad run is even accompanied by a Shad Derby. Running along a 5-mile stretch of the Connecticut is the former Windsor Locks Canal towpath, now a greenway perfect for leisurely strolling or biking. Finally, for a different perspective on things in this largely flat landscape, visit Penwood State Park, where a densely forested basalt ridge yields valley views in two directions.

History

In 1633 a party of traders from Plymouth, Massachusetts, under the leadership of Lt. William Holmes, built a fort at Windsor just upstream of a Dutch fort built a few months earlier at what is now Hartford. Land on both sides of the river was inhabited by several Indian tribes. In fact, one of the largest Indian habitations in Connecticut was a Podunk village on the river in present-day East Hartford, and some accounts have it that a Podunk representative traveled to Plymouth in 1631 to request that the English settle in the valley. The Podunks saw in the English possible allies against raiding Pequots.

Windsor was a palisaded fort (hence the references to it as the Palisado), but whether the stockade was built for protection against the Dutch, the Pequots, wild animals or some combination of these is not clear. The settlers passed a miserable first winter in the wilderness, with many English and Indian deaths from a smallpox epidemic, and Windsor went on to have a rather confused early history due to the arrival of a second band of settlers from Dorchester, Massachusetts, and a third conflicting claim.

By virtue of it being the first town in Connecticut, Windsor dominates the state's early history. One of the town's earliest residents was John Mason, who led the colonists in the Pequot War of 1637 in response to a Pequot attack at Wethersfield. In 1636 land east of the river was purchased from Indians and made part of the town. In 1642 John Bissell established the first ferry across the Connecticut River to allow the proprietors to farm their east bank land and return home to the west bank at night. Twenty years later Bissell's family became the first English to settle perma-

nently east of the river. Another Windsor first came in 1647 when resident Alice Young became the first person to be tried and executed for witchcraft in North America.

The Revolutionary War period was notable both for what it took from and brought to the area. It is said that in some towns every eligible man served the Patriot cause. But Tories were sent here en masse when a copper mine in East Granby (then Simsbury) was converted to use as a prison and named Newgate after an infamous British jail. The inmates continued to work the copper veins and were then employed making nails and other goods, but eventually all such activity stopped because of an undesirable side effect: the prisoners spirited away sharp metal objects to use as weapons.

Tobacco cultivation began in 1640 with seed from Virginia, and the crop eventually dominated the economy of the whole upper Connecticut River Valley. In 1921 over 30,000 acres were devoted to tobacco. The figure is about one-tenth that today, although it's increasing again. It's been estimated that at least one town in the area, South Windsor, was 90% dependent on the tobacco crop when the market for it collapsed in 1953 after the development of a cheaper substitute (the tobacco equivalent of fiberboard) for the high-quality leaf grown here. Only an upsurge of industry in the Hartford area and the demand for land for new housing as a result of the post–World War II baby boom saved the area from economic disaster.

Different types of tobacco were grown in the valley over the years, but eventually local farmers specialized in a broad-leaf type that was used to bind and wrap cigars. One Mrs. Prout of East Windsor is credited with rolling the first U.S.–made cigar in 1801, and the first cigar factory in the country opened in West Suffield in 1810.

Tobacco is responsible for the North Central area's two most singular landmarks—the tobacco tent and the tobacco barn. Around the turn of the 20th century, local tobacco farmers met stiff competition from tobacco leaf grown in Sumatra and responded with a most innovative solution: growing their leaf under gauze

133

tents that simulated the warm, humid Sumatran climate. They still do it the same way, and you can see tobacco tents in use simply by taking a drive through the area in early summer. The tobacco barn has unique slatted sides of various designs to allow for controlled ventilation during the critical drying stage of tobacco production. Tobacco also altered the ethnic makeup of the valley. Migrant laborers from Jamaica and Puerto Rico came to the area to help with the harvest just as Mexicans currently do in California, and some stayed.

River topography gave rise to another local landmark: Windsor Locks Canal. It was built in

1827–1829 in order to take river traffic (principally southbound from Springfield, Massachusetts, to Hartford) around a rocky portion of the river 5.5 miles long known as the Enfield Rapids. The canal worked effectively but was closed in 1845, not coincidentally only one year after the opening of the railroad in 1844. Opposite the southern tip of the locks is Warehouse Point in Enfield. This was as far as one could sail up the river prior to construction of the canal, and warehouses were located here for about 200 years to hold goods as they made the transition between boat and cart.

Many other notable people and events are associated with the area. A Shaker community flourished for a time in Enfield just after the Revolution, but it died out and little trace of it remains. Windsor Locks is the birthplace of Ella T. Grasso, the first woman governor of any state who did not succeed a husband in office. East Windsor is the birthplace of John Fitch, who developed the steamboat design that Robert Fulton patented after Fitch's untimely death. And native to South Windsor (then East Windsor) was Jonathan Edwards, the foremost preacher of the Great Awakening that rocked the Congregational Church in the 1740s.

In recent years suburbanization has fueled a great deal of the development in the North Central towns. The pattern, though, has been such that in many places new housing and old farms are still interspersed, which makes the area a nice place to live and a pleasant place to tour.

Major Attractions

New England Air Museum

Aircraft buffs will not want to miss this, the largest aviation museum in the Northeast. It has a good mix of civilian and military craft from the beginning of the age of flight right up to the present day, from an 1870s Silas Brooks balloon basket (the oldest surviving American aircraft anywhere) to an A-10 Warthog flown in Desert Storm. They have a very comprehensive exhibit on the life and work of Igor Sikorsky,

best known as the developer of the first practical helicopter. One highlight is the oldest surviving Sikorsky aircraft, an S-39 flying boat made in Bridgeport in 1932. The display was built and donated by the company Sikorsky founded, which is now headquartered in Stratford. Another strength of the museum's collection is their World War II–era aircraft. Perhaps the best way to enjoy the museum is by attending one of their frequent special events. The most popular are the Open Cockpit Days held several times during the year, when you can climb into the cockpit of more than a dozen aircraft. There's also a scale model show in Nov. and an antique auto show in June; call for a schedule. Admission: $6.50 adults, $5.50 seniors, $3 children 6–11. Hours: 10:00 A.M.–5:00 P.M. daily, year-round; closed on Thanksgiving and Christmas. Located **off Rte. 75 approximately 2.5 miles north of Rte. 20 (follow the signs), Windsor Locks, 06096; (860) 623-3305.**

Northwest Park and Nature Center

Any town would be lucky to have a municipal recreation area offering everything Northwest Park in Windsor provides. There are trails for walking and cross-country skiing, a half-mile Braille Trail, woods roads for mountain biking, a museum documenting the local tobacco growing industry, barnyard animals, a picnic pavilion, free family programs on weekends, demonstration gardens, an operating sugarhouse, an annual fair and even a coffeehouse series. On your first visit, make a point of stopping by when the nature center is open so you can get a good overview of all the recreational and educational opportunities here. Access to all facilities is free, although there can be a charge for programs and special events. Nature Center hours (Sept.–June): Mon.–Thu., noon–5:00 P.M.; Sat., 10:00 A.M.–4:00 P.M. July/Aug. hours: Mon.–Fri., 9:00 A.M.–5:00 P.M. Grounds hours: dawn–dusk daily, year-round. **145 Lang Rd., Windsor, 06095; (860) 285-1886.**

Old Newgate Prison and Copper Mine

Established in 1707, the first chartered copper mine in the colonies served a more sinister function as a prison beginning in 1773. The Patriot governing authorities were especially fond of confining Tories in Newgate's dank tunnels during the Revolutionary War. It was named for a prison in London notorious for its awful conditions—features they shared. Connecticut's Newgate remained open for 54 years, despite numerous successful breakouts. Exhibits focus on both the industrial and penal aspects of the site. There are aboveground ruins with some excellent displays, but the most fascinating part of your visit will be your self-guided tour of the mine itself. The atmosphere is as chilling as it was two centuries ago; make sure to wear a sweater and even a slicker, because the temperature in the mines is in the forties, and moisture drips from seams in the rock at every turn. Delightfully creepy, Old Newgate Prison would make an especially enjoyable Halloween season outing. In fact, a local fife and drum corps has recently begun hosting a special Halloween party at the site. The event may become an annual one; call for details. Admission: $3 adults, $1.50 seniors and children. Hours: Wed.–Sun., 10:00 A.M.–4:30 P.M., mid-May–Oct. **115 Newgate Rd. (north of Rte. 20), East Granby, 06027; (860) 653-3563.**

Windsor Historical Society Museums

Windsor is the oldest English settlement in Connecticut, and as such it has a large number of historic buildings. Many are clustered around a green on Palisado Ave. north of downtown, where the society keeps three museums, all of which can be visited for one admission price. The **Lt. Walter Fyler House** (ca. 1640) was built by Fyler, who came to the New World on the *Mary and John* from Plymouth, England, in 1630. He spent five years in the Massachusetts Bay Colony and then came to Connecticut in 1635 as part of the

Getting There

Connecticut's principal airport, **Bradley International,** is located in Windsor Locks in the heart of the North Central area. Several ground transportation options are available at the airport. I-91 runs north-south through the area, making access by automobile easy.

second group to populate Windsor. Fyler's 1683 estate inventory, compiled by local officials after his death and from which the museum's curators know exactly what he owned, is on display in the house. The furnishings are period pieces, although not Fyler's original belongings.

The second museum property is the **Dr. Hezekiah Chaffee House,** a brick Georgian colonial dating from 1765. In keeping with its builder's profession, there are exhibits of medical instruments from the Revolutionary War period.

The modern **Wilson Museum** contains a variety of displays on Windsor history, including Indian artifacts and documents such as the list of local men who responded to the alarm in Lexington. There's also a handwritten survey of the Palisado, Windsor's original stockaded settlement, measured in rods and drawn by the second town clerk. The extensive library of genealogical and other records is also open to the public by appointment. Admission: $3 for adults, free to students and children under 18. Summer (Apr.–Oct.) hours: Tue.–Sat., 10:00 A.M.–4:00 P.M. Winter (Nov.–Mar.) hours: Mon.–Fri., 10:00 A.M.–4:00 P.M. Closed national holidays. **96 Palisado Ave. (Rte. 159), Windsor, 06095; (860) 688-3813 or (860) 298-9203.**

When you visit these museums, also take a moment to explore the historic district in which they're located. The oldest marked gravestone in Connecticut can be found in the cemetery next to the First Congregational Church across the street. Ephraim Huit's marker is dated 1644, and it's still readable. There are about twenty 17th-century gravestones here. Also look for the Founders Monument on the green. Engraved on it are the names of 125 of the first European families to settle in Windsor, and hence the state.

Festivals and Events

Shad Derby and Festival
May

Connecticut's rivers are a spawning ground for shad, an important indigenous food fish. Both the Indians and the colonists relied upon it, and it's still a seasonal favorite, although not to everyone's taste. Shad run in midspring at about the same time it starts to get warm and pleasant out of doors, so they provide a good excuse for a festival with truly regional flavor spread out over several weeks. The main event is probably the festival and craft fair held on the town green the third Sat. of the month, but there's also a fishing tournament, a parade and a formal ball. Call or look through a local paper for a schedule of the current year's happenings; most are free. For more information call the **L.P. Wilson Community Center** at **(860) 285-1990.**

Eastern States Exposition
Sept.

This huge regional agricultural fair that takes place just over the border in Massachusetts is the biggest in the East, drawing participants from across New England and spectators from far and wide. It begins the second Fri. after Labor Day and runs for 17 days. Major events include a horse show, a circus and musical entertainment. The Avenue of the States features large replicas of the capitol buildings of the six participating states, and each state has one day of the expo devoted to it. On that day special events occur in that state's building, so make a point of visiting on Connecticut Day. Admission: $10 adults, $8 children 6–12. Hours: 8:00 A.M.–10:00 P.M. daily. **1305 Memorial Ave. (Rte. 149), West Springfield, MA 01089.** Take I-91 to exit 3 and follow the

signs. A brochure with a schedule of events is available beginning in June. For more information call **(413) 737-2443.**

Northwest Park Country Fair
last Saturday in Sept.

Northwest Park's scaled-down version of a traditional New England agricultural fair has a special emphasis on family-oriented fun and games. You can take part in three-legged races and tests of strength, pie-eating and scarecrow-making contests, pumpkin carving, apple cider pressing, storytelling, hayrides, crafts and more. There's parking on-site, but bus transportation is also available from several lots around town. Admission: $1 per person. Hours: 10:00 A.M.–4:00 P.M. For more information about all the things to see and do at the park, see the listing under Major Attractions. **145 Lang Rd., Windsor, 06095; (860) 285-1886.**

Outdoor Activities

Biking

The Connecticut River cuts right down the middle of the North Central region, but luckily there is bicycle access to several bridges. You can cross at the Bissell Bridge (I-291) between Windsor and South Windsor. Pick up the separate bike/pedestrian lane from E. Barber St. off Rte. 159 on the Windsor side or from Main St. on the South Windsor side. On Rte. 140 between Windsor Locks and East Windsor, there is a raised sidewalk separated from automobile traffic for bikes and pedestrians. At the western end of the bridge in Windsor you can ride right on to the Windsor Locks Canal towpath described below. There is no bicycle access to the Dexter Coffin Bridge where I-91 crosses the river, but the Rte. 140 crossing is close by. Farther north you can cross on Rte. 190 between Enfield and Suffield, but you must approach the bridge from an unpaved path on the far side of a railing separating the path from the main traffic lanes. You cannot ride on Rte. 190 itself.

Mountain Biking

The best place to mountain bike for miles around is the **Metropolitan District Commission** reservoir areas described in the **Hartford** chapter. The terrain is challenging and the setting beautiful.

For a less strenuous ride head to **Northwest Park,** described under Major Attractions, where mountain bikes are allowed on several miles of flat woods roads. This is an especially good place to ride with children because of the easy terrain and the wide range of activities for them.

A third option is **Penwood State Park,** a tall, narrow tract of land atop the Metacomet Ridge. There are two roads and a bike path running north-south through the park. The main road is rather narrow because it used to be half of a 3.5-mile, one-way loop. The return loop has been closed to auto traffic, but cyclists can use it. The dedicated bike path branches off the main road a short way past the entrance, rejoining the main road at the picnic area. Some portions of roadway may be in poor repair, but you can negotiate them on a mountain bike with ease and on a road bike with care. Trails (except the blue-blazed Metacomet Trail) in the park are also open to mountain bikers. For more information, see the listing under Hiking.

Road Biking

A portion of the former towpath of the **Windsor Locks Canal,** described under History, has been paved for use as a hiking/biking trail. The surface is suitable for any type of bike, although it's a bit rough. The path is open to the public from the Rte. 140 bridge in Windsor Locks to the Rte. 190 bridge in Suffield, a distance of about 4.5 miles. It's lined with trees, and the scenery is especially beautiful in autumn when the fiery colors of turning leaves are reflected in the calm waters of the canal. Under no circumstances should you try to enter the canal itself, no matter how inviting it is and how calm it looks. There are dangerous undercurrents, and there may not be anyone nearby to help if you get in trouble. Heading north on Rte. 159 from Windsor, follow these directions to find parking: At the light at Rte. 140 turn right, cross the railroad tracks and the canal but do not cross the bridge. At the first light, which will be only a few yards down the road, turn left onto the driveway running between the canal and the old Montgomery tinsel factory. Drive completely past the buildings on your right and you'll come to a small parking lot. Park at the far end near the gated entrance to the towpath. The other end of the towpath is accessible from Canal Rd. in Suffield by the broken Enfield Dam.

Boating

Connecticut River

A state boat launch is located in Windsor Meadows State Park in Windsor. The entrance is at the end of East Barber St., and the parking lot was recently improved. Another launch in Enfield is co-owned by the state and Northeast Utilities. It's located on Parsons Rd. off Bridge Rd. A third possibility is a town launch at the end of Vibert Rd. in South Windsor. You can launch anything from a canoe on up at all these facilities, and there's no charge.

Farmington River

Above the Rainbow Dam, the Farmington is almost as wide across as the Connecticut. The area is often referred to as Rainbow Reservoir, although there is no strict upriver obstruction defining the other boundary. There's a hydroelectric plant here owned by Stanley Works, the tool manufacturer. This plant used to supply power to Stanley's New Britain factory directly; now the wattage they generate is traded against their Connecticut Light & Power bill. The water level in the reservoir can fluctuate by several feet when the plant is in operation. A boat launch is located one-quarter mile down Merriman Rd. off Rainbow Rd. in Windsor. A fee is charged in summer. The only restriction is a 35 m.p.h. speed limit. The reservoir is appropriate for any type of boat, including canoes.

137

There's also a boat launch below Rainbow Dam where Rte. 159 in Windsor crosses the river. This area is known as Bart's, in reference to a tackle shop/restaurant nearby. Water height is good here regardless of power generation at the dam because the Farmington is essentially an arm of the Connecticut River here. This is an especially nice starting point for a canoe trip. It's flatwater a short distance on the Farmington before it spills out into the broad Connecticut. There's an island to ride alongside; then you float gently until reaching a good take-out point at Riverside Park north of downtown Hartford. This whole trip takes only about an hour and a half. For powerboat access to the lower Farmington, you're better off launching at Windsor Meadows State Park on the Connecticut River and coming upriver; see the previous listing for details.

Fishing

Connecticut River

The Connecticut is an important spawning ground for anadromous fish (species that live as adults in saltwater but return to freshwater to breed) in early spring. Anglers can find American shad, blueback herring, and ale-wives (as well as the striped bass that feed on them) and white perch. Later in the year, there are good fisheries for smallmouth and large-mouth bass, primarily from a boat. From shore try going for white and channel catfish or, in protected bays, calico bass. The best place to fish in the upper river is at (but not on!) the broken Enfield Dam at the top of Windsor Locks Canal. From the large parking lot at the end of Canal Rd. in Suffield, walk down the canal towpath a short distance to get access to the riverbank. Then walk back up to the dam. Or, fish from anywhere on the riverbank beside the canal. There is a consumption advisory on carp taken in the Connecticut; see the *Connecticut Angler's Guide* for more information.

East Branch and West Branch Salmon Brook

These two streams that flow through Granby before joining and continuing southeast through East Granby are both stocked with trout. To access the East Branch, use the large parking area off Canal Rd. in Granby just east of the river off Rte. 20. Mechanicsville Rd., which runs between Rte. 189 and Rte. 10/202, also provides easy access. For West Branch access, park along Simsbury Rd. just south of Rte. 20 where the street parallels the river.

Farmington River

Although the Farmington is a major trout stream upriver, its lower portion is a much better fishery for other species. In Rainbow Reservoir in Windsor you'll find largemouth and smallmouth bass, rock bass, calico bass (in still water) and white and yellow perch. The best fishing here is from a boat; see the Boating section for information on access.

For a few miles below the dam the water flow is highly variable depending on whether power is being generated at the dam. Given sufficient water, there's good car-top boat and shore access at a small park in the Poquon-nock section of Windsor. Traveling southbound on Rte. 75, you'll find the park on the right just before crossing the river.

Even farther down there's shore access and a boat launch at Rte. 159 where it crosses the river. If you need supplies, nearby **Bart's (860-688-9035)** is a tackle shop inside a deli/restaurant and specializes in outfitting shad anglers. The shop is also a sponsor of the annual Shad Derby described in Festivals and Events. In spring this area is flush with shad, blueback herring and striped bass. Year-round you'll find northern pike, largemouth and smallmouth bass, channel catfish and white perch.

Hiking

McLean Game Refuge

This private preserve was established in 1932 according to provisions in the will of former senator George P. McLean; it is free to the public. A fairly complex trail system negotiates undulating, sometimes steep terrain through the Barndoor Hills, intrusive rock formations composed of lava that never broke the surface of the earth (like the traprock of the Metacomet Ridge) but instead hardened underground. On the more rigorous trails there are overlooks; signs mark the way to the summit. The red, orange and blue loops, ranging in length from just over 1 mile to just over 2 miles, would be appropriate for short hikes. Hours: 8:00 A.M.–dusk. There are actually several entrances to the refuge, but the one with the best access to the short loops is on Rte. 10/202 just north of Canton Rd. in Granby.

Metacomet Trail
See the **Farmington** chapter for details on this 51-mile trail that runs from Meriden to the Massachusetts line, following the Metacomet Ridge for much of its length. The easiest place to pick up the trail in this area is at Penwood State Park, described below.

Northwest Park
There are over 10 miles of trails through easy, mostly flat and wooded terrain at this municipal park. If you want to take small children on a "real" hike without leaving civilization too far behind, Northwest Park is ideal, although by no means boring for more rugged types. A map, along with numerous guides to the flora and fauna of the area, is available at the nature center and in a map box outside the center. There is a half-mile Braille Trail for the visually impaired. For more information, see the listing under Major Attractions.

Penwood State Park
Although neighboring Talcott Mountain State Park is more well known because of its lookout tower, Penwood State Park is every bit as lovely and actually accommodates more types of activity. There's an extensive system of hiking trails on its 800 acres, including a stretch of the Metacomet Trail. Although the park is located atop the Metacomet Ridge, the trails are not especially strenuous since they lie on the ridge's gently sloping eastern side. The access road is open to auto traffic Apr.–Nov. only, but you can hike in any time conditions permit. Maps are posted both at the entrance and at the picnic area where the long entrance road ends. The Pinnacle and Cedar Ridge Overlooks marked on the map do indeed provide great views of the western half of the Central Valley. Unfortunately, the Veeder Cabin also

marked on the map was lost to a fire a few years ago. There's also a nature trail that goes around Lake Louise and follows boardwalks through a bog. Numbered stations on the nature trail correspond to a guide you can pick up at the maintenance building near the picnic area when it is staffed. Park hours: 8:00 A.M.–dusk daily, year-round. The entrance to the park is on Rte. 185 between Rtes. 10 and 178 in Bloomfield at the top of the Metacomet Ridge. The entrance to Talcott Mountain State Park is almost directly opposite. Park office: **(860) 242-1158.**

South Windsor Wildlife Sanctuary
Tucked between two back roads in South Windsor is a 160-acre sanctuary with an extensive system of easy blazed trails through forest and meadows. The preserve contains the highest point in South Windsor (420 feet), from which you can view the surrounding valley, and plaques at stations around the sanctuary identify many plants. A map box at the entrance is stocked with trail guides. Pets and picnicking are not allowed. Hours: dawn–dusk daily, year-round. The entrance is on Niederwerfer Rd. For more information call the **South Windsor town hall** at **(860) 644-2511, ext. 253.**

Windsor Riverwalk
This brand new, mile-long walkway accessible from downtown Windsor is part of an effort to link all the riverside towns in the Hartford area with recreational corridors. It will eventually connect with paths leading to Hartford, Windsor Locks and the other side of the river. The path takes you along the last stretch of the Farmington River before it spills into the Connecticut. Park at the commuter parking lot off Central St. in Windsor. The path starts on the far side of the pond.

In the Air

Airventures does hot-air ballooning with departures from several locations in North Central Connecticut, depending on weather conditions. See the listing in the **Farmington** chapter for complete details.

139

Skiing

Cross-Country

Cedar Brook Farm

The smallest cross-country ski area in the state has 6 miles of groomed trails on 200 acres. Most are novice to intermediate difficulty. Maps are available at the warming hut, where they also sell new and used equipment. Bring your own equipment, and you can ski as cheaply as $5 on weekdays or $8 on weekends. With rentals, rates begin at $12. They also offer instruction. Open daily when conditions permit, 9:00 A.M.–dusk. **1481 Ratley Rd., W. Suffield, 06093; (860) 668-5026.**

Northwest Park

This Windsor municipal park has over 10 miles of ungroomed trails blazed according to difficulty, with most being easy. There's a warming hut, and in Feb. and Mar. a stop at the sugar-house is a must. The park rents equipment for $7.50 a half day, $10 a full day. For more information, see the listing under Major Attractions.

Penwood State Park

The main access road into Penwood, which is closed to traffic and left unplowed in winter, is appropriate for cross-country skiing when conditions allow. For variety, loop back on the gated portion of the road that is used by bicyclists and hikers in warm weather. There's a bit of a climb at the start of the return portion, but otherwise the terrain is gently rolling. For more information, see the listing under Hiking.

South Windsor Wildlife Sanctuary

All the trails at this town preserve are open to cross-country skiers when conditions are appropriate. You can also cut tracks across the open fields. For more information, see the listing under Hiking.

Seeing and Doing

Museums

In addition to the listings below, the Windsor Historical Society operates several museums described under Major Attractions, and the Wintonbury Historical Society keeps the **Old Farm School Museum** in Bloomfield. The second floor of this 1794 two-room schoolhouse still contains built-in desks dating from the 1830s, and artifacts from Bloomfield families are exhibited on the lower floor. The museum, located at the **corner of Park Ave. and School St. in Bloomfield,** is open Sun., 1:00 P.M.–4:00 P.M., mid-May–mid-Oct.

Connecticut Trolley Museum

The highlight of this attraction is a half-hour ride in vintage trolley cars on 3 miles of track. Buy a ticket and ride all day if you want. Two cars of different vintages leave about every 30 minutes with special theme rides for Halloween and Christmas. A new visitors center houses some vintage cars that you can explore rain or shine, and more trolley cars from 1894 to 1949 in various stages of restoration are scattered across the grounds, including an ornate beauty from Toronto that is one of only four in the world. Major improvements are planned, so don't be surprised if lots of construction is evident. Admission: $6 adults, $3 children 5–12 years. Hours: 10:00 A.M.–5:00 P.M. daily, Memorial Day–Labor Day; Labor Day–Dec. 31, open 10:00 A.M.–5:00 P.M. on Sat. & noon–5:00 P.M. on Sun. Special evening hours for holiday theme rides. **58 North Rd. (Rte. 140), East Windsor, 06088; (860) 627-6540.** The **Connecticut Fire Museum** at the same location, which displays a collection of fire engines and fire-fighting artifacts as well as transit buses, is open daily during summer and on weekends in spring and fall. For more information call **(860) 623-4732.**

Enfield Historical Society Properties

The Martha Parsons House, located on Enfield's lovely main street, is a local history museum furnished with the heirlooms of one prominent Enfield family acquired over a span of 180 years. Parsons, who bequeathed the house to the Society in 1962, was an exceptional businesswoman around the turn of the century. One highlight is a wallpapered hallway done in a rare memorial George Washington pattern made in 1800, the year after his death, and said to be extant in only one other house in the country. You'll also see many fine examples of period furniture, silver and other crafts.

The Old Town Hall Museum began life as a church and later served as the Enfield town hall from 1848 to 1892, one of the centers of town life for more than a century. It's a fitting locale for the Historical Society's collection of items documenting Enfield life, agriculture and industry. **The Parsons House** is located at **1387 Enfield St. (Rte. 5) in Enfield.** The **Old Town Hall Museum** is at **1294 Enfield St.** Hours for both are Sun., 2:00 P.M.–4:30 P.M., May–Oct., and admission is free. For more information call **(860) 745-6064.**

Hatheway House

The Hatheway House, which sits demurely behind a picket fence on Suffield's exquisite Main St., is the most impressive of the Antiquarian and Landmarks Society properties in Connecticut. It is renowned for its antique wallpapers. There's also a great deal of decorative woodwork such as small and large dentil molding, opulent paneling and fireplace mantels. Perhaps the oddest thing about Hatheway House is that one of its rooms was removed and sold in its entirety, floorboards and all, to the Winterthur Museum in Delaware in the 1950s before the house became a museum. The agreement stipulated that an exact copy of the room be built by Winterthur and installed as a replacement. Hatheway House is actually rather like two houses. The original 1760s center-chimney structure was expanded in the late 1700s in such a way that the older portion became one wing of a center hall layout, which had become the style. The property also features a huge restored barn for special events and a spectacular 300-year-old sycamore shading the house. A guided tour takes about one hour. Admission: $4 adults, $1 children under 18. Hours: Wed., Sat. & Sun., 1:00 P.M.–4:00 P.M., mid-May–mid-Oct.; open Wed.–Sun. in July/Aug.; also open in late Nov. for an annual Holidayfest. **55 S. Main St., Suffield, 06078; (860) 668-0055** or **(860) 247-8996.**

King House Museum

The King House is one of the best historical society museums in Connecticut and should be

The Hatheway House in Suffield has the most extensive collection of 18th-century wallpapers in the country. Photo courtesy Antiquarian and Landmarks Society.

high on anyone's list of local places to visit. This center-chimney colonial house (ca. 1764) was built by Dr. Alexander King, a medical doctor and representative to the Connecticut General Assembly who worked on ratification of the U.S. Constitution. The house features high-quality woodwork including a shell-carved corner cabinet, wainscoting, paneling and decorative fireplace surrounds. The house has been restored to a beautiful condition over the course of 50 years by benefactors Samuel R. and Helena Spencer, who were also able to acquire many old Suffield pieces with which to furnish it before giving it to the Suffield Historical Society in 1960. Be sure to ask about the reproduction mural.

On the second floor there are displays of toys, family artifacts and more exceptional furnishings. King's Revolutionary War–era military commissions, bearing the signatures of John Hancock and Connecticut governor Jonathan Trumbull, are on display. A rear ell contains a large and exceptional exhibit of Bennington pottery, humorous wedding anniversary tinware and tobacco industry memorabilia. Admission: $1 adults, free to children and students. Hours: Wed. & Sat., 1:00 P.M.–

Central Valley

4:00 P.M., May–Sept., & by appointment; also open in early Dec. for an annual Holidayfest. **232 S. Main St. (Rte. 75), Suffield, 06078; (860) 668-5256.**

Luddy/Taylor Connecticut Valley Tobacco Museum

I highly recommend a stop at this museum documenting the fascinating history of tobacco agriculture in the Central Valley (see the History section). Displays with background information, photographs and artifacts can be found in a modern building next to a restored barn where you can see the tools and techniques used by tobacco growers. Admission is free. Hours: Tue.–Thu. & Sat., noon–4:00 P.M., Mar.–Dec. 15; closed holidays. Located in **Northwest Park, 145 Lang Rd., Windsor, 06095; (860) 285-1888.**

Noden Reed House

The Windsor Locks Historical Society operates this local history museum on a 1762 farm property. Dating from the mid-1800s, the house contains displays of vintage clothing and uniforms, period utensils and furnishings. A barn dating from 1826 is the only one built of brick still standing in New England and is on the National Register of Historic Places. It's used to exhibit old tools and tobacco farming implements. It is said that the first Christmas tree in the New World was put up here by a Hessian soldier, Hendrick Roddemore, captured during the Revolutionary War. There are also walking trails on the 22-acre site. Admission is free. Hours: Sun., 1:00 P.M.–5:00 P.M., May–Oct., & by appointment. **58 West St., Windsor Locks, 06096; (860) 627-9212.**

Oliver Ellsworth Homestead

The man for whom this historic home museum is named was Connecticut's first senator, attended the Constitutional Convention, and later served as ambassador to France and Chief Justice of the U.S. Supreme Court. He lived all of his life in or around Windsor, building this home in 1780. It was restored in 1990. A tour of the house focuses on Ellsworth's life, lifestyle and career. It features some original Ellsworth furniture and other period furniture, original and reproduction 18th-century wall-

papers and mementos of Ellsworth's career. Admission is by a $2 donation, free to children under 12. Hours: Tue., Wed. & Sat., 10:00 A.M.–5:00 P.M., May 15–Oct. 15. **778 Palisado Ave. (Rte. 159), Windsor, 06095; (860) 688-8717.**

Salmon Brook Settlement

Salmon Brook was the original name of Granby before it was taken from Simsbury and incorporated in 1786, and the Salmon Brook Historical Society tells the story of how Granby lived over the course of two centuries at this museum. When you visit you'll be guided through a cluster of buildings. The 1753 saltbox home of Abijah Rowe, furnished with mid-18th-century pieces, is original to the property. Two rooms are devoted to Victorian toys and dolls. A 1790 home used for a Victorian parlor display and a Civil War–era schoolhouse were moved to the site. The centerpiece of it all is an authentic tobacco barn that houses a reconstructed country store, shoemaker's shop and milking room, a Civil War exhibit and vintage farm tools. Admission: $2 adults, $1 seniors and children under 12. Hours: Sun., 2:00 P.M.–4:00 P.M., mid-May–mid-Oct. A genealogical library is open by appointment. **208 Salmon Brook St., Granby, 06035; (860) 653-9713.**

Scenic Drives

Despite the proximity of Hartford, quiet country roads are more characteristic of the North Central region than crowded suburbs. As with many parts of the state, you can pretty much wander at will and see beautiful foliage in autumn, old tobacco barns and fields still under cultivation. If you prefer to be more destination-oriented, some recommended rides include the following: Rte. 159 north of downtown Windsor heading into that town's historic district, where you'll find several historical society museums; Rte. 185 in Bloomfield toward Simsbury, which will take you up and over the Metacomet Ridge and past the entrances to Penwood and Talcott Mountain State Parks; past the stately homes of Main St. (Rte. 75) in Suffield or through more of the same in the historic district of South Windsor along Main St. below Rte. 5; out Rtes. 20 and 219 through Granby headed toward Old Newgate Prison (a museum) and the long stretches of unbroken woodland as you approach Barkhamsted and Kennedy Rd. in Windsor, where tobacco tents and barns come right up to the edge of a multilane thoroughfare, and a turn onto Old River Rd. will bring you to a great farm market.

Seasonal Favorites

Although just a hop, skip and jump from Bradley International Airport, it looks like country when you're picking strawberries at **Brown's Strawberry Harvest (Rte. 75 at Rainbow Rd., Windsor; 860-683-0266)** in June. Hours are 8:00 A.M.–6:00 P.M. daily.

You can pick fruit all summer long at **Dzen Farms (Barber Hill Rd., South Windsor; 860-644-2478)**; the name is pronounced "zen." The season starts with strawberries in June, continuing with raspberries in July and ending with blueberries in Aug. You can also cut your own Christmas trees beginning the day after Thanksgiving. Call for hours.

Also see the listing for **Northwest Park** under Major Attractions. In Feb. and Mar. maple sap is boiled down at the sugarhouse there, and the syrup is available for purchase.

Tours

A free walking-tour guide to Suffield's Main St. is available from the Hatheway House and the King House Museum in town during their regular hours and also from the public library in the center of town. The brochure gives details of the architectural style and elements of many of the homes on a stretch about eight blocks long. Suffield has one of the most beautiful main streets in all of Connecticut, so this is a very worthwhile walk.

By advance arrangement you can get a guided tour of Windsor's historic green, the site of the first colonial settlement in Connecticut, by a member of the **Windsor Historical Society.** For more information on what there is to see here, read the listing for the society's

properties under Major Attractions. The cost is $3 per person. Call **(860) 688-3813** or **(860) 298-9203** at least a few days in advance of your visit.

Where to Stay

Bed & Breakfasts

Charles R. Hart House—$$$

Originally a farmhouse, this B&B was converted to a Victorian in the 1860s by the owner for whom it is named. From the veranda with its wicker furniture to the lace curtains and coverlets, it offers a genuine Victorian atmosphere with modern amenities like central air-conditioning. Victorian home fans will find soul mates in hosts Dorothy and Bob McAllister, an engaging couple happy to show off the Hart House's features. Five guest rooms, each with a private bathroom and something unique to offer, are on the upper floors. One room with a queen bed has a working fireplace. The turret and former billiard room have been converted into a guest room with twin beds, a little sitting area and beautifully hand-stenciled and -papered walls. You'll find cast iron, brass and carved wood bed frames, period antiques and extra long mattresses in every room. **1046 Windsor Ave., Windsor, 06095; (860) 688-5555.**

Hotels, Motels & Inns

Because Bradley International Airport is nearby, there are lots of accommodations in this region. If you want to be close to the airport, choose a hotel with a Windsor Locks address. For even more options, contact the **North Central Tourism Bureau** at **(800) 248-8283** or **(860) 763-2578.**

Courtyard by Marriott—$$$ to $$$$

Geared toward the value-conscious business traveler but suitable for anyone, this pleasant, tasteful hotel has two categories of accommodations: standard rooms with one king or two double beds and an in-room refrigerator and suites that are similarly furnished but twice

143

the size. Furnishings are better than average and in very good condition. Health facilities include an indoor pool, exercise equipment and a whirlpool. There's a full-service restaurant serving breakfast and dinner on-site. The hotel is very convenient to I-91. **One Day Hill Rd., Windsor, 06095; (800) 321-2211** or **(860) 683-0022.**

Harley Hotel—$$$ to $$$$

Part of the Helmsley chain of hotels, this Harley offers three categories of accommodations. At the low end there are standard rooms with two double beds. Corner king rooms are somewhat larger and come with one king bed. At the top end of the price range are Ambassador rooms on a concierge floor, which come with kings beds, steam bath units, split bathrooms, an expanded Continental breakfast, hors d'oeuvres and cocktails served daily in a private lounge and a morning newspaper. There's a full-service restaurant and lounge on-site, and room service is available. With indoor and outdoor pools, saunas, a whirlpool, some resistance equipment, and outdoor basketball, volleyball and tennis courts, it has a broader range of exercise facilities than most hotels. Guests also have access to a local gym at a discounted rate. **One Bright Meadow Blvd., Enfield, 06082; (800) 321-2323** or **(860) 741-2211.**

Holiday Inn—$$$ to $$$$

Standard rooms at this Holiday Inn, which was renovated in 1995, are identical except for bed size: some have two doubles, some have a king, some have a king and a pullout queen sofa. There are also two suites with a separate living area and wet bar. Rooms have a business traveler orientation and are equipped with an iron, ironing board and hair dryer, and you'll find lower rates on the weekends. There is a 24-hour shuttle to the airport. Between the restaurant and the lounge you can get three meals a day and room service. An indoor pool, sauna and whirlpool comprise the on-site health facilities, and guests get a free pass to a nearby full-service gym. **16 Ella Grasso Tpke. (Rte. 75), Windsor Locks, 06096; (800) 465-4329** or **(860) 627-5171.**

Homewood Suites Hotel—$$$ to $$$$

Most of the rooms at Homewood are king suites with a separate living area, bath and fully stocked kitchen with all appliances. A few master suites also have a fireplace and a little more square footage. Two-bedroom suites could very comfortably accommodate a four-person family. Free beverages and light food are served during an evening social hour as well as a Continental breakfast. The Jacuzzi and pool are seasonal, but the small exercise room is open 24 hours a day. The hotel caters to business travelers, so you'll actually get a lower rate on the weekend and a location about 1 mile from the airport. **65 Ella Grasso Tpke. (Rte. 75), Windsor Locks, 06096; (800) 225-5466** or **(860) 627-8463.**

Residence Inn—$$$ to $$$$

Part of the Marriott chain of hotels, Residence Inns look like condominium complexes. This one offers two types of rooms: a studio suite with kitchen, living room, bedroom and bath, and a penthouse suite, which is the same but has a loft bedroom and an additional bathroom. Some units have fireplaces for Duraflame logs. Free passes are available to a nearby Gold's Gym, there's a tennis court and an outdoor pool on the property and guests can also use the indoor pool at the Courtyard by Marriott just a few minutes away. This hotel enjoys a wooded setting that is quiet yet only one minute off I-91. **100 Dunfey Ln., Windsor, 06095; (800) 331-3131** or **(860) 688-7474.**

Holiday Inn Express—$$$

For Holiday Inn–type accommodations (see the listing above) without amenities like a restaurant and lounge, try Holiday Inn Express. All the rooms have one king or two queen beds, but otherwise it's very similar, and prices are lower. **60 Main St. (Rte. 5), East Windsor, 06088; (800) 432-0504** or **(860) 627-6585.**

Red Roof Inn—$$ to $$$

If you are traveling on a budget, this motel offers comfortable, clean, utilitarian rooms with double, queen and king beds and standard

144

amenities. It's located within walking distance from restaurants and shopping, is very convenient to I-91 and would make a good choice for overall value and convenience. **5 Hazard Ave., Enfield, 06082; (800) 843-7663 or (860) 741-2571.**

Best Western—$$ to $$$

For budget accommodations and convenience to the interstate, this hotel, a former Ramada, will satisfy most customers. Standard rooms have one king or two double beds, and some have whirlpools. There are also a few suites. It offers a 24-hour shuttle service to the airport and to a local gym that guests can use for a fee. Its Park, Ride & Fly program allows you to leave your car up to two weeks in the lot. There's a full-service restaurant providing room service, a lounge with pool tables and an outdoor pool on-site. Rates include a Continental breakfast. **161 Bridge St., East Windsor, 06088; (800) 528-1234 or (860) 623-9411.**

Other

Windsor Youth Hostel—$

This home hostel affiliated with American Youth Hostels (AYH) can accommodate up to four travelers, and as with all AYH hostels, you'll find an informative host accustomed to welcoming visitors from all around the globe. The setting is a casual house in a residential neighborhood. Accommodations are basic: two rooms, both with two twin beds, and a couple of couches. Sleeping arrangements are flexible depending on the number and gender of guests. Bring sheets or a couple of extra bucks for linens; towels are free. There's one shared bathroom. Guests have full house privileges including use of a deck, washer/dryer and kitchen. You'll be given the address when you make your reservation. For more information call **(860) 683-2847.**

Where to Eat

The Eatery—$$$ to $$$$

An atmospheric 50-year-old house is the setting for this American steakhouse that's always high on everyone's list of recommended restaurants. Several rooms, including the former library and the porch, have been pressed into service as dining areas, and no two are alike. The menu features steaks and chops, filet mignon, rack of lamb, fish and seafood. You can come casual or dressed up and feel comfortable either way. Reservations are recommended on the weekends. Lunch is served Mon.–Fri., 11:30 A.M.–2:30 P.M. Dinner hours are Mon.–Sat., 5:00 P.M. until 8:00 or 9:00 P.M. **297 S. Main St. (Rte. 5), East Windsor, 06088; (860) 627-7094.**

Madeleine's—$$$ to $$$$

For a special evening meal, Madeleine's offers several options. You could simply dine off the large menu of French dishes or the spa menu of low-fat, low-salt, low-cholesterol choices, ordering à la carte or building a six-course dinner for a $39 per person fixed price. Or, add a few more courses with everything chosen by the chef and you've got the Mystery Dinner for $49 per person. Gastronomes will enjoy the opportunity (for $65 per person, six people maximum) to sit right in the kitchen to watch chef Warren Leigh prepare the meal. The dining room has a great river view. Low light, heavy silverware and nice table linens all contribute to a romantic ambiance. Proper attire is requested. Also see the write-up for Bistrot Gabrielle, owned and operated by Leigh and right next door. Hours: Mon.–Sat., 5:00 P.M.–9:00 P.M. (until 10:00 on weekends). **1530 Palisado Ave., Windsor, 06095; (860) 688-0150.**

Albert's Restaurant—$$$

Open every night of the week for Continental/American dining, Albert's is casual but nice and moderately priced. For air travelers it's conveniently located very close to the airport. It serves steaks and chops, seafood ranging from beer-battered shrimp to lobster Newburg pie to baked Boston scrod, many surf 'n' turf combinations, some Italian dishes, even barbeque, and it offers a Fri.–Sun. prime rib special for $10.95. Reservations recommended on weekends. Hours: Mon.–Sat., 4:00 P.M.–10:00 P.M.; Sun., noon–9:00 P.M. **159 Ella**

T. Grasso Tpke. (Rte. 75), Windsor Locks, 06096; (860) 292-6801.

Bank Street Bistro—$$$

Located in the center of Granby and especially convenient for lunch or dinner if you're visiting Old Newgate Prison, Bank Street Bistro is a relatively new restaurant with a casual, modern look. The lunch menu is mostly overstuffed cold sandwiches, grilled sandwiches and salads. At dinner the menu is split fairly evenly between Italian and American entrées. Hours: lunch served Tue.–Fri., 11:30 A.M.–2:00 P.M.; dinner served Mon.–Thu., 5:00 P.M.–9:00 P.M., & Fri.–Sat., 5:00 P.M.–10:00 P.M. **9B Bank St. (in Geissler's Shopping Plaza), Granby, 06035; (860) 844-8180.**

Jonathan Pasco's—$$$

Situated in a 1784 house with several dining rooms upstairs and down (several with fireplaces), a deck for summertime use and wheelchair-accessibility, Jonathan Pasco's has a lot of seating choices, including private rooms for larger parties. The Continental/American menu consists of a large number of chicken and seafood entrées, steaks and chops from the grill and numerous pastas, all complemented by a wine list of mostly California vintages. On Sun. it offers a $10.95 brunch from a set menu, including cocktail, dessert and beverage. Dress is casual. Hours: Mon.–Fri., 4:00 P.M.–10:00 P.M.; Sat., 5:00 P.M.–10:00 P.M.; Sun. brunch 11:00 A.M.–2:30 P.M., & dinner 3:00 P.M.–9:00 P.M. **31 S. Main St. (Rte. 5), East Windsor, 06088; (860) 627-7709.**

The Mill on the River—$$$

The Mill on the River's name refers to its historic setting at a mill site on the Podunk river. The Continental menu with an emphasis on seafood is especially popular with the older crowd. There is outdoor seating in good weather. Lunch/bruch hours: Mon.–Sat., 11:30 A.M.–2:30 P.M.; Sun., 11:00 A.M.–2:00 P.M. Dinner served Mon.–Fri., 5:00 P.M.–9:30 P.M.; Sat. until 10:00 P.M.; and Sun., 3:00 P.M.–8:00 P.M. **989 Ellington Rd., South Windsor, 06074; (860) 289-7929.**

Bistrot Gabrielle—$$ to $$$

Sharing an address and a kitchen with Madeleine's, Bistrot Gabrielle is a new venture combining a pretty riverside setting with traditional bistro cuisine at bargain basement prices. Beef Bourguignon, lobster bisque and other hearty but uncomplicated fare are served in a comfortable but polished atmosphere enhanced in winter by a wood-fired oven used as a fireplace. Hours: Tue.–Sat., 5:00 P.M.–9:00 P.M. (until 10:00 on weekends). **1530 Palisado Ave., Windsor, 06095; (860) 688-2616.**

Services

Local Visitors Information

Farmington Valley Visitors Association, P.O. Box 1015, Simsbury, 06070; (860) 651-6950 or (800) 493-5266.

North Central Tourism Bureau, 111 Hazard Ave., Enfield, 06082; (800) 248-8283 or (860) 763-2578.

State Welcome Centers

Tourism information is available at Bradley International Airport terminals A and B, 9:00 A.M.–9:00 P.M. daily, year-round. There's also a seasonal welcome center in Windsor Locks at the entrance to the commuter parking lot off I-91 northbound and southbound exit 42. The center is staffed 8:00 A.M.–6:00 P.M., Memorial Day–Labor Day.

Transportation

Interstate bus service to East Windsor is provided by **Peter Pan/Trailways;** call **(800) 343-9999** for schedule and fare information. Regional bus service between towns in the North Central and Hartford region is provided by the **Greater Hartford Transit District** at **(860) 247-5329** and **CT Transit** at **(860) 525-9181.**

Wethersfield

History is the reason to come to Wethersfield. Its 17th- and 18th-century homes, Congregational church and early graveyard are its main attractions, and unlike so many towns where the historic district is no longer a center of community life, Old Wethersfield has restaurants, shops and a bed & breakfast all within a three-block walk, making the town ideal as a destination.

Wethersfield's museums reflect the important role the town played in the state's development. The Webb-Deane-Stevens Museum and Buttolph-Williams House consist of four historic homes that illustrate a period stretching from European settlement of the Connecticut River Valley to the Industrial Revolution. You can tour them on a combined ticket and get an overview of two centuries of American life.

For a change of pace, you need only walk a block for some shopping, a couple of casual restaurants and the farm-store environment of Comstock, Ferre & Co., the oldest continuously operating seed company in the country.

History

Wethersfield, the second-oldest town in Connecticut, was settled in 1634 by a group from Watertown, Massachusetts, and named Watertown. English occupation came as a result of a trading expedition to the same site a year earlier by a small party led by John Oldham. The native Wongunk Indians called the meadow-filled lowlands here Pyquag, meaning "clear land" or "cleared land." The English name was changed to Wethersfield in 1637.

As with the settlers of Windsor, the colonists were evidently encouraged to stay by the Indians, who had been suffering from incursions by the Pequots, a circumstance that presaged a seminal event in state history that occurred in Apr. 1637. Several colonists and some livestock were killed by Pequots. The Wethersfield Massacre provoked the Pequot War, when the Pequot fort at present-day Mystic was burned and the tribe almost wiped out.

Although the notoriety of being the first town in the New World to try and execute a witch belongs to Windsor, Wethersfield also experienced one of the earliest witchcraft scares. Accusations began to fly in 1648, 50 years before the infamous trials at Salem, Massachusetts.

Wethersfield was perhaps the first real shipping and shipbuilding center in Connecticut. The town had a deep-water port prior to a flood in the early 1690s that changed the course of the Connecticut River. The port was located at a shallow inlet now known as Wethersfield Cove. In those days the port would have been lined with warehouses full of goods for the West Indies trade. Wethersfield exported red onions, livestock, flax seed, pork, salt beef, lumber and more, taking in return molasses, cane sugar, rum and cotton.

One of the most important conferences between Gen. George Washington and the Comte de Rochambeau, the leader of French forces during the Revolutionary War, took place in Wethersfield in May 1781. At this meeting (in one of the houses comprising the Webb-Deane-Stevens Museum) the two commanders formulated plans for what would become the final stage of the conflict.

Wethersfield is situated on a fertile plain that is ideal for agriculture. Historically two crops have been associated with the town: red onions and garden seeds. There are numerous early accounts of the pungent aroma the sizable onion crop released into the Wethersfield air and the sight of tens of thousands of onions curing in the field. The onion is still used as a symbol for the town. The heyday of the seed industry was 1820–1900, and it was complemented by many small factories manufacturing all kinds of gardening and agricultural implements. At least eight seed companies were located here at the industry's peak, but with westward expansion and competition from states with longer growing seasons, it began to die out. Two growers remain, however—Comstock, Ferre & Co. and Hart Seed Co.—the former maintaining a wonderful retail store on Main St.

With the growth of nearby Hartford in the 20th century, Wethersfield became more suburbanized and remains so today. It's a picturesque town where history is integrated into contemporary life in a most pleasant way.

Major Attractions

Comstock, Ferre & Co.

Although it was not the first seed company to be founded in Wethersfield, Comstock, Ferre &

Co. is the longest lived, founded in 1820. Many old fixtures remain in the store, giving it an atmosphere of things past. In addition to flower and vegetable seeds, it sells a full range of gardening supplies, books and a great selection of potted plants. Inquire about the Sat. lecture series. If you garden with perennials, don't pass up a stop at the nursery. Hours: Mon.–Sat., 9:00 A.M.–6:00 P.M. (Thu. until 8:00 P.M.); Sun., 10:00 A.M.–5:00 P.M. **263 Main St., Wethersfield, 06109; (860) 529-3319.**

Historic Sites and Museums

Webb-Deane-Stevens Museum

The Colonial Dames operate this museum, consisting of three houses from different decades around the time of the Revolutionary War. By comparing the 1751 Webb House, 1766 Deane House and 1788 Stevens House, you can see plain evidence of the advent of the Industrial Revolution and the growing wealth of the country through the years.

Georgian in style, the Webb House was built by Joseph Webb, a well-to-do merchant in the West Indies trade. Its most remarkable feature is a series of murals inspired by an event that occurred there in May 1781, when Gens. Washington and Rochambeau met to lay plans for the final campaigns of the Revolutionary War. In 1914–1915 Colonial Revivalist Wallace Nutting converted the house into one of his series of New England museums that romanticized "old" America. Aware of the historic events that had transpired there, he commissioned murals depicting significant events of the war for the parlor walls, but he took some liberties. For instance, Washington is shown accepting the surrender of Cornwallis at Yorktown, but in fact Cornwallis was not even present at the occasion. The murals are all the more remarkable because for years they were covered up on the rationale that they were not original to the house. Only in 1995 were they restored to public view.

The Deane House was built by Silas Deane, a wealthy and politically active merchant around the time of the Revolutionary War. It is fateful that the Deane and Webb houses stand next to one another, because even as Washington and Rochambeau were meeting in the Webb House, Deane was serving as commissioner to France, his job to procure the very military assistance that allowed the Patriot victory.

The Stevens House was built by Isaac Stevens, a leather worker and a farmer. Unlike his two neighbors, he was decidedly middle class. In an earlier period when everything was handmade, he would not have been able to afford many of the items he owned: wall-to-wall carpeting, a product of New England's burgeoning textile industry; a mantel clock from Terryville, one of the centers of Connecticut clock making; printed fabric used for bed hangings that would have been prohibitively expensive if hand-blocked in the old way.

One-hour guided tours of the houses start on the hour. Admission: $6 adults, $5 seniors, $2.50 students and children 6–16. Combined ticket price (including Buttolph-Williams House): $7 adults, $6 seniors. Summer (May–Oct.) hours: Wed.–Mon., 10:00 A.M.–4:00 P.M., Nov.–Apr. the museum is open Sat. & Sun. only. **211 Main St., Wethersfield, 06109; (860) 529-0612.**

Buttolph-Williams House

Built around 1720, the Buttolph-Williams House has the central chimney, exposed joists and summer beams, wideboard flooring and small casement windows typical of early New England architecture. It has been little altered over the years, no heat or plumbing ever having been added, and it is furnished with late-1600s pieces. The house was the setting for the children's classic *The Witch of Blackbird Pond* by Elizabeth Speare, who was a Wethersfield resident at the time she wrote it. Her choice of the house as a setting reflects the fact that Wethersfield was the site of one of the first witchcraft scares in North America in 1648, but there is no connection between the house and any of the real witchcraft trials that took place in the area, all of which transpired

Getting There

Wethersfield is a 15–20 minute drive by car or bus from Hartford, connected to the city by both surface roads and I-91. Follow signs from I-91 exit 26 to the corner of Main and Marsh Sts., and you're in the center of the historic district. Bradley International Airport, also off I-91, is approximately 30 minutes away.

before the house was even built. Admission: $2 adults, $1 children. You can tour this house and the Webb-Deane-Stevens Museum for a combined ticket price of $7 adults, $6 seniors, $2.50 children 6–16. Hours: same as for Webb-Deane-Stevens Museum. **249 Broad St., Wethersfield, 06109; (860) 529-0612.**

Ancient Burying Ground

One of the oldest cemeteries in Connecticut since the time of European occupation is located behind the First Church of Christ at the corner of Main and Marsh Sts. Rubbings are permitted if taken with care. The oldest stone here is dated 1648, although there are certainly older graves. A printed guide called "The

Experience the 17th century at the Buttolph-Williams House. Photo courtesy Antiquarian and Landmarks Society.

Stone and the Spirit" is available through the Wethersfield Historical Society for $8.95. It highlights about 20 stones and several carvers and also lists stones by family name and location. The society office is in the **Keeney Memorial Cultural Center** at **200 Main St.;** **(860) 529-7656.** The church is open 9:00 A.M.–5:00 P.M. daily.

Cove Warehouse

As you go through Wethersfield and learn about its history as a commercial center, you might be perplexed by all the early references to a deep-water harbor in town. The Cove, Wethersfield's connection to the Connecticut River, isn't very large or deep. That's because a flood in 1692 changed the Connecticut River's course, moving it eastward. Prior to that point, the Cove was a deep-water harbor, lined with warehouses filled with goods waiting for shipment or distribution. This former warehouse, on the site of a 1690 structure but probably more modern than that, now holds museum exhibits on Wethersfield's role in the West Indies trade. Admission: $1, free to children 16 and under. Open mid-May–mid-Oct. Hours: Thu.–Sun., 10:00 A.M.–4:00 P.M., from July 4 to Labor Day. During other open times, Sat., 10:00 A.M.–4:00 P.M.; Sun., 1:00 P.M.–4:00 P.M. Located at the **northern end of Main St.** For more information call **(860) 529-7656.**

Hurlbut-Dunham House

This historic home sharing Georgian and Italianate qualities was built by sea captain John Hurlbut in 1804 but is interpreted to the early 20th century (1907–1935), when it was inhabited by the socially prominent Howard and Jane Dunham. Guided tours, lasting about 50 minutes and given as needed, start from the Wethersfield Museum in the Keeney Memorial Cultural Center at 200 Main St. Admission: $3 adults, free to children 16 and under. Hours: Thu.–Sat., 10:00 A.M.–4:00 P.M.; Sun., 1:00 P.M.–4:00 P.M., mid-May–Dec.; also

open weekends mid-Mar.–mid-May. **212 Main St., Wethersfield, 06109; (860) 529-7656.**

Wethersfield Museum at the Keeney Memorial

This museum of the Wethersfield Historical Society covers the whole spectrum of town history. There is one permanent gallery and two devoted to changing exhibits. Their holdings include artifacts from the farming and seed industries, clothing, portraits, furniture and more. Occasionally artisan guilds are invited to mount exhibits of their work. The society also maintains an important genealogical library nearby; inquire for details. Admission: $2, under 16 free. Hours: Tue.–Sat., 10:00 A.M.–4:00 P.M.; Sun., 1:00 P.M.–4:00 P.M. Located in the **Keeney Memorial Cultural Center** at **200 Main St., Wethersfield; (860) 529-7656.**

Festivals and Events

In addition to the listings below, there's a new celebration in the works that may become an annual event. The **Wethersfield Weekend Festival,** which took place for the first time in mid-May 1997, has many components. There's a historical aspect focusing on the period 1775–1800, including reenactments of a Revolutionary War battle, various small historical vignettes and children's games, plus an antique show and an international food and entertainment festival. For more information call **(860) 529-7656.**

Old Wethersfield Craft Fair
first Sat. in Oct.

Just as the leaves start to turn every year, 130 exhibitors gather at Cove Park for a juried craft show. The weather is cool and comfortable for browsing all day long, and this is a perfect leisure activity to combine with a visit to Wethersfield's historic home museums. Admission: $3, free for children under 12. Hours: 10:00 A.M.–4:00 P.M. Enter on State St. near Hartford Ave. For more information call **(860) 529-7656.**

Lantern Light Tours of Old Wethersfield
late Oct.

One weekend per year "historical encounters" take place all around Wethersfield. These dramatic role-playing events—some fictional, some historical—always include visits to the Ancient Burying Ground and the historic home museums in town. You'll walk the easy route led by a lantern-carrying guide, so wear comfortable shoes. The one-hour tours start at dusk (about 5:30 P.M. at that time of year) and keep going until about 8:30 P.M. Cost: $7 adults, $3.50 children under 12. For more information call **(860) 529-7656.**

Outdoor Activities

Boating

There is a town boat launch at the **Cove,** Wethersfield's one-time deep-water harbor. From here you go through a 100-foot channel under I-91 out to the Connecticut River. It can accommodate pretty much any size pleasure craft, and there's plenty of parking. The town charges a launch fee in summer. Located at the northern end of Main St.

Fishing

At picturesque **Cove Park** you can fish from shore for striped bass, catfish, white and yellow perch and northern pike. Anglers frequent the channel leading to the **Connecticut River** under the I-91 bridge. You can also launch a boat for fishing on the Connecticut River. Located at the northern end of Main St.

Hiking

The only real trails in Wethersfield are at **Wintergreen Woods,** a 120-acre preserve in the center of town. The land is low-lying and flat, so the trails are easy, and there's really no way to get lost. The entrance and parking area are on Folly Brook Blvd. a short distance north of Wells Rd. Hours: dawn–dusk daily, year-round. For more information call the **Wethersfield Nature Center** at **(860) 721-2953.**

Horseback Riding

Meadowgate Farm's one-hour-long, guided trail rides through private farmland along the Connecticut River are a nice way to enjoy the outdoors in Wethersfield. The cost is $15/person, and rides are offered daily, year-round, conditions permitting. Children can enjoy a pony ride in a corral on the farm on weekends 10:00 A.M.–4:00 P.M. Or, get behind a team of Belgian horses on a hay wagon or sleigh; there's a $105 minimum and 25-person maximum capacity. Call for reservations. **250 Elm St., Wethersfield, 06109; (860) 257-9008.**

Seeing and Doing

Children and Families

When your kids need a break, take them to **Fun Zone,** an indoor amusement park where they can enjoy laser tag, carnival rides and arcade games. There's a full-size basketball court for adults. Pay either a flat fee or by the ride. Hours: Mon.–Thu., 11:00 A.M.–9:00 P.M.; Fri., 11:00 A.M.–11:00 P.M.; Sat., 10:00 A.M.–11:00 P.M.; Sun., 10:00 A.M.–9:00 P.M. **1178 Silas Deane Hwy. (Rte. 99), Wethersfield, 06109; (860) 563-0000.**

Nature Centers

Animal exhibits, a log cabin, taxidermy and Native American artifacts make the **Wethers-**

field **Nature Center** worth a visit if you've got young children. Admission is free. Hours: Mon. & Wed., 3:00 P.M.–5:00 P.M.; Tue. & Thu., 9:00 A.M.–noon; Sat., 10:00 A.M.–1:00 P.M. **30 Greenfield St., Wethersfield, 06109; (860) 721-2953.**

Tours

In the Visitors Information Center at Keeney Memorial Cultural Center, pick up a copy of a free brochure called "A Tour of the Old Village," which gives extensive background information on many of the buildings in the square mile or so around the historic center of town. Use the brochure to design your own walking tour. In addition, the Wethersfield Historical Society offers occasional walking tours covering either general history or the Ancient Burying Ground. They're given one Wed. and one Sat. per month in spring, summer and fall; call for a schedule. The cost is $2 per person, free to society members.

Where to Stay

Bed & Breakfasts

Chester Bulkley House—$$$
Located in Wethersfield's idyllic old town center, this B&B (the only one in town) is found in a whitewashed brick Greek Revival house (ca. 1830). From here it's a half-block to all of Wethersfield's museums. It's virtually across the street from a couple of restaurants, yet still in a quiet neighborhood and ideally located for visitors to Hartford, who can hop on I-91 and be downtown in 15 minutes yet return to the peace and calm of Wethersfield at night. There are three guest rooms with private baths and two that share a bath. The rooms are bright and cluttered in a homey way, and furnished with dark, substantial pieces. A full breakfast is included. **184 Main St., Wethersfield, 06109; (860) 563-4236.**

Hotels, Motels & Inns

Wethersfield has only a few places to stay, but neighboring towns such as Rocky Hill and Cromwell also have hotels and are just minutes away on I-91. Hotel listings for those towns and others can be found in the **Middletown** chapter.

Ramada Inn—$$$
Wethersfield's principal hotel has 112 rooms, all identically outfitted with one king or two double beds. Extras include a coin-operated laundry, same-day dry cleaning service, complimentary breakfast and afternoon snacks and free guest passes to a health club with an indoor pool and exercise facilities within walking distance from the hotel. Rates are reasonable even in summer. **1330 Silas Deane Hwy. (Rte. 99), Wethersfield, 06109; (860) 563-2311.**

Where to Eat

Sweet Gatherings—$$
An old-time interior and an ice cream fountain in the back give this restaurant the feel of a pleasant small-town luncheonette. It serves three meals a day featuring items such as quiche, veggie lasagna, light and hearty sandwiches, burgers and four or five entrées at dinner. Its soup and salad or soup and sandwich specials are a good bargain. Hours: Tue. & Thu.–Sun., 8:00 A.M.–9:00 P.M.; Wed., 8:00 A.M.–10:00 P.M. **219 Main St., Wethersfield, 06109; (860) 563-1040.**

Village Pizza & Grinders—$$
Old Wethersfield's Italian restaurant is a casual, family-friendly place where your kids will feel right at home and the whole family can fill up for a fair price. Hours: Mon.-Thu., 10:00 A.M.–11:00 P.M.; Fri.-Sat., 10:00 A.M.–midnight; Sun., 10:00 A.M.–10:00 P.M. **233 Main St., Old Wethersfield, 06109; (860) 563-1513.**

Services

Local Visitors Information

Keeney Memorial Cultural Center, 200 Main St., Wethersfield, 06109; (860) 529-7161. Hours: Tue.–Sat., 10:00 A.M.–4:00 P.M.; Sun., 1:00 P.M.–4:00 P.M.

Transportation

Local bus service with connections throughout the Hartford area is provided by **CT Transit** at **(860) 525-9181.**

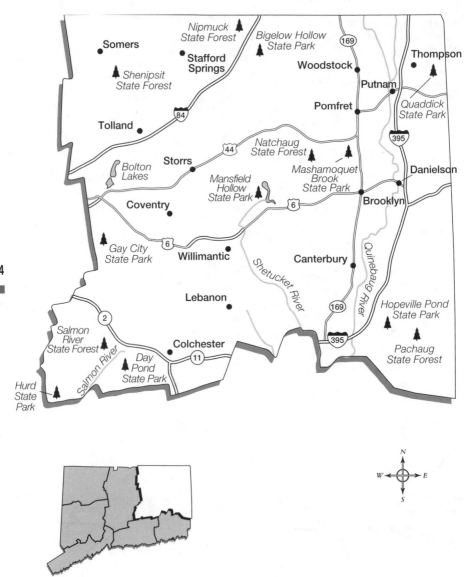

154

The Quiet Corner

155

Far Northeast

This chapter covers the largest geographic area of any in this book, a broad region whose common history was recently recognized with the naming of the Quinebaug-Shetucket National Heritage Corridor. The Quinebaug and the Shetucket are the two principal rivers that drain this upland of gentle hills, and their water power drove the textile mills that are so much a part of the area's historical identity.

Windham County has been traditionally referred to as the Quiet Corner of Connecticut. Indeed it is—Union is the least populated town in the state—but not necessarily more quiet than other predominantly rural parts of the state, such as the Litchfield Hills. In fact, unlike the Northwest, the Quiet Corner has an interstate highway running like a spine right up its middle and making travel between all the towns along it fast and easy.

One of the highlights of the Far Northeast is its history. You can take a little piece of it home when you make purchases in Putnam's burgeoning antiques district, or examine it more closely with a museum visit. The best place to get a sense of what life was like in the state's innumerable factory towns is at the Windham Textile & History Museum in Willimantic, operating out of buildings that were formerly part of a huge textile complex. A very different experience is in store at Woodstock's landmark Roseland Cottage, a pink Gothic Revival architectural treat whose builder was no less flamboyant than his creation. Whereas the former contrasts the lives of working-class people and their wealthy employers, the latter focuses squarely on the life of one upper-class family in Victorian-era Connecticut.

Although the valleys of the Far Northeast supported manufacturing, the area has remained home to many large tracts of mountainous near-wilderness. At least one town here has more state forest than private land within its bounds. Nowhere are the opportunities to fish, boat and hike more concentrated, and miles of old logging roads offer extensive terrain for mountain biking and horseback riding. If camping is your preferred method of overnight accommodation, this is the right place to go. North of Norwich is Connecticut's camping country, with lots of choices of both commercial and state-owned campgrounds. There are even unique horse camps in two state forests. If you prefer the B&B experience, Pomfret has what may be the largest cluster of such accommodations in the state.

Walking Weekend is the perfect event around which to plan a trip to the Far Northeast. It's a series of organized hikes and tours highlighting the history and natural beauty of more than 25 towns. It's always scheduled when the fall foliage is at its finest and the air is crisp. The local tourism district, which also does an exceptional job of producing informational materials with a very specific focus, is the place to find out more. Make sure to contact them at the address given under Services.

History

When English settlers arrived in northeast Connecticut, they found Quinebaug, Nipmuck and other Indians living in the area, and few conflicts ensued. Much local land was deeded to settlers by Owaneco and Joshua, sons of the Mohegan chief Uncas. One local land trust is even called Joshua's Trust, in reference to one such parcel of land that came to be known as Joshua's Tract. Most towns were settled in the first two decades of the 18th century, although many were not incorporated under their current names until later.

For an entire century this corner of the state was strictly agricultural. Textile manufacturing, which would dominate local economies for the next 150 years, sprang up practically overnight, the result of a convergence of events. Eastern Connecticut, next to Rhode Island where Samuel Slater had established the first cotton mill in the country

around the turn of the 19th century, was perfectly situated to absorb the growth of that industry. It had the water power, and it had the labor. The embargo of 1807–1809 and the War of 1812 brought trade with England to a virtual standstill. The demand for domestic textiles soared.

The first cotton mill in Connecticut was built in 1806 in Putnam by Smith Wilkinson, a relative of Samuel Slater. In less than a decade, Windham County was a textile-manufacturing center. Killingly Cotton Manufacturing Co. was founded in 1814, and by 1818 there were three competitors in town. Until the Ponemah Mills in Norwich were founded, Killingly was the center of cotton manufacturing in Connecticut. Willimantic's textile history began with the founding of Willimantic Linen Co. in 1854. The world's largest mill, the first one built on one level and the first lit by electricity, was built in that town, which is now the site of a museum documenting Connecticut's textile industry. Eventually more than half the towns in the region would see mills established, and many communities that are quiet backwaters today had bustling factories that employed thousands.

Even in 1950 textiles were still thriving here. Yet 20 years later many companies had closed up shop, and 40 years later there was little more than a handful of survivors. What happened? Textiles were among the first industries to develop in the young United States and one of the first to be lost to global competition. Today manufacturing in this area is done on a smaller and more diversified scale. With the passage of the giant mills into history, the Far Northeast has once again become an area that visitors associate not with an industry but with an exceptional scenic heritage.

Major Attractions

Roseland Cottage

Henry C. Bowen was a Woodstock native who went to New York City as a young man, made a fortune in the dry goods business and returned

to his hometown to build a most unusual summer residence. Architect Joseph Collins Wells designed for Bowen a Gothic Revival home based on the ideas of noted American landscape architect Andrew Jackson Downing. Roseland may be the only example of this remarkable architectural style open to the public in Connecticut.

One trait typical of the style is an immodest exterior color scheme, and Roseland is no exception: it's painted bright pink, hence the name. In fact, it's on its 14th coat of pink paint. Inside are stained-glass windows and hand-painted Lincrusta wall coverings made

Roseland Cottage, a Gothic Revival mansion and one of Woodstock's most "colorful" landmarks. Photo by David Bohl, courtesy Roseland Cottage, Woodstock/The Society for the Preservation of New England Antiquities.

to imitate tooled leather. The original furnishings are intact because family members lived in the house until 1968. Outside is a restored garden in which plants are bedded out each year in Victorian fashion.

Roseland Cottage is also the site of numerous special events. From June to Sept. you can attend Sun. afternoon program teas, which include a presentation on a Victorian subject ranging from tea-leaf readings to 19th-century stories for children. The first Sat. in Aug. (rain date: Sun.) is the date for an annual Children's Lawn Party featuring Victorian games and a peanut hunt. Bowen himself began this tradition for the community's children, but now everyone is welcome. Children are encouraged to come dressed to the nines. Pink lemonade and cookies are provided, and you can bring a picnic lunch. The adult counterpart of this event is the evening Garden Party, held the last Sat. in June with a light supper on the lawn under a tent and dancing to Big Band music. Guided tours of the house and grounds are given on the hour; the last tour begins one hour before closing. Admission: $3 adults, $2.50 seniors, $1.50 children under 12. Hours: Wed.–Sun., 11:00 A.M.–5:00 P.M., June–Oct. 15; always open on July 4 & Columbus Day. **556 Rte. 169, Woodstock, 06281; (860) 928-4074.**

Thompson International Speedway

NASCAR Pro Stocks division racing takes place on **Thompson International Speedway**'s five-eighths-mile oval track on Wed. nights, mid-June–Labor Day, at 7:00 p.m. It also features Busch Grand Nationals and Modified Tour events. Ticket prices: $12 adults, $6 children for weekly racing; $25–$35 adults and $12 children for special events. Located on **E. Thompson Rd., Thompson, 06277; (860) 923-9591.**

Windham Textile & History Museum

This excellent museum tells the powerful story of the company town and the rise and decline of manufacturing in Connecticut. In the early part of the 20th century Willimantic's main employer was the American Thread Company, a textile concern that built the mills, now empty, directly opposite the museum. As the company grew it built a huge complex of worker housing and other facilities and was considered the model of a progressive manufacturer. Much of that housing is still standing and visible on Main St. east of the museum. The Victorian homes of successive mill bosses are also still visible, across the river on Windham Rd. (Rte. 32).

American Thread Co. left Willimantic in 1989 to go to South Carolina, leaving 1,500 people without jobs. Willimantic has struggled with the loss and has done a beautiful job documenting the era in which it was known as Thread City. Leave at least an hour and a half for the guided tour, which gives you a real feel for the ways in which 18th- and early-19th-century manufacturers shaped whole communities and the lives of individual workers.

Next door in a former warehouse you get a close look at water-powered carding and bobbin-winding machines and a flying shuttle loom. Originally all the mills on this site were powered by the waters of the Willimantic River, but one of the mills was designed by Thomas Edison as the first in the world to be lit (not driven) by electricity. Admission: $4 adults, $2 students, seniors and children 7–18. Hours: Fri.–Sat., 10:00 A.M.–5:00 P.M.; Sun., noon–5:00 P.M. **157 Main St. at Union St., Willimantic, 06226; (860) 456-2178.**

Festivals and Events

Ceilidh
May

Pronounced something like "kaylee," this small Scottish heritage festival featuring music, dancing, storytelling and more is an annual scholarship fund-raiser. It has been described as a hootenanny, where audience members are encouraged to bring their musical instruments and dancing shoes and join in. It is always held on a May evening, but the date changes from year to year. The festival is sponsored by the Highland Festival Association of Scotland and held at the **V.F.W. Hall, 263 Taylor Hill in Jewett City.** For more information call **(860) 546-6862** or **(860) 423-1880.**

Spring Farm Day
first Sat. in May

This family event features barnyard animals for children to pet, demonstrations of colonial crafts and chores and tours of the Waldo House, a local museum. Admission charged. Hours: 9:00 A.M.–3:00 P.M. The Waldo House is easy to find—it's the only house on Waldo Rd. in Scotland. For more information call **(860) 456-0708.**

Blue Slope Country Museum Open House
weekend after Fourth of July and weekend after Columbus Day

This two-day-long, twice-a-year colonial heritage festival takes place on a 380-acre working dairy farm on which the Staebener family keeps registered Holsteins. The festival is basically an open house of the Blue Slope Country Museum, which normally opens only for

Getting There

Because this chapter covers such a broad area, the best route into it depends on your ultimate destination. Towns in the Far Northeast are anywhere from one to two hours away from Hartford by car. Communities at the southern end of the region are best accessed by taking Rte. 2 southeast out of East Hartford all the way to I-395 and then the appropriate secondary highway. To get to the northern end, take I-84 east out of Hartford and then a smaller road. Rtes. 44 and 6 are east-west roads that cut through the center of the region, and I-395 goes north-south straight up the middle from Norwich to the Massachusetts state line.

groups. There are demonstrations of working horses and oxen, butter making, basket weaving, loom and tape weaving, spinning and more. Admission: $5 adults, free for children 12 and under. Hours: 10:00 A.M.–4:00 P.M. **138 Blue Hill Rd., Franklin, 06254; (860) 642-6413.**

Brooklyn Fair
weekend before Labor Day weekend (Thu.–Sun.)

The oldest country fair in Connecticut offers the classic combination of agricultural events and a carnival atmosphere. Come early to see livestock judging, farm machinery and all the traditional aspects of a country fair (which go on throughout the day), or arrive after noon when the midway gets going. On Sat. night there's a series of children's games such as "the cows are out," in which kids race to dress in farm clothes and pen loose calves. Another exceptional event is Sat. afternoon harness racing—the only horse racing in Connecticut—on a half-mile track between 1:00 P.M. and 4:00 P.M. Other attractions include a circus, food vendors, crafts and both headliner and regional musical entertainment. Parking is available across the street for $2. Admission:

$5 adults, free for children 12 and under. Hours: Thu., 4:00 P.M.–11:00 P.M.; Fri.–Sat., 8:00 A.M.–11:00 P.M.; Sun., 8:00 A.M.–6:00 P.M. Held at the **Brooklyn Fairgrounds on Rte. 169 in Brooklyn.** For more information call **(860) 779-0012.**

Woodstock Fair
Labor Day weekend (Fri.–Mon.)

The second of the Northeast's major country fairs follows the Brooklyn Fair by one week and makes a great way to end summer with a splash. Bring the kids to see baby animals, or watch working livestock demonstrations where animals from oxen to ponies and their drivers vie to pull the heaviest load. It's late enough in the year for the fair to be an honest-to-goodness harvest celebration with judging for produce, flowers, canning, baking and more. There's a midway with carnival rides and games, entertainment ranging from country, folk and pop music to dance to magic and children's acts, crafters giving demos and selling their wares and dozens of food vendors. If you have the competitive spirit, register a couple of weeks in advance and bring your best SPAM cuisine to compete in the annual SPAM contest on Fri. night. Parking is available for about $3 on many private lots within walking distance of the fairground; there is also minimal parking at the fairground. Admission: $6 adults, free for children under 12. Gate hours: Fri., 4:00 P.M.–9:00 P.M.; Sat.–Mon., 9:00 A.M.–9:00 P.M. Ticket sales stop when the gate closes, but many events continue until 10:00 or 11:00 P.M. Held at the **Woodstock Fairgrounds at the junction of Rtes. 169 and 171 in Woodstock.** For more information call **(860) 928-3246.**

Walking Weekend
Columbus Day weekend

Back in 1991 when a group of people in the northeast were trying to have a 25-town region designated the Quinebaug-Shetucket National Heritage Corridor (they have since been successful), one woman had the idea of encouraging people to learn about the history of the area by having a weekend full of organized walks and tours. That was the genesis of Walking Weekend. It has grown to the point where upward of 55 hikes occur in conjunction with numerous local celebrations and special, one-time events. Many of the hikes are a straightforward opportunity to see some beautiful countryside, but others occur in urban or village areas and focus on architecture, local history, bridges, rivers and falls, mill sites, gardens, cemeteries and more. You'll find rambles of all difficulty levels, and maybe even a night hike or two. All hikes are free, although donations are often gratefully accepted to benefit historic sites or organizations whose members have volunteered their time as hike leaders. A schedule of the current year's walks becomes available in late summer and can be obtained from the **Northeast Connecticut Visitors District, P.O. Box 598, Putnam, 06260; (860) 928-1228.**

Thompson Illumination Night
Sat. of Columbus Day weekend

Thompson's biggest annual event came about when the steeple of the Congregational Church at one end of the town green burned down in 1987. The steeple had been lit at night, creating a beautiful scene, and was sorely missed. The Village Improvement Society devised a fund-raiser whose centerpiece was an evening tour around the green with the surrounding historic homes brightly lit for the occasion. Funds raised the first year went toward rebuilding the steeple, which makes a pretty picture at night once again, and in subsequent years the funds have gone toward a variety of other town improvement projects. The event is currently held in conjunction with Walking Weekend, so you can easily combine it with other activities throughout the Northeast, but there is a possibility the date will be changed, so call before going.

Toward evening there are free guided candlelight walks around the green with a focus on the architecture of the houses that surround it. Thompson is notable for having examples of architectural styles ranging from early colonial to Gothic Revival on its green. The day finishes with supper and a concert at the Congregational Church. The exhibits open around noon. Tours of the green start up around 6:00 P.M. Dinner runs about $6 and the concert $10. Thompson green is located at the **intersection of Rtes. 200 and 193.** For more information call **(860) 923-9661.**

Highland Festival
Sun. of Columbus Day weekend

Held in—where else?—the town of Scotland, the Highland Festival includes pipe band performances, dancing, athletic competitions and genealogical exhibits and Scottish food. Admission: $7 adults, $5 seniors, free to children under 12. Hours: 10:00 A.M.–5:00 P.M. Held at the **Edward Waldo Homestead on Waldo Rd. in Scotland; (860) 456-8627.**

Festival at Roseland Cottage
weekend after Columbus Day

Every year when the fall foliage is in its glory, the grounds of Roseland Cottage play host to a two-day arts and crafts fair with 125 vendors, live entertainment and plenty of food. Proceeds benefit restoration efforts at the cottage. Admission: $4 adults, $3 seniors, $2 children. Hours: 10:00 A.M.–5:00 P.M., rain or shine. Roseland Cottage is on **Rte. 169, Woodstock, 06281; (860) 928-4074.**

Windham Lighter Than Air Balloon Festival
third weekend in Oct. (Fri.–Sun.)

This benefit for the Hole in the Wall Gang children's camp features musical entertainment, amusement park rides (charge applies), a kid's tent with games and activities geared toward young ones, a juried art show, a beer tent and, of course, hot-air balloons. If you want to see the balloons, come early or late; they are only on view at dawn or just before

Pipers at Scotland's Highland Festival.

dusk. At midday they're packed up and put away. About 30 balloons are in attendance, and you can take a ride in several. Inquire about rates. There are also lots of food vendors. Admission to the festival site is free. Hours: Fri., noon–10:00 P.M.; Sat., 6:00 A.M.–10:00 P.M.; Sun., 6:00 A.M.–5:30 P.M. The balloons are out at 6:00 a.m., and most other activities start up around 10:00 A.M. The festival takes place at **Jillson Square on Main St. at Jackson in Willimantic.** Park free at Willimantic Plaza (Rte. 32 half a mile south of Rte. 6) and take the shuttle bus to the site; call for other parking options. For more information or to make balloon ride reservations call the Lighter Than Air Fund at **(860) 456-7666.**

Thompson Christmas Festivities
Dec.

In Dec. Thompson hosts two holiday events that combine the religious and secular aspects of Christmas. The Old Town Hall Christmas Concert is held the first Sat. in Dec. at 7:30 P.M. Community musicians, both children and adults, perform a selection of holiday music in a historic town hall built in 1842. A Candlelight Caroling and Live Crêche celebration is held the second Sun. of the month at 4:00 P.M.

Children dress up in costume to participate in a nativity display with live animals, and there is a tree-lighting ceremony followed by caroling at nearby Vernon Stiles Inn. Both events are free. The Thompson green is located at the **intersection of Rtes. 200 and 193.** For more information call **(860) 923-3738.**

Outdoor Activities

In addition to all the great state parks and forests in the Northeast, there's one outdoor recreational facility that's a little hard to pigeonhole. The centerpiece of **West Thompson Lake Recreation Area** is 200-acre West Thompson Lake, the result of an Army Corps of Engineers flood-control project damming the Quinebaug River. The lake is a good spot for boating and fishing, and 1,800 acres of protected land around it offer opportunities for snowmobiling, hunting, hiking and camping. Tours of the dam are offered on selected summer Sun. from June to Aug. at 11:00 A.M. For more on all these activities, see the appropriate sections below. In addition, every Sat. in June, July and Aug. the staff offers free, family-oriented nature programming for both campers and the public. For a fee and by reservation only, organized groups can use the open fields for activites. The same policy applies to two picnic shelters, one with electric and water, both with grills. It's also possible to arrange organized remote model float plane and airplane flying, bass tournaments and powerboat racing on the lake. Swimming is not allowed. The recreation area (except for the campground and the boat ramp) is open during daylight hours year-round; only fishing is allowed at the boat ramp during nighttime hours. West Thompson Lake is located on **Reardon Rd. in Thompson.** For more information or to make reservations call **(860) 923-2982.**

Biking

Mountain Biking

Airline State Park Trail

This partially rebuilt trail follows the track of an old railroad bed for 30 miles or more across northeast Connecticut. Some portions are well maintained, but others may be in poor condition. A good access point is from the James L. Goodwin Conservation Center on Rte. 6 in Hampton. Park in the Conservation Center lot and hike up the entrance road (Potter Rd.) to the trail. You will have to backtrack to return to your car unless you want to use public roads.

Moosup Valley State Park Trail

Yet another trail that follows an abandoned railroad bed (this was a stretch of a Hartford to Providence line), the Moosup Valley Trail is ideal for both mountain biking and walking. Mostly flat and straight, it runs for about 8 miles from the town of Plainfield into the town of Sterling, never straying far from the course of the Moosup River, which provides many pretty views. To get to it, find River Rd. in the village of Moosup. It's right at a red brick mill on Main St. (Rte. 14). Turn on River Rd., cross the small bridge and park in the dirt pullout you'll see immediately on the right. The trail is across the street. If you follow it all the way to the end you'll wind up on Main St. in Sterling. Turn right to get to **Main St. Variety & Deli (860-564-3695)** where you can pick up a basic breakfast or lunch. You'll have to backtrack to the start or leave a second vehicle near the trailhead in Sterling.

Natchaug/Pachaug State Forests

You can bike on broad gravel and dirt roads on these expansive tracts of land, but only if you're prepared to be polite and dismount for equestrians. These multiple-use areas are popular for horseback riding because of dedicated horse camps inside the forests. If you plan to tear around, go to Moosup Valley instead. In addition, riding on blue-blazed hiking trails, such as the Natchaug and Nehantic Trails, is forbidden. The entrance to the Natchaug is located on Rte. 198, 3 miles south of Rte. 44 in Eastford. The entrance to Pachaug is located on Rte. 49 a short distance north of Voluntown.

Quaddick State Forest

A few miles of woods roads and an abandoned town road crisscross this small state forest in

Thompson. Parking is available on Baker Rd. at the bridge on Quaddick Reservoir. Head east on Baker Rd. to ride into the forest.

Road Biking

The *Northeast Connecticut's Bike Guide* available from the Northeast Connecticut Visitors District includes rides in Killingly, Putnam, Thompson, Sterling, Canterbury/Scotland, Pomfret/Woodstock and Ashford/Eastford. They range in length from under 5 to nearly 25 miles. The guide lists highlights of each ride as well as mileages, lodging suggestions and the location of some stores. See Services.

Birding

In addition to the properties listed below, there is a handicapped-accessible observation deck on **Pine Acres Lake** at the James L. Goodwin State Forest good for watching herons, ducks and geese. If the Conservation Center there is open, you can pick up a list of bird species that have been sighted in the area. The forest entrance is located on Rte. 6 in Hampton.

Pomfret Farms

This 280-acre tract owned by the Connecticut Audubon Society is a conglomeration of three former farms. It contains 5 miles of trails through fields and woods where over 150 bird species have been documented. The society offers frequent bird walks in spring and fall on both weekdays and weekends, as well as weekend workshops. There are two good spots from which to access trails at Pomfret Farms. To get to the first, go east on Day Rd. from Rte. 169. At the stop sign 1 mile down, turn right. There is a pullout for parking between two white houses on the right and a trailhead. To reach the other, go north three-tenths of a mile from the junction of Rtes. 169 and 101 and park at the Bosworth Farm barn. A sign saying "Connecticut Audubon Society" is at the spot. Both of these starting points are in Pomfret. Boxes at the trailheads contain maps, bird checklists and program information. Hours: dawn–dusk, year-round. For more information call **(860) 928-4041.**

Trail Wood

Also owned by the Connecticut Audubon Society, Trail Wood is the 130-acre farm of the late naturalist-author Edwin Way Teale. Teale won a Pulitzer Prize for his 1964 book *Wandering Through Winter*, the fourth installment in a tetralogy about the seasons. Teale is perhaps best known, however, for his book about Trail Wood, entitled *A Naturalist Buys an Old Farm*.

The trails cross a number of habitats including forest, meadow and beaver pond. Old foundations and a remnant of a colonial road make pleasant "discoveries." Birds commonly sighted include ducks, geese and herons, juncos, woodpeckers and red-tailed hawks. Special programs with a natural science, history or literary focus are offered one or two Sat. per month, Jan.–Nov., and there are spring and fall bird walks led by ornithologists.

There is also a small museum here (open May–Nov., second and fourth Sun. of the month, 1:00 P.M.–4:00 P.M.), exhibiting Teale memorabilia and taxidermy. Hours: dawn–dusk daily, year-round. Look for a Connecticut Audubon Society sign at the entrance to Trail Wood; the driveway leads to a visitor parking lot. Signs there direct you to an old cow barn with maps and other information. **93 Kenyon Rd., Hampton, 06247; (860) 455-0759.**

Boating

For canoeing, try some of the ponds where motors are prohibited or restricted to electric and the only wake you'll have to worry about is from occasional groups of swimmers. There is a car-top boat ramp at **Green Falls Reservoir** in Voluntown located off Rte. 138, 3 miles east of Voluntown. A parking fee is charged here on weekends and holidays in summer. **Pine Acres Lake** in James L. Goodwin State Forest on Rte. 6 in Hampton is free and moderately large at 136 acres. There's a paved parking area by the Conservation Center nearby. **Wauregan Reservoir,** also called Quinebaug Pond on some maps, is quite lovely. The easy-to-miss entrance is on Shepard Hill Rd. off Rte. 12 in Killingly.

For motorboating, consider **Beach Pond** in Voluntown, where you can launch your boat from a concrete ramp accessible from North Shore Rd. In neighboring Griswold there's a public boat launch on 830-acre **Pachaug Pond** accessible off Rte. 138 as well as a paved ramp at **Hopeville Pond,** where there's an 8 m.p.h. limit. See the *Connecticut Boater's Guide* for information on waterskiing restrictions on Beach Pond and Pachaug Pond. A parking fee is charged on weekends and holidays at Hopeville Pond, which is a state park, but you'll also have access to a sandy beach, concessions, rental canoes and paddleboats and toilets. Also consider **West Thompson Lake** in Thompson (5 m.p.h. limit), described at the start of the Outdoor Activities section.

Mashapaug Pond and **Bigelow Pond** are two lovely bodies of water at Bigelow Hollow State Park in Union. Motors are prohibited on the former, and there is a 10 m.p.h. speed limit on the latter. A parking fee is charged in summer. For more information and directions, see the listing under Hiking. Finally, boating is one of the primary attractions at Quaddick State Park, which consists almost entirely of 466-acre **Quaddick Reservoir.** The reservoir is quite shallow, having an average depth of 4.5 feet, but waterskiing is allowed. Canoes and paddleboats are available for rent from the concession stand, which is usually open weekends in May and then daily June–Labor Day. The park is on Quaddick Town Farm Rd. in Thompson. A parking fee of $5 for Connecticut vehicles and $8 for out-of-state vehicles is charged on weekends and holidays, Memorial Day–Labor Day. Park hours: 8:00 A.M.–dusk daily, year-round. For more information call the park office at **(860) 928-9200.**

Fishing

Fishing opportunities abound in the Far Northeast. Check the *Connecticut Angler's Guide* for a complete list of all the public fishing spots in the area. If you would like to learn more about Connecticut's fish hatcheries and fish-stocking programs, visit the **Quinebaug Valley Trout Hatchery,** one of the largest hatcheries in the East. Brown, brook and rainbow trout are raised here for release into Connecticut's wa-

terways. Hours: 10:00 A.M.–4:00 P.M. daily. Located on **Trout Hatchery Rd., Central Village, 06332; (860) 564-7542.**

Natchaug River
The Natchaug is perhaps the best river in the Northeast for trout fishing. It's stocked with browns, brooks and rainbows. Easiest access is from within the Natchaug State Forest in Eastford, described under Hiking. Also within the forest is **Hampton Reservoir,** where you can catch bass and panfish, and **Pine Acres Lake** in adjacent James L. Goodwin State Forest is good for the same. You can access the reservoir from Kenyon Rd. off Rte. 97 and Pine Acres Lake from the main entrance to James L. Goodwin State Forest on Rte. 6, both of them in Hampton.

Pachaug State Forest
Voluntown, which is two-thirds state land, is an angler's paradise. Several ponds in Pachaug State Forest are notable fishing spots. **Beachdale Pond** is small but stocked with trout. You'll also find pickerel, smallmouth bass and largemouth bass here. There is a handicapped-accessible fishing pad and wheelchair ramp, and a boat ramp if you want to launch something small. An 8 m.p.h. speed limit is in effect. The pond is located across from the main entrance to Pachaug State Forest on Rte. 49 less than 1 mile north of Voluntown.

Beach Pond is a large body of water where you'll also encounter water-skiers and swimmers. Fishing is perhaps best by boat, although you could park at the launch and fish from the shore. You'll be able to reel in trout and bass. The entrance is on North Shore Rd. in Voluntown.

Green Falls Reservoir is a very good smallmouth and largemouth bass fishing area that is also stocked with trout. Fish from the shore or a rowboat; motors (except electric) are not allowed. You'll also find picnic facilities and a rustic campground. If the day is hot you can take a dip in the reservoir. A parking fee is collected here on weekends and holidays, Memorial Day–Labor Day. If you decide you'd like to camp nearby, check out Green Falls Campground, an inexpensive, rustic state facility. Green Falls Reservoir is on a forest road off Rte. 138. The turnoff is 3 miles east of Voluntown. For more information on Pachaug State Forest facilities call **(860) 376-2920.**

West Thompson Lake Recreation Area

This shallow artificial lake is one of the best spots for smallmouth and largemouth bass in the state. It is also stocked with trout upstream. You can fish from anywhere along the shore or from a boat (5 m.p.h. limit), and launch facilities are available free of charge. See the listing at the start of the Outdoor Activities section for directions and more information.

Other Lakes and Rivers

Mashapaug Pond and **Bigelow Pond** in Bigelow Hollow State Park, detailed under Hiking, are known for their excellent trout and bass fishing. Mashapaug is also a favorite ice-fishing spot. A parking fee is charged in summer.

In **Hopeville Pond State Park,** described under Swimming, a dammed section of the Pachaug River yields trout in spring, then bass and perch later in the year when the water warms. There's a paved ramp so you can fish from shore or from a boat (8 m.p.h. speed limit) and access to other amenities. A parking fee is charged on summer weekends and holidays.

Quaddick Reservoir, described under Boating, is shallow, yielding mostly warmwater species such as bass, pickerel, perch and sunfish. To enter Quaddick State Park, you have to pay a fee on weekends in summer, but most people just park at the bridge on Baker Rd. in Thompson and fish from the bridge, where it's free and there's less of a crowd.

The **Shetucket River** around the hamlet of Baltic in Sprague is stocked with brood stock Atlantic salmon in the fall. You can access the river from Rte. 138 near its junction with Rte. 97, where there's a big gravel parking lot on the north side of the road.

Your best bets in shallow **Wauregan Reservoir** are largemouth bass and chain pickerel. The entrance is on Shepard Hill Rd. off Rte. 12 in Killingly. There's a dirt ramp for

nonmotorized boats, or you can fish from shore.

Finally, the **Moosup River Trout Management Area** is a portion of the Moosup River restricted to fly fishing only. It begins where Rte. 14 crosses the river in Plainfield and reaches to the Moosup's confluence with the Quinebaug.

Hiking

In addition to the listings below, the **Moosup Valley State Park Trail** is a wonderful wooded linear trail with some great river views. Its overall flatness makes it ideal for folks who would be too taxed by lots of elevation changes. For details, see the listing under Biking.

Bigelow Hollow State Park/ Nipmuck State Forest

The tracts of land that make up Bigelow Hollow State Park and Nipmuck State Forest lie adjacent to one another with no distinguishable boundary, forming a total block of over 8,000 mostly forested acres in the least populous town in Connecticut. An extensive network of trails and paved and unpaved roads make for numerous hiking possibilities. Trails encircle two ponds and border the southern shore of a third. You can also pick up the blue-blazed Nipmuck Trail here, full details of which can be found in the *Connecticut Walk Book.* Hikers are requested not to use parking areas intended for boaters. The parking lot at the top of Bigelow Pond about halfway down the main park road gives access to the greatest number of trails while avoiding boater areas. On weekends and holidays, Memorial Day–Labor Day, there is a parking fee of $5 per car for vehicles with Connecticut plates, $8 for vehicles with out-of-state plates. Located on **Rte. 171 east of Rte. 190 in Union; (860) 928-9200.**

Mashamoquet Brook State Park

As for the name, don't even waste time thinking about how to pronounce it. As long as you come close to Mush-MUCK-et or MASH-ma-ket, folks will know what you mean. Several blazed trails and a broad dirt road (Wolf Den Rd.) that cuts diagonally through the park make it possible to hike several loops of varying distances at mountainous Mashamoquet Brook. Both the red and the blue trail lead to the Wolf Den, where a plaque marks the spot where Israel Putnam (a Connecticut farmer who had an esteemed career as a Revolutionary War general) killed what is said to have been the last wolf in Connecticut in 1742 after years of her feeding on local livestock. Bring a flashlight if you want to crawl to the back of the "den," a low, narrow cave a good half-hour hike from the main entrance. To get to the trails, cross the small footbridge you'll pass on the right on your way to the parking areas. Take the rightmost leg of either trail to get to the Wolf Den most quickly. Alternatively, the wolf den is only a five- or ten-minute walk from a parking area on Wolf Den Dr. Access to this parking area is easier from Jericho Rd. to the south. Wolf Den Dr. is dirt at this point.

Other attractions at the park include swimming, picnic facilities and a neat little museum right at the entrance. On weekends and holidays, Memorial Day–Labor Day, a fee of $5 per car is charged for vehicles with Connecticut plates and $8 for vehicles with out-of-state plates. Park hours are 8:00 A.M.–dusk daily, year-round. Located on **Rte. 44 about 1 mile west of Rte. 169 in Pomfret; (860) 928-6121.**

Natchaug and James L. Goodwin State Forests/Natchaug Trail

The Natchaug Trail is a blue-blazed trail 20 miles long, beginning at the James L. Goodwin Conservation Center in Hampton and ending at the Nipmuck Trail in Westford. In between it passes through the adjacent parcels of land that make up Natchaug and James L. Goodwin State Forests. Natchaug State Forest alone is over 12,000 acres in size, with the lovely Natchaug River running along its western edge. The trail terrain is mountainous and mostly wooded, passing several marshes, a few hilltop valley lookouts and an old mill dam. The best place to pick up the Natchaug Trail is in Natchaug State Forest, where you can also avail yourself of a network of gravel and logging roads that make loop hikes possible, convenient picnic areas and rest rooms. A map is posted at the entrance on Rte. 198 in the town

of Eastford, approximately 3 miles south of Rte. 44. You can also start from the James L. Goodwin Conservation Center parking lot on Rte. 6 in Hampton. For more information about trails at either forest call **(860) 928-6121.** Full details on the Natchaug Trail can be found in the *Connecticut Walk Book.*

Old Furnace and Ross Pond State Parks

This 3-mile trail across two small and largely undeveloped state parks takes you through a quiet hemlock forest, right alongside a marsh and eventually close to the shore of Ross Pond at the foot of some impressive granite ledges. In autumn hoarfrost on the marsh grass is an exquisite early morning sight, but you have to get there before the sun burns it off. To get to the Old Furnace entrance, take Rte. 6 going east. After crossing under I-395, keep an eye out for the first road on the right; there should be a sign for Old Furnace. Take this country road about a quarter-mile to a large dirt parking lot on the right. A short path at the far end of the lot leads to a clearing. At the opposite end of the clearing look for blue blazes at a stream crossing (not the blaze on the rock) to get on the right section of trail. Backtrack to return to your car.

Pachaug State Forest/ Nehantic and Pachaug Trails

The Nehantic Trail is a 13-mile, blue-blazed trail starting at a pond in Voluntown and ending at another pond in Griswold, giving hikers swimming opportunities at both ends. The Pachaug Trail is another blue-blazed path on which you can hike a giant loop up into the town of Sterling and connect with the Quinebaug Trail. These trails form a rather complex spidery network that connects most of the outdoor recreational sites in this neck of the woods. The Nehantic and the Pachaug come together at Green Falls Reservoir, where side trails and connectors make it possible to do quite a bit of hiking without backtracking. There's even a first-come, first-served rustic campground. Park at Green Falls Reservoir (also called Green Fall Pond) in Pachaug State Forest off Rte. 138, 3 miles east of Voluntown.

A parking fee is charged on summer weekends and holidays. Take either the Nehantic or the Pachaug Trail heading north away from the pond. From either one you can take the Nehantic Crossover or the Laurel Loop Trail to connect with the other and return to the pond. There's also a loop around the pond with side trails, one of which heads east into Rhode Island where there's another pond loop. If you're ambitious, hike the whole Nehantic Trail, which comes out at Hopeville Pond State Park on Rte. 201. For more information on hiking in this area call **(860) 376-2920.**

Horseback Riding

Airline State Park Trail
This linear trail, named for a railroad line that once operated along its route, is popular with equestrians, but it's not easy making a loop back to your trailer, so plan to backtrack. And be prepared to encounter mountain bikers and hikers—this is a multiple-use area. You can access the Airline Trail at the James L. Goodwin Conservation Center in James L. Goodwin State Forest on Rte. 6 in Hampton. Park your trailer in the Conservation Center lot and ride a short distance north on the main park road to the trailhead.

Diamond A Ranch in Dayville
Diamond A Ranch is perhaps the only stable in Connecticut to offer Western-style cookouts. On this trip you ride out in late afternoon across the fields and woods of their 107-acre property, cook a kielbasa and beans-style dinner by campfire, then ride back in the moonlight. Overnight and picnic lunch rides are also available, as well as an outing to Bluff Point Reserve in Groton for a ride on the beach. One-hour rides start at $15 per person. There is no strict age cutoff; children under 5 can ride double with one parent. **975 Hartford Tpke. (Rte. 101, 2 miles east of I-395 exit 93), Dayville, 06241; (860) 779-3000.**

Natchaug and Pachaug State Forests
These two state forests are perhaps the premier places in the state to ride. Miles of wide forest roads with gentle grades allow you and

companions to ride side-by-side. Horse camps are located right in the forests, and the campground in Natchaug is free. Both areas are also used for hiking and mountain biking, so be prepared to share the roads, and note that blue-blazed hiking trails, such as the Natchaug and Nehantic Trails, are off-limits to equestrians. Natchaug State Forest is located in the town of Eastford on Rte. 198 approximately 3 miles south of Rte. 44. Pachaug State Forest is located on Rte. 49 less than 1 mile north of Voluntown. For more information on the horse camps, see the Camping section.

Skiing

When snow cover is adequate, the numerous gravel and dirt roads through **Bigelow Hollow State Park, Natchaug State Forest** and **Pachaug State Forest** are ideal for cross-country skiing. For directions and more information, see the listings under Hiking. Another possible destination is **Trail Wood,** a nature sanctuary with 4 miles of trails that is described under Birding. The open areas and trails of **West Thompson Lake Recreation Area** are also appropriate for skiing. See the listing at the start of the Outdoor Activities section for details. All of these areas are ungroomed, and access is free.

Snowmobiling

Natchaug State Forest offers what is probably the single-longest run of any snowmobile trail in Connecticut. One very long trail runs almost the entire height of the forest, and a couple of large loops branch off from it. The entrance is on Rte. 198 in the town of Eastford, approximately 3 miles south of Rte. 44.

Over at **Nipmuck State Forest,** a small trail system has one small loop incorporated into a second, larger loop. Access is through the entrance to Bigelow Hollow State Park on Rte. 171 east of Rte. 190 in Union.

The moderately sized system of interconnecting loops at **Pachaug State Forest** makes it possible to design a trip here ranging from quite short to at least half a day. The entrance to the state forest is on Rte. 49, 1 mile north of Voluntown.

Finally, snowmobiling is allowed at **West Thompson Lake Recreation Area** as long as there are 4 inches of hard-packed snow on the ground. Here, 1,800 acres of land surround a 200-acre lake, and you may go on any trail as well as through open areas. For directions and more information, see the listing at the start of the Outdoor Activities section. For a report on conditions, contact the park office at **(860) 923-2982.** All of these areas are ungroomed.

Swimming

For all of the facilities listed below, a parking fee of $5 for Connecticut vehicles and $8 for out-of-state vehicles is charged on weekends and holidays Memorial Day–Labor Day. Lifeguards, where available, are usually on duty weekends in May, then daily June–Labor Day between 10:00 A.M. and 6:00 P.M. All state parks and forests are open 8:00 A.M.–dusk daily, year-round.

Green Falls Reservoir
If you don't require lifeguards and lots of facilities, Green Falls Reservoir (also known as Green Falls Pond) is a nice place for a dip. The pond is ringed by hiking trails, and a rustic campground is nearby. It's located on a forest road through Pachaug State Forest. Take Rte. 138 about 3 miles east of Voluntown and look for a sign at the turnoff.

Hopeville Pond State Park
Hopeville Pond is a dammed portion of the Pachaug River that forms a long, narrow body of water where there's a large, sandy, guarded beach for swimming. There's also a paved boat ramp, a concession stand, a picnic area with tables and fireplaces, flush toilets and a campground, but no bathhouses. Baseball diamonds, horseshoe pits and a large open field for kite flying or Frisbee are all available at no extra charge. In addition, the park is the starting point of the blue-blazed Nehantic Trail, on which you can hike 13 miles to Green Falls Reservoir. The park entrance is on Rte. 201 in Griswold about 1.5 miles east of I-395 exit 86. For more information call **(860) 376-2920.**

Mashamoquet Brook State Park
You can swim at Mashamoquet Brook State Park in a small, artificial pond with a sandy, guarded beach surrounded by forested mountains. There are concessions and a huge, beautiful, open-air picnic shelter built of stone with a fireplace at its center. One state park campground is a short walk away, and another is on the opposite side of the park. The entrance to the park is on Rte. 44 about 1 mile west of Rte. 169 in Pomfret. For more information call **(860) 928-6121.**

Quaddick State Park
Quaddick Reservoir sports a sandy, guarded beach with bathhouses, concessions and picnic areas with grills or cement fireplaces. The entrance is on Quaddick Town Farm Rd. about three-quarter-mile north of Quaddick Rd. in Thompson. For more information call **(860) 928-9200.**

Seeing and Doing

Antiquing

Antiquing Weekend is a fledgling event held annually the first weekend (Fri.–Sun.) in Nov. One highlight is the series of appraisals, refinishing and reproduction demonstrations and special events that go on Sat. and Sun. Most of the participating shops, some of which are normally open by appointment only, commit to keeping 10:00 A.M.–5:00 P.M. hours on all three days. There is at least one designated information center open 9:00 A.M.–9:00 P.M. each day, so maps, brochures and information are always available. Package rates and special rates at some area lodging providers are available. Call **(860) 928-1228** for a calendar.

Antiques stores are scattered here, there and everywhere throughout the Far Northeast, but the undisputed center of activity is Putnam. It's a fairly new trend that caught on at the urging of one dealer who made a big commitment to retail space in town. You can obtain maps of the Putnam Antiques District by calling the **Putnam Antiques District**

Association at (800) 514-3448 or **Playhouse Supply Company** at (860) 963-9030.

Art Galleries

The **New England Center for Contemporary Art** is the private mission of a Brooklyn art lover. It's in an unconventional, warehouselike space and run rather informally, but you can see excellent work here. Admission by donation. Hours: Tue.–Fri., 10:00 A.M.–5:00 P.M.; Sat.–Sun., 1:00 P.M.–5:00 P.M. Located on **Rte. 169 a short distance north of the town center, Brooklyn, 06234; (860) 774-8899.**

Greenhouses

Plant lovers will not want to miss the opportunity to visit Logee's Greenhouses, a highly unusual retail nursery. When you step inside one of the greenhouses that form the **Logee's** complex **(141 North St. in Danielson; 860-774-8038)**, it's like entering another world. The air is warm and moist, and it smells like the tropics. Virtually everything on display is for sale, and the selection is astonishing. It's really worth the trip from anywhere, and it has a mail-order business too. Hours are Mon.–Sat., 9:00 A.M.–4:00 P.M.; Sun., 11:00 A.M.–4:00 P.M., year-round.

Museums and Historic Sites

Aside from Roseland Cottage and the Windham Textile & History Museum (described under Major Attractions), there are also many smaller museums worth stopping at. Two of them in Scotland are currently open by appointment only. The **Waldo House** is a center-chimney colonial home built in 1714 and lived in by seven generations of the Waldo family until 1975. It is furnished with numerous antiques, all of them made in eastern Connecticut. To arrange a tour call **(860) 456-0708.** The other museum is the birthplace of **Samuel B. Huntington,** one of only four Connecticut signers of the Declaration of Independence. Currently unrestored, the building is a National

Historic Landmark and a good example of how early colonial homes evolved from two-room structures into saltboxes. The oldest part of the house dates from the 1720s. It is usually open only on national holidays. To arrange a tour and get directions call **(860) 423-6862.**

The **Connecticut Eastern Railroad Museum (Bridge St. [Rte. 32 between Main and Pleasant Sts.], Willimantic; 860-456-2221),** a project of the local chapter of the National Railroad Historical Society, has a rail yard, a former station and five vehicles, including a 1940s diesel locomotive, two passenger cars (ca. 1905) and a wooden-sided freight car that was used until the 1960s by the Central Vermont Railroad. Planned hours are Sat., 9:00 A.M.–1:00 P.M., May–Oct.

The **Brayton Grist Mill** and **Marcy Blacksmith Museum** at the entrance to Mashamoquet Brook State Park on Rte. 44 in Pomfret preserves a couple of slices of that town's past. The mill was operated by Billy Brayton from 1890 until 1928. The milling equipment is still intact, although the power generation machinery is not. Free admission. Hours: Sat.–Sun., 2:00 P.M.– 5:00 P.M., May–Sept.

The personal passion of Bill Glazier, a retired priest with a concern about stewardship of the environment, the **Photomobile Model Museum (1728 Rte. 198, Woodstock; 860-974-3910)** features solar-powered model cars, boats and magnetic levitation vehicles that Glazier designed himself. Admission: $3 adults, $2 children under 16. Hours are usually Sat., 10:00 A.M.–5:00 P.M., & Sun., noon–5:00 P.M., but call before going.

Prudence Crandall Museum

In 1831 young Prudence Crandall was asked by a committee of Canterbury citizens to become headmistress of a private school for the area's youth. With the support of the townspeople and elected officials, the school was established the following year. In only the school's second semester, Crandall accepted as a student a young girl of mixed race. To express their displeasure with this, the parents of the white students withdrew them from classes. Left with the problem of how to continue operation of the school with few students, Crandall decided on a logical, if inflammatory, solution: to run an academy exclusively for the education of black girls.

The museum, operated by the Connecticut Historical Commission, is situated in the house where Crandall attempted to run her school. It is a beautifully restored (ca. 1805) example of Federal architecture. The rooms house changing exhibits on a variety of subjects that have included Canterbury history, the designation of Rte. 169 (which passes just outside the museum) as a scenic road, the story of Crandall's difficult struggle to keep the school open, black history and women's history.

The museum offers special programs often having to do with social reform, education, interracial and intercultural relations and archaeological work at the house. It hosts an annual tea in early Nov. in which a dramatist plays Crandall delivering an impassioned monologue, as well as a tree-trimming party in early Dec. The gift shop has an excellent series of books on Connecticut history. Admission: $2 adults, $1 seniors and children 6–17. Hours: Wed.–Sun., 10:00 A.M.–4:30 P.M.; closed Dec. 15–Jan. 31. Located at the **corner of Rtes. 14 and 169, Canterbury, 06331; (860) 546-9916.**

Nature Centers

The **James L. Goodwin Conservation Center** offers an impressive variety of programs year-round, from full-moon cookouts to birdhouse building to wildlife tracking; call for a schedule. There is also a small museum with mounted animals, some live animals and 55-gallon aquariums in warm weather. The museum is usually open Sat., 10:00 A.M.–1:00 or 2:00 P.M., spring–fall. It is located in the **state forest of the same name on Rte. 6 in Hampton; (860) 455-9534.**

Performing Arts

Break-a-Leg Productions at QVCTC
Looking for a show your kids will enjoy? This new theatrical group stages shows with casts made up of local children age 8–18. They stage

two shows per year, one in mid-July and one in mid-Nov. The summer show is a musical and the autumn one a cabaret. Tickets run $6 adults, $4 seniors and children 12 and under. Performances at 7:00 P.M. are given Thu.–Sun. in the **Quinebaug Valley Community Technical College Auditorium** at **742 Upper Maple St. in Danielson.** For more information call the **Continuing Education Office of QVCTC** at **(860) 774-1133.**

Opera New England
This volunteer organization brings professional performers into the area to perform opera and occasional musicals. Ticket prices are in the $20–$25 range. Its venue is the Hyde Cultural Center at the **Hyde School, 150 Rte. 169 in Woodstock.** For more information call **(860) 928-2946.**

Theatre of Northeastern Connecticut
Bradley Playhouse in Thompson is home to this very active amateur theater company that presents about seven shows during a season stretching Feb.–Dec. A season's offerings can run the gamut of styles, but usually includes one major musical, one children's show and a production of *A Christmas Carol* during the holidays. The historic playhouse, which was once used for vaudeville and silent movies, is pleasantly quirky and holds about 400 audience members in auditorium-style seats. Each show runs two to three weeks with performances Fri. & Sat. at 8:00 P.M. & one Sun. matinee at 2:00 P.M. Tickets prices are $11 for adults, $8 for seniors and students. Dinner/theater ticket packages are available in conjunction with several area restaurants, as well as a ticket/accommodation package with King's Inn, which also serves as the box office. For a schedule of upcoming performances call **King's Inn** at **(800) 541-7304** or **(860) 928-7961,** or call the theater directly at **(860) 928-7887. 30 Front St. (Rte. 44), Putnam, 06260.**

Scenic Drives

The rolling hills of northeastern Connecticut make ideal terrain for a scenic drive. Look for the beauty close at hand in stretches of farmland, curving stone walls and stunning foliage in autumn. Rte. 169 from the Massachusetts/ Connecticut state line south to Newent is a designated scenic drive that strings together little towns like beads on a necklace, and I-395 is the prettiest stretch of interstate in Connecticut, with great views of rolling hills in the distance. In autumn it's like driving through blazing pincushions.

If you happen to be visiting in late June, don't miss the Nipmuck State Forest **Laurel Sanctuary** in Union. The mountain laurel is Connecticut's state flower—appropriate enough since the plant is a native and grows profusely in this part of its range. Its flower trusses are ordinary looking from a distance, but individual blossoms seen up close have an almost alien beauty, a strict geometry and angularity rare in the macroscopic plant world. Their season is short—roughly two weeks beginning in mid-June. At the sanctuary you can drive a broad, flat woods road and view the plants that line it from your car. Another option is to park at the main entrance and take a leisurely walk, which will enable you to get close enough to appreciate the unique beauty of this unusual flower. The main entrance and a small parking area are on Rte. 190 about one-tenth of a mile west of Rte. 89. At the opposite side of the sanctuary, turn around and exit the way you came. Don't try to drive the continuation of the road unless you have a 4-wheel-drive vehicle.

Seasonal Favorites

Northeastern Connecticut is blanketed with farms where you can pick your own apples and pumpkins in autumn, as well as other fruits and vegetables at other times of year. A few representative ones are **Buell's Orchard (108 Crystal Pond Rd., Eastford; 860-974-1150), Lapsley Orchard (Rte. 169, Pomfret; 860-928-9186)** and **Woodstock Orchards (Rte. 169, Woodstock; 860-928-2225).** If you have time, request the "Farms & Family Fun in Eastern Connecticut" brochure from the **Northeast Connecticut Visitors District (NCVD)** by writing to **P.O Box 598, Putnam, 06260,** or calling them at **(860) 928-1228.**

This guide suggests all sorts of places to have on-the-farm experiences. Below are a couple of other interesting places with seasonal attractions.

Whipple's Christmas Wonderland
What began 30 years ago as a memorial to Mervin Whipple's son has become a widely publicized holiday event drawing tens of thousands of spectators annually. Whipple's property is decorated with over 108,000 lights and vignettes containing hundreds of animated figures including Father Christmas and a life-sized manger scene. He keeps the lights on from the first Sun. after Thanksgiving through New Year's night from 5:00 P.M. to 9:30 P.M. and greets people as they arrive. Free admission. The Wonderland is located at **101 Pineville Rd. in Ballouville,** a hamlet of Killingly. For more information call his home at **(860) 774-2742.**

Wright's Mill Farm
Wright's Mill Farm features many different things according to the season, including a crafts barn with a spiral staircase and an observation deck in the silo; tractor-drawn Pumpkin Hunt hayrides on weekends, mid-Sept.–Oct., and Christmas caroling hayrides Thanksgiving–Christmas. This is a nice place to pick out a pumpkin in fall, pick up gifts in the Christmas shop or tag and cut your own Christmas tree. Hayrides are $3 per person during the times specified but can be given for a $40 minimum by appointment at other times. Guests are also welcome to picnic and hike on the farm's 250 acres. Open Apr.–Dec. 24, 9:00 A.M.–5:00 P.M. daily. **63 Creasey Rd., Canterbury, 06331; (860) 774-1455.**

Wagering
Plainfield Greyhound Park
Connecticut's first greyhound track offers wagering on greyhound racing on-site as well as simulcast jai-alai, thoroughbred racing and greyhound racing from other tracks. A heated track surface allows for daily racing year-round. There are inside and outside viewing areas, two full-service restaurants open Fri.

evenings and weekends and casual dining facilities. Doors open at 11:30 A.M. each day. Post time is 1:00 P.M. on Sat.–Tue. & Thu. & 7:30 P.M. on Wed., Fri. & Sat. By law you must be at least 18 years old to enter the park. **137 Lathrop Rd., Plainfield, 06374; (800) 722-3766 or (860) 564-3391.** The park also participates in a greyhound adoption program. For more information call **Plainfield Pets** at **(860) 564-5640.**

Wineries

One of Connecticut's newest wineries, **Heritage Trail Vineyards (291 N. Burnham Hwy. [Rte. 169], Lisbon, 06351; 860-376-0659)** opened in Dec. 1996. Over the course of several years vintner Diane Powell has planted 6 acres of pinot noir, merlot, cabernet franc, horizon, ravat and vignoles grapes on her 40 acres and is just beginning to produce wines for public release. A tasting room with a fireplace and an outdoor deck overlooking a pond are attached to the back of her renovated 1790 colonial farmhouse home. Open Fri.–Sun., 11:00 A.M.–5:00 P.M., May–Jan. 1, & by appointment.

172

Where to Stay

Bed & Breakfasts

There are lots of B&Bs in this large geographic area. The greatest numbers are found in Pomfret because the town has three academies, and visiting parents need accommodation. The B&Bs listed here represent a sampling of the whole, ranging from the modest to the luxurious. For additional possibilities call the **Northeast Connecticut Visitors District** at **(860) 928-1228.**

Corttis Inn—$$$$
First and foremost, the Corttis Inn offers privacy. It's situated on 900 acres that afford guests the opportunity to hike, bike and cross-country ski without ever having to leave the property. The 18th-century farmhouse with one guest suite has been in the Corttis family for 200 years. The suite's arrangement of two bedrooms that share a bath and private dining area is ideal for a family. **235 Corttis Rd., North Grosvenordale, 06255; (860) 935-5652.**

Friendship Valley—$$$ to $$$$
The name of this B&B on Brooklyn's main road is attributed to local heroine Prudence Crandall, who stayed here as a guest of a prominent abolitionist family. In a letter she referred to the house as "friendship's valley," and it has been known by that name since. The oldest part of the structure, in which the honeymoon suite is located, dates from about 1740. This room features a queen mahogany bed, a private bath with a whirlpool tub and a private entrance. Two other "suites" have multiple beds and are suitable for families. All the bathrooms are on the small side. Antique furnishings, refinished pine floors and fireplaces in the majority of rooms accentuate the house's traditional feel. Guests can enjoy several common rooms, and a glassed-in porch, heated in winter, is used for breakfast service. **60 Pomfret Rd. (Rte. 169), Brooklyn, 06234; (860) 779-9696.**

Karinn—$$$ to $$$$
This sprawling, 20-room, three-story Victorian home was once Miss Vinton's School for Girls (ca. 1885–1890) but was shut down because the boys at nearby Pomfret Academy were felt to be an "unwholesome influence." Its five guest rooms range in size from a couple of two-bedroom suites, one with a working fireplace, to a small room with a gender-neutral decor that can accommodate one guest comfortably. A sofa bed in a sitting room can accommodate an extra person in any party. Most bathrooms (some private; others shared) have claw-foot tubs with shower attachments. There are countless common rooms at Karinn, most of them grand in scale and furnishings, but guests will probably gravitate to the two rooms more in keeping with modern proportions: the cozy library and the hall-like game room where you can enjoy billiards along with a complimentary cocktail and snacks. A full

breakfast is included in the rate, and there's a lovely veranda and gardens. Children are welcome. **330 Pomfret St. (Rtes. 169/44), Pomfret, 06259; (860) 928-5492.**

Lord Thompson Manor—$$$ to $$$$

Manorial indeed, this 30-room mansion built in 1917 is situated on 44 wooded acres with walking trails. It was the summer home of a mercantile family from Providence, Rhode Island. Hard to categorize, it seems to fall halfway between inn and B&B. The number of rooms—eight—is small, but this is a favorite spot for weddings and banquets. The interior and exterior bespeak a different time and a pedigree of wealth. The staff stresses a high level of service, with little extras like bubble baths, fresh-squeezed orange juice and the flexibility to accommodate your schedule and special requests. Of the eight rooms, four are minisuites with private baths, and four are smaller rooms with shared baths. They all share an equestrian decorative theme and feature a wood-burning fireplace. The bathrooms are equipped with vintage claw-foot tubs and shower attachments. A full breakfast is included. Located on **Rte. 200 just east of I-395 exit 99, Thompson, 06277; (860) 923-3886.**

Chickadee Cottage—$$$

This B&B is less a cottage and more a capehouse (ca. 1910) situated on 10 acres with both modern and traditional decorative aspects that hosts Tom and Sandy Spackman have artfully combined. One very desirable room has a beamed ceiling, a four-poster double bed with a canopy of lace tatting and a private attached bath. A private entrance opens onto a garden in back. A small sofa converts to a single bed to accommodate a third person. The second guest room upstairs has a double bed, a foldout cot and a shared bath. In warm weather guests can enjoy their Continental breakfast in either a screened porch or a stunning tiled atrium overlooking a perennial garden. Children age 4 and over can be accommodated. Payment by cash or check only. Birding and hiking opportunities are across the street. The proximity of Chickadee Cottage

to Golden Hill Farm B&B next door makes it possible for the two together to accommodate a larger party. **375 Wrights Crossing Rd., Pomfret, 06259; (860) 963-0587.**

Clark Cottage at Wintergreen—$$$

This is a cottage only in the Victorian sense of being smaller than a mansion. Doris and Stanton Geary's large and lovely gray-shingled 1880s home looks much more modern than its years both inside and out. The best room has an unusual and ornate queen Italian "green bed," a private attached bath, a bright eastern and southern exposure and a working fireplace. The second room has two twin beds; the third is a suite made up of two bedrooms and a shared bath that makes a good value for a family. The house has a screened veranda overlooking a large lawn with wicker furniture for lounging. A full breakfast is included. **354 Pomfret St. (Rte. 169/44), Pomfret Center, 06259; (860) 928-5741.**

173

Felshaw Tavern—$$$

True to its name, this Georgian farmhouse was a tavern in pre-Revolutionary times. Current owner and host Herb Kinsman, a talented woodworker, handcrafted much of the reproduction furniture in the house. Two upstairs bedrooms both have queen four-poster beds and wood-burning fireplaces. The modern baths are detached but private. You'll enjoy a full breakfast in an east-facing dining area with a bay window and cathedral ceiling that lets the sun pour in. Outside are lawns and a garden sitting area for guests to enjoy. Located at the **corner of Five Mile River Rd. and Rte. 21, Putnam, 06260; (860) 928-3467.**

Golden Hill Farm—$$$

This pretty B&B on a quiet back road offers a lot of privacy because of its unique arrangement. The two guest rooms are located in a small "half cape" house, separate from the main house where hosts Nancy and Jim Weiss live. Dating from the 1790s the house is restored and nicely furnished, featuring painted wideboard floors, two working fireplaces (one in the downstairs bedroom), a galley kitchen and a living room with the second fireplace and a couple of big, inviting wing chairs. Nancy leaves the fixings for an expanded Continental breakfast for guests to prepare when they want it. The Weisses maintain a mile-long path through fields around the property on which guests can walk and enjoy the views. More birding and hiking opportunities are across the street. The proximity of Golden Hill to Chickadee Cottage B&B next door makes it possible for the two together to accommodate a larger party. **389 Wright's Crossing Rd., Pomfret, 06259; (860) 928-5531.**

Stoughton Brook Farm—$$$

Guy and Sandra Farnsworth have a beautiful, spacious house with portions dating from 1740 and 1815. If you enjoy antique furnishings, you'll like going from room to room to see what they've collected. The downstairs bedroom has a Victorian air, rich with red velvet and a working fireplace. The French Room upstairs is ornate and flowery. Both of these have queen beds and private baths with tubs. The two remaining bedrooms, each with two twin beds, form a suite with private bath or accommodations for a family or group of friends. There is also a beautiful small yard and garden for relaxing outside. **510 Buckley Highway (Rte. 190), Union, 06076; (860) 684-6510.**

Woodchuck Hill—$$$

The guest accommodations at Woodchuck Hill consist of a nice chalet apartment separate from the main house in a wooded setting on 13 acres. This is a place where you can have total privacy in a rustic setting. The apartment has a cathedral ceiling, a modern, neutral interior with comfortable furnishings, a telephone, a TV and a galley kitchen stocked with dishes, utensils, a coffeemaker and beverages. A king bed can be converted into two twins. A Continental breakfast is brought to you each morning. Because of the private setup, hosts Frank and Joan Vincent can accommodate children of any age. **256 Cemetery Rd., Canterbury, 06331; (860) 546-1278.**

Nathan Fuller House—$$ to $$$

This 18th- and 19th-century farmhouse looks appropriate in its setting on a quiet country lane perfect for long strolls. Owners Georgia

and Bruce Stauffer are from Pennsylvania Dutch country, and their background is reflected in the Shaker-like simplicity of the house's furnishings. There are two upstairs guest rooms, one with a double bed and a view over fields out back, the other with a raised four-poster queen bed and a working fireplace. Guests have the use of two baths, one upstairs and one down. Georgia serves a full breakfast in the house's original parlor where a fire is kept going in winter. Very reasonable rates. **147 Plains Rd., Scotland, 06264; (860) 456-0687.**

Isaac Shepard House—$$

This yellow colonial (ca. 1730) situated on a hilltop with views of the surrounding countryside offers comfortable and casual accommodations in an authentic old farmhouse. Host Betty Kemp's policy of pricing per person rather than per room makes this an ideal spot for single travelers on a budget. There are three rooms and two baths in the main house, plus a room in a converted barn behind the house that kids might especially like. Guests have use of the washer and dryer and a comfortable common room with a large fireplace. Kemp serves a full breakfast. There is a TV and telephone in every room and a half-mile-long walking path on the property. **165 Shepard Hill Rd., Plainfield, 06332; (860) 564-3012.**

Hotels, Motels & Inns

The Inn at Woodstock Hill—$$$ to $$$$

This pretty inn is a white clapboard Colonial Revival structure set on 14 acres, yet convenient to the main road. There are 19 rooms in the main house and 3 in the former caretaker's cottage, all traditionally furnished. Six of the rooms are minisuites with distinct sitting areas. All rooms come with TV, telephone and private bath. You might request one of the two rooms having cathedral ceilings or one with a fireplace. An expanded Continental breakfast is included. **94 Plaine Hill Rd. (enter on Rte. 169), S. Woodstock, 06267; (860) 928-0528.**

King's Inn—$$$

King's Inn is a moderately priced, moderately sized hotel. There are 20 rooms with a queen bed and walk-in shower, and 20 rooms with a full bed and full bath. One suite is an efficiency apartment with a king bed and a fully equipped kitchen. Furnishings are traditional, and there is a restaurant on the premises. King's Inn offers some package rates that include tickets to local theater performances in Putnam. **5 Heritage Rd., Putnam, 06260; (800) 541-7304** or **(860) 928-7961.**

Camping

In addition to the state campgrounds listed below, there are many commercial campgrounds in this area. The *Connecticut Campgrounds* directory published by the Connecticut Campground Owners Association (CCOA) is a good, inexpensive resource for identifying some of them. It contains a chart of member campground's amenities and a locator map. The directory costs $2 by mail, or you can get it free at member campgrounds, some visitors information centers and the occasional restaurant or convenience store. Contact the **CCOA** at **P.O. Box 27, Hartford, 06141; (860) 521-4704.**

Hopeville Pond State Park Campground—$

Hopeville Pond offers 82 wooded sites near a pond with a large, sandy, guarded beach for swimming. If you are a campground guest, there's no extra charge for access to the beach. In fact, there's a beach in the campground itself open to campers only. Fishing and boating are also allowed. The sites are shaded but not particularly private, and each one has a picnic table and fire pit. Amenities include flush toilets, hot showers, a concession stand at the beach and a dump station. Located on **Rte. 201 in Griswold.** Campground office: **(860) 376-0313.** Park office: **(860) 376-2920.**

Mashamoquet Campground—$

One of the two campgrounds associated with Mashamoquet Brook State Park (the other one

is Wolf Den), this small and lovely campground is just a few hundred feet west of the entrance to the park on Rte. 44. There are 20 sites along a short access road with a loop at the end. All sites are wooded, with picnic tables and grills. They are flat, nearly ideal tent sites, although RVs are accommodated. The only facilities are pit toilets, but during summer campers can use flush toilets at the swimming area in the park a short walk away. There is a dump station nearby. Admission to the swimming area is free to campers. There's also a small museum on the park grounds open summer weekends. Located on **Rte. 44 in Pomfret; (860) 928-6121.**

Pachaug State Forest Campground—$

There are actually three campgrounds in the Pachaug State Forest. All three are rustic, with no flush toilets or showers. Reservations are not accepted—the policy is first-come, first-served. The **Frog Hollow Horse Camp** has 18 wooded sites with facilities comparable to those at the Silvermine Horse Camp described below, but there is a small charge of $9 per night here. This campground is accessed via the main entrance to Pachaug State Forest on Rte. 49 about half a mile north of Voluntown. For nonequestrians, there is the **Green Falls Campground** ($10 per night), which has 18 wooded sites near swimming and excellent fishing in the Green Falls Reservoir. Both activities are free to campers. Every site has a picnic table and fire pit. This campground is located off Rte. 138 about 3 miles east of Voluntown. **Mt. Misery Campground** ($9 per night) is similar to Green Falls. Here you'll have access to excellent canoe fishing for trout in Mt. Misery Brook, and several other great fishing spots—Edward's Pond, Phillip's Pond and Loudon Brook—are nearby. Like Frog Hollow, this campground is located off the main entrance to the forest on Rte. 49. For more information call **(860) 376-4075.**

Silvermine Campground/Natchaug State Forest Horse Camp—no charge

This unique free campground for the exclusive use of campers traveling with horses is lo-

175

cated in a state forest riddled with old gravel and dirt roads that make great equestrian trails. Campsites (14 in all) and parking areas are extralarge to accommodate horse trailers and the animals, and each campsite has a hitching post. There are no facilities other than outhouses and water pumps, and you must pack out your own garbage. Campsites are available on a first-come, first-served basis only. The entrance to the state forest and the campground is on Rte. 198 in Eastford about 3 miles south of Rte. 44. For more information call **(860) 974-1562.**

West Thompson Lake Recreation Area Campground—$

This Army Corps of Engineers–run campground offers 27 partially wooded sites, all of which have a picnic table and fire ring. Basic sites are $10; sites with an Adirondack Shelter (an open-air structure having three sides and a roof) are $16 and sites with water and electric are $20. Recreational facilities include a playground, a horseshoe pit, staff-led nature programming on Sat. evenings and occasional tours of the dam. The campground is equipped with rest rooms, hot showers and a dump station. Campsites are available on a first-come, first-served basis only. The campground does fill up in summer, so the staff recommends that you arrive by 7:00 P.M. on Fri. to be reasonably assured of getting a site for a summer weekend. The camping season extends from the third Fri. in May through the Sun. after Labor Day. Located on **Reardon Rd. off Rte. 12 in Thompson.** Park office: **(860) 923-2982.** Campground office: **(860) 923-3121.**

Wolf Den Campground—$

The second of the two campgrounds associated with Mashamoquet Brook State Park offers 35 sites in a large open field with flush toilets, hot showers and a dump station. Sites are flat and grassy, with some juniper and spruce for privacy and shade. There is direct access to the park's trails, but the other facilities (see the Mashamoquet Campground listing for details) are a good hike or a short drive away. The entrance is on Wolf Den Dr.

near the intersection of Rtes. 44 and 101 in Pomfret. For more information call **(860) 928-6121.**

Where to Eat

Golden Lamb Buttery—$$$$

Consistently booked solid and consistently a winner of readers' choice awards and high ratings from critics, the Golden Lamb Buttery could easily be the highlight of a stay in Windham County. Hosts Jimmie and Bob Booth have perfected the art of concept dining. The concept is simple: good food, lots of entertainment and an extraordinary country setting. The fixed price of $60 (tax included, but not gratuity, wine or beer) might be a little hard to swallow at first, but once you're here you find yourself thinking it's not really unreasonable. After all, you could pay that much for dinner and concert tickets.

The food is American with a heavy emphasis on fresh produce from the Booths' gardens. The meal is served in four courses. Guests generally have a choice of four entrées and five side dishes per night. Entertainment is provided— a singer/guitarist who circulates from table to table, performing from a music menu. The country setting is a barn on 1,000-acre Hillandale Farms, surrounded by white rail fences, a pond, fields, pastured animals and stunning views from the deck where lunch is served in summer. All the dining rooms have a country decor; ask for the "bird's nest" if you want a cozy table for two.

Reservations are essential. For dinner you'll need to call weeks or months in advance; for lunch you may be able to get a seat the same day. Lunch is à la carte with prices in the $15 range. Payment is by cash or check only. Lunch is served Tue.–Sat., noon–3:00 P.M. Dinner is Fri.–Sat., 7:00 P.M.–"whenever." The restaurant is on **Bush Hill Rd. at the corner of Wolf Den Rd. in Brooklyn; (860) 774-4423.**

The Inn at Woodstock Hill—$$$ to $$$$

This American restaurant housed on the main floor of a 22-room inn serves classic dishes in

176

a traditional setting replete with table linens, silverware, wine goblets and a rosy decor, with piano music on holidays. In summer you can dine on a canopied outdoor deck. The menu is small but varied. The restaurant can be closed because of functions, so call ahead. Reservations recommended. Breakfast is served Mon.–Fri., 7:00 A.M.–9:00 A.M.; Sat.–Sun. & holidays, 8:00 A.M.–10:00 A.M. Lunch/Sun. brunch hours: Tue.–Sun., 11:00 A.M.–2:00 P.M. Dinner hours: Mon.–Sat., 5:00 P.M.–9:00 P.M.; Sun., 3:30 P.M.–7:00 P.M. **94 Plaine Hill Rd. (enter on Rte. 169), S. Woodstock, 06267; (860) 928-0528.**

Golden Creek—$$$

This family-style restaurant offers a little bit of everything, from seafood casserole, fettucine carbonara and steak Diane to finger food, sandwiches, burgers, pizza, grinders, salad plates and kid's portions. The setting is casual, and the place is usually jam-packed on weekend nights. Hours: 11:00 A.M.–10:00 P.M. daily; take-out until 11:00 P.M. on Fri. & Sat. Located on **Rte. 12 just south of Rte. 21, Attawaugan, 06241; (860) 774-0167.**

Main Street Café—$$$

For lunch or dinner in a casual tavern atmosphere, Main Street Café is a good choice. There's an extensive list of hot and cold sandwiches, some on the unusual side. They also offer a full menu of American chicken, seafood and beef dishes, pastas, soups and salads, several vegetarian options and a kid's menu. Or try one of their large selection of microbrewery beers and some finger food. Hours: Sun.–Mon., 4:00 P.M.–10:00 P.M.; Tue.–Thu., 11:00 A.M.–10:00 P.M.; Fri.–Sat., 11:00 A.M.–11:00 P.M. Pub open until midnight Sun.–Wed. & 1:00 A.M. Thu.–Sat. Pub menu served until midnight most nights. **877 Main St., Willimantic, 06226; (860) 423-6777.**

Modesto's—$$$

Modesto's is one of the more frequently recommended restaurants in the Norwich area. Most people think of it as specializing in Italian food, but I recommend choosing from the Mexican offerings, the steaks or the seafood. The atmosphere is subdued, and quiet solo

entertainment is offered some nights. Hours: from 11:30 A.M. daily, closing Mon.–Thu. at 10:00 P.M., Fri.–Sat. at 11:00 P.M., Sun. at 9:00 P.M. **10 Rte. 32, Franklin, 06254; (860) 887-7755.**

Vernon Stiles Inn—$$$

Once a busy stagecoach stop, this old establishment (ca. 1818) has lots of character and does staunchly American cuisine (roasts, broiled fish, etc.) quite well. The lunch menu is a bit lighter, with hearty salads and hot sandwiches in addition to full entrées. There is an all-you-can-eat Fri. lunch buffet for $7.25. In fall and winter they sometimes offer "stew and story" evenings, which are a combination of dinner and entertainment. The meal is not necessarily a literal stew and can be anything hearty and not too complicated. Stew and story begins around 6:30 P.M. and lasts about two hours. Lunch/brunch hours: Wed.–Fri., 11:30 A.M.–2:00 P.M. (Fri. buffet starts at noon); Sun., 11:00 A.M.–2:00 P.M. Dinner hours: Sun.–Mon. & Wed.–Thu., 4:30 P.M.–8:00 P.M.; Fri.–Sat., 4:30 P.M.–9:30 P.M. Located at the **intersection of Rtes. 200 and 193, Thompson, 06277; (860) 923-9571.**

The Vine Bistro—$$$

The Vine Bistro gets my award for most cosmopolitan restaurant in the Northeast. It has a bright, neutral interior with white walls, blonde wood flooring and furniture and nice lighting. The tables for two and four have faux marble tops, and abstract paintings adorn the walls. Having the waitstaff—whose service is stylish and quick but friendly—dressed all in casual black lends an air of hipness to the place. Freshness is the key to their culinary approach, as the menu boasts, and the name of the restaurant (as in "fresh from the vine") was chosen to reflect that. It also has one of the better selections of vegetarian food in the area. Hours: Tue.–Sat., 11:00 A.M.–9:00 P.M.; Sun., 11:00 A.M.–8:00 P.M. **85 Main St., Putnam, 06260; (860) 928-1660.**

Brom's—$$ to $$$

This relatively new restaurant serves an area that sorely needed a good, family-style, three-meal-a-day place. It serves a

The Quiet Corner

little bit of everything from steaks to salads, grinders, seafood and more, and breakfast from an early hour. Hours: open 6:00 A.M. year-round, closing at 10:00 P.M. Mon.–Thu. (9:00 P.M. in winter); 11:00 P.M. Fri.–Sat. (10:00 P.M. in winter); 8:00 P.M. Sun. **180 Westminster Rd. (Rte. 14 west of Rte. 169), Canterbury, 06331; (860) 546-9409.**

J. D. Cooper's—$$ to $$$

J. D. Cooper's is a moderately priced establishment that tends to be the choice of locals meeting for a casual lunch. It was a golf clubhouse before its conversion into a restaurant. The cuisine is American—steaks, seafood, pasta, salads—plus a few odds and ends like fajitas. There is also a cozy lounge and a sports pub with pool tables, a wide-screen TV and games. Hours: 11:30 A.M.–10:00 P.M. daily (the kitchen stops serving around 9:00). **146 Park Rd., Putnam, 06260; (860) 928-0501.**

Stoggy Hollow General Store and Restaurant—$$ to $$$

Miles from anywhere but worth the drive, Stoggy Hollow offers casual family dining in a house dating from 1836. It serves three meals daily, and the bakery turns out breads, pies (about a dozen flavors at any one time), oversized muffins, pastries and cookies for eating in or taking home. The menu, which changes frequently, is broad-based American, ranging from prime rib to gussied-up home-style dishes like meatloaf Florentine. There are three dining areas: the house's original parlor with a fireplace, an enclosed atrium (a modern addition) with skylights and heating in winter and the open-air porch. Hours: Sun.–Thu., 7:00 A.M.–8:00 P.M.; Fri.–Sat., 7:00 A.M.–9:00 P.M. **492 Rte. 198 (a quarter-mile north of Rte. 171), Woodstock Valley, 06281; (860) 974-3814.**

Fox Hunt Farms—$$

Fox Hunt Farms is basically a deli whose strength is in its selection of fillings—everything from bologna and American cheese to pâtés and duck—plus a fairly wide choice of breads to wrap around them. You'll also find soups, salads and a few hot items. There are small tables inside and a deck outside, plus a

sweet shop next door. Hours: Tue.–Fri., 10:00 A.M.–7:00 P.M.; Sat.–Sun., 10:00 A.M.–5:00 P.M. **292 Rte. 169, S. Woodstock, 06267; (860) 928-0714.**

Traveler Restaurant and Book Store—$$

"The food and book people," as they call themselves, have a nifty gimmick: they give away a hardcover book to every customer. To supply their library, they scour auctions and buy out bookstores and libraries. Anywhere from 2,000 to 3,000 books fill the shelves in the dining areas, and there's also a used bookstore with 20,000–30,000 titles for sale in the basement. As for the food, it's American with a turkey specialty. They serve the noble bird five ways: pot pie, traditional Thanksgiving-style dinner and as a hot, cold or club sandwich. Other menu items range from steaks to seafood to grilled cheese sandwiches. Hours: 7:00 A.M.–9:00 P.M. daily. **1257 Buckley Hwy. (Rte. 171 at I-84 exit 74), Union, 06076; (860) 684-4920.**

The Vanilla Bean—$$

The Vanilla Bean is a casual, mostly self-serve student hangout capable of delivering great food and lively entertainment. Even if it weren't the only restaurant in town, kids from Pomfret Academy probably would still choose it over anything else. The dining areas are simply furnished, airy and inviting. There are umbrella-topped tables outside for enjoying a cool breeze on a warm day. In summer they grill up burgers and other items out here. Inside you order at the counter from selections on huge blackboards and are given a card to take to your table. When your meal is ready, it is brought to you. The Vanilla Bean is renowned for its sandwiches, but there's also a choice of several hot entrées daily, such as baked pasta or burritos, as well as salads and soups that are meals in themselves. There are usually as many vegetarian as meat-based dishes, and the desserts are really a treat. Hours: Mon.–Tue., 7:00 A.M.–3:00 P.M.; Wed.–Fri., 7:00 A.M.–8:00 P.M.; Sat.–Sun., 8:00 A.M.–8:00 P.M.; in summer open until 9:00 P.M. Fri. & Sat. Located at the **corner of Rtes. 44, 169 and 97, Pomfret, 06258; (860) 928-1562.**

Zip's—$$

A classic diner from both culinary and aesthetic standpoints, Zip's is fun, and inexpensive and offers the sort of comfort food that is especially welcome when you're on the road. Its rounded exterior is straight out of the 1950s. Inside it's largish and comfortable, with lots of booths and a spacious lunch counter. Folks are friendly if you are. And the food? Lots of breakfast items, sandwiches, burgers, straightforward entrées like broiled fish and pot roast and, of course, homemade desserts. If you like diners, you'll love Zip's. Credit cards not accepted. Hours: 6:00 A.M.–9:00 P.M. daily. Only a stone's throw from I-395 exit 93, Zip's is located at the **intersection of Rtes. 101 and 12 in Dayville; (860) 774-6335.**

Bill's Bread and Breakfast—$

This great little bakery is one of the best choices in the area for a satisfying, inexpensive breakfast or lunch. They make the breads and baked goods they serve with their meals, and their cinnamon rolls are nearly perfect. They have a full breakfast menu as well as sandwiches and soups for lunch. Hours: Tue.–Fri., 6:00 A.M.–3:00 P.M.; Sat.–Sun., 7:00 A.M.–2:00 P.M. (breakfast only). **149 Providence St. (Rte. 171), Putnam, 06260; (860) 928-9777.**

Coffeehouses, Sweets & Treats

The Grapevine—$$

This combination tearoom/gift shop serves a small menu of lunch items such as focaccia, soups and salads as well as delectable Jamaican meat and veggie pies. They offer 80–90 teas ranging from popular and uncommon true teas to herbal blends. They also stock a wide range of gifts, clothing and tea paraphernalia. Hours: Tue.–Sat., 10:00 A.M.–5:30 P.M. **861 Main St., Willimantic, 06226; (860) 423-1109.**

Olde English Tea Room—$$

At this reservation-only tearoom you can enjoy a tea in the setting of an old center-chimney colonial home. Make sure to take a look at the tea-related art and collections of tea items scattered about. Owner Pearl Dexter also publishes a national tea magazine. **3 Devotion Rd., Scotland, 06264; (860) 456-8651.**

The Fox's Fancy Sweet Shoppe—$

This great little place for ice cream and sweets is located right next door to Fox Hunt Farms, so you can get a real meal and then walk over for dessert. Hours vary according to the season, but are usually Tue.–Fri., noon–9:00 P.M., & Sat.–Sun., 11:00 A.M.–9:00 P.M.; closed Jan.–Mar. **290 Rte. 169, S. Woodstock, 06267; (860) 928-2558.**

Services

Local Visitors Information

Northeast Connecticut Visitors District, P.O. Box 598, Putnam, 06260; (860) 928-1228.

Transportation

Interstate bus service to Danielson and Willimantic is available through **Bonanza Bus Lines.** Call **(800) 556-3815** or **(860) 456-0440** for schedule and fare information. Regional bus service is provided by the **Windham Transit District** at **(860) 456-2221** and the **Northeastern Connecticut Transit District** at **(860) 774-1253.** For taxi service in the local area call **Colchester Cab** out of Willimantic at **(860) 423-5700** or **Community Cab** out of Pomfret at **(860) 963-0690** or **(860) 774-9484.**

179

Lebanon

The Lebanon area is a part of the state to which few tourists venture, not for lack of worthiness but because all the major highways except one miss it, and big attractions on the Connecticut River or in New London or Mystic or Hartford capture their time and attention. Yet it is a place of unusual importance in the state's history. Although many Connecticut natives today might not know where Lebanon is, in 1776 the name would have been on everyone's lips. Lebanon was the home of Connecticut's Revolutionary War governor Jonathan Trumbull, the only colonial governor to serve through and after the war from 1769 to 1784. Many colonial governors, such as William Franklin, governor of New Jersey and son of Benjamin Franklin, were avowed Tories and were removed from office or resigned.

Trumbull was a close confidant of Gen. George Washington, who referred to him affectionately as "Brother Jonathan." He mustered troops, food, munitions and supplies for Washington's needy troops many times over, perhaps literally saving Patriot soldiers from starvation at Valley Forge and earning Connecticut its wartime nickname "the Provision State." Washington wrote in a postwar letter that "but for Jonathan Trumbull, the war could not have been carried to a successful conclusion."

Today Lebanon is trying to make its story known. Several historically significant buildings are open to the public, including the homes of Jonathan Trumbull and his son Jonathan Trumbull, Jr. (also a governor of the state and Gen. Washington's private secretary), and the so-called Revolutionary War Office (the elder Trumbull's general store from which the war effort was run locally). Lebanon's most prominent feature is a mile-long green that is still in agricultural use. By tradition, property owners around it can make hay on the portion of the green in front of their house. Many people want the tradition to continue, so the grass is allowed to grow, and on dry days in June the meadow is mowed.

Although Revolutionary War history is one of the best reasons to come to the area, it isn't the only reason. Several exceptional golf courses take advantage of the rolling, uncluttered landscape, as do several beautiful state parks and forests that offer some of the best fishing in the state, plus swimming and hiking. The Old Comstock Covered Bridge is a scenic landmark, and Marlborough Country Barn is the ultimate shopping experience for folks trying to get the colonial look in their home.

History

The towns in this area were established on land deeded by or purchased from various Native American groups beginning in the 1660s. In most cases settlement occurred around 1700. Located at the crossroads of routes connecting New York, Boston, Hartford and Norwich, Lebanon grew rather quickly to become the sixth most populous community in the state by 1756. Nonetheless, "populous" is a relative term, especially since the Lebanon of 1756 also included present-day Columbia. The Duc de Lauzun, a French officer who wintered in town with his Legion of Horse in 1780–1781, put it in perspective when he wrote, "Siberia alone can be compared to Lebanon, which is composed only of some cottages scattered in the midst of a vast forest."

But this Yankee Siberia was a hive of activity. In May 1775 the Council of Safety (also called the War Council of Connecticut) was appointed to perform all necessary functions relating to the war effort when the General Assembly was not in session. It held over 1,200 meetings in both Lebanon and Hartford. Those in Lebanon occurred in the War Office, the converted general store of Governor Jonathan Trumbull. In it Trumbull received a parade of notable figures, including Americans George Washington, Thomas Jefferson, Samuel Adams, Benjamin Franklin and John Jay, as well as French commanders Rochambeau and Lafayette.

After the war people turned their attention to developing the area's resources. The outlet of Lake Pocotopaug in East Hampton was a natural place for industry to arise. Early on there was an iron forge and a scythe factory there. William Barton began manufacturing sleigh bells and hand bells in 1808, and soon East Hampton (which was called Chatham until 1915) was known as "Bell Town." One manufacturer—Bevin Bros.—remains. The lake was also used for recreation: in the mid-1800s horse races were held on it when it froze in winter, and in the early 20th century there was a casino on the shore. Today it's really only accessible to residents.

In the 1800s textiles were king throughout eastern Connecticut, and this area was no exception. Woolens, cottons and silks were woven at mills in Hebron, Marlborough and elsewhere. Down in Colchester the Haywood Rubber Co., in business from 1847 to 1893, was famed for its "spading boots." These goods and others were transported to market after 1873 on the New York and Boston Railroad, more commonly called the Airline.

The Airline was built as a high-speed passenger line between New York and Boston. Its "Ghost Train"—so called because it was painted white—was *the* fashionable way to travel in its time. Because it followed a straighter line than previous routes, the Airline shaved more than two hours off the travel time. But to do so it had to cross some difficult country. The Airline was remarkable for the geographic obstacles it overcame, necessitating long trestles over rivers and valleys. The ride was supposed to be quite breathtaking. Unfortunately, these elevated portions of the line were filled in with gravel in the early 1900s to allow the structures to support heavier trains. Passenger service ceased in 1927, and all service stopped in 1965. The Airline is now under development as a linear hiking/biking trail.

Major Attractions

Governor Jonathan Trumbull House

Jonathan Trumbull, Sr., served as Connecticut's enormously popular governor from 1769 to 1785 and is said to be the only colonial governor who supported the Patriot cause. More than 65 years old when the Revolutionary War began, he led the state with remarkable energy and bears no small responsibility for the American victory.

The Trumbull House, which has been moved from its original site about a block away, was built by Jonathan's father Joseph between 1735 and 1740 and has been run as a museum by the Connecticut Daughters of the American Revolution since 1935. Some of the furnishings are original Trumbull pieces. Tours focus on Trumbull's family life and professional accomplishments, and if you wish to see it, the grave of this most influential of Connecticut's native sons is located in Trumbull Cemetery less than 1 mile east of town on Rte. 207. The Wadsworth Stable next to the house (moved from its original location in Hartford) holds a collection of ironware and horse- or ox-drawn vehicles. Admission: $2 adults, free to children under 12. Hours: Tue.–Sat., 1:00 P.M.–5:00 P.M., mid-May–mid-Oct. Located on **W. Town St., Lebanon, 06249; (860) 642-7558.**

Marlborough Country Barn

If you are in the market for the New England look in home furnishings, there's really no more pleasant or complete place to visit in Connecticut than Marlborough Country Barn. The variety of goods it carries—furniture, textiles, hearth accessories, lighting, hardware and more—and a picturesque pondside location in a small town make this cluster of shops well worth seeking out. There's also a Christmas shop and a good little restaurant (Sadler's Ordinary) at which to have lunch. Hours: Tue.–Sat., 10:00 A.M.–5:30 P.M.; Sun., noon–5:00 P.M. **61 N. Main St., Marlborough, 06447; (800) 852-8893** or **(860) 295-8231.**

Other Attractions

Old Comstock Covered Bridge

Eastern Connecticut's only remaining major covered bridge crosses the Salmon River on the edge of the Salmon River State Forest at the East Hampton/Colchester town line. Open to pedestrian traffic only, it's a good starting point for the nice walk described under Hiking. It's also suitable for a picnic or just taking souvenir photos, despite the fact that it sometimes gets graffitied. Located on the corner of Rte. 16 and Comstock Bridge Rd. Follow the orange blazes to pick up the Comstock Bridge Connector Trail.

Festivals and Events

Hebron Maple Festival
second weekend in Mar.

The Hebron Maple Festival is a good place to discover just how good Connecticut maple syrup is. Stop at any local business to get a map of six sugarhouses open for self-guided tours. There's also a quilt show at the Old Town Hall, a book sale at the library, pony rides for kids, sled dog and crafts demos and food vendors. Hours: 10:00 A.M.–5:00 P.M. both days. For more information call **(860) 228-9317.**

Hebron Historical Society Doll and Miniature Show and Sale
first Sat. in June

The longest-running and probably largest doll show in the state features antique and collectible dolls plus everything related to them: dollhouses, clothing, wigs, repair services and more. About 75 exhibitors set up in the gymnasium of the RHAM high school on **RHAM Rd. off Rte. 85 in Hebron.** Admission: $3 adults, $.50 children under 12. Hours: 10:00 A.M.–4:00 P.M. For more information call **(860) 228-8471.**

Colchester Historical Society Craft Fair and Connecticut Valley Field Music Muster
late July

Similar to the Marlborough muster listed below but on a smaller scale, the Colchester event always takes place the Sat. after the Deep River Muster described in the **Old Saybrook/Old Lyme** chapter. The parade of a dozen or so corps begins at noon, and the music lasts until 3:00 P.M. Meanwhile, upward of 125 crafters exhibit their wares on Colchester green 10:00 A.M.–4:00 P.M. Craft fair admission: $2 adults, children under 12 free, the muster is free. For more information call **(860) 267-2640.**

Lebanon Country Fair
second weekend in Aug.

This medium-sized fair has a small-town flavor with "big fair" activities. Highlights include fireworks late Sat. night, historical society and farm museum exhibits with demonstrations of old-time crafts, an antique machinery display, short helicopter rides during daylight hours (most years), a horseshoe tournament and silly contests on Sat. for adults and kids. On all three days you'll find agricultural exhibits and competitions, plus a midway and stage entertainment. On-site and remote parking is free; shuttle buses are provided. Admission: $5 adults, $4 seniors, children under 12 free; $1 off admission on Fri. Hours: Fri., 6:00 P.M.–11:30 P.M.; Sat., 9:00 A.M.–midnight; Sun., 9:00 A.M.–10:30 P.M. The Lebanon Fairground is on **Mack Rd. in Lebanon.** For more information prior to the fair call **(860) 423-4886.** During the fair call **(860) 642-6012.**

Hebron Harvest Fair
weekend after Labor Day (Thu.–Sun.)

The third-largest country fair in Connecticut is four days of harvest celebration as summer draws to a close. The agricultural and home-making exhibits take center stage, with three days of horse shows, working draft animal demonstrations and ongoing competitions and judging in the barns. The week's livestock competitions culminate in a premium showmanship award on Sun. afternoon for the best animal in the fair. On the entertainment side there are stage performers, a midway with rides and games plus a carnival area for small children age 6–10. Kids will also enjoy participating in the Farm Games on Fri. & Sat. On-site and remote parking is free; shuttle buses are provided. Admission: $5 adults ($6 Sun.), $3 seniors, children 12 and under free. Hours: Thu., 6:00 P.M.–10:00 P.M.; Fri., noon–11:00 P.M.; Sat., 9:00 A.M.–11:00 P.M.; Sun., 9:00 A.M.–10:00 P.M. Hebron Fairground is on **Rte. 85 in Hebron; (860) 228-0892.**

Getting There

Lebanon is about half an hour southeast of Hartford by car. Pick up Rte. 2 south or east in East Hartford and take it all the way to exit 18 in Colchester. Rte. 16 east to Rte. 207 east will bring you directly to Lebanon green.

Marlborough Junior Ancient Muster
weekend after Labor Day

The Marlborough Junior Ancient Fife & Drum Corps hosts this, the third-largest ancient muster in the southern New England region. Thirty to forty corps from all over the Northeast participate in the parade and extended jam session at Blish Park on Park Rd. at Lake Terramuggus in Marlborough. In even years the event happens Fri. & Sat.; in odd years it takes place Sat. & Sun. It starts with a military tattoo—an opening ceremony at which up to five corps perform—7:00 P.M.–midnight on the first night. The parade begins on day two at noon, and the music continues until evening. For more information call **(860) 295-0749** or **(860) 295-9426.**

Outdoor Activities

Biking

Mountain Biking

Gay City State Park
Mountain biking is allowed on the network of trails at Gay City, which provide a nice variety of climbs, wet areas, bridges and rocky, rutted stretches. The only exception is the section of the blue-blazed Shenipsit Trail that leads west out of the park, which is off-limits to bikes. For more information, see the entry under Hiking.

Hurd State Park
The woods roads leading into this park make for good riding, as do the interconnected trails,

but be forewarned that the steep paths leading down to the river are daunting. For more information, see the listing under Hiking.

Meshomasic State Forest

This large parcel of state forest is peppered with drivable dirt roads and smaller trails that have been cut through the woods. Be aware that there are rattlesnakes in this area. They are protected but dangerous, so avoid them and do not disturb any you encounter. Enter the forest by driving south on Clark Hill Rd. across the Glastonbury/Portland town line. Park along the side of the road and ride wherever it looks interesting.

Salmon River State Forest/
Airline Trail

The Airline State Park Trail follows 7 miles of the route of the defunct New York and Boston Railroad. It can be hard riding because portions of the trail are covered with crushed stone and maintenance is minimal (although increasing as funds become available), but it's notable for gravel fills around the original trestles as high as 150 feet. You can access one of the better sections of trail from River Rd. in Colchester. For much of its length River Rd. parallels a section of the Salmon River. It's quiet and nice for biking. Somewhere near the middle, you'll find a fairly big parking lot and a stone railroad trestle where you can pick up the Airline Trail. You'll come out on Smith St. in East Hampton.

Road Biking

This whole area is generally hilly, but the back roads of Lebanon, especially around Red Cedar Lake, are quite suitable for touring. The *Northeast Connecticut's Bike Guide* available from the Northeast Connecticut Visitors District suggests a 25-mile loop through Lebanon and Columbia that can be modified to make it a few miles shorter.

Boating

The main recreational body of water in the area is **Pickerel Lake** on Pickerel Lake Rd. in Colchester. There's a public boat launch and

an 8 m.p.h. speed limit except on summer days after 11:00 A.M., so you can water-ski here. The 8 m.p.h. speed limit at **Holbrook Pond** in Hebron is in effect at all times and the shoreline is undeveloped, so it's a better place to bring a canoe or rowboat. To find the boat launch, follow signs from Rte. 85 north of Hebron town center.

Fishing

Lakes and Ponds

Largemouth bass and several kinds of panfish are what you'll find in most of the ponds in this area open to the public for fishing. If you plan to fish from a motorboat, the best choice is **Pickerel Lake** in Colchester. The only shore access is at the state boat launch on Pickerel Lake Rd. Pickerel Lake is a bass management area where specific limits are in effect that anglers should check on in advance. A quiet spot where you can fish from a boat or from anywhere on shore is **Holbrook Pond** off Rte. 85 in Hebron. It's in the middle of a small patch of state forest, so the shoreline is totally undeveloped. Another peaceful place to fish from shore is **Red Cedar Lake** in Lebanon near the "Four Corners," where Lebanon, Bozrah, Colchester and Salem meet. Park in the pullout at the top of the lake on Camp Moween Rd.

If it's trout you're after, **Day Pond** in the state park of the same name is stocked. Boats are prohibited, but you can fish from anywhere on shore except the beach area. At this park there's also a concrete pad for wheelchair fishing access and reserved parking close by.

Rivers and Streams

The **Salmon River Trout Management Area** is extremely picturesque and heavily stocked with Atlantic salmon as well as brown, brook and rainbow trout. Anglers are limited to fly fishing only. You'll find the area along River Rd. off Comstock Bridge Rd. in Colchester. Look for signs announcing the trout management area and park in any of the pullouts nearby. Physically challenged anglers can use a special access area with a paved ramp down to the water's edge and two concrete pads that extend out into the river. There's even a picnic table here with one seat removed so a wheelchair can be rolled up to it.

The **Connecticut River** is accessible from Hurd State Park on Hurd Park Rd. off Rte. 151 in East Hampton. You have to walk a short distance down some steep trails—too steep for carrying a boat—to get to the riverbank, but it's an especially lovely spot when you do get there. Expect to find northern pike, bass, white perch and channel catfish.

Golf

Connecticut magazine recently rated both of the courses below among the top ten in the state. When they host tournaments, they are closed for public play, so call ahead for a tee time. They begin taking reservations one week in advance for weekday times and Mon. beginning at 8:00 A.M. for the following weekend.

Blackledge Golf Course
With three 9-hole courses that can be played individually or in combination for a full round of 18, Blackledge has a unique setup. From the white tee, yardages are in the 6,200-foot range. The combination known as Links is noted for tight fairways and water on four holes. Blackledge is closed to the public for league play Mon.–Thu., 3:30 P.M.–5:30 P.M., mid-Apr.–Aug. It has a pro shop, practice areas for putting, chipping and driving, showers, lockers, a restaurant and a lounge. Rentals and lessons are available. Season: Mar.–Dec. **180 West St., Hebron, 06248; (860) 228-0250.**

Tallwood Country Club
Fans of this 18-hole course applaud the attractive setting, fast greens and a layout that is playable yet challenging for both novice and expert golfers. From the white tee it is a 72 par, 6,126-yard course. The course closes to the public for league play on weekdays, 3:30 P.M.–5:45 P.M. It offers all rentals, lessons, a pro shop and a snack bar. Season: Mar.–snow cover. **91 North St. (Rte. 85), Hebron, 06248; (860) 646-1151.**

Hiking

Day Pond State Park/ Salmon River State Forest
The blue-blazed Salmon River Trail is a nice 4-mile loop through woodland with an orange-blazed connector (another 4 miles round-trip) that takes you directly to the Old Comstock Covered Bridge described under Major Attractions. There's also a swimming area on the pond itself. A parking fee of $5 for in-state vehicles and $8 for out-of-state vehicles is charged on summer weekends and holidays. To get to the park, follow the signs from Rte. 149 north of Rte. 16 in Colchester. Park office: **(860) 295-9523.**

Gay City State Park
This beautiful 1,500-acre park set amid rolling mountains is named after the Gay family who settled here in 1796 along with several other adherents of a religious sect. The foundation of the sawmill they built, which provided the lumber for their homes, can still be seen along the Outer Loop Trail. Beaver activity can be extremely evident below the swimming pond, and it's interesting for children to see the signs of beaver habitation. Iron in the surrounding soil and rock causes the streams to have a reddish cast in places. The hiking trails here are a nice length for an afternoon hike. One highlight of the park is a swimming area on a dammed portion of a river. A parking fee of $5 for in-state vehicles and $8 for out-of-state vehicles is charged on summer weekends and holidays. Located on **Rte. 85 in Hebron; (860) 295-9523.**

Hurd State Park
Hurd is the largest and perhaps the wildest of the state parks on the Connecticut River. It contains an extensive network of trails, and the maps posted at the trailheads color-code the trails according to the difficulty of the terrain, so you can pick a route to correspond to your level of fitness and be fairly assured of not having to turn back. Unfortunately for those hoping for an easy hike and an opportunity to get close to the water, most of the flat trails are on the inland side of the park. The

185

slopes descending into the valley are fairly precipitous and not recommended for the inexperienced. Located on **Hurd Park Rd. off Rte. 151 in East Hampton; (860) 526-2336.**

Shenipsit Trail

A short distance up this blue-blazed trail described and mapped in the *Connecticut Walk Book*, you can enjoy a noted overlook of Great Hill Pond and the Connecticut River. It starts in East Hampton off Gadpouch Rd., a continuation of Great Hill Rd. The overlook is a white-blazed side trail less than half a mile from the start. This is a linear trail, so return the way you came or park a second vehicle at the first road crossing (Dickinson Rd. in Glastonbury).

Skiing

The trails at several area state parks and forests are excellent for cross-country skiing when there is adequate snow cover. At **Gay City State Park** some trails are winding and narrow, whereas others are broad and straight; use discretion. The trails at **Hurd State Park** are even more challenging, but they are blazed according to difficulty, and maps posted at several spots provide the legend. The Comstock Bridge Connector Trail at **Day Pond State Park** is broad, straight and most suitable for less experienced skiers. For directions to these parks, see the listings under Hiking.

Swimming

Day Pond and **Gay City State Parks** have very similar swimming facilities on small ponds, and they're both exceptionally pretty. In addition to the beaches, you'll find lots of picnic tables with grills, bathhouses and hiking trails. For more information on and directions to either park, see the listings under Hiking.

Seeing and Doing

Museums and Historic Sites

All of Lebanon's principal historic buildings open to the public are within easy walking distance of one another, clustered around Lebanon's prairielike green. Three of them (the Governor Jonathan Trumbull House, the Jonathan Trumbull, Jr., House and the Revolutionary War Office) are tied to the Trumbull family and the Revolutionary War period. All three are run by different organizations, and in the past they have not always kept similar hours, but there are plans afoot to coordinate them, so check beforehand the hours of any you plan to visit. The Governor Jonathan Trumbull House is described under Major Attractions.

In addition to the listings here, a new museum focusing on all aspects of Lebanon's history is being built on the green by the local historical society. It should be open by the time this book appears but may be a bit of a work in progress for a while. For more information call the town hall at **(860) 642-6100.**

Dr. William Beaumont House

Visitors knowledgeable about the history of medicine may known the name of Dr. William Beaumont, called the "father of the physiology of digestion." This house (ca. 1760) in which Beaumont lived before he became an Army doctor has a small room furnished as an early 19th-century doctor's office and exhibits explaining an extraordinary set of experiments he conducted that led to our first understanding of digestion. Admission by donation. Hours: Sat., 1:00 P.M.–5:00 P.M. **169 W. Town St., Lebanon, 06249; (860) 642-6744.**

Jonathan Trumbull, Jr., House

This house (ca. 1769) is named for its most prominent resident, the son of Connecticut's Revolutionary War governor Jonathan Trumbull. Trumbull, Jr., served in many capacities in the fledgling U.S. government, including Speaker of the House and senator, and was also governor of Connecticut during 1798–1809. The interior of his house has several features of architectural interest dating from a modification by master joiner Isaac Fitch. The museum is a work in progress. Plans call for period reproduction furnishings, a historically accurate design for the grounds and exhibits on Trumbull and Fitch. Admission: $2 adults, children free. Hours: Sat., 1:00

P.M.–5:00 P.M., mid-May–mid-Oct. Located on **Rte. 87 about a quarter-mile north of Rte. 207 in Lebanon.** For more information call the town hall at **(860) 642-6100.**

Revolutionary War Office

When the Revolutionary War began, Governor Jonathan Trumbull's two-room general store was converted into the principal meeting place of the Council of Safety, a committee that co-ordinated the war effort on a day-to-day basis. It now houses artifacts such as an interesting musket with a 1777 inscription and written materials giving background on the Trumbull family and Lebanon. Hours: Sat., 1:30 P.M.–5:00 P.M., June–Sept.; Sun., 1:30 P.M.–4:30 P.M., June–Aug. Located on **W. Town St., Lebanon, 06249; (860) 642-7558.**

Where to Stay

Bed & Breakfasts

Olivia's Garden—$$$

Named in reference to both the daughter of hosts Carol and Tom Puckett and the self-service fruit and vegetable stand they operate outside their home, Olivia's Garden is a re-laxed, comfortable B&B on one of Columbia's main streets with two guest rooms in a modern family home. The rooms each have a double bed, and they share a bathroom. A Continental breakfast is included. Kids will find the pick-your-own strawberry patch, the cider mill and everything else a blast. **256 Rte. 66 (1 mile west of Rte. 87), Columbia, 06237; (860) 228-8070.**

Camping

Sites for campers arriving by canoe are avail-able at Hurd State Park in East Hampton. For details, see the listing on River Camping in the **Old Saybrook/Old Lyme** chapter. There are also several commercial campgrounds in the area. The *Connecticut Campgrounds* directory published by the Connecticut Campground Owners Association (CCOA) is a good, inex-pensive resource for identifying some of them.

It contains a chart of each member camp-ground's amenities and a locator map. The directory costs $2 by mail, or you can get it free at member campgrounds, some visitors information centers and the occasional restau-rant or convenience store. Contact the **CCOA** at **P.O. Box 27, Hartford, 06141; (860) 521-4704.**

Cottages

Cottages around Columbia Lake are occasion-ally available for rental. The best way to find one is to check for ads in the Sun. *Hartford Courant.*

Spas

The Spa at Grand Lake—$$$$

This spa and weight-loss center with basic overnight accommodations is located on 75 acres next to Lake Williams. Rates include al-most everything except salon services: daily massage; participation in all the exercise pro-grams from aerobics to yoga; use of all the facilities (indoor and outdoor pools, weight-training equipment, tennis courts, sauna and more); three low-fat, low-calorie meals each day; evening entertainment and ac-commodations. **1667 Exeter Rd. (Rte. 207), Lebanon, 06249; (860) 642-4306** (in Con-necticut) or **(800) 843-7721** (out-of-state).

Where to Eat

Marlborough Tavern—$$$

Both the food and the atmosphere are good reasons to visit this restaurant in a historic colonial building that was a tavern as far back as 1740 and is still very much the gathering place for locals. Ancient wooden beams, pan-eling and fireplaces make for a cozy feel in the dining rooms, and the pub is an appealing place to meet with friends. The menu is basi-cally American but ranges from fish 'n' chips to teriyaki, with light fare available in the pub. Mon.–Sat. each night's specials have a theme. An excellent all-around choice for couples, families and groups. Casual to moderately dressy attire. Lunch: Mon.–Sat., 11:30 A.M.–2:30 P.M. Dinner: Mon.–Thu., 5:00 P.M.–9:30 P.M.; Fri.–Sat., 5:00 P.M.–10:30 P.M. Open continuously on Sun., 11:30 A.M.–9:00 P.M., serving brunch until 3:00 P.M. and dinner thereafter. Located at the **corner of Main St. and Rte. 66, Marlborough, 06447; (860) 295-8229.**

NuNu's Bistro—$$ to $$$

A real sleeper tucked away off Colchester's green, NuNu's attempts to bring a little dining flair to this underserved area while also offering a children's menu to satisfy kids who prefer the familiar. At lunch you can expect to find frittatas and numerous sandwiches, pastas and a few meat-and-potato entrées. The last category is expanded at dinner and complemented by a number of specials. The menu is basically Italian-American, and you are invited to bring your own beer or wine. A little hard to find, it's in a former carriage house behind another house on the green. Keep an eye out for signs. Lunch hours: Mon.–Sat., 11:00 A.M.–2:00 P.M. Dinner served Mon.–Wed., 5:00 P.M.–8:00 P.M.; Thu.–Sat. until 9:00 P.M. **45 Hayward Ave., Colchester, 06415; (860) 537-6299.**

Sadler's Ordinary—$$ to $$$

This casual restaurant at Marlborough Country Barn is worth stopping at even if you're not on a shopping spree. It's a something-for-everyone kind of place serving good food and especially handy because they serve breakfast, lunch and dinner and sell bakery items. It features lots of light dishes such as salads, sandwiches, soups and quiche, but they also serve full entrées of seafood, pasta and comfort food such as pot pies and meatloaf. Hours: Tue.–Thu., 6:00 A.M.–8:30 P.M.; Fri.–Sat., 7:00 A.M.–9:00 P.M.; Sun., 7:00 A.M.–7:00 P.M. **61 N. Main St., Marlborough, 06447; (860) 295-0006.**

Benjamin's—$ to $$$

Benjamin's is a family-style restaurant/lounge. The menu of daily specials has dishes presented with more flair than the items on the small regular menu, which consists of meat-and-potatoes American fare. Mon. nights the restaurant offers a special menu of "home cooking" dishes (spaghetti, liver and onions, etc.) at rather low prices, and there's always a Fri. fish fry. Benjamin's also has a deserved reputation for good, hearty soups and substantial portions. Lunch: Mon.–Sat., 11:00 A.M.–3:00 P.M. Dinner: 4:00 P.M.–9:00 P.M. nightly. Located on **Rte. 85, about 1 mile south of the town green, Colchester, 06415; (860) 537-5218.**

Services

Local Visitors Information

Greater Hartford Tourism District, 234 Murphy Rd., Hartford, 06114; (860) 244-8181 (in Connecticut) or **(800) 793-4480** (out-of-state).

Mystic & More, a.k.a. Southeast Connecticut Tourism District, 470 Bank St., New London, 06320; (800) 863-6569 or **(860) 444-2206.**

Northeast Connecticut Visitors District, P.O. Box 598, Putnam, 06260; (860) 928-1228.

Transportation

Regional bus service between towns in the northeast is provided by the **Windham Transit District** at **(860) 456-2221** and the **Northeastern Connecticut Transit District** at **(860) 774-1253.**

Storrs

Home to the largest campus in the state postsecondary system, Storrs is UConn Husky country and a place where many aspects of life revolve around the schedule of semesters and school breaks.

UConn is an agricultural college. The traditional area of expertise of local farmers—dairy cattle—gave rise to a delicious tradition: visiting the UConn Dairy Bar to sample the school's own ice cream. In fact, you could practically make an activity out of sampling and comparing ice cream at UConn, Fish Family Farm, Shady Glen Dairy and other small makers. But Storrs (and Mansfield, the larger town in which the community of Storrs is found) is no hick backwater. With two museums and a major performing arts complex, the campus is a center of cultural life for northeastern Connecticut.

Next door to Storrs is Coventry, the heart of Nathan Hale country. Born in Coventry, Hale was the Revolutionary War firebrand designated Connecticut's official state hero. Nearly every American schoolchild can recite Hale's immortal last words: "I only regret that I have but one life to lose for my country." He is said to have uttered this phrase just prior to his death at the hands of the British in New York after he had been captured while on a spying mission. He was only 21 years of age. His body was unceremoniously buried in an unmarked grave in central Manhattan, but a massive monument to Hale was erected in 1846 in Coventry Cemetery, where it still can be seen today. The Nathan Hale Homestead at the site of his birthplace is one of Connecticut's major historical museums.

Given the proximity of Coventry to Storrs, it's only natural that it too should have an attraction of horticultural interest. Caprilands is a mecca for gardeners who come to stroll the specialty herb gardens created over the years by noted author Adelma Grenier Simmons.

(Note: Because business life in Storrs revolves around the student clientele, restaurants and other establishments may have

shortened hours in summer. The high season in this area is Sept. through May. Museums and major attractions, however, have the same "summer on" schedule as elsewhere in Connecticut.)

History

Mansfield, a part of the huge 1675 land deed by the Indians to the English known as Joshua's Tract, was settled sometime in the last quarter of the 17th century. It was originally part of Windham but was incorporated as a separate town in 1702. Neighboring towns such as Coventry, which was originally known as Wangumbaug (meaning "crooked pond," a reference to the body of water that still bears that name), were settled at about the same time.

Nathan Hale (1755–1776) is the most famous native son of the region, but there is no actual record of how Hale looked because he died at such a young age. The statue of Hale outside Connecticut Hall on the Yale campus in New Haven (from which he graduated in 1773) is modeled after an anonymous student. The only real indicator of how he might have looked is a silhouette of him painted on the back of a door at the Nathan Hale Homestead, which gives only the barest suggestion of his features.

Before and after the Revolutionary War this part of Connecticut was humming with activity. Five major rivers flowing through the area meant there was ample water to power mills. A gristmill in Gurleyville, part of Mansfield, is among the most complete in the state and is open to the public as a museum. It was in operation until the 1930s and was run briefly by the family of Wilbur Cross, Connecticut's immensely popular, four-term Depression-era governor and a native of Mansfield.

Of all the goods that were manufactured here early on, probably none was more important than silk. Although the silk industry would be most lasting in neighboring Manchester, it got its start in Mansfield. Silkworm culture was introduced to the town in the 1760s by one Dr. Nathaniel Aspinwall. The wife of a local minister had observed the process of reeling silk from cocoons in France and was able to duplicate the results. From an output of 265 pounds of raw silk in 1793, Mansfield's production grew to 25,000 pounds in 1850.

The manufacture of silk thread and fabric in the state continued until well into the 20th century. On Hanks Hill Rd. by Hanks Hill Pond in Mansfield, a small plaque identifies the spot where the first silk mill in America was built in 1810 by Rodney Hanks. There is nothing more to see of it today since the building was sold in 1931 to the Henry Ford Museum in Dearborn, Michigan.

Coventry had at least 17 mills on the appropriately named Mill River. The one best remembered today manufactured commemorative glass from 1830 to 1848 that is now collectible. Samples of it are displayed at the Strong-Porter House Museum, and there are long-range plans to develop a museum of Connecticut glass in Coventry.

After its silk heyday Mansfield returned to its agricultural roots. Storrs would probably be a small village today if not for a fortuitous gift. Two brothers by the name of Storrs gave land to the state in 1881 to establish an agricultural school. Storrs Agricultural College, as it was first known, was slow getting off the ground and remained small until after World War II, when it became a state university. Today it is one of the biggest employers in eastern Connecticut. It and the town have experienced a tremendous burst of growth since 1950, but both retain a down-to-earth quality based on a heritage of drawing livelihood from the soil.

Major Attractions

Caprilands Herb Farm

Caprilands is the combination showcase garden, shop, plant nursery, tearoom and school where renowned herb gardener and author Adelma Grenier Simmons has lived and gardened for decades. The grounds are extensively planted, and you are invited to stroll through them at no charge. There are also shops selling plants, dried herbs, specialty foods, craft items, seeds, books, baskets and all sorts of gardening and cooking paraphernalia. If you are able to make plans ahead of time, however, try to attend a luncheon. By reservation only, these can fill up weeks in advance, so call early. Tables are set inside Simmons's old colonial home, and all the food is prepared according to one of her own recipes using herbs and other ingredients from the grounds. Numerous other events and lectures go on throughout the year, so call for a schedule. Shop hours: 9:00 A.M.–5:00 P.M. daily, year-round; closed some major holidays. **534 Silver St., Coventry, 06238; (860) 742-7244.**

Nathan Hale Homestead

At the tender age of 21, a young Continental army captain, Coventry native and Yale graduate named Nathan Hale volunteered for a dangerous espionage mission on Long Island, then in British hands. Disguised as a schoolteacher, he gathered vital statistics about British forces and their movements but was discovered and later hanged. His bravery was acknowledged by his designation as Connecticut's official state hero. The house in which he was most probably born no longer stands, but parts of it were incorporated by his parents into this farmhouse. Admission: $4 adults, $1 children under 18. Hours: 1:00 P.M.–5:00 P.M. daily, mid-May–mid-Oct. **2299 South St., Coventry, 06238; (860) 742-6917.** Dedicated Hale buffs may also want to stop at the cemetery on Lake St. (one block from Rte. 31) to see the Nathan Hale Monument, a gargantuan stone obelisk right by the entrance that was erected by townspeople in his honor.

University of Connecticut at Storrs

The UConn campus is home to many attractions, including the William Benton Museum of Art, the Connecticut State Museum of Natural History, several performance venues, Huskies basketball games (plus soccer and football) and the renowned Dairy Bar where you can sample this agricultural college's own ice cream. If you'll be visiting anything on campus, note that parking is controlled on weekdays 8:00 A.M.–4:30 P.M. Follow signs for parking services from Rte. 195 in front of the campus to a control gate where you can pick up a campus map and get a visitors pass. A shuttle bus system operates on campus between 7:30 A.M. and 10:00 P.M. every day that classes are in session during the normal school year. For information about parking or getting around the campus call **(860) 486-4930.**

Getting There

Storrs is located almost due east of Hartford about half an hour by car. From Hartford take I-84 east to I-384 east to Rte. 44 east. This will take you to Mansfield Four Corners. A short drive south on Rte. 195 will bring you to the University of Connecticut at Storrs campus and the commercial district.

Other Attractions

Red Goose Farm and Gardens

If you're in the area to visit Caprilands, you'll also want to know about Red Goose Gardens. Louise Wisnewski, a Master Gardener, gives lectures about gardening topics and keeps a shop stocked with heirloom seeds, teas, herbal products, specialty foods and decorative items. High tea is served with lectures, and visitors are invited to enjoy the perennial gardens, pond and meadow walk on the grounds. Scheduling is such that you could

191

The Nathan Hale Homestead, Coventry, is where Connecticut's state hero was raised.

manage both luncheon at Caprilands and tea at Red Goose Farms plus two lectures all in one day. Call for the lecture schedule. Shop hours are Thu.–Sun., 11:00 A.M.–5:00 P.M., Apr.–Dec. Gardens closed on Sun. Located on **Goose Ln., Coventry, 06238; (860) 742-9137.**

Festivals and Events

Caprilands Events
year-round

The renowned luncheon and lecture program at Caprilands (see the listing under Major Attractions) is offered Mon.–Sat., Apr.–Dec. High tea is served Sun. year-round, plus Sat. in winter. Other high points of the Caprilands calendar include May Day (celebrated the Sat. or Sun. closest to May 1), when a traditional dance troupe performs, and Memorial Day, when Quiet Corner Artists give a fine art show and sale. Call for a complete schedule. **534 Silver St., Coventry, 06238; (860) 742-7244.**

Nathan Hale Homestead Events
throughout summer

Several special events take place during summer on the grounds of the Nathan Hale Homestead. Probably the biggest is the colonial encampment and ancient muster on a weekend in late July. For two days reenactors live like Patriot and British soldiers, engaging in a mock battle on Sat. in the early afternoon. On Sun. the Nathan Hale Ancient Fifes and Drums host a muster that starts around 12:00 P.M. and lasts the afternoon.

Another big draw is the annual antiques show noted for the high quality of its pieces. It takes place outdoors, rain or shine, and includes a lecture. The date is variable, so call to check. Admission is charged. There is also a day of children's games and activities on the weekend closest to June 6 in commemoration of Hale's birthday, a play or commemoration of

his death on the weekend closest to Sept. 20 and walking tours through Nathan Hale State Forest, plus crafters giving demonstrations of hearth cooking, soap making, candle making and spinning on Columbus Day weekend. **2299 South St., Coventry, 06238; (860) 742-6917.**

Walking Weekend
Columbus Day weekend

Most of the towns in this area participate in this three-day extravaganza of guided tours and walks through northeastern Connecticut's most beautiful and historically significant places. See the **Far Northeast** chapter for details.

Outdoor Activities

Biking

Mountain Biking

The **Hop River State Park Trail** is an abandoned railroad line that's popular with mountain bikers. The trail remains largely undeveloped, so conditions can be rough and sometimes wet, especially on the northern end. The trail is noted for some high trestles that can be exciting to cross. At times you may have to take detours around missing bridges. Total length is about 12 miles. The book *Great Rail-Trails of the Northeast* by Craig Della Penna gives a mile-by-mile description of this trail with suggested resting points.

If you're looking for something a little less rigorous, see the description of **Mansfield Hollow State Park** under Hiking. The paved top of the levee described there makes a great place for riding. You can also ride on the dirt roads that cross the low promontory that juts out into Willimantic Reservoir, water levels permitting, and on the southern portion of the levee. If you are willing to register with the Mansfield Parks and Recreation Dept., there are some town park trails available for mountain biking. Contact the office at **(860) 429-3321.**

Road Biking

The *Northeast Connecticut's Bike Guide* available from the **Northeast Connecticut Visitors District** at **(860) 928-1228** includes a 16-mile loop in Mansfield that can be chopped in half if you aren't up for that long a distance, plus an 11-mile loop in and around Coventry beginning and ending at the Hale Homestead. A second option is the booklet "Trails for the Future: Twelve Scenic and Historic Tours for Bikers and Hikers in Mansfield," available from the **Mansfield Parks and Recreation Dept.** Call **(860) 429-3321** for details.

Coventry has many back roads that are quiet and ideal for road biking. Some parts are quite hilly, but Silver St. and South St. are largely flat. Silver St. will take you right past Caprilands Herb Farm, where you can take a break and walk through the gardens at no charge, and South St. cuts through Nathan Hale State Forest and past the Hale Homestead and Strong-Porter House. Parking is available at the Hale Homestead and at Patriot's Park on Lake St. about a quarter-mile from the Rte. 275/Rte. 31 intersection.

Boating

If you continue past the main entrance to Mansfield Hollow State Park on Bassett Bridge Rd., you will soon come to a boat ramp from which you can launch your craft on either portion of **Mansfield Hollow Reservoir,** an Army Corps of Engineers flood-control project also known as Naubesatuck Lake. The undeveloped shoreline is quite pretty, and an 8 m.p.h. speed limit keeps it nice for small sailboats and canoes.

Another reservoir with a summer resort look to it is **Bolton Lakes,** one body of water broken into three parts by two causeways. There are public boat launches onto all three. Access the lowest and largest section from Rte. 44 near the North Rd./South Rd. intersection in Bolton. Access the other two from Cedar Swamp Rd. just over the town line in Coventry. Turn on Vernon Branch Rd., and you'll find the launches on either side of the road just west of the causeway. Motors are limited to 6 HP.

Lake Wangumbaug is a center of public recreation in Coventry, busy but still very attractive. There's a public boat launch near the intersection of Cross and Lake Sts. a few feet away from the entrance to Patriots Park.

Finally, there's a car-top launch on **Eagleville Lake,** a tall and narrow dammed portion of the Willimantic River. To get there, follow signs from Stonehouse Rd. off Rte. 32 at the Coventry/Mansfield town line.

Fishing

Lakes and Ponds

Mansfield Hollow Reservoir is the largest and most accessible body of water in this area, and an undeveloped shoreline and restricted boat speed make the atmosphere very appealing for anglers. You can fish from anywhere on shore or from your boat. Largemouth bass, trout, northern pike and panfish are all found here.

The **Bolton Lakes** are an attractive fishery shared by the towns of Bolton and Vernon where you'll find yellow perch, largemouth bass, chain pickerel and brown bullhead. Fish from the causeway on Vernon Branch Rd. in Vernon or see the listing under Boating for directions to the boat launches.

Lake Wangumbaug is a good spot to try for trout, largemouth and smallmouth bass and yellow perch from your boat. There's also limited shore access from the boat launch on Lake St. in Coventry and at Patriots Park, a town park next door.

Largemouth bass, chain pickerel and trout are found in **Eagleville Lake.** The listing under Boating gives details about the boat launch, which is also the only viable shore access point.

Rivers and Streams

For trout fishing, you can access the lowest reaches of all three rivers that feed Mansfield Reservoir—the **Fenton, Mt. Hope** and **Natchaug Rivers**—from upriver bridges that are still within the state park. These are found on Warrenville Rd., Atwoodville Rd. and Bates Rd. in Mansfield. The Fenton River is also accessible from Old Turnpike Rd. farther north.

193

Park and walk south along the riverbank to find a good spot. You can also fish the Mt. Hope River from anywhere along Rte. 89 where roadside parking is available and no restrictions are posted.

Two other major trout streams are the Skungamaug and the Willimantic Rivers. The former can be remote and very quiet thanks to the large blocks of forested land it crosses, including portions of the Nathan Hale State Forest. The bridge on River Rd. in Coventry may be the best point of entry. As for the latter, Brigham Tavern Rd. in Coventry along its west bank is one of the nicest sections.

Hiking

Joshua's Trust

This private land trust owns and maintains preserves in a ten-town region in the Northeast corner. In the late 1600s Joshua, a son of the Mohegan leader Uncas, deeded a huge parcel of land in this area to English settlers. Many towns in the Northeast were settled on this land, which was known as Joshua's Tract. The trust's large walk book describing trails in its preserves is sold for $10 at the **Mansfield Historical Society Museum.** For more information call the trust at **(860) 429-9023.** The Knowlton Pond Trail is included here.

Another guide, "Trails for the Future: Twelve Scenic and Historic Tours for Bikers and Hikers in Mansfield," is available for $1 in person or $2.25 by mail from the **Mansfield Parks and Recreation Dept.** Stop by their office at **4 S. Eagleville Rd. (Rte. 275 at Rte. 195) in Mansfield** Mon.–Fri., 8:30 A.M.–4:30 P.M., or call **(860) 429-3321** for mailing instructions.

Knowlton Pond

This pleasant walk in one of the preserves in Joshua's Trust takes you across an estate, down to the shore of a pond, through woods and an open hayfield. From the intersection of Knowlton Rd. and Wormwood Hill Rd. in Mansfield, go north on Knowlton Rd. about half a mile. On the right you'll see an open field and a big estate house. Just before the driveway to this house is a parking area on the right. The

trail—a mowed grass path—starts right there. Once you hit the woods, follow the yellow blazes. Whatever way you go you will eventually loop back to Knowlton Rd.; turn left to return to your car.

Nipmuck Trail

The Nipmuck Trail is one of the blue-blazed trails described and mapped in the *Connecticut Walk Book*. It stretches all the way from Mansfield to the Massachusetts state line. You can pick it up at several points in Mansfield. The first is at the pullout on Crane Hill Rd. just southwest of Brown's Rd. A half-mile walk brings you to Wolf Rock, a 10-foot-high boulder perched on an exposed ledge from which there are nice views of the countryside toward Willimantic. You can continue another 2 miles to the southern terminus of the trail at Puddin' Ln.

In the opposite direction, the trail leads to the town park called Schoolhouse Brook on Clover Mill Rd., another good access point where there's a whole network of trails. One of them, Bryon's Trail, is a six-tenths-mile path designed specifically for the moderately handicapped. Maps are posted at the trailheads.

The third spot to pick up the Nipmuck Trail is in Mansfield Hollow State Park, where one of its two southern branches starts. Enter at the sign on Bassett Bridge Rd. and look for the blue blazes on the woods side of the picnic area. The top of a levee, part of the Mansfield Hollow Dam fortifications, is paved and closed to vehicles. It extends for about 1 mile on the north side of the dam and continues as a dirt road. You can access the southern arm of the levee at the parking area on Rte. 6 about 1 mile east of Rte. 66.

Ice Skating

The **UConn Ice Rink** is open for public skating at least three hours a day, Fri.–Sun., mid-Oct.–mid-Mar. The rink is covered but not enclosed, so the season is variable. Skate rentals ($1.50) and lessons are available. Admission is $3 per person. Located on **Stadium Rd. on the UConn-Storrs campus.** For more information call **(860) 486-3808.**

Skiing

The hiking trails at two Mansfield town parks, **Schoolhouse Brook** on Clover Mill Rd. and **Shelter Falls** on Bone Mill Rd., make great ungroomed cross-country ski terrain in winter. Those at Shelter Falls tend to be narrow with hills and turns and are more appropriate for skilled skiers. A third choice is **Mansfield Hollow State Park** on Bassett Bridge Rd. in Mansfield, where there are trails through the woods as well as large fields near a scenic reservoir.

Swimming

The principal public swimming beach in the area is at Patriots Park on Lake St. in Coventry, where you can enjoy beautiful Lake Wangumbaug. Facilities include a playground, picnic area and changing rooms. A boat launch next door and a small fishing area make this a good destination for groups whose members have different interests. Admission is $3 per car on weekdays, $7 per car on weekends and holidays. Season: mid-June–Labor Day. Hours: noon–7:00 P.M. on weekdays; 10:00 A.M.–5:00 P.M. weekends and holidays. For more information call **Coventry Parks and Recreation** at **(860) 742-4068.** Coventry town beach on the same lake, but located on Rte. 31, is available for the use of guests at any of Coventry's B&Bs or inns; ask your innkeeper.

A second, smaller beach is at **Barrows Pond** in Schoolhouse Brook Park on Clover Mill Rd. in Mansfield, where admission is $3 per person on weekends ($2 weekdays) for nonresidents of Mansfield. Hours: 10:00 A.M.–7:00 P.M. daily in summer.

Seeing and Doing

Antiquing

Memory Lanes Countryside Antique Center (2224 Boston Tpke. [Rte. 44 at Rte. 31], Coventry; 860-742-0346), a multidealer shop housed in an old house and barns, is the type of store that people make a point of stopping at again and again whenever they're in the area. The inventory includes furniture, linens, jewelry and decorative and household items, and the atmosphere is pleasant in a way few shops can match. Open Wed.–Sun., 10:00 A.M.–5:00 P.M.

Museums and Historic Sites

Connecticut State Museum of Natural History

The manageable size of this small museum— it's basically housed in one large room—and the child-oriented nature of many of its exhibits make it a good place to introduce a young one to the study of the natural world. Major installations include exhibits on the Long Island Sound ecosystem, sharks, mounted birds and Algonquian Indian culture. You can see most or all of the exhibits in a couple of hours, and admission is free (although donations are "gratefully accepted"). Hours: Thu.–Mon., noon–4:00 P.M. Located in **the Wilbur Cross building on the grounds of the UConn-Storrs campus; (860) 486-4460.** See the UConn listing under Major Attractions for parking information.

Gurleyville Gristmill

This 19th-century water-powered mill, which produced flour and meal for local families until 1941, is remarkable for the fact that all its innards are original. You can walk down into the lower level to see the gears and shafts that transmitted power from the water wheel (later a turbine) to the grinding stones above and the mechanism for adjusting the fineness of the grind. On the main level you can inspect the hoppers, elevators, sifter and other devices for turning out the finished product. Because of the fragility of the old parts, the mill is nonoperational. Open Sun., 1:00 P.M.–5:00 P.M., late May–mid-Oct. Located on **Stone Mill Rd. off Chaffeeville Rd. in Storrs; (860) 429-9023.**

Mansfield Historical Society Museum

In the realm of local history museums, this one is near the top. The choice of subject matter is creative and the execution of the exhibits admirable. Be sure to check out the permanent

195

The intact interior of the 19th-century Gurleyville Gristmill, Storrs.

exhibit on town offices of the colonial period. It's quite a hoot from a vantage point of 200–300 years. Admission by donation. Hours: Thu. & Sun., 1:30 P.M.–4:30 P.M., June–Sept. **954 Storrs Rd. (Rte. 195), Storrs, 06268; (860) 429-6575.**

Strong-Porter House

The Coventry Historical Society's museum, located in a farmhouse (ca. 1730), has permanent displays on Coventry glass (one of the state's first major glass factories was located in town, and its work is now collectible), ammunition, household crafts and restoration of the house itself. A huge barn full of tools, farm implements and artifacts from a variety of local mills is out back. You can buy a combined ticket for this and the Hale Homestead at a savings. Admission: $1, children under 18 free. Hours: Sat.–Sun., 1:00 P.M.–5:00 P.M., mid-May–mid-Oct. **2382 South St., Coventry, 06238; (860) 742-7847.**

William Benton Museum of Art

This small museum has two galleries for displaying changing exhibits of new work in various media and items from the museum's collection, which is strong in 20th-century American Impressionist and realist painting.

The New York City scenes of Reginald Marsh, works by German artist Käthe Kollwitz and Cuna Indian molas are also especially well represented. There is a short downtime between exhibits, so call before going. Admission is free. Located on **the UConn-Storrs campus; (860) 486-4520.** See the UConn listing under Major Attractions for parking information.

Nightlife

With a student population to satisfy, Storrs has a small selection of bars and clubs. Go looking down Rte. 195, the main drag, and you'll find them. Bulletin boards at the student union are a good source of information about local after-hours events. One notable club is **Husky Blues (1254 Storrs Rd. [Rte. 195], Mansfield; 860-429-2587),** where jazz and blues are offered most nights. It's also a restaurant; see the Where to Eat section for more. For a more old-fashioned night out, see a flick at the **Mansfield Drive-In Theatre (junction of Rtes. 31 and 32, Mansfield; 860-423-4441).** It has three features on three screens nightly during summer break, on weekends the rest of the year.

Performing Arts

The Jorgensen Auditorium, the Harriet Jorgensen Theatre, the Studio Theatre and the Von der Mehden Recital Hall are four venues on the UConn-Storrs campus offering four different atmospheres for theater (musicals, comedies and dramas), popular and ethnic music, symphonic and chamber music, dance, children's shows and cinema. Among them you'll find just about anything that would take place on a stage or a screen, and the season isn't limited to the school year. For information on events at the first two venues call the **Jorgensen box office** at **(860) 486-4226.** For Studio Theatre events call the box office or **Connecticut Repertory Theatre** at **(860) 486-3969.** For information on recital hall events call **(860) 486-2260.**

Shopping

A favorite Sun. pastime for locals is visiting either or both of two big flea markets. If that sounds like your cup of tea, check out eastern Connecticut's oldest and largest, the Eastern Connecticut Flea Market at **Mansfield Drive-In Theatre (junction of Rtes. 31 and 32, Mansfield; 860-456-2578).** Parking is $1, and hours are Sun., 9:00 A.M.–3:00 P.M., spring–Thanksgiving. The **Indoor/Outdoor Flea Market (Lake St., Coventry; 860-742-1993)** is open Sun., 9:00 A.M.–4:00 P.M., year-round. Admission charged.

And if you're a UConn Huskies fan, the **UConn Co-op (860-486-3537)** on the UConn-Storrs campus is the place to go for T-shirts, coffee mugs and other items advertising your allegiance. They're open year-round, but hours change, so call before going.

Sports

The UConn women's basketball team, the Huskies, made history in 1995 when they achieved a perfect season and won the NCAA Division I basketball championship. Ever since then, there's been a tremendous upsurge in interest in college basketball and college sports in general. UConn home games in football, men's and women's basketball and men's and women's soccer are ticketed events. You can get information on all these events and buy tickets through one central phone number: **(860) 486-2724.**

Tours

Appropriately enough for an agricultural college, the UConn-Storrs campus is an arboretum with many beautiful tree specimens. If the idea of strolling the grounds and admiring them appeals to you, stop by the **Connecticut State Museum of Natural History** in the Wilbur Cross Building on campus (see the listing under Museums for hours) to pick up a copy of the free "Tree Walking Tour" guide. This substantial brochure identifies and maps 166 tree species, points out highlights of the plantings by season and contains one suggested walk. Don't overlook the "special gardens" section, which directs you to 15 unique gardens and monuments scattered around the campus, each with a special theme.

Wineries

Nutmeg Vineyards Farm Winery (800 Bunker Hill Rd., Coventry; 860-742-8402) is a small vineyard with a yearly production of under 1,000 cases, making a broad mix of table wines and dessert wines from the staple Connecticut varietal, chardonnay, as well as seyval, foch and hybrids. Their tasting room is open Sat.–Sun., 11:00 A.M.–5:00 P.M., and visitors may also take a self-guided tour of the vineyard.

Where to Stay

Bed & Breakfasts

Bird-in-Hand—$$$

In the evening you'll find your bed turned down and a glass of brandy on your night table at this B&B in an old colonial that's been unobtrusively modernized where necessary yet retains all the rugged flavor of an 18th-century house. Two guest rooms have wideboard floors, canopy beds, working fireplaces and private baths. They share a library for reading or watching TV. There's also a detached cottage with kitchen, sofa bed, fireplace and TV available both nightly and for longer stays. A full breakfast is served on weekends and a lighter one on weekdays. If you're looking for a unique dining experience in fall or winter, ask about their hearth-cooked meals. Get directions in advance. Payment by cash or check only. **2011 Main St. (Rte. 31), Coventry, 06238; (860) 742-0032.**

The Fitch House—$$$

This 1836 Greek Revival house was built by a fledgling architect to showcase his skills. There are three guest rooms, two of which can be connected to form a suite, and private bathrooms. A full breakfast is served by candlelight in front of a downstairs fireplace in winter and

197

in a solarium in warm weather. The large lawn and garden is a beautiful place to relax. The Holts both come from longtime northeast Connecticut families and can answer many questions about the area. Payment by cash or check only. Closed July 15–Aug. 15 & Christmas–Jan. 15. **563 Storrs Rd. (Rte. 195), Mansfield Center, 06250; (860) 456-0922.**

Maple Hill Farm—$$$

This rambling 18th- and 19th-century center-hall farmhouse is located in a rural setting, surrounded by several acres of lawns, woods, pastures and a community of horses and farm animals. The five or so guest rooms are all completely different. Most rooms have double beds, and baths are shared or private depending on the number of guests. A full breakfast is served by candlelight because the dining room is not electrified. Guests also get to enjoy two common rooms with fireplaces, a large screened porch, a solarium with hot tub and tropical plants, an outdoor pool and a hammock on the back lawn. There's even barn dancing one Sat. a month in one of the outbuildings, and bikes are available for those who would like to explore the neighborhood free of their automobile. Ask about hearth-cooked meals in fall and winter. **365 Goose Ln., Coventry, 06238; (800) 742-0635 or (860) 742-0635.**

Jared Cone House—$$ to $$$

The traditional furnishings, huge fireplaces and wood floors in Jeff and Cinde's Georgian farmhouse make for a homey atmosphere at this relaxed B&B, and their policy of welcoming children makes it very family-friendly. There are three appealing guests rooms with queen beds, two with a shared bath and one with a private bath. A full breakfast is served in a formal dining room or, in warm weather, on the porch. The downstairs living room is shared with the family. The B&B is steps away from a nice town park with trails, open spaces and a playground. **25 Hebron Rd., Bolton, 06043; (860) 643-8538 or (860) 649-5678.**

Mill Brook Farm—$$ to $$$

Mill Brook Farm is described by owners Rose and Joe Fowler as "Coventry's laid-back B&B."

The atmosphere is indeed casual, and the Fowlers are very tolerant, accommodating smokers and children of any age. Their 1850s farmhouse is situated on a quiet back road with barns and paddocks for their animals. Two guest rooms have double beds and share a bathroom. You can rest on the veranda or in a comfortable library/TV room on the main floor. Guests are welcome to use the washer, dryer and ironing board or to accompany Joe as he feeds the animals. Inquire about Rose's made-to-order teddy bears and weekend workshops in which you can learn spinning, make teddy bears, comb the countryside for bargains (Joe runs Coventry's flea market) or learn about the history of the area. A light breakfast is included. **110 Wall St., Coventry, 06238; (860) 742-5761.**

Special Joys B&B—$$ to $$$

At Special Joys, dolls are clearly the love of one of the hosts, Joy Kelleher, and gardening the passion of the other, Joy's husband Bill. This attractive modern home shares quarters with a small doll shop and museum. Dolls and toys line the hallways and adorn the three guest rooms. Of the two larger rooms with queen beds and private baths, one has a Victorian theme and the other a colonial theme. A third bedroom in another part of the house has two twin beds and a bath shared with the owners. All guest rooms have wall-to-wall carpeting, hideaway TVs and air-conditioning. A full breakfast is served in a cheerful sunroom, and at the rear of the house a covered patio (heated in winter) overlooks the garden. The Kellehers accommodate "well-behaved" children. **41 North River Rd., Coventry, 06238; (860) 742-6359.**

Hotels, Motels & Inns

Basic rooms in the $$$ price range are available at the **Best Western Regent Inn (123 Storrs Rd. [Rte. 195 just north of Rte. 6], Mansfield Center, 06250; 860-423-8451)** and in the $$ to $$$ price range at the **Altnaveigh Inn (957 Storrs Rd. [Rte. 195], Storrs, 06268; 860-429-4490).** The former has a small indoor heated pool and a coin-op washer/dryer. Rooms are in great shape and come with a microwave and refrigerator. The latter is a family-run inn in a modified 18th-century farmhouse with a popular restaurant on the main floor (see the Where to Eat section for details). Some have a private bath, others shared, and they all come with a Continental breakfast.

Where to Eat

Altnaveigh Inn—$$$ to $$$$

The nicest place in the area for a special night out is Altnaveigh, where the specialty is classic dishes such as filet mignon, lobster Newburg and beef Wellington. The dining rooms and a sitting room/lounge are located on the main floor of an 18th-century house with inn rooms upstairs. The setting is equally enjoyable for lunch, when you can get hearty sandwiches, meal salads, pastas and seafood. A stone terrace is occasionally available for dining in good weather. Sun. brunch is served as well. Lunch hours: Mon.–Fri., 11:30 A.M.–2:30 P.M. Dinner hours: Mon.–Thu., 5:00 P.M.–9:00 P.M.; Fri.–Sat., 5:00 P.M.–10:00 P.M.; Sun., 2:00 P.M.–8:00 P.M. Sun. brunch served 11:00 A.M.–2:00 P.M. **957 Storrs Rd. (Rte. 195), Storrs, 06268; (860) 429-4490.**

Bidwell Tavern—$$ to $$$

Although Bidwell Tavern has a notable setting, it's the huge menu that really sets it apart. There's a page each of appetizers, chicken and seafood, somewhat less of beef and veal, a vegetarian section and no less than 22 kinds of chicken wings. Even the salad dressing selection beats all, and there is a good selection of wines, including several Connecticut vintages. Food is of mixed inspiration with a few regional classics like Yankee pot roast for contrast. Portions are so large here that bread and salad alone could make a meal. As for the ambiance, this beautiful old brick structure was once the office of a mill and later the town hall. It's a lively place with a bar, a small stage (live music is offered most nights) and seating in several dining rooms, including a solarium and an outdoor terrace by a small stream.

Hours: Mon.–Thu., 11:00 A.M.–1:00 A.M.; Fri.–Sat., 11:00 A.M.–2:00 A.M.; Sun., 11:30 A.M.–1:00 A.M. The kitchen stops serving dinner at 10:00 P.M. (9:00 on Sun.), but a late-night sandwich menu is available until closing. **1260 Main St. (Rte. 31), Coventry, 06238; (860) 742-6978.**

Homestead Restaurant—$$ to $$$

This Italian-American restaurant has both a main dining room tastefully decorated with quilts and subdued colors and a large casual pub, both of which are suitable for family dining. The menu runs the gamut from award-winning prime rib to salads, sandwiches, grinders and burgers. Lunch hours: Mon.–Fri., 11:30 A.M.–2:30 P.M. Dinner hours: Mon.–Thu., 4:30 P.M.–9:00 P.M.; Fri.–Sat., 4:30 P.M.–10:00 P.M.; Sun., 3:00 P.M.–9:00 P.M. There is a seasonal Sun. brunch; call for hours. **50 Higgins Hwy. (Rte. 31), Mansfield, 06250; (860) 456-2240.**

Husky Blues—$$ to $$$

The only drawback of this combination restaurant and jazz/blues nightclub is that it can get loud. The menu is a strange mix of down-to-earth foods with some rather highbrow items. It's not often that pizza, barbeque and pecan pie come out of the same kitchen as crème brûlée and house-smoked fish. There are even some veggie pastas and a children's menu. Tickets are $3–$12 per person in addition to the cost of the meal, but you can go for a meal alone without paying extra since acts usually don't start until around 9:00 P.M. Husky Blues is located in a strip mall opposite the southern end of the UConn campus and is a little hard to find unless you drive slowly. Enter at the back of the building. Open Mon.–Thu., 5:00 P.M.–1:00 A.M.; Fri.–Sat., 4:00 P.M.–2:00 A.M.; Sun., closed in summer but open during the school year 4:00 P.M.–11:00 P.M. **1254 Storrs Rd. (Rte. 195), Storrs, 06268; (860) 429-2587.**

Netto's at the Depot—$$ to $$$

This unique restaurant is located in a converted train depot (with a red caboose tacked on for good measure) alongside tracks that still carry freight traffic. When trains roll through, the place really shakes, and diners in

199

the glassed-in porch converted from a loading bay get a close view. The menu includes stone pies (individual pizzas baked in a stone oven), salads, pastas, light grilled meats and fish and some veggie entrées—all with a basis in Italian cuisine. There is a fair selection of wines and live jazz on Thu. nights. Lunch hours: Mon.–Fri., 11:30 A.M.–2:30 P.M. Pub menu offered Mon.–Fri., 2:30 P.M.–5:00 P.M. Dinner served Mon.–Wed., 5:00 P.M.–9:00 P.M.; Thu.–Sat., 5:00 P.M.–10:00 P.M.; Sun., 4:30 P.M.–9:00 P.M. Sun. brunch is 11:00 A.M.–2:30 P.M. Closed Mon. during summer. **57 Middle Tpke. (Rte. 44), Mansfield Depot, 06251; (860) 429-3663.**

Vito's Birch Mountain Inn—$$ to $$$

More than a century old, Vito's (née Villa Louisa) offers good value in Italian dining and a family-friendly atmosphere for dinner or Sun. brunch. There's also a steak and chop portion of the menu, plus interesting vegetarian pasta dishes, and all pastas are available in half portions. Hours: Tue.–Sun., 4:00 P.M.–8:30 P.M.; Sun. brunch served 11:00 A.M.–2:00 P.M. **60 Villa Louisa Rd., Bolton, 06043; (860) 646-3161.**

Cup o' Sun—$ to $$

Located directly opposite the southern end of the UConn-Storrs campus, this restaurant/bakery is a student hangout with a coffee shop interior and very low prices. A good place to get a filling but inexpensive breakfast or lunch, it also serves dinner two nights a week during the school year. Wed.'s dinner selections are all pasta dishes, and Fri. is fish night. Breakfast hours: Mon.–Fri., 7:00 A.M.–11:00 A.M. (open at 8:00 A.M. in summer); Sat.–Sun., 9:00 A.M.–2:00 P.M. Lunch hours: Mon.–Fri., 11:00 A.M.–3:00 P.M. Dinner hours: Wed. & Fri., 4:30 P.M.–7:30 P.M., during the school year only. **1254 Storrs Rd. (Rte. 195), Storrs, 06268; (860) 429-3440.**

Hale's Kitchen—$ to $$

In the words of one customer, Hale's is "what Coventry does on Sunday mornings." Indeed, this lively and friendly luncheonette is probably where most town business transpires. Even if you're not a local, it's a great place to get a hearty breakfast or lunch (plus dinner on Fri.).

Open Mon.–Thu., 5:30 A.M.–2:00 P.M.; Fri., 5:30 A.M.–9:00 P.M.; Sat., 6:00 A.M.–noon; Sun., 7:00 A.M.–noon (breakfast food only). **1203 Main St. (Rte. 31), Coventry, 06238; (860) 742-5771.**

Shady Glen Dairy Store—$ to $$

Shady Glen is a luncheonette/ice cream store with a real 1950s flavor. The waitresses wear crisp uniforms with white collars and frilly aprons; the waiters wear white shirts, black bow ties and little folding caps. This is strictly sandwich and "platter" fare. It's crowded even on weekdays, so come early or be prepared for a short wait. Hours: Mon.–Sat., 7:00 A.M.–11:30 P.M.; Sun., 10:30 A.M.–11:30 P.M. **840 Middle Tpke. (Rte. 6/44 east of Rte. 85), Bolton, 06043; (860) 649-4245.**

Reggie's—$

When you want to enjoy the classic combination of a burger and a shake or a hot dog and ice cream, head to Reggie's. It's a small place that draws the early morning breakfast crowd as well as the late-night ice cream addicts. Hours: Mon.–Sat., 6:30 A.M.–9:00 P.M.; Sun., 6:30 A.M.–3:00 P.M. Located on **Daly Rd. at Rte. 31, Coventry, 06238; (860) 742-9596.**

Coffeehouses, Sweets & Treats

Café Earth—$

Head here when you get that midafternoon coffee-and-something-sweet craving, because it's the desserts that shine, especially their vast slices of baklava. Hours: open at 7:00 A.M. daily, closing Sat.–Wed. at 10:00 P.M., Thu.–Fri. at 11:00 P.M. **1244 Storrs Rd. (Rte. 195), Storrs, 06268; (860) 429-5304.**

Fish Family Dairy Farm—$

In an informal newspaper review, the ice cream at this unique farm store got a three-cone rating for flavor, out of a possible four. Suffice it to say, the ice cream is very good, made from the rich milk of Jersey cows raised on the property. Hours: Mon.–Sat., 10:00 A.M.–8:00 P.M. When you turn at the entrance, take the right-hand driveway and at the top of the hill pull up to the barns. **20 Dimock Ln., Bolton, 06043; (860) 646-9745.**

Munson's Chocolates—$

Perhaps it's the Jersey milk they buy from Fish Family Farm up the road, but the chocolate here is incredible, and with their mail-order service (in cool weather only), you can keep the taste of Connecticut on hand. Hours: Mon.–Fri., 9:00 A.M.–8:00 P.M.; Sat.–Sun., 10:00 A.M.–6:00 P.M. Located on **Rte. 6 just south of Rte. 44, Bolton, 06043; (860) 649-4332.** For telephone orders call **(800) 321-7008** (in Connecticut) or **(800) 322-7008** (out-of-state).

University of Connecticut Dairy Bar—$

The ice cream here, made on campus with student assistance, is quite good and cheap by today's gourmet ice cream shop standards. The dairy bar is a tad hard to find. From Storrs Rd. (Rte. 195) at the northern end of campus, look for signs on the east side of the road directing you to the Dairy Products Sales Room. Park in the first lot on the right and climb the stairs next to the loading dock to enter. Hours: weekdays, 10:00 A.M.–6:00 P.M.; weekends, noon–6:00 P.M. Labor Day–Memorial Day it closes at 5:00 P.M. Phone: **(860) 486-2634.**

Services

Local Visitors Information

Coventry Visitors Center, 1195 Main St., Coventry, 06238; (860) 742-1085. Open mid-May–mid-Oct. Hours: Mon.–Fri., 9:00 A.M.–2:00 P.M.; Sat.–Sun., 10:00 A.M.–3:00 P.M.

Northeast Connecticut Visitors District, P.O. Box 598, Putnam, 06260; (860) 928-1228.

Transportation

Bus transportation from Hartford directly to the Storrs campus is provided by **Arrow Bus Lines (800-243-9560)** on a limited basis during summer and an expanded basis during the school year. You can transfer to Arrow from any of the major bus carriers serving Hartford **(Greyhound** at **800-231-2222** and **Peter Pan/Trailways** at **800-343-9999)** and **Amtrak (800-872-7245).**

Tolland

Although the high-speed excitement of NASCAR racing at Stafford Motor Speedway is the biggest attraction in these parts, as a whole the area is supremely tranquil, the true Quiet Corner of Connecticut.

Geologically this area is made up mostly of the rolling mountains and valleys of the Tolland Range. At the western edge there's a belt of more rugged mountains called the Bolton Range, which includes Soapstone and Bald Mountains. Soapstone is the centerpiece of Shenipsit State Forest, where trails and a road climbing to a lookout tower give visitors one of the best views in the state. Finally, the westernmost edge of towns such as Somers, Ellington and Vernon dip down into the Central Valley.

Tolland itself is a pretty village with a cluster of history museums, some of which reflect the activity it saw as the seat of Tolland County back when Connecticut had an active county government. The Tolland County Jail has been the home of the Tolland Historical Society ever since prisoners vacated in 1968 and is one of only two former prisons open to the public in Connecticut. Before coming to the jail more than a few people probably made a visit to the Old Tolland County Courthouse across the street. Built in 1822 it still has all its original fixtures and possesses such an elegant simplicity that it was the subject of research for a courthouse reconstruction in Virginia's Colonial Williamsburg.

Also in Tolland, the Hicks-Stearns House focuses on the Victorian era and interprets displays to involve visitors in a most engaging way. Rounding out the Tolland quartet of museums, the Daniel Benton Homestead represents the colonial and Revolutionary War era.

Virtually every town in the area also has a small historical society museum. Most keep limited hours, so if you find yourself here on a weekday in summer, visit the Civilian Conservation Corps Museum or the Somers Mountain Museum of Natural History and Primitive Technology, which are open on a more extended basis.

Several events in and around Tolland are worth planning a trip around. Two wartime encampments are put on yearly by the historical society, the Victorian Lantern Light Weekend in Dec. is like theater in the streets of the town and there are weekly polo and occasional horse shows at Shallowbrook Equestrian and Polo Center in Somers. With one inn and two B&Bs, Tolland also makes a good, quiet home base if you want to stay in the country and make daytime excursions to Hartford, Storrs or Massachusetts attractions such as Sturbridge Village or the thrice-yearly antiques shows in Brimfield.

History

Towns in this area, which comprises roughly the upper half of Tolland County, were settled in the early 1700s, with most families coming east from the Connecticut River. Ellington, for example, was taken from East Windsor in 1786 and Somers (pronounced like "summers") was part of Enfield until 1734.

The land is hilly and a little rough for farming, so with one exception, the area did not come into its own until the Industrial Revolution, when local rivers were harnessed for water power. The exception is Stafford Springs, a village named for two mineral springs—one high in iron content, the other in sulphur—that were known to and valued by the native Podunk and Nipmuck Indians for their supposed curative properties. When Europeans arrived, they found the same to be true. The first hotel was built in 1802 and called the Stafford Springs House. The village remained a viable resort until well into the 20th century. In 1959 a fire destroyed the hotel, and an era came to an end. The capped iron spring can still be seen on Spring St. One remnant of those days is a small, local soda bottler descended from the Stafford Springs Mineral Water Co.

Presumably the same underlying geology that gave rise to the mineral springs was also responsible for the deposits of iron in Stafford, because it existed in sufficient quantities to be mined from 1734 on. Blast furnaces to smelt the ore followed in 1779 and 1796. Cannon and shot were made here for the Continental army, and the industry persisted until 1840.

Tolland, designated the county seat in 1785, did a brisk business in food, drink and sleeping quarters for visitors to its courthouse. Other towns developed their water resources, so that in the 1800s nearly every village had its mills turning out woolens, cottons, silks, boots and shoes, woven hats, trunks, wagons and leather goods such as harnesses. Shenipsit Lake, where it is drained by the Hockanum River in the Rockville part of Vernon, was an especially suitable spot for a water-powered mill, and from humble beginnings in about 1809 the spot became Connecticut's center of woolens manufacturing. Fabric from the Hockanum Mills is said to have clothed three presidents—Harrison, McKinley and Theodore Roosevelt—at their inaugurations.

Most of the mills are gone, having succumbed to the economics of a global marketplace. One holdout is Warren of Stafford, a small textile operation making cashmeres and other high-quality fabrics. The Hockanum Mills did not go out of business but were moved down south in the 1950s. In some cases higher-tech firms have filled the employment gap. Printed circuit boards are now made locally, a hospital provides many jobs and some businesses rely on the traffic generated by I-84. Although Tolland is no longer the principal community in the area, the neighborhood around its wide green retains a stately air that bespeaks its former significance.

Major Attractions

Hicks-Stearns House Museum

The Victorian-era focus of this museum is a bit unusual for Connecticut, where most museums concentrate on the colonial period. Actually, the Hicks-Stearns House is colonial too, having been built in the 1750s. It was Victorian-

ized when a local legislator owned it and wanted it to look more fashionable. Guides in Victorian dress give engaging tours, which have themes such as the life of a Victorian child, family roles and a Victorian Christmas. During Sept. the theme is Clue, and a brief tour of the house is followed by an activity based on the board game of the same name. A series of concerts, magic shows and other family activites are held on the grounds on selected weeknights in July and Aug., and a special Christmas event is held the first weekend in Dec. Admission to the house and to concerts: $2 adults, $1 children 6–12. Hours:

NASCAR/Winston Racing Series Modifieds compete every Fri. night at Stafford Motor Speedway. Photo by Dave Manlouganes/Stafford Motor Speedway.

open the second Sun. of the month, 1:00 P.M.–4:00 P.M., mid-May–mid-Sept., & for holiday events in Dec. Three tours a day are given at 1:00, 2:00 & 3:00 P.M. **42 Tolland Green, Tolland, 06084; (860) 875-7552.**

Soapstone Mountain

The best view in this area is found atop Soapstone Mountain, a 1,075-foot peak in Shenipsit State Forest in the Bolton Range. A lookout tower here affords an excellent view of the boundary between the Central Valley and the Eastern Uplands, often called the Eastern Wall. There is a paved road to a parking lot at the top from which you hike about a minute to the tower. A half hour before sunset is the best time to visit. There's also a string of picnic tables along the road near the top.

If you want to hike, pick up the Shenipsit Trail at the summit. From the summit you can hike about 5 miles to the south and 3 to the north, and it's pretty much downhill in both directions. The access road is off Gulf Rd. in Somers. Forest office: **(860) 928-9200.**

Stafford Motor Speedway

This NASCAR/Winston Racing Series facility offers auto racing in five divisions on a half-

mile track Apr.–Sept. The program consists of Modifieds, Pro stocks, Late Model stocks, DARE stocks and Legends. There are also Four Modified Tour events and two NASCAR/Busch North Series events during the season. The Speedway began life as a fairground that drew large crowds who came by trolley to see horse racing. Auto racing started shortly after World War II, although the track wasn't paved until the early 1960s. Today Stafford is considered one of the more challenging tracks in the country. There's one race per week on Fri. The gates open at 5:30 P.M., and racing begins at 7:00 P.M. Adult admission ranges from $12.50–$35, $2 for children 6–14. **55 West St., Stafford Springs, 06076; (860) 684-2783.**

Festivals and Events

Tolland Historical Society Special Events

This local preservation society holds three annual events—two historic and one just for the fun of it—on the grounds of the Daniel Benton Homestead in Tolland. The historic ones are two period encampments. During the first, held the third weekend of Apr., it is 1756 once again and the French and Indian War is in full swing. The second, held in late summer, depicts a scene that might have occurred a few years into the Revolutionary War. At both encampments you can also witness demonstrations of 18th-century ways of cooking and making basic products. These are very interactive events in which the participants are eager to answer questions from spectators. Admission: $2. Hours: Sat.–Sun., 10:00 A.M.–5:00 P.M.

The third event, held the last Sun. in Oct., is "an afternoon of family fun" with a Halloween theme, featuring a fortune-teller, face painting, mask making, a mad scientist cooking up trouble in the basement and games such as skeleton croquet and a slime run. Admission: $1. Hours: 1:00 P.M.–5:00 P.M. All three events take place at the homestead on **Metcalf Rd. half a mile from Grant Hill Rd. in Tolland; (860) 872-8673.**

Strawberry Moon Powwow
third weekend in June

This is very similar to the Connecticut River Powwow described under the **Middletown** chapter, but on a smaller scale. Admission: $6 adults, $4 seniors and children 6–12. Hours: Sat.–Sun., 11:00 A.M.–7:00 P.M. The location is the Four Town Fairground on Egypt Rd. in Somers. Confirm dates for the current year at **(860) 684-6984.**

Four Town Fair
second weekend after Labor Day (Thu.–Sun.)

Somers, Enfield, East Windsor and Ellington are the four towns that participate in the Four Town Fair. This was one of the first agricultural fairs to be organized in Connecticut back in 1838. The unquestioned highlight of the event is three nights of doodlebug (a farm vehicle—usually an old pickup truck—reinforced and rebuilt for strength) pulls, a variation on the horse and oxen pulls that are common at country fairs. There's also a gymkhana (barrel-racing and other maneuvers on horseback), a midway, entertainment, food and all the agricultural exhibits and activities you would expect at a country fair. Four Town Fairground is located at **56 Egypt Rd. (off Rte. 83) in Somers.** For more information immediately prior to and during the fair call **(860) 749-6527.** The rest of the year call **(860) 749-3340** or **(860) 749-2485.**

Chili Festival
last weekend in Sept.

This big chili cookoff is an International Chili Society–sanctioned event in two parts. A Connecticut state competition takes place the first day. Sat.'s winner goes on to compete the next day in the New England regional contest. Activities for spectators include live music and children's entertainment, pony rides and a petting zoo. There's lots of food to sample, and it's not limited to chili. If you have the stomach for multiple doses of fiery food, you can taste

Getting There

The village of Tolland is only about 20–25 minutes northeast of Hartford. From the capital it's a straight shot on I-84 to exit 68 and then a couple of minutes into town. From there you can access all the towns in upper Tolland County on smaller highways and back roads.

samples of the chilis cooked up each day and cast your vote for the winner of the People's Choice award. Admission charged. Hours: 11:00 A.M.–5:00 P.M. The cookoff takes place at the **Shallowbrook Equestrian Center on Hall Hill Rd. in Somers.** For more information call the **Development and Community Relations Department** of event sponsor **Johnson Memorial Hospital** at **(860) 684-8109.**

Victorian Lantern Light Weekend
mid-Oct.

Recently initiated, Lantern Light Weekend may become an annual event in Tolland. The idea is for a mystery to unfold around you as you take a one-hour tour of the historic sites and buildings near the town green. Costumed guides lead the activity, and the green and surrounding buildings are specially decorated for the occasion. Tours begin every half hour from 5:30 P.M. to 8:30 P.M. Tickets: $8. Reservations required. For information or reservations call **(860) 875-7552** or **(860) 870-9599.**

Outdoor Activities

Biking

Mountain Biking

Soapstone Mountain
Several broad dirt roads on the west side of Soapstone Mountain (described under Major Attractions) in Somers provide some mountainous and challenging mountain biking terrain. They are labeled Parker Rd. and Webster

Rd. on maps. You may have to dismount frequently unless you're an expert rider because the roads are severely eroded in places. It's pretty much a straight climb to the 1,075-foot summit with few or no breaks. The paved main entrance road off Gulf Rd. in Somers will give you the same elevation challenge without the rough road surface, so you could also make this trek on a road bike. On the way up just keep reminding yourself that there is a reward at the top: the view from the tower atop the mountain is incredible. Make sure your brakes and wrists are in good shape for coming back down.

Road Biking

This part of Connecticut varies dramatically in terrain. The western part of the area is at the very edge of the relatively flat Central Valley landscape. As you travel over the Eastern Wall the terrain gets mountainous rather quickly, subsiding somewhat into the gentle Tolland Range of rolling hills that covers most of the region. Be prepared for hills wherever you go. Here's a ride that will take you on a mix of back roads and highways with a moderate amount of automobile traffic. From the green in Tolland, take Old Stafford Rd. to the center of Stafford Springs. Go east briefly on busy Rte. 190 to River St. (Rte. 32) and make a right. This road runs directly alongside the Willimantic River for several miles before heading under I-84. At Rte. 74, turn right. There are a few picnic tables in a little patch of state forest land on the river here that make a nice stopping point. A few miles down the road you will return to your starting point. Total round-trip: 10–12 miles.

Boating

Pretty much the only lake in the region with public access, **Crystal Lake** is understandably popular and can be crowded. A free public boat launch (concrete, with pads) is located on the west side of the lake off Rte. 30 in Ellington, but there are many speed limit and other regulations. Check the *Connecticut Boater's Guide* for details.

Fishing

Lakes and Ponds

The largest and least developed body of water in this area is Connecticut Water Company's (CWC) **Shenipsit Lake.** It's open to the public for fishing through CWC's recreational use program. You need a valid Connecticut fishing license but no special permit. Trout are stocked, and there are also sizable populations of largemouth and smallmouth bass and panfish. You may launch your own boat (gasoline engines prohibited), but it must remain there in dry dock for 48 hours prior to use because of the zebra mussel alert. Loaner boats are available on a first-come, first-served basis. For a brochure showing designated shore-fishing areas, check with the lake activities monitor on-site sunrise–sunset at the boat storage area on Ellington Rd. in Tolland. The boating portion of the program ends Oct. 31; shoreline fishing continues until Dec. 15. For more information call **(800) 286-5700.**

Crystal Lake is a heavily stocked Trophy Trout Lake that also has a substantial population of largemouth bass. The shore is virtually all private, but there's access at the boat launch on the west side of the lake off Rte. 30 in Ellington, as well as from a stretch of that road at the northern tip of the lake. Of course, you can also fish from your boat.

The two Walker Reservoirs, East and West, are located on Reservoir Rd. right by I-84 exit 67 in Vernon. There's a handicapped fishing platform on Walker East, where trout are stocked. Walker West is a natural bass fishery. These are also recommended as spots to take small children fishing.

Rivers and Streams

In the **Belding Wild Trout Management Area** on the Tankerhoosen River, anglers are restricted to barbless, single-hook artificial lures and barbless, single-hook flies for catch-and-release fishing only. Park on tiny Bread and Milk Rd. in Vernon, then walk around the corner and look for a gate on Vernon Rd. marking the entrance.

State forest land surrounds a portion of **Roaring Brook,** a stocked trout stream, making for a quiet setting in which to fish. There's parking and good access on Fenton Rd. in Stafford.

There's also a trout management area limited to fly fishing on the **Willimantic River** from the mouth of Roaring Brook downstream to the Rte. 74 bridge on the Tolland/Willington town line. The land on either side of the river for most of this stretch is part of undeveloped Nye Holman State Forest. One good access point is from the I-84 westbound rest area, where you can leave your car. Look for a gate and a sign for the Cole W. Wilde Trout Management Area. Another entry point is Pero Rd. in the state forest off Rte. 74 on the Tolland side of the river. If you want to keep your catch, park at the commuter lot on Rte. 32 just south of Stafford Springs, and fish right there.

Snowmobiling

The paved access road up Soapstone Mountain and some other dirt roads form a rather linear network of designated snowmobile trails through Shenipsit State Forest. The terrain here is pretty much up or down. Access is off Gulf Rd. at the base of the Soapstone Mountain access road. To the east side of Gulf Rd. a straight section of trail leads to a small loop perhaps 2 miles long. The access road goes over the summit of Soapstone to some roads forming a long, narrow loop. The last portion of trail dead-ends at Rte. 83.

Seeing and Doing

Antiquing

One of the biggest antiques confabs in the Northeast happens three times each year just over the border in Massachusetts. One weekend each in May, July and Sept. bargain hunters make a beeline for Brimfield, where about 20 different shows go on simultaneously each with its own admission and parking fees and hours. The original and still the biggest of them all, with 500–800 exhibitors,is the J & J Promotions Auction Acres show, which was

started in 1959 by the grandfather of one of the current organizers. Admission to the J & J show is $5 on Fri. and $3 on Sat.; parking is $5. Their hours are 6:00 A.M.–5:00 P.M. on Fri.; 8:00 A.M.–5:00 P.M. on Sat. Other shows may run as early in the week as Tue. and as late as Sun. To get to Brimfield from Connecticut, take I-84 north or east to Sturbridge and pick up Rte. 20 west. Go approximately 6 miles to Brimfield. For more information, check the Antiques and the Arts Weekly annual calendar or weekly magazine **(c/o Newtown Bee, P.O. Box 5503, Newtown, CT 06470; 203-426-8036).**

Museums

Also see the listing for the Hicks-Stearns House Museum under Major Attractions, and consider a visit to one of the area's local history museums. The Ellington Historical Society maintains the **Nellie E. McKnight Museum,** a Federal-style house built in 1812 and modernized in the 1920s. In addition to the house and its furnishings, you can see exhibits of items from local residents, including a Venetian glass collection. Hours: Sat., noon–4:00 P.M., May–Oct., & by appointment. **70 Main St. (Rte. 286), Ellington, 06029.** For more information call **(860) 875-1136.**

There is a museum in Stafford Spring's former railroad depot at the corner of Rtes. 32 and 190. Its holdings include a large postcard collection, a video on local history and products made in Stafford, such as pearl buttons, stoves and woolens. The museum is open the second Sun. of each month, 2:00 P.M.–4:00 P.M., Sept.–June, & Thu., 2:00 P.M.–4:00 P.M., in July & Aug. For more information call **(860) 684-3646** or **(860) 684-5115.**

Somers's museum is housed in the town's first library, which was recently moved to the town green. For more information call **(860) 763-8205.**

Daniel Benton Homestead
The Tolland Historical Society gives visitors to this cape house (ca. 1720) a feel for 18th-century farm life. Architectural highlights of the homestead include large fireplaces with

ovens, original wainscoting and painted floors. Several period rooms are filled with appropriate furnishings, and two cases display pre-1780 artifacts excavated from the property. Special events include two encampments and a Halloween activity day each year (see the listing under Festivals and Events), in addition to numerous lectures and demonstrations. Admission: $2. Hours: Sun., 1:00 P.M.–4:00 P.M., mid-May–mid-Oct., & by appointment. Located on **Metcalf Rd. half a mile from Grant Hill Rd. in Tolland; (860) 872-8673.**

Northeast States Civilian Conservation Corps Museum

This museum documents the activities of the Depression-era agency responsible for developing so much of the national and state park system in the northeastern states. Although it existed for only nine years, the Civilian Conservation Corps left an indelible mark on our public lands. The museum interprets their work through photographs, artifacts and the written word. Admission is free. Hours: noon–4:00 P.M. daily, Memorial Day–Labor Day, & by appointment in May, Sept. & early Oct. **166 Chestnut Hill Rd., Stafford Springs, 06076; (860) 684-3430.**

Old County Jail Museum and Tolland County Courthouse

Because the village of Tolland was once the Tolland county seat, the Superior Court met here and the County Jail was here. The courthouse saw its last case in the late 1800s and later served as the town library. The jail ceased operation in 1968, when the building was taken over by the Tolland Historical Society. The jail building is unique, having a Victorian house attached to the front in which the warden lived. The complex now houses artifacts from Tolland's past: clothing, household goods, furniture, tools, a large collection of Indian arrowheads and more.

The cell blocks in the back of the structure have been retained so you can see the sort of conditions county prisoners could expect. Opposite them are numerous newspaper stories and other paraphernalia having to do with the jail, which was regarded as one of the "nicest"

jails at which one could hope to do time. When you are done here, walk across the street to the old County Courthouse to see an excellent example of a 19th-century courthouse with all its fixtures still intact. Admission: $2. Hours: Sun., 1:00 P.M.–4:00 P.M., Mar.–Dec. **52 Tolland Green, Tolland, 06084; (860) 870-9599.**

Somers Mountain Museum of Natural History and Primitive Technology

What used to be called the Somers Mountain Indian Museum, in reference to its large collection of arrowheads, buckskins, war clubs and other Native American artifacts, is small but unique in its mission of preserving early technologies and knowledge. The collection contains items from across the country, and the exhibits are expanded upon in a series of workshops in skills such as bow making, hide tanning, drum building, bead and quill work, pottery and so on. Call for a schedule of classes. Admission: $2 adults, $.99 children 5–16. Hours: the first weekend in Apr.–Memorial Day & Labor Day–Jan. 1, open Sat.–Sun., 10:00 A.M.–5:00 P.M.; Memorial Day–Labor Day, open Wed.–Sun., 10:00 A.M.–5:00 P.M. **332 Turnpike Rd., Somers, 06071; (860) 749-4129.**

Sports

Horse shows and polo meets take place at **Shallowbrook Equestrian and Polo Center** year-round thanks to extensive indoor and outdoor facilities. The highlight of the polo season is the National Arena Open, the highest-rated polo tournament in the country, which takes place in late Apr. each year. There are also polo meets every Sun. at 2:30 P.M., year-round, & league polo on Fri. at 7:30 P.M. in winter (Oct.–Apr.) & 5:00 P.M. in summer. Annual horse shows (hunters and jumpers) are held in Nov., Dec., Feb., Mar. and the first weekend in June. Admission to most events is $5 per person. Seating is on bleachers indoors; for summer meets bring a lawn chair or blanket. **247 Hall Hill Rd., Somers, 06071; (860) 749-0749.**

Tours

A century ago the textile industry was *the* industry in northeastern Connecticut. Most of the mills have been silent for years, but one holdout is Warren of Stafford, makers of specialty fabrics such as cashmeres and camel hairs, and it gives free, 90-minute factory tours to groups of five or more. It has a mill store on-site where you can buy fabrics off the bolt as well as some garments made from its fabrics, and it offers custom tailoring, so you can have a garment made to your measurements in 4–6 weeks. To get the full tour you do need to have a means of getting around (part of the tour is at a different location), and you must be able to climb lots of stairs. Tours can be given Tue.–Fri., 10:00 A.M.–5:00 P.M.; reserve at least one week in advance. The store is open Tue.–Sat., 10:00 A.M.–5:00 P.M. **29 Furnace Ave., Stafford, 06075; (860) 684-2766.**

Where to Stay

Bed & Breakfasts

English Lane—$$$
The name of this B&B, owned by Tracey and Lane Aubin, is derived from the fact that she is English and his name is Lane. Their recently restored 1840 colonial is in tip-top shape, looking like a new house although much of it is original. There are two guest rooms with private but unattached baths. Robes are provided for making the trip across the hallway. One room is done in Laura Ashley florals with a queen brass bed. The second is done in Waverly patterns and has a bathroom/sitting room with a daybed that could accommodate a third person. A full breakfast is served. **816 Tolland Stage Rd. (Rte. 74), Tolland, 06084; (860) 871-6618.**

Old Babcock Tavern—$$ to $$$
If you love restored colonials, you'll love the Old Babcock Tavern. Not only is it a beautiful example of an early-18th-century center-chimney home, but the proprietors Stu and Barbara Danforth actually did the restoration

themselves and documented much of it, which you can see in the form of a slide show transferred to video. The house was first licensed as an inn at least as early as 1794, and the original taproom is still an area for guests to enjoy a drink. All rooms have private (sometimes separate) baths and double beds. There is a small "overflow" room with a twin bed for an extra person. A full breakfast is served by candlelight to classical music. Rates are very reasonable. **484 Mile Hill Rd. (Rte. 31 at Cedar Swamp Rd.), Tolland, 06084; (860) 875-1239.**

Hotels, Motels & Inns

The Tolland Inn—$$$ to $$$$
Whatever room is yours for the night at The Tolland Inn, you'll probably sleep on or otherwise use furniture crafted by one of your hosts. Stephen Beeching is a talented woodworker who makes only custom pieces. He and his wife keep an inn that feels like a large B&B. Their home on the Tolland green features seven unique rooms, traditionally furnished, some simply and some more ornately. One ground-floor room has a private entrance, a fireplace, a hot tub inside the bathroom and a canopied bed. All rooms have air-conditioning and private baths. A full breakfast and afternoon tea are served in a formal dining room or on a glassed-in porch with a fireplace that is lit in winter. **63 Tolland Green, Tolland, 06084; (860) 872-0800.**

Where to Eat

Chez Pierre—$$$$
Housed in a Victorian building with a mansard roof, Chez Pierre is an unexpected find on the main street of Stafford Springs. Expect a very traditional restaurant experience and traditional French cuisine with offerings such as Chateaubriand and cassoulet. It offers both fixed-price and à la carte dining and a complete wine list. Proper attire is required; jacket preferred for gentlemen. Hours: Wed.–Sat., 5:00 P.M.–closing; also open on Mother's Day. **111 Main St. (Rte. 190), Stafford Springs, 06076; (860) 684-5826.**

The Quiet Corner

The Somers Inn—$$$ to $$$$

With its beautifully set tables and country inn atmosphere, the Somers Inn is the most traditional setting for an American/Continental meal in the area. At lunch, in addition to reduced portions of most of their dinner entrées, it offers sandwiches, salads and a choice of unusual omelets. Lunch/brunch hours: Tue.–Fri., 11:30 A.M.–2:30 P.M.; Sun., 10:30 A.M.–2:30 P.M. Dinner served Tue.–Sat., 5:00 P.M.–9:00 P.M. (10:00 P.M. on weekends); Sun., noon–8:00 P.M. **585 Main St. (corner of Rtes. 83 and 190), Somers, 06071; (860) 749-2256.**

Baker's Fare—$$ to $$$

Baker's Fare is one of the best options for family dining in this area, especially if you're visiting Stafford Motor Speedway. It serves only breakfast and lunch on some days, and three meals on others, focusing on made-from-scratch casual American food. Lunch is soups, salads, sandwiches and grinders. The dinner menu ranges from prime rib to a fried fish platter to pasta. One specialty available lunch and dinner is a stuffed pie somewhat like a tall pizza. The restaurant is situated in an old house with wood floors and a colonial look. All the furnishings are from the Baker's Country Furniture store next door, which is run by the same family. Hours: Tue.–Thu. & Sun., 7:00 A.M.–4:00 P.M.; Fri.–Sat., 7:00 A.M.–9:00 P.M. **42 W. Main St., Stafford Springs, 06076; (860) 684-2040.**

Lotus Restaurant—$$ to $$$

Vietnamese cuisine, for those who are unfamiliar with it, is perhaps closest in taste to Thai food, relying heavily on the flavors of lemongrass, chilis, scallions, tamarind and gingerroot. Vegetarians will find a large number of possibilities here, and lunch dishes are an exceptional bargain. Hours: Tue.–Sat., lunch served 11:30 A.M.–2:00 P.M.; dinner served 5:00 P.M.–9:00 P.M. **409 Hartford Tpke. (Rte. 30 off I-84 exit 65), Vernon, 06066; (860) 871-8962.**

Rein's New York Style Deli—$$ to $$$

Got a craving for brisket or noodel kugel? How about smoked fish on a bagel or a huge Reuben sandwich? For miles around, the only place you'll find New York–style deli food is at Rein's. In addition to selling everything by the pound or the piece for take-out, it's also a full-service restaurant with a liquor license, serving three meals, seven days a week. The same family has been preparing much of what they serve on the premises for more than 25 years. The atmosphere is bright and family-friendly. Hours: 7:00 A.M.–midnight daily. **435 Hartford Tpke. (Rte. 30 off I-84 exit 65), Vernon, 06066; (860) 875-1344.**

Willington Pizza—$$ to $$$

Pizza parlors proliferate elsewhere, but not in Tolland County. Maybe it's because the competition from Willington Pizza is too stiff. Their red potato pizza—more like a potato skin than anything Italian—is the biggest seller. The seafood casino pizza was also recognized at a national competition. And with the recent addition of a grill, it has expanded beyond pies and Italian entrées to surf 'n' turf and other American classics. To complement it all, it has 20 beers on tap. The restaurant is located in an 18th-century building with exposed beams in the main dining room and every square inch of wall space occupied with stuff ranging from Americana to UConn sports memorabilia. Hours: 11:00 A.M.–11:00 P.M. daily. **25 River Rd. (Rte. 32 one-quarter mile north of Rte. 195), Willington, 06279; (860) 429-7433.**

La Petite France—$

Not a place to eat per se, La Petite France is a bakery where you can stock up on baguettes for a picnic or pastries to satisfy a sweet tooth. It's pretty easy to find: head down the main road through Stafford Springs and look for the French flag. Open Tue.–Sun., 6:00 A.M.–6:00 P.M. **88 W. Main St. (Rte. 190), Stafford Springs, 06076; (860) 684-9408.**

Track Nine Diner—$

If you're looking for a fun breakfast and lunch place, especially if you're traveling with kids, visit this restaurant decorated on a railroad theme. It's located on a stretch of functioning track, so a freight train might pass by during the meal to shake the walls and spark young imaginations. The food is straightforward:

eggs, cereals and pancakes in the morning with breakfast specials on the weekend; burgers, dogs and sandwiches at lunch. Hours: 6:00 A.M.–2:00 P.M. daily. **12 Tolland Tpke. (Rte. 74 a quarter mile from I-84 exit 69), Willington, 06279; (860) 487-1619.**

Services

Local Visitors Information

Greater Hartford Tourism District, 234 Murphy Rd., Hartford, 06114; (800) 793-4480 or **(860) 244-8181.**

North Central Tourism Bureau, 111 Hazard Ave., Enfield, 06082; (800) 248-8283 or **(860) 763-2578.**

State Welcome Centers

A state welcome center is located on I-84 westbound at exit 70 in Willington. Hours: 8:00 A.M.–6:00 P.M. daily during spring & summer, 9:00 A.M.–5:00 P.M. daily in fall & winter. The facilities, including picnic tables, barbeques, rest rooms, vending machines and parking, are open 24 hours, and the center was recently renovated to increase accessibility.

Transportation

Regional bus service between towns in the northeast is provided by the **Windham Transit District** at **(860) 456-2221** and the **Northeastern Connecticut Transit District** at **(860) 774-1253.**

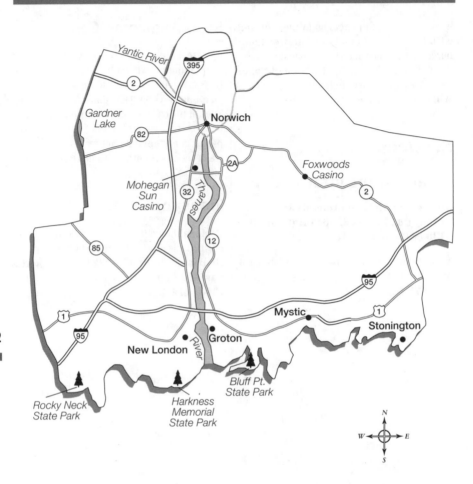

Yantic River

395

2

Gardner
Lake

Norwich

82

2A

Foxwoods
Casino

Mohegan
Sun
Casino

32

Thames

2

85

12

95

1

Mystic

1

95

Stonington

New London

Groton

River

Bluff Pt.
State Park

Rocky Neck
State Park

Harkness
Memorial
State Park

N

W ← → E

S

Seafaring Southeast

Seafaring
Southeast

Mystic

The Mystic coast attracts more visitors than any other part of Connecticut, largely because of the presence of Mystic Seaport, the noted maritime museum in the setting of a 19th-century whaling village on the banks of the Mystic River, and the Mystic Marinelife Aquarium. The village of Mystic is among the most picturesque in Connecticut and very strongly oriented toward tourists, with lots of shops and restaurants, an excellent art association gallery and a downtown area ideal for strolling. It is also completely unique in one odd respect. Most Connecticut villages lie entirely within the bounds of one town, but Mystic is shared by two towns: Stonington and Groton. Mystic's famed bascule bridge joins the two halves of the community, which are separated by the Mystic River. Because of this anomaly and other reasons, it's a good idea to get specific directions to any local destination.

If the bustle of Mystic gets to you, head for the borough of Stonington, the prettiest seaside village in Connecticut. Two blocks of interesting stores and restaurants plus two museums are among the attractions, but the best thing to do there is simply walk through the streets admiring the colorful houses and breathing the salt air. At the end of Water St. (the main drag) you'll find a parking lot, a picnic table (count your blessings if you're lucky enough to get it), a small lawn and du Bois beach. After Labor Day there is no fee for swimming, and it's a slice of heaven on a sunny day in early Sept. after the summer crowds are gone.

History

Mystic was the site of an early and decisive event in European-Indian relations in Connecticut. The Pequots who figured so prominently in the early political history of the area had a fort here in the 1630s. As a result of a Pequot raid at Wethersfield in which several settlers were killed and of prior conflicts with neighboring Indian tribes, an alliance of colonists under the command of Maj. John Mason, Mohegan Indians loyal to the sachem Uncas and a number of Narragansett Indians participated in a merciless attack on the fort in 1637. Many hundreds of Pequots were killed, and Mason, in his history of what came to be called the Pequot War, referred to "[God] crushing his proud enemies and the enemies of his people."

The virtual destruction of the Pequots left land in southeastern Connecticut up for grabs. Massachusetts lay claim to some because it had provided men and ammunition for the 1637 raid. In 1658 it was given jurisdiction of the area from the Mystic River east past what would eventually become the Rhode Island line and called it Southerton. Massachusetts control was short-lived, however. The royal charter of 1662 set definite bounds for Connecticut, and they included Southerton.

Under Connecticut jurisdiction, the entire town was at first called Mystic. Despite its resemblance to a bona fide English word, the name is actually a corruption of an Indian term that sounded something like "misstuck," meaning "large tidal river." Only one year later, though, the town name was changed to Stonington, which is quite descriptive of the native soil. Now only the village is called Mystic.

One of the more famous episodes in Stonington history took place in 1814 during the War of 1812. Long Island Sound was blockaded by the British, who engaged in some threatening posturing off the coast at Stonington village. The captain in command of the British fleet sent a note warning the residents that they had one hour to leave town. The townspeople replied defiantly that they would defend themselves, and the Battle of Stonington commenced. The British bombarded Stonington for three days with Congreve rockets and other munitions. The villagers' original one-hour supply of cannonballs was replenished from New London and, with only three cannon, Stonington did far greater damage to the British than the British inflicted on Stonington. One of the cannon fired in the battle still sits facing seaward in Cannonball Square.

Shipbuilding was a natural occupation for villagers in Mystic and Stonington where there was easy access to Long Island Sound. The first mention of shipbuilding dates back to about 1680. Shipbuilding also dovetailed perfectly with whaling, which rose to a peak in the mid-1800s when whale oil was the preferred fuel and lubricant for many uses. The lamps in early lighthouses along the Connecticut shore were all lit with whale oil. Both shipbuilding and whaling gave rise to innumerable small and large supply businesses, but manufacturing was also important, even as late as the mid-20th century. Some of the first plastics were made in Stonington at a Monsanto factory, and the village was also known for its pottery.

One of the more important 20th-century events in Stonington, at least from the perspective of a visitor today, was the establishment of the Maritime Historical Association in 1929. Now known as Mystic Seaport, this non-profit institution is dedicated to preserving and interpreting American maritime heritage with an emphasis on the 19th century and the Atlantic coast. Mystic Seaport has been the number-one tourist attraction in Connecticut for many years, and although Foxwoods Casino might draw more in sheer numbers, Mystic Seaport is undoubtedly still the most popular destination in the state for families and among the most worthwhile in the entire Northeast.

Major Attractions

Mystic Marinelife Aquarium

One of Connecticut's two major aquaria, Mystic Marinelife Aquarium features numerous indoor tanks, outdoor penguin and seal habitats and a "marine theater" where beluga whales, bottlenose dolphins and their trainers put on shows several times daily. My favorite exhibit is the New England Coastal Waters display, an open-topped, plastic-sided tank with a water depth of only about 14 inches. Inside is a whole community of flounder, catfish, hake, skate, crabs, starfish, sea anemones and more. The tank is supported at kid's-eye-view height, with little platforms so even really small children can look at these native New England sea creatures eye-to-eye. Admission: $10.50 adults, $9.50 seniors, $7.50 children 3–12. Hours: 9:00 A.M.–6:00 P.M. daily, July 1–Labor Day; 9:00 A.M.–5:00 P.M. daily the rest of the year. **55 Coogan Blvd., Mystic, 06355; (860) 572-5955.**

Mystic Seaport

When you read about Mystic Seaport, you can't help but wonder if it will be little more than a glorified theme park. Happily, the museum's administrators seem to trust in the ability of

Interpreters help make Mystic Seaport come alive; this one is explaining the cooper's trade.

216

visitors to appreciate the inherent value of the museum's exhibits without making them into a circus. It is the most-visited attraction in Connecticut for good reason.

Mystic Seaport's collection of maritime artifacts includes a whole village of historic buildings and workshops as well as vintage watercraft, all explained and enhanced by a huge variety of daily and seasonal public programs for both adults and children. The museum bills itself as "The Museum of America and the Sea," and it manages to cover that broad claim pretty thoroughly with displays about shipbuilding, life at sea and on shore, sailors' skills, fishing (everything from oysters to whales) and much more. Interpreters are on hand at many locations to answer questions and give demonstrations. Where there are no helpers, drawings, documents and audiovisual materials do the job.

When you arrive, you'll be given a map and a schedule of the day's events. Do take a few minutes to scan them. Mystic Seaport is not especially large, but there is a lot in a small space, and taking part in the special programming can enhance your experience tremendously. Deciding beforehand what's most important to you will help you have a satisfying visit, but if you run out of time, you'll be happy to know that

your ticket is also good for the next calendar day. Just ask for a validation when you leave.

First on my "be sure to see" list is the docked exhibit vessel *Charles W. Morgan*, the last surviving American wooden whaling ship. Built in 1840–1841 in New Bedford, Massachusetts, it is a National Historic Landmark. Don't miss the chance to climb below deck to see the sailors' quarters and hold. There are also two other tall ships open for boarding.

Once you've explored these beautiful old vessels, you'll probably find yourself all pumped up for a ride on the water. Excursion options run the gamut from the *Sabino*, "the last coal-fired passenger steamer in operation in the United States," to a simple rowboat. All daytime boat excursions involve a charge over and above museum admission, but museum admission is not required for evening trips on the *Sabino*. To make same-day reservations for evening cruises on *Sabino* (reservations are not taken for daily half-hour cruises) call **(860) 572-5351** after 10:00 A.M. Same-day reservations for daytime rentals and rides on other vessels can be made at **(860) 572-0711, ext. 4233.** The season for boat trips and rentals is mid-May–mid-Oct.

On the way over to the excursion boats, stop for a quick look at the Mystic River scale model, where you can orient yourself to the sights you'll see from the water. Later on, explore the village; the cooperage is my favorite stop. Other attractions include a planetarium with daily shows and a bookstore with a huge selection of titles on maritime subjects. The Seamen's Inne is a full-service restaurant on-site. Admission: $16 adults, $8 children 6–15. Hours vary by season but are generally 9:00 A.M.–5:00 P.M. in summer (until 6:00 P.M. in July & Aug.) & 10:00 A.M.–4:00 P.M. in winter. Open daily except Christmas Day. **75 Greenmanville Ave. (Rte. 27), Mystic, 06355; (860) 572-0711.**

Mystic Village

Regardless of what brings you to the Mystic area, don't leave without visiting the village itself. Its appeal can be attributed to a concentration of nifty shops, restaurants and lodgings on Main and W. Main Sts. and a landmark bascule drawbridge that opens hourly in summer to let vessels pass on their way up and down the beautiful Mystic River that divides the village in two. The bridge was built in 1922 and is the oldest of its type in the country. Its twin "hammerheads" are counterweights that provide the poundage needed to hoist the bridge's considerable mass. You can see it operate every day in summer at a quarter past the hour (except 12:15) between 7:15 A.M. and 7:15 P.M.

You can take a cruise right from the center of town, peruse fine art by regional talent at the Mystic Art Association, enjoy a coffee at an outdoor café and sample some of the best ice cream made in Connecticut at Mystic Drawbridge Ice Cream Shoppe, where they also have a great wooden deck overlooking the river. During summer a trolley runs between the downtown, Mystic Seaport, Mystic Marinelife Aquarium and several hotels.

Festivals and Events

Mystic Seaport Events

Mystic Seaport has at least one major event every month between Apr. and Dec. There are too many to list separately, but the Lobsterfest (three days in late May), the Sea Music Festival (four days in early June), the Antique Boat Show (three days in late June), the Chowderfest (three days in mid-Oct.) and Dec. Lantern Light Tours are some highlights. Lobsterfest and Chowderfest are really all about eating. At the Sea Music Festival you'll be treated to traditional songs of the sea performed live. Over 100 vessels are docked at Mystic Seaport for the Antique Boat Show, completely filling the waterfront. Finally, on a Lantern Light Tour you watch a traveling Victorian drama while touring the museum after dark (see the Tours section). All events take place at **Mystic Seaport, 75 Greenmanville Ave. (Rte. 27), Mystic, 06355; (860) 572-0711.**

Getting There

Mystic is located in the most southeastern town in Connecticut, just a few miles from the Rhode Island border and right on Long Island Sound. From Hartford the easiest route by car is south on I-91, south on Rte. 9 and east on I-95 to exit 90. The trip will take about an hour and a half under good conditions. Train and air service are also available; see the Services section for more.

Spring Crafts Festival
Memorial Day weekend

Kick off the summer with a visit to this juried craft show with more than 100 exhibitors displaying their work both indoors and out. Unlike the Outdoor Art Festival that also takes place in Mystic (but at a different location), this

An interpreter taking apart a barrel at Mystic Seaport; a member of the audience helped reassemble it.

show is 100% crafts. Admission: $2 adults, children under 12 free. Hours: Sat., 10:00 A.M.–5:00 P.M.; Sun., 11:00 A.M.–4:00 P.M. The show takes place at the **Mystic Community Center off Mason's Island Rd., Mystic, 06355; (860) 536-3575.**

North Stonington Agricultural Fair
second full weekend in July (Thu.–Sun.)

North Stonington's celebration of its farm heritage is one of the state's moderately sized country fairs where you'll find all the classic activities: draft animal and tractor pulls, a horse show, tests of prowess in pie eating and nail driving, antique farm machinery, judging of all things agricultural, a petting zoo, entertainment and a midway. On Sun. around midday there are kid's contests, such as bubble blowing, wheelbarrow races and a softball toss, that don't require advance registration—anyone can participate. The early morning hours tend to be filled with animal judging and other purely agricultural events; the midway opens late morning. Plenty of free, on-site parking is available. Admission: $5 adults, $3 seniors (Sat. only), children under 12 free. Hours: Thu.–Fri., 5:00 P.M.–midnight; Sat., 9:00 A.M.–midnight; Sun., 9:00 A.M.–8:00 P.M. The fairgrounds are located on **Wyassup Rd. (1 mile from Rte. 2) in North Stonington.** For more information call the fair secretary at **(860) 599-8498.**

Blessing of the Fleet
last weekend in July

A tradition in many coastal communities like Stonington, the annual blessing of the fishing fleet here has grown to become a town celebration. Strictly speaking, it's not just the fishing fleet that gets blessed; many pleasure boats also take part in the ceremony. The timing, however, reflects that fact that late July is a slack period for lobstering. The event starts with a Sat. night lobster feast (5:00 P.M.–midnight) and musical entertainment at Stonington town dock at the end of Front St. The next morning at 10:30 A.M., a fisherman's mass is

held at St. Mary's Church in town. A parade beginning at 1:00 P.M. features floats, a statue of St. Peter and local bands and organizations marching through the streets of the borough to the site of the blessing at the dock, which starts around 3:00 P.M. A Catholic bishop of the Norwich diocese blesses each boat individually as it passes by, after which they form a procession out into the harbor to hold a memorial service for lost sailors. For more information call **(860) 535-3150.**

Mystic Outdoor Art Festival
second weekend in Aug.

This juried arts and crafts festival takes place on the sidewalks of downtown Mystic. Over 250 artists exhibit painting, photography, sculpture and other fine arts, complemented by the jewelry, pottery, textiles and other creations of more than 60 craftspeople. The event is free. Hours: 10:00 A.M.–dusk both days. For more information call the **Mystic Chamber of Commerce** at **(860) 572-9578.**

A Taste of Connecticut
weekend after Labor Day (Fri.–Sun.)

One of the bigger "Taste of ..." events in Connecticut every year takes place in Mystic but features restauranteurs from around the state. Over 30 of the best eateries offer samples of their culinary creations from booths up and down Cottrell St. in downtown. There's live music and activities for children. Pay as you eat. Hours: Fri., 5:00 P.M.–10:00 P.M.; Sat., 10:00 A.M.–10:00 P.M.; Sun., noon–5:00 P.M. For more information call the **Mystic Community Center** at **(860) 536-3575.**

Santa Arrives in Mystic by Tugboat
Sat. after Thanksgiving

Foregoing the conventional sleigh, Santa arrives in this coastal town aboard a vehicle better suited to the water: Mystic Seaport's tugboat *Kingston II*. He rides up the Mystic River to the drawbridge at Main St., where he disembarks around 2:00 P.M., greets children and hands out candy canes. The occasion is preceded by caroling and a daytime tree-lighting ceremony at 1:30 P.M. For more information call the **Mystic Chamber of Commerce** at **(860) 572-9578.**

First Night
New Year's Eve

Mystic puts on a good show to ring in the new year. Between 6:00 P.M. and midnight more than 100 performances of all sorts take place at about 18 locations. There's sure to be a lot of music and children's activities, but you might also be treated to dance, comedy, theater—it changes from year to year. The festivities culminate in a fireworks display over the Mystic River at midnight. Admission to all events comes with a button that you can purchase in advance ($7 before Dec. 25, $10 after Dec. 25) or on Dec. 31. Children 4 and under are admitted free. For more information call **(860) 536-3575.**

Outdoor Activities

Biking

Road Biking

The Mystic area is rather congested, but there are a few places where you can bike safely yet still be close to the activities in the center of town. The Masons Island area is a beautiful community of private homes and quiet streets with occasional glimpses of Mystic Harbor and Long Island Sound. There's a marina in the northwest corner with a restaurant. The lower part of Mason Pt. is private. It's okay to bike Mon.–Thu., but Fri.–Sun. from May to mid-Oct. guards are posted to keep out all but local traffic. If you're in Mystic during the right hours, though, Masons Island is a great place for a very low-key ride.

Another spot yielding excellent water views is River Rd. in Mystic on the west side of the

Mystic River. You'll enjoy the best view around of Mystic Seaport on the opposite bank. You can take this all the way up to Burnetts Corner, where you can cross the river on Rte. 27. Stay on the west side of the river to have access to the quiet back roads of Ledyard; on the east side you can ride for miles into North Stonington. To avoid auto traffic just stay away from any numbered highway, and be aware that it gets hilly quite fast as you move inland.

A third place to ride where the terrain is flat and you can cover a fair distance without having to make many turns is Green Haven Rd. in Stonington east of Stonington borough. The road runs for about 6 miles through very quiet neighborhoods and undeveloped land in the southeast corner of town. Palmer Neck Rd., a dead end leading to a state boat launch, makes an interesting detour. If you start in Wequetequock you'll end up in Pawcatuck, a large town on a river of the same name directly across from Westerly, Rhode Island. The surroundings get a bit industrial-looking as you approach Pawcatuck, but once you're there you can get a bite to eat or a beverage at any number of places. Return the same way you came or, if you don't mind traffic, complete a loop on Rte. 1.

If you need a rental, try **Mystic Cycle Center** at **7 Williams Ave. in Mystic; (860) 572-7433.** They'll rent by the day and longer periods, with a discount for every additional bike you rent.

Birding

Barn Island Wildlife Management Area, a large coastal preserve in Stonington, is an unstructured environment for catching a glimpse of shorebirds such as egrets and herons. Access is via Palmer Neck Rd. If you prefer a more "developed" site, head to the **Denison Pequotsepos Nature Center** and pick up the flyer listing all 169 species that have been sighted at this 125-acre sanctuary. Some birds of prey made unreleasable by injury are also in residence. Birding books, optics and more are available in an excellent gift shop. For more information, see the listing under Nature Centers.

219

Boating

Freshwater

Anderson Pond (also known as Blue Lake) is a small, shallow body of water good for small powerboats and ideal for canoes and rowboats. There's a public boat launch off Cossaduck Hill Rd. in North Stonington, but parking is limited.

Although **Billings Lake** (105 acres) is suitable for small powerboats, car-top boats present fewer launching problems. The access road here is narrow, the turnaround is small, the ramp is steep and parking is limited. The lake is quite pretty, though, with very clear water. There are several tiny islands out in the center, two of which are state-owned. They are open for exploration, but you cannot camp or picnic. The launch is located at the end of Billings Lake Rd. in North Stonington.

At 97 acres, **Wyassup Lake** is on the small side and enjoys an undeveloped western shore of state forest land. It is suitable for both car-top and small powerboats. Speed limits are in effect here at times; check the *Connecticut Boater's Guide* for details. The launch is located off Wyassup Lake Rd. in North Stonington. Follow signs from Rte. 2.

Pretty **Lake of Isles,** 87 acres in size, has a largely undeveloped shoreline and a dam on private property at the northern end. There are indeed several small islands out in the middle. Although motors are allowed, there is an 8 m.p.h. speed limit. This should be an enjoyable spot for exploring in a canoe or rowboat. Lake of Isles Rd. is off Watson Rd. off Rte. 2 in Preston. Follow it to the end; signs there direct you to the boat launch, which is actually in North Stonington. Pit toilets are provided. The boat launch here may become private in coming years but is currently state-owned, so just go and see how it's posted. If it has become private, the other lakes listed here are close by.

Saltwater

If you'll be using a lot of marine services, obtain a copy of the "Mystic Waterfront Directory," a brochure published by the **Mystic Chamber of Commerce (16 Cottrell St.; 860-572-9578).** It lists marinas, charter fishing and cruise operators, boat liveries and more (much of the information is included here under the Boating, Fishing and Tours sections).

Be aware of the bridge opening schedule if you'll be traveling up the Mystic River. There are two bridges: a railroad swing bridge at the mouth of the river that is usually open (the bridge tender can be reached at **860-444-4908** or on VHF 13 if it is not), and a bascule drawbridge where Main St. crosses the river. The bascule bridge is normally closed, opening at one-quarter past the hour from 7:15 A.M. to 7:15 P.M. (except 12:15) daily and on demand at other times May–Oct. During winter you must give eight hours notice by calling the bridge tender at **(860) 536-7070** or on VHF 13. The passage is narrow; boats traveling with the tide have right-of-way.

If you want to rent a boat, give **Shaffer's Boat Livery** a call. They have a fleet of 16-foot fiberglass skiffs with 6 HP engines. Call for pricing and details. Shaffer's is located at **106 Mason's Island Rd., Mystic, 06355; (860) 536-8713.**

The best access to Long Island Sound is at the public boat launch at Wequetequock Cove in the Barn Island Wildlife Management Area. You'll find it at the end of Palmer Neck Rd. off

Long Island Sound's protected waters draw sailors like this man in a catamaran. Photo courtesy Connecticut's Mystic and More!

Green Haven Rd. in Stonington. It's crowded on weekends, but a double ramp helps accommodate demand. A fee is charged in summer.

Marinas

Mystic River Marina (800-344-8840 or **860-536-3123;** VHF 9) on Masons Island has 50 transient slips and offers the broadest range of amenities and facilities in the area of Mystic proper, but is open only seasonally. Although it's not walking distance from Mystic village, it has most of the services you want on-site. To the west side of Mystic Harbor on Willow Pt. is **Mystic Shipyard (860-536-9436;** VHF 9), and right along the river above the railroad bridge but below the bascule bridge are **Fort Rachel Marine Service (860-536-6647;** VHF 68), **Mystic Harbor Marine (860-536-1210;** VHF 9), **Seaport Marine Inc. (860-536-9681)** and many more. With an advance reservation (call months ahead of time) you can even dock right at **Mystic Seaport (860-572-5391;** VHF 16), although this still puts you a distance from Mystic village. Admission to the museum is included in the dockage fee. At Stonington village across town, the principal marina is **Dodson's Boat Yard (860-535-1507;** VHF 78). **Harbor View (860-535-2720)** is a waterfront restaurant that has historically offered dockage for customers. Call to find out its current status.

Fishing

Freshwater

Anderson Pond (Blue Lake) is a very small, shallow body of water that is stocked with trout in spring and is also good for smallmouth and largemouth bass and pickerel. **Billings Lake** is a deep body of water that is stocked with trout and also yields several species of panfish and some big bass. Smallmouth and largemouth bass, in addition to panfish such as yellow perch and sunfish, are found at **Wyassup Lake.** It's also stocked with trout in spring. State forest land on the western shore provides excellent access for anglers. **Lake of Isles** is a panfish lake, with little in the way of game fish. Pickerel and black crappie are two predominant species. All of these ponds have a

public boat launch, so you can fish from shore or from a boat. See Boating for directions.

Saltwater

Saltwater fishing in the Mystic/Stonington area is by charter only. For party boats you have to go to New London, which is only about 20 minutes away. The **Blue Heron (860-535-3387)** departs from Stonington for striped bass June–Oct. The **Lorna Anne (860-423-9121)** departs Mystic for full- and half-day outings late Apr.–Oct. for "whatever's running"— blues, bass, flounder, fluke, blackfish and more. Capt. Art Goodwin of the **Magic** out of Mystic Harbor Marina does mostly inshore fishing for blues and bass, half days and full days as well as nights. He is also currently setting up a small boat especially for light tackle/saltwater fly fishing. There's also the **Karen Ann (860-345-2570)** out of the same marina. Capt. Jeff Eckert specializes in 12-hour offshore trips for shark, tuna and marlin, but also goes after inshore species for full and half days.

Also consider the cluster of operators that depart from Noank, which is just a stone's throw from Mystic. For inshore and offshore fishing, give the **Mataura** a call at **(800) 605-6265** or **(860) 536-6970.** You can charter it for a half day or a full day to go for blues, bonita, bass, tuna and shark. Capt. Tom also caters to customers interested in saltwater fly fishing. Another Noank inshore/offshore specialist is **Trophy Hunter Sportfishing (860-536-4460).** Half-day, full-day and 12-hour trips are all available.

If you're willing to go farther west, see the **New London** chapter for more fishing options. Call **Mystic & More** at **(800) 863-6569** for a complete and up-to-date list of area charter operators. The free *Connecticut Vacation Guide*, available by calling **(800) 282-6863,** also contains a list.

Golf

Ben Jackson's
New England Golf Academy

This golf school at private Stonington Golf Course offers classes ranging from mini-

221

sessions to two-day programs. The emphasis is on developing both mental and motor skills to increase retention and enable the student to continue learning on his or her own. Call for fees and schedule. **394 Taugwonk Rd., Stonington, 06378; (800) 790-6342.**

Elmridge Golf Course

The only 27-hole, fully irrigated course in the area is par 71 and 6,082 yards. Greens fees are $21 weekdays ($18 after 3:00 P.M.), $25 weekends for 18 holes. Weekends after 2:00 P.M. or any time Mon.–Fri., 9-hole play is available. Facilities include driving and putting ranges and a chipping practice area, a pro shop and a clubhouse with restaurant and full bar. All rentals and lessons from a PGA pro are available. Call Mon. after 7:00 A.M. for weekend tee times, Fri. after 7:00 A.M. for weekday tee times. Proper attire is required. Season: Mar.–Dec. **229 Elmridge Rd., Pawcatuck, 06379; (860) 599-2248.**

Pequot Golf Club

This 18-hole, par 70, 5,903-yard course has tight fairways and small greens that make it easy to walk, and it's accommodating to beginner golfers. The cost for 18 holes is $18 weekdays, $23 weekends ($17 after 1:00 P.M.); 9 holes are $12 weekdays only. Weekday discounts are given to seniors. There's a chipping practice area, putting green, pro shop for sales and repair work, a restaurant and bar and full rental and lesson availability. The course is given over to league play Mon.–Thu., 4:00 P.M.–5:30 P.M. Call one week in advance for tee times. Season: Mar.–Nov. **127 Wheeler Rd., Stonington, 06378; (860) 535-1898.**

Hiking

Seven miles of trails of all lengths take you past a variety of habitats at the **Denison Pequotsepos Nature Center.** It's only five minutes from the main attractions in Mystic. Trails are blazed, and a map is available in the gift shop. Some of the center's members have formed a hiking club offering organized outings to other local hiking spots; inquire for details. For directions and more information, see the listing under Nature Centers.

Sleigh and Carriage Rides

Established in 1654, **Davis Farm (576 Greenhaven Rd., Pawcatuck, 06379; 860-599-5859)** is one of the last Revolutionary War–era farms in Connecticut still run by the same family. Its old name is Osbrook, short for Oyster Brook, and you may still see it referred to by that name. For its Haunted Hayrides in Oct., teams of Belgian horses draw wagons holding up to 20 people on a 2-mile trek across the farm. Rides take place after dark and last 35–40 minutes. They are scheduled on weekends the first two weeks of the month and then nightly through Halloween, with wagons leaving every 15–20 minutes. Or try a Santa's Ln. ride in Dec., on which the trail to Santa's cabin is decorated with 150 decorated Christmas trees, 30,000 lights and nativity scenes. At the cabin, Santa comes out to greet the children and distribute small gifts. Santa's Ln. rides start about the day after Thanksgiving and run through New Year's (with a break for Christmas itself, and after Dec. 25 Santa has returned to the North Pole). Haunted Hayrides are $6 per person; children under 4 free. Santa's Ln. rides are $7.50 adults, $5 children 4–12, under 4 free. Reservations required. There is a $100 minimum for daytime rides the rest of the year. Davis Farm is also a great place to stop during autumn for cider and pumpkins.

Swimming

There is no more beautiful place to swim in Long Island Sound than **du Bois Beach** at Stonington Point. The beach here is very small, and the whole area is rocky, but the setting is exquisite. Don't expect the same sort of facilities you'll find at a state park, however. The beach is guarded Labor Day–Memorial Day (weekends only early and late in the season, daily in July/Aug.). Admission is $2 per person or $5 per family on weekdays, $3 per person or $6 per family on weekends. Located at the end of Water St. in the borough of Stonington.

For more information call the **Stonington Community Center** at **(860) 535-2476.**

Seeing and Doing

Antiquing

Walking distance from the center of Mystic village, you'll find **Mystic River Antiques Market,** a multidealer co-op with 7,000 square feet of antiques, collectibles and artwork. It's open 10:00 A.M.–5:00 P.M. daily, year-round. Free parking is available at the rear of the building. **14 Holmes St., Mystic, 06355; (860) 572-9775.**

Art Galleries

The **Mystic Art Association Gallery** shows exceptional work in all media in a museumlike exhibit space. It's a short walk from downtown Mystic, so you can easily combine it with a cruise, dining and shopping. Everything on display is original work by regional artists, often depicting or inspired by the look and history of Mystic, and it's all for sale. The Art Association also offers classes and workshops (mostly in painting and drawing) and cosponsors about six performing arts events per year. Admission to the museum is by donation. Hours: 9:00 A.M.–5:00 P.M. daily except when shows are changing; call ahead. Tickets for special events are $7–$10 per person, with discounts for children. All events take place in or on the grounds of the gallery on Sun., from 4:00 P.M. to 6:00 P.M., followed by a reception. **9 Water St., Mystic, 06355; (860) 536-7601.**

Children and Families

Maple Breeze Park

This small amusement park got its start as a miniature golf course in 1969. Since then it has added two 350-foot water slides, a quarter-mile go-cart track and bumper boats to keep young ones entertained. Snack food is available. Entrance into the park is free; admission is on a per-ride basis. Hours and season: 10:00 A.M.–10:00 P.M. daily, late June–Labor Day, but some rides close earlier. Call for early season hours. **350 Liberty St. (Rte. 2 in between I-95 and Rte. 78), Pawcatuck, 06379; (860) 599-1232.**

Mystic Carousel

This indoor fun center features a carousel with music provided by a vintage Wurlitzer calliope, a child-sized train with pigs for cars, arcade games and other diversions. Pay as you play, or get an all-day pass for $6.95. Adults ride free with children too young to ride alone. Concessions are available, and the Carousel Museum of Mystic is next door. Hours: 10:00 A.M.–9:00 P.M. daily, year-round. **Rte. 27 opposite the I-95 southbound exit 90 off-ramp, Mystic, 06355; (860) 572-9949.**

Museums

Captain Nathaniel B. Palmer House

Palmer, who with his brother built this house in 1851–1853 as a residence for both their families, is best known for discovering the Antarctic landmass in 1820. In his later years he was a renowned designer of clipper ships. The Italianate mansion, supposedly built by shipwrights, is in beautiful condition. Before the house was purchased by the Stonington Historical Society, it was used by a developer as a designer showcase, and many remnants of that episode are still visible. Guided tours, about 45 minutes in length, focus on Palmer's life and the Stonington of his time. Admission: $4 adults, $2 children 6–12. A combined ticket is available for the Palmer House and Old Lighthouse Museum for $6 adults, $3 children 6–12. Hours: Tue.–Sun., 10:00 A.M.–4:00 P.M., May–Oct., & by appointment. **40 Palmer St., Stonington, 06378; (860) 535-8445.**

Carousel Museum of Mystic

This museum, with a restoration shop and exhibits on the history and styles of carousel art, is a branch of the New England Carousel Museum in Bristol. This is one attraction that really has the potential to be equally engaging for adults and children. The museum is located in the same building as Mystic Carousel, and the two complement one another nicely. Hours: Mon.–Sat., 10:00 A.M.–5:00 P.M.; Sun., noon–5:00 P.M.; closed major holidays & Mon.–Wed., Dec.–Mar. **Rte. 27 opposite the I-95 southbound exit 90 off-ramp, Mystic, 06355; (860) 536-7862.**

Old Lighthouse Museum

Back in 1823 when this became the first federally operated lighthouse in Connecticut, lamps were fueled by whale oil. Functional until 1889 the lighthouse has been the museum of the Stonington Historical Society since 1927. It was moved a short distance from its original position out on the point because of erosion around its base. The history of Stonington is documented here by whaling and fishing gear, swords, cannonballs, toys and photographs, as well as pottery, plastics and other items manufactured in town. Climb

224

The Old Lighthouse Museum in Stonington.

the tower for a view out over Long Island Sound. Admission: $4 adults, $3 children 6–12. A combined ticket is available for the Lighthouse Museum and the Capt. Nathaniel B. Palmer House for $6 adults, $3 children 6–12. Hours: Tue.–Sun., 10:00 A.M.–5:00 P.M., May–Oct.; also open Mon. in July/Aug. **7 Water St., Stonington, 06378; (860) 535-1440.**

Other Museums

At **Mystic's Denison Homestead (Pequotsepos Rd.; 860-536-9248)** (ca. 1717), you can see documents, artifacts and heirlooms tracing one family's history for 11 generations. Many of the most interesting items are in the display case at the entrance. The furnishings of five rooms in the house are interpreted to different periods between 1717 and 1941. Admission: adults $4, seniors $3, children under 12 $1. Hours: Thu.–Sun., 1:00 P.M.–5:00 P.M., Memorial Day weekend– Columbus Day weekend, & by appointment. The last tour begins no later than 4:30 P.M.

Portersville Academy (76 High St., West Mystic, 06355; 860-536-4779) is a small museum that is half re-created 1840s schoolroom, half gallery with exhibits pertaining to the history of Mystic. Admission is free. Hours: Tue., 10:00 A.M.–noon (late May–early Oct. only); Thu., 1:00 P.M.–3:00 P.M.

Nature Centers

The **Denison Pequotsepos Nature Center (109 Pequotsepos Rd., Mystic; 860-536-1216)** offers lovers of the outdoors 7 miles of trails crossing 125 acres and a variety of habitats, a nice gift shop and bookstore, exhibits on the natural world and an extensive schedule of field trips and organized activities for all ages, year-round. Admission: $4 for adults, $2 for children 6–12. Hours: Tue.–Sat., 9:00 A.M.–5:00 P.M., year-round. Also open Mon., 9:00 A.M.–5:00 P.M. (Memorial Day–Labor Day), & Sun., 1:00 P.M.–5:00 P.M. (May–Dec.).

Performing Arts

Professional, non-Equity **Odyssey Dinner Theater** stages musical comedies that sometimes involve spirited audience participation. They give evening performances at the Copperfield Lounge in the Best Western Sovereign Hotel. Tickets are in the $30 range with a discount for advance purchase. The price includes a four-course dinner at the lounge. Dinner is served at 6:30 P.M., and show time is 8:00 P.M. Inquire about show dates, seating arrangements and menu details. The hotel is located at **9 Whitehall Ave. (Rte. 27), Mystic, 06333; (800) 718-1945, (860) 536-7469** or **(860) 434-5644.**

Scenic Drives

For a pleasant drive in the Mystic area, head inland; the river and shoreline areas are better explored on foot. All of Rte. 234 through Stonington is beautiful. Turn off on Taugwonk Rd. and head north to Stonington Vineyards for a wine tasting and a chance to stretch your legs. On Northwest Corner Rd. in North Stonington you can stop in at Maple Lane Farms for some pick-your-own summer fruit, and in autumn Clyde's Cider Mill on Old Stonington Rd. in Old Mystic is another quaint destination. This is an area best experienced by wandering at will. Just carry a map and follow whatever road beckons.

Seasonal Favorites

See also the listing for Davis Farm under Sleigh and Carriage Rides.

Clyde's Cider Mill

For a special autumn treat, stop to watch apple cider being pressed at the last steam-powered cider mill in New England. The Clyde family has been making cider here since 1881, and this mill and its machinery date from 1898. They never sell sweet cider that's more than 24 hours old, so from late Sept. through the day before Thanksgiving they press cider every day. On weekends they have demonstrations at set times: 1:00 P.M. & 3:00 P.M. In addition to sweet cider and hard cider (they're the oldest maker of hard cider in the country), you can purchase seasonal baked goods and produce, jams, jellies, honeys and cornmeal ground in their own gristmill. Hours: 9:00 A.M.– 6:00 P.M. daily in season. **129 N. Stonington Rd. in Old Mystic; (860) 536-3354.** In the off-season, they can be reached at **(860) 536-0722.**

Maple Lane Farms

For pick-your-own strawberries, raspberries, blueberries, peaches, apples and pumpkins, head to this farm in an exceptionally beautiful corner of North Stonington. You can also cut your own Christmas trees beginning the day after Thanksgiving. There is a picnic area for customers, and half-hour hayrides at $1 per person run on weekends late Sept.–Oct. **57 Northwest Corner Rd., North Stonington, 06365; (860) 889-3766** to reach the farm or **(860) 887-8855** for 24-hour pick-your-own information.

Shopping

The little stores in downtown Mystic are a great place to shop for souvenirs, nice clothing and decorative items for the home. If you want a souvenir that's above average but still within the means of a modest budget, try **The Emporium (15 Water St.; 860-536-3891).** This mixed-bag store in a Victorian house has three floors filled with stuff that's mostly inexpensive but not tacky. And if you can't resist a Christmas decoration, you've come to the right place. Several Christmas shops are in Mystic, including **Mystical Christmas (90 Greenmanville Ave.; 860-572-9772),** open virtually year round, and the **Holly Wreath Christmas Shop (26 Old Stonington Rd. 1A; 860-536-0700),** open mid-Apr.–Christmas Eve.

Mystic Factory Outlets

Two dozen outlet stores including Izod, Bass, L'Eggs and Corning are clustered in two complexes opposite Olde Mistick Village. Hours: Mon.–Fri., 10:00 A.M.–9:00 P.M.; Sat., 10:00 A.M.– 7:00 P.M.; Sun., 11:00 A.M.–6:00 P.M. **Coogan Blvd., Mystic, 06355; (860) 443-4788.**

225

Seafaring Southeast

Olde Mistick Village

Olde Mistick Village is an outdoor shopping center designed to look quaint and villagelike. Sixty stores carry goods ranging from souvenirs to high-quality handcrafts, and there is a movie theater, a laundromat, a grocery store, banks and a visitors information center on-site. Concerts, dancing and other special events are held May–Christmas at the gazebo or the meetinghouse. Call for a one-page map, directory and calendar of events, or pick one up when you visit. Store hours: Mon.–Sat., 10:00 A.M.–6:00 P.M. (8:00 P.M. during summer & the end-of-year holiday period); Sun., noon–5:00 P.M. Located on **Coogan Blvd., Mystic, 06355; (860) 536-4941.**

Tours

A walking tour brochure of Mystic entitled "Curbstones, Clapboards & Cupolas" describes four walks in the downtown area. It's available for $3 from the **Mystic River Historical Society (74 High St., West Mystic 06388; 860-536-4779)**, the public library and at selected stores around town. At the Old Lighthouse Museum in Stonington, described under Museums, you can also pick up an inexpensive guide to the town's old cemeteries.

Mystic Seaport Lantern Light Tours

At Mystic Seaport on Dec. evenings, 19th-century costumed characters lead you through the museum as scenes from a traveling drama unfold around you. Tours leave every 15 minutes, 5:00 P.M.–9:00 P.M., and last one hour. Tickets: $18 adults, $10 children. Reservations required. You can order tickets beginning in early Oct. by calling **(800) 522-1841.** Inquire about other tours of Mystic Seaport. **75 Greenmanville Ave. (Rte. 27), Mystic, 06355; (860) 572-0711.**

Cruises

Mystic Whaler Cruises

The 83-foot reproduction schooner *Mystic Whaler* sails from Mystic seasonally for three-hour lobster dinner cruises, day sails and regularly scheduled overnight cruises lasting two to five days. You can either sit back and relax or take part in the sailing experience. Dinner cruises ($50 per person, lobster dinner included) take place Wed.–Sun., 4:30 P.M.–7:30 P.M. Day sails ($65 per person, lunch included) depart at 9:30 A.M., returning at 3:30 P.M., every day that the ship is in port. The *Mystic Whaler* holds up to 65 people and sleeps 36. Reservations required. Cruises depart from **7 Holmes St. in Mystic.** For more information call **(800) 697-8420** or **(860) 536-4218.**

Sylvina W. Beal Cruises

The *Sylvina W. Beal* goes out on weekend, three- and five-day trips along the New England coast from Mystic to Block Island, Long Island, Newport or Martha's Vineyard. This authentic 1911 schooner was originally a working sailboat built to catch cod off Maine. Now she travels under sail power with an auxiliary motor. Her fish holds have been converted to cabins with simple bunk beds that allow her to accommodate 18 people. Season: May–Oct. Fares run $285–$500, meals included. Departures are from the West Mystic Wooden Boat Yard on the Groton side of the Mystic River. Reservations required. Transportation available from the train station to the departure point. **120 School St., Mystic, 06355; (800) 333-6978** or **(860) 536-8422.**

Voyager Cruises

If traveling along the shore has piqued your interesting in sailing, indulge it with a morning, afternoon or evening cruise on the 81-foot *Argia*, a gaff-rigged schooner and a replica of a type of working sailboat popular in the 1800s. With Capt. Frank Fulchiero at the helm, *Argia* sails daily (weather permitting), mid-Apr.–Oct. in the quiet waters of Fishers Island Sound. Daytime trips run 10:00 A.M.–1:00 P.M. & 2:00 P.M.–5:00 P.M. Evening trips are two hours long and begin at 6:00 P.M. (5:30 in autumn). Sound Experience cruises, offered Tue. and Thu. afternoons in July and Aug., are part pleasure sail and part marine education. Fulchiero trawls with a net, then brings up what was caught—usually lobster, crabs, flounder and seahorses—for passengers to examine. A staffer from Mystic Marinelife Aquarium is on hand to answer questions, and the creatures are released back into the sound. Snacks and drinks are available onboard or BYO beverages (alcohol okay) and food. Fare: $30–$32 for adults with a $5 discount for seniors, $20 for children. *Argia* holds 49 people; reservations are recommended. Board at **Steamboat Wharf, Mystic, 06355; (860) 536-0416.**

Wineries

Fieldstone Vineyards

Under new owners and getting back on its feet, the former Crosswoods Winery is just starting to release product. A hard cider will be the first offering, possibly to be followed by an apple wine. The winery is a 1980s replica of an 1850s original with a tasting room open to the public. This is a young operation, and it's hard to say what it will have to offer in coming years, so call for details and hours. **75 Chester Maine Rd., North Stonington, 06359; (860) 535-4221.**

Haight Winery and Wine Education Center

An outlet of the Haight Winery in Litchfield, this shop is primarily a retail store that also offers wine tasting and features displays concerning the history of wine and wine making. Hours: Mon.–Sat., 10:00 A.M.–6:00 P.M.; Sun., noon–5:00 P.M.; open until 8:00 P.M. some nights in summer. Located in **Olde Mystick Village, Coogan Blvd., Mystic 06355; (860) 572-1978.**

Stonington Vineyard

When you visit Stonington Vineyard, start with a tasting in the gift shop. The vineyard makes five or six wines in a normal year, specializing in whites. Its flagship vintage is a chardonnay. Take a walk among the varieties of grapes that grow in a beautiful rural setting or tour the winery and hear an explanation of the wine-making process. Tours are given daily at 2:00 P.M. Hours: 11:00 A.M.–5:00 P.M. daily, year-round; closed some major holidays. **523 Taugwonk Rd. (about 2 miles north of I-95 exit 91), Stonington, 06378; (860) 535-1222.**

Where to Stay

There is a high demand for rooms in the Mystic area seven nights a week during the high season and weekends for much of the rest of the year. Mystic sees more tourism than any other part of the state, so be prepared for high rates. Also, to avoid disappointment, you must make advance reservations. I'd recommend booking at least a month ahead for summer weekends, and don't restrict yourself to accommodations right in Mystic. Check the **Norwich** and **New London** chapters for additional listings. Distances between Mystic and the towns that surround it are small.

If you feel the need to work out while you're on vacation, you can use the facilities of the Mystic Community Center for a mere $8 a day. Many hotels without exercise facilities provide guests with free passes to the center, so check with yours. Facilities include Nautilus and cardiovascular equipment, free weights, an indoor pool and a sandy beach for saltwater swimming in summer. Hours change seasonally but are generally 6:00 A.M.–9:00 P.M. For more information call them at **(860) 536-3575.**

Bed & Breakfasts

One service that can help in the search for the right room is **Bed & Breakfasts of the Mystic Coast:** 27 B&Bs from Bozrah to Westerly, Rhode Island, participate in this availability line, sharing their booking information for the coming week. A different B&B staffs the phone line each day, but you call only one central number: **(860) 892-5006.** Please note that many of the participating B&Bs are described in the **Norwich** and **New London** chapters. Only B&Bs with addresses in Stonington, North Stonington, Mystic and West Mystic (technically in the town of Groton) are described here.

Antiques & Accommodations—$$$$

Owners Tom and Ann Gray, who started this B&B in the late 1980s, are frequent visitors to antiques auctions and will occasionally part with one of the pieces they've used to furnish the guest rooms in these two houses dating from 1860 and 1820, both on the same property. The 1860 house has three guest rooms, one with a fireplace, each with a modern, private bath. Each floor of the 1820 house is a suite, the upper one with two bedrooms and two baths, a common room with fireplace and a library; the lower one with three bedrooms (one with fireplace), living room, kitchen, one bathroom, covered porch and patio. Almost all the beds in both houses are queen, canopied four-posters. The B&B is noted for its breakfast by candlelight, and the Grays will accommodate children of any age as long as they are capable of respecting the antique furnishings. **32 Main St., North Stonington, 06359; (800) 554-7829 or (860) 535-1736.**

High Acres—$$$$
High Acres is situated in a 1740s farmhouse with an 1840s addition overlooking 150 acres of rolling hills and horse pasture on a picture-perfect country road. Four guest rooms are decorated in an informally elegant style that comfortably blends old and new. The queen and king bedsteads are outfitted with feather beds and down comforters. There are a couple of comfortable parlors, one with a fireplace, that serve as common rooms, and a full breakfast is served in the morning. Owners Peter and Liz Agnew keep horses and can provide short-term boarding. **222 Northwest Corner Rd., North Stonington, 06359; (860) 887-4355.**

House of 1833—$$$$
Opulent and grand come to mind first as words to describe the House of 1833. The ceiling in the entryway of this meticulously decorated Greek Revival mansion soars above your head, setting up high expectations that the guest rooms fulfill. All of the rooms are beautifully and uniquely decorated, and if you enjoy a great soak as much as a comfy bed, you'll appreciate the effort that's gone into the bathrooms. All the rooms except one have fireplaces, and fire logs are provided. Some of the rooms also have private porches. The common rooms are all spectacular, and a gourmet breakfast is served. Guests are invited to use the swimming pool, 18-speed

bikes and tennis court. Hosts Carol and Matt Nolan will accommodate children on weeknights by prior arrangement. **72 North Stonington Rd., Mystic, 06355; (800) 367-1833 or (860) 536-6325.**

Pequot Hotel—$$$$
This Greek Revival house on 23 acres has three rooms with private baths. Two of the guest rooms, one with a double bed and the other with a queen, feature 12-foot coved ceilings and working fireplaces. One also has a whirlpool bath. The third room, a suite with two bedrooms (one double and two twin beds) and a connecting bathroom, might work well for a family. The house is furnished in country style, with braided rugs, ceiling fans, rockers and quilts. A full breakfast is served at 8:30 A.M. Innkeeper Nancy Mitchell can provide services like laundry or picnic lunches at a modest charge. **711 Cow Hill Rd., Mystic, 06355; (860) 572-0390.**

Red Brook Inn—$$$$
Two historic buildings side-by-side on 7 acres are the setting for this B&B with a colonial feel. Almost a dozen rooms are split between the former Haley Tavern (ca. 1740) and the Crary Homestead (ca. 1770). Rooms are divided into three rate categories: quaint chambers that are on the small side, with a double bed and no fireplace or whirlpool; deluxe chambers in the Crary House with a double bed and fireplace and superior chambers in the Haley Tavern with four-poster, queen beds, fireplaces and (in one case) a whirlpool bath. A full breakfast is included. Inquire about their package deals. **2750 Gold Star Hwy., Mystic, 06355; (860) 572-0349.**

Adams House—$$$ to $$$$
Six rooms in the main house of this 18th-century colonial are quite nice with private baths, queen beds and quilts. The two downstairs rooms have fireplaces and open onto the dining room, which is the common area for both family and guests. The upstairs rooms offer a little more privacy but do not have fireplaces. The cottage is a separate building whose rooms have open-beamed cathedral

ceilings and views onto the garden. The house is on a main road, but room air-conditioners allow you to keep windows shut if moderate traffic noise bothers you. **382 Cow Hill Rd., Mystic, 06355; (860) 572-9551.**

Arbor House—$$$ to $$$$

A 1900 hilltop Victorian farmhouse on a working vineyard is the setting for one of the newest B&Bs in southeastern Connecticut. Four guest rooms feature queen beds and country furnishings. One room is a suite with a separate sitting area. Some rooms have a private bath, others shared; ask for details. The grounds form a large part of the appeal of Arbor House. Many of the 37 acres are planted with grapes and other fruits, and a tasting room is just steps away from the house. There is a pond where guests are invited to do catch-and-release fishing for largemouth bass. An equestrian trail rings the property, and guests' horses can be boarded overnight in a stable with three stalls. Breakfast is served. The owners have two young children and welcome guests with the same. **75 Chester Maine Rd., North Stonington, 06359; (860) 535-4221.**

Brigadoon—$$$ to $$$$

This sprawling old farmhouse with many additions has eight guest rooms and a relaxed, hospitable atmosphere. The rooms all have queen or king beds, a few of them four-posters, and air-conditioning. Bathrooms are all modern and private. Wideboard floors grace a couple of rooms located in the oldest part of the house dating from 1740. There's also a large "honeymoon suite" with a cathedral ceiling and a brass and iron bed. A full country breakfast is served in the morning, tea late in the afternoon and wine in the evening. The dining room gives you the choice of eating breakfast privately at your own table or family-style with other guests. Inquire about corporate rates, discounts and transportation from Mystic train station. **180 Cow Hill Rd., Mystic, 06355; (860) 536-3033.**

Old Mystic Inn—$$$ to $$$$

Old Mystic Inn is actually two buildings: a 1794 colonial and a modern "carriage house." Rooms are evenly split between the two but have a common decorative theme based on simple Shaker-style pieces, including pencil-post canopy beds (queen). Three of the four rooms in the main house have small fireplaces in which guests can burn fire logs. Two of the rooms in the carriage house have whirlpool tubs. Bathrooms are all modern, and a full breakfast is served between 8:30 and 9:30 A.M. **58 Main St., Old Mystic, 06372; (860) 572-9422.**

Boat & Breakfast

With a Boat & Breakfast, you stay overnight on a vessel that remains docked or moored, usually at a marina. Space is limited on boats, so always inquire about the dimensions and nature of the sleeping accommodations and bathing facilities. It's not uncommon for showers to be provided onshore. Some boats can accommodate only two people; others can sleep four or more.

Coastline Yacht Club—$$$$

When not being used for sailing charters, a small fleet of 30- to 50-foot sailboats is available for Boat & Breakfast. Your overnight stay can be combined with a sunset sail at a package price, and a Continental breakfast is brought aboard in the morning. The boats dock at **Spicer's Marina** in Noank. For more information call **(800) 749-7245** or **(860) 536-2689.**

Stonecroft—$$$$

Stonecroft is a B&B in the nearby town of Ledyard that plans to add a Boat & Breakfast aspect to its business. Stonecroft's vessel is a restored 1949 Baltzer Seamaster, a 40-foot wooden powerboat that will be docked at Old Mystic Marina (a.k.a. Mystic Marine Basin). Restoration was still under way at the time of this writing, so call for details. The B&B is located at **515 Pumpkin Hill Rd., Ledyard, 06339; (860) 572-0771.**

Hotels, Motels & Inns

Mystic has several chain hotels offering standard hotel and luxury rooms at a reasonable price *for this area*. They all offer a high standard of accommodation, and all things considered often represent the best value. Expect rates to *begin* at $60 per night on winter weekends and twice that in summer. In Mystic even hotels that you wouldn't expect to have suites or luxury rooms often do, so always inquire, especially if you're visiting in the off-season. Hotels right in Mystic include **Best Western (9 Whitehall Ave.; 860-536-4281), Comfort Inn (48 Whitehall Ave.; 800-228-5150 or 860-572-8531), Days Inn (55 Whitehall Ave.; 800-325-2525 or 860-572-0574)** and **Residence Inn (40 Whitehall Ave.; 800-331-3131 or 860-536-5150)**. By the way, Whitehall Ave. is Rte. 27 north of I-95. There is also an excellent **Hilton (20 Coogan Blvd.; 800-445-8667 or 860-572-0731)**. Currently the only place to stay in Stonington borough is an in-law cottage with three basic rooms. For details contact **Lasbury's Guest House, 24 Orchard St., Stonington, 06378; (860) 535-2681**. For additional listings call the local tourism district, **Mystic & More**, at **(800) 863-6569**.

Steamboat Inn—$$$$

The Steamboat Inn's setting is amazing—literally at the bascule bridge in Mystic so you can walk out your door and be steps from the vibrant main street of the village. But instead of overlooking the noisy street or a parking lot, the rooms face the relative quiet of the river. The rooms are exceptionally spacious, and all but one have a river view. Some rooms have special amenities such as two-person baths, so ask for a full description of each. Second-floor rooms have wood-burning fireplaces; first-floor rooms have efficiency kitchens with a small refrigerator, a coffeemaker and a small stock of dinnerware. All rooms have a whirlpool bath, TV, telephone and individual climate controls. A self-serve Continental breakfast is served in an upstairs café room. **73 Steamboat Wharf, Mystic, 06355; (800) 364-6100 or (860) 536-8300**.

Whitehall Mansion—$$$$

Whitehall Mansion is a former colonial home and one-time headquarters of the Stonington Historical Society that has been converted into

a five-room inn. The rooms have all the trappings of a B&B, such as working fireplaces and queen, four-poster canopy beds, but they also have hotel amenities such as telephones and modern bathrooms with whirlpool tubs. One room is handicapped-accessible. Unfortunately, the rooms do not have much in the way of a view. The house is part of the Residence Inn complex and is surrounded by a parking lot. **42 Whitehall Ave. (Rte. 27), Mystic, 06355; (860) 572-7280**.

The Inn at Mystic—$$$ to $$$$

There are four accommodation options at this sprawling complex overlooking Mystic Harbor: the Inn building, a converted 1904 mansion with five rooms; the East Wing, a separate building with 12 rooms, built and decorated to resemble the Inn; the Gatehouse, the original guest house on the property with four rooms and the motor inn, which contains rooms like those at the Inn as well as budget rooms. This cluster of buildings and a fine restaurant are located on 15 acres. The rooms range from a suite with wet bar, deck and fireplace taking up the entire second floor of the Gatehouse to motel accommodations with two twin beds and simple furnishings. Prices vary accordingly, so call for details. Recreational facilities include an outdoor heated pool, hot tub, tennis court, canoes, rowboat and paddleboat. Guests are given passes to the small beach and exercise equipment at Mystic Community Center nearby. Inquire about package deals. At the **junction of Rtes. 1 and 27, Mystic, 06355; (800) 237-2415 or (860) 536-9604**.

Randall's Ordinary—$$$ to $$$$

Randall's Ordinary offers 15 inn rooms in two buildings and a restaurant serving exclusively hearth-cooked food three times a day. Rooms are found in the colonial-era Randall Homestead, which also houses the restaurant, and in an 1819 dairy barn. The highlight is the Silo Suite, built into the silo attached to the barn. It's a small apartment that can accommodate five people, featuring a queen Adirondack bed in the master bedroom, gas fireplace and a staircase around the perimeter of the silo winding upstairs to a Jacuzzi. The rate includes a full breakfast for two. The Silo is booked months in advance, so call early if you want it.

The dairy barn rooms are all different, with queen or double beds (four-posters, canopies, brass and trundles) and original wideboard flooring in most rooms. All of them have a private, modern bath, TV and telephone. The three rooms in the Randall Homestead have queen canopy beds and private, modern baths. There's also a log cabin for up to six people with limited availability; inquire for details. A Continental breakfast is served in the restaurant, but there's also à la carte service. See the listing under Where to Eat for more about the restaurant. Inquire about the lodging/dinner-for-two package. Located on **Rte. 2, North Stonington, 06359; (860) 599-4540.**

Taber Inne & Suites—$$$ to $$$$

As the name implies, Taber Inne & Suites offers various accommodations. There is a modernized 1829 house, eight two-bedroom townhouses, a guest house for up to five people and a motor inn with 16 rooms. Many of the more expensive rooms feature queen canopied four-poster beds, wet bars, gas fireplaces, whirlpool tubs and decks or balconies. Guests have access to the exercise and swimming facilities at Mystic Community Center about two blocks away. **66 Williams Ave. (Rte. 1), Mystic, 06355; (860) 536-4904.**

The Whaler's Inn—$$$ to $$$$

The Whaler's Inn is actually a complex of four different buildings located right at the eastern end of the bascule bridge in Mystic village. The Inn building houses the lobby. Here and in the 1865 House (my favorite), the rooms open onto interior hallways, but in the Noank and Stonington Houses the rooms open onto outdoor walkways. Some rooms in the Inn are quite large and furnished in traditional or contemporary style. Those in the 1865 House are attractively old-fashioned. The other two are rather more like motels. If noise is a concern, ask for a room away from the street. Inquire about special packages. **20 East Main St., Mystic, 06355; (800) 243-2588** or **(860) 536-1506.**

Camping

There's little in the way of camping right in or very near Mystic, but if you travel just a couple of towns to the north you'll find many commercial and state campgrounds. For more information, see the **Far Northeast** chapter.

Where to Eat

The Mystic area is positively awash in good restaurants. It's impossible to describe all the ones worth visiting, but below you'll find a sampling of places that offer everything from a quick bite to fine dining. **Drawbridge Inn (34 W. Main St.; 860-536-9653)** and **41° North (21 W. Main St.; 860-536-9821)** are local favorites right in Mystic village. **Go Fish (Olde Mistick Village, corner of Coogan Blvd. and Rte. 27, Mystic; 860-536-2662)** is a new seafood restaurant with a very trendy aquatic-themed interior. **One South Café (201 N. Main St., Stonington; 860-535-0418)** is a critic's favorite noted for hearty soups, signature grilled mussels and food with international influences. **Sea Swirl Seafood Restaurant and Ice Cream (at the junction of Rtes. 1 and 27 in Mystic; 860-536-3452)** is widely recognized as "the best of the best clam shacks"—a place to go for very informal, mostly fried "fast" seafood. If you're out Stonington borough way, also try **Water St. Café (142 Water St.; 860-535-2122)**, serving American, French and Asian dishes in an elegant but casual and intimate setting. Finally, **Nutmeg Crossing (One W. Broad St., Pawcatuck; 860-599-3840)** is located practically on the Connecticut/Rhode Island state line in Pawcatuck and offers a broad-based American menu in a nice family dining atmosphere with a downtown setting right on the Pawcatuck River.

The Flood Tide Restaurant—$$$$

The restaurant on the grounds of The Inn at Mystic serves Continental cuisine that was voted the best in its category statewide by readers of *Connecticut* magazine in 1996. It offers tableside service in which dishes, such as rack of lamb Dijonaise and Chateaubriand, are finished before your eyes. The Flood Tide is also a good choice for breakfast or lunch in a nice setting, for which you'll pay only a little more than you might elsewhere. For the hungry but budget-conscious, it offers breakfast and lunch buffets daily in summer for $8.95 and $10.95. The latter is also available on Fri. in winter. Reservations recommended. Hours: breakfast served 7:00 A.M.–10:30 A.M. daily; Sun. brunch 11:00 A.M.–2:00 P.M.; lunch available Mon.–Sat., 11:30 A.M.–2:00 P.M.; lounge menu served between lunch & dinner; dinner served Sun.–Thu., 5:30 P.M.–9:30 P.M., & Fri.–Sat. until 10:00 P.M. Located at the **junction of Rtes. 1 and 27 in Mystic, 06355; (860) 536-8140.**

Randall's Ordinary—$$$$

Specializing in hearth-cooked food served by colonially garbed waitstaff, Randall's Ordinary is housed in a colonial farmhouse with inn rooms upstairs and in an adjacent building. It serves three meals a day, and you do not have to be an overnight guest to enjoy breakfast here, which includes such unusual items as codfish cakes and venison sausage in addition to griddle cakes and such. Breakfast and lunch are à la carte. Dinner is a fixed-price ($30 per person) affair with only one or two seatings nightly. The multicourse meal includes cheese and crackers and popcorn, soup and breads, your choice of three entrées, dessert and beverage. The decor is fairly rustic, with antique furniture of mixed styles. There's also a small taproom where you can see for yourself the origin of the term "bar." The hearth-baked bread is available for purchase. Hours: breakfast served 7:00 A.M.–11:00 A.M. daily; lunch served noon–3:00 P.M. daily; dinner seatings Sun.–Fri. at 7:00 P.M. & Sat. at 5:00 P.M. & 7:30 P.M. Located on **Rte. 2, North Stonington, 06359; (860) 599-4540.**

Bravo Bravo—$$$ to $$$$

Almost like two restaurants in one, Bravo Bravo has a small inside dining room with fewer than 20 tables and a large tented terrace for outdoor dining May–Oct., weather permitting. The terrace is the only bistrolike setting where you can get a full meal in Mystic.

The two areas keep somewhat different hours and even have different menus, with slightly less elaborate, less expensive dishes offered on the terrace. The food is a mix of Italian, Continental and American, with many seafood offerings. At lunch there are a number of meal salads and grilled sandwiches. From Sept. to June hours for the indoor restaurant are as follows: lunch served Tue.–Sat., 11:30 A.M.–2:30 P.M; dinner served Tue.–Thu., 5:00 P.M.–9:00 P.M.; Fri.–Sat. until 10:00 P.M. In July & Aug. you can dine on the outdoor terrace from 11:30 A.M. until closing daily; lunch is served outdoors only and indoor dinner hours are the same as in winter with the addition of Sun. **20 E. Main St., Mystic, 06355; (860) 536-3228.**

Boatyard Café—$$$

Located at Dodson Boatyard, this café offers delicious local seafood right off the dock. It also serves breakfast and lunch and good housemade desserts. It's a shore restaurant that can be casual or dressy, as you please. Hours: Wed.–Mon., 8:00 A.M.–2:30 P.M. for breakfast & lunch; Wed.–Sun., 6:00 P.M.–9:00 P.M. for dinner. **194 Water St., Stonington, 06378; (860) 535-1381.**

Captain Daniel Packer Inne—$$$

Situated in an 18th-century house, this restaurant draws large crowds because of its atmospheric first-floor pub. In winter when things are slower, the pub is cozier, thanks in part to a large fireplace. You can wait for your table here or order from a substantial pub menu that equals the regular menu at many other restaurants. There are two dining rooms with five fireplaces on the upper floors of the house, mostly set with small tables. The menu is Continental/American with a few Asian dishes for variety. At lunch the menu reverts almost entirely to cold and grilled sandwiches, salads and individual pizzas. Reservations are essential on summer weekends, and leave plenty of time to find a parking space on the street because their lot is inadequate. Hours: lunch served 11:00 A.M.–4:00 P.M. daily; dinner served Mon.–Sat., 5:00 P.M.–10:00 P.M., & Sun., 2:00 P.M.–10:00 P.M. Bar open Sun.–Thu. until 1:00 A.M.; Fri.–Sat.

232

until 2:00 A.M. **32 Water St., Mystic, 06355; (860) 536-3555.**

J. P. Daniels—$$$

One great thing about J. P. Daniels is that fully half of its menu items are available in light portions, so you don't have to pass up a good meal just because you're not ravenous. The menu is small yet offers pasta, poultry, fish and seafood, veal and beef, supplemented by daily specials. The setting is a one-time dairy barn with old carriages and farm implements decorating the woody, rustic interior. There are three dining rooms: an intimate sunken one by the bar, the main one with an open ceiling in the center that allows you to look up into the rafters and a balcony ringing the main dining room one floor above. Hours: dinner from 5:00 P.M. nightly & Sun. buffet brunch 11:00 A.M.–2:00 P.M. Located on **Rte. 184, Old Mystic, 06372; (860) 572-9564.**

The Mooring—$$$

The restaurant at the Mystic Hilton was voted the best hotel restaurant in New London County by readers of *Connecticut* magazine. The cuisine is Continental/American, with a focus on seafood and steak. It serves three meals a day, including a breakfast buffet. Although the dining room is on the large side, it's broken up into three levels to keep it more intimate. Decorated with a nautical theme, it features a bay window overlooking a garden and a specially commissioned whale sculpture. The Soundings Lounge is also used for mealtime seating and makes a good meeting place. Reservations suggested. Hours: breakfast served Mon.–Sat., 6:30 A.M.–10:30 A.M., & until noon on Sun.; lunch available Mon.–Sat., 11:30 A.M.–2:30 P.M., & 11:00 A.M.–midnight on Sun. in Soundings Lounge; dinner served Sun.–Thu., 5:30 P.M.–9:30 P.M., & Fri.–Sat. until 11:00 P.M. **20 Coogan Blvd., Mystic, 06355; (860) 572-0731.**

Noah's—$$$

The linen-clad walls, pressed-tin ceiling, ceiling fans and lacquered wooden tables at this excellent restaurant combine to create an atmosphere that will immediately put you at ease. It offers everything from soups to noodles to a bohemian rice, beans and fish dish. Noodles are made in-house, and half-portions are available. In the evening Noah's takes on the feel of a friendly bistro, and the menu shifts toward excellent American fare with international aspects, often featuring seafood. Open Tue.–Sun. for breakfast, 7:00 A.M.–11:00 A.M.; lunch, 11:30 A.M.–2:30 P.M.; dinner 6:00 P.M.–9:00 P.M. (Fri.–Sat. until 9:30). **113 Water St., Stonington borough, 06378; (860) 535-3925.**

S&P Oyster Co.—$$$

For a sit-down dining experience that is still family-oriented or just plain casual and fun for a group, give this waterside restaurant a try. Window tables have a great view of the Mystic River and the drawbridge. Crayons are provided for drawing on the paper that covers the tables. The menu is solidly devoted to seafood, covering the spectrum from clam and oyster rolls and a half-lobster special at lunch to all kinds of steamed, fried and broiled seafood platters on the dinner menu, which is available all day. A few pasta, steak and chicken dishes round it out, and the bar will keep the daiquiris and margaritas coming with regularity. Hours: open Mon.–Sat. at 11:30 A.M. & Sun. at noon, serving until 9:00 P.M. Sun.–Thu. & 10:00 P.M. weekends. **One Holmes St., Mystic, 06355; (860) 536-2674.**

Seamen's Inne—$$$

As you might expect from its location next to Mystic Seaport, the menu at Seamen's Inne is mostly seafood, and not just New England style. Preparation is as varied as Maryland crabcakes, shrimp Creole, fried catfish, seafood pot pie, shrimp scampi, a raw bar, chowders, lobsters and fish and chips. Seafood comes with the pasta; oysters come with the steak. The lunch menu has lighter fare such as seafood rolls and salads. The restaurant is also locally famous for its Dixieland Country breakfast buffet (Sun. brunch), currently priced at $9.95 (free for children 6 and under), which has a live Dixieland jazz band. Reservations are suggested, especially during the summer. Lunch hours: Mon.–Fri., 11:30 A.M.–2:00 P.M.; Sat. until 3:00 P.M.; Sun. brunch, 10:30 A.M.–2:00 P.M. Dinner hours: Mon.–Sat.,

4:30 P.M.–9:00 P.M.; Sun., 3:30 P.M.–8:30 P.M.; open Fri.–Sat. in summer until 10:00 P.M. **105 Greenmanville Ave. (at Mystic Seaport), Mystic, 06355; (860) 536-9649.**

Steak Loft—$$$

This large, popular, family-oriented steak house has a rustic, woody, Bonanza-like barn interior. The menu tends toward sandwiches at lunch and meat-and-potato entrées at dinner, supplemented by a salad bar and an extensive selection of finger food. There are a couple of dining rooms. The most atmospheric is the one with the bar, which has a loft displaying antique carriages, farm implements, old license plates and such, and a small corner stage where country music bands play almost nightly. Hours: lunch served Mon.–Sat., 11:30 A.M.–2:30 P.M.; dinner served Mon.–Sat., 5:00 P.M.–10:30 P.M. (until midnight on Fri.), & all day on Sun. from 11:30 A.M. In Olde Mistick Village at the **corner of Coogan Blvd. and Rte. 27, Mystic, 06355; (860) 536-2661.**

Pizzaworks—$$

This eatery is one of a small chain of three restaurants across southeast Connecticut that are repeatedly recognized for having the best pizza in the region. The only drawback is that they don't do slices. This one has an open kitchen near the entrance where you can see everything being made up. It has the pleasing ambiance of an old factory building with exposed brick walls, two-story ceilings and neon signs. In addition to pizza, they offer salads, a couple of pastas and a selection of over 75 beers. Park in the lot across the street, and they'll validate your ticket. Hours: Sun.–Thu., 4:00 P.M.–9:00 P.M.; Fri.–Sat., noon–10:00 P.M. **12 Water St., Mystic, 06355; (860) 572-5775.**

Steamers—$$

"Steamers" are, of course, clams, but that's just the tip of the iceberg at this informal little eatery that specializes in serving up simple seafood dishes mostly steamed and fried and usually served with corn, fries and cole slaw on the side. The atmosphere is biergartenlike, with umbrella-shaded tables on a cool, walled terrace and a few formica-topped tables inside. If you're a novice at lobster eating, you might want to come here for your inaugural experience; the "how to eat lobster" placemats will be your coach. BYOB. Call for hours and season. **13 Water St., Mystic, 06355; (860) 536-1168.**

Under Wraps—$$

The name of this high-quality fast-food restaurant is a cute reference to the fact that everything they serve comes tucked inside a tortilla. But these are all the things you've never seen served in a tortilla before: blackened chicken with corn salsa and Spanish rice, grilled lamb, Moroccan curried vegetables and couscous, jerk chicken, teriyaki tofu and more. The frozen smoothies are just the thing for a hot day. For something a little adventurous, nutritious and easy on the budget, this is a great choice. Hours: 11:00 A.M.–9:00 P.M. daily. **7 Water St. (enter in back), Mystic, 06355; (860) 536-4042.**

2 Sisters Deli—$ to $$

Only a half-block from W. Main St. and yet easy to overlook, 2 Sisters offers award-winning sandwiches, deli salads, soups, bagels and a few entrées for reheating. It works better for take-out than eating in. Hours: Mon.–Sat., 8:30 A.M.–7:00 P.M.; Sun. 9:00 A.M.–5:00 P.M.; closing time is one hour earlier in winter. **4 Pearl St., Mystic, 06355; (860) 536-1244/2068.**

The Yellow House—$ to $$

This coffee and tearoom serves a wide variety of hot and cold breakfast items and good sandwiches, soups and inexpensive baked stuffed potatoes (although they are reheats) at lunch. Its location on the main street of Stonington borough makes it a natural for a quick bite if you're strolling through town. It carries all the beverage paraphernalia you'd expect at a tearoom. Hours: Mon.–Thu., 6:30 A.M.–3:00 P.M.; Fri.–Sun., 7:00 A.M.–4:00 P.M.; open later in summer. **149 Water St., Stonington borough, 06378; (860) 535-4986.**

Coffeehouses, Sweets & Treats

Green Marble Coffeehouse—$

The only thing approaching a sidewalk café in Mystic village is located down Peacock Alley between the Company of Craftsmen and the Army/Navy store on W. Main St. The outdoor tables are pleasant for enjoying a cup of java roasted locally by Mystic Coffee Roasters. It also serves light food such as soup and bagels and offers live acoustic folk music most Fri. & Sat. evenings and occasionally on Sun. Hours: Open at 7:00 A.M. daily, closing Sun.–Thu. at 9:30 P.M. & Fri.–Sat. at 10:00 P.M. Phone: **(800) 367-5282** or **(860) 572-0012.**

Mystic Drawbridge Ice Cream Shoppe—$

Unlike a lot of places that advertise having "the best," Mystic Drawbridge Ice Cream probably does, at least as far as ice cream goes in these parts. Not only that, but no one can beat the view from its tiny wooden deck—the river with its boats and drawbridge is only feet away. Call for hours and season. **2 W. Main St., Mystic, 06355; (860) 572-7978.**

Services

Local Visitors Information

Mystic & More! (a.k.a. **Southeastern Connecticut Tourism District**), **470 Bank St., P.O. Box 89, New London, 06320; (800) 863-6569** or **(860) 444-2206.**

Mystic and Shoreline Information Center, Olde Mistick Village, Mystic, 06355; (860) 536-1641. High season (May–Aug.) hours: Mon.–Sat., 9:00 A.M.–6:00 P.M.; Sun., 10:00 A.M.–6:00 P.M. Off-season (Sept.–Apr.) hours: Mon.–Sat., 9:00 A.M.–5:00 P.M.; Sun., 10:00 A.M.–5:00 P.M.

Mystic Chamber of Commerce, 16 Cottrell St., Mystic, 06355; (860) 572-9578. Hours: Mon.–Fri., 9:00 A.M.–5:00 P.M. They have literature and a computerized visitors information

service available outside 24 hours a day. Using the computer, you can contact selected hotels and other advertisers directly.

Mystic Coast & Country; (800) 692-6278.

SNET Visitor Information Center. Located off I-95 southbound near exit 92; **(860) 599-2056.** Hours: 8:00 A.M.–6:00 P.M. daily, Memorial Day–Columbus Day; 8:30 A.M.–4:30 P.M. daily the rest of the year.

Tourist Information Depot of Mystic, Rte. 27 directly opposite the I-95 exit 90 southbound off-ramp, Mystic, 06355; (860) 536-3505. Hours: 7:00 A.M.–9:00 P.M. daily, year-round. Discounted admission to some area attractions available, as well as discount coupons for area lodging and dining. Public rest rooms available.

Transportation

Mystic is a stop on **Amtrak**'s Washington-Boston route. For schedule and fare information call **(800) 872-7245.** Regional bus service to Stonington is provided by **South East Area Transit (SEAT)** at **(860) 886-2631.**

Commuter flights to and from the New London area land at **Groton/New London Airport (860-445-8549). Yellow Cab** provides local taxi service 24 hours a day, year-round, between all the major transportation centers, hotels, casinos and attractions. You can reach it at **(860) 536-8888.**

The **Mystic Trolley** runs Memorial Day–Columbus Day between Mystic Marinelife Aquarium, Mystic Seaport and the downtown with stops at Mystic hotels. Hours are 9:00 A.M.–8:00 P.M. daily. Pay per ride or purchase a day pass. For more information call the **Mystic Chamber of Commerce** at **(860) 572-9578.**

New London

New London and Groton lie opposite each other on the Thames River, the principal waterway of eastern Connecticut. Nowhere else is the state's maritime heritage more evident than in these two cities—not even Mystic, because far from being just an aspect of the past, here seafaring is still very much a part of the present. The U.S. Coast Guard Academy is situated on a beautiful riverside campus in New London, an active U.S. Naval Submarine Base is located in Groton and Electric Boat Co., a submarine manufacturer, is (despite defense cutbacks) a major Groton employer. Part of the charm of New London is the presence of men and women in Navy and Coast Guard uniforms around town and the sight of submarines slowly making their way up and down the Thames. New London also sees more ferry activity than any other Connecticut city, with regular service to Long Island, Fishers Island and Block Island.

The river and Long Island Sound dominate recreation in the area in the same way they dominate the economy. Parts of the Coast Guard Academy are open to the public, and although the submarine base itself is not, at the nearby Nautilus Memorial you can board the first nuclear-powered sub ever built and learn about the distinguished history of the U.S. submarine fleet. Boating, fishing, tour boats on the river and educational cruises on the Sound are all big attractions. Even New London's annual street festival, Sailfest, has a nautical theme, with tall ships and fireworks over the river.

Unlike some parts of the state, there is a lot of public access to the shoreline here. Ocean Beach Park in New London is a seaside amusement park with modern facilities set within an old-fashioned context. Rocky Neck State Park in East Lyme offers saltwater swimming, camping and hiking, and a renowned summertime music festival takes place each year on the oceanside lawns of Harkness Memorial State Park in Waterford.

One personality that will forever be linked to New London is Eugene O'Neill. One of America's greatest playwrights, he lived in New London during his childhood and for many summers thereafter. A statue of O'Neill as a boy is located at City Pier right behind Union Station. Monte Cristo Cottage (O'Neill's boyhood home) was the setting for his semiautobiographical *Long Day's Journey into Night* and is now a museum open for tours. The Eugene O'Neill Theater Center contributes greatly to the cultural life of the area, as do the Lyman Allyn Art Museum, the Garde Arts Center and Connecticut College with its art galleries, Palmer Auditorium and historic chapel.

The broader strokes of history are also painted here. One of the two Hempstead Houses, a pair of historic homes that together form a museum, is among the oldest wood-frame houses in the state, and Fort Griswold in Groton is probably Connecticut's foremost Revolutionary War monument, commemorating the bloodiest battle of the war on state soil. Although to out-of-towners New London may not have the name recognition of a Hartford or a New Haven, the area has a rich, accessible history and a high concentration of things to see and do that make it well worth visiting.

History

New London was first laid out in 1646 by John Winthrop, Jr., son of the governor of Massachusetts. It was first called Pequot, but the name was officially changed to New London in 1658. The excellence of the Thames River for shipping led to fast growth in the area and a great deal of prosperity. Maritime traffic demanded construction of the first lighthouse on the Connecticut shore around 1760. The local economy was enhanced by privateering and supply activities during the Revolutionary War. With its warehouses bulging from booty seized from British ships, the city was a tempting target. Perhaps more of the energy the privateers

showed at sea should have been devoted to fortifying New London and Groton, because when the British took action to stem the tide of losses, the Americans were found lacking. The British landed large forces on both sides of the river on a Sept. morning in 1781 and proceeded to burn New London and quickly gain control of the fort in Groton. Fort Griswold is now a state park and a fascinating stop for history buffs.

After the war New London continued to prosper from maritime activities such as fishing, shipbuilding, whaling, sealing and shipping. One indicator of the sheer flow of money and goods through the city is the fact that in 1807 it was the only city in Connecticut with two banks. The Thames was blockaded during the War of 1812, but neither New London nor Groton suffered as they had in the Revolutionary War. In fact, when the war reached its conclusion, the British officers in the harbor were invited ashore for a Peace Ball.

By the mid-19th century New London was second only to New Bedford, Massachusetts, in the size of its whaling industry. In time a thriving resort community also developed, especially in areas such as Pequot Ave. in New London and Groton Long Point in Groton, where houses had wonderful water views.

Land for the naval base in Groton was set aside in 1868. After much wooing of the Navy, a submarine base was finally established in 1916. At about the same time a shipyard was being built for Electric Boat Co., now a division of General Dynamics. During World War II this plant supplied the U.S. Navy with almost 75 submarines, and in 1954 it launched the first nuclear-powered U-boat in the world. The *Nautilus* set records everywhere it went, and today, in retirement, it is the centerpiece of the Nautilus Memorial, a museum.

The Coast Guard Academy conducted training in the area from 1910 on and finally built its academy here in 1932 on land donated by New London. It is currently one of only four military academies in the nation. Although the area has felt both the boom and the bust of its dependence on defense industries, the sub base and the Coast Guard Academy together with Connecticut College have provided a lot of

stability. In recent years New London has seen major redevelopment with an eye toward tourism, and with increased traffic through the area from the proximity of the casinos to the north in Ledyard and Montville, its attractions should only increase.

Major Attractions

Harkness Memorial State Park

The mansion that was the Harkness family's seaside summer residence, Eolia, is currently under restoration and not open to the public. But the grounds are reason enough to go. A pretty system of paths is popular with early-morning walkers and joggers. There are numerous picnic tables, sweeping ocean vistas to contemplate and a small beach to comb. You can fish from the promontory or enjoy a concert at an annual summer music festival held in July and Aug. An adjacent beach/picnic area is reserved for handicapped use. The park is open year round, 8:00 A.M.–dusk. A parking fee is charged Memorial Day–Labor Day. (Note: Because of the danger of erosion, it is essential not to walk on the sand dunes.) **275 Great Neck Rd. (Rte. 213), Waterford, 06385; (860) 443-5725.**

Ocean Beach Park

This beautiful, well-maintained city park is an oceanside attraction that offers saltwater and pool swimming, a water slide, a miniature golf course, a games arcade, picnic areas, concessions and the longest boardwalk in Connecticut. The park and beach are open year-round, but all of the other facilities are seasonal, opening the Sat. before Memorial Day and closing on Labor Day. The golf course alone keeps a longer season. During summer, parking is $2 per hour per car, with a maximum of $6 per day Mon.–Thu. and $12 per day Fri.–Sun. and holidays. There are additional charges for use of the pool, golf course, water slide and lockers. Off-season access is free. The park is open daily 9:00 A.M.–10:00 P.M.; in season all facilities except the golf course are open 10:00 A.M.–5:00 P.M. Course hours: 10:00 A.M.–10:00 P.M. To get there, go south on Ocean Ave. in New London until you can go no farther. Turn right on Neptune Ave., and the entrance is straight ahead. For more information call **(800) 510-7263, (800) 962-0284** or **(860) 447-3031.**

Rocky Neck State Park

One of Connecticut's best state-owned shoreline parks has a long, sandy beach for swimming, bathhouses, a nice campground, an extraordinary picnic pavilion, woodland trails for hiking, a salt marsh with an observation deck and a handicapped-accessible fishing and crabbing area and a great little promontory for fishing in the surf.

Rocky Neck is sliced in half by Bride's Brook, a stream that forms a salt marsh as it nears Long Island Sound. There's a famous story about a couple in colonial times who were anxious to get married but stymied by the floodwaters of this stream that separated them from the nearest minister. According to legend, the couple arranged to stand on one bank of the raging waterway while the minister bellowed the wedding ceremony from the other, and henceforth the stream has been known as Bride's Brook. A parking fee is charged Memorial Day–Labor Day: weekdays, $5 for in-state vehicles and $8 for out-of-state vehicles; weekends, $7 and $12, respectively. Rocky Neck is on **Rte. 156 just east of the Old Lyme/East Lyme town line.** For more information call **(860) 739-5471.**

USS Nautilus Memorial/ Submarine Force Library and Museum

If you think submarines are a 20th-century invention, think again—they were first deployed to place mines during the Revolutionary War. If that surprises you, or if you've always been fascinated by subs, this is the place to learn more. The *USS Nautilus,* a National Historic Landmark, was the world's first nuclear-powered sub. *Nautilus* set a slew of speed and distance records and was the first ship to reach the geographic North Pole back in 1958. You enter through a museum where models, timelines and photos trace the history of the U.S. submarine fleet. Try out a periscope or watch a film before proceeding to the *Nautilus* itself, where you can take a self-guided tour. Because of the small spaces, handicapped access to the sub is minimal. Admission is free. Summer (Apr. 15–Oct. 14) hours: Wed.–Mon., 9:00 A.M.–5:00 P.M.; Tue., 1:00 P.M.–5:00 P.M. On busy days during summer, arrive by 3:30 P.M. if you want to tour the sub. Winter

(Oct. 15–Apr. 14) hours: Wed.–Mon., 9:00 A.M.–4:00 P.M.; closed Tue. Also closed some major holidays, the first full week of May and the first two weeks of Dec. Located at the **U.S. Naval Submarine Base on Crystal Lake Rd. off Rte. 12, Groton, 06349; (800) 343-0079** or **(860) 449-3174.**

Other Attractions

City Pier

City Pier at the foot of State St. is the hub of New London. It's where the ferries come in from Long Island, Block Island and Fishers Island. It's where trains and buses unload their travelers from Boston or New York. It's where the statue of Eugene O'Neill as a boy reminds visitors of the inspiration this city provided a great American dramatic talent, and the historic Nathan Hale Schoolhouse is just a few steps away. It's great fun to just hang out here and watch the boats go by. You might see a sub on its way up to the Naval Submarine Base in Groton, an excursion boat showing tourists the local sights or explorers in kayaks heading out to open ocean. Lots of folks fish from the end of the pier. These are considered marine waters, so you don't need a permit. And from City Pier, it's no more than a 15-minute walk to many of New London's historic attractions.

U.S. Coast Guard Academy

This sprawling complex on the New London side of the Thames River is one of the nation's four military academies the Coast Guard began in 1790 as the Revenue Cutter Service, given the responsibility of enforcing maritime customs and tariffs. That entity combined with the Life Saving Service in 1915 to create the Coast Guard of today.

There are several things to see and do on the grounds. Stop at the Visitors Center (open 9:00 A.M.–5:00 P.M. daily May–Oct. and weekends 10:00 A.M.–5:00 P.M. in Apr.) for a self-guided walking tour brochure. Visit the museum (open weekdays 9:00 A.M.–4:30 P.M.

Getting There

New London and Groton are both located about an hour and a half southeast of Hartford by car. The easiest way to get there is to take I-91 south to Rte. 9 south to I-95 east and follow the signs. For other transportation options, see Services at the end of this chapter.

[Thu. until 8:00]; Sat., 10:00 A.M.–5:00 P.M.; Sun., noon–5:00 P.M.; closed major holidays) for a look at maritime and Coast Guard artifacts. If the tall ship and cadet training vessel *Eagle* is in port, you can take a self-guided tour of its topside any time sunrise–sunset on weekends and 1:00 P.M.–sunset on weekdays. The *Eagle* is a barque, a term that defines its mast structure and rigging. The *Eagle* is the only working ship of its kind in the country. Tours are free, but the *Eagle* is typically not in

239

Board the world's first nuclear submarine at the Nautilus Memorial in Groton.

port between May and Aug., so opportunities are limited. Because it's a working ship, access can be further restricted depending on the day's activities. Check on its schedule before going by calling **(860) 444-8595.**

In spring and fall you might also catch a dress parade, in which cadets march in formation and are reviewed by commanders or occasionally an important guest. They take one hour and are generally held on Fri. afternoons. **15 Mohegan Ave. (Rte. 32; follow signs from I-95 exit 82A), New London, 06320; (860) 444-8270.**

Festivals and Events

Summer Music at Harkness

This very popular series of summertime concerts features classical, pop, jazz and family music performances on the grounds of beautiful Harkness Memorial State Park. The spreading lawns, ocean views and formal gardens of Harkness are the perfect setting for arts events. Concerts take place on Sat. at 8:00 P.M., rain or shine, with special events some Thu. The grounds open at 6:00 P.M. Bring a blanket or lawn chair, or enjoy a real seat under a tent. There are concessions, and you can get a catered buffet dinner for $12 if you order 48 hours in advance by calling the number below. Otherwise, pack a picnic. Tickets are $14 for lawn "seating" or $21–$28 for a spot under the tent. The park is at **275 Great Neck Rd. (Rte. 213) in Waterford.** For information on the concert series call **(800) 969-3400.**

SubFest
Fourth of July weekend (Thu.–Sun.)

This big Fourth of July celebration takes its name more from its location on the Naval Submarine Base in Groton than from any connection to submarines. The highlight is a big fireworks display on the Fourth. Other evenings are filled with musical entertainment by name talent under a tent with seating for 3,000 people. During the days there's a boat

show, a business expo, wandering entertainers, contests for kids and hot-air balloon rides (at dusk only; extra charge applies). The low entrance fee of $4 for adults (children under 12 free) includes concert admission. Hours vary by day; call for details. Parking is free. To get to the base entrance, take Crystal Lake Rd. off Rte. 12 in Groton and stay straight. For more information call **(860) 449-3238.**

SailFest
second weekend in July (Fri.–Sun.)

New London's biggest street and harbor festival occupies the whole downtown area for one summer weekend. Much of State and Bank Sts. is closed to traffic for the event. A tall ship visits the harbor, and the public is invited to tour it. The highlight of the event is a gigantic fireworks display over the Thames River on Sat. night, sponsored by the Mashantucket Pequots. Many people arrive by boat, docking at the marina at City Pier or simply dropping anchor in the harbor to watch the show, and the Cross Sound Ferry runs a special excursion boat that night. Other activities include children's games, antique-looking carnival rides for kids and adults, regional musical talent, crafts and souvenirs for sale, food vendors and, of course, the downtown's merchants, who stay open late. Admission is free, but there is a charge for games, rides and food. Hours: Fri., noon–10:00 P.M.; Sat., 10:00 A.M.–close of fireworks; Sun., noon–6:00 P.M. For more information call the **Downtown New London Association** at **(860) 444-1879.**

Outdoor Activities

Biking

Mountain Biking

Bluff Point Coastal Reserve
Bluff Point is a huge undeveloped tract of wooded land right on Long Island Sound, surprisingly remote and wild considering its location next to a major urban area. It's largely flat

and crisscrossed by numerous trails that are great for mountain biking as long as you don't mind getting sand in your gears. For directions, see the listing under Hiking.

Haley Farm State Park

A portion of a designated bike route from Mystic to New London passes through this pretty off-road area for several miles. Enter via Haley Farm Rd. off Brook St. in Groton. Haley Farm Rd. probably doesn't appear on any map, but Brook St. does, and it's short, so you shouldn't have too much trouble finding the turnoff. Bikes are allowed on all the trails at Haley Farm, but bikers should slow down or dismount for hikers and joggers. The designated bike trail is blazed as such. It comes out on Midway Oval, a Groton street. From there take Depot Rd. to Rte. 1 to go farther, or backtrack to return to your car. Park hours: 8:00 A.M.– sunset daily, year-round.

Road Biking

The New London area is rather built-up, but there are places to ride and get an ocean view without encountering too much traffic. Rte. 213 in Waterford near Harkness Memorial State Park is flat, pretty and excellent for biking. In the park itself, an oceanside estate under restoration, there are a few paths, both paved and unpaved, that go right up to the water's edge. Leave your car at Harkness or at the state boating access area on Shore Rd. Depending on the day and season, a parking fee might be collected. Street parking may also be available in the Pleasure Beach area off Shore Rd.

The Groton Long Pt. area is picture-perfect, and a network of small streets here is nice for a leisurely ride, but you'll have to park in the small lot at Haley Farm State Park off Brook St. and then ride back down Rte. 215, which can be quite busy, to the point.

If you want to cross the Thames River on your bike, you're in luck. There is bicycle and pedestrian access to Goldstar Bridge, which carries the traffic from I-95 between New London and Groton. Follow signs from surface streets on either side of the bridge.

Birding

Although New London is a heavily developed urban area, there are several places where you can see substantial numbers of birds. Bluff Pt. is a large undeveloped tract of wooded land right on the shore where songbirds and raptors are easily sighted. Harkness Memorial State Park is a good spot for observing shorebirds. For more information on these two areas, see the listings under Hiking and Major Attractions.

Boating

Boat Launches

Long Island Sound

There's a state boat ramp between Avery Pt. and Jupiter Pt. at the southern tip of Groton. Take Rte. 349 south to Bayberry Ln., where you'll find a large lot. A fee is charged on weekends in summer. In addition, the Dock Rd. state access area is at the end of Dock Rd. off Shore Rd. in Waterford. You'll know you're in the right place if you can see Millstone Nuclear Power Plant, now out of commission, on the opposite shore.

Niantic River

To get to this free state access area from Niantic, travel east on Rte. 156 and cross the drawbridge between Niantic (East Lyme) and Waterford. Take the first left-hand turn you can after the bridge; the road should be marked West St. Go to a stop sign and turn left again. Go to a second stop sign and turn right. Drive about a block and turn right at Hillyer's Tackle Shop; the parking area will be straight ahead. A fee is charged in summer. Sea kayakers will find this a good spot to access both the open water of Long Island Sound and the protected waters of Niantic Bay.

Poquonnock River

At Bluff Pt. Coastal Reserve there's a launch area into the Poquonnock River suitable for canoes, kayaks and larger craft at high tide. Downriver there's a mile-long sand spit separating the mouth of the river from the open water of Long Island Sound. Swimming and picnicking are allowed on the spit, but the beach is unguarded. Cooking and campfires are not permitted.

Thames River

A heavily used state access area is located at State Pier (a commercial pier) in New London. Follow signs for State Pier from Crystal Ave. off Main St. The launch is a stone's throw from I-95. On the opposite side of the river in Groton, the Kenneth E. Streeter boat launch is located on the south side of Fairview Ave. off Bridge St. under the Goldstar Bridge. This area is designed to accommodate wheelchair-bound visitors. Both of these launches can accommodate any size boat, and a fee is charged in summer.

Cruises

New London Ledge Lighthouse

This special summer program for adults and families is run by **Project Oceanology** (see the Children and Families section for more). You'll board a 55-foot ship for a two-hour trip down the Thames and out into New London harbor with (weather permitting) a stop at New London Ledge Lighthouse, an impressive structure, reminiscent of a mansion, dating from 1909. It's still operational but automated and undergoing restoration. For safety reasons children under age 6 are not allowed to disembark at the lighthouse. Reservations required; appropriate attire (sneakers and a windbreaker) suggested. Fare: $13 adults, $9 children 6–11. The cruise is offered Tue., Thu., Sat. & Sun. at 4:00 P.M. , mid-June–Labor Day. The ship departs from the **University of Connecticut campus at Avery Point, Shennecossett Rd., Groton, 06340.** For more information call **(860) 445-9007** (in Connecticut) or **(800) 364-8472** (out-of-state).

Thames River Cruises

The tour boat *Patriot* makes daily sightseeing excursions up and down the Thames River July–Oct., departing from New London's City Pier at the foot of State St. You can choose from several rides with narrative themes such as Lighthouses and More, See Subs by Boat and River Ramble. During fall they also offer an upriver foliage tour. Each ride follows a

different route, taking you past local landmarks while an onboard guide gives historical background. There are five departures per day between 9:00 A.M. and 5:00 P.M.; call for the current schedule. Ticket prices are $10–$15 for adults and $6–$10 for children 4–13. For more information call **(860) 444-7827.**

Whale Watching

On Tue., Thu. and Sun. in July and Aug., board the 100-foot *Sunbeam Express* for a trip out into open ocean for whale watching. The boat departs at 9:00 A.M. and returns at 4:00 P.M. A naturalist is onboard to answer questions. Reservations suggested. Ticket prices: $35 adults, $30 seniors, $20 children 5–12, children 4 and under free. The boat departs **Capt. John's Dock** at **15 First St., Waterford, 06385.** For more information and directions call **(860) 443-7259.**

Marinas

Three of the larger marinas in New London geared toward transient visitors are **Burr's Yacht Haven (860-443-8457), Crocker's Boatyard (860-443-6304)** and **Thamesport Marina (800-882-1151).** You can also reach them on VHF 9. They all sell gas, have in the neighborhood of 25–30 transient slips and can accommodate boats of nearly any size; Burr's and Thamesport also have moorings. Burr's and Crocker's operate year-round and can repair nearly anything. Thamesport probably offers the greatest number of amenities overall, but call the marinas for specific details.

There's no lack of marina facilities in Niantic Bay, either. **Bayreuther Boat Yard, Inc. (860-739-6264;** VHF 9), **Boats, Inc. (860-739-6251;** VHF 71), **Niantic Bay Marina (860-444-1999;** VHF 9), **Port Niantic (860-739-2155;** VHF 9) and **Waddy's Mago Point Marina (860-442-2710;** VHF 88) are among those that offer the greatest range of services and facilities. If you just want a meal, **Sunset Rib Co. (860-443-7427;** open seasonally) provides dockage for patrons.

In Noank both **Noank Shipyard (860-536-9651;** VHF 9) and **Spicer's Noank Marina (860-536-4978;** VHF 68) have a large number of transient slips and offer a lot in the way of facilities and repairs, although only Noank sells fuel. At **Abbott's Lobsters in the Rough (860-536-7719)** you can dock alongside and dine or have seafood packed in ice for preparation onboard.

Kayak rentals

The same people who offer parasailing rides also rent two-person kayaks and an inflatable raft with an 8 HP motor for use on Niantic Bay. Rates begin at $25 for a half day. **ParaSail USA is at Capt. John's Dock, 15 First St., Waterford, 06385; (860) 444-7272.**

Fishing

The New London area is the saltwater fishing capital of Connecticut. There are approximately two dozen charter operators out of these waters—too many to list here. For the names and numbers of current ones, your best bet is to call one of the tourist information sources listed under Services.

Several operators offer regularly scheduled excursions on large vessels known as party boats. Each one has its own schedule of departure times and fees, and some may offer special trips that others do not, such as night fishing or outings on which they seek a particular type of fish. Each operator will be glad to fill you in on what you can expect to hook. Seabass, bluefish, flounder, blackfish, porgies and mackerel are all possibilities depending on the season. Half-day party boat trips generally run about $25 for adults, exclusive of tackle rental, and some will allow you to ride as a sightseer for a discounted price. Most operators provide bait free of charge. Arrive at least one half hour before your departure time, and allow extra time for traffic. See the Introduction for more information on saltwater fishing.

The *Hel-Cat II* **(860-535-2066** or **860-535-3200)** out of Groton is the largest party fishing boat on the Connecticut coast. It runs a fishing contest weekly with prizes awarded for the biggest fish caught onboard. The **Sunbeam Fleet (860-443-7259)** out of Waterford offers both party boat and charter service with summer Wed. devoted to fluke fishing and night bass fishing May–Oct. Its staff will clean any fish

you've caught free of charge on the way back to the dock. The *Black Hawk II* **(800-382-2824** or **860-443-3662)** and the *Mijoy 747* **(860-443-0663)** are two other options.

You can also try for bluefish, striped bass, blackfish and flounder from shore at any state boat launch. Harkness Memorial and Rocky Neck State Parks (see the listings under Major Attractions) both have suitable spots. At Rocky Neck there's even a handicapped-accessible crabbing area at the edge of a picturesque salt marsh. **Hillyers Tackle Shop (860-443-7615)** at Mago Pt. near the Niantic River state boat launch is a good place to get outfitted for either fresh- or saltwater fishing and pick up a tide chart.

Although most people come to this area to do saltwater fishing, largemouth bass can be had at **Pattagansett Lake** in East Lyme, which is stocked with rainbow trout, largemouth and smallmouth bass and perch. Access is off Rte. 1 about 2 miles west of I-95 exit 75.

Golf

Shennecossett Golf Course

Shennecossett offers perhaps the best views of any public, 18-hole golf course near the Sound in Connecticut. This par 72, 6,142-yard course is located at Avery Pt., on even terrain where wind is always a factor. It is $21–$25 for a full round, with 9-hole play available after 3:00 P.M. and discounted 18-hole play after 2:00 P.M. The course is closed to the public for league play 3:30 P.M.–5:30 P.M. on weekdays. To get a weekend tee time, call after 7:30 A.M. on Tue. for Sat., ditto on Wed. for Sun. Facilities include practice areas for putting and chipping, a pro shop, lessons, a full-service restaurant and bar and all rentals. **93 Plant St., Groton, 06340; (860) 445-0262.**

Handicapped Access

Camp Harkness

Adjacent to Harkness Memorial State Park is another, little-known state park specifically designed for the use of the disabled and their families and friends. Access to the park is free, but you must send away for a pass in advance.

Facilities include a beach with wooden ramps to the water's edge, a picnic area, an exercise trail and heated cabins available by advance reservation Labor Day–Memorial Day (not the other way around; they are reserved for group use during summer). There are also therapeutic programs in horseback riding, swimming and raised-bed gardening. Hours: 8:00 A.M.–dusk daily, year-round. For more information, contact the Camp Director at **Camp Harkness, 301 Great Neck Rd., Waterford, 06385; (860) 443-7818** or **(860) 443-8806 (TDD).**

Hiking

Also see the listing for Haley Farm State Park under Biking.

Bluff Pt. Coastal Reserve
The main trail at this large shoreline property is flat, straight and a bit boring, but a good place to stroll if you don't want to encounter many elevation changes or tree roots to trip you up. It's popular with joggers. This path takes you past a rocky shoreline, a little sandy spit and finally up to a low bluff from which you have a nice view of the Sound and planes taking off and landing at Groton/New London Airport across the Poquonnock River. There are also broad, flat rocks at water level (depending on the tide), perfect for stretching out in the sun. No map is posted at the entrance, and this is a large area, so be careful not to overextend yourself. Unless you know your way around, the side trails are best avoided. The entrance to Bluff Pt. is a bit tricky to find. Take Depot Rd. south from Rte. 1 in Groton, go under the railroad tracks and continue straight to the large parking area and boat launch site. For more information call **(860) 445-1729.**

Rocky Neck State Park
Although most people probably come here to swim, Rocky Neck has 7 miles of beautiful trails crisscrossing wooded hills running right down to the ocean, a beach and grassy promontories for strolling and a dedicated bike/walking path between the campground and the beach. For directions and more information about Rocky Neck, see the listing under Major Attractions.

Ice Skating

Dayton Arena, the skating rink at Connecticut College, is open for occasional public skating Oct.–mid-Mar. Admission is $4 per person, and rental skates are available. To get to the rink from the center of New London, take Mohegan Ave. (Rte. 12) north past the main entrance to the Connecticut College campus. At the next light, turn right and follow signs. For a recorded message with current hours call **(860) 439-2575.**

Swimming

The New London area is blessed with two of the best public shoreline swimming areas in Connecticut, **Ocean Beach Park** and **Rocky Neck State Park,** and both of them offer a range of activities in case you get tired of surf and sand. For more information, see the listings under Major Attractions. A third possibility is **Bluff Pt. Coastal Reserve,** but you'll have to hike to earn your swim. If you follow the main trail here out toward the point, you'll eventually come to a mile-long sand spit on the right-hand side. Swimming is permitted at your own risk. Bring a picnic of prepared food (cooking is not permitted) and make a day of it.

Seeing and Doing

Art Galleries

The **Cummings Art Center at Connecticut College (Mohegan Ave. [Rte. 32], New London; 860-439-2740)** comprises three adjoining galleries with 3,000 square feet of exhibit space devoted to contemporary work. It's open during the school year (roughly Sept.–May) Mon.–Fri., 9:00 A.M.–5:00 P.M., & by appointment on Sat. Three to four exhibits are mounted each semester, including shows of the Connecticut College faculty in fall and the students in spring. Every other year in late winter, there's a symposium and special exhibit on the theme of the arts and technology.

Right in downtown New London, you'll find the **New London Art Society & Gallery (147**

State St.; 860-443-0632), three floors of exhibit space in a converted office building. There are three juried shows yearly showcasing a wide range of media and styles. Admission is free. Hours: Wed.–Sat., 11:00 A.M.–3:00 P.M.

Also see the listing for the Lyman Allyn Art Museum under Museums, and consider stopping at the **East Lyme Art Gallery (6 Grand St., Niantic; 860-739-3263),** a small, seasonal, artist-run gallery. Hours can be erratic, so call before going.

Children and Families

Described as a "marine science center and advanture camp" for kids, the **Ocean Quest Interactive Science and Learning Center** is a major new attraction under development that should be of great interest to families with young children. For more information call **(860) 437-6590.** If you or your child wish to learn about the process of nuclear power generation, visit **Millstone Information and Science Center (278 Main St., Niantic; 800-428-4234** or **860-691-4670),** an educational effort of Northeast Utilities, which owns the Millstone nuclear power plant nearby. Admission is free. Hours: Mon.–Fri., 9:00 A.M.–4:00 P.M. with some extended hours in summer. And if you're visiting the last weekend in April, attend the **Connecticut Storytelling Center's Annual Storytelling Festival** at Connecticut College, where tales for both adults and children are told. The center also organizes **Telebration,** an event the weekend before Thanksgiving at multiple locations around the state, with a focus on stories for adults. For details on either event call **(860) 439-2764.**

Children's Museum of Southeastern Connecticut
Targeted squarely at children under the age of 10, this facility is not so much a museum as a hands-on activities center. Kids can mess around with computers, do arts and crafts, operate model trains, put on puppet shows, do some role playing in a child-size village and more. Admission: $3 per person. Hours: Tue.–Sat., 9:30 A.M.–4:30 P.M. (Fri. until 8:00); Sun.,

noon–4:00 P.M.; also open Mon. in summer & Mon. holidays. **409 Main St. (Rte. 156), Niantic, 06357; (860) 691-1255.**

Project Oceanology
Between mid-June and Labor Day, you and your children can take a two-and-a-half-hour cruise on a 55-foot research vessel dedicated to scientific education. Under the guidance of instructors, you'll take core samples, bring fish up into an onboard holding tank, perform tests on ocean water, learn to navigate and more. There are departures daily at 10:00 A.M. & 1:00 P.M., plus Mon. & Wed. at 4:00 P.M. Cost: $17 adults, $12 children under 12. Suggested for children age 6 and above. Reservations essential. The same folks run trips out to New London's Ledge Lighthouse in summer; see the Cruises section for more information. The boat leaves from the **University of Connecticut campus at Avery Point on Shennecossett Rd., Groton, 06340; (860) 445-9007** (in Connecticut) or **(800) 364-8472** (out-of-state).

Science Center of Eastern Connecticut
Half community resource, half tourist attraction, this is a "touch me" museum with 57 workstations that allow visitors to experiment with mechanical systems, biology, energy, light, sound and more. Programs are given daily in a small science theater. There is a complete range of exhibits for very young children to adults. There's also a shaded picnic grove on-site, as well as access to Connecticut College Arboretum trails for hiking or plant study. Admission: $6 adults, $4 for seniors and children 2–16. Hours: Mon.–Sat., 9:00 A.M.–5:00 P.M.; Sun, 1:00 P.M.–5:00 P.M.; closed major holidays. Call before going to verify hours. **33 Gallows Lane, New London, 06320; (860) 442-0391.**

Gardens and Arboreta

Do not expect manicured gardens or flower beds at **Connecticut College Arboretum,** a 425-acre showcase for Connecticut College's native tree and shrub collection. This is a

245

naturalistic planting much more akin in spirit to New York City's Central Park, only on a smaller scale. There are easy hiking trails, ponds and pleasant vistas. Admission is free. Hours: dawn–dusk daily. Free tours are given on Sun. at 2:00 P.M., late Apr.–late Oct. For more information on tours call **(860) 439-5020.** The entrance to the arboretum is on Williams St. in New London directly opposite the back entrance to the campus. For general information about the arboretum call **(860) 439-2140.**

Historic Sites

Fort Griswold Battlefield State Park

Revolutionary War buffs will love this site of an infamous 1781 battle. Not only is it one of the few battles Connecticut experienced during that war, but the ignominious turncoat Benedict Arnold played an important role in it. His familiarity with the area (he was native to neighboring Norwich) was invaluable to the British, and Arnold even led one of the two corps of troops that made the attack.

Fort Griswold was not retired until after World War II, so the park contains remains from several periods. At the 18th-century fort site you can still see large earthen embankments and stonework and walk through a "sallée port," a tunnel that allowed access to the powder magazine. Visitors are asked not to climb on the stonework or the earthen embankments for the sake of their preservation. A 134-foot granite obelisk memorializes the men who fought in the 1781 battle. A spiral staircase with 166 steps leads to an observation platform at the top. In the Monument House Museum next door you can see Col. Ledyard's sword, a model of the fort as it is believed to have looked at the time of the battle and other artifacts. Completing the attractions is the Avery House, a center-chimney home to which the American wounded were brought for doctoring. On Labor Day weekend, either a battle reenactment or a commemoration sponsored by the 2nd Connecticut Regiment of the Continental Line takes place at the park. Call the **Monument House Museum** at **(860) 449-6877** for details on the current year's activities.

Admission to the park and all of its buildings is free. Hours for the Monument House Museum and the obelisk are 10:00 A.M.–5:00 P.M. daily, Memorial Day–Labor Day, then weekends only until Columbus Day. The Avery House is open the same hours, but only until Labor Day. Park hours are 8:00 A.M.–sunset daily, year-round. Park on Fort St. for easiest access to the Avery House, and on Park Ave. for everything else. The park is located at **Monument St. and Park Ave. in Groton; (860) 445-1729.**

National Submarine Memorial

Dedicated to the memory of all the U.S. submariners (over 3,600 in number) who lost their lives in World War II, this monument is a poignant landmark. It's located in a rather busy spot next to an auto body shop at the intersection of Bridge and Thames Sts. in Groton, but visitors will find it moving nonetheless. Two memorial services are held here

The remains of Fort Griswold are still visible in the state park of the same name, Groton.

yearly, on the Sun. preceding Memorial Day and Veteran's Day. For more information call U.S. Sub Veterans of World War II members Joe Holmes at **(860) 464-8200** or Andrew Feindt at **(860) 464-0268**.

Ye Townes Antientist Burial Ground

The oldest graveyard in New London County contains marked stones from as far back as the mid-1600s. One unusual thing about it is the large number of markers carved from non-native stones and displaying a broad range of decorative styles. It seems that the relatively prosperous early inhabitants of New London could afford to have stones "imported" from Newport, Boston and elsewhere. Hence, these stones represent the work of more than your usual two or three local stonecarver families. When you visit, park on Bulkeley Pl. in New London and enter the graveyard on Huntington St.

Museums

In addition to the listings below, there are a few other museums you might try. Some have hours restricted to the summer season. Call the **Noank Historical Society** at **(860) 536-7026** or **(860) 536-3960**, the **Waterford Historical Society** at **(860) 442-2707**, the **East Lyme Historical Society** at **(860) 739-0761** and the **Robert Mills U.S. Custom House Museum** at **(860) 447-2501**.

Hempsted Houses

The Hempsted Houses are two historic homes, one rather typical of early Connecticut architecture and the other very atypical. The Joshua Hempsted House (ca. 1678) is the oldest house in New London and one of the oldest houses in New England. The exposed beams, projecting porch, steeply pitched roof and casement windows (not original, although their placement is) are all classic examples of 17th-century architectural and building practices. A 1728 addition sports sash windows and other signs of advancing style. Joshua kept a renowned diary from 1711 to 1758 documenting everyday life in the new colony that was also an important resource for 20th-century antiquarians trying to understand the nomenclature of 17th-century homes.

In contrast, the Nathaniel Hempsted House just across the lawn is very unusual. It was built in 1759 with 2-foot-thick stone walls and some unique interior details. Family and period furnishings are interesting enough, but the real attraction here is the houses themselves. Admission: $3 adults, $2 students. Hours: Tue.–Sun., 1:00 P.M.–5:00 P.M., mid-May–mid-Oct., & by appointment. **11 Hempstead St. at Jay St., New London, 06320; (860) 443-7949.**

Jabez Smith House

This center-chimney house (ca. 1783), little changed since it was built, is named for the man who built it and shows how a typical Groton family might have lived in the town's early years. The house is furnished with many Smith family antiques since it remained in their hands until relatively recently. A cutaway of an interior wall allows visitors to see how the house was constructed. The grounds are pleasant for strolling. Admission by donation. Hours: Sat.–Sun., 1:00 P.M.–5:00 P.M., Apr.–Dec. **259 North Rd. (Rte. 117), Groton, 06340; (860) 445-6689.**

Lyman Allyn Art Museum

Showcase great art and artifacts in a stunning, classically inspired building, give it all an estate setting overlooking New London and you've got the Lyman Allyn Art Museum. The highlight is the American Collection on the first floor, an all-encompassing exhibit of paintings, silver, china, glass, furniture and more, including some American Impressionist works. Move counterclockwise through the outer "ring" to get the story of the development of American styles of decorative and fine arts from the late 1600s to the late 1800s. This exhibit alone makes the museum worth a visit, but there are several other galleries of permanent and changing exhibits and a lecture program. Wheelchairs are available, as is an American Sign Language interpreter by prior arrangement. Admission: $3 adults, $2 teens and seniors, free for children 12 and under. Hours: Tue. & Thu.–Sat., 10:00 A.M.–5:00 P.M.; Wed., 10:00 A.M.–9:00 P.M.; Sun., 1:00 P.M.–5:00 P.M. **625 Williams St., New London, 06320; (860) 443-2545.**

Explore the life, times and work of playwright Eugene O'Neill at Monte Cristo Cottage, New London. Photo by A. Vincent Scarano/Monte Cristo Cottage, New London.

248

Monte Cristo Cottage

The boyhood home of Nobel and Pulitzer Prize–winning playwright Eugene O'Neill is now a museum focusing on O'Neill's life, family and New London surroundings, and how all three were expressed in his work. The cottage was named for the stage role that made O'Neill's actor father famous. Your visit starts off with a video giving background on O'Neill and New London in the early 1900s. Following that, you take a guided tour through the Victorian house. A visit to Monte Cristo Cottage makes an excellent prelude to a performance of an O'Neill work at the Eugene O'Neill Theater Center in nearby Waterford. Groups can make advance arrangements for a bus tour of Eugene O'Neill's New London by calling the number below. Tours of the house begin at designated times; call for the current schedule. Admission charged. Summer (Memorial Day–Labor Day) hours: Tue.–Sat., 10:00 A.M.–5:00 P.M.; Sun., 1:00 P.M.–5:00 P.M. Fall (mid-Sept.–mid-Oct.) hours: Mon.–Fri., 1:00 P.M.–5:00 P.M. Closed early Sept. **325 Pequot Ave., New London, 06320; (860) 443-0051.**

Shaw Mansion

The museum of the New London County Historical Society documents the city and two of its most prominent families during the 18th and 19th centuries. It was built by Capt. Nathaniel Shaw, a monied merchant and ship owner, as a family home in 1756. When Shaw's son Nathaniel, Jr., became Connecticut's Naval War Agent during the Revolution, the house was his headquarters. From this address Shaw organized Connecticut's contributions to the Continental navy and oversaw local privateering efforts. Guided tours are given as needed, with an emphasis on the Shaw family, the West Indies trade and early New London history. Admission: $4 adults, $3 seniors, $1 children under 12. Hours: Wed.–Fri., 1:00 P.M.–4:00 P.M.; Sat. 10:00 A.M.–4:00 P.M. **11 Blinman St., New London, 06320; (860) 443-1209.**

Thomas Lee House and Little Boston School

Sitting side-by-side unobtrusively on Rte. 156 are these two structures dating from 1660 and 1734, respectively. The former has been called "one of the two or three best preserved 17th-century houses in the region and a remarkable primer of vernacular architecture in New England." Its age makes it one of the state's oldest wood-frame houses. Its condition is relatively unaltered since the late 1700s, and portions are original to the 1600s. One highlight is the frame of an old casement window (one of only a handful in Connecticut) still extant in an upstairs chamber.

The schoolhouse, although built in 1734, is set up as it might have been about 100 years ago. Kids especially might find it interesting, and adults will probably enjoy the stories told of some of the school's more famous pupils. Admission: $2 adults, $1 children. Hours: Tue.–Sun., 1:00 P.M.–4:00 P.M., Memorial Day–Labor Day, & by appointment. **230 W. Main St. (Rte. 156 opposite N. Bride Brook Rd.), Niantic, 06357; (860) 739-6070.**

Nightlife

New London is one of the few areas in Connecticut that can be said to have a real nightlife, although it's still pretty low-key. There are many pubs and coffeehouses as well as seasonal restaurants offering live music. A walk down Bank St. and up State St. will take you past many of the year-round ones. For something more upscale, check the listings under Performing Arts, and remember that there is always something going on at the Garde Arts Center.

A couple of suggestions include **Burke's Tavern (13 Hope St., Niantic; 860-739-5033)**, where there's blues Thu.–Sat. nights around 9:30 P.M. and an open blues jam every other Sun. around 6:00 P.M. The **El 'n' Gee Club (86 Golden St., New London; 860-437-3800)** is the major dance club/hangout of eastern Connecticut, featuring rock 'n' roll, metal, reggae, alternative music—a little bit of everything, depending on the night. For a quieter alternative, **Niantic Cinema (279 Main St., Niantic; 860-739-6929)** is a four-screen cinema showing art and foreign films for bargain basement prices.

Performing Arts

One of the smallest but most beautiful venues in New London is **Harkness Chapel** on the grounds of Connecticut College. This is a functioning chapel offering services for students and the general public during the school year, but it's also the site of concerts such as an annual winter solstice celebration in early Dec. that's always packed, and it hosts some of the Early Music Festival performances listed separately below. To see if there will be an event during your stay in the area call **(860) 439-2450.**

Concert & Artist Series
Half a dozen or more classical music, opera and dance performances by nationally acclaimed artists comprise this series held at Connecticut College's Palmer Auditorium. The season coincides with the school year, Sept.–May. The auditorium is on the campus of Connecticut College at **270 Mohegan Ave., New London, 06320.** For more information call **(860) 439-2787.**

Early Music Festival
The **Connecticut Early Music Society** sponsors these performances of music, primarily from the 18th century, in which the musicians perform in a historically informed style on antique and replica period instruments. These are mostly small ensembles, which allow the concerts to be held at some of the most intimate and charming venues in the area. Concerts take place the last three weekends of June. For more information call **(860) 444-2419.**

Eastern Connecticut Symphony Orchestra
Led by conductor Dr. Paul Phillips, this regional orchestra performs four concerts of orchestral classics during an Oct.–May season. Its annual pops concert during the first week in Dec. often features Broadway numbers. All performances take place at the Garde Arts Center at **329 State St. in New London.** For more information call **(860) 443-2876.**

Eugene O'Neill Theater Center
The Eugene O'Neill Theater Center (named for the famed playwright who grew up in and was inspired by nearby New London) is dedicated to the presentation of new works for the theater. A series of conferences takes place here every year in which untested plays are presented to the public while being evaluated by established professionals for the benefit of the budding artists. Because the focus is on feedback, sets and costumes are minimal and actors often carry their scripts, so don't expect this to look and sound like Broadway. But if you're excited about the development of American theater, few places could be more exciting than this "incubator" of new voices in the art. Call for details on the current season. **305 Great Neck Rd., Waterford, 06385; (860) 443-5378.**

Garde Arts Center
Built in 1926 as a studio-owned movie palace and vaudeville playhouse, the Garde Arts Center is now an entertainment complex presenting national and international touring companies for short theatrical engagements, a film series, performances of the Eastern Connecticut Symphony Orchestra, country and pop music concerts and children's theater. The big theatrical shows tend to have a run of only one or

two shows, usually on weekend nights, so make reservations early. When there isn't a live performance, first-run independent and foreign films are shown nightly on the largest movie screen in southeastern Connecticut. **329 State St., New London, 06320; (888) 644-2733, (860) 444-7373** or **(860) 437-2314.**

Seasonal Favorites

Halloween Haunted Trail

For one or two weekends before Halloween a path through the woods at the Nautilus Community Center in Groton is transformed into a Haunted Trail. The ghouls and goblins make their appearance on Fri. and Sat. evenings and are even persuaded to come out during the day on Sun. There's a reservation system that allows you to purchase a ticket when you arrive and then enjoy entertainment (a storyteller, a puppet show, clowns and rides) without having to wait in line until it's your turn to enter. Babysitting is available for children under 6. Admission: $3 adults, $2 children. The community center is off Gungywamp Rd. about 1 mile south of the Naval Submarine Base; follow the signs from Rte. 12. For more information call **(860) 449-3238.**

Scenic Drives

When they come to the New London area, most folks want water views. A pleasant drive that will reveal a few begins in downtown Niantic. Take Rte. 156 east over the East Lyme/Waterford bridge. A couple miles down, turn right on Rte. 213. This takes you past Harkness Memorial State Park, where you can walk right down to the shore. Continue on Rte. 213 until it hangs a sharp left at Ocean Ave. Go right on Ocean, left on Neptune and then left again on Pequot Ave. This is a long road that hugs the shoreline for quite a distance before heading inland a few blocks. Along Pequot you'll see the old Pequot Ave. Lighthouse (privately owned; please do not trespass) and Monte Cristo Cottage, the boyhood home of playwright Eugene O'Neill. At this point you'll be approaching the busy heart of New London.

Near a railroad overpass make a left onto Shaw St. and then a right on Bank St. You're in the center of the city, a short walk from all its attractions.

Sports

Harvard/Yale Regatta

The oldest collegiate sporting event in the country takes place during the first two weeks of May, but the date changes from year to year. You can get a close view from an excursion boat or watch the competition from City Pier at the foot of State St. in New London. The regatta consists of three races beginning around 5:00 P.M., but related events take place from noon onward at several sites in New London. Shuttles run to these locations from parking garages in the downtown. For more information call **(860) 437-6313.**

Waterford Speedbowl

Stock car auto racing on a one-third-mile oval track is the feature event at Waterford Speedbowl every Sat. night at 6:00 P.M., Apr.–Oct. It offers racing in four divisions: SK Modifieds, Late Models, Strictly Stocks and Mini Stocks. There are also occasional special events such as stunt shows. Parking is free. Ticket prices begin at $12 for adults, $2 for children 6–12. Located on **Rte. 85, Waterford, 06385; (860) 442-1585.**

Tours

Create your own walking tour with the "Map of Downtown New London, Connecticut" brochure distributed at all the local visitors information centers (see the Services section for locations). One side has a map showing the locations of the major attractions, and the other contains information on the attractions and all sorts of local shops, restaurants and services.

For a backstage look at a 1920s movie palace, call the **Garde Arts Center box office (888-664-2733** or **860-444-7373)** one week in advance to make a reservation. The tour (for groups of ten or more only; fee charged) focuses on the history of movie palaces and the restoration of the Garde, which is described under Performing Arts.

The Thames River Valley Heritage Tour is a paired audiocassette and booklet produced by the **New London County Historical Society** that will lead you on a self-guided drive past historic sites in New London. There is no charge; you are asked only to return the materials. Pick them up at the Trolley Information Station at the corner of Eugene O'Neill Dr. and Golden St. For more information call **(860) 444-7264.**

Finally, if you're in town at the right time, visit the U.S. Coast Guard barque *Eagle*, a training vessel that can be toured when it is in port. For more information, see the listing for the U.S. Coast Guard Academy under Other Attractions.

Where to Stay

The New London area is chock-a-block with overnight accommodations. You'll be hard-pressed to find anything truly inexpensive, since the demand for rooms is very high, but there is a reasonable **Motel 6** in **Niantic (860-739-6991)** along with several other budget motels along Flanders Rd. (Rte. 161). There are quite a few hotels and motels clustered along Goldstar Highway (Rte. 184) in Groton, but they're not necessarily cheap. The accommodations listed below are a sampling of places where most visitors would be happy to stay. For additional listings, contact the **Southeastern Connecticut Tourism District (Mystic & More!)** at **(800) 863-6569** or **(860) 444-2206.**

Bed & Breakfasts

The Palmer Inn—$$$$
The only B&B in the tiny village of Noank offers visitors a quiet home base from which to walk the area's picturesque streets or venture into the bustle of Mystic a short distance away. A turn-of-the-century mansion built by ship-wrights in the Federal style with a grand, two-story portico, it was recently restored and furnished somewhat incongruously with Victo-

rian pieces. There are six guest rooms featuring solid oak, mahogany and brass bedsteads and private baths. A Continental breakfast is included. It's a tad pricey, but the location is unbeatable if you're looking for peace and quiet. **25 Church St., Noank, 06340; (860) 572-9000.**

Queen Anne Inn—$$$$
This urban inn located on central Williams St. is a Victorian "painted lady" whose ten guest rooms (including a suite in the tower) are richly furnished with antiques. Many of the rooms have a four-poster or brass bed, a fireplace, TV and telephone. Most of the bathrooms are private. The front rooms might experience a distracting level of traffic noise, but air-conditioning allows you to keep the windows shut. A full gourmet breakfast and afternoon tea is included, and a Jacuzzi is available for private use by appointment. **265 Williams St. (at Fremont), New London, 06320; (800) 347-8818 or (860) 447-2600.**

Shore Inne—$$$
The strong point of this seasonal B&B is its location on Groton Long Point, an exceptionally beautiful little community to which nonresidents otherwise have limited access. There are five guest rooms with private bathrooms in this casual family residence. Arrangements can be made to dock your boat nearby. A Continental breakfast is included. **54 E. Shore Ave., Groton Long Point, 06340; (860) 536-1180.**

Hotels, Motels & Inns

East Lyme Inn—$$$ to $$$$
The excellent condition and tasteful interior of East Lyme Inn place it in a higher class than many of the other moderately priced hotels in the area and make it suitable for all travelers. The weekend rates during the high season are a bit pricey, but the weekday rates are such a good value that they balance out if you're staying longer than just Fri. and Sat. All rooms have two double beds or a king, and most have a tiny refrigerator. Extras include a coin-op laundry, outdoor pool, free Continental breakfast and access to a town beach on Long Island

Sound. **239 Flanders Rd. (Rte. 161), East Lyme, 06357; (860) 739-3951.**

Holiday Inn—$$$ to $$$$

This Holiday Inn gets a three-diamond rating from AAA. Deluxe rooms, for only a few dollars more than standard ones, come with some or all of the following extras: coffeepot, refrigerator, bathrobes, hair dryer and whirlpool tub. Several rooms are especially outfitted for the convenience of handicapped guests. A family-style steak house on-site serves breakfast and dinner daily, and there's a sports bar/deli for lunch and a gathering place. It has an outdoor swimming pool, an exercise facility, room service and a free evening shuttle to and from Mohegan Sun Casino. Located on **Frontage Rd., New London, 06320; (800) 465-4329** or **(860) 442-0631.**

Lighthouse Inn—$$$ to $$$$

This restored 1902 mansion one block from Long Island Sound is not actually a lighthouse, but it is a stone's throw from one. There are rooms in two buildings: the mansion itself and a carriage house. The former has 12-foot ceilings, antique furnishings including canopied four-poster beds and whirlpool bathtubs. All these rooms are different; some are more spacious and romantic than others, so it really pays to specify what you want. The five minisuites are the most luxurious. Rooms on the outside of the crescent (the mansion was built in the shape of an arc) may be lighter and brighter than those on the other side. The carriage house rooms are more like ordinary hotel accommodations in terms of both size and furnishings. Breakfast served in the mansion and access to the hotel's private beach are included. The Mansion Restaurant on the main floor of the inn is one of New London's best, and is especially noted for its Sun. brunch. Inquire about their theme weekends. **6 Guthrie Pl., New London, 06320; (800) 678-8946** or **(860) 443-8411.**

Niantic Inn—$$$ to $$$$

Utilitarian-looking from the outside, this is a good all-around hotel on the inside. The rooms have standard but nice hotel furnishings in good condition. Each room has a small refrig-

erator, microwave, coffeepot and sitting area. The building has security doors and a coffee lounge on the second floor as a gathering place. It's conveniently located on the main drag of Niantic but set back and shielded from noise by the hotel office. **345 Main St., Niantic, 06357; (860) 739-5451.**

Radisson—$$$ to $$$$

The 120 rooms at this hotel were recently renovated, and every standard room has one king or two double beds. Three suites also have a living area, wet bar, microwave and refrigerator. Rooms on the business-class floor are wired with data ports. Amenities include a full-service restaurant, pub, heated indoor pool, Jacuzzi, room service, complimentary passes to a nearby gym and complimentary shuttle to and from both casinos nightly. By advance arrangement, they'll also transport you to and from trains and ferries in New London. **35 Governor Winthrop Blvd., New London, 06320; (800) 443-7000** or **(860) 443-7000.**

The Sojourner Inn—$$$ to $$$$

Sojourner Inn offers four categories of suites ranging from singles sized like conventional hotel rooms to luxury whirlpool units having an open floor plan with a sunken sitting area, a separate but unpartitioned sleeping area, a whirlpool tub on a step-up alcove off the sitting area and a private full bathroom. All of the rooms have a kitchenette, and all but the singles have a pullout sofa. A Continental breakfast is included. Amenities include fax and valet service, movie rental, coin-op laundry facilities and complimentary passes to Mystic Community Center where guests can use exercise facilities and a small saltwater beach. Inquire about the suites modified for greater handicapped-accessibility, discounted tickets to area attractions and package deals. **605 Goldstar Hwy. (Rte. 184), Groton, 06340; (800) 697-8483** or **(860) 445-1986.**

Camping

Rocky Neck State Park Campground—$

Rocky Neck offers the lovely and unusual campground combination of woodland and

252

shore. There are five camping circles that can accommodate RVs (no hookups) as well as designated tent sites. Hot showers and flush toilets are available at the camping circles, but pit toilets only at the tent sites. The landscape is fairly open but surrounded by trees. If you want a fire, you must bring your own container. A bike path provides a shortcut to the beach from the campground, and there's an amphitheater and nature center for public programs. Reserve your spot well in advance; Rocky Neck fills up for holiday weekends by Mar. Located on **Rte. 156 in East Lyme.** Campground office: **(860) 739-5471.**

Where to Eat

Mansion Restaurant—$$$ to $$$$

The in-house restaurant at Lighthouse Inn serves classic American shore cuisine in an elegant setting: a 1902 mansion with tall ceilings, wood paneling and chandeliers. Seafood is prominently featured, from clam and lobster bisques to bouillabaisse and grilled swordfish. The small menu is completed by a few classic meat and poultry dishes. The fixed-price Sun. brunch buffet is huge, with a carving station, waffles, omelets and numerous entrées. It also has a Wed. night all-you-can-eat pasta special in the lounge. Casual dress is acceptable in the lounge, but in the restaurant gentlemen must have a collar or jacket. Reservations recommended. Lounge hours: 4:30 P.M.–1:00 A.M. daily. Dining room hours: Wed.–Sun., 5:00 P.M.–close, last seating at 9:00 P.M. **6 Guthrie Pl., New London, 06320; (860) 443-8411.**

Constantine's—$$$

Family-run for three generations, this local restaurant gets high marks for its large menu and numerous daily specials, fast service and good food at reasonable prices. Seafood is the star here, but there are many other dinner choices based on steaks, chops, chicken, veal and pasta. There are always several soups, salads and a few homemade desserts. Arrive early on weekends if possible; they don't take reservations (except for groups of six or more), and there is often a line. Hours: Tue.–

Thu., 11:30 A.M.–9:00 P.M.; Fri.–Sat., 11:30–A.M.–10:00 P.M.; Sun., noon–9:00 P.M. Mon. hours (summer only): 4:00 P.M.–9:00 P.M. **252 Main St., Niantic, 06357; (860) 739-2848.**

Lorelei—$$$

This favorite of both locals and tourists has hardwood floors, tin ceilings and a great old bar that create a casual atmosphere families love. It serves American food—seafood, steaks, pasta, soups and salads—and is known for homemade pecan and apple pies and pecan-orange cake. Hours: Mon.–Thu., 11:30 A.M.–9:00 P.M.; open Fri.–Sat. until 10:00 P.M.; Sun., 4:00 P.M.–9:00 P.M. **158 State St., New London, 06320; (860) 442-3375.**

Timothy's—$$$

Timothy's is regarded by many as the best place to eat in downtown New London. As such, plan for crowds on weekend nights and make a reservation. The cuisine is Continental, focusing on grilled meats, poultry and fish lightly sauced and served with fruity or savory accompaniments. The lobster and mushroom crêpe appetizer and lobster and crabmeat bisque are specialties of the house. Several pastas are available in both appetizer and entrée portions at dinner. Lunch offerings include pasta, hamburgers, sandwiches, salads and seafood. Lunch is served Mon.–Fri., 11:30 A.M.–2:30 P.M. Dinner hours: Mon.–Thu., 5:30 P.M.–9:00 P.M.; Fri.–Sat., 5:30 P.M.–10:00 P.M. **181 Bank St., New London, 06320; (860) 437-0526.**

Upper Deck—$$$

This small restaurant with seating for only about 24 in its main dining room is named for the seasonal deck with a view of the Thames River that provides supplemental seating Memorial Day–Labor Day. The atmosphere is casual, but the tables are decked out with linens for lunch and dinner. Lunch offerings include burgers, meal salads, classic sandwiches and a few odds and ends like eggs Benedict and beef stew. The dinner menu features such dishes as roast duckling, pot roast, petite beef Wellington and chicken parmesan. Reservations recommended; no smoking. Breakfast served Sat.–Sun., 8:00 A.M.–1:00 P.M. Lunch hours: Wed.–Fri., 11:00 A.M.–2:00 P.M. Dinner served Wed.–Sat., 5:00 P.M.–9:00 P.M. **123½ Pequot Ave., New London, 06320; (860) 439-0884.**

Bangkok City—$$ to $$$

The kitchen at this reliable Thai restaurant turns out quite good food, and the dining room is comfortable and casual, making Bangkok City a worthwhile first choice of dinner destination as well as a good standby on weekend evenings when there's no chance of getting a table without a reservation at the handful of trendy eateries in the area. If you like Thai food, you won't be disappointed. Lunch is served Mon.–Fri., 11:00 A.M.–3:00 P.M. Dinner hours: Mon.–Thu., 5:00 P.M.–9:00 P.M.; Fri.–Sat., 4:00 P.M.–10:30 P.M. **123 State St., New London, 06320; (860) 442-6970.**

Don Juan's International Combat Style Cuisine—$$ to $$$

Pseudopolitical statements on the menu make the point that this is not a restaurant dedicated to a cuisine—unless international is a cuisine. You'll find Jamaica in the jerk chicken, New Orleans in the dirty rice, Japan in the teriyaki, Tex in the barbequed ribs and Mex in the burritos. BYOB. The food presentation, decor and crowd are casual, but they're not the point here. This is a hangout for a young crowd with strong stomachs. Lunch served Tue.–Fri., 11:30 A.M.–2:00 P.M. Dinner hours: Mon.–Sat. from 5:00 P.M. **405 Williams St., New London, 06320; (860) 437-3791.**

Pedo's Tavern—$$ to $$$

Offering a self-described "seafood Cajun-American" menu, Pedo's is a popular family-oriented, family-run eatery. The interior is publike, featuring three large windows affording a view of the Thames River. About half of the dinner items are Cajun dishes, such as crawfish prepared several ways, catfish and ribs barbequed in a Louisiana hot sauce. The remainder of the menu is casual American cuisine ranging from burgers and sandwiches to steak and tortellini, with daily seafood specials in summer. There's a fairly high percentage of fried dishes here, but the meal salads make it possible to eat reasonably light. Lunch

hours: 11:00 A.M.–3:00 P.M. daily. Dinner hours: Sun.–Thu., 5:00 P.M.–9:00 P.M.; open Fri.–Sat. until 10:00 P.M. **2 State St., New London, 06320; (860) 447-3951.**

Recovery Room—$$ to $$$

The Recovery Room is one of a small chain of three local and exceptional pizzerias. They've won the best pizza in New London County readers' poll award from *Connecticut* magazine for many years running, and reviewers agree. Although all three of their restaurants serve pizza, this is the only one to have a full menu with pasta, sandwiches, salads and children's items. It also has a full bar and a selection of 40-plus beers. Hours: Mon.–Fri., 11:30 A.M.–9:00 P.M.; Sat.–Sun., 4:00 P.M.–9:00 P.M. **445 Ocean Ave., New London, 06320; (860) 443-2619.**

The Shack—$ to $$

If you're looking for a place to get home-style cooking at reasonable prices, you probably won't find a better spot in this area than The Shack. But it's not just a breakfast and lunch place. In the evening it serves comfort food like pot roast, lasagna and open-faced turkey sandwiches with all the fixings. There's a daily all-you-can-eat fish fry. The atmosphere is very casual and dineresque with booths, tables and a lunch counter. The Shack is also incredibly convenient to the interstate. Hours: Mon.–Sat., 5:30 A.M.–8:00 P.M.; Sun. (breakfast only), 6:00 A.M.–1:00 P.M. Located on **Flanders Rd. (Rte. 161) immediately north of I-95 exit 74 in East Lyme; (860) 739-8898.**

Coffeehouses, Sweets & Treats

With coffee, as with most things in New London, you can find it by walking down Bank St. and up State. At **Greene's Books & Beans (140 Bank St.; 860-443-3312)** it's combined with an "alternative" bookstore. If it's tea you're after, call the **Queen Anne Inn (265 Williams St.; 860-447-2600).** Jan.–Apr. the innkeepers offer Sun. afternoon high teas at 3:30 and 5:00 P.M. You have your choice of tea with sandwiches and desserts or desserts only, and you do not have to be an overnight guest. The setting is a beautiful Victorian house right near the center of town. Reservations required.

Services

Local Visitors Information

East Lyme Tourist Information Center, exit 74 off I-95, East Lyme; (860) 739-0208. Summer (July 1–Labor Day) hours: 9:00 A.M.–5:00 P.M. daily. Spring and fall hours: 10:00 A.M.–4:00 P.M. daily.

Mystic & More!, 470 Bank St., P.O. Box 89, New London, 06320; (800) 863-6569 or **(860) 444-2206.**

Trolley Information Station, Eugene O'Neill Dr. at Golden St., downtown New London; (860) 444-7264. Hours: 10:00 A.M.–4:00 P.M. Open daily June 15–Sept. 15 & Fri.–Sun., May 1–June 14 & Sept. 16–Oct. 31.

Transportation

Commuter flights to and from the New London area land at **Groton/New London Airport (860-445-8549).** If you need a cab to get you into town, try **A-1 Taxi** at **(860) 443-1563** or **Harry's Taxi** at **(860) 444-2255.**

Shore Line East Commuter Rail offers Mon.–Fri. service along the shore between New London and New Haven. For fare and schedule information call **(800) 255-7433.** New London is also a stop on **Amtrak**'s Washington-Boston route. For information on trains into Union Station call **(800) 872-7245.**

Greyhound buses also stop at Union Station. Call **(800) 231-2222** for fares and schedules. For details on regional bus service call **South East Area Transit (SEAT)** at **(860) 886-2631.**

New London sees more ferry activity than any other port in Connecticut. Most ferries can accommodate autos, bikes, walk-on passengers and pets at all times, but you should inquire about the policy regarding oversized vehicles and trailers. There may be limitations, or you may have to reserve in advance. (Note: When taking a ferry you should always arrive 30 minutes prior to departure. They *do* fill up.) Some ferries have food service and diversions such as arcade games; others do not. The rides can be long, so find out in advance about services you think you'll need and bring along anything not provided.

Cross Sound Ferry offers year-round service between New London and Orient Point, Long Island (New York). Locally it operates out of a terminal at **2 Ferry St.** on the north side of Union Station near, but not at, City Pier. Schedules change with the season, but there are always several round-trips daily. The crossing normally takes one and a half hours one-way, but Apr.–Dec. there are also high-speed, passenger-only (no vehicles) ferries in service that make the crossing in 45 minutes. They offer a package deal, good only for certain departures and only for walk-on passengers departing from Long Island, that includes a shuttle up to Foxwoods Casino and $25 worth of vouchers and other incentives good at the casino. Reservations are taken for parties with vehicles only. For schedule and fare information call **(860) 443-5281.** For information only (no reservations) from Long Island call **(516) 323-2525.**

Block Island is a popular but very seasonal vacation destination belonging to Rhode Island, so Block Island Ferry transportation from the Connecticut shore is available only during the summer, roughly Memorial Day–Labor Day. Service to the Rhode Island shore, however, is year-round; call for details. During its season of operation from Connecticut, **Block Island Ferry** makes two round-trips on Fri. and one on all other days. The daily departure from New London is at 9:00 A.M., but schedules are subject to change, so call to confirm. You don't want to miss it, because you'll have to wait 24 hours for another or drive to Rhode Island. The second Fri. departure is at 7:15 P.M. Reservations are recommended for passengers with vehicles. The crossing takes two hours. The ferry departs from the terminal at **2 Ferry St.** in New London on the north side of Union Station near, but not at, City Pier. For more information call **(860) 442-7891** or **(860) 442-9553.** To make a reservation call **(401) 783-4613.**

Fishers Island Ferry offers transportation between Fishers Island (a largely private island that is part of New York state) and City Pier in New London. There are at least four round-trips daily, year-round except Christmas Day. The crossing time is 45 minutes. Reservations are accepted only for passengers with oversized vehicles. For a recorded message giving the current season's schedule call **(860) 443-6851.** To make a reservation call **(860) 442-0165.** You can reach the island office at **(516) 788-7463.**

Montauk Ferry shuttles passengers between Montauk, Long Island (New York) and New London Fri. & Sun. only, Memorial Day–Labor Day. Early in the season there is one round-trip per day; later in the season there are two. The crossing takes about one and three-quarter hours. Tickets purchased in New London must be paid for with cash. For fare and schedule information call **(800) 666-8285.**

Norwich and Casino Country

Although Norwich is the largest city in this area, and nearby Mystic alone was the tourist draw that filled the B&Bs for many years, it is the casino towns of Ledyard and, more recently, Montville where changes are fast and furious. In 1983 the Mashantucket Pequots received official recognition as an Indian tribe from the U.S. government, and a drive began to bring members who had drifted away back to the reservation in Ledyard. Since the opening of Foxwoods Resort Casino, growth has been explosive. It is currently the largest casino in the world. If you find its size intimidating, Mohegan Sun Casino, operated by the Mohegans in Montville, might suit you better. A lot of effort has gone into making both casinos family-oriented places that are worth visiting even if you don't gamble. They both have entertainment, dining, shopping and child-care facilities. They are well maintained and attractive, similar to the best Las Vegas has to offer. As an interesting contrast to the activity of the casinos, both towns also have quietly striking historic sites such as the 19th-century water-powered sawmill in Ledyard, which may be the state's only one still in operation.

Norwich itself is a distinctive-looking city with a prominent waterfront. The Quinebaug and the Shetucket, the two principal rivers of northeastern Connecticut, join near the Taftville section of town and continue southward to a confluence with the Yantic River, which forms the Thames. American Wharf, which includes a marina, is located at this point, and the downtown, known as Chelsea, is situated on a hill overlooking it.

If you love architecture, Norwich should be high on your list of Connecticut destinations. When the city was growing by leaps and bounds in the 19th century, beautiful homes

257

went up one after another, and most of them are still extant, lining the streets as if standing at attention for review. A Queen Anne might stand next door to an Italianate villa, both of them facing a Second Empire across the street. Norwichtown, the colonial-era center of Norwich, is rich in houses of that period and has a notable cemetery and a historic home museum.

Some of the city's best attractions are municipal recreational facilities: one of the best golf courses in Connecticut, a new, year-round ice-skating rink with lots of public access and a huge, mountainous municipal park (Mohegan Park) for swimming, biking, hiking and picnicking. This park contains a noted rose garden in recognition of Norwich's sobriquet, "The Rose of New England." In addition to the marina, American Wharf also has family activities such as miniature golf and bumper boats, plus a seasonal restaurant. Howard T. Brown Memorial Park a few feet away is the site of several annual festivals and a beautiful place to watch the sun set on a summer evening.

Festivals are another good reason to come to town. Norwichtown Days in Norwich and the Colonial Craft Fair in Ledyard both celebrate the skills and way of life of the area's 18th- and early-19th-century residents. For an insight into Native American heritage and culture, attend the Mohegan's Wigwam Festival or the Mashantucket Pequot's intertribal Schemitzun.

As for the future, growth is still in the air. Foxwoods continues to expand, and right next door the Pequots plan to open a major new museum documenting the heritage of northeast Woodlands Indians. The success of the casinos is sure to spin off other attractions and bring more people into the area.

History

The modern history of the Norwich area would have to start with the 1638 peace treaty signed by the Mohegans, the Narragansetts and the English following the Pequot War in 1637. The agreement soon fell apart as differences arose between Uncas (leader of the Mohegans and traditionally friendly toward the white settlers) and Miantonomo (a leader of the Narragansetts and traditionally hostile toward the newcomers). Miantonomo is alleged to have tried secretly to build an Indian alliance to move against the English, but Uncas learned of his doings and shared his knowledge with the colonists. But when the English investigated the allegations, Miantonomo was acquitted. In 1643 the Narragansetts actually invaded Mohegan territory, but despite superior numbers they were driven back; Miantonomo was captured and eventually killed.

Two years later the Narragansetts once again invaded, this time in revenge for the killing of Miantonomo, and besieged the Mohegans at their fort, called Shantok. Uncas's friendliness toward the settlers paid off when Lt. Thomas Leffingwell, then resident at Saybrook (now Old Saybrook), came to the tribe's aid with food to withstand the siege. This episode was probably a motivating factor behind Uncas's 1659 gift of 27 square miles of land for the settlement of Norwich by families from Saybrook.

With three of the major rivers of northeastern Connecticut coming together at Norwich, water power was plentiful, and the city was a natural place to build mills. One of Norwich's most important inhabitants in this regard was Christopher Leffingwell. He built the first paper mill in Connecticut locally, and its output was used in part for bullet cartridges during the Revolutionary War. He was said to have been one of the wealthiest men in eastern Connecticut during his lifetime, and he financed many Patriot military campaigns, including the seizure of Fort Ticonderoga in New York state by Ethan Allen and the Green Mountain Boys. He also manufactured woolen stockings and chocolate, which first came into popular use as a substitute for English tea boycotted by the Americans just prior to the war.

As the domestic textile industry developed during the early 1800s, it became centered in the Quinebaug and Shetucket valleys, and major factories sprang up in dozens of localities. The Ponemah Mill in Taftville, chartered in 1866, was the largest cotton mill complex in the world. The textile industry in New England would eventually collapse, although a small remnant of it survives. The Ponemah Mill still stands, largely vacant now and mansionlike in its grandeur on the west bank of the Shetucket. A small portion has been redeveloped into retail space; perhaps all the buildings will one day be put to a new use.

Today Norwich is a working-class city that has managed, even through hard economic times, to preserve much of value, such as the city's incredible architecture. Recent redevelopment projects are slowly transforming the downtown, which still has some empty warehouses and factories. The beautiful wharf at the head of the Thames, which replaced a rather grimy coal distribution plant, is a prime example.

The opening of the casinos in Ledyard and Montville has wrought major changes in everything from traffic patterns to land ownership. Their success, the proximity of Norwich to the tremendous tourism resources of New London and Mystic and plans for future recreational development in nearby towns spell only growth for the entire area.

Major Attractions

Foxwoods Resort Casino

Foxwoods is billed as the largest gaming facility in the world and was the only casino in New England until the opening of Mohegan Sun in 1996. It has hundreds of game tables for everything from blackjack to baccarat, thousands of slot machines, a bingo hall and a simulcast facility called Race Book where you can view and bet on horse and greyhound races from tracks around the country. If you're a novice, you might want to start with some free poker instruction before you try your "hand" at the real thing.

When you want a break from the gaming activity, check out the Cinetropolis entertainment complex, a "city of specialty theatres." The Cinedrome 360 Theatre shows short films on a wraparound screen during the day, then becomes a dance club showing music videos at night. The Fox Theatre also does double duty, showing giant screen movies early on, then becoming a venue for name entertainment at night. Turbo Ride is a "motion theatre" with hydraulic seats that make you feel as if you're engaging in the on-screen action, and Virtual Adventures takes teams of participants on an "underwater" search for Loch Ness monster eggs. You can

Norwich is little more than an hour's drive southeast of Hartford. Getting there is a snap. Pick up Rte. 2 in East Hartford and stay on it—it'll take you all the way to downtown Norwich. See the listings for the casinos for details on transportation directly to those attractions.

buy a day pass for Cinetropolis or purchase tickets individually.

Other diversions include numerous restaurants and an extensive shopping concourse. The Foxwoods complex is filled with large-scale sculptures of Native American figures. If you are curious about the artwork, pick up a copy of the Alan Houser and Bruce LaFountain exhibits guide booklet at the concierge desk. A child-sitting service (prepayment and reservations are required, but there is no age cutoff) and overnight accommodations are available on-site.

There are several ways of getting to the casino if you don't have a car. **Amtrak (800-872-7245)** serves New London on its Washington-to-Boston route, and when you make your train reservation you can also purchase an inexpensive ticket for a connecting bus up to the casino. Package tickets are available covering ferry transportation from Orient Point, Long Island, to New London and a connecting bus to the casino. Call the **Cross Sound Ferry** directly at **(860) 443-5281** or **(516) 323-2525** for details. **Greyhound (800-231-2222)** and regional **South East Area Transit (SEAT; 860-886-2631)** buses run between New London and the casino several times daily, and **Peter Pan/Trailways (800-343-9999)** provides some service from Massachusetts and New Hampshire. Foxwoods is located on **Rte. 2 in Ledyard, 06339.** For general information or restaurant reservations call **(800) 752-9244** or **(860) 885-3000.** The box office number is **(800) 200-2882.** The **Cinetropolis Hotline** number is **(860) 885-4009.** Child-care reservations can be made at **(860) 447-4829.**

Mohegan Park and Memorial Rose Garden

At 385 acres, Mohegan Park is larger than some state parks and is certainly one of the most beautiful municipal open spaces in Connecticut. The center of the park is developed with great public attractions that are clean and well maintained, but the majority of the acreage is hilly, undeveloped forest rich in pine trees. At the Rockwell St. entrance is a locally famous rose garden containing 2,500 bushes that reach their peak in June. A map of the park is also posted here. Up the road you'll find Spaulding Pond ringed by a jogging path, a children's petting zoo, a beach with lifeguards, two playgrounds and a picnic grove. Petting zoo hours: 10:00 A.M.–7:00 P.M. daily, Memorial Day–Labor Day; until 3:00 P.M. in the off-season. The beach is open 10:00 A.M.–7:00 P.M. from the week after Memorial Day until Labor Day. Swimming has been free in years past, but that situation may change for nonresidents. Park hours are dawn–dusk. The main entrance is on Rockwell St. opposite Platt Ave. You can also enter from the west on John Edwards Dr., from the northwest on Ox Hill Rd., and from the northeast on Mohegan Park Rd. For more information call **(860) 823-3755.**

Mohegan Sun Casino

Connecticut's second casino opened in autumn 1996 with 3,000 slot machines, 170 game tables, several restaurants, a lounge, a fully licensed and supervised child-care facility, an arcade for teenagers and a 1,500-seat bingo hall that can also accommodate sporting and musical events. The atmosphere at Mohegan Sun is distinctly different from that at Foxwoods, and the complex is smaller. The casino can provide you with information on regularly scheduled buses that run to and from Mohegan Sun daily; call **(888) 770-0140** for schedules, fares and information on charters. Located on **Mohegan Sun Blvd.** (follow the signs from Rte. 2A in either direction), **Uncasville, 06382; (888) 226-7711.**

Festivals and Events

Chelsea Street Festival
third Sat. in May

This family-oriented festival was established a few years ago simply to bring folks to downtown Norwich, historically known as Chelsea, for a day of fun for parents and children. It takes place at Howard T. Brown Memorial Park on Chelsea Harbor Dr. opposite the marina. Adults will enjoy browsing booths of high-end crafts and fine arts; kids will probably gravitate to the entertainment, such as face painting, clowns and jugglers. Admission is free, although activities may involve a fee. Hours: roughly 10:00 A.M.–5:00 P.M. For more information call **(860) 886-4683.**

Eastern Connecticut Antique Auto Show
third weekend in July

This big event draws tens of thousands of automobile enthusiasts, some of whom come to compete, most of whom come to appreciate the hundreds of vintage cars on display. Sat. the focus is on street rods and custom cars; the emphasis shifts to antique and show cars on Sun. You'll also find antique farm equipment. Sometime during the weekend there's an auto parade and a tractor parade, as well as ongoing raffles and giveaways, vendors with everything from antique parts to T-shirts and lots of food. Admission: $3 adults, $2 seniors, free for children 11 and younger accompanied by an adult. Hours: 8:00 A.M.–5:00 P.M. both days. The show takes place at the **Norwich Regional Vocational Technical School, 590 New London Tpke., Norwich, 06360.** From I-395 exit 80 (Rte. 82), follow the signs to shuttle parking lots. For more information call **(860) 887-1647.**

Wigwam Festival
third weekend in Aug.

Historically the most significant community event of the Mohegan year, the Wigwam Festival is a celebration of thanksgiving for the corn harvest. The festivities go on from noon until 6:00 P.M. each day, kicked off by the Grand Entry (an entrance procession) at noon on Sat. There are dancers, singers, storytellers and vendors. Admission is charged. The festival is held at **Fort Shantok State Park, Fort Shantok Rd. in Montville.** For more information call **(860) 848-6100.**

Harbor Day
last Sunday in Aug.

Harbor Day came about as an attempt to draw attention to the marina in downtown Norwich, which was built in the 1980s. As such, a lot of the activities are water-oriented. There are musical performances throughout the day and many food vendors. Evening fireworks close this last big bash of summer. It all takes place at **Howard T. Brown Memorial Park on Chelsea Harbor Dr. in Norwich.** Admission is free. Things start around 11:00 A.M. and keep going until the last sparkler is used up. For more information call **(860) 886-4683.**

Historic Norwichtown Days
first weekend in Sept.

This celebration of colonial arts and life takes place at the Norwichtown green, which is lined with historic colonial-era homes. For two days there are costumed reenactors, displays of old-time skills, such as spinning and candle dipping, lectures and tours. There is always a parade on Sat. with fife and drum corps and other groups in costume. This is primarily a daytime festival (hours run 10:30 A.M.–4:30 P.M.), but there may be a few nighttime events. The annual Taste of Italy festival takes place in Howard T. Brown Memorial Park the same day, and a free shuttle bus runs between the two. For more information call **(860) 886-4683.**

Schemitzun
Sept. (Wed.–Sun.)

The Mashantucket Pequot's annual Feast of Green Corn and Dance is one of the largest Native American cultural and educational festivals anywhere. Dancers, drummers, singers and artisans from tribes across the continent convene for five days of competitive performance and cultural expression. There are demonstrations of basketry, beadwork, silverwork, weaving and pottery; hand games; storytelling and music. Schemitzun's location and exact dates change from year to year and can be as far away as Hartford; call for the current year's information. Daily admission: $6 adults, $4 children and seniors. A $15 five-day pass is available. Hours: 10:00 A.M.–11:00 P.M. each day. For a recorded message giving general information call **(800) 224-2676.**

Colonial Craft Fair
fourth Sun. in Sept.

This exploration of colonial life is held on the grounds of the Nathan Lester House in Ledyard. Approximately 40 crafters sell wares and give demonstrations of hearth cooking, velvet and linen stenciling, weaving, quilting and more. Hours are 11:00 A.M.–5:00 P.M., rain or shine. Admission: $4 for adults, $3 teens and seniors, under 12 free. Park at the Ocean State Job Lot discount store on Rte. 12 in Gales Ferry and take a shuttle bus to the site. For more information call **(860) 464-1865.**

Walking Weekend
Columbus Day weekend

Walking Weekend is a huge event that covers the whole northeast corner of Connecticut. For three days, dozens of walking tours and hikes take place throughout a 27-town area, including many at historic and beautiful spots in and around Norwich. For more information, see the listing in the **Far Northeast** chapter.

Oktober Family Fest
third weekend in Oct.

Despite the intentional similarity of its name to Oktoberfest, this event is not rows of picnic tables, polka bands and massive beer consumption (although beer is available). Oktober

Family Fest is three days of very kid-centered activities: children's music, amusement park rides, pony rides and more. There are also many food vendors and evening fireworks. General admission is free; pay as you go. Much of the festival takes place in the open-air but covered promenade of Dodd Stadium, so it's on rain or shine. Dodd Stadium is at **14 Stott Rd. in Norwich Industrial Park, Norwich, 06360.** For more information call **(860) 886-4683.**

Outdoor Activities

Biking

Road Biking

The key to cycling in the Norwich area is staying away from urban areas and the approaches to the casinos. Back roads in Bozrah, Preston and western Montville will take you through some very pretty country. The southern half of Ledyard is also quite tranquil east of Rte. 12. Make stops at the Ledyard Water-Powered Up-Down Sawmill on Iron St. and the Nathan Lester House at the intersection of Long Cove and Vinegar Hill Rds., respectively described under Historic Sites and Museums.

Boats docked at the marina at American Wharf, downtown Norwich. Photo courtesy the American Wharf.

West of Rte. 117 you'll find lovely Rosemond Lake on Sandy Hollow Rd. There's no access to the lake itself or the land around it, but a ride by it is enough, and a beautiful old cemetery on Sandy Hollow is a great spot to rest.

The paved roads of Mohegan Park are a great place to bike if you can handle rolling hills. Because the park is located on a high point, all the roads leading into it climb at the start, but the ring around Spaulding Pond is pretty easy. For more information, see the listing under Major Attractions. (Note: There is no bicycle access to Rte. 2A over the Thames River. You must cross at the head of the river in Norwich.)

Boating

Boat Launches

Despite being fairly developed, the shore of **Amos Lake** is still quite pretty. To get to the launch, look for the boat launch sign on Rte. 164 in Preston. The dirt road leads to a paved road and ramp. See the *Connecticut Boater's Guide* for speed limit and other restrictions.

A pretty lake that's not too intensively developed, **Long Pond** has a tall, thin shape that makes it interesting. There's a state boat launch area with a concrete ramp on the west side of Lantern Hill Rd. in Ledyard at the very top of the pond. A 5 m.p.h. speed limit is in effect.

Stoddard Hill State Park on Rte. 12 in Ledyard has a car-top boat launch for putting small craft into the **Thames River.**

Marinas

If you're arriving in Norwich by boat, the Marina at **American Wharf (860-886-6363; VHF 68)** will be able to accommodate just about all your needs. Plus, there's a seasonal restaurant right on the wharf, and you're walking distance from a few dining and shopping options in the downtown. If you want to get somewhere (like the casinos) in style, a local coach operator will pick you up at the marina in a stretch Lincoln Town Car.

For navigational details, charts and complete lists of marine facilities throughout this area, your best source of information is

Embassy's Complete Boating Guide & Chartbook to Long Island Sound. Contact the publisher at **142 Ferry Rd., Old Saybrook, 06475; (860) 395-0188.**

Fishing

A centrally located tackle shop where you can get the scoop on fishing in the area as well as stock up on all your supplies is **The Fish Connection (127 Rte. 12, Preston; 860-885-1739).** Hours change seasonally, but it's open daily, year-round. It also operates a saltwater fly fishing and light tackle charter vessel for up to three people. For $275, you can go out for a full day of fishing for striped bass, bluefish, bonito and false albacore.

Lakes and Ponds

See the Boating section for information on access to **Amos Lake,** a small body of water stocked with trout and also good for largemouth bass and pickerel. Fish from your boat or from shore at the boat launch.

Brown bullheads and sunfish are plentiful in **Avery Pond,** a small, pretty lake with a fairly undeveloped and open shoreline. Access is via the upper part of Lynn Dr. off Rte. 164 in Preston at the boat launch sign. When Lynn Dr. starts to curve to the right, stay arrow-straight onto a dirt road that looks like a driveway. Most likely there will be no sign indicating that this is the road to the launch. Fish either from shore near the launch or put in a boat; an 8 m.p.h. speed limit is in effect.

Gardner Lake is one of only a handful of lakes in the state where walleye are stocked. It's also good for smallmouth bass, trout, perch and pickerel. The only real access area for shore fishing is undeveloped Hopemead State Park on Cottage Rd. in Bozrah. Park in the lot at the entrance and walk the gated road to the water's edge. Alternatively, put in a boat at a state-owned launch area on the opposite shore, accessible from Rte. 354 in Salem.

Appealing **Long Pond** on Lantern Hill Rd. in Ledyard is stocked with trout and is also good largemouth bass and pickerel habitat. Fish from your boat (see the Boating section for information) or from shore at the ramp.

Finally, **Spaulding Pond** at the center of Mohegan Park in Norwich (described under Major Attractions) is stocked with several kinds of trout, and, thanks to a jogging path encircling the pond, you can fish from anywhere on shore except in the beach area.

Rivers and Streams

Striped bass is the favorite sport fish in the tidal **Thames River.** For access, use the small pier at Howard T. Brown Memorial Park on Chelsea Harbor Dr. in downtown Norwich. Parking is available at low cost in a municipal lot only a block away. You can also fish from shore at Fort Shantok State Park on Fort Shantok Rd. in Montville. Stoddard Hill State Park on Rte. 12 in Ledyard features a handicapped-accessible fishing area and a car-top boat launch area.

The **Yantic River** is stocked heavily with trout and limited to fly fishing upriver of the bridge where Fitchville Rd. crosses it near Schwartz Rd. in Bozrah. Anglers usually just park on the shoulder of the road. Stockhouse Rd., which parallels the north side of the river, is another good spot. If you need supplies, **Colonial Sports (860-889-4901)** is just a tad to the west at **431 Fitchville Rd.** It stocks fly fishing gear only. Hours are Mon.–Fri., 9:30 A.M.–5:30 P.M.; Sat. until 4:30 P.M.

Golf

Norwich Golf Course

Connecticut magazine considered this one of the state's ten best public golf courses in 1995. It's a 6,200-yard, 18-hole course dating from the 1920s, with very walkable distances between tees and greens. The greens are small and the course hilly. Weekday tee times are taken same day only, beginning at 6:30 A.M. in person and 7:00 A.M. by phone. Weekend tee times are by a lottery system; call on Wed. for Sat. times and Thu. for Sun. times, beginning at 7:00 A.M. The fee is $21.25 weekdays and $25.50 weekends, with discounts after 5:00 P.M. and for active military on weekdays. There are practice areas for putting and chipping, a golf pro is available to give lessons and a full-service restaurant and clubhouse are located

263

on the premises. Pull carts, motorized carts and clubs can be rented. **685 New London Tpke., Norwich, 06360; (860) 889-6973.**

Hiking

In addition to wilderness hiking, there are a number of excellent urban walking tours available in Norwich. The **Heritage Walkway** is especially appropriate for folks who want to get some exercise while they sightsee. See the Tours section for details.

Lantern Hill
The very thing that makes the summit of Lantern Hill so interesting also makes it extremely dangerous. The rock here has been turned vertically, 90 degrees from its orientation when it was formed millions of years ago, making the footing very unsure. The view to the south is blocked somewhat by trees, but to the east the view is totally unobstructed because there's a sheer drop-off. Exercise caution, especially with children. To access Lantern Hill, park in the small pullout on Wintechog Hill Rd. two-tenths of a miles from Rte. 2 in Ledyard. The blue blazes mark the start of the Narragansett Trail. A short distance up this path another trail comes in from the right. Stay to the left to climb Lantern Hill, and return the same way you went up.

Horseback Riding

Leaning Birch Equestrian Center is set on 10 wooded acres adjoining a preserve, and riding trails crisscross both properties. It has numerous mounts, indoor and outdoor arenas so you can ride whatever the weather and a pony for small children. Reservations required; call for pricing. **463 Pumpkin Hill Rd. just north of Lambtown Rd., Ledyard, 06339; (860) 572-0305.**

Ice Skating

Norwich Municipal Ice Rink is one of the best places to skate in Connecticut. The facility is new, and there are public skating sessions daily (including one for adults only), as well as "stick times" several days a week, instructional programs, skate rental and a well-stocked pro shop on the premises. Admission is $3–$4 per session; call for hours. **641 New London Tpke., Norwich, 06360; (860) 892-2555.**

Swimming

There is a guarded beach on **Spaulding Pond** in Mohegan Park, Norwich's huge municipal green space. For more information, see the listing under Major Attractions. In addition, see the entry for **Hopeville Pond State Park** under the **Far Northeast** chapter. If you're looking for something less crowded and developed, take a drive to Hopemead State Park on the eastern shore of **Gardner Lake.** A gated road leads down to the water's edge where you can go swimming, but there's no beach, no lifeguards and no facilities. The entrance is on Cottage Rd. in Bozrah. There's also a private park on Gardner Lake where swimming is available for a fee; see the **Old Saybrook/Old Lyme** chapter for details.

Seeing and Doing

Art Galleries

Although it is small, the caliber of work on display at the **Norwich Arts Council Gallery (60 Broadway, Norwich; 860-887-2789)** is professional. Exhibits change every four–six weeks, and you never know what you'll get: painting, photography, sculpture, pottery or something that defies categorization. Around the corner you'll find **Main St. Place Gallery (154 Main St., Norwich; 860-887-9449),** a moderately sized commercial gallery that always has a broad variety of work in-house.

Children and Families

Putts Up Dock, a miniature golf course and bumper boat pond in the pretty setting of American Wharf on the Thames River, is a good place for some silly family fun. The course has such oddities as a volcano that "erupts" every 20 minutes. It is open daily 9:00 A.M.–10:00 P.M. (11:00 P.M. on Fri. & Sat.), late June–Labor Day, and during more limited hours early and late in the season. Parking is available in lots at the Wharf (enter from W. Main St.) and on Water St. in downtown Norwich. For more information call **(860) 886-7888.**

Historic Sites

Fort Shantok State Park

In the mid-1600s this patch of land above the Thames River was the site of a Mohegan fort. It was on this spot that the last major conflict between the Mohegans and the Narragansetts took place in 1645. Colonists with whom Uncas was allied came to his aid, and the Narragansetts were defeated. There are no remains of the fort, but there is a burial ground still in use by the Mohegans; be respectful if you choose to look around. The entrance is on Fort Shantok Rd. in Montville.

Ledyard Water-Powered Up-Down Sawmill/Sawmill Park

Connecticut is rich in water-powered mill sites, but it's very unusual for a mill to still be in operating condition. But here in Ledyard, a sawmill has been restored to how it probably was in 1869, and is demonstrated for visitors on Sat. in spring and late fall. Operation is seasonal because spring and fall are when water levels are highest, and powering a mill can drain a pond quickly. There are also grist and shingle mills and a functioning blacksmith's shop on-site. Admission is free. Hours: Sat., 1:00 P.M.–4:00 P.M., during Apr., May, the latter half of Oct. & Nov. Located on **Iron St. (Rte. 214) in Ledyard; (860) 464-8888.**

Norwichtown Cemetery

This lovely old cemetery is incredibly peaceful and attractive. Some of its many old stones are well preserved, and some have hexlike decorative work that is very beautiful. If you want to photograph, come in the afternoon since most

of the stones face west and do not have light on their faces until late in the day. One entrance is on Old Cemetery Ln., a short, dead-end street that can be a little tricky to enter by car. Park on Elm Ave. and walk to the entrance.

Ponemah Mill

Except for a couple of retail stores in one building, what was once the largest cotton cloth mill complex in the world is not really open to the public but worth a drive past. Ponemah Mill is absolutely grand—five stories tall with a mansard roof. A dam on the Shetucket River behind the mill powered Ponemah's looms. The mill is located on Norwich Ave. in the Taftville section of Norwich.

Royal Mohegan Burial Grounds

This small graveyard on a residential street, a fraction of its original size, is most notable as the resting place of Uncas, the controversial

This headstone at Norwichtown Cemetery records the 1660 birth of "ye first born of males in ye town" of Norwich.

Indian leader whose alliance with the English colonists divided his people into the Mohegan and Pequot tribes of today. An obelisk marks his grave. Located on Sachem St. about a block from Chelsea Parade in Norwich.

Museums

Leffingwell House Museum

This house (ca. 1675), one of Norwich's oldest, was the home of the Leffingwells, one of Norwich's original colonist families. A Leffingwell came to the aid of Uncas and his warriors at Fort Shantok in 1645 when the Mohegans were warring with the Narragansetts. Although many members of the family were notable, it is Christopher Leffingwell, one of the first American industrialists and a Revolutionary War financier, who gets the most attention. He anticipated the growth in demand for domestically produced goods that resulted from boycotts of British goods and built factories turning out paper, stockings and chocolate. Most of the house is restored to how it might have looked when he lived there in the late 1700s. Admission: $3 adults, $1 children under 12. Hours: Tue.–Sun., 1:00 P.M.–4:00 P.M., May 15–Oct. 15, & at other times by appointment. **348 Washington St. at the junction of Rtes. 2 and 169, Norwich, 06360; (860) 889-9440.** The best approach to this busy intersection is from the north on West Town St.

Mashantucket Pequot Museum and Research Center

Located a stone's throw from Foxwoods Resort Casino, this new museum focuses on northeast Woodlands Indians with an emphasis on the Mashantucket Pequot experience. There are permanent and changing exhibits on the art, history and culture of Native Americans, lecture space, research facilities and a library. For more information call **(860) 572-6800.**

Nathan Lester House and Farm Tool Museum

The Lester House is a local museum documenting life in Ledyard over the years. The colonial home of the Lester family (ca. 1793) is filled with antique furnishings donated by local people. The Farm Tool Museum in an outbuilding features implements dating from as early as 1800. A set of fossilized dinosaur footprints (not native to the property) given to the museum by the state are on display out back. There is also a moderately sized trail system and a worthwhile garden. The house and tool museum are open Memorial Day–Labor Day only, but the grounds are open year-round. Admission charged. House and museum hours: Tue. & Thu., 2:00 P.M.–4:00 P.M.; Sat.–Sun., 1:00 P.M.–4:30 P.M. Located at the **intersection of Long Cove Rd. and Vinegar Hill Rd., Gales Ferry, 06355; (860) 464-1865.**

Powerhouse Museum

One of the most spectacular gorges in Connecticut is on the Yantic River about 2 miles upstream of the marina in downtown Norwich. A few hundred yards upstream of that is Upper Yantic Falls, where the rushing water invited industrial development quite early in the town's history. The museum is located in a one-room brick building that formerly regulated the supply of energy to a downstream mill that is still standing and has been converted into housing. Inside the museum you'll find a brief overview of the manufacturing history of the site, and you can view some preserved machinery.

The spot is also the start of the Heritage Walkway, a 1.8-mile path along the river and down neighborhood streets, ending at Howard T. Brown Memorial Park in downtown. The path of the walkway is marked with street signs and shown on the "Tourist Guide to Historic Norwich," available from the **Norwich Tourism Office, 69 Main St., Norwich, 06360; (860) 886-4683.** The entrance to the Powerhouse Museum is on Sherman St. just east of the Yantic River. Admission is free. Hours: Tue.–Sat., 10:00 A.M.–4:00 P.M. Operation is seasonal, so call before going.

Slater Memorial Museum

The Slater Museum is a stunning Romanesque building housing a real mixed bag of items, most notable among them a collection of plaster casts of some of the greatest artwork of the classical world and Renaissance Europe, ranging from Michelangelo's *Pietà* to Greek temple pediments. Walking amid these massive sculptures, you feel as if you've wandered onto the set of an epic movie. The attached Converse Art Gallery hosts changing exhibits of contemporary art. Located on the **campus of Norwich Free Academy, 108 Crescent St., Norwich, 06360; (860) 887-2505/6.**

Tantaquidgeon Indian Museum

This small museum, almost a family project of an elderly Mohegan couple, is filled with artifacts of eastern Woodlands Indians. Admission by donation. Operation is seasonal; call for hours. **1819 Norwich–New London Tpke., Montville, 06353; (860) 848-9145.**

Nightlife

With the opening of Foxwoods and Mohegan Sun Casinos, evening entertainment options in the Norwich area have grown tremendously. At Mohegan Sun, the Wolf Den is a nightclublike space in the very center of the game floor where acts perform, and there's also a 1,500-seat hall for concerts. Foxwoods hosts big-name entertainers in its Fox Theatre and has a dance club. The facilities at both casinos are described in the listings under Major Attractions.

Occasional live concerts take place at **Dodd Stadium,** which can handle really large crowds. Call the stadium at **(860) 887-7962** for details. If you're looking for a local hangout with live music, try **Billy Wilson's Ageing Still** at **78 Franklin St. (860-887-8733)** in downtown Norwich. It's a small bar with a very casual atmosphere. There are occasionally poetry readings and folk music at the **Liberty Tree (Two Market St., 860-886-4465),** a bohemian restaurant downtown, plus cover bands on the weekends at **Americus on the Wharf (on American Wharf off W. Main St. in Norwich; 860-887-8555).**

Performing Arts

Free concerts take place at the gazebo in Howard T. Brown Memorial Park (Chelsea Harbor Dr. in downtown Norwich) on some summer afternoons and evenings in July and Aug. A great way to enjoy one would be from a reserved table at the seasonal restaurant Americus on the Wharf in the marina opposite the park. In addition, Fri. evening concerts take place on the green in Norwichtown. For a schedule call the **Norwich Arts Council** at **(860) 887-2789.**

Seasonal Favorites

If you like apples but you're bewildered by all the different kinds, you'll want to stop at **Holmberg Orchards (Rte. 12 in Ledyard; 860-464-7305 or 860-464-7107).** They grow over a dozen varieties and are one of the few farm stores to sell them by the pound rather than just by the peck or bushel, so you can try them all without having to buy them in quantity. You can also pick your own blueberries, peaches, raspberries, apples, pears and pumpkins in season. Pick-your-own hours are generally Tue., Thu. & Sat., 9:00 A.M.–noon during summer, & then daily 10:00 A.M.–5:00 P.M. once the apples start coming in. There's also a cider mill open to the public when cider is being made, usually Mon. & Thu. mornings in fall and one day a week until the supply of apples runs out. Hours are not cast in stone; call before going.

Sports

Check out the boys of summer at brand-new **Dodd Stadium,** the 6,200-seat home of the Norwich Navigators. The 'Gators are a AA Eastern League affiliate of the New York Yankees. Their season runs Apr.–Sept. with 71 home games. In Apr. & May, weeknight (Mon.–Fri.) games are at 6:35 P.M. & weekend games are at 2:05 P.M. From June on, Mon.–Sat. games are at 7:05 P.M. & Sun. games are at 2:05 P.M. There's a store on-site where you can get Yankees and Navigators merchandise all year round, and Stott's at Bat Ice Cream Bar and Batting Range just down the road is a great place to let the kids live out their fantasies of becoming pro baseball players. Tickets are only $4–$8. Dodd Stadium is also host to college baseball in the form of the Big East

267

Tournament, a four–five day series of elimination games in the middle of May. **14 Stott Rd. in Norwich Industrial Park** (enter via Connecticut Ave. off West Town St.), **Norwich, 06360; (800) 644-2867** or **(860) 887-7962.**

Tours

The Norwich Tourism Office has developed several fantastic walking tour guides to Norwich's historic neighborhoods. If you love architecture, this is *the* thing to do here. Four guides were in print at the time of this writing. Two of them cover 19th-century structures, and a third showcases pre-1785 homes. The fourth (Heritage Walkway) focuses not on architecture but on manufacturing history and the natural beauty of the Yantic River. Call the **Norwich Tourism Office** at **(860) 886-4683.**

268

Where to Stay

Accommodations around the casinos and neighboring Mystic are on the expensive side. Rather than wasting time comparing rates, you're better off picking a place that sounds really interesting to you and enjoying the experience. For additional listings, see the **Mystic** and **New London** chapters.

One service that can help in the search for the right room is **Bed & Breakfasts of the Mystic Coast:** 27 B&Bs from Bozrah to Westerly, Rhode Island, participate in this availability line, sharing their booking information for the coming week. A different B&B staffs the phone line each day, but you only have to call a central number: **(860) 892-5006.** Please note that many of the participating B&Bs are described in the **Mystic** and **New London** chapters.

Bed & Breakfasts

Applewood Farms Inn—$$$$
A stately center-chimney colonial (ca. 1826) filled with period furniture is the setting for five guest rooms at Applewood Farms. One

unusual highlight is a putting green, and smokers will rejoice to know that puffing is allowed in the common rooms of the house (the owners smoke), although the bedrooms are still off-limits. Four of the rooms have fireplaces and private baths, and all share a country feel. One room is a suite that can be combined with a couple of the other rooms to provide separate sleeping quarters for a party of people traveling together. A full breakfast is served. Children are accommodated by prior arrangement, and they'll also take pets, even horses; inquire for details. **528 Colonel Ledyard Hwy., Ledyard, 06339; (860) 536-2022.**

Blueberry Inn—$$$$
Many modern houses do not lend themselves well to B&Bs, but the large, new country cape house of Ray and Jackie Dows is an exception. The house is set on 17 meticulously maintained acres on a country road. Of the three rooms, the Studio is the most distinctive with a cathedral ceiling, skylights, great views, a queen bed and an attached bath. There's also a sunny great room and a deck with an outside hot tub available year-round. A full breakfast is included. **40 Bashon Hill Rd., Bozrah, 06334; (860) 889-3618.**

Stonecroft—$$$$
This restored Georgian colonial surrounded by stone walls has a historic, peaceful and romantic feel. Four guest rooms (three with fireplaces) each offer something unique, including one with wraparound murals and another with extensive modifications for wheelchair-accessibility. A full breakfast is served fireside on winter weekends or outside in summer. There are plans in the works to build luxury "country inn" rooms in a barn on the property, and their new Bed & Boat operation is described in the **Mystic** chapter; inquire for details. **515 Pumpkin Hill Rd., Ledyard, 06339; (860) 572-0771.**

Abbey's Lantern Hill Inn—$$$ to $$$$
This rambling contemporary home near Foxwoods Resort Casino has seven rooms and a lot of personality. All the rooms are nice,

ranging from two moderately priced ones with a shared bath to several large, rustic ones, which make for a nice romantic weekend. No two are alike, so call for details. A full breakfast is served on weekends (weekdays it's Continental), and the kitchen is open 24 hours a day. There's also a large deck and lawn for a barbeque or relaxing. Families with small children are welcomed. Payment by cash or credit card; checks accepted only in advance. **214 Lantern Hill Rd., Ledyard, 06339; (860) 572-0483.**

Captain Grant's—$$$ to $$$$

Ask innkeepers Carol Collette and Glen Vonasek to fill you in on the colorful history of this colonial (ca. 1754) once owned by a ship captain who made his living in the West Indies trade. The house features a grand central staircase, exposed oak and chestnut beams, refinished pine flooring, a lot of original doors, gun-stock posts and other reminders of its vintage. Four guest rooms have been outfitted with modern, private baths. A full breakfast is served as well as wine in the afternoon, and the recent addition of a three-story deck gives guests an outdoor dining and socializing area. **109 Rte. 2A, Preston, 06365; (860) 887-7589.**

Fitch-Claremont House—$$$ to $$$$

The older parts of this late 1700s house are so well restored that the interior looks like a beautiful reproduction, and all four guest rooms are in a recent addition that manages to meld very naturally with the 200-year-old part. The guest rooms all have private baths, gas fireplaces, 9-foot ceilings and quilts, with beautiful furnishings that range from four-posters to sleigh beds. The Fitch-Claremont also has a small whirlpool tub. Breakfast is extensive, served in a sunroom, and guests will probably find themselves gravitating to the library/common room, which has a gas fireplace, a sound system and a selection of CDs. The grounds are planted with 2.5 acres of grapes, the raw material for co-owner Warren Strong's hobby of amateur wine making. A complimentary bottle comes with each room, and he offers special two-part wine-making

overnight stays; call for details. **83 Fitchville Rd., Bozrah, 06334; (860) 889-0260.**

Roseledge Farm B&B—$$$ to $$$$

This B&B stands out in several ways: the hearth-cooked breakfast and afternoon tea served every day; the policy of accommodating children of any age (who will be enthralled by the farm animals in residence); special events held throughout the year and theme weekends, most of them focusing on cooking or crafts. The rooms are all authentically colonial, with pencil-post bedsteads, feather beds, original 18th-century doors and wideboard flooring and wood-burning fireplaces. **418 Rte. 164 at Burdick Rd., Preston City, 06365; (860) 892-4739.**

Hotels, Motels & Inns

Foxwoods Resort Hotel—$$$$

Foxwoods's rooms fill up virtually every night. Call months in advance to reserve for a weekend, and weeks in advance for a weeknight stay. Plans for a new hotel may eliminate the wait by the time you read this, but be prepared. Of the existing rooms, the two options are one-bedroom suites and standard rooms. The new hotel will also have many ultraluxurious presidential suites. The one-bedroom suites feature a king or two double beds, a sitting area with sleeper couch, a combination safe for protecting valuables, a refrigerator, a wet bar, an oversized TV and a very spacious bath with marble floor, a glassed-in shower and a two-person whirlpool tub as well as a half-bath with a telephone. Standard rooms are more like what you'd expect at any good-quality hotel. A concierge floor is available. There is a salon and a health club on-site, free valet parking, 24-hour room service and wheelchair-accessibility. Located on **Rte. 2, Ledyard, 06339; (800) 369-9663.**

Norwich Inn & Spa—$$$$

The key word here seems to be flexibility. You can stay here without ever partaking of the spa facilities, use the spa without staying overnight or pick from an array of package deals that combine the two. Accommodations boil down to about four options ranging from standard hotel rooms to two-bedroom condominium-like villas that come with free access to gyms and outdoor pools. There is also a restaurant on the premises. **607 W. Thames St., Norwich, 06360; (800) 275-4772** or **(860) 886-2401.**

Two Trees Inn—$$$$

The second hotel to be built at Foxwoods Resort Casino is separate from the casino but still within walking distance. Rooms come in two classes: a two-room suite with a sitting area and sleeper sofa in addition to one king or two double beds and a standard room with the same choice of beds. What distinguishes it from the Foxwoods Resort Hotel are lower prices and the absence of "resort" amenities such as room service. Other features of Two Trees include a large pool, a gym and a good restaurant. Continental breakfast is included. The wait for a room here is not as long as it is at the resort hotel, but you still need to call well in advance. Shuttle service is available. **240 Lantern Hill Rd., Ledyard, 06339; (800) 369-9663.**

Ramada Hotel—$$$ to $$$$

The Ramada offers standard rooms with queen or double beds and executive rooms with king beds and extra amenities such as hair dryers, coffeemakers, ironing boards and irons. Huntington's, the in-house restaurant, gets good reviews, and there's also a tavern with live musical entertainment on weekends. The hotel operates a free evening shuttle bus to Foxwoods Resort Casino and Mohegan Sun Casino, and you can also catch an inexpensive private shuttle during the day. **10 Laura Blvd., Norwich, 06360; (800) 272-6232** or **(860) 889-5201.**

Camping

Also see the listings for **Hopeville Pond State Park** and **Pachaug State Forest** campgrounds and information on private campgrounds in the **Far Northeast** chapter.

Strawberry Park—rates vary

One of the nicer private campgrounds in Connecticut, Strawberry Park is set on 77 acres. It accommodates RVs and tents, offers on-site RV rental and has a seasonal camping program that allows you to keep your own RV there year-round. Facilities include swimming pools, a camp store, a laundry, an exercise room, a recreation center and all kinds of playing fields. There are a range of organized activities and musical entertainment and an area for hiking and horseback riding. Call for rates and reservation information. Located on **Rte. 165, 1 mile east of Rte. 164 in Preston; (860) 886-1944.** Mailing address: **P.O. Box 830, Norwich, 06360.**

Where to Eat

Even if you're not a casino-goer, do consider eating at them. Both casinos have three fine restaurants whose specialties parallel each other: Italian, Chinese and American steak house. These casino restaurants are extremely busy, so always make a reservation. And certainly don't ignore all the local restaurants that have been serving Norwich for years.

Norwich Inn & Spa—$$$ to $$$$

The Prince of Wales restaurant at Norwich Inn & Spa serves both spa and American cuisine at all three meals, so dieters and nondieters can eat together and both be happy. There are even spa dessert choices. Breakfast is a buffet, whereas lunch and dinner are à la carte, but special requests for cooked-to-order items are always accommodated. Across the lobby, Jack's lounge has a great "hunt club" atmosphere in which to enjoy a before- or after-dinner beverage. Breakfast/brunch hours: 7:00 A.M.–10:30 A.M. daily. Lunch hours: Mon.–Fri., noon–2:00 P.M.; Sat.–Sun., noon–3:00 P.M. Dinner hours: Sun.–Fri., 6:00 P.M.–9:00 P.M.; Sat. until 10:30 P.M. A light menu is served between lunch and dinner each day. **607 W. Thames St., Norwich, 06360; (860) 886-2401, ext. 334.**

Norwich and Casino Country

Foxwoods Resort Casino—$ to $$$$

There are too many dining choices at Foxwoods to list all the restaurants separately, but rest assured that several of them are worth coming to Foxwoods for even if you would not otherwise be visiting the casino. Cedars Steakhouse, the most recommended restaurant in this area, serves Angus beef and boasts a grill room with a raw seafood bar. Chinese in a formal atmosphere is available at Han Garden, and Al Dente serves Southern Italian cuisine. Appropriate semiformal attire is requested at all three, which are open for dinner only from 5:00 P.M. daily. Reservations are essential, even on weeknights. For more casual dining, there are at least four other restaurants, including a buffet, a deli, a 24-hour grill and The Bistro, serving brick-oven pizza in a smoke-free setting. All the fast-food options you could want can be found in a huge food court. Two Trees Inn also has a restaurant (Branches) whose cozy dining room is warmed by a fireplace, featuring a menu of sandwiches, steaks and salads. Located on **Rte. 2, Ledyard, 06339; (800) 369-9663.**

Mohegan Sun Casino—$ to $$$$

Mohegan Sun Casino is replete with restaurants. Of the three fine dining eateries, the Longhouse features steak and seafood; Pompeii & Caesar gets high marks for its Italian and Bamboo Forest serves Chinese cuisine. Chief's Deli, Seasons (a buffet) and Mohegan Territory (the latter open 24 hours) fill in the middle ground. For a really casual and quick bite, there are ten fast-food outlets in a food court. The three better restaurants are fronted by display kitchens offering smaller portions of a sampling of menu items. The display kitchens keep longer hours than the main dining rooms, opening at 11:30 A.M. & serving until 1:00 or 2:00 A.M. most nights, until 6:00 A.M. at Bamboo Forest on weekends. At The Cove bar you can sample items from all three of these restaurants. The Longhouse, Pompeii & Caesar and Bamboo Forest are open for dinner 5:30 P.M.–11:00 P.M. daily; the Longhouse also serves lunch Mon.–Sat., 11:30 A.M.–2:00 P.M.; & Sunday brunch 11:00 A.M.–

3:00 P.M. with dinner service from 3:00 P.M. on. Appropriate dress is nice casual or better. Reservations essential. Located on **Mohegan Sun Blvd. off Rte. 2A, Uncasville (in Montville), 06382; (888) 226-7711.**

Americus on the Wharf—$$ to $$$

Located on a prime spot on American Wharf right at the head of the Thames, this nautically themed restaurant has a decor that reflects the locale: a boat hanging above the bar spouts fog; a foghorn sounds last call; windows open and close with line (ropes) and the day's specials are displayed out front through a porthole window. There are also tables on an outdoor patio. Operation is seasonal (roughly Apr. 15–Sept. 30, weather permitting) to coincide with summertime activity at the marina. Because a lot of people come in right off their boats, dress is casual. The cuisine is American, with virtually identical lunch and dinner menus. You'll find a selection of grilled items, pastas, seafood, sandwiches, soups and individual pizzas. Reservations recommended on weekends. Serving lunch and dinner from 11:30 A.M. daily, until 9:30 P.M. Sun.–Thu., until 10:30 P.M. Fri.–Sat. Located at **American Wharf in Norwich, 06360;** enter from W. Main St. where it crosses the Yantic River; **(860) 887-8555.**

Engine No. 6 Pizza Co.—$$ to $$$

A pizza parlor housed in the former Independence Hose No. 6 firehouse, inside you'll find casual seating at cafeteria-type tables and a sizable menu of calzones, grinders, pizza, pasta, soups and salads. Hours: Mon.–Thu., 10:30 A.M.–10:00 P.M.; Fri.–Sat., 10:30 A.M.–11:00 P.M.; Sun., 11:00 A.M.–9:00 P.M. **195 W. Thames St. (Rte. 32 South), Norwich, 06360; (860) 887-3887.**

Huntington's—$$ to $$$

This in-house restaurant at the Ramada Hotel serves reliably good American food, with the Sat. prime rib buffet dinner being especially popular. There is also a breakfast buffet daily, expanded on weekends, in addition to à la carte offerings. Reservations recommended.

Breakfast is served from 6:30 A.M. every day ending at 11:00 A.M. Mon.–Fri., noon on Sat. & 1:00 P.M. on Sun. Lunch hours are Mon.–Fri., 11:30 A.M.–2:00 P.M.; Sat., noon–5:00 P.M.; Sun., 1:00 P.M.–5:00 P.M. Dinner is served from 5:30 P.M. each night, ending at 10:00 P.M. on Sat. & 9:00 P.M. other days. **10 Laura Blvd., Norwich, 06360; (860) 889-5201, ext. 172.**

Pagoda Chinese Restaurant—$$ to $$$

A perennial favorite among locals, Pagoda has a nicer interior than most Chinese restaurants, serving excellent MSG-free food. There are the usual inexpensive luncheon specials, more elaborate chef's specials that are served in larger portions and a small menu of steamed foods for those on a low-calorie, low-fat diet. A little hard to find, Pagoda is located in a strip mall called The Meadows Center opposite the Caldor/Stop & Shop plaza in Norwichtown. Hours: Mon.–Thu., 11:00 A.M.–10:00 P.M.; Fri.–Sat., 11:00 A.M.–11:00 P.M.; Sun, noon–10:00 P.M. **47 Town St., Norwich, 06360; (860) 887-7500.**

Yantic River Inn—$$ to $$$

Yantic River Inn is very much a meat-and-potato, hometown restaurant that has a loyal following of mostly older customers who like their food cooked and presented in a very straightforward manner. The regular menu stresses steaks and broiled and fried fish. There's also a small selection of pasta and other items, a salad bar and daily specials. Sun. family specials, such as roast turkey and lamb, are offered at very reasonable prices. Hours: Tue.–Sat., 11:30 A.M.–3:30 P.M. for lunch & 4:00 P.M.–9:00 P.M. for dinner; Sun. dinner, noon–8:00 P.M. **270 W. Town St. (Rte. 32), Norwich, 06360; (860) 887-2440.**

Liberty Tree—$$

This casual coffeehouse/bohemian restaurant is housed in an 1861 building with high ceilings, chandeliers, brass detail work and massive wooden booths with marble tabletops. The Norwich memorabilia on the walls is from the co-owner's personal collection. The menu, serving lunch and dinner, consists mostly of sandwiches, soups and salads, with several veggie items. Order at the counter, and your meal will be brought to you. There's also a separate coffee bar and some comfy furniture for reclining with your java and dessert. Hours: Mon.–Fri., 8:30 A.M.–11:00 P.M.; Sat., noon–midnight. **Two Market St., Norwich, 06360; (860) 886-4465.**

Olde Tymes—$$

"Home is just a taste away" is the slogan at this eatery known for comfort food, a rustic, family-friendly atmosphere and good service. The floors and walls are wood, the table bases are made from old treadle sewing machines and antiques adorn the walls. Some of the most popular items are roast turkey, pot roast, prime rib and fish 'n' chips. Breakfast is served until 2:00 P.M. every day. Hours: Sun.–Thu., 7:00 A.M.–9:00 P.M.; Fri.–Sat., 7:00 A.M.–10:00 P.M. **360 W. Main St., Norwich, 06360; (860) 887-6865.**

Ledyard Country Breakfast—$ to $$

The rustic-looking, weathered wood board-and-batten exterior of Ledyard Country Breakfast should put you in the right frame of mind for the bright, informal interior and diner menu. As the name suggests, this is a place to come for an inexpensive eggs-and-biscuits breakfast or a tuna-melt lunch. The only night it's open for dinner is Fri., when it offers a fish fry (or fish broil for the health-conscious). LCB is also an ice cream stand during the warm-weather months. Hours: Tue.–Thu., 7:00 A.M.–1:30 P.M.; Fri., 7:00 A.M.–1:30 P.M., & 4:00 P.M.–8:00 P.M. for dinner; Sat.–Sun., 7:00 A.M.–1:00 P.M. (breakfast only on Sun.). **680 Colonel Ledyard Hwy., Ledyard, 06339; (860) 464-1055.**

Services

Local Visitors Information

Norwich Tourism Office, 69 Main St., Norwich, 06360; (860) 886-4683. Hours: Mon.–Fri., 9:00 A.M.–4:00 P.M.

Transportation

See the listing for the casinos under Major Attractions for information on transportation to the casinos through New London. For **Peter** **Pan/Trailways** bus service to and from Foxwoods Casino from New Hampshire and Massachusetts call **(800) 343-9999.** For details on regional bus service call **South East Area Transit (SEAT)** at **(860) 886-2631.**

Salmon River

Gardner
Lake

11

E. Haddam

Devils
Hopyard
State Park

85

Haddam
Meadows
State Park

9

82

Connecticut River

Cockaponset
State Forest

Gillette Castle
State Park

Chester

Lake
Gaillard

Chatfield Hollow
State Park

Deep River

Rogers
Lake

Essex

1

Lake
Saltonstall

Old
Saybrook

95

1

Old
Lyme

95

Guilford

Madison

The
Thimble
Islands

Hammonasset Beach
State Park

N
W   E
S

Lower Connecticut River Valley

Lower Connecticut River Valley

Central Shore

Between New Haven and Old Saybrook, there's a series of towns just off the Boston Post Rd. strung out like pearls on a necklace. Although their boundaries reach quite far inland, their dominant feature is shoreline, including the single largest public stretch of sand in the state: Hammonasset Beach State Park in Madison, 2.25 miles long. It is visited by tens of thousands of sunbathers and swimmers every year. With a large campground, a nature center offering an incredibly wide range of public programming to educate and entertain both kids and adults, a bike path and a boat launch, Hammonasset is designed to be a family destination.

The area's second great seaside attraction is The Thimble Islands in Stony Creek Harbor, Branford. Local tour operators, who make regular excursions in summer from the town dock, like to say there are 365 total—one for each day of the year. The Indians gathered food here, colonist farmers grazed livestock here and everyone from Revolutionary War rebels to pirates (including Capt. Kidd) used the islands as blinds and hideouts. A leisurely boat trip through The Thimbles today is little different from how it was a quarter-century ago: equal parts blue sky, blue water, fresh air and colorful narrative.

Also not to be missed are the area's beautiful inland parks and preserves. Near the shore but without any seaside frontage are wooded Stony Creek Quarry and Westwoods with trails for hiking and biking. Further afield but similar in feel is Guilford's Timberlands. Chatfield Hollow State Park has superb freshwater swimming and an upland, forested atmosphere that makes a wonderful contrast with the beach.

In addition to the great outdoors, the Central Shore has many other attractions. Guilford, first colonized in 1639, has the third-largest collection of 17th- and 18th-century dwellings in New England, three of which are open for tours. One of them, the Henry Whitfield State Museum, is the oldest stone house in New England. Neighboring towns also have architecturally and historically significant homes that are run as museums.

Shopping is fast becoming a full-fledged activity here. Two large outlet malls in Clinton and Westbrook draw people from miles around who want to stock up on favorite brand-name items. For handmade, limited production arts and crafts, visit the Guilford Handcraft Center or Branford Craft Village. The former is a combination gallery and school recognized for the excellence of its shop, which carries work in just about every known medium. It also organizes the Guilford Handcrafts Exposition arts and crafts show and sale every July. Branford Craft Village nearby is a cluster of studios and shops where you may be able to catch artists at work.

Great dining is a necessity for any great destination, and the Central Shore is a winner in that respect too. Area restaurants serve everything from French to fried clams, and many have desirable locations overlooking a town green or a quiet patch of harbor. The single greatest concentration of restaurants is on Branford green, where a recent facelift has made the neighborhood exceedingly pleasant for strolling. For a different kind of refreshment, visit the tasting room at Chamard Vineyard in Clinton to sample their critically acclaimed chardonnay and other vintages.

In the end the Central Shore is a place where you define the role the shore will have. You can spend your days doing nothing but lying on the beach listening to the pulse of wind and wave, or you can search out other activities against a background of superb seafood dinners and water views.

History

Settlement of the Central Shore by the English began around 1640. Old Saybrook was already in existence to the east and New Haven to the west, although both communities were young. One group of colonists arrived from England at Guilford in 1639, and another from Wethersfield at Branford in 1644. Land was purchased from the Hammonasset and other Indians. The Guilford party was led by Reverend Henry Whitfield, whose stone house, begun in 1639, still stands and is currently a museum.

One of Branford's claims to a piece of Yale history is a meeting that took place in 1701, at which a number of clergymen pledged a precious gift of books with which to begin the school's library. Clinton, meanwhile (at that time part of Killingworth), can rightfully be said to have had Yale's first classroom (no longer in existence), because the first president of the college, Abraham Pierson, taught students in his home for the first few years.

At about the same time visits by Capt. Kidd, a British privateer turned pirate who was captured and hanged in England in 1701, gave rise to what would become a powerful legend: that treasure is buried at several locations on the Connecticut shore, but most especially in The Thimble Islands. The islands are a natural hiding place for small ships and were used by both the British and the rebels for that purpose during the Revolutionary War.

David Bushnell, a native son of Westbrook, left his mark on history during that war when he developed the first practical submarine. He called it a "new invention for annoying ships," since his purpose in building it was to devise a way to attach underwater mines to British vessels. He called his invention *American Turtle* for its resemblance to two turtle shells attached to form a "bubble." A replica is on display at the Connecticut River Museum in Essex. Little could Bushnell have imagined the submarine base and Electric Boat shipyard that would eventually grow up in Groton a few miles away as a result of his experimentation.

A variety of industries sustained people here over the years. Shipbuilding of the conventional sort was a main pursuit from roughly 1700 to 1860. Along the shore, straw bonnets were made from the plentiful grasses, and fish were rendered for oil. Inland where the elevation of the land gave streams enough momentum to provide better water power, mills for

cider, flour, flaxseed oil and the fulling and dyeing of fabric were built. In the 1800s John Beattie, a Scotsman, operated quarries in Guilford from which stone was taken for the Brooklyn Bridge and the base of the Statue of Liberty. And from 1860 on, tin toys and other wares were manufactured in large quantities in Clinton.

Summer colonies developed pretty early on. In the late 1800s there were regular pleasure boat excursions to The Thimble Islands from New Haven, and resorts on the largest islands flourished. Strangely, though, Hammonasset Beach was not made into a public

A working undershot waterwheel at Chatfield Hollow State Park, Killingworth.

park as soon as one might think. Around the turn of the 20th century it was a rifle-testing range for the Winchester Repeating Arms Co. of New Haven. Similarly, ammunition was tested there during World War I. By 1920, however, the area was a state park. It hadn't seen the last of gunfire, though. During World War II it became a firing range once again. You can imagine the shape it was in when the war ended and the state was faced with the task of rebuilding it as a public facility.

Over the past few decades the Central Shore has undergone a transition from resorts that doubled or tripled in size every summer to towns with a sizable year-round population. Although June, July and Aug. will always be the high season, the consequent growth in services, such as restaurants, means that the Central Shore is no longer a summer-only destination.

Major Attractions

Chatfield Hollow State Park

Chatfield Hollow is a wonderful recreation area for hiking, cross-country skiing, freshwater swimming and picnicking. A guarded swimming area on a picturesque pond overhung with tall pines is a great place to escape

summer's heat. Over 350 picnic tables are scattered throughout the park. The loveliness of the woodland setting makes this a favorite spot for locals taking a morning walk on both the paved roads and an extensive trail system. A yellow-blazed, half-mile nature trail located near the park entrance is designed for families with small children, and a small, seasonal nature center is located in the Oak Lodge Shelter (staffed Sat.–Mon., noon–3:00 P.M. during summer). Inquire about public programs. Finally, a small covered bridge (for foot traffic only) and a working undershot waterwheel fed by an exquisite pond are located at the very end of the main park road. A parking fee of $4 weekdays, $5 weekends for state residents and $5 weekdays, $8 weekends for nonresidents is charged Memorial Day–Labor Day, but if you are just hiking or strolling, use the free parking lot outside the gate and hoof it from there. Hours: 8:00 A.M.–sunset daily, year-round. Located on **Rte. 80 about 1 mile west of Rte. 81, Killingworth; (860) 663-2030.**

Hammonasset Beach State Park

Hammonasset Beach, with 2.5 miles of uninterrupted prime sandy realty, is the largest of about half a dozen public shoreline parks. Ocean swimming is not the only attraction here, however. Willard's Island Trail is a wheelchair-accessible series of paved paths through a large salt marsh where numbered stations along the way correspond to descriptive entries on a map available at the trailhead. Meig's Point Nature Center has great displays on the wildlife and history of the area that both children and adults will enjoy, as well as public programs. There is a boat launch, concessions, bathhouses, an unpaved bike path and a boardwalk. Special wheelchairs for going through sand and surf are available at no charge. A 560-site campground is walking distance away. Admission for Connecticut residents is $5 per car weekdays, $7 Sat., Sun. and holidays. Nonresident fees are $8 and $12, respectively. Open 8:00 A.M.–sunset year-round. Lifeguards and naturalists on duty Memorial Day–Labor Day. Entrance on Rte. 1

approximately 2 miles east of the center of Madison; **(203) 245-2785.**

Henry Whitfield State Museum

If you've seen even a few of New England's oldest houses, you'll be struck immediately by an obvious difference between them and the Henry Whitfield House: most old houses are built of wood, but this one is built of stone. Stone houses were the castles of the New World, serving not only as residences for the community's most well-to-do and learned leaders but also as fortresses in times of danger when most of the new immigrants were living in little better than lean-tos. Very few of these stone houses (and none of the settlers' original lean-tos) remain, and this one, originally built in 1639, has a long story of alteration, near destruction and ultimate restoration to tell. It's interesting not only for its focus on the earliest period of Connecticut's colonial history, but also because of the story it tells about historic preservation. Admission: $3 per adult, less for seniors and children. Open Wed.–Sun., 10:00 A.M.–4:30 P.M.; closed on Thanksgiving & Dec. 15–Jan. 31 except by appointment. **248 Old Whitfield St., Guilford, 06437; (203) 453-2457.**

The Thimble Islands

The Thimble Islands are a series of outcroppings off the coast of Branford that range from boulders barely big enough to accommodate a few seagulls to honest-to-goodness islands that support up to two dozen households. They are rich in history and lore. Capt. Kidd, the famous privateer gone bad, is said to have hidden here when the British put a price on his head for piracy. Residents of the largest island, Kidd's Island (really High Island), all paint their homes "pirate black" (a charcoal color), and some of them fly the skull and crossbones to keep the legend alive.

Cruising The Thimbles, which takes only about 45 minutes, should be at the top of your list of things to do here. Catch any one of three launches (the *Sea Mist II*, the *Islander* and the

Getting There

The Central Shore is about an hour due south of Hartford by car, and any direct route will take you on some very pretty back roads. I-91 south to Rte. 9 south to Rte. 17 south will take you to Rte. 77 south straight to Guilford. You could also continue on Rte. 9 to Rte. 81 south, which will take you to Clinton. Once you're on the shore, I-95 provides the fastest east-west corridor between towns. Public transportation between towns is also quite good. For details, see the Services section at the end of this chapter.

Volsunga IV) that make several journeys daily from Stony Creek town dock in Branford. Each captain takes a slightly different course through the islands and has a personal take on the goings-on of residents past and present. Memorial Day–Labor Day, the first trip of the day is generally 10:00-ish and the last trip 4:30-ish. All departures are subject to weather conditions and the required eight-person minimum. The *Sea Mist II* also keeps an abridged schedule on weekends in May as well as Labor Day–Columbus Day, and the others may also

279

A New World fortress, the Henry Whitfield State Museum was first built in 1639. Photo courtesy Henry Whitfield State Museum, Guilford.

have an extended season. The boats can be chartered for dinner cruises or for daytime use (call for rates; some captains will arrange catering for an additional charge, or you can bring your own food). The 45-minute sightseeing cruise costs $6 per adult, $5 for seniors and $3 for children under 12. Stony Creek town dock is at the **terminus of Thimble Islands Rd. in Branford, 06405.** You can reach the **Sea Mist II** at **(203) 488-8905,** the **Islander** at **(203) 397-3921** and the **Volsunga IV** at **(203) 481-3345.**

Festivals and Events

Civil War Living History Encampment & Battle
first weekend in May

Every May the campground of Hammonasset Beach State Park is the scene of a Civil War battle replete with infantry, artillery and cavalry. This massive reenactment involves 600–650 participants and draws a crowd of 10,000 spectators. There are period civilian activities for adults and children, such as Maypole dancing, a tea party with Mrs. Lincoln and performances of both military and nonmilitary music. There is one full-scale battle per day, Sat. at 1:00 P.M. & Sun. at 2:00 P.M. Admission: $6 adults, $4 seniors, $3 children 3–18. Hours: Sat., 9:00 A.M.–4:00 P.M.; Sun., 9:00 A.M.–3:00 P.M. The park is on **Rte. 1 approximately 2 miles east of the center of Madison.** For advance ticket purchase or for more information call **(860) 526-4993.**

Guilford Handcrafts Exposition
third weekend in July (Thu.–Sat.)

With more than 125 exhibitors, the Guilford Handcrafts Exposition is one of the largest crafts shows in the state. It's held on Guilford's picturesque town green, noon–9:00 P.M. for three days. Admission: $5. The Guilford Art League has a simultaneous art sale, also on the green. For more information call the

Guilford Handcraft Center at **(203) 453-5947.**

Guilford Antiques Festival & Sale
last Sat. in July

For nearly 40 years the Guilford Keeping Society has held this antiques show to benefit restoration and upkeep of the **Thomas Griswold House** museum. About 100 dealers display their goods at booths set up on the lawn outside the museum at **171 Boston St. (Rte. 146) in Guilford.** Hours: 9:00 A.M.–4:00 P.M., rain or shine. Admission: $4. For more information call the museum at **(203) 453-3176.**

Bluefish Festival
mid-Aug. (Fri.–Sun.)

Over 20 years old, Clinton's annual family festival got its name from a fish common in Long Island Sound waters. Musical entertainment has become the big draw, with everything from blues to big band going on at some point over the festival's three days. Peruse the booths of arts and crafts vendors, take a turn at tube racing in the harbor or throw your muscle into a tug-of-war on the beach. Special activities for kids take place on Sat. at the nearby town beach on Waterside Ln. Admission charged. Hours: Fri., 6:00 P.M.–10:00 P.M.; Sat., noon–10:00 P.M.; Sun., noon–6:00 P.M. For more information call **(203) 664-3900** or the **Clinton Chamber of Commerce** at **(860) 669-3889.**

Westbrook Ancient Muster
fourth Sat. in Aug.

Smaller and more controlled than the Deep River muster (see the **Old Saybrook/Old Lyme** chapter for details and some background on musters), the Westbrook event follows the same pattern: a parade of fife and drum corps down the main street followed by informal performances and demonstrations. Be there early to get a parking space and a good spot for the 11:00 A.M. start. For more information call **(860) 399-6436.**

Guilford Fair

third weekend in Sept. (Fri.–Sun.)

One of the oldest fairs in Connecticut, this fair has traditional events centered around agriculture and livestock and is unique in being the only fair in the state to incorporate a circus. Musical entertainment is also a big draw. An oldies concert with a big-name 1950s or 1960s band always takes place Fri. night, and a current Nashville artist is featured on Sat. Admission: $5 adults, $1 children 6–12, discounted three-day pass available. Parking at the fairground is $2, other lots are free and there is free shuttle bus service. Hours: Fri., 1:00 P.M.–11:00 P.M.; Sat., 9:00 A.M.–11:00 P.M.; Sun., 9:00 A.M.–8:00 P.M. Enter Guilford Fairgrounds from Stone House Lane. For more information call **(203) 453-3543.**

Outdoor Activities

Biking

The best place around to mountain bike is The Timberlands in Guilford, a network of multiple-use trails through 600 forested inland acres where bikers may encounter equestrians and hikers. There are a couple of options for rides with views of Long Island Sound, all of which are appropriate for any type of bike. At Hammonasset Beach State Park, guided one-and-a-half-hour "bike hikes" are given by park staff along a bike path with commentary on the history and ecology of the area. The terrain and pace are easy, but keep in mind that sand will get in your gears. For more information, see the listing under Major Attractions.

The Sachem Head area of Guilford is a quiet, secluded residential neighborhood where you can escape automobile traffic almost entirely. Head down Sachem's Hill Rd. to Vineyard Point Rd., which will take you out to the Sound. Park in the pullout for the Westwoods trail system where Sam Hill Rd. meets Rte. 146 at the top of Sachem's Head Rd. and bike from there.

A rather short clockwise loop in Madison that takes you right along the water for a stretch starts at the Stop 'n' Shop complex on Samson Rd. Ride south on East Wharf Rd., take Middle Beach Rd. and Middle Beach Rd. West to West Wharf Rd., then return via Rte. 1 to the starting point.

You can also bike the length of Neck Rd. in Madison, which is paved for most of its length but becomes dirt toward the end. It goes through a neighborhood of resort houses clustered along the shore, but yields nice views of the water at very close range, and at the end of the road there is a row of a dozen or so interesting stilt houses.

Finally, Rte. 146 from the Indian Neck part of Branford east to the green in Guilford is extremely pretty. On this ride you'll be treated to a variety of views including some of the Sound and salt marsh, and you can easily dip down into the village of Stony Creek for a bite to eat or a tour of the Thimble Islands.

Birding

Hammonasset Beach State Park is probably the best year-round birding spot in Connecticut, in part because of its tremendous diversity of habitat: salt marsh, woodland, coastline with a promontory and open fields. Birders sight 240–260 species each year. For directions and more details on the park, see the listing under Major Attractions.

While you're in the area, you may want to stop in at **The Audubon Shop,** a unique store devoted to birds and birders that carries everything from telescopes and birdseed to guidebooks and binoculars for rent. Open Mon.–Sat., 10:00 A.M.–5:00 P.M.; Sun., noon–4:00 P.M. **871 Boston Post Rd. (Rte. 1), Madison, 96443; (203) 245-9056** (in Connecticut) or **(800) 776-5811** (out-of-state).

Boating

A unique way to experience the Sound is in a sea kayak from **Stony Creek Kayak (203-481-6401).** Christopher Hauge offers hourly instruction and tours by the half day and day, mid-May–Oct. He also leads trips on the Connecticut River, Quonnipaug Lake and elsewhere.

Lower Connecticut River Valley

Boat Launches

Freshwater boating options in this area are pretty limited, but what's accessible is very pretty. The public boat launch on **Quonnipaug Lake** in North Guilford is located on Rte. 77 about one-third mile north of the town beach. A 6 HP limit is in effect.

Several public launches are available for access to **Long Island Sound.** Hammonasset Beach State Park has one; see the listing under Major Attractions for more information. Another state boat launch is located on the Branford River at the end of Goodsell Pt. Rd. in Branford. A fee is collected on weekends. You can try your luck with a third state launch on the East River in Guilford that is reached by driving down Neck Rd. in Madison and looking for signs. If you find the entrance gated, call the phone number posted to have it opened.

Guilford's town launch at the mouth of the East River is located at the end of Old Whitfield St. It's open Apr.–Oct. The launch fee is $5 per day or $30 per season for residents and $10 per day or $60 per season for non-residents. There's also a certified mooring field up the East River. Call the dockmaster at **(203) 453-8092** for more information. The town of Clinton also has a public launch located next to the town dock on Riverside Dr. Season: Apr.–Nov. A fee is charged. For more information call the **First Selectman's office** at **(860) 669-9333.**

Marinas

Facilities for transient boaters in this part of the Connecticut shore get larger and more numerous as you travel east toward Old Saybrook. In Branford Harbor you'll find **Bruce & Johnson's Marina (203-488-8329;** VHF 9), with 25 transient slips and the best all-around array of services and facilities in the area. Clinton's **Cedar Island Marina (860-669-8681)** has 70 transient berths plus a pool, a hotel and every service you could want. They're also the only source for fuel in Clinton Harbor. **Clinton Yacht Haven (860-669-7716), Old Harbor Marina (860-669-8361), Port Clinton Marina (860-669-4563)** and **Riverside Basin Marina (860-669-1503)** all

have ten transient slips apiece and monitor VHF 9.

Westbrook has even more facilities plus tons of services for boaters at the waterfront, which is a few miles distant from the center of town. **Brewer's Pilot's Pt. Marina (860-399-7906)** has 90 transient berths at three locations and recreation such as a swimming pool, tennis and golf in addition to a full range of repairs and services. **Pier 76 (860-399-7122),** a small boat specialist with no hookups, has 50 transient berths on hand as well as a bait and tackle shop and a restaurant where you can practically tie your boat to your table. You can reach all the marinas here on VHF 9.

For navigational details, charts and complete lists of marine facilities throughout this area, your best source of information is *Embassy's Complete Boating Guide & Chartbook to Long Island Sound.* Contact the publisher at **142 Ferry Rd., Old Saybrook, 06475; (860) 395-0188.**

Fishing

Freshwater

The **Hammonasset River** is stocked with trout below the Lake Hammonasset reservoir dam on the Clinton/Madison line. The portion of the river from the dam (just north of Rte. 80) downstream to Chestnut Hill Rd. is a Trout Management Area where anglers are limited to catch-and-release only during the normal closed season and the number of fish you can take is limited during the normal open season. You can access this whole section of the Hammonasset via a riverside trail. Use pullouts off Rte. 80 for parking.

Schreeder Pond in Chatfield Hollow State Park, described under Major Attractions, is also heavily stocked. A loop road circles the pond, so shoreline access is easy. **Chatfield Hollow Brook,** also within the park, is a good spot for stream fishing.

Lake Quonnipaug is tall, narrow and deep in the manner of glacial lakes and very good for trout fishing. In fact, it's a Trophy Trout lake with near-ideal trout habitat. You'll also find largemouth bass here. Put in a boat at the town launch (fee charged) on Rte. 77 in Guilford.

For largemouth bass try **Messershmidt's Pond,** where there's a car-top launch right off Rte. 145 on the Westbrook/Deep River town line, and good shore access from the state-owned land surrounding the water.

Finally, two of the South Central Connecticut Regional Water Authority properties in this area, **Big Gulph** in North Branford and **Gene-see** in North Madison and North Guilford, allow stream fishing. For more information, see the listing under Hiking.

Saltwater

For charter fishing in this area try the *Catch 'Em* (860-223-1876 or 860-399-5853 on summer weekends) captained by Richard J. Siedzik or the *Gypsy VI* (860-388-2664 or 860-391-3346) captained by Jack Mise-rocchi. They both depart from Pilot's Pt. Marina in Westbrook and offer inshore fishing for bluefish, striped bass and the like. The season runs approximately May–Oct.

If you've got your own boat and are just looking for supplies, try **Stony Creek Marine & Tackle (203-488-7061)** on the town dock at the end of Thimble Island Rd. in Stony Creek.

Hiking

Chatfield Trail
This short (under 5 miles) section of blue-blazed trail starts immediately opposite the entrance to Chatfield Hollow State Park, traversing ledges with good views and following a course through Indian caves and past glacial erratics. It is described in detail in the *Connecticut Walk Book*. Park at the lot outside Chatfield Hollow's control gate on Rte. 80 in Killingworth.

Land Trusts
The Madison Land Conservation Trust maintains 14 different trails in that town. One of the most highly recommended for its beauty is the Bailey Memorial Trail down the west side of the Hammonasset River. It follows the

hemlock-shaded riverbank for about 3 miles. Near the northern end is an overlook loop that climbs Buck Hill, where a ledge affords views of Long Island Sound (4–5 miles away) on clear days. The stone mansion visible downriver, which belonged to the inventor of Silly Putty, lies atop a high point called Legend Hill. To access the trail, park in the pullout where Rte. 80 crosses the river. Copies of the *Madison Trail Guide,* which includes maps of this trail and 13 others, can be purchased for $2 at **The Audubon Shop** at **871 Boston Post Rd. (Rte. 1), Madison; (203) 245-9056.**

The Killingworth Land Conservation Trust's trail book also describes this trail, as well as the Chatfield Trail, Chatfield Hollow State Park trails and two others. To get a copy, write them care of the **Platt Nature Center, P.O. Box 825, Killingworth, 06419.**

SCCRWA Properties
The South Central Connecticut Regional Water Authority owns four beautiful watershed properties in Guilford, Madison and North Branford that are open for recreational use by permit only for a small charge. There are paved walking paths and hiking trails ranging from an easy loop around a reservoir to a rigorous climb up Totoket Ridge in the Farm River valley and everything in between. Stream fishing is also available at two properties. Permits cost $35 per year and provide access for one couple and their children under age 21. Information on access is provided when you obtain the permit. Call **(203) 624-6671** for details.

The Timberlands
The Timberlands is 600 acres of town-owned prime woodland in the midst of a suburban community. There are two great things about The Timberlands: easy access from several points, including a main road (Rte. 80), and moderate size. The Timberlands is located south of Rte. 80 and east of Rte. 77 in northern Guilford. One access point is from the North Guilford Archery Range parking lot on the north side of Rte. 80 just east of Maple Hill Rd. Park, then cross the road to pick up the white-blazed trail. The Guilford Lakes Golf Course

parking lot at the intersection of North Madison and Maupas Rds. is an easy-to-find starting point at the southern end of this trail system. From that point walk up Maupas Rd. a short distance to a trailhead on your right. Most trails are easy; look for the orange- and blue-blazed paths if you want more of a workout. An excellent map of these trails, with helpful notes on parking, is available from the **Westwoods Trails Committee, Guilford Land Conservation Trust, P.O. Box 200, Guilford, 06437.** The map is also sometimes available at the visitors information desk at the Henry Whitfield State Museum on Whitfield St. in Guilford.

Westwoods and
Stony Creek Quarry Preserve
Highlights of these two interconnected trail systems in Guilford and Branford include waterfalls, Indian caves (overhanging rocks), vistas, an abandoned quarry and more. The Westwoods half is so dense with trails it's almost mazelike; you should definitely hike with a map. The whole system is described in detail in the *Connecticut Walk Book,* and the same map published in brochure form is often available for $1 from the visitors information center at the Henry Whitfield State Museum, the town clerk's office and Bishop's Orchards, all in Guilford. The best entrances, all with parking for a few cars, are on the Westwoods side. One is located at the intersection of Rte. 146 and Sam Hill Rd. in Guilford. Another is at the end of Dunk Rock Rd., two more are on Moose Hill Rd. and a fifth is off Peddlers Rd.

Swimming

For more on saltwater swimming at **Hammonasset Beach State Park,** Connecticut's largest developed shoreline park, see the listing under Major Attractions.

Clinton Town Beach
In season you can swim at this municipal beach on Waterside Ln. for a daily fee of $7 per car from the third week in June until Labor Day. Facilities include a playground, bathhouses and two picnic pavilions with barbeques. For more information call the **Clinton Recreation Dept.** at **(860) 669-6901.**

Jacobs Beach
Jacobs Beach is a town-owned shoreline swimming area located at the end of Seaside Ave. in Guilford. It's guarded and fully developed with facilities such as changing rooms, showers, a playground, beach volleyball courts and a picnic area with a few grills. Admission is $2 per car for residents and $3 for nonresidents on weekdays; $4 and $6 on weekends. For more information call the **Guilford Parks Dept.** at **(203) 453-8068.**

Quonnipaug Lake
For freshwater swimming, the town of Guilford offers a small, sandy beach on this pretty inland lake. It's open weekends only from Memorial Day until mid-June, then daily until Labor Day. There are lifeguards, a picnic area, showers, changing rooms and a small craft launch area for windsurfers and canoes. Both resident and nonresident season passes are available, or you can pay by the day: $2 weekdays and $3 weekends per person for town residents; $4 and $6 for nonresidents. Resident children under age 12 admitted free. Buy passes from the **Guilford Parks Dept.** at **32 Church St.** in town. Beach hours: 9:00 A.M.–8:00 P.M. Located on **Rte. 77, 3 miles north of Rte. 80.** For more information call **(203) 453-8068.**

Seeing and Doing

Crafts Centers

Branford Craft Village
At times you may be able to see a glassblower, sculptor, potter or other artist at work in this cluster of studios and shops. Mixed in with the fine-quality decorative work and an herb store is some souvenir-quality merchandise. Crafts festivals are held on the grounds twice a year, on the first weekend in July and Oct., and Dec. brings Christmas festivities that change from year to year. There's also a decent restaurant on the premises. Store hours: Tue.–Sat., 11:00 A.M.–5:00 P.M.; Sun., noon–5:00 P.M. **779 East Main St. (Rte. 1), Branford, 06405; (203) 488-4689.**

Guilford Handcraft Center

There's lots to choose from and be inspired by at this combination shop, gallery and school. Two galleries present a wide range of work formally, and in the shop you can find glassware, jewelry, textiles, turned wood, quilts, photography, rugs, paintings and more. In early Nov. the store's inventory rises dramatically and spills over into one of the galleries for the center's annual Holiday Exhibit & Sale. Normal shop hours: Mon.–Sat., 10:00 A.M.–5:00 P.M.; Sun., noon–4:00 P.M.; closed major holidays. Call for their holiday exhibit hours. **411 Church St., Guilford, 06437; (203) 453-5947.**

Museums

The Central Shore area is of special interest to history buffs. Guilford bears the distinction of having the third-largest number of homes built prior to 1800 still standing in the country. The three historic home museums in Guilford complement one another well—the Whitfield State Museum illuminates the 1600s, Hyland House the 1700s and the Thomas Griswold House the 1800s—and their proximity makes them ideal to visit as a trio.

Allis-Bushnell House

This beautifully restored home is fascinating both for the contrast between the two halves of the downstairs interior, one of which is colonial and the other Victorian in flavor, and for the rich collection of artifacts it houses, from a queer Victorian hearing aid to the original petition to the State Assembly to make Madison a separate town. An outbuilding is the de facto Madison town museum, and there's an attractive formal garden out back. The house's name reflects its ownership by Cornelius Bushnell, financier of the ironclad ship the USS *Monitor.* Admission is free. Open Wed., Fri. & Sat., 1:00 P.M.–4:00 P.M. **853 Boston Post Rd. (Rte. 1), Madison, 06443; (203) 245-4567.**

Deacon John Grave House

Madison's oldest house (ca. 1685) is in the midst of restoration, having been acquired as a museum only recently. It was lived in for nearly 300 years by descendants of the builder, and few changes were made, making

Hyland House, one of Guilford's many 17th-century homes, is open for tours.

this an especially interesting stop for those who would like to see the nuts and bolts of an old structure. This is also one of the best-documented houses in Connecticut, thanks to a ledger of household expenses kept from 1678 to 1895. Inquire about the hearth cooking and weaving demonstrations, the summer dinner and auction held the second Sat. in Aug. and the early Dec. Holiday House Tour of homes in Madison. Admission: $2 adults, $1 students. Hours: Wed.–Sun., noon–3:00 P.M., late spring–mid-fall; also by appointment & for occasional special winter exhibits; call before going. **581 Boston Post Rd. (Rte. 1), Madison, 06443; (203) 245-4798.**

Harrison House

Although the original center-chimney structure here was built in 1724, later modifications have been retained, so that today the Harrison House exhibits traits of several different periods. It's an interesting case study in restoration efforts of the early 20th century. One upstairs room is set aside for the display of the Branford Historical Society's collection of local artifacts. A genealogical library occupies the rear. Admission by donation. Open Thu.–Sat., 2:00 P.M.–5:00 P.M., June–Sept. **124 Main St., Branford, 06405; (203) 488-4828.**

Hyland House

This saltbox (ca. 1660) belonged to clock maker Ebenezer Parmelee, noted for being the first person to put a clock in a church steeple (the Second Congregational Church on Guilford green) in Connecticut Colony. The house is architecturally significant for its external overhang and extremely rare original casement window that was simply built over when the lean-to portion of the structure was added. Inside you'll find several examples of very early, locally made furnishings and decorative arts. Admission: $2 per adult, children under 12 free with adult. Hours: Tue.–Sun., 10:00 A.M.–4:30 P.M., first Mon. in June–Labor Day weekend, then weekends only until Columbus Day & by appointment. **84 Boston St. (Rte. 146), Guilford, 06437; (203) 453-9477.**

Stanton House

The Stanton family, after whom this house is named, was important to Clinton's history. In the late 1700s a Stanton established a business supplying goods and services to sailors whose ships docked at the foot of Waterside Ln. nearby. He did well enough to buy this property. Stanton House is filled exclusively with family furnishings, so you can see how a well-established Yankee family really lived over the centuries. Admission by donation. Hours: Tue.–Sat., 2:00 P.M.–5:00 P.M., June–Sept. **63 E. Main St., Clinton, 06413; (860) 669-2132.**

Thomas Griswold House

The Guilford Keeping Society maintains this 1774 lean-to saltbox that has been restored, furnished and interpreted to the early 1800s. In addition to the permanent display of furnishings and artifacts, you'll find changing exhibits here that can focus on any aspect of Guilford history. A working blacksmith shop and other outbuildings are open occasionally. Call for a schedule of the biweekly hearth cooking, weaving and other demonstrations. Admission: $2 adults, $1 seniors and students. Hours: Tue.–Sun., 11:00 A.M.–4:00 P.M., June–mid-Sept.; weekends until the end of Oct. & occasionally in Nov. & Dec. & by appointment. **171 Boston St. (Rte. 146), Guilford, 06437; (203) 453-3176.**

Other Museums

Totoket Historical Society's **Center School** is a multiroom schoolhouse used for the display of changing exhibits on North Branford history and industry. Its collection of greeting cards reflects the town's one-time status as "the greeting card capital of the world." Located behind town hall on Foxon Rd. in North Branford. Admission is free. Hours: Wed., 2:00 P.M.–4:00 P.M., year-round. For more information during open hours call **(203) 488-0423.**

The **Westbrook Historical Society** keeps a museum building on the town green open the third Sat. of every month, 10:00 A.M.–4:00 P.M., year-round. Free tours focus on the Westbrook families whose belongings are on display. For more information call **(860) 399-7361.** A few feet away on N. Main St., you'll find the **Military Historians Museum (860-399-9460),** whose holdings include the largest collection of American military uniforms in the United States and a number of working military vehicles. Admission is free. Hours: Tue.–Fri., 8:00 A.M.–3:30 P.M., & by appointment.

Clinton Historical Society keeps a museum room at the town hall housing a large collection of Clinton artifacts. Open July–Aug., Mon.–Fri., 2:00 P.M.–4:00 P.M., & Sept.–June, Fri. only. If you're more interested in historic buildings, visit the **Captain Elisha White House** (ca. 1750), a.k.a. the Old Brick, at **103 E. Main St.** It was the first brick house built between New London and New Haven. Hours: Sat.–Sun., 2:00 P.M.–4:00 P.M., July & Aug. Guided tours are free. For more information call the historical society at **(860) 669-2148.**

Nature Centers

By virtue of its exceptional location, as well as the quality and quantity of its free exhibits and programs, **Meigs Point Nature Center** at Hammonasset Beach State Park is one of the best nature centers in Connecticut. There are numerous displays on Long Island Sound ecology, including native animals and plants and human use of the land and water. Public programs include canoe trips, naturalist presentations for kids age 6 and up, bird and nature walks, bike hikes and even some nighttime activities. The nature center is located in the weathered clapboard building near the eastern edge of the park. Programs run late June–Labor Day; closed on Mon. All programs are free, but park entrance fees apply. Call **(203) 245-8743** to request a program schedule. For directions and more details on the park, see the listing under Major Attractions.

Performing Arts

One of Connecticut's most unique stages is the **Stony Creek Puppet House Theatre (128 Thimble Island Rd., Branford, 06405; 203-488-5752)**. This intimate, 90-seat venue was built as a silent movie house around 1900 and was at one time the home of Orson Welles's Mercury Theatre. Now you can see semiprofessional and amateur productions staged by the in-house Thimble Island Theatre Company and by guest artists. The season runs Mar.–Dec. and typically includes comedies, dramas and musicals. The playhouse is also the site of summertime acoustic folk and bluegrass concerts, children's theater and regular playwright forums with staged readings of new work by Connecticut authors. The theater takes its name from a collection of 90-year-old Sicilian rod puppets on display in the lobby; occasional productions feature the puppets. Show nights are usually Thu.–Sun. with tickets in the $5–$10 range; call for details.

Andrews Memorial Town Hall Theater on **E. Main St. (Rte. 1) in Clinton** is the home of the Opera Theater of Connecticut and the Nutmeg Players. You can reach the **Opera Theater** at **(860) 669-8999** and the **Nutmeg Players** at **(800) 688-6343** or **(860) 388-3932**. The latter is a community theater group that has been bringing stage plays to the shore area for over three decades. It does two or three Broadway musicals or other big shows Nov.–May and presents a weekend one-act drama festival every Feb.

Finally, the **Shoreline Alliance for the Arts** is a group very active in keeping the arts alive on the shore, sponsoring (among other things) a series of summer Sun. concerts on Guilford green every year. Check local papers for events listings or call **(203) 453-3890**.

Scenic Drives

Rte. 77 north of Guilford to the Middlesex county line and Rte. 146 from Guilford west halfway across Branford are designated scenic roads and among the prettiest in the area, but they are far from the only ones. Rtes. 79 and 81 heading inland are also beautiful and surprisingly light on traffic north of I-95. Rte. 148 through Killingworth and Rte. 80 across North Guilford and North Madison are exceptional as well. Other than outdoor recreation, there's not much in these areas to do, so go for the woodland scenery and rolling hills alone.

If the shore is more to your liking, you must visit Stony Creek, a picturesque village at the end of Thimble Islands Rd. in Branford. From the town dock you can take a short, inexpensive boat tour of the islands. That and lunch at Stony Creek Market should make half of a perfect day.

Seasonal Favorites

Bishop's Orchards is a large and locally famous produce and specialty food market, but the real reason to visit is for the pick-your-own fruit experience. It's great fun for kids who get to search for the perfect apple or peach, and relaxing for adults. They offer strawberries, blueberries, peaches, pears, raspberries and apples, listed in the order in which they become available, beginning in June. Store hours: Mon.–Sat., 8:00 A.M.–6:00 P.M.; Sun., 9:00 A.M.–6:00 P.M. Pick-your-own hours vary with the season and are posted in the store at **1355 Boston Post Rd. (Rte. 1), Guilford, 06437; (203) 453-6424.** The orchards are located off New England Rd. a couple of miles away.

Shopping

The Central Shore offers several genuinely pleasant shopping opportunities. Make the Guilford Handcraft Center and Branford Craft

Village (both described under Crafts Centers) tops on your list. Between them you'll find everything from fine art to fine food. You'll enjoy an equally unique atmosphere at **The Pink Sleigh (860-399-6926),** a Christmas shop and more housed in a converted barn straight out of a fairy tale. It's open mid-July–Christmas Eve. Located on **Rte. 153 half a mile north of I-95 exit 65 in Westbrook.**

Both Guilford and Madison have nice downtown shopping districts. The west side of Guilford green is lined with boutiques, a couple of art galleries, restaurants, bakeries, a chocolatier and a coffee bar. Don't neglect to explore the alleys, which lead to more storefronts. You can easily stroll from one to the other while getting fresh air and stop for refreshment whenever you want to. Parking is heavily restricted, but if you go just one block away you can avoid the annoying necessity of moving your car before you get a ticket. The green is bounded by Broad, Park, Water and upper Whitfield Sts.

In Madison the shopping experience is similar, except that the shops are not located on the green but rather on two blocks or so of the Boston Post Rd. (Rte. 1) east of Rte. 79.

Fifty or so retailers are located at **Westbrook Factory Stores (860-399-8656),** a complex of outlets on **Rte. 153 right at I-95 exit 65 in Westbrook.** It proved so popular that **Clinton Crossing (860-664-0700),** a second outlet mall with a focus on "premium" brand names, was developed. Clinton Crossing is on **Rte. 81 about two-tenths of a mile north of I-84 exit 63.**

Wineries

A leader in this nascent Connecticut industry, **Chamard Vineyard (115 Cow Hill Rd., Clinton, 06413; 860-664-0299)** specializes in dry, European-style wines. Owner William Chaney is CEO of Tiffany & Co., and he takes an active role in running the vineyard. The beautiful tasting room enjoys an extremely scenic setting overlooking 20 acres planted with chardonnay, merlot, pinot noir and other grapes. It's open Wed.–Sat., 11:00 A.M.–4:00

P.M., year-round. Tours are also given during those hours as needed.

Where to Stay

Bed & Breakfasts

The relatively small number of B&Bs in this area range from fairly luxurious to somewhat utilitarian, and several choices are described below. Some other options include **Acorn B&B (628 Rte. 148, Killingworth, 06419; 860-663-2214),** the brand-new **Guilford Corners B&B (133 State St., Guilford, 06437; 203-453-4129), Honeysuckle Hill (116 Yankee Peddler Path, Madison, 06443; 203-245-4574)** and **Westbrook Inn (976 Boston Post Rd. [Rte. 1], Westbrook, 06498; 860-399-4777).**

Tidewater Inn—$$$ to $$$$
Three of the guest rooms at this beautifully kept B&B really stand out. The two on the ground floor feature fireplaces, and the very largest and most expensive room in the main house has a king bed, lots of space, exceptional furnishings, a refrigerator and a tub in the bathroom. The level of luxury in the other rooms varies, but all have private baths with shower, air-conditioning and TV, and some have a VCR. Guests also have the use of a refrigerator, iron and ironing board in a shared area. For total privacy, reserve the newly remodeled private cottage, which features a king suite, galley kitchen and Jacuzzi bath. A full breakfast is served in a sumptuous combination dining/sitting room. **949 Boston Post Rd. (Rte. 1), Madison, 06443; (203) 245-8457.**

Welcome Inn—$$$ to $$$$
This turn-of-the-century farmhouse B&B has been thoroughly modernized and furnished in a warm, homey manner. The decor is a combination of traditional and modern that includes both rustic furniture and wall-to-wall carpeting. For the sake of privacy only two of the three guest rooms are rented at any given time, unless all three are required by a large party. There's one shared primary bathroom, but a

second one is available in a pinch. Common areas include a large den with a working fireplace and a wooden deck and garden for warm-weather enjoyment. A full breakfast is included. Payment by cash or check only. **433 Essex Rd. (Rte. 153), Westbrook, 06498; (860) 399-2500.**

B&B at B—$$$

This B&B, located about two minutes by car from Guilford green, is in a modern raised ranch set back from the road. The owners live downstairs, giving guests in the two bedrooms the run of the entire upstairs. Enjoy ocean-swimming privileges at Jacobs Beach or use of an in-ground pool in the yard. Rates include a full breakfast. American Express is the only credit card accepted. **279 Boston St., Guilford, 06437; (203) 453-6490.**

Binder's Farm—$$$

Everything about this B&B, from its rambling layout to its country decor, spells farmhouse. Hosts Anna and Ed Binder raise garden and field vegetables, which they sell at the farm stand a few feet down from their driveway, and chickens kept out back provide fresh eggs for the table. The four guest rooms have queen or double beds and private baths. The arrangement of rooms and furniture is such that groups of three or parties that require separate beds in the same or adjoining rooms can be accommodated easily. A cozy music room serves as a common area for guests to get to know each other or the Binders. They serve a full breakfast in the morning. Payment by cash or check only. **593 Essex Rd. (Rte. 153), Westbrook, 06498; (860) 399-6407.**

Captain Dibbell House—$$$

A bargain for the price, Captain Dibbell House is one of the most appealing B&Bs around. Hosts Helen and Ellis Adams used to vacation in this area and liked it so much they finally moved here to establish the B&B. Any of the four airy, comfortable, lovely rooms with private baths in this 1866 Victorian will please. In warm weather you can enjoy a full breakfast in a gazebo with a view of flower gardens. You can even get breakfast in your room, a rarity at B&Bs. Guests have access to the town beach

on Long Island Sound. You'll appreciate lots of small touches and friendly attention, such as fresh flowers from their garden throughout the house, bathrobes in the rooms and afternoon and morning treats baked fresh by Ellis himself. Located half a block from the main street of Clinton on a quiet road. **21 Commerce St., Clinton, 06413; (860) 669-1646.**

Hotels, Motels & Inns

The Inn at Café Lafayette—$$$$

Positioning themselves squarely for luxury-minded and business travelers, the owners recently remodeled and have gone haute decor and high tech. There are five rooms, each with queen or king bed, private marble bathroom, cable TV, VCR, telephone with fax port, voice mailbox, meeting facilities and even business services such as secretarial support and audiovisual equipment. The linens, bathrobes and antique furnishings are decidedly European in style and feel. A fruit basket and Continental breakfast are included in the room rate, and room service is available from the fine restaurant downstairs. The inn is conveniently located right in the middle of the main shopping block of town. **725 Boston Post Rd. (Rte. 1), Madison, 06443; (800) 660-8984 or (203) 245-7773.**

Water's Edge Inn & Resort—$$$$

Water's Edge is a combination time-share condominium complex and vacation resort that is indeed right at the water's edge and large enough to be a small community of its own. For the traveler just passing through, there are several options: one- and two-bedroom villas (condominium units that can accommodate either four or six), hotel rooms with or without a water view and small suites. Facilities include an acclaimed restaurant, a lounge with live entertainment, tennis courts, indoor and outdoor swimming pools, a spa and fitness center and a small private beach on Long Island Sound. Weekly rates and package deals are available. **1525 Boston Post Rd. (Rte. 1), Westbrook, 06498; (800) 222-5901 or (860) 399-5901.**

289

Lower Connecticut River Valley

Guilford Suites Hotel—$$$ to $$$$
If you're looking for a nice, spacious place to stay and don't care about being on the water, this hotel could be one of the best choices around for a group of three or four people, especially midweek when rates are very reasonable. All the rooms are identical suites with a king bed, a convertible queen sofa in the living room, a kitchenette, TV and telephone. You won't find a swimming pool or any real amenities outside the rooms, but the hotel is comfortable and in excellent condition. **2300 Boston Post Rd. (Rte. 1), Guilford, 06437; (800) 626-8604 or (203) 453-0123.**

The Madison Beach Hotel—$$$ to $$$$
This is the type of hotel that you see in old photographs of summer people frolicking at the shore. It's long, tall and thin so all the rooms have a water view. It also has a covered porch with rockers facing out to sea. The accommodations are simple and uncomplicated, well suited to swimming, strolling and dozing. There are only a handful of places like this left in New England. It has fewer than three dozen rooms, a few of which are suites. Wicker and rattan furniture evokes the feel of Victorian-era seaside summer cottages. The windows of rooms on the first floor open directly onto the public porch, but rooms on upper floors have private balconies. There's a restaurant on the main floor and a private sandy beach right out the front door. Open Mar.–Dec. only. **94 West Wharf Rd., Madison, 06443; (203) 245-1404.**

Maples Motel—$$ to $$$$
Basic rooms at Maples Motel have twin, double and queen beds and are very moderate in price. There are also several two-bedroom, two-bathroom efficiency cottages available by the week (which accounts for the four dollar signs). The latter are very popular and booked for summer months in advance. The motel is about a five-minute walk from the beach. Guests have beach privileges and use of an outdoor pool at the motel. **1935 Boston Post Rd. (Rte. 1), Westbrook, 06498; (860) 399-9345.**

Dolly Madison Inn—$$$
This inn has a massively popular restaurant and bar on the ground floor, which is convenient for your own enjoyment but makes noise levels a bit high and parking tight. It's only a two-minute walk from the water, and guests have access to a town beach for swimming and sunbathing (a small returnable deposit is required to get the beach pass). Consider one of the half-dozen newly remodeled rooms in the main building. These are small but cute, with queen or twin beds and private baths. **73 West Wharf Rd., Madison, 06443; (203) 245-7377.**

Ramada Limited—$$$
Of the midpriced hotels in the area that are not on the water, the Ramada Limited is among the best. All the rooms have a king or two double beds. Minisuites have a double bed, convertible sofa/daybed and kitchenette with refrigerator and microwave. There's a small indoor pool, weight room and sauna for exercise and relaxation and a coin-op laundry. Its location is very convenient to I-95 exit 56. **3 Business Park Dr., Branford, 06405; (800) 950-4991 or (203) 488-4991.**

Motel 6—$$
This Motel 6 is one of the least expensive accommodation options in this area, and yet nicer than some of the hotels that charge more. It's set back from the road and perfectly adequate for anyone looking for a basic place to stay. For the safety-conscious, there are security doors that require a card key for entry. **320 E. Main St., Branford, 06405; (203) 483-5828.**

Camping

Hammonasset Beach State Park—$
The campground at Connecticut's largest shoreline state park has 560 sites. You won't find privacy here, but you will find a slew of facilities (a camp store, hot showers and flush toilets at most sites, and a dump station) plus family programs in an amphitheater at the edge of the campground and a comfortable atmosphere. Your kids will not have any prob-

lem finding playmates! The site is open and grassy with some juniper and scrub brush growing all around. A very small number of sites have shade trees. There's no additional charge for access to the beach, and Meig's Point Nature Center, located within the park, offers great kid's programs. The park and campground entrance are one and the same, located on **Rte. 1 in Madison.** Campground office: **(203) 245-1817.** Park office: **(203) 245-2785.**

Where to Eat

This area enjoys an abundance of fine eating establishments. Of special note is Branford green, an undiscovered jewel among mealtime destinations. There must be a dozen or more varied and worthwhile restaurants spanning a wide price spectrum in a stretch of a few blocks. Come early and stroll past them all to have a look. In addition to fine dining establishments, there are several pizza and ice cream parlors open late in summer, some with sidewalk seating. Give the kids (or yourself) a treat and stop in at **Branford Candy Shop (1036 Main St.; 203-488-6626)** before dinner (it probably won't be open after) or go earlier in the day and get an ice cream creation at the vintage soda fountain.

For quick and inexpensive meals and snacks, here are a few more suggestions. At breakfast or lunch, try the **Madison Coffee Shop (765 Boston Post Rd. [Rte. 1], Madison; 203-245-4474)** or the **Waiting Station (1048 Main St. on the green, Branford; 203-488-5176).** For any meal of the day, you can always head to **Parthenon Diner (374 E. Main St. [Rte. 1], Branford; 203-481-0333).**

You can get specialty coffees, teas and baked goods at **Willoughby's Coffee & Tea (752 Boston Post Rd. [Rte. 1], Madison; 203-245-1600), Madison Beanery (712 Boston Post Rd. [Rte. 1], Madison, 203-245-1323)** or **Common Grounds (1096 Main St. on the green, Branford; 203-488-2326). Cilantro Coffee Roasters (85**

Whitfield St. on the green, Guilford; 203-458-2555) also offers an appetizing array of breads, cheeses and prepared foods.

Le Petit Café—$$$$
Overlooking Branford green, this small, lively restaurant has been called one of the ten best bistros in Connecticut and defies most people's expectations of French restaurants. Although it is not inexpensive, there is a recognition that without good value patrons will not return. Plus, food here is not presented elaborately. Rather, it's served family-style and you help yourself, which keeps it hotter and encourages sharing. Dinner is a fixed-price ($21.50), four-course affair consisting of appetizer, soup, your choice of six or seven entrées (bistro classics such as beef Burgundy and chicken chasseur) and dessert. Hours: Wed.–Thu. from 6:00 P.M.; Sun. from 5:00 P.M.; on Fri. & Sat. there are two seatings at 6:00 P.M. & 8:30 P.M. Closed Mon. & Tue. **225 Montowese St., Branford, 06405; (203) 483-9791.**

Water's Edge—$$$ to $$$$
The restaurant at the resort of the same name is worth serious consideration even if you're not staying there. A beautiful main dining room with a soaring ceiling and a view of Long Island Sound through two-story windows is a lovely setting for any meal, and it serves all three. There's also a lounge and an informal terrace grill and bar during warm weather. The dinner menu is split between Mediterranean-inspired pastas, risotto and seafood and very American meat and poultry dishes. The Sun. brunch buffet is notable—pricey but truly a combination of two meals. Breakfast served Mon.–Fri., 7:00 A.M.–11:00 A.M.; Sat., 8:00 A.M.–11:00 A.M.; Sun., 8:00 A.M.–10:00 A.M. with brunch 10:00 A.M.–3:00 P.M. Lunch available Mon.–Sat., 11:30 A.M.–2:30 P.M. Dinner hours: 5:30 P.M.–9:00 P.M. (Fri.–Sat. until 10:00). **1525 Boston Post Rd. (Rte. 1), Westbrook, 06498; (860) 399-5901.**

The Bistro on the Green—$$$
The name of this informal bistro refers to Guilford green, over which it looks. It is truly a neighborhood restaurant, serving three meals a day, offering uncomplicated yet satisfying

291

fare ranging from crêpes and sandwiches to steak au poivre and Mediterranean-inspired pasta and chicken. The interior is cheery, cool and comfortable with about 15 tables. Hours: Mon.–Thu., 10:00 A.M.–9:00 P.M.; Fri. until 10:00 P.M.; Sat., 8:00 A.M.–10:00 P.M.; Sun., 8:00 A.M.–9:00 P.M.; closed Mon. & Tue. nights in winter. **25 Whitfield St. (Rte. 77; on the green), Guilford, 06437; (203) 458-9059.**

Café Bella Vita—$$$

This Northern Italian restaurant, located about a block east of Branford green, is a small and intimate place with low lighting and local art on the walls. It specializes in fish, pasta and Black Angus beef, sometimes prepared in a more health-conscious way than usual. Lunch served Mon.–Fri., 11:30 A.M.–2:30 P.M.; dinner Tue.–Sun. from 5:00 P.M. (winter) or 5:30 P.M. (summer) until 9:00-ish. **2 E. Main St., Branford, 06405; (203) 483-5639.**

Café Lafayette—$$$

This restaurant, located in the center of the main shopping block of Madison, was once a church, and if the tables on the porch are un-occupied in the middle of the afternoon it still looks like one. The menu is broad-based, with Continental and American elements, some-times mixed in one dish. Choices range from the simplicity of meatloaf (albeit no ordinary meatloaf, and topped with brie) to a sophisti-cated entrée version of the famous salade niçoise. The golden gazpacho was beautiful in the bowl and the only soup I've ever had whose texture could honestly be described as crisp. The café also serves Sun. brunch and offers evening entertainment: a pianist on Thu. and contemporary jazz on summer Sat., with no cover. Lunch/brunch hours: Tue.–Sat., 11:30 A.M.–2:30 P.M.; Sun. until 3:00 P.M. Dinner served Tue.–Thu. 5:30 P.M.–9:00 P.M.; Fri.–Sat. until 10:00. Bar menu available for half an hour after the kitchen closes & Sat. until 11:30 P.M. **725 Boston Post Rd. (Rte. 1), Madison, 06443; (203) 245-7773.**

Dolly Madison—$$$

This massively popular restaurant has a con-genial, tavernlike atmosphere and is an espe-cially nice place to dine if you want to go for a stroll down oceanside streets after eating. It's about half a block from the water in a pretty section of Madison. The bar is the liveliest spot in town and definitely a local gathering place. The menu is American, featuring pasta, prime rib and seafood. The baked stuffed shrimp is a specialty. Reservations are a must. Hours: Mon.–Thu., 11:30 A.M.–9:00 P.M.; Fri–Sat. until 10:00; Sun., 9:00 A.M.–8:30 P.M. with brunch available until 12:30 P.M. **73 W. Wharf Rd., Madison, 06443; (203) 245-7377.**

Friends & Co.—$$$

This popular restaurant has found success striking a balance between fine dining and family friendliness. A section of the menu con-sists of straightforward steak, pasta and chicken dishes. The health-conscious "pyra-mid dinners" are named in reference to the USDA's food pyramid and emphasize grains and vegetables over meats and fats. There is a kid's menu, and a vegetarian could get by here with relative ease. The interior is rather classy—like a wood-paneled parlor—and soft music plays on the sound system, elevating the dining experience a notch. Lunch hours: Tue.–Fri., noon–2:30 P.M.; Sun. brunch, 11:00 A.M.–2:30 P.M. Dinner hours: Mon.–Thu., 5:00 P.M.–10:00 P.M.; Fri.–Sat. until 11:00 P.M.; Sun., 4:30 P.M.–9:00 P.M. **11 Boston Post Rd. (Rte. 1 just east of the Guilford town line), Madi-son, 06443; (203) 245-0462.**

Sea Breeze—$$$

A few years back Sea Breeze started offering a promotional dinner special for two with wine for $24.24, and it was so successful they just kept doing it. You get a pair of one-and-a-quarter-pound lobsters along with a bottle of California cabernet, chardonnay or white zinfandel. It's been called the best lobster deal on the shore. Lobster is usually available all summer, but sometimes the spe-cial is prime rib, shrimp or another popular entrée, so call ahead if it matters. The rest of the menu has a general Mediterranean focus. Hours: noon–9:00 P.M. (Fri.–Sat. un-til 10:00) daily. **525 Boston Post Rd. (Rte. 1 just west of Rte. 146), Guilford, 06437; (203) 453-6715.**

Steamers—$$$

As you might guess from its name and its location at Guilford marina, the menu at Steamers has a definite focus on seafood. Windows encircling the restaurant yield good views of the marsh, water and boats, and there are 15 beers on tap. Smokers won't feel like second-class citizens here: a large enclosed porch serves as the smoking area. Hours: Mon.–Sat., 11:30 A.M.–10:00 P.M.; Sun., noon–10:00 P.M. **505 Whitfield St., Guilford, 06437; (203) 458-1757.**

The Wharf—$$$

From its name to its seaside location, everything about The Wharf (the in-house restaurant at The Madison Beach Hotel) spells seafood, prepared American-style, baked, broiled, fried and stuffed. Lobster, clam and oyster rolls and a seafood casserole are very popular. From the outdoor seating area upstairs, there are great views of the beach in front of the hotel. An enclosed dining room downstairs provides protection from the elements. Before or after your meal, go for a stroll on the hotel's private beach. Open Apr.–Nov. only. Hours: Mon.–Sat., 11:30 A.M.–10:00 P.M.; Sun., 10:30 A.M.–8:30 P.M., with brunch served 11:30 A.M.–2:30 P.M. **94 West Wharf Rd., Madison, 06443; (203) 245-1404.**

Darbar India—$$ to $$$

Darbar is a welcome complement to the abundance of bistros and seafood specialists on the coast. Vegetarians will be pleased to see a very broad range of choices, and Darbar features one thing you won't see on the menu at most Indian restaurants: a trio of Nepalese dishes, a reflection of the chef/owner's Nepalese heritage. The all-you-can-eat Fri.–Sun. lunch buffet for $7.95 is a great bargain. A quiet mood is set by a running fountain, Indian statuaries and a friendly waitstaff. Hours: 11:30 A.M.–2:45 P.M. daily for lunch; 5:00 P.M.–10:30 P.M. nightly for dinner. **1070 Main St., Branford, 06405; (203) 481-8994.**

Lenny & Joe's Fish Tale—$$ to $$$

Ask someone where to get seafood in this area, and the name Lenny & Joe's is sure to come up. Actually, it's two restaurants: a full-service, family-oriented place where you can get seafood baked, stuffed, broiled and fried (plus some steak and chicken for folks who don't eat fish) and a very casual drive-in BYOB spot selling mostly fried seafood supplemented by a lobster and steamer stand in summer. The latter is located very close to Hammonasset Beach and pulls in lots of families looking for somewhere you can eat without changing out of your swimsuit. Prices at both places are comparable and very moderate. Hours: 11:00 A.M.–9:00 P.M. (Fri.–Sat. until 10:00) daily; the drive-in closes a half hour earlier. The drive-in is at **1301 Boston Post Rd., Madison, 06433; (203) 245-7289.** The full-service restaurant is at **86 Boston Post Rd., Westbrook, 06433; (860) 669-0767.**

Noodles—$$ to $$$

The inland regions of central shore towns offer little in the way of dining options, but happily there are a few restaurants around like Noodles in North Madison, which is especially convenient if you've spent the day at Chatfield Hollow State Park. The specialty here is pastas (hence the name), most of which are available in both entrée and appetizer portions. There's also an "Un-Noodles" section of the menu with meats and fish, as well as casual fare such as fish 'n' chips and burgers. Daily specials are a strength, so check them out. Hours: dinner only from 5:00 P.M. until 9:00 P.M. during the week, 10:00 P.M. on Fri. & Sat. & 8:30 P.M. on Sun.; food served a half hour later in their lounge. Located in the mall at the **northwest corner of the junction of Rtes. 79 and 80 in North Madison; (203) 421-5606.**

Stony Creek Market—$$ to $$$

Stony Creek Market is a combination restaurant and bakery under one roof that has the best setting of any restaurant in the Guilford/Branford area. The view from the deck is picture-perfect: out into the water of the Sound with the Thimble Islands in the distance, small boats moored near shore and a cluster of houses hugging the coast. This west-facing deck is the place to be at sunset on a summer night, chowing down on Stony Creek's renowned pizza (available at dinner only).

Because they serve three meals a day, you can enjoy this beautiful spot in all its moods early and late. If you can afford the calories, indulge yourself with a sticky bun or something else from the bakery. Open Mon.–Fri., 6:00 A.M.–3:00 P.M. & Sat.–Sun., 8:00 A.M.–3:00 P.M. for breakfast & lunch. Dinner is served Tue.–Sun., 5:00 P.M.–9:00 P.M.; closed Mon. night. **178 Thimble Islands Rd., Branford, 06405; (203) 488-0145.**

Su Casa—$$ to $$$

Su Casa has won the Best Mexican countywide (New Haven) award in the annual *Connecticut* magazine readers' poll for nearly a decade now, testament to its popularity. The menu features both Tex-Mex and more "authentic" Mexican cuisine, plus daily specials. It's a sprawling, rustic place with several small dining rooms, two bars, stucco walls, tile floors, lots of wooden booths and Aztec and Mayan art on the walls. A guitarist plays anything from jazz to flamenco every night except Mon. starting as early as 6:30 P.M. Hours: Mon.–Thu., 11:30 A.M.–10:00 P.M.; Fri. until 11:00 P.M.; Sat., noon–11:00 P.M.; Sun., 4:00 P.M.–10:00 P.M. **400 E. Main St. (Rte. 1), Branford, 06405; (203) 481-5001.**

Anna's Temptations—$$

For a late breakfast pastry pick-me-up or a light lunch of soup, sandwich or salad, stop at this little bakery/restaurant/gift shop. You can also pick up deli salads by the pound or coffee from the self-serve bar. Seating is at cute Parisian café tables inside or on an outdoor brick patio in the rear, where there's also an herb garden for strolling. Hours: Mon.–Sat., 9:00 A.M.–5:00 P.M.; Sun., 10:00 A.M.–5:00 P.M. **1004 Boston Post Rd. (Rte. 1), Guilford, 06437; (203) 453-1046.**

Perfect Parties—$$

This self-described "not quite a restaurant" just a block from Madison's main drag features deli salads, prepared foods, noodles, sandwiches and soups for take-out or consumption at one of the small tables in the lively dining room. The format is very casual: you order at the counter and then have a seat. It also has a selection of good coffees (self-serve), fresh

breads, cheeses and extravagant desserts. Since many of the foods are prepared in advance, this is a good place to get something hearty and a little unusual for lunch or dinner without a long wait. Open Mon.–Sat., 8:00 A.M.–8:00 P.M.; Sun., 8:00 A.M.–6:00 P.M. **885 Boston Post Rd. (Rte. 1), Madison, 06443; (203) 245-0250.**

Shoreline Diner and Vegetarian Enclave—$$

Shoreline Diner's split-personality menu—standard diner fare as well as a dozen or so "creative vegetarian" selections—will allow both vegetarians and meat-eaters to coexist peacefully, and with two Culinary Institute of America graduates wearing chef's hats, you can expect very good quality food. Some offerings are vegan, including two desserts. Hours: 8:00 A.M.–11:00 P.M. daily. **345 Boston Post Rd. (Rte. 1), Guilford, 06437; (203) 458-7380.**

Judie's European Baked Goods—$

The "home of the handcrafted breads" is a specialty bakery that also does breakfast and lunch on weekends. Each day Judie, who started the business more than 20 years ago because of frustration with store-bought bread, turns out three to five unique types of loaves and several fine pastries. Breakfast features baked goods and items like French toast made with the bread, plus old-fashioned, slow-cooked oatmeal and omelettes. Lunch fare consists of hearty soups and sandwiches, and Judie will prepare custom picnic baskets too. If you get hooked, you'll be relieved to know she does mail order. Open Tue.–Sat., 7:00 A.M.–5:30 P.M.; Sun., 6:30 A.M.–1:30 P.M. **126 Shore Dr., Branford, 06405; (203) 488-2257.**

Services

Local Visitors Information

Connecticut River Valley and Shoreline Visitors Council, 393 Main St., Middletown, 06457; (800) 486-3346 or **(860) 347-0028.** Hours: Mon.–Fri., 8:30 A.M.–4:30 P.M., year-round.

There are small tourist information centers in Guilford, Madison and Clinton. The Guilford desk is located at the **Henry Whitfield State Museum** at **248 Old Whitfield St.; (203) 453-2457.** Information is available during the museum hours given in the listing under Major Attractions.

Madison's office is in a tiny building called the Powderhouse next to the old town hall at the light at the eastern end of the green. The petite structure looks like an addition to the town hall but is actually a separate one-story building. Someone is usually there to help visitors 9:00 A.M.–3:00 P.M. on summer weekends. For more information call **(203) 245-5659.**

In Clinton you can get travel information at the **1630 House on E. Main St. (Rte. 1)** directly opposite the police station. Call **(860) 669-8500** for hours. The State Welcome Center is located off I-95 northbound between exits 65 and 66; **(860) 399-8122.** This free rest area has shaded picnic tables and grills, rest rooms and a visitors information center. Information is available 8:00 A.M.–6:00 P.M. daily, Memorial Day–Oct. 31.

Transportation

Shore Line East Commuter Rail offers Mon.–Fri. (except major holidays) service along the shore between New Haven and New London, with stops in Branford, Guilford, Madison, Clinton, Westbrook and Old Saybrook. For fare and schedule information call **(800) 255-7433.**

Old Saybrook/ Old Lyme

The stretch of the lower Connecticut River valley from Haddam and East Haddam to Old Saybrook and Old Lyme represents the pinnacle of natural beauty where mountain, river and saltwater join. Elsewhere rivers of this proportion (the Connecticut is the largest in New England) have become heavily urbanized and industrialized, but the river that lent the state its name was saved from despoilment by a sandbar at its mouth that limits its usability. Make an effort to experience the river firsthand in some way. A wide variety of cruises are available, and the Connecticut River Museum in Essex is the place to go if you want to know more about its history.

Art galleries are scattered informally up and down the valley, but the undisputed center of the scene is Old Lyme, the site of a turn-of-the-20th-century Impressionist art colony that is remembered at the Florence Griswold Museum. That museum, the Lyme Art Association, the Lyme Academy of Fine Arts and two fine inn/restaurants are all within one block's walk.

Gillette Castle is the valley's principal landmark, a stone mansion built between 1914 and 1918 as the private home of William Gillette, a noted stage actor. It is now one of Connecticut's most frequented state parks. A visit is memorable for the curiosities of the mansion itself, the breathtaking views from its hilltop perch and the details of Gillette's extraordinary life.

Excursions take two forms: by water and land—and you can even combine the two. By water the choices range from small and large riverboats on the Connecticut to schooners on Long Island Sound, plus the river and shoreline are lined with marinas if you'll be bringing your own. By land there's the Valley Railroad.

Formerly a full-fledged passenger and freight line, it now makes sightseeing runs up the west side of the valley. You can ride the rails from Essex to Deep River and then connect to a riverboat on a combined ticket.

The area has many excellent restaurants offering everything from dockside family dining to fine French cuisine to traditional American fare in one of the state's oldest inns. Going hand-in-hand with these culinary riches are several outstanding theaters. The historic Goodspeed Opera House is a late-19th-century architectural gem that has built a reputation as a theater where Broadway hits are both born and revisited. No less enjoyable are Ivoryton Playhouse and the Norma Terris Theatre (a.k.a. Goodspeed-at-Chester).

Other highlights include hiking and swimming; special celebrations, such as the Deep River Ancient Muster and the Quinnehtukqut Festival; scenic drives; luxury spa experiences and the most unique camping spots in the state—on islands out in the middle of the Connecticut River.

History

The traditional inhabitants of what is now Old Saybrook were Nehantic Indians who, it is believed, were subjugated by the Pequots around the year 1600. The first English appeared on the scene when, in the early 1630s, a group of wealthy "lords and gentlemen" obtained royal permission to settle in the area. They were seeking a place to which they might repair in case their efforts at bringing about a Puritan revolution in England turned sour. They sent ahead a small army, money and a governor (John Winthrop, Jr.) to act on their behalf in establishing their new colony. They also sent an English soldier by the name of Lion Gardiner to construct a fort for them.

The Dutch had been the first Europeans to explore the area when Adriaen Block sailed past Saybrook Point on his famed journey up the Connecticut River in 1614. In 1633 the Dutch bought land from the Indians and built a trading post or fort near Saybrook Point but neglected to establish a permanent settlement. The English ignored their claim, and an armed contingent of the Winthrop party took possession of the area in Nov. 1635. From the fort Gardiner constructed, the English were able to repulse the Dutch and the Pequots, who tried to retake the land.

Saybrook was at first a colony completely independent of Connecticut Colony, centered up the river at Hartford. In 1644, when it became evident that the lords on whose behalf Saybrook had been settled would not be coming to the New World, Saybrook was sold to Connecticut Colony and was thereafter administered from Hartford. In 1647 the fort Lion Gardiner had built burned, and a pale shadow of it was constructed at the current site of Fort Saybrook Monument Park, where a series of plaques gives a detailed history of the town's earliest days. No trace of either fort remains.

Shipbuilding was a natural industry for the area. It was established as early as 1648 and remained viable until 1900 or so. The *Oliver Cromwell*, Connecticut's first warship, was built in Essex and launched in 1776. At one time there were more than 50 shipyards on the Connecticut River between Saybrook and Springfield, Massachusetts. That Essex is the pleasure boating capital of the state is evidence of this heritage.

In 1701 Saybrook was made the official location of the Collegiate School, later to become Yale University. Classes were held in Clinton at first, that being the residence of the first instructor, Abraham Pierson. Classes were held in Old Saybrook beginning in 1707, and commencements were always held there, but in 1716 the college (with resistance on the part of locals) was moved to New Haven.

Despite many threats, the British did little damage to the area during the Revolutionary War. The War of 1812 was somewhat different, however. The British sailed up to Essex in Apr. 1814, set fire to all the anchored ships and then cut them loose in flames. To this day a quirky festival is held in town commemorating the event.

In the 1800s small mills were built on the Pattaconk River in Chester, Deep River in Deep River and Falls River in Essex. Auger bits,

crochet needles, buttonhooks, brushes, ivory combs, ivory piano keys and stop knobs for organs were made in these towns. Three-fourths of the ivory exported from Zanzibar in 1884 is said to have been shipped to Deep River and Ivoryton where Pratt, Reed & Co. and Comstock & Cheney Co. were the two big manufacturers.

In 1867, just a year after William H. Goodspeed began construction of the opera house that bears his name, Valley Railroad was chartered, built in part because ice on the Connecticut River in winter made transportation by water difficult. When the line ran all the way from Hartford to the Fenwick portion of

The Florence Griswold Museum, Old Lyme, was the site of a 19th-century Impressionist art colony. Photo by William Hubbell/Florence Griswold Museum.

Old Saybrook, it had more miles of trestle (3) than any other line in the state. It passed over long stretches of water at several spots, including North and South Coves in Old Saybrook. Valley Railroad was in regular operation until 1968, after which it became the scenic line it is today.

Also in the late 1800s a trio of sisters and their mother who ran a boardinghouse in Old Lyme began attracting a regular crowd of resident artists each summer. The painters were of the Barbizon and Impressionist schools, and they came in such numbers that Old Lyme gained a reputation as an art colony. The Florence Griswold Museum in Old Lyme, which documents that period, is named for the daughter most responsible for succoring the colony and is located in the very boardinghouse the Griswolds ran. Perhaps the arts had even deeper roots in the area, because one Phoebe Griffin Noyes (b. 1797) is said to have started one of the first art schools in the country in Old Lyme, operating out of her home. She was herself a noted painter of miniatures, and her relative William Noyes built the home in which the Griswolds later entertained their artist friends and customers. Although, of course, there has been a lot of development in the 20th century, much of the lower Connecticut River Valley is now as it was then—dominated by salt marsh, riverbank and shoreline, and a constant inspiration for the appreciative mind.

Major Attractions

Florence Griswold Museum

There is something at the Florence Griswold Museum to satisfy lovers of art, architecture and history. In fact, they refer to themselves as an art *and* history museum. The setting is a late-Georgian mansion where Florence Griswold, daughter of an affluent sea captain, opened her home to board some of the scores of artists that flocked to the Connecticut shore each summer around the turn of the 20th century to paint. For decades her house and hospitality played an important role in the development of American art. Guided tours of the house cover its history, Griswold's life and the personalities and work of the artists who boarded with her. Wonderful period paintings hang in the museum downstairs, and the upstairs has been converted into galleries for contemporary work. Also on-site is the studio of Impressionist painter William Chadwick, set up as it was during his lifetime. The museum gift shop and perennial gardens on the grounds are both exceptional. Admission: $4 adults, $3 seniors and students, children under 12 free. Summer (June–Oct.) hours: Tue.–Sat., 10:00 A.M.–5:00 P.M.; Sun, 1:00 P.M.–5:00 P.M. Winter (Nov.–May) hours: Wed.–Sun., 1:00 P.M.–5:00 P.M. **96 Lyme St., Old Lyme, 06371; (860) 434-5542.**

Gillette Castle State Park

Looking at the massive fieldstone structure that is the main attraction at this unusual state park, you can't help but think to yourself that its builder, actor William Gillette, really took to heart the old saying, "A man's home is his castle." Gillette was a Hartford native best known for his stage portrayals of Sherlock Holmes in the early 1900s. Gillette designed the castle and all of its interior details himself, supposedly taking inspiration from an 11th-century Norman fortress. It took five years and half a million dollars to complete.

The house is full of marvelous innovations and decorative as well as functional details.

When Gillette was living there, a narrow-gauge railway ran between the house and the ferry at the river below on 3 miles of track. Gillette and his guests actually used the train for transportation. Presentations by staff are given every quarter hour, after which you can wander at will, but the talk will add to your experience immeasurably. In addition to the house, there are several miles of winding trails. Horses and carriages for hire on the grounds will take you on a leisurely ride through the grounds. A picnic area, concession stand, rest rooms and gift shop round out the facilities. Castle admission: $4 adults, $2 children 6–11; admission to the grounds is free. Castle hours: 10:00 A.M.–5:00 P.M., daily, Memorial Day–Columbus Day; weekends only Columbus Day–the fourth weekend after Thanksgiving. Park hours: 8:00 A.M.–dusk daily, year-round. **67 River Rd. in East Haddam; (860) 526-2336.**

Goodspeed Opera House

Perched precipitously on a cliff overlooking a particularly beautiful stretch of the Connecticut River, the Goodspeed Opera House looks like it could be made from frosting and candy fluff. It was built by theater lover and businessman William Henry Goodspeed, who made a fortune in finance and shipping. Its first run, from 1876 until the early 1900s, had a steamboat terminal to accommodate both talent and patrons who came up the river from New York. After Goodspeed's death the opera house did not receive much attention, and it eventually closed. It was almost demolished in the late 1950s, but thankfully local preservationists saved and restored the magnificent structure.

Since its reopening in 1963, it has served as the showcase for revivals of old musicals as well as a testing ground for new ones. *Annie, Man of La Mancha* and *Shenandoah* all premiered here before going on to Broadway. Currently three shows are staged each year between Apr. and Dec. Evening/twilight performances are Wed., Thu., Fri. at 8:00 P.M., Sat. at 4:00 P.M. & 9:00 P.M. & Sun. at 6:30 P.M. Matinees are given Wed. at 2:30 P.M. & Sun. at 2:00 P.M. There's also one audience discussion session with the cast of each of the season's three musicals on selected dates; inquire for details. The Gelston House next door is the ideal place for a before- or after-show meal, and season ticket/dining packages are available. Half-hour tours ($2 adults, $1 children 6–11) highlighting the architecture and interior design of the

Old Saybrook on the shore is about an hour from Hartford by car. The fastest way there is via I-91 south to Rte. 9 south, which ends at I-95 in Old Saybrook. Rte. 9 runs down the west side of the river, and secondary highways run into the villages of Haddam, Chester, Deep River and Essex. The east side of the river is considerably quieter, with no highway like Rte. 9. There are year-round river crossings at Rte. 82 between Haddam and East Haddam and I-95 between Old Saybrook and Old Lyme. A seasonal ferry completes Rte. 148 between Chester and Hadlyme.

See a play before it gets to Broadway at the Goodspeed Opera House, East Haddam.

opera house are given as needed Sat., 11:00 A.M.–1:30 P.M., & Mon., 1:00 P.M.–3:00 P.M. **6 Main St. (Rte. 82), East Haddam, 06423; (860) 873-8668.**

Valley Railroad/Essex Steam Train

Valley Railroad, built in part because there was a need for reliable transportation up and down the Connecticut River Valley when the river froze over in winter, began operation in 1871. It carried freight and passengers along the corridor from Hartford to Old Saybrook for nearly a century, but now the olive green and gray cars have an easier job: carrying vacationers on a scenic 12-mile round-trip upriver from Essex. At the far end you can board a riverboat for an excursion up the Connecticut River as far as the Goodspeed Opera House in East Haddam, returning the way you came. The train-only trip is just over an hour, and the train/boat trip is two and a half hours. For information on the North Cove Express dinner train, see the listing under Where to Eat. Fares: $15 adults, $7.50 children 3–11 for train and boat; $10 adults, $5 children 3–11 years for train only. For a few dollars more you can ride in the parlor car. Season: Memorial Day–late Oct. & late Nov.–late Dec. Trains run Wed.–Sun. in spring and fall, daily in summer, Fri.–Sun. in Dec. Call for the schedule, and arrive 30 min. before departure. The depot is **on Rte. 154 a quarter-mile west of Rte. 9 in Essex; (800) 348-0003 or (860) 767-0103.**

Other Attractions

Sundial Herb Garden

Sundial offers wonderful experiences for tea or garden lovers. Proprietors Tom Goddard and Ragna Tischler Goddard are husband-and-wife connoisseurs who hope to both educate and delight their visitors on the subject of tea. She makes the tea presentation, and he is the pastry chef whose creations complement the beverages. The schedule of Sun. afternoon

teas, given Apr.–Sept., becomes available in early spring. Reservations are essential. Appropriate dress is expected, and on-time arrival is important. Teas take about two and a half hours. Before or after you'll want to peruse the Goddard's shop where they sell imported teas, high-quality tea accoutrements, books, foods and herbal products.

The garden at Sundial is an attraction in and of itself. It has taken the Goddards 20 years to build this lovely series of interrelated formal gardens inspired by 17th- and 18th-century gardening principles. They incorporate knots, topiary, avenues, boxwood-lined parterres and statuary, all on a reduced scale appropriate to that of their nearby home. You may take a self-guided tour of the garden for $1.

Finally, the Goddards give in-depth Sat. seminars (Feb.–Apr.) on topics ranging from fine foods, medicinal herbs and gardening to, of course, tea. Inquire in Jan. for the schedule. Shop and grounds hours: Sat.–Sun., 10:00 A.M.–5:00 P.M., year-round; closed the last two weeks of Oct. & major holidays. **Brault Hill Rd., Higganum, 06441; (860) 345-4290.**

Festivals and Events

The lower Connecticut River Valley is rich in annual events that attract large crowds. In addition to the ones described below, Old Saybrook hosts a Boat Show on Father's Day weekend in mid-June with all the latest craft, accessories and services; a Taste of Saybrook festival in mid-July featuring the culinary expertise of more than a dozen local restaurateurs and an arts and crafts show the last weekend of July that draws 100 artists, 100 crafters and 25,000 visitors to Old Saybrook green. For information call the **Old Saybrook Chamber of Commerce** at **(860) 388-3266.**

Old Lyme has its share of festivities too. Highlights of the annual **Midsummer Festival** held all along Lyme St. include a free outdoor pops concert, a petting zoo, art shows, children's games and storytelling. For more information call the **Florence Griswold Museum** at **(860) 434-5542.**

Essex has so many wacky parades you wonder how the residents have time for anything else. It starts early with a Groundhog Day Parade (held on Feb. 2 if it falls on a weekend, otherwise the Sun. following) involving a fiberglass rodent named Essex Ed who stands in for the real critter. The Burning of the Ships Parade in early May commemorates an attack during the War of 1812 in which enemy British troops set boats afire and sent them downriver. There's also a shad bake the first Sat. in June, a clambake the first Sat. in Aug. and a Halloween Parade. The Essex town clerk **(860-767-4344)** should be able to provide information on these events. Finally, the Hot Steamed Jazz Festival, similar to but smaller than The Great Connecticut Traditional Jazz Festival described below, is held the third weekend of June at Valley Railroad in Essex. For more information call **(800) 348-0003** or **(860) 767-0103**.

National Theater for the Deaf Storytelling Series
Sun. in June

The National Theater for the Deaf is a touring company based in Chester. The company spends many months of the year on the road, but June is always devoted to performances for the hometown crowd. Each Sun. people gather on Chester's town green to enjoy a family-oriented story that is both told aloud and signed for the hearing impaired. Spread a blanket under the shade trees, bring a picnic lunch and prepare to be entertained. Performances start at 1:00 P.M. and last about one hour. Even if it rains you won't be disappointed—the whole production moves into a meetinghouse nearby. Located on **Chester's Meetinghouse Green, Goose Hill Rd., Chester, 06412; (860) 526-4971** or **(860) 526-4974 (TTY)**.

Deep River Ancient Muster
third Sat. in July

Two centuries ago the sound of fifers and drummers setting the pace for militia drills

rang out every week over every town green in Connecticut, and this colonial musical heritage is still celebrated in a number of annual musters. A muster is a "gathering of the troops"—a parade of costumed fife and drum corps after which each participating company plays a brief, five- to ten-minute concert, followed by other activities and demonstrations. The "ancient" in the name refers to a regional style of fifing and drumming that remained popular in New England after largely having died out elsewhere.

The event in Deep River is the largest annual muster in Connecticut, drawing 60–80 corps and perhaps 8,000 spectators in recent years. If you come, plan to arrive in Deep River at least an hour and a half before the parade's start time (noon), because streets along the parade route are cordoned off late in the morning. The parade begins at the corner of Main and Kirkland Sts. and ends 1 mile later at Devitt Field on the the corner of Main and Southworth Sts., where postparade activities take place. Expect to pay about $5 for parking; viewing the parade is free.

301

The Great Connecticut Traditional Jazz Festival
first full weekend in Aug. (Fri.–Sun.)

Over a dozen bands playing Dixieland, blues and ragtime keep crowds enthralled at this annual three-day music fest on the grounds of Sunrise Resort in Moodus. There are five stages and five dance floors, all covered so the event is on rain or shine. You can also take part in a Saturday Morning Jazz Breakfast Cruise on the Connecticut River and a nondenominational Sun. morning gospel hour (arrive early, because it always fills up). Ticket prices are $20 per session or $64 for a three-day pass. Bring a usable musical instrument (no junk or marginal items, and horns are a priority) for free admission. Sessions run Fri., 6:00 P.M.–1:00 A.M.; Sat., noon–6:00 P.M. or 7:00 P.M.–1:00 A.M.; Sun., 9:30 A.M.–5:00 P.M. Sunrise Resort is on **Rte. 151, 1 mile northwest of Rte. 149 in Moodus.** For more information call **(800) 468-3836** or **(203) 483-9343**.

At the Quinnehtukqut Festival in Haddam, a participant in regalia does the Navajo hoop dance.

Quinnehtukqut Festival
third full weekend in Aug. (Fri.–Sun.)

Billed as a "Rendezvous and Native American Festival," half of this split-personality event is devoted to Native American dance, singing and crafts and the other half to a colonial encampment. The Native American half of the celebration includes a Grand Entry (a parade of dancers and musicians in regalia) each day, dance and drum competitions, storytelling, lots of food vendors and arts and crafts tents. This is an intertribal event with participants from across the United States and Canada.

The rendezvous portion of the Quinnehtukqut Festival is a pleasantly low-key event in which participants engage in colonial role playing. They dress in pre-1840s clothes, set up camp, cook over open fires and answer questions from onlookers. They may sell handmade items ranging from baubles to leather work or wooden toys. You might see a muzzle-loading rifle shooting competition or hear period songs performed on period acoustic instruments. Admission: $8 adults, $6 seniors, $4 children 6–12. Hours: Fri., noon–8:00 P.M.; Sat., 9:00 A.M.–8:00 P.M.; Sun., 9:00 A.M.–6:00 P.M. The festival takes place in a large, flat, grass-covered field (Haddam Meadows State Park on Rte. 154 in Haddam), so wear appropriate footwear. Parking is in an adjacent field. For more information call **(860) 282-1404** or **(800) 486-3346.**

Chester Fair
fourth weekend in Aug. (Fri.–Sun.)

In recent years Chester's annual agricultural fair has really expanded in the area of children's activities, making it especially appealing to families with youngsters. A series of old-fashioned games and contests is held in the early afternoon on Sat. and Sun. There's no advance registration and no additional charge for your child to take part in three-legged races, finger painting and other fun. Of course, these are in addition to farm displays and livestock shows, a midway and other entertainment. Admission: $5 adults, $3 seniors, children under 12 free. Hours: Fri., 6:00 P.M.–11:00 P.M.; Sat., 8:00 A.M.–11:00 P.M.; Sun., 8:00 A.M.–9:00 P.M. Parking is on-site and free. Chester Fairground is on **Rte. 154 a quarter-mile north of Rte. 148 in Chester.** For more information call **(860) 526-5947.**

Haddam Neck Fair
Labor Day weekend (Sat.–Mon.)

What better way to say good-bye to summer than at a country fair? This one features one of the best horse pulls in the Northeast. Another highlight is a Mon. afternoon baby contest in three age categories between 0 and 18 months. Prizes are awarded for both boys and girls in all categories, including prettiest, chubbiest and best personality. For older kids, Mon. is Children's Day, with contests and fun activities. Be sure to stop in at the Haddam Neck Products booth to see what local entrepreneurs are selling. Admission: $4 adults, children under 12 free. On-site parking is free. Hours: Sat., 9:00 A.M.–10:00 P.M.; Sun., 7:30 A.M.–10:00 P.M.; Mon., 7:30 A.M.–6:00 P.M. Haddam Neck Fairground is on **Quarry Hill Rd. off Haddam Neck Rd. in Haddam on the east side of the Connecticut River.** For more information call **(860) 267-4671.**

Traditional Vessels Weekend
mid-Sept. (Fri.–Sun.)

See more than 30 boats of wooden construction or traditional design at this annual maritime festival at the Connecticut River Museum. On Fri. evening during a welcoming cocktail party some of the boats may be available for boarding. The big event on Sat. is races. Small boats compete off the dock at the festival site, and the Governor's Cup Regatta for big sailboats takes place on Long Island Sound. Inquire about a spectator boat to watch the latter. All the participating boats take part in a Sun. parade. Other highlights of the weekend include an auction of marine items, period music, dancing, a clambake and a barbeque. Admission may be charged. The museum is at **Steamboat Dock at the bottom of Main St. in Essex.** Museum hours are 10:00 A.M.–5:00 P.M., but the festival has its own schedule. For more information call **(860) 767-8269.**

Saybrook Stroll and Torchlight Parade
early Dec.

These two holiday events take advantage of Old Saybrook's old-fashioned, broad Main St. The Saybrook Stroll is principally a merchant's Christmas open house. The town decorates the street, and shopkeepers decorate their stores and stay open until 9:00 P.M. on the first Fri. in Dec. Santa and Mrs. Claus receive young visitors in the lobby of a local bank, and there are hayrides, caroling, jazz bands and a slew of activities.

In the Torchlight Parade more than 30 uniformed fife and drum corps, flanked by torchbearers, parade down Main St. while spectators carrying makeshift "torches" of their own—flashlights, lanterns, lighters—fall in behind and follow them to the site of a Christmas carol sing that goes on through the evening. It takes place the second Sat. in Dec. beginning at 6:00 P.M. For more information call **(860) 395-3123.**

Essex Christmas Festivities
throughout Dec.

The event known as Trees in the Rigging and the Santa Parade, the biggest of many Christmas fetes in Essex, begins with a caroling procession starting at town hall and ending at Steamboat Dock with several stops in between. The date varies, but it's usually the second Sun. in Dec. around 4:00 P.M. Come early to visit the Connecticut River Museum at Steamboat Dock, where the annual holiday show always involves model trains. Other activities during the month include a tree lighting and a Tea Time in Essex Village event around the 15th. For more information on any of them call **(860) 767-4348.**

Outdoor Activities

Biking

Mountain Biking

Cockaponset State Forest is a hilly, wooded tract with both paved roads suitable for any type of bike and gravel roads where you'll need a mountain bike. When you've worked up a sweat and need to cool off, ride over to Pattaconk Reservoir for a swim in a mountain lake. Stick to the roads and trails blazed any color but blue. Enter via Cedar Lake Rd. off Rte. 148 in Haddam and park at the reservoir. Hours: 8:00 A.M.–dusk daily, year-round. Park office: **(860) 345-8521.**

Biking is also allowed on the rather poor park roads and on woods roads at **Nehantic State Forest,** but not on the blue-blazed Nayantaquit Trail. For more information, see the listing under Hiking.

Road Biking

There are great opportunities for road biking in the lower Connecticut River Valley and along the shore at the mouth of the river, but there are also some congested areas to be avoided. In general, roads on the east side of the river carry less traffic than those on the west side.

303

Lower Connecticut River Valley

All the back streets of Lyme and Old Lyme are quite pretty and very suitable for biking. The further north you go the quieter and hillier it gets.

A counterclockwise loop that will show you a good bit of the valley without exposing you to too much auto traffic is formed by Rte. 154 on the west side of the river, Rte. 148 crossing the river via ferry at the southern end, River Rd. (which passes Gillette Castle State Park), Town St. up the east side of the river and Rte. 82 past Goodspeed Opera House and over the river on a historic swing bridge. Gillette Castle would make a good starting point, since you can park there for free and the climb back up to the parking lot from the river will be the last thing you do.

The Cornfield Pt. and Saybrook Pt. areas of Old Saybrook are also beautiful places to ride where you can plan a route past several attractions and there are plenty of places to stop for refreshment. Bikes can cross the Connecticut River on the Baldwin Bridge (I-95) between Old Saybrook and Old Lyme, on the Rte. 82 bridge between Haddam and East Haddam and on the ferry at Rte. 148 between Chester and Hadlyme.

Boating

Freshwater

Connecticut River

In the area above the mouth of the river there are two state boat launches that see heavy use in summer. One is located off Rte. 149 about 1.5 miles north of the village of East Haddam where the Salmon River joins the Connecticut. The other is at Haddam Meadows State Park off Rte. 154 in Haddam. A fee is charged at both.

A car-top launch is located at the small picnic area north of Rte. 148 on the east side of the river right where the Chester-Hadlyme ferry departs. If you don't have your own canoe, you can rent from **North American Canoe Company (860-739-0791),** Memorial Day–Labor Day. They have a four-canoe minimum, but they deliver right to this spot. Reservations required.

If you plan to explore the lower Connecticut River by canoe or kayak, contact **The Nature Conservancy (55 High St., Middletown, 06457; 860-344-0716)** to request their "Tidelands of the Connecticut River" brochure, which describes several excursions. Note that primitive campsites are available on the river; see the Camping section for details.

Pattaconk Reservoir

Although the beach is crowded on summer weekends, this is still one of the nicest spots around to launch a car-top boat. Motorboats are allowed, but internal combustion engines are forbidden in July and Aug., and there's an 8 m.p.h. speed limit. Enter from Cedar Lake Rd. off Rte. 148 in Chester.

Uncas Pond/Norwich Pond

Uncas and Norwich Ponds are two exceptionally lovely bodies of water in Nehantic State Forest, where the surrounding land is still wild and undeveloped. Motors are prohibited on both lakes, making them ideal for exploration by canoe or rowboat. Access is via Keeney Rd. off Rte. 156 in Lyme. There is no road sign here; just turn at the sign for Nehantic State Forest. You'll come to Uncas Pond first, where there's a small, unguarded beach and a picnic area. There are no picnicking or swimming facilities at smaller Norwich Pond.

Other Lakes and Ponds

There are several options for boating on both sides of the Connecticut River. Motorboaters will probably want to head for **Gardner Lake, Moodus Reservoir** or **Rogers Lake,** all of which are on the east side of the valley. Gardner, the largest freshwater body in this region, is located inland in Salem on the Montville line. There's a state boat launch on Rte. 354 just northwest of Rte. 82 that can be quite crowded. Moodus Reservoir's upper and lower halves in East Haddam are friendly to motor boaters and water-skiers yet still good for canoeing and fishing. Both have state boat launches. Access to the upper portion is directly off Haddam-Colchester Tpke., the road that splits the reservoir in two. Access to the lower portion is on Launching Area Rd. Rogers Lake, shared by Lyme and Old Lyme, has a

Old Saybrook/Old Lyme

public boat launch with toilets and a large gravel lot with plenty of easy parking and room to maneuver. Engines are limited to 135 HP and speeds to 6 m.p.h. until 10:00 A.M.; check the *Connecticut Boater's Guide* for other regulations. The access area on Grassy Hill Rd. is well labeled.

Lake Hayward in East Haddam is 189 acres and has a developed shoreline, but internal combustion engines are forbidden. There's a public boat launch at the top of the lake off Lake Hayward Rd.

There are fewer boating choices on the west side of the Connecticut River, but **Cedar Lake**'s beauty amply makes up for that limitation. It has a largely undeveloped shoreline except for a public beach on the southern end. Motors are allowed, but there's a 6 m.p.h. speed limit. Access the state boat launch via Cedar Lake Rd. off Rte. 148 in Chester.

One final choice is tiny (32 acres), tall and narrow **Higganum Reservoir** in Haddam. There's a car-top launch with access from Rte. 81.

Saltwater

There are three state launches from which you can access Long Island Sound. One is at the mouth of the Four Mile River opposite Rocky Neck State Park. Take Rte. 156 to Oakridge Dr. in Old Lyme, take the first right and follow it to the ramp at the end. On the other side of town there's a public launch at the end of Smith Neck Rd. The third one is on Ferry Rd. in Old Saybrook under Baldwin Bridge where I-95 crosses the mouth of the Connecticut River. A fee is charged at the latter two spots in summer. For canoe and small craft rental in the lower valley call Saybrook Marine Service at **(860) 388-3614.**

Cruises

African Queen

Yes, this is the boat in which Katharine Hepburn rode in the 1951 movie of the same name. The 30-foot steam launch is captained by Jim Hendricks, who gives sightseeing rides to the mouth of the Connecticut River in Old Saybrook July–Labor Day. Hendricks narrates

the tour with background about the boat and the movie. Fare: $15, half-price for children under 12. Hendricks will also offer half-hour trips on *The Thayer*, the 22-foot mahogany runabout used by Henry Fonda in *On Golden Pond*. Departing Saybrook Pt. near the Saybrook Point Inn & Spa on the hour, 10:00 A.M.–4:00 or 5:00 P.M., Tue.–Sun. For more information call **(860) 395-2125.**

Camelot Cruises

The biggest cruise operator on the Connecticut River offers trips on which you can enjoy Sun. brunch, Dixieland jazz, a murder mystery, fall foliage, banjo music or rock 'n' roll oldies entertainment. Departure times and prices vary, with fares ranging from $15 to $50 and trip time ranging from two hours to all day. They also do full-day vacation cruises to Sag Harbor and Greenport Village, Long Island. Reservations suggested. **One Marine Park** (directly opposite the Connecticut River from Goodspeed Opera House), **Haddam, 06438; (860) 345-8591.**

Eagle Watch

The season for eagle watching on the Connecticut River is Feb.–mid-Mar. A boat departs Dock and Dine restaurant on Saybrook Pt. Sun. at 9 A.M., returning at noon. The fare is $25 adults, $21 seniors, $15 children under 12, free for children under 4. Dress warmly. For more information call **(860) 443-7259.**

Riverboat Cruises

Deep River Navigation Company offers cruises on small riverboats up and down the Connecticut River from Hartford to Old Saybrook. (For information on departures from **Hartford** and **Middletown,** see those chapters.) Locally they operate the Silver Star out of Essex for eagle watch cruises on Sat., mid-Jan.–Feb., at 10:00 A.M. Once a year, on Sat. of Memorial Day weekend, they do a full-day 50-mile cruise from Essex upriver to Hartford. Fares are in the $20–$25 range, half-price for children 3–11 and discounted for seniors. These both leave from the dock at the Connecticut River Museum at the bottom of Main St. There is no designated parking lot; park wherever you can in Essex.

Lower Connecticut River Valley

They also offer cruises out of Saybrook Pt. next to the Dock and Dine restaurant, late June–Labor Day. These run daily, leaving at noon for a two-hour run up the Connecticut River to Essex, at 2:30 P.M. for two hours in Long Island Sound and at 5:00 and 6:00 P.M. for one-hour trips to the Outer Lighthouse. Fares are in the $6–$10 range with the same discounts as noted above. Free parking is available in a large lot by the restaurant. For more information call **(860) 526-4954.**

Schooner, Inc.

The home port of the 91-foot replica schooner *Quinnipiack* is New Haven's Long Wharf, but on occasion it sails out of Saybrook Pt. in Old Saybrook and the Connecticut River Museum in Essex on both educational and sunset cruises. For more information, see the listing under the **New Haven** chapter.

Marinas

An abundance of marinas serve the lower Connecticut River Valley, with the greatest concentration by far on the west bank. Moving north from the lighthouses at Lynde Pt. in the Fenwick section of Old Saybrook, the first facilities you'll come to are at Saybrook Pt., a peninsula lying south of Old Saybrook proper. **Harbor One Marina (860-388-9208;** VHF 9) and **Saybrook Point Inn & Spa** marina **(860-669-9613;** VHF 9) both have 20 transient slips. The former offers the broadest range of strictly marine services (plus a swimming pool), but Saybrook Point Inn is a luxury resort with a great restaurant, wonderful rooms and a health spa. Although Saybrook Pt. is not what most people would consider walking distance from town, a trolley does run in summer, and the point is not without attractions. At Fort Saybrook Monument Park a few steps away you can read the most complete history of the town that you'll find anywhere, and there's a miniature golf course located right at water's edge. **Dock and Dine (860-388-4665),** the restaurant with perhaps the best water views of any on the river, is also located here. There is free dockage for customers.

Just north of Saybrook Pt. you'll find **North Cove,** where the town of Old Saybrook dedi-cates ten free guest moorings to transient boaters; contact the Harbormaster at **(860) 388-4002** or VHF 9 for more.

Most of the marinas in Old Saybrook are clustered around the I-95 (Baldwin) Bridge. **River Landing Marina (800-783-6257** or **860-388-1431;** VHF 9) is foremost among them in transient berths, services and facilities (including a pool, a restaurant and fuel), although it is seasonal. Two alternatives are year-round **Oak Leaf Marina (860-388-9817;** VHF 9) and seasonal **Ferry Point Marina (860-388-3260).** Here too you'll need to take the trolley or other ground transportation to get to the center of town.

If you want to put in on the opposite bank of the river, you have two choices: year-round **Old Lyme Marina (860-434-1272)** and seasonal **Old Lyme Dock Co. (860-434-2267),** the only one of the two to sell fuel. Hail them both on VHF 9.

Farther upriver, Essex is and probably always has been the yachting capital of Connecticut. For a transient berth, gas or repairs you'd be equally well served by **Essex Island Marina (860-767-1267),** the **Chandlery at Essex (860-767-8267)** or **Brewer's Dauntless Shipyard (860-767-2483).** The former two also have transient moorings. Brewers is the only one to offer pump-out service. In Essex the marinas are actually in the town, only steps away from several excellent restaurants and limited overnight accommodations. You won't need transportation here.

Continuing northward, you'll find the broadest range of services and facilities at **Deep River Marina (860-526-5560)** in Deep River, **Chrisholm Marina (860-526-5147;** VHF 9) in Chester and **Andrews Marina (860-345-2286)** in Haddam. Headed for a play at Goodspeed Opera House? They have limited docking available for patrons, free to members, at a fee to nonmembers. Call **(860) 873-8668** to make a reservation.

For navigational details, charts and complete lists of marine facilities throughout this area, get *Embassy's Complete Boating Guide & Chartbook to Long Island Sound.* Contact the publisher at **142 Ferry Rd., Old Saybrook, 06475; (860) 395-0188.**

Fishing

The best source of fishing information is local tackle shops, and the most complete outfitter in this area is **Rivers End Tackle** at **141 Boston Post Rd. (Rte. 1), Old Saybrook, 06475; (860) 388-2283.** It can provide supplies, rental equipment and advice for freshwater or saltwater fishing.

Freshwater

Connecticut River

The lower river is a very popular area for striped bass. White perch is also good, especially in Hamburg Cove, and so is northern pike up toward Haddam. Largemouth bass are found in protected coves, and catfish throughout. Put in a boat at any of the state launches described under Boating. If you prefer fishing from shore, Steamboat Dock in Essex may be the most picturesque spot you've ever tried. There's also shore access at Haddam Meadows.

Other Rivers, Lakes and Ponds

Eight Mile River is heavily stocked with trout, and Devil's Hopyard State Park provides easy access to it. There's even a handicapped access area right below the falls at water's edge. For directions and more information, see the listing for Devil's Hopyard under Hiking.

Several of the ponds described under Boating are excellent for trout. These include **Uncas** and **Norwich Ponds** (there are also largemouth bass in the former), **Higganum Reservoir,** and **Pattaconk Reservoir.** There are car-top launches at all three, and plenty of undeveloped state-owned land for shore access. **Cedar Lake** is another good trout spot where you'll also find largemouth bass. Launch a boat or fish from shore along Cedar Lake Rd.

The bass lakes in this area are best fished from a boat, although they all have minimal shore access at boat launches. **Moodus Reservoir** is considered one of the best largemouth bass lakes in the state. **Bashan Lake** nearby has good largemouth bass as well as smallmouth bass and trout, and it's less busy. Largemouth bass, sunfish and trout are found at **Lake Hayward. Rogers Lake** also fits this pattern, and in addition it's one of only three lakes in the state stocked with walleye. For information on **Gardner Lake,** see the **Norwich and Casino Country** chapter.

Saltwater

Perhaps because of the competition in New London, the charter fishing business in this area is small. Try Peter Wheeler, captain of the **Sea Sprite** out of Saybrook Point Inn & Marina in Old Saybrook **(860-669-9613).** He does both inshore and offshore trips including light tackle and night bass.

Hiking

Canfield Woods/
Meadow Woods Preserve

These two contiguous preserves containing a dense network of blazed trails across woodland and wetland are accessible from the heart of both Essex and Deep River. The best entrance is the one on Book Hill Woods Rd. in Essex, where you'll find boxes stocked with trail maps (also available at the public library and the town clerk's office). Hours: dawn–dusk daily, year-round.

Cockaponset State Forest

If you're going to hike at this mountainous state forest, be sure to bring a towel, because after a few hours on the trail a swim in cold, clear Pattaconk Reservoir will be just the ticket. There's one central, north-south, blue-blazed trail—the Cockaponset—with several other ancillary trails coming off it. Enter via Cedar Lake Rd. off Rte. 148 in Chester and follow signs to the reservoir. You can pick up either the Pattaconk Trail or the Cockaponset Trail just beyond the parking lots. Forest office: **(860) 345-8521.**

Devil's Hopyard State Park

Noted for its rugged beauty, Devil's Hopyard's hemlock-shrouded hills are crossed by 15 miles of trails that intertwine to make possible hikes of a variety of lengths. After a jaunt, relax by the cool air that wafts up from 60-foot-tall Chapman Falls. Some stories credit the park's name to a corruption of Dibble's Hopyard, where a farmer named Dibble is supposed

307

to have grown hops, or Devlin's Hop, where another man is supposed to have operated a dance hall. Devil's Hopyard also offers excellent picnicking, fishing and camping. Located on Hopyard Rd. (Rte. 434) in East Haddam. Park office: **(860) 345-8521.**

Gillette Castle State Park

There are about 10 miles of mixed terrain trails at this state park described under Major Attractions. Three miles of flat, easy-to-negotiate paths follow the bed of a former narrow-gauge railway. Trails that descend to the river are the steepest.

Hartman Park

This town park provides an interesting opportunity to hike through a formerly active farming and industrial site that has reverted to the wild. A guide called "The Heritage Trail: A Walk in Hartman Park" (on sale for $2 at Lyme town hall on Rte. 156) gives in-depth information about the homestead, charcoal kiln, mill and other structures that were once here, of which only meager traces remain. Several miles of blazed trails here go through some pretty rugged terrain. A map is posted at the entrance on Gungy Rd. in Lyme north of Beaver Brook Rd. Picnicking is allowed and tables are provided, but fires are forbidden and you need to pack out all trash. Hours: dawn–sunset daily, year-round.

Honey Hill Preserve

Looking for a place to take small children for a hike? This self-guided, mile-long nature trail is just the ticket. An interpretive guide describing the flora and other features visible at 16 stations along the way is available at Lyme town hall. The entrance is on Clark Rd. north of Rte. 82 in Lyme at the East Haddam town line. Hours: dawn–dusk daily, year-round.

Nature Conservancy Preserves

The Nature Conservancy owns several tracts of land in this area that are often managed by local land trusts. A hike at Pleasant Valley Preserve will take you through former orchards and pasture as well as woodland along the Eight Mile River. To get to Pleasant Valley, take McIntosh Rd. off Rte. 156 in Lyme. Go over a bridge and look for a dirt driveway and

a gate on the right. Pass through the gate and follow the path until it forks. Take the right fork and follow the green and white signs.

Another preserve offering good hiking is Selden Creek, notable for its views of Selden Island State Park, which is accessible only by boat, and marshland at the edge of the Connecticut River. The entrance is on Joshuatown Rd. in Lyme 1.4 miles north of Mitchell Hill Rd. For more information call **(860) 344-0716.**

Nehantic State Forest

The blue-blazed Nayantaquit Trail makes a 3-mile loop on easy terrain within this forest, and by taking a crossover trail you can halve the distance. Look for the parking lot on Keeney Rd. off Beaver Brook Rd. in Lyme. Forest office: **(860) 739-5471.**

In the Air

The Connecticut River Valley is beautiful from the air, and you can see it from that perspective when you take a scenic flight in a three- or six-passenger plane with **Eagle Aviation.** Trips are 20–60 minutes in length. The pilot overflies the Connecticut River and surrounding attractions such as the Goodspeed Opera House and Gillette Castle. Prices start at $40 per person. Hours: 8:00 A.M.–6:00 P.M. daily, year-round. **Goodspeed Airport, Creamery Rd., East Haddam, 06423; (800) 564-2359 or (860) 873-8568.**

Sleigh and Carriage Rides

Allegra Farm, the folks who provide the beautiful horses and carriages to Gillette Castle and Mystic Seaport, offers private rides in restored Victorian horse-drawn carriages and sleighs by appointment. The beautiful farm setting makes this an especially nice place to treat your child to a pony ride, and it's inexpensive. Or, for $5 you can take a self-guided tour of more than two dozen sleighs and carriages in various stages of restoration. Although it is incongruous, the farm also offers chuck-wagon dinners for groups; inquire for details. Located on **Rte. 82, East Haddam, 06423; (860) 873-9658.**

Snowmobiling

A block of the **Cockaponset State Forest** around the Deep River/Chester town line contains several woods roads that make good snowmobile trails. Pine Ledge Rd. and Hoopole Hill Rd. cross, forming four arms for exploration. To get to the entrance, take Cedar Swamp Rd. off Rte. 80 in Deep River. The starting point and parking lot are just inside the forest boundary.

Swimming

Freshwater

Cedar Lake/Pelletier Park

Nonresidents of Chester are charged $4 per person or $10 per family per day to swim at this pretty yet easily accessible lake. It's got a sandy beach, a designated swimming area and lifeguards. Located on Rte. 148 in Chester just east of Cedar Lake Rd. For more information call the **Chester Parks and Recreation Dept.** at **(860) 526-0017**.

Gardner Lake Park

This private park on Gardner Lake in Salem has been serving the local community for 60 years. It has a 350-foot beach, kiddie rides, an arcade, a snack bar, rest rooms and changing rooms. Admission: $2 adults, $1 children under 6. Hours: 10:00 A.M.–7:00 P.M. daily, Memorial Day–Labor Day, weather permitting. **38 Lakeview Ave., Salem, 06420; (860) 859-3340.**

Pattaconk Reservoir Recreation Area

The beach at this lovely little lake nestled among forested hills is small and the imported sand on the coarse side, but there are no buoys restricting you, so you can swim out as far as you'd like. Because it's free, Pattaconk can be packed on summer weekends, but on weekdays you're likely to have very little company. You'll find it off Cedar Lake Rd. off Rte. 148 in Chester. For more information call **(860) 345-8521**.

Uncas Pond

The exquisite little beach on tranquil Uncas Pond in Nehantic State Forest is free and un-guarded, and the only boats allowed on the lake are nonmotorized. It can get busy on summer weekends. You'll find it on Keeney Rd. off Rte. 156 in Lyme. Follow signs to the picnic area, where the beach is also located.

Saltwater

Soundview Beach

Pretty much the only old-fashioned free public beach left in Connecticut is Soundview Beach at the end of Hartford Ave. in Old Lyme. The surrounding neighborhood is filled with casual eateries and rudimentary seasonal cottages where people while away relaxed summers. Park in the lots; street parking is minimal. Alcohol, coolers and pets are forbidden. For more information call **(860) 434-7275** or **(860) 434-1605**.

Seeing and Doing

Antiquing

Old Saybrook is gaining a reputation as an antiquing destination. Request the "Old Saybrook Antiques" brochure from one of the visitors information centers listed in Services. This map and directory describes the specialties of ten shops and shows you where to find them. All ten are located on or just off Rte. 154 north of Main St., with most of them north of Rte. 9. Hours and days vary by store, but nearly all are open Wed.–Sun., 11:00 A.M.–5:00 P.M.

Art Galleries

Old Lyme was the site of one of Connecticut's three Impressionist art colonies in the early 20th century and continues to draw both students and aficionados of fine art thanks to three excellent art galleries, one of which is also a school. The history of the town as an art colony is told at the Florence Griswold Museum, described under Major Attractions.

The art at all of the galleries listed below is usually for sale. Other places to look for art to buy include **Spring Street Studio & Gallery**

(One Spring St., Chester; 860-526-2077), the showroom of husband-and-wife painters Leif and Katherine Nilsson, where you'll find Impressionist landscapes in oil and pattern-oriented watercolors, or **Saybrook Colony Artists** (at Saybrook Pt. by the miniature golf course, Old Saybrook; **860-388-5010**), the place to go for maritime scenes in all media.

James Gallery
This unique combination of art gallery/soda fountain is housed in a former general store and pharmacy. On the gallery side you'll find fine art for sale. There are also a number of fine duck and goose decoys. Sept.–June hours: Mon.–Fri., 3:00 P.M.–9:00 P.M.; Sat.–Sun., 10:00 A.M.–9:00 P.M. July–Aug. hours: 10:00 A.M.–10:00 P.M. daily. **2 Pennywise Lane at Main St., Old Saybrook, 06475; (860) 395-1406.**

Lyme Academy of Fine Arts
An accredited art school emphasizing drawing, painting and sculpture, the Lyme Academy of Fine Arts was founded in 1976 by artists. The on-site gallery is housed in the historic John Sill House (ca. 1817), a colonial home and National Historic Landmark. You'll find mostly representational work with rare but occasional downtime between shows. Admission by donation. Tue.–Sat., 10:00 A.M.–4:00 P.M.; Sun., 1:00 P.M.–4:00 P.M. **84 Lyme St., 06371; (860) 434-5232.**

Lyme Art Association
Regional representational artists are showcased in five major exhibits at the Lyme Art Association annually. It also keeps an active schedule of demonstrations, workshops and lectures. There is downtime between shows, so call before going. Admission: $3 suggested donation. Hours: Tue.–Sat., noon–4:30 P.M.; Sun., 1:00 P.M.–4:30 P.M., May–Dec. Also open for special exhibits Feb.–Apr. **90 Lyme St., Old Lyme, 06371; (860) 434-7802.**

Museums and Historic Sites

Connecticut River Museum
The Connecticut River Museum's location is ideal for an institution that focuses on the his-tory and wildlife of New England's greatest waterway. Steamboat Dock at the waterfront end of the main street of Essex overlooks the river and has a rich history of use stretching back centuries. A downstairs area houses changing exhibits, while the upstairs is devoted to permanent displays concerning ship-building, privateering and a variety of subjects connected with the river. In a separate boathouse there is a replica of "America's first practical submarine," built during Revolutionary War times. The museum also hosts a variety of special events, including its annual holiday show, which begins the day after Thanksgiving with two days of storytelling and a railroading exhibit that stays up until early Feb. Museum admission: $4 adults, $2 children age 6–11; children under 6 free. Hours: Tue.–Sun., 10:00 A.M.–5:00 P.M. **67 Main St., Essex, 06426; (860) 767-8269.**

Fort Saybrook Monument Park
The site of a 17th-century fort is now a passive park marked by a series of plaques that tell the story of Saybrook Colony's establishment and growth. Located at the **intersection of College St. and Bridge St. in Old Saybrook.** Open year-round during daylight hours.

Historic Home Museums
The oldest historic home museum in the area is the **Pratt House (West Ave., Essex; 860-767-1191),** fascinating for its evolution from a half cape into a full cape into a colonial. It was built in sections beginning in 1701. Guided tours focus on how the building and its furnishings (ca. 1800) reflect the lives of the Pratt family, who were founders of the town. A post-and-beam reproduction barn in the rear holds changing exhibits on Essex history. Admission: $3 adults, free to children under 12. Hours: Sat.–Sun., 1:00 P.M.–4:00 P.M., June–mid-Sept.

The 1767 Georgian-style **General William Hart House (350 Main St., Old Saybrook; 860-388-2622)** built by the merchant and Revolutionary War general of the same name, is now the headquarters of the Old Saybrook Historical Society. Its corner fireplaces are unusual, and the house is rich in structural and aesthetic details that reflect Hart's wealth and status. There are also local history exhibits and an extensive herb garden out back. Admission: $2 donation. Hours: Fri.–Sun., 1:00 P.M.–4:00 P.M., mid-June–mid-Sept.

Named for one of its original inhabitants, the **Thankful Arnold House (corner of Hayden and Walkley Hill Rds., Haddam; 860-345-2400)** is a gambrel-roofed home built in sections between 1794 and 1810. On display are local artifacts and period furnishings, including several Connecticut River Valley pieces. Plant lovers will find the garden a high point. A 40-year correspondence between father and son Arnold family members is among the historical society's holdings; they hope to have a transcript of the Civil War years on display soon. Admission: $2. Hours: Sat.–Sun., 2:00 P.M.–4:00 P.M., Memorial Day–Columbus Day, & by appointment.

The Antiquarian and Landmarks Society maintains the 1816 **Amasa Day House (junction of Rtes. 151 and 149, Moodus; 860-873-8144 or 860-247-8996),** a Federal home furnished with late-19th-century furniture and featuring some rare stairwell stenciling. The East Haddam Historical Society's museum in a barn behind the house showcases a collection of artifacts documenting local life and industry. Admission charged. Hours: 1:00 P.M.–5:00 P.M. on weekends Memorial Day–June & Wed.–Sun., July–Labor Day.

Aptly named, the **Stone House (245 Main St., Deep River; 860-526-1449 or 860-526-5684)** was built in 1840, probably from locally quarried stone. You'll see original furnishings, a collection of Obadiah Dickinson portraits, plus exhibits on local industries such as shipbuiding, lace and ivory piano keys. Admission is free. Hours: Sat.–Sun., 1:00 P.M.–4:00 P.M., July and/or Aug.

Other Museums

The materials at the **Nathan Hale School House** provide a good quick introduction to the man who is Connecticut's state hero. This is a reproduction of the structure where Hale taught briefly during the school year 1773–1774, moved here from the original site. Hours: Sat., Sun. & holidays, 2:00 P.M.–4:00 P.M., Memorial Day–Labor Day. Admission free,

but contributions welcome. Located on **Rte. 149 behind St. Stephen's Church, East Haddam; (860) 873-9547.** Look for the small sign by the road, and then follow signs back to the schoolhouse.

Fife and drum music, which once had a critical military role, has had a resurgence in recent years as musters and battle reenactments have gained popularity. The history of the genre is documented at the **Museum of Fife and Drum (62 N. Main St. at Highland Tr., Ivoryton; 860-767-2237)** through instruments, uniforms and photographs. Recorded and written fife and drum music is for sale, and there are occasional Tue. night concerts in summer. Admission: $2. Hours: Sat.–Sun., 1:00 P.M.–5:00 P.M., June–Sept.

Performing Arts

American Magic-Lantern Theater

A popular diversion in Victorian times, magic-lantern theater is a combination show of storytelling by a costumed dramatist, live music, singing in which the audience is invited to participate and hand-painted Victorian slides projected on-screen. Although it's not a kiddie show, it will appeal to children as young as 6. This particular company is the only magic-lantern theater in the country. It tours and plays to home audiences at Ivoryton Playhouse in Essex, Cheney Hall in Manchester, Chester Meetinghouse in Chester and the Little Theater in New Haven. Regularly scheduled performances include the Halloween Show in late Oct., Christmas Show in early Dec. and Valentine Show in early Feb. Performances last about 90 minutes with an intermission. Admission is about $10 for adults, $4 for children. For more information and ticket sales call **(860) 345-7578.**

Goodspeed-at-Chester/ Norma Terris Theatre

Affiliated with the Goodspeed Opera House in East Haddam (described under Major Attractions), this intimate, 200-seat theater was specifically developed to showcase new musicals. Located on **N. Main St., Chester, 06412; (860) 873-8668.**

Lower Connecticut River Valley

Ivoryton Playhouse

The River Rep is the in-house company at this small theater presenting a mix of new and established plays June–Aug. It's the sort of cultural institution that can make a small town something special. Evening performances take place Tue.–Sat., with early matinees Wed. & Sat. & "twilight" matinees on Sun. Ticket prices are $15–$19. **Main St., Ivoryton, 06442; (860) 767-8348.**

Scenic Drives

Almost any road outside the developed parts of this area yields rewarding views. The one drive you must do is the Connecticut River loop described under Biking, which takes you past a couple of the area's major attractions and through some exquisite scenery. It even includes a ferry ride. The western portions of Haddam, Chester and Deep River, as well as all of Lyme and East Haddam, are filled with scenic roads and nothing in particular to head for except the scenery or the hiking and swimming spots described above.

Shopping

Of all the towns that dot the west bank of the lower Connecticut River Valley, Chester is the visual jewel. With its main street curving fluidly into a hillside and the pleasant façades and brimming shop windows looking like a movie set, the town seems to have been transported from a storybook. Shops change frequently, but you can find everything from fine textiles to hardware. Essex also has excellent shopping, with many stores that carry fine accessories for the home.

In Old Saybrook, **Marlborough Country Barn (14 Main St.; 860-388-0891)** is packed to the gills with everything for the "Americana" home, from fake fruit to furniture, including window treatments.

Goodspeed's Station in Haddam **(22 Bridge Rd.; 860-345-7322)** is a gift shop housed in an old train depot with an above-average selection of gifts and some reasonably priced antiques in very good condition thrown

in for good measure. Also, try **Merchant House (junction of Rtes. 154 and 82; 860-345-4195),** a huge gift and collectibles shop spread out on two floors of an old colonial house. For Goodspeed Opera House memorabilia, stop in at **Goodspeed Two (860-873-8664),** a "theatrical gift shop" located off the lobby of Gelston House next door to the Opera House in East Haddam.

Spinners and weavers will take special interest in **Sankow's Beaver Brook Farm (139 Beaver Brook Rd., Lyme; 860-434-2843),** a sheep farm with a retail shop selling woolen goods, yarn, spinning wheels and meat. Come the Sat. after Thanksgiving for the free open house (11:00 A.M.–4:00 P.M.) with demonstrations of sheep shearing and spinning, plus hayrides at no charge for the kids. The spring Shearing Day, always held on an afternoon in mid-May, 1:00 P.M.–4:00 P.M., focuses exclusively on shearing and fleece handling. Shop hours: 9:00 A.M.–4:00 P.M. daily.

Where to Stay

Bed & Breakfasts

Deacon Timothy Pratt House—$$$$

This 18th-century, central-chimney colonial was restored to beautiful condition recently. It has two large guest rooms, the Library and the Suite. The Suite is notable for its curtained double doors separating the main sleeping area from a small room with a daybed for a third person. Both rooms have working fireplaces and private attached baths. Children are welcome—they can even bring sleeping bags to spread on the floor, and a cot is available. There's a backyard with a hammock for seclusion, or you can walk a few blocks into town. Guests have access to two sandy town beaches, and old home buffs will enjoy looking through the scrapbook documenting the restoration. **325 Main St., Old Saybrook, 06475; (860) 395-1229.**

Bishopsgate Inn—$$$ to $$$$

Located on the main road through East Haddam, Bishopsgate is the only B&B within walking distance of the Goodspeed Opera House. The center-hall colonial (ca. 1818) has six guest rooms, most of which have a country colonial look. Four of the rooms have wood-burning fireplaces, and all of them have private baths. You'll be served a full breakfast in a cozy, family kitchen with a huge fireplace. By special arrangement you can also enjoy a candlelight dinner for two or a custom picnic lunch. Located on **Rte. 82, East Haddam, 06423; (860) 873-1677.**

Hidden Meadow—$$$ to $$$$

This nicely restored and maintained rambling structure, located on one of Lyme's quiet residential roads that are so nice for strolling and bicycling, contains parts as early as 1760 and as late as the 1930s, yet retains a strong colonial ambiance. Some of the five guest rooms capitalize on the features of an older part of the house, but others have more modern aspects, such as wall-to-wall carpeting. Most have traditional furnishings, light and airy color schemes, queen or king beds and private baths. The attractive outdoor spaces at Hidden Meadow, including gardens and terraces for breakfast in good weather, are a real plus. **40 Blood St., Lyme, 06371; (860) 434-8360.**

Indian Ledge—$$$ to $$$$

When you want to get away from it all without straying too far from civilization, head for Indian Ledge. Located at the top of a long driveway with nothing but trees for neighbors, the lovely house is a modern adaptation of a traditional center-chimney colonial with a light and airy layout. Most guests will probably gravitate to the sunroom, overlooking the back garden, where a full breakfast is served. There are two exceptionally nice upstairs guest rooms and one basement suite with a unique barn door entrance. All rooms have a queen, four-poster canopy bed and a private bathroom. Trudy Lombard, who runs the B&B with her husband Ray, is from Switzerland. Foreign travelers may appreciate her fluency in German and Swiss dialects. Payment by cash or check only. **411 Hamburg Rd. (Rte. 156 just below Beaver Brook Rd.), Lyme, 06371; (860) 434-9566.**

Riverwind—$$$ to $$$$

Located in a rambling farmhouse packed with beautiful antiques and collectibles, Riverwind's eight rooms are unique, comfortable and come with private baths. Multiple fireplaces add to the rustic atmosphere. There are sitting and game rooms where guests can read, relax and be social. Barlow, who runs the B&B with her husband Bob Bucknall, is also a justice of the peace and occasionally marries guests, many of whom then stay in the Champagne and Roses room, which comes with a bottle of champagne. Breakfast always features Smithfield ham (Barlow is originally from Smithfield, Virginia) and southern biscuits. **209 Main St., Deep River, 06417; (860) 526-2014.**

Woodbridge Farm—$$$ to $$$$

Woodbridge Farm is a rambling, late-18th-century, center-chimney colonial set on 120 acres with trails for hiking and horseback riding. Owner Marian Bingham can board horses overnight in her barn, making this a destination in and of itself if you just want to get away for a weekend of riding. There are six rooms, three with private baths with footed tubs. The two most expensive rooms have wood-burning fireplaces and king or queen beds. The two smallest rooms are suitable for solitary travelers. Breakfast is Continental, served buffet-style 8:00 A.M.–9:00 A.M. Bingham will occasionally accommodate small children in certain rooms; call for details. **30 Woodbridge Rd., Salem, 06420; (860) 859-1169.**

Hotels, Motels & Inns

Copper Beech Inn—$$$$

Locally famous for its French restaurant (see Where to Eat for more), Copper Beech Inn has nine rooms in a restored carriage house, each of which feature four-poster beds, traditional furnishings, modern bathrooms with whirlpool baths, cathedral ceilings with exposed beams (in the upper-story rooms) and small balconies. **46 Main St., Ivoryton, 06442; (860) 767-0330.**

313

Gelston House—$$$$

This longtime inn preceded the Goodspeed Opera House next door by a good 150 years, although it is thoroughly modernized. Plush and well-appointed rooms, a grand lobby and an excellent restaurant on the main floor (see Where to Eat for more) combine to create a feel of exclusive luxury at Gelston House. Prices for the six spacious and elegant rooms are in direct proportion to the window view. All rooms have a private bath. Breakfast is self-serve—there are coffeemakers in the rooms and a hospitality basket of fresh fruit and baked goods is provided. **8 Main St., East Haddam, 06423; (860) 873-1411.**

The Inn at Chester—$$$$

Although visually the inn's buildings are a blend of old and new, this modern hotel has over 40 rooms that are, for the most part, traditionally furnished. In addition, there is a three-bedroom guest house, available weekly, built in an old center-chimney farmhouse with several fireplaces. An exercise room, sauna and tennis courts are available, and massages can be arranged. The in-house restaurant, The Post and Beam, is beautifully rustic and very good (see Where to Eat for more). **318 W. Main St. (Rte. 148, about 3 miles west of Rte. 9), Chester, 06412; (860) 526-9541.**

Saybrook Point Inn & Spa—$$$$

Possibly the most luxurious accommodations on the Connecticut coast are to be found at this inn built on the site of the once (in)famous Terra Mar Hotel. The amenities at this waterfront resort are legion: large, well-furnished rooms, wet bars, refrigerators, fireplaces or marina views in some rooms, dining tables and whirlpool baths in the suites, an on-site spa where you can receive head-to-foot pampering, an excellent restaurant, indoor and outdoor pools, a fitness center and a marina steps away. Docking is available for overnight guests. A seasonal lighthouse apartment (queen bedroom, sitting room, kitchenette and dining area) above the dock office is available on a weekly basis. Spa packages are available. **2 Bridge St., Old Saybrook, 06475; (800) 243-0212 (outside Connecticut) or (860) 395-2000 (in state).**

Bee and Thistle Inn—$$$ to $$$$

One of two inns within walking distance from the "art district" of Old Lyme, the Bee and Thistle has 11 small rooms with older, very traditional furniture. Bathrooms are all private and on the old-fashioned side. In addition there's an innkeeper cottage with a kitchen, a sitting room with a fireplace, a queen bedroom, country furnishings and a deck. There's an excellent restaurant on the main floor, so there will be a certain amount of traffic during lunch and dinner hours. Breakfast is not included. **100 Lyme St., Old Lyme, 06371; (800) 622-4946 or (860) 434-1667.**

The Griswold Inn—$$$ to $$$$

The Griswold is one of Connecticut's truly historic inns, having been open to the public since 1776. Comprising several buildings on the main street of Essex, in which there are over two dozen rooms, this inn practically defines the category. The regular rooms are adequate, but pay a little extra and get one of the suites. Some of them feature sliding wooden doors to separate the sleeping from the sitting quarters and wood-burning stoves to help set a homelike mood. All the rooms have a private bath and a telephone. The Griswold's restaurant is quite famous locally (see Where to Eat for more). A Continental breakfast is included. **36 Main St., Essex, 06426; (860) 767-1776.**

Old Lyme Inn—$$$ to $$$$

This restored 1850s farmhouse with modern additions has 13 rooms with traditional, 18th-century-style furniture (including four-poster or canopy beds in some rooms), private baths and subtle decorative schemes. There are essentially three price categories for rooms. The ones in the middle are more spacious than the least expensive rooms (which are still quite nice) and just as attractive as the higher-priced ones. All rooms have air-conditioning, TV and telephone. A wheelchair ramp and ground-floor rooms make the Old Lyme Inn very accessible despite its vintage. Pets are allowed, and a Continental breakfast is served. Closed the first half of Jan. **85 Lyme St., Old Lyme, 06371; (800) 434-5352 or (860) 434-2600.**

Sandpiper Motor Inn—$$$ to $$$$

In the motel category, this is one of the best around, with a complimentary breakfast, coin-op laundry and VCR rental. There are four room types ranging from queen single to double deluxe (with refrigerator, wet bar and pullout sofa), and rates that range from quite reasonable to average for the area. Guests have free access to any of several town beaches as well as the on-site swimming pool. **1750 Boston Post Rd. (Rte. 1), Old Saybrook, 06475; (800) 323-7973** or **(860) 399-7973.**

Resorts

Sunrise Resort—$$$$

Families looking for organized activities should take a look at Sunrise Resort. Activities range from musical entertainment, games and nightly movies to exercise and dance classes and horseback riding. Some of these involve an extra charge. Lots of activities for kids are supervised so parents can have some time alone, and baby-sitters are available in the evening for a fee. Accommodations are all summer-camp caliber: twin or double beds, two or four to a unit, and very basic. Meals, served in a dining hall with designated seatings, are also family-oriented: barbeque, burgers, lasagna and so forth. Facilities include swimming pools, playgrounds, ball fields, picnic groves, a barbeque pavilion, a spa with exercise equipment, a small beach and boats for use on the river. Sports equipment is provided in many cases. Prices vary depending on the length of stay and type of accommodation. Open May–Sept. Inquire about theme weekends and camping. Located on **Rte. 151 (1 mile north of Rte. 149), Moodus, 06469; (860) 873-8681.**

Camping

Devil's Hopyard State Park—$

Of course, there is nothing devilish about Devil's Hopyard—just 21 semiwooded sites and basic facilities such as water pumps and

This covered bridge crosses a stream at Devil's Hopyard State Park. Photo courtesy Connecticut Department of Environmental Protection.

pit toilets. Stream fishing and hiking are two activities for which the park is ideally suited. The campground entrance is on Foxtown Rd. a short distance east of Hopyard Rd. (Rte. 434) in East Haddam. Campground office: **(860) 873-8566.** Park office: **(860) 345-8521.**

River Camping—$

The most unique camping experience in Connecticut is to be found on the Connecticut River itself. There are three riverside state parks where primitive campsites are available for boaters May–Sept.: Hurd, Gillette Castle and Selden Neck. You must arrive by boat (in fact, Selden Neck is an island and only accessible by boat), and there are no slips or moorings. Only boaters in canoes may stay overnight at Hurd and Gillette Castle, and they must break camp by 9:00 A.M. since the campgrounds are otherwise public areas. The fee is an incredible $4 per person per night. The stay is limited to one night at each park. You must make a reservation two weeks in advance or purchase the permit in person at Gillette Castle during its normal open hours. Drinking water is available at Hurd and Gillette Castle but not at Selden Neck; it's always advisable to bring your own. Outhouses, picnic tables and fireplaces are provided. For more information call **Gillette Castle State Park** at **(860) 526-2336,** or request the river camping pamphlet from the **DEP State Parks Division** at **79 Elm St., Hartford, 06106; (860) 424-3200.**

Where to Eat

If you plan to visit any of the finer restaurants along the Connecticut River, be aware that there's a more consistently high standard of evening dress here than anywhere else in Connecticut. There is certainly an abundance of casual restaurants where shorts and sandals are appropriate, but the white-tablecloth restaurants openly encourage better attire. This part of the world is a good place to refamiliarize yourself with the pleasure of dressing up.

In addition to the listings below, a few more places to try include **Saybrook Fish House (99 Essex Rd., Old Saybrook; 860-388-4836)**, an award-winning restaurant with a fresh fish focus; the **Terra Mar Grill (2 Bridge St., Old Saybrook; 860-395-2000)**, the in-house restaurant of the Saybrook Point Inn & Spa where virtually all the tables have a marina view and **Saigon City (1315 Boston Post Rd. [Rte. 1], Old Saybrook; 860-388-6888)**, a Vietnamese/Thai restaurant in a colorful old Victorian house that nicely contrasts the menus most local dining establishments feature.

Bee and Thistle Inn—$$$$

This much-altered 18th-century farmhouse is consistently awarded recognition as one of the most romantic places to dine in Connecticut. There's one innlike dining room with a large fireplace and two narrow sunrooms on either side of the entryway. The menu is a mix of American and Continental specialties, mostly hearty roasted and grilled dishes. Homemade sausage is a specialty. Lunch is a little lighter but does not revert to a menu of sandwiches. Reservations strongly suggested. Proper attire requested at dinner; jacket required of gentlemen on Sat. **100 Lyme St., Old Lyme, 06371; (800) 622-4946 or (203) 434-1667.**

Copper Beech Inn—$$$$

This French country restaurant is a local institution, widely considered to offer one of the most exceptional fine dining experiences in the state. The setting is the onetime private home of the ivory comb and piano key manufacturer from whose business the local township took its name. Three dining rooms on the main floor hold a smattering of beautifully set and candlelit tables, attended by an efficient staff. Dress your best. Reservations recommended. Hours: Tue.–Thu., 5:30 P.M.–8:00 P.M.; Fri.–Sat., 5:30 P.M.–9:00 P.M.; Sun., fixed-price lunch served 1:00 P.M.–3:00 P.M., à la carte dinner served 1:00 P.M.–7:00 P.M. **46 Main St., Ivoryton, 06442; (860) 767-0330.**

North Cove Express Dinner Train— $$$$

In a twist on the dinner cruise, the North Cove Express train allows you to dine and ride aboard restored Pullman cars pulled by a diesel engine. Special "theme" trains feature entertainment by barbershop quartets, a murder mystery and a rail-to-river rendezvous on which you transfer to a riverboat in Deep River for a cruise up to Goodspeed Opera House and back. The menu is limited, but the food is only part of the whole experience. You get a selection of three entrées: barbequed baby-back ribs, chicken or fish. Regularly scheduled trains run May–Oct. only, and later in the season by private charter. Trains depart Thu.–Sun. at 6:30 or 7:00 P.M., returning between 8:30 and 10:00 P.M. There are also special Mother's Day and Father's Day afternoon excursions. Prices range from $32.95 to $42.95 excluding tax and gratuity; for $5 more you can ride in air-conditioned comfort in a first-class car. All cars are heated during colder months. Reservations required. Board at the Valley Railroad/Essex Steam Train depot at **One Railroad Ave. in Essex; (800) 398-7427.**

Old Lyme Inn—$$$$

Old Lyme Inn offers a real mix of atmosphere. The elegant main dining room, with tall ceilings, heavy draperies, velvety upholstered chairs and beautifully set tables, looks the way all banquet halls should. But there's also a casual tavernlike grillroom where you can have lunch, a light supper or a full dinner in front of a fire while enjoying mellow jazz guitar or piano music on Fri. & Sat. nights. The cuisine is American, heavy on classics such as roasts and shore dinners. At lunch there are several substantial entrées in addition to soups, salads and sandwiches. Closed the first half of Jan. Lunch served Mon.–Sat., noon–2:00 P.M.; Sun. brunch 11:00 A.M.–3:00 P.M. Dinner served Mon.–Sat., 6:00 P.M.–9:00 P.M.; Sun., 4:00 P.M.–9:00 P.M. **85 Lyme St., Old Lyme, 06371; (800) 434-5352 or (860) 434-2600.**

Restaurant du Village—$$$$

This acclaimed French restaurant has been around for years, and despite a change in ownership a few years ago its reputation continues to be sterling. Its small size creates a feeling of privilege at having garnered one of the few tables, and nothing could be more charming than a windowside seat here overlooking the storybook main street of Chester. The menu is small, but there are always several daily specials from which to choose. There is no strict dress code. Hours: Wed.–Sat., seatings every 15 minutes, 5:30–6:45 P.M. & 8:15–9:00 P.M.; Sun., seatings every 15 minutes, 5:00–6:00 P.M. & 7:30–8:15 P.M. **59 Main St., Chester, 06412; (860) 526-5301.**

Dock and Dine—$$$ to $$$$

Dock and Dine's location on Saybrook Pt. is as close to the water as you can get without being in a boat. It's lined with windows on three sides so there are water views from virtually all the tables. The menu consists of casual American-style seafood, steaks, chicken, pasta and a salad bar. It offers docking privileges to customers, but make a reservation if at all possible to avoid disappointment. Hours: Apr.–Columbus Day, open 11:30 A.M.–9:30 P.M. (Fri.–Sat. until 10:00) daily; open Wed.–Sun., 11:30 A.M.–9:00 P.M. the rest of the year. **Saybrook Pt., College St., Old Saybrook, 06475; (860) 388-4665** (in Connecticut) or **(800) 362-3625** (out-of-state).

Glockenspiel—$$$ to $$$$

Desperately seeking a Berliner Weisse (unpasteurized wheat beer served with raspberry syrup) or Späten Oktoberfest on tap? You're in luck. Glockenspiel serves up German beer as well as food. Specialties are pork and veal, schnitzels, sausages from mild to spicy and traditional side dishes such as red cabbage, potato pancakes and spätzle. The menu also

features a number of American and Continental favorites such as chicken cordon bleu, blackened swordfish, game and pastas available in half and full portions. Look for the monthly wine special, which is always something that makes a good value by the glass. Hours: Mon.–Thu., 5:00 P.M.–9:00 P.M.; Fri.–Sat., 5:00 P.M.–10:30 P.M.; Sun., 2:30 P.M.–9:00 P.M. Tavern opens at 4:00 P.M. (2:30 P.M. on Sun.) & stays open a couple hours later than the kitchen. On **Killingworth Rd. (Rte. 81) one-tenth mile from Rte. 154, Higganum, 06441; (860) 345-4697.**

The Post and Beam—$$$ to $$$$

The in-house restaurant of The Inn at Chester, The Post and Beam is located in an authentic converted barn that juxtaposes rustic and elegant looks in an appealing manner. A romantic loft overlooking the main dining room is very desirable for parties of two, and the tavern next door makes a convenient spot for meeting friends. The cuisine is straightforward American/Continental. The tavern and lunch menu is an abridged version of dinner with the addition of pizzas and sandwiches. An à la carte Sun. brunch features some unusual choices such as smoked salmon Benedict, grilled lamb and sun-dried tomato sausage and even a fish of the day. Inquire about dinner and theater packages. Hours: lunch served daily 11:30 A.M.–2:00 P.M. (until 2:30 for Sun. brunch); dinner served Mon.–Sat., 5:30 P.M.–9:00 P.M., & Sun., 4:00 P.M.–8:30 P.M. The tavern menu is available between lunch and dinner. **318 W. Main St. (Rte. 148, about 3 miles west of Rte. 9), Chester, 06412; (860) 526-9541.**

Aleia's—$$$

Pronounced "A-LEE-uz," this self-billed "innovative bistro" is simply one of the best restaurants around. Many of the dishes have a Mediterranean flavor, and pastas are a mainstay of the menu, but it also does upscale comfort food such as a delectable roasted chicken with whipped potatoes. Come casual or dressed up. Hours: Tue.–Sun., 5:30 P.M.–9:00 P.M. (Fri.–Sat. until 10:00). **1687 Boston Post Rd. (Rte. 1), Old Saybrook, 06475; (860) 399-5050.**

Lower Connecticut River Valley

Anne's Bistro—$$$

Here you'll find a hodgepodge of Italian, American, Cajun, vegetarian and other dishes. The baked-in-house breads are great. Baked goods and a tiny menu of breakfast foods are served in the morning. Lunch is light, consisting mostly of sandwiches and deli salads, and the full-fledged meals come out at dinner. Mon.–Sat. hours: breakfast served 8:00 A.M.–11:00 A.M.; deli open 11:00 A.M.–4:00 P.M.; lunch served 11:30 A.M.–2:00 P.M.; dinner available 5:30 P.M.–9:00 P.M. Sun. brunch in summer, 8:00 A.M.–12:30 P.M. **Old Lyme Marketplace (in the A&P shopping center), Rte. 1, Old Lyme, 06371; (860) 434-9837.**

Chart House—$$$

The Chart House is part of a chain of steak house restaurants in one-of-a-kind properties that deliver far more than chain restaurant ambiance. This particular Chart House is housed in the renovated Rogers & Champion Brushworks mill, situated in a picturesque ravine by the Pattaconk River. Inside, a few relics of the mill's active days are still on display. There are several dining rooms, but arrive early for a table with a river view. The menu is American, with a wide selection of steaks, fish and pasta. Hours: Mon.–Fri., 5:00 P.M.–9:30 P.M.; Sat., 5:00 P.M.–10:00 P.M.; Sun., 4:00 P.M.–9:30 P.M. **129 W. Main St. (Rte. 148 just east of Rte. 9), Chester, 06412; (860) 526-9898.**

Cuckoo's Nest—$$$

The area's best Mexican/southwestern restaurant also dishes up Cajun/Creole food. And if you're tired of the same old brunch options, try theirs: it's all-you-can-eat for $9.95 and not a Belgium waffle to be found. Hours: open daily at 11:30 A.M., closing Sun.–Thu. at 9:30 P.M. & Fri.–Sat. at 11:00 P.M.; brunch served until 3:00 P.M. **1712 Boston Post Rd. (Rte. 1), Old Saybrook, 06475; (860) 399-9060.**

Fiddlers Seafood Restaurant—$$$

One word sums up Fiddlers: seafood. Ninety percent of the menu is devoted to it. They'll prepare any of their fresh fish (the selection changes daily) one of six ways: mesquite grilled, poached, pan sautéed, broiled, baked or Cajun spiced. Or, select from more than a dozen classic preparations such as bouillabaisse, whole lobster, crabcakes and stuffed sole. All of the fresh fish offerings are also available at lunch. Located behind the shops at the lower end of Chester's main street. Lunch hours: Tue.–Sat., 11:30 A.M.–2:00 P.M. Dinner hours: Sun. & Tue.–Thu., 5:30 P.M.–9:00 P.M.; Fri., 5:30 P.M.–9:30 P.M.; Sat., 5:30 P.M.–10:00 P.M. **4 Water St., Chester, 06412; (860) 526-3210.**

Gelston House—$$$

If you are seeing a musical at Goodspeed, make dinner at Gelston House the prelude. It is the only fine-dining type of restaurant in the vicinity of the Opera House (located next door), and certainly the one with the best view, since it sits astride a low mountain overlooking a beautiful stretch of the Connecticut River. The cuisine is fine American with some international touches. Lunch dishes are in a similar vein, and the à la carte Sun. brunch selections are also rather sophisticated. Reservations are essential. However, windowside tables are first-come, first-served, so if you want one your best bet is to have dinner around 5:00–5:30 P.M. Attire is dressy. Hours: open Wed.–Sun., 11:30 P.M.–2:30 P.M. for lunch/brunch; 5:30 P.M.–9:00 P.M. (10:00 Fri.–Sat.) for dinner. **8 Main St., East Haddam, 06423; (860) 873-1411.**

The Griswold Inn—$$$

The Griswold is an institution that knows its clientele and keeps on satisfying it year after year. It's very popular, especially among the older crowd, who make a ritual out of Sun. attendance at the Hunt Breakfast. This smorgasbord of brunch foods is available for $12.95—about two-thirds the price you'd pay at the handful of other restaurants that offer similar spreads. At other meals the menu is meat-and-potato-oriented, plus overstuffed sandwiches and the Griswold's signature sausages at lunch. Prime rib is a house specialty. If you visit in Dec., you can partake of a special game menu while being entertained by strolling performers. The Griswold's decor deserves special mention. One dining room contains parts of a real covered bridge and is anchored by a massive fireplace at the far end. Maritime artwork reflecting the shipbuilding heritage of Essex lines the walls of the Wardroom. Another room is a small, intimate library with a fireplace and, of course, bookshelves. Reservations are recommended for all meals. Lunch hours: Mon.–Fri., 11:45 A.M.–3:00 P.M.; Sat., 11:30 A.M.–3:00 P.M. Dinner hours: Mon.–Thu., 5:30 P.M.–9:00 P.M.; Fri., 5:30 P.M.–10:00 P.M.; Sat., 5:00 P.M.–10:00 P.M.; Sun., 4:30 P.M.–9:00 P.M. Sun. brunch (Hunt Breakfast): 11:00 A.M.–2:30 P.M. Happy Hour with complimentary finger food: Mon.–Fri., 4:00 P.M.–6:00 P.M. **36 Main St., Essex, 06426; (860) 767-1776.**

Hideaway Restaurant & Pub—$$$

The variety and accessibility of the menu at the Hideaway make it a good choice for families with many tastes to satisfy, yet the food is good enough to please a more discriminating eater. The menu is exceedingly large, including finger food, Mexican dishes, light soup and salad lunches, pasta, steak and more. The atmosphere is pleasant, with whimsical birdhouses strategically positioned just outside a trio of bay windows on the main floor. Hours: 11:00 A.M.–9:30 P.M. in the restaurant and 10:30 P.M. in the pub daily. Located in **Old Lyme Shopping Center, Rte. 1, Old Lyme, 06371; (860) 434-3335.**

Mad Hatter Bakery & Café—$$$

The dinner menu here shows a strong Mediterranean influence, which means French, Italian, even African. Moroccan chicken stew, redolent of cinnamon and fruit, coexists happily with pasta puttanesca and lamb seasoned with herbes de Provence. Breakfast relies heavily on the output of the bakery: breads, muffins, croissants, sticky buns and French toast made from challah, as well as frittatas, multigrain pancakes and cereals. Breakfast hours: Sat.–Sun., 8:30 A.M.–1:00 P.M. Lunch: Wed.–Fri., 11:30 A.M.–3:00 P.M.; Sat.–Sun., noon–3:00 P.M. Dinner served from 5:30 P.M., closing Thu. at 8:00 P.M., Fri.–Sat. at 9:00 P.M. Also open between meals & until 6:00 P.M. on Wed. for dessert and coffee. **23 Main St., Chester, 06412; (860) 526-2156.**

Riverwalk Café—$$$

The pleasant but rather ordinary interior at Riverwalk Café (which, by the way, does not give one a view of any river) belies above-average competence and imagination on the part of the kitchen. The menu is moderately sized, featuring straightforward barbecue pork ribs and sirloin steak as well as more creative treatments of chicken, fish, beef and pasta. The warm goat cheese salad appetizer and grilled chicken with roasted chiles entrée have proved to be consistently excellent. Lunch is a scaled-down dinner menu with the addition of numerous sandwiches and burgers. Lunch served Tue.–Sun., 11:30 A.M.–5:00 P.M.; dinner served Sun.–Thu., 5:00 P.M.–9:30 P.M., & Fri.–Sat., 5:00 P.M.–10:00 P.M. **184 Main St. (Rte. 154), Deep River, 06417; (860) 526-8148.**

Stella D'Oro—$$$

Despite its innocuous strip mall location, Stella D'Oro serves some of the best Italian food in the county. It's small but comfortable on the inside with both table and booth seating. The menu is made up of boiled and baked pastas, chicken, seafood and a very wide selection of veal dishes. Two signature creations—Rigatoni alla Stella D'Oro and Gamberetti alla Stella D'Oro (containing shrimp, spinach and a brandy cream sauce)—are highlights. Reservations suggested. Open nightly 5:00 P.M.–10:00 P.M. (Fri.–Sat. until 11:00). **210 Main St., Hoyts Cinema Plaza, Old Saybrook, 06475; (860) 388-6590.**

Steve's Centerbrook Café—$$$

This is a classic chef-owned restaurant, where a mixed bag of offerings includes several dishes of Tuscan and Asian inspiration. Pastas are available in half-portions for light eaters, and there's a large wine list including 15 selections at $15 per bottle. Set in an old Victorian building, the interior is light and bright, with some small, private romantic alcoves. Hours: Tue.–Sun., 5:30 P.M.–9:00 P.M. Also closed in Feb. & Mar. **78 Main St., Centerbrook (at the intersection of Rtes. 154, 602 and 604), 06409; (860) 767-1277.**

Wine and Roses—$$$

As you enter through a foyer lined with sterling reviews, Wine and Roses looks like a health-food restaurant until your eyes settle on the long bar and the menu. The fare emphasizes freshness, seasonality and the personal

319

expressiveness of the chef. You'll find steaks, a lot of fish and seafood, pastas, veal, lamb, salads and complex appetizers, supplemented by salads and sandwiches at lunch. There is also an upstairs lounge where longtime local keyboard talent, Al DeCaro, plays show tunes and requests on Sat. evenings. Lunch hours: Tue.–Sat., 11:30 A.M.–3:00 P.M. Dinner hours: Sun. & Tue.–Thu., 5:00 P.M.–9:00 P.M.; Fri.–Sat., 5:00 P.M.–10:00 P.M.; closed Mon. **150 Main St., Old Saybrook, 06475; (860) 388-9646.**

Hale 'n' Hearty Restaurant—$$ to $$$

This casual restaurant and pub serves a large menu of family-style American food—salads, sandwiches, pasta, broiled and baked seafood, chicken, steaks and home-style favorites such as pot roast, roast turkey and meatloaf. The biergarten for warm-weather use is a great place to hang out after a day of canoeing or hiking. Hours: Tue.–Sun., 11:30 A.M.–9:30 P.M., with a pub menu available Wed.–Sat., 9:30 P.M.–11:00 P.M., late May–Oct. **381 Town St. (Rte. 151 at Rte. 82), East Haddam, 06423; (860) 873-2640.**

Caffè Toscana—$$

Not just a coffeehouse, Toscana serves a small menu of lunchtime items that are perhaps best described as refined grinders: sweet sausage and Italian peppers, meatballs and shredded beef roasted with wine, vegetables and herbs. Cold sandwiches are also available, as well as baked goods and Italian ice treats. Hours: Mon.–Thu., 7:00 A.M.–4:00 P.M.; Fri.–Sat., 7:00 A.M.–10:00 P.M. **25 Main St., Old Saybrook, 06475; (860) 388-1270.**

PizzaWorks—$ to $$

True to its name, award-winning pizza is the specialty here. The beer selection is exceptional, consisting of more than 150 brews. Kids will love the working model trains that make a circuit above the dining room and in the upstairs seating area. Hours: Mon.–Thu., 4:00 P.M.–9:00 P.M.; Fri.–Sun., noon–9:00 P.M. **455 Boston Post Rd. (Rte. 1), Old Saybrook, 06475; (860) 388-2218.**

Vanderbrooke Bakery—$ to $$

Vanderbrooke is *the* bakery in Old Saybrook, where the food is as lovely to behold as it is to eat. The real strength here is the bread: full-size and miniloaves as well as beautifully fashioned individual rolls, in an array of surprising flavors. Of course, there are also cakes and tarts, as well as various deli salads sold by the pound, and at midday a couple of simple hot lunch items such as baked macaroni and cheese or little open-face sandwiches on crusty bread. Two or three tables handle the eat-in crowd. Hours: Tue.–Fri., 8:30 A.M.–5:30 P.M.; Sat., 8:00 A.M.–5:00 P.M.; Sun. (Memorial Day–Labor Day only), 8:30 A.M.–12:30 P.M. **65 Main St., Old Saybrook, 06475; (860) 388-9700.**

Wheatmarket—$ to $$

Despite its health-food store name, Wheatmarket is a place to visit if you want something fast and filling for $5. The hot prepared foods, such as macaroni and cheese, chicken pot pie, shepherd's pie and veggie lasagna, are all hearty and familiar and come with a salad on the side. Or choose from soups, deli salads and sandwiches. Wheatmarket is also the home of a popular and monstrous 10-inch-tall, 15-pound apple pie specialty. Hours: Mon.–Sat., 9:00 A.M.–6:00 P.M. **4 Water St., Chester, 06412; (860) 526-9347.**

Whistle Stop Café—$ to $$

This very informal but cheerful neighborhood diner serves a full range of breakfast foods as well as salads, burgers and sandwiches at midday, all for what you'd pay at a take-out deli without table service. Two nights a week it also does full dinners. Hours: Breakfast & lunch served 7:00 A.M.–2:30 P.M. daily; dinner served Fri.–Sat., 6:00 P.M.–9:00 P.M. **108 Main St. (Rte. 154), Deep River; 06417; (860) 526-4122.**

Coffeehouses, Sweets & Treats

In Old Saybrook, **James Gallery** (described under Art Galleries) is a most unusual ice cream and light lunch destination. **Paperback Café (Hoyts Cinema Plaza, 196 Main St.; 860-388-9718)** is a plain-Jane coffeehouse and eatery with plenty of reading material sitting around for patrons to enjoy with a light breakfast or lunch. They have live jazz Fri. & Sat. nights 8:00 P.M.–11:00 P.M. & on Sun. 11:00 A.M.–2:00 P.M. For chocolates by the piece or pound, as well as other candies, visit **Sugarplum's (235 Main St.; 860-388-6188)**, the "sweets of Saybrook" shop that sells Burnham & Brady chocolates, made in South Windsor, Connecticut.

Between them, next-door neighbors **Ken's Coffeehouse** and **Sweet Martha's (Main St. in the square opposite the Griswold Inn, Essex; 860-767-8454 and 860-767-0632)** serve all the foods you are likely to crave after a few hours of trotting around the streets of Essex shopping or visiting the Connecticut River Museum: coffee, chocolate, baked goodies and ice cream. Farther north and on the opposite side of the river near the Goodspeed Opera House, **Caffe Pronto (2 Norwich Rd. [Rte. 82], East Haddam; 860-873-8100)** is a convenient place to grab a cup of good coffee and dessert or a "gourmet" sandwich. **Salem Valley Farms Ice Cream (at the junction of Rtes. 82 and 11, Salem; 860-859-2980)** is a popular spot to stop for a cool cone or a packed quart.

Services

Local Visitors Information

Connecticut River Valley & Shoreline Visitor's Council, 393 Main St., Middletown, 06457; (800) 486-4446 or (860) 347-0028. Hours: Mon.–Fri., 8:30 A.M.–4:30 P.M., year-round.

The **Old Saybrook Chamber of Commerce** runs a tourist information booth out of a little red shed at the foot of Main St. next to the firehouse. It's open 9:00 A.M.–2:00 P.M. daily, Memorial Day–Labor Day. Outside of that season visit their office at **146 Main St.**, open Mon.–Fri., 9:00 A.M.–5:00 P.M., or call **(860) 388-3266.**

Transportation

Although it is just another form of transportation, the **Chester/Hadlyme Ferry** is an attraction in and of itself. Bridge crossings can be exciting too, of course, but there's something even more special about being able to get out of your car and ride within a few feet of the water, and this ferry is among the oldest in the country, having been in continuous operation since 1769. This ferry carries only about ten cars at a time, all on one deck. Crossing the river takes under five minutes, but if you happen to arrive just as a ferry is leaving the wait can increase your crossing time to 20 minutes or more. Fares at the time of this writing were $2.25 per car and driver plus $.75 for each passenger and $1.50 for a trailer. Pedestrians, bicyclists and moped drivers could cross for $.75. The ferry operates Apr.–Nov., weather permitting, Mon.–Fri., 7:00 A.M.–6:45 P.M.; Sat.–Sun., 10:30 A.M.–5:00 P.M. For more information call **(860) 443-3856.**

Regional bus service as far east as Old Lyme, as far west as Clinton and as far north as Chester is provided by the **Estuary Transit District** at **(860) 388-3497.** The **Old Saybrook Trolley** operates in a more limited range. This mechanized bus made to look like an authentic 1930s trolley does a one-hour loop serving the beach communities, several marinas and the shopping district, connecting with a bus in Westbrook that'll take you to many destinations in that town including the Westbrook Factory Stores (an outlet mall). Most merchants in town have schedules, and they're also published in local newspapers. Fare: $1 per ride or $3 per day. Season: weekends Memorial Day–late June, then daily until Labor Day. For more information call the **Chamber of Commerce** at **(860) 388-3266.**

Shore Line East provides weekday commuter rail service between New London and New Haven with stops in Old Saybrook and other shore towns. For schedule and fare information call **(800) 255-7433.** For details on long-distance train travel out of Old Saybrook call **Amtrak** at **(800) 872-7245.**

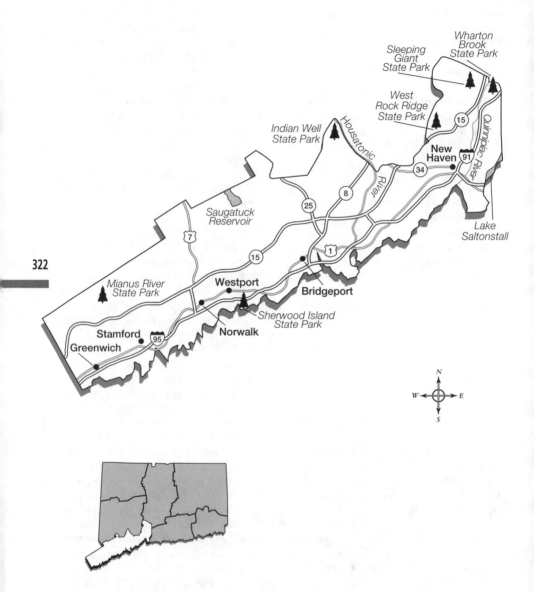

Wharton Brook State Park

Sleeping Giant State Park

West Rock Ridge State Park

Indian Well State Park

Housatonic

River

New Haven

Quinnipiac River

Lake Saltonstall

Saugatuck Reservoir

Mianus River State Park

Westport

Bridgeport

Sherwood Island State Park

Stamford

Norwalk

Greenwich

N
W E
S

Southwest Coast

323

Bridgeport

A one time industrial titan and still a bustling port handling the distribution of goods to and from New England, Bridgeport is Connecticut's largest city. Despite the lingering effects of hard times, one notable feature of Bridgeport's attractions is their strong family orientation. Connecticut's only full-fledged zoo, the Beardsley, is situated here with the beauty of a large urban park as a backdrop (Bridgeport's nickname is Park City). The Discovery Museum is one of the largest and best children's museums in the state. And who has brought more delight to children than P. T. Barnum, founder of "The Greatest Show on Earth" and the subject of a fun but thoughtful retrospective at the Barnum Museum?

The performing arts remain vibrant as well. Bridgeport's next-door neighbor, Stratford, shares with the English city of the same name a connection with William Shakespeare. For many years it was the site of the renowned American Shakespeare Theatre, whose rebirth as the Stratford Festival Theater is imminent. The Quick Center for the Arts at Fairfield University and the Klein Auditorium in Bridgeport are excellent venues for all sorts of cultural activities, and Bridgeport has an active symphony orchestra and cabaret theater. During summer there are also many pop music performances at Captain's Cove, a seaport-themed shopping area at Black Rock Harbor.

Despite the fact that a large portion of the area is solidly urban, you can still get close to nature. Milford Point is second only to Hammonasset Beach on the opposite side of the state for viewing shorebirds, and in addition to the Audubon Society property at the point, there are two others close by. Shore swimming and fishing are also available.

History

What is today Bridgeport was first inhabited by Native Americans who called the area Pequonnock, meaning "cleared field," in reference to their own cultivation of the land north of Black Rock Harbor. In 1637 during the Pequot War, members of the Pequot tribe being pursued by colonists fled down an east-west trail through the region. The bloody defeat of the Pequots came in a swamp in what was then called Uncoway (now Fairfield). Starting in 1639 or so Europeans began settling here, making Stratford and Fairfield among Connecticut's earliest towns. The parts of those towns (the dividing line was Park Ave.) that would later become downtown Bridgeport were called Newfield.

Because of the proximity of Stratford and Fairfield to British-held Long Island, they were fortified during the Revolutionary War by order of the General Assembly. There were also a fair number of Tories in the area, and Bridgeport Harbor was used to smuggle supplies to the enemy. Tories notwithstanding, British general Tryon's troops burned Fairfield in July 1779. Those who suffered losses were compensated in 1792 by land in Connecticut's Western Reserve (now Ohio), and for years that tract was known as the Fire Lands.

With several harbors to its credit, the area grew. Whereas Newfield at the start of the Revolution had perhaps a dozen houses, a quarter-century later it had more than quadrupled in size, and the first bridge across the Pequonnock River had been built, financed by a lottery. So, the community had a bridge and a port, and in 1800 Bridgeport was born as a borough of Stratford and was finally incorporated in 1821. Soon thereafter the history of the area was changed forever with the arrival of an expert showman, native to Bethel, Connecticut, but late of New York City. P. T. Barnum, who founded "The Greatest Show on Earth," was drawn to Bridgeport because of the city's fast growth and future potential, which he must have seen as paralleling his own rise in fame and fortune.

Bridgeport was becoming an industrious place. *Industria Crescimus*, Bridgeport's motto, means "By Industry We Live." And indeed, its history has been defined by the peaks and valleys of the industries that employed its immigrant masses. Its harbors plus the termination of the Housatonic Railroad at Bridgeport in 1836 (ditto the Naugatuck Railroad in 1848, followed by a connection to New York City in 1849) clinched Bridgeport's position as the transportation nexus in southwestern Connecticut. Manufacturers poured into East Bridgeport, and immigrants followed the jobs. A short list of their output in the last century and a half includes ammunition and guns that supplied troops in the Civil War and both world wars, gramophones and long-playing (LP) records, sewing machines, corsets, Frisbee pie plates and an endless assortment of gears and machine parts. One floor of the Barnum Museum is devoted to Bridgeport's incredible productivity.

The area played an important role in aviation history thanks to the ingenuity of Russian emigré Igor Sikorsky. Sikorsky's career began in czarist Russia where he built the first four-engine airplane in the world. He continued his career in the United States, specializing in building large flying boats, before developing the world's first practical helicopter. Rotary wing flight is a concept he is said to have been fascinated with since reading Jules Verne as a boy. Stratford is still the home of Sikorsky Aircraft and the local airport bears the Sikorsky name.

Bridgeport is notable for the 24-year tenure of its socialist mayor, Jasper McLevy, from 1933 to 1957. Just prior to his election, corruption in Bridgeport, long a problem, had grown so egregious that the state actually took over the city's finances for two years. Early in his reign McLevy was adept at dealing with Bridgeport's wasteful patronage system and instituting real reform, but by the 1950s his pecunious methods were perhaps not the right approach to the city's problems. The height of Bridgeport's prosperity had come during World War I when, during the course of one year, the population increased by 50% in response to job availability. Forty years later, however, the aftermath of two boom-and-bust cycles was catching up to Bridgeport in the form of substandard schools and housing that simply encouraged flight to the suburbs. Just as Bridgeport had once eclipsed the towns

325

that gave birth to it, those towns were now growing at Bridgeport's expense.

In its 200-year history Bridgeport has experienced a crushing volume of activity equivalent to that of a city several times its age. Today it is engaged in a fight for economic rejuvenation. Some urban renewal has taken place, including the completion of a minor league baseball park for the Bridgeport Bluefish, an AA Atlantic League team. It remains to be seen just how Bridgeport will be restored to its former health, but its history as a city of indomitable spirit is an encouraging heritage to contemplate as its leaders face the task.

Major Attractions

Barnum Museum

Named after and dedicated to preserving the legend of Phineas Taylor (P. T.) Barnum, creator of "The Greatest Show on Earth," the Barnum Museum documents the life and exploits of its founder as well as the city whose fate was inextricably linked with his. A little bit of Barnum history seems in order. He began his show business career in Manhattan in 1842 with what we would now call a freak show. One of his finds, a midget by the name of Charles Stratton, was metamorphosed under Barnum's guidance into General Tom Thumb, an actor who entertained the courts of Europe and became quite wealthy in his own regard.

Barnum was a man of seemingly contradictory traits. As a showman he had no compunction against perpetrating hoaxes, yet he served the public sincerely and honestly as both mayor of Bridgeport and a state representative. His twin barometers of acceptability when it came to some new exploit seem to have been whether his audience would find a scheme amusing and whether there was money to be made in it! He pulled off his deceptions with humor, and the audience laughed with him. As a flamboyant, daring and

shrewd arbiter of public taste, Barnum has probably never been equalled.

The museum that honors him is a spectacular brownstone with Byzantine influences, as grandiose as its namesake. The first floor is devoted to the story of Barnum's life. The second level serves as a museum of Bridgeport history, including a homage to its past manufacturing glory. The top floor focuses on Barnum's work: the people he made famous, the hoaxes he concocted and his genius at promotion. Admission: $5 adults, $4 seniors, $3 children 4–18. Hours: Tue.–Sat., 10:00 A.M.–4:30 P.M.; Sun., noon–4:30 P.M.; open half days on Mon. in July & Aug. **820 Main St. (1 block south of State St.), Bridgeport, 06604; (203) 331-1104.**

Beardsley Zoological Gardens

You won't see elephants and rhinoceroses at Connecticut's only accredited zoo. With a few exceptions, such as the trio of Siberian tigers, the focus is on animals native to our own hemisphere. The Beardsley is intimate in size and very family-oriented, making it ideal for an outing with young children. Strolling at an easy pace and spending a bit of time at each exhibit, you can see everything in an hour and a half. But add in musical entertainment, a ride on the stunning enclosed carousel, a meal in the picnic grove and browsing at the gift shop, and a visit could easily fill an afternoon. Admission: $4 adults, $2 children age 5–15, $1 children age 3–4. Parking: $3 for Connecticut vehicles, $5 for out-of-state vehicles. Hours: 9:00 A.M.–4:00 P.M., year-round; closed major holidays. **1875 Noble Ave. (in Beardsley Park), Bridgeport, 06610; (203) 576-8082.**

Other Attractions

Captain's Cove Seaport

Captain's Cove is a small complex of shops together with a marina and a restaurant on the shore of Bridgeport's Black Rock Harbor. The

Shoppers at Captain's Cove, Black Rock Harbor, Bridgeport. Photo by Stuart Smith/Coastal Fairfield Convention and Visitors Bureau.

326

postage-stamp-size stores lining the boardwalk sell mostly souvenirs. Captain's Cove restaurant serves seafood in an atmosphere that bridges the gap between fast food and a full-service eatery. At the marina just steps away, charter vessels are available for saltwater fishing. Concerts and special events are frequently scheduled on summer weekends.

Black Rock Harbor is also the home port of the HMS *Rose,* "the largest operational sailing vessel in the world" and "the only example of a Revolutionary [era] warship afloat today," according to the placard at her dock. The *Rose,* which was built in 1970, is a replica of a British frigate dating from the 1750s. *Rose* travels the world, representing the United States in tall-ships festivals around the globe. If you visit Bridgeport during the one week or so out of every year when she is in port and open for tours (usually in May), make it a point to go. The lightship *Nantucket,* the largest ever built and one of only 12 extant, is permanently docked at the Cove and available for guided tours on a more regular basis; call for a schedule and pricing. The season for the attractions at Captain's Cove is roughly Apr.–Oct. Store hours are 11:00 A.M.–6:00 P.M., but on rainy days the shops often stay shuttered, so call before going if there's any question. Located at the **end of Bostwick Ave. in Bridgeport;** (203) 335-1433.

Festivals and Events

Dogwood Festival
mid-May

More than 200 years ago a Fairfield resident began transplanting Connecticut native dogwood trees from the woods to his private property. Their beauty inspired others, and today it is estimated that over 30,000 dogwoods grow in Fairfield, putting on a spectacular show when they bloom in May. The festival consists of walking tours of Fairfield's historic neighborhoods, crafts vendors, an art show, a plant sale, luncheon (by reservation) and more. It takes place Mother's Day weekend and contin-

Getting There

Bridgeport and the communities that surround it are located about an hour and a half southwest of Hartford by car. From Hartford take I-91 south to the Merritt Parkway (Rte. 15) if you're headed for the north side of Bridgeport or inland suburbs such as Trumbull. If your destination is downtown Bridgeport or neighboring shore towns, take I-91 all the way to New Haven and pick up I-95 west to the appropriate exit. For other transportation options, see the Services section at the end of this chapter.

ues through the following Tue. Admission is free. Hours: Sat., 10:00 A.M.–5:00 P.M.; Sun., 11:30 A.M.–5:00 P.M.; Mon.–Tue., 10:00 A.M.–3:30 P.M. Start from **Greenfield Hill Congregational Church, 1045 Old Academy Rd., Fairfield; (203) 259-5596.**

Stratford Day
Sat. after Father's Day (June)

This family street festival features a real grab bag of activities, with 110–125 crafters displaying their work, children's games, a small carnival, an antique and classic auto show, musical and magical entertainment, street performers, pony rides and recitations of Shakespeare (a tie-in to the American Shakespeare Theatre). The festival proper takes place on **Main St. between Stratford Ave. and Church St.** Admission is free. Hours: 10:00 A.M.–6:00 P.M. For more information call **(203) 377-0771.**

Trumbull Day
last weekend in June (Sat. or Sun. but not both)

The "largest single-day event in Fairfield County" is basically a big party for no particular reason. It started about 30 years ago as a town picnic and just kept getting bigger. Now it draws 60,000 people annually. Attractions include numerous carnival rides, continual entertainment on stage as well as strolling performers in the crowd, a crafts market, food vendors and a massive fireworks display after dark. Admission: still only a buck! Hours: 11:00 A.M.–midnight. Held at Hillcrest Jr. High School at **Daniels Farm and Strobel Rds. in Trumbull.** For more information call **(203) 377-2858** during business hours.

P. T. Barnum Festival
Fourth of July weekend

Although the Barnum Festival culminates with a parade, fireworks and concerts on Fourth of July weekend, the festival is actually a two-month-long series of events around the city. Throughout May and June there are balls, dances, a banana boat party (in recognition of the fact that more bananas are handled through the Cilco Terminal in Bridgeport than through any other on the East Coast), the Wing Ding parade featuring kids in costume and on floats, a Jenny Lind concert/competition (in real life Lind was a light operatic star Barnum promoted), the crowning of the Barnum king and queen and more.

Finally, on the last weekend there's a huge fireworks display Fri. night, shot off from Seaside Park, and people gather all along the shore to watch. Sat. evening there's a marching band battle of the bands called Champions on Parade, and the final event is a parade on Sun. at 10:00 A.M. following a route up Park Ave., down Capitol Ave. and ending at the reviewing stands on Lincoln Blvd. For more information call **(203) 367-8495.**

New England Arts & Crafts Festival
early July

Usually held on the weekend following the Fourth of July, this juried festival is known for the high quality of the merchandise. There's musical entertainment both days, as well as readings, other performances and a food court. The show takes place on the **Milford green between N. Broad and S. Broad Sts.** Admission is free. Hours: 9:00 A.M.–5:00 P.M.

both days. For more information call **(203) 878-6647.**

Milford Oyster Festival
third Sat. in Aug.

Taking its name from the fact that Milford was a busy oyster-harvesting area for hundreds of years, used first by the Indians and then by the colonists, this festival is a celebration of the harbor and the downtown. Two hundred or so arts and crafts vendors set up on the green. A tall ship gives rides (reserve in advance by calling **203-876-1501** during daytime hours), as does the tour boat *Liberty Belle*, which comes over from New Haven for the occasion. There's a music stage, children's entertainment and plenty of food, including but definitely not limited to oysters. The festival takes place on the **Milford green between N. Broad and S. Broad Sts.** Admission is free. Hours: 9:00 A.M.–5:00 P.M. For more information call **(203) 878-4225.**

Outdoor Activities

Biking

Mountain biking is permitted on the abandoned railroad bed at Pequonnock Valley Park in Trumbull, described under Hiking. The main trail is 2.5 miles long, and many side trails branch off it. In Fairfield, try the trails surrounding Lake Mohegan on Morehouse Highway. For details call the **Fairfield Conservation Dept.** at **(203) 256-3071.**

Birding

Connecticut Audubon Society Birdcraft Museum and Sanctuary
The oldest private bird sanctuary in America is located on 6.5 acres in an almost urban setting one block from Milford's train station and Rte. 1. One point of the exhibits is to show how wildlife can thrive in urban areas. There are demonstration gardens for attracting birds and butterflies, a boardwalk across a small pond,

a bird observation area, a museum with diorama exhibits on birds and Connecticut habitats and a small gift shop. Museum admission: $2 adults, $1 children 12 and under. Admission to the grounds is free. Museum hours: Tue.–Fri., 10:00 A.M.–5:00 P.M.; Sat.–Sun., noon–5:00 P.M. Grounds hours: dawn–dusk daily. **314 Unquowa Rd., Fairfield, 06430; (203) 259-0416.**

Connecticut Audubon Society Center at Fairfield

Of the three Audubon properties in the area, this one has the most extensive hiking trail system, with 6 miles of paths through woodland and salt marsh. Because of the mix of habitats, birders can see everything from shorebirds and songbirds to turkeys. Admission: $2 adults, $1 children under 12, free for members and Fairfield residents. The trails are open dawn–dusk daily. Pets and picnicking are not allowed. Gift shop hours: Tue.–Sat., 9:00 A.M.–4:30 P.M.; open seasonally on Sun. **2325 Burr St., Fairfield, 06430; (203) 259-6305.**

Milford Point Coastal Center

This Connecticut Audubon Society preserve is located on 800 acres of salt marsh on Long Island Sound, making it a great area for viewing shorebirds spring through fall and migrating hawks in autumn. Visitors can walk along the shore, then visit the new Coastal Center, an educational facility featuring a touch tank filled with Long Island Sound fauna, scopes for getting a close-up view of birds on the marsh, computerized information on birds and more. Free bird walks are offered Sat. mornings 9:00–10:00 A.M., year-round, and other programming takes place regularly. Admission: $2 adults, $1 seniors and children under 12, or $5 for a family group. Hours: Tue.–Sat., 10:00 A.M.–4:00 P.M.; Sun., noon–4:00 P.M. Located at the **end of Milford Pt. Rd., Milford; (203) 878-7440.**

Boating

Housatonic River/Long Island Sound

A state boating access area is located near the mouth of the Housatonic River in Milford under the I-95 bridge between Milford and Stratford. The parking lot and ramp are on Naugatuck Ave. north of Rte. 1. From here you can explore upriver to the first dam at Derby or go south past the huge nature preserve at Milford Pt. and out into Long Island Sound. A parking fee is charged in summer.

Cruises

The home port of the 91-foot replica schooner *Quinnipiack* is New Haven's Long Wharf, but on occasion it sails out of Milford Dock on both educational and sunset cruises. For more information, see the listing under the **New Haven** chapter.

Marinas

Bridgeport Harbor is a largely commercial deep-water harbor, but none of the marinas can accommodate pleasure boats much above 50 feet. **Ryan's Marine Services (203-579-1319;** VHF 10) offers a few transient slips, repair services, rest room and pump-out facilities, but no gas. Try **Lou's Boat Basin (203-336-9809;** VHF 6) or **Riverside Marine (203-335-7068;** VHF 9) if you just need to refuel. **Hitchcock Marine (203-334-2161)** also offers complete repair service.

Black Rock Harbor, also in Bridgeport, is a little more attuned to the needs of the transient visitor but still somewhat industrial in appearance. **Captain's Cove Seaport (203-335-1433;** VHF 18) is a marina cum tourist attraction (see the listing under Other Attractions) with 20 transient berths, a full range of services and facilities, and the ability to accommodate even the largest boats. **Cedar Marina (203-335-6262;** VHF 9) also offers 20 transient berths for boats up to 60 feet in length and a number of services, but no gas.

Milford Boat Works, a.k.a. Milford Harbor Marina **(203-877-1475;** VHF 68), and **Port Milford Marina (203-877-7802;** VHF 9) are two full-service commercial facilities in Milford ready to serve transient boaters. The latter has a little more in the way of conveniences, such as a restaurant and grocery store, but only the former sells gas. There's also a brand-new municipal facility called **Milford Landing (203-874-1610;** VHF 9) that is completed geared toward transient visitors. It has 40 slips, hourly and overnight docking rates, showers, a laundromat, hookups, car and bicycle rental and access to town recreational facilities a few steps away.

Finally, over Stratford way **The Marina at the Dock (203-378-9300)** and **Stratford Marina (203-377-4477;** VHF 9) both have plenty of transient berths and most services you could want. Stratford Marina also sells gas.

For navigational details, charts and complete lists of marine facilities throughout this area, your best source of information is *Embassy's Complete Boating Guide & Chartbook to Long Island Sound*. Contact the publisher at **142 Ferry Rd., Old Saybrook, 06475; (860) 395-0188.**

Fishing

Several small charter fishing vessels operate out of area harbors mid-Apr.–Nov. The *Carol Marie* (203-264-2891), the *Daystar* (203-876-2910) and the *Somertime* (203-438-5838) depart from Captain's Cove Seaport at Black Rock Harbor in Bridgeport; the *Reel Joy III* (203-877-7164) is based at Spencer's Marina in Milford and the *Mako* (203-261-8821) docks at Birdseye Ramp in Stratford. For a completely current list, contact the local chambers of commerce or the **Coastal Fairfield County Tourism District** (see Services). The office at **Captain's Cove (203-335-1433)** can provide you with a complete list of charter operators at its dock, but it does not arrange charters. You must call the captains of the vessels directly.

During the third weekend of Aug. Captain's Cove sees a lot of action as a weigh station for the annual Bluefish Festival, a massive fishing derby with cash prizes of up to $25,000. For more information call the derby organizer, local radio station **WICC 600 AM**, at **(203) 366-2583.**

Hiking

In this urban area, open spaces are principally town-owned and maintained. Call the **Fairfield**

Recreation Dept. at **(203) 256-3010** and the **Trumbull Recreation Dept.** at **(203) 452-5060** for details on numerous small parks with free hiking and nature trails in addition to those listed below. In Stratford you can hike 350-acre **Roosevelt Forest** for a small fee. Call **(203) 385-4052** for details.

Paugussett Trail

You can pick up this blue-blazed trail at Indian Well State Park on Indian Well Rd. in Shelton. The trail traverses the park, which is a tall, linear one hugging the west bank of the Housatonic River, crosses Webb Mtn. Park in Monroe, then turns inland around Stevenson Dam before terminating at East Village Rd. in Monroe about 5 miles from the starting point. A parking fee is charged in summer.

Pequonnock Valley Park

The long and fascinating history of a section of the Pequonnock River Valley is described in detail in a wonderful guide to its hiking trails available from the **Trumbull Recreation Dept.** at **(203) 452-5060.** Mills, dams, a railroad and an amusement park are just some of the things that were once in the valley, and remains of some can still be found. Open dawn–dusk, year-round. Enter from Mine Hill Park off Old Mine Rd. or from Indian Ledge Park on Indian Ledge Park Rd. in Trumbull.

Ice Skating

Two area rinks—seasonal **Milford Ice Skating Pavilion (291 Bic Dr., Milford; 203-878-6516)** and year-round **Wonderland of Ice (123 Glenwood Park, Bridgeport; 203-576-8110)** offer public skating hours weekly. Call for hours and rates. Rental skates are available at Wonderland, which also offers stick time on weekday afternoons and regular pickup hockey games.

Swimming

Freshwater

Indian Well State Park

At Indian Well you can take a dip in Lake Housatonic, the widened portion of the Housatonic

River above Derby Dam. There's a picnic pavilion as well as individual tables with grills, space for field sports, horseshoe pits (bring your own horseshoes), access to the blue-blazed Paugussett Trail for hiking, a boat launch and lifeguards. Located on **Indian Well Rd. off Rte. 110 in Shelton; (203) 735-4311.**

Saltwater

Jennings Beach/Penfield Beach
Collectively known as Fairfield Beach, Jennings and Penfield are the two principal public beaches in Fairfield. Jennings is located at the end of S. Benson Rd. and Penfield is on Fairfield Beach Rd. A parking fee of $10 per car on weekdays and $15 per car on weekends is charged Memorial Day–Labor Day. Season passes are $50. For more information call **(203) 256-3010.**

Seaside Park
Bridgeport's principal beach runs for nearly 2 miles along Fayerweather Island, which is no island at all but more of a long, thin stretch of land tapering off into Long Island Sound. Seaside is packed in summer with a real cross-section of Bridgeport life, and a fee is charged for entry. The main swimming area is in the center below Barnum Dyke. The roads that run along the beach can be confusing because of a one-way system. You can enter only from certain north-south streets, such as Park Ave. and Iranistan Ave.

Short Beach
This Stratford town beach and recreation complex is available to nonresidents for a $3 per car fee. In addition to a sandy beach on Long Island Sound there are picnic tables, tennis and platform tennis courts, a playground, a volleyball area and miniature golf and a 9-hole municipal golf course. Hours: dawn–dusk daily. Located on **Short Beach Rd. in Stratford.** For more information call **(203) 385-4052.**

Walnut Beach
The largest of Milford's public shoreline beaches is currently available to nonresidents for $5 per car. Early and late in the season (Memorial Day–July 1 and mid-Aug.–Labor Day) the beach is open weekends only, 11:00 A.M.–3:00 P.M.

During the height of summer, hours are 10:00 A.M.–4:00 P.M. daily. From Walnut Beach you can access an undeveloped state-owned shoreline property known as Silver Beach, from which you can walk to outlying Charles Island at low tide and explore, but don't get stuck out there with the tide coming in! Located at the **corner of Viscount Dr. and E. Broadway in Milford.** For more information call **(203) 783-3280.**

Seeing and Doing

The most current and comprehensive guide to upcoming events, concerts, art shows and more in this area is the *Fairfield County Weekly,* a free periodical available at newsstands, convenience stores and many attractions. Also check the *Connecticut Post* for listings.

Antiquing
Stratford Antique Center is a huge warehouse filled with the displays of 200 dealers in antiques and collectibles. It's open daily 10:00 A.M.–5:00 P.M., keeping late hours on Thu. before Christmas. **400 Honeyspot Rd., Stratford, 06497; (203) 378-7754.**

Art Galleries
Part of the Quick Center for the Arts at Fairfield University, the **Walsh Art Gallery** is open to the public free of charge Tue.–Sat., 11:00 A.M.–5:00 P.M., & Sun., noon–4:00 P.M. Shows change about every six weeks, with a short break between shows, so call before going. Enter the Fairfield University campus from N. Benson Rd. between Black Rock Tpke. and Boston Post Rd. (Rte. 1) in Fairfield. For more information call the **Quick Center** at **(203) 254-4010.**

At the **Housatonic Museum of Art,** part of the Housatonic Community-Technical College, the holdings consist primarily of 20th-century paintings and graphics, including works by Warhol, Lichtenstein, Matisse and Picasso. About 500 pieces are distributed throughout the building. Call for hours and directions. **900 Lafayette Blvd. (at State), Bridgeport, 06604; (203) 332-5200.**

Other galleries are at the Discovery Museum (described under Children and Families) and the Housatonic Museum of Art (described under Museums).

Children and Families

The Discovery Museum (4450 Park Ave. between Eckart and Geduldig Sts., Bridgeport, 06604; 203-372-3521) is a hands-on science center—the perfect place to take kids who are at that stage where they're curious about how things work. Major exhibits include displays on electricity, nuclear energy, light and sound and the rules of perspective and color theory in art. There is a hand-eye coordination game with a space mission theme and a small planetarium with daily shows. The main floor also contains a large gallery—by itself worth a trip to the museum—for changing art exhibits.

The museum offers a plethora of programs: art and science classes for tots on up (adults included), a "Museum Magic Hour" (story time followed by a project appropriate for preschool children) and the ambitious Challenger Learning Center, in which kids and adults take part in a simulated space mission for the better part of a weekend afternoon. Advance reservations are required for this once-a-month program, but miniversions of it take place each Sat. & Sun. at 3:00 P.M. Call to confirm the hours of any special programs before going. Admission: $6 adults, $4 children 3–18. Hours: Tue.–Sat., 10:00 A.M.–5:00 P.M.; Sun., noon–5:00 P.M.

Museums

Several area groups run museums of local history. Call the **Stratford Historical Society (203-378-0630)**, the **Shelton History Center (203-925-1803)** and the **Trumbull Historical Society (203-377-6620)** for details on the historic sites they maintain. Most museums are open during summer and early autumn only. Also see the listing for the Barnum Museum under Major Attractions.

Boothe Park

The unique collection of buildings and artifacts at Boothe Park in Stratford was mostly built or acquired by the wealthy and eccentric Boothe family, who farmed on the site for over 300 years. Structures include a homestead (ca. 1900), an Americana Museum and a redwood "cathedral," among others. Many exhibits focus on 19th-century farming and domestic life. Free guided tours of two of the buildings are given Tue.–Fri., 11:00 A.M.–1:00 P.M., & Sat.–Sun., 1:00 P.M.–4:00 P.M., June–Oct. During that season the other buildings are open daily for self-guided exploration, approximately 8:00 A.M.–3:00 P.M. Located in **Boothe Memorial Park on Main St. Putney in Stratford; (203) 381-2046.**

Fairfield Historical Society

Fairfield has an extremely active historical society that maintains the Ogden House (ca. 1750), and a museum with three galleries exhibits items pertaining to Fairfield History. The museum is open weekdays 9:30 A.M.–4:30 P.M. & weekends 1:00 P.M.–5:00 P.M. The Ogden House can be toured Sat.–Sun., 1:00 P.M.–4:00 P.M., mid-May–mid-Oct. For more information call **(203) 259-1598.**

Milford Historical Society Wharf Ln. Complex

This trio of historic buildings is named for the lower part of High St. connecting the town dock with the town green, which used to be called Wharf Ln. One of the properties is believed to be the oldest house in Milford. Another is the first one built outside the town stockade. The Bryan-Downs House contains a collection of artifacts, some of them 10,000 years old, gathered by a local amateur archaeologist. Admission by suggested $2 donation. Hours: Sat.–Sun., 2:00 P.M.–4:00 P.M., Memorial Day–Columbus Day. **34 High St., Milford, 06460; (203) 874-2664.**

Nightlife

Although there are plenty of small bars and music clubs in this area where you can while away the wee hours, the scene isn't dominated by any one place. Two recommendations are **Boston Billiards (111 Black Rock Tpke., Fairfield; 203-335-2255)** and **Black Rock Castle (2895 Fairfield Ave., Bridgeport; 203-336-3990)**. The former is an authentic billiards club similar to the Boston Billiards in **Danbury**; see that chapter for details. Black Rock Castle, a restaurant and bar specializing in Irish food, beer and music, is described under the Where to Eat section.

Performing Arts

Greater Bridgeport Symphony/Klein Memorial Auditorium

The programming is frequently a combination of something popular combined with something classic. Most performances take place at **Klein Memorial Auditorium, 910 Fairfield Ave., Bridgeport, 06604.** For more information call **(203) 576-0263.**

In addition to being home to Bridgeport's orchestra, the Klein also hosts guest artists such as the Hartford Ballet and the Connecticut Grand Opera. It's an older venue known for its excellent sight lines and good sound from any seat in the house. Parking is free. For a schedule of upcoming events call **(203) 576-8115.**

Downtown Cabaret Theatre

Bridgeport's unique BYOB dinner theater mounts productions of classic and new musicals as well as children's shows. Seating is at tables or booths; bring your own food and drink. Call for show times and ticket prices. Secure parking is available for only $2. Enter the theater from the brick terrace on the side of **263 Golden Hill St. in Bridgeport; (203) 576-1636.**

Quick Center for the Arts

This comprehensive cultural center brings national and international talent to town for broad-based programming including theater, music and children's entertainment. Several big events include a St. Patrick's Day performance, a Mardi Gras party in mid-Feb. with New Orleans jazz, late spring Pops concerts and Christmas shows with the Fairfield University Glee Club and a Young Audience series of music, storytelling and more. Located on the campus of Fairfield University. Enter on **N. Benson Rd. between Black Rock Tpke. and Boston Post Rd. [Rte. 1] in Fairfield; (203) 254-4010.**

Stratford Festival Theater

From its construction in the mid-1950s until its closure in 1982 after a loss of funding, the American Shakespeare Theatre in Stratford exposed legions of schoolchildren to the works of William Shakespeare. Now the private non-profit Stratford Festival Theater plans to renovate the existing theater building as well as build new venues to accommodate year-round programming, including Shakespearean works, musicals, family-oriented shows, lectures and special events. The goal is to attract the same caliber of talent that made the American Shakespeare Theatre renowned in its first incarnation. At the same time, they intend to continue the theater's original educational mandate. **1850 Elm St. (at Ferry Blvd. and Stratford Ave., Stratford, 06497; (203) 378-1200.**

Sports

The major area sports attraction is the Bridgeport Bluefish, an AA Atlantic League baseball team playing in a new 5,300-seat stadium off I-95, exit 27, within walking distance from downtown. Tickets are $4–$15 with discounts for seniors and kids. For more information call **(203) 334-8499.**

Fans of BMX racing will find a quarter-mile track in Indian Ledge Park in Trumbull where races are offered Tue. nights, 7:00 P.M.–10:00 P.M., May–Aug. Admission is free. Grandstand seating and refreshments are available. Enter via Indian Ledge Park Rd. off Whitney Ave. For more information call **(203) 452-0315.**

Wagering

Milford Jai-Alai

Milford Jai-Alai has daily performances six days a week and an off-track betting parlor with live calling from thoroughbred and grey-

333

hound tracks around the country. Jai-alai performances are given at 12:15 P.M. Sat.–Mon. & Wed. & at 6:30 P.M. Wed.–Sat. & Mon. Dining available. You must be 18 years old to enter the facility. **311 Old Gate Ln., Milford, 06460; (800) 972-9650 (in Connecticut), (800) 243-9660** (out-of-state) or **(203) 877-4242.**

Shoreline Star Greyhound Park

Shoreline Star offers live greyhound racing May–Nov. on an outdoor track and simulcast thoroughbred and greyhound racing year-round. Post time during the racing season is 1:00 P.M. on Wed., Sat. & Sun. & 7:30 P.M. on Mon. & Wed.–Sat. Free parking; dining available. You must be 18 years old to enter the facility. **255 Kossuth St., Bridgeport, 06608; (888) 463-6446.**

Where to Stay

Bed & Breakfasts

Nathan Booth House—$$$ to $$$$

The only B&B in the area is located in a restored Greek Revival farmhouse near Boothe Memorial Park. The house is furnished with period antiques and reproductions to complement the wideboard floors and other original features of the property. There are four guest rooms, some with private bath, some with shared. Downstairs there is a guest parlor with a fireplace and TV for socializing. Innkeepers Ken and Jean Smith serve a full breakfast in a formal dining room. **6080 Main St. Putney, Stratford, 06497; (203) 378-6489.**

Hotels, Motels & Inns

In the Bridgeport area room rates tend to be lower on weekends, since most of the hotel clientele are business travelers staying over on weeknights. The price of accommodation can vary widely; always inquire about special discounts. It can be possible to stay at some of the better hotels for little more than you'd pay at a budget hotel with far fewer amenities. The listings below represent some of these better

hotels. For more listings call the **Coastal Fairfield County Tourism District** at **(800) 866-7925** or **(203) 854-7825.** Milford, especially, has a large number of moderately priced places.

Additionally, inn rooms are planned for **Rainbow Gardens (117 N. Broad St., Milford, 06460; 203-878-2500),** the new and well-received restaurant in Milford. This mid-1800s house was at the end of a two-year restoration at the time of this writing, and the rooms had not yet been completed, but there will be three of them with a shared bath. Call for details.

Residence Inn—$$$$

For long-term visitors or folks who just want to stretch out a little more than an ordinary hotel room allows, Shelton's Residence Inn would be a good choice. This is one of the Marriott chain of "all-suite" hotels with the flavor of a small condominium complex. They all have a fully equipped galley kitchen and most have small wood-burning fireplaces. They offer a laundry room, a valet laundry service, a free buffet breakfast, an outdoor swimming pool, a heated outdoor spa, a barbeque and picnic area and a multipurpose sports court. Guests can avail themselves of Nautilus equipment and an Olympic-size pool at Shelton Community Center at no charge. Pets can be accommodated. **1001 Bridgeport Ave., Shelton, 06484; (203) 926-9000.**

Holiday Inn—$$$ to $$$$

The only major hotel in downtown Bridgeport has everything you'll need for a short stay on-site: a workout room, an indoor pool, a full-service restaurant serving three meals a day and a lounge for meeting friends or colleagues. The accommodations include several suites in addition to standard hotel rooms. The Holiday Inn is walking distance from the train, bus and ferry terminals, but free shuttle service is available to those locations as well as Sikorsky Memorial Airport in Stratford. Secure garage parking is available behind the hotel; enter from Middle St. **1070 Main St.** (near I-95 exit 27 northbound, exit 29 southbound), **Bridgeport, 06604; (203) 334-1234.**

Ramada Hotel—$$$ to $$$$

The Ramada is a good place to take advantage of the perks normally accorded only business travelers. All rooms have an iron and ironing board, hair dryer and coffeemaker. There are also several classes of suite, some with kitchenette or whirlpool tub. A number of rooms are equipped for handicapped-accessibility. Other facilities and services include two restaurants, room service, an indoor pool, a sauna, exercise equipment and a complimentary shuttle service to any destination within a 12-mile radius of the hotel. **780 Bridgeport Ave., Shelton, 06484; (800) 272-6232** or **(203) 929-1500.**

Trumbull Marriott—$$$ to $$$$

The Trumbull Marriott offers a broad range of services and facilities on-site, making it a favorite with local people putting up family members from out of town. There are two full-service restaurants on the premises, one of which was recognized for best hotel dining in Fairfield County by *Connecticut* magazine. There's also a piano bar, a dance club and a seasonal poolside bar and grill. Other amenities include indoor and outdoor pools, a sauna, an exercise facility, a game room, safe deposit boxes, a baby-sitting service and a car rental desk in the lobby. **180 Hawley Ln., Trumbull, 06611; (800) 221-9855** or **(203) 378-1400.**

Where to Eat

In addition to the eateries listed below, the in-house restaurants at the **Trumbull Marriott** (see the listing under Where to Stay) are worth your consideration, and the Holiday Inn's **Parc 1070** offers moderate prices, a central location **(1070 Main St., Bridgeport, 06604; 203-334-1234)** for breakfast, lunch or dinner and easy parking in the hotel's garage.

Jeffrey's—$$$ to $$$$

Jeffrey's has an elegant but comfortable atmosphere in keeping with its Continental/American menu. Nice table linens, candlelight, a surprising view out over salt marsh and Long Island Sound and piano music Thu.–Sat. set the mood. Several dinner choices are available at lunch, in addition to sandwiches and salads. The restaurant won *Connecticut* magazine's readers' poll award for Best Continental in New Haven County. Reservations recommended. Lunch is served Mon.–Fri., 11:30 A.M.–3:00 P.M. Dinner hours: Mon.–Thu., 5:30 P.M.–9:00 P.M.; Fri–Sat. until 10:00 P.M.; Sun. dinner only 2:00 P.M.–8:00 P.M. **501 New Haven Ave., Milford, 06460; (203) 878-1910.**

Scribner's—$$$ to $$$$

Scribner's *is* seafood in the Bridgeport area. New England, Rhode Island and Manhattan clam chowder are all available every day. Steaks and the surf-and-turf combination are also popular; plus there's a menu of spicier, more elaborate daily specials. The interior is woody, with two moderately sized dining rooms and a small lounge with a few intimate booths. Lunch hours: Mon.–Fri., 11:30 A.M.–2:30 P.M. Dinner served from 5:00 P.M. daily. **31 Village Rd., Milford, 06460; (800) 828-7019.**

Arizona Flats—$$$

If you guessed Tex-Mex, you're right. There's evidence of all manner of cuisines in the menu, including a rack of lamb with a blue cornmeal crust served with Creole mustard. The bar is a crowded hangout, but the restaurant is calmer and firmly southwestern in decor. Lunch served Mon.–Sat., 11:30 A.M.–3:00 P.M. Dinner hours: Mon.–Sat., 5:00 P.M.–11:00 P.M.; Sun., 4:00 P.M.–11:00 P.M. The bar stays open considerably later. **3001 Fairfield Ave., Bridgeport, 06605; (203) 334-8300.**

Black Rock Castle—$$$

This is one place you really can't miss as you're driving down the street. It's the only black castle in town, modeled after an authentic castle of the same name in Cork, Ireland, and it is the local outpost of Irish food, beer and music. It has 24 beers on tap, including Bass, Harp, Foster's and its own Castle Rock Ale, as well as German, Scottish and domestic brews. It serves traditional foods such as imported smoked Irish salmon. Live music Thu.–Sat.

begins around 9:00 P.M. Entertainment ranges from rock 'n' roll to traditional Irish sing-alongs; call for specifics. Every Sun. at 6:30 P.M. there's an Irish jam session that anyone with an instrument and a familiarity with Irish music is invited to join. In honor of St. Patrick's Day, the month of Mar. is filled with special events. Restaurant open Sun.–Thu., 11:30 A.M.–9:00 P.M.; Fri.–Sat., 11:30 A.M.–11:00 P.M. Bar open Fri.–Sat. until 2:00 A.M., other nights until 1:00 A.M. **2895 Fairfield Ave., Bridgeport, 06605; (203) 336-3990.**

Centro's Ristorante & Bar—$$$

Centro's offers fresh and upscale Italian food in a family-oriented setting. Pasta is the reason to come here, and it's all homemade. There are also cold and grilled sandwiches and thin-crust pizzas. Lunch hours: Mon.–Sat., 11:30 A.M.–3:00 P.M. Dinner hours: Mon.–Thu., 5:30 P.M.–10:00 P.M.; Fri.–Sat., 5:30 P.M.–11:00 P.M.; Sun., 5:00 P.M.–9:30 P.M. **1435 Boston Post Rd. (Rte. 1), Fairfield, 06430; (203) 255-1210.**

The Metropolitan—$$$

The former Ocean Sea Grill is now the Metropolitan, located on the 11th floor of the Wright Financial Building. It's a large place with views of downtown Bridgeport and Long Island Sound. The cuisine is American/Continental with the choices evenly divided between four categories: grilled meats, fish and seafood, pastas and sandwiches. Lunch served Mon.–Fri., 11:30 A.M.–3:00 P.M. Dinner hours: Wed.–Sat., 5:00 P.M.–10:00 P.M. **1000 Lafayette Blvd., Bridgeport, 06604; (203) 331-9701.**

Rainbow Gardens—$$$

This new restaurant in Milford is a full-service counterpart to a rather bohemian self-service cousin in New Haven, and it's getting rave reviews. The "rainbow" in the name seems to imply spectrum, as in a wide range of cuisines. You'll find Asian stir-fry, "Texarcana" burgers, salmon seasoned with lemongrass but served over couscous and a "new-fashioned" turkey dinner (leaner, with no candied yams in sight). About half of the menu is vegetarian items. Owner Meg Profetto has been running a local catering business for years and might very well be able to pull off this hodgepodge of

styles with aplomb. The setting is a restored old home furnished country-style with antiques and reproductions. Reservations strongly recommended on weekends. Lunch hours: 11:00 A.M.–3:00 P.M. daily. Dinner served Wed.–Thu., 5:00 P.M.–9:00 P.M.; Fri.–Sat., 5:00 P.M.–10:00 P.M. **117 N. Broad St., Milford, 06460; (203) 878-2500.**

Ralph & Rich's—$$$

This Italian/Continental restaurant is one of downtown Bridgeport's principal restaurants for both lunch and dinner. It specializes in veal chops and Black Angus steak, but also serves lighter sandwiches at lunch and runs daily specials to keep it interesting. On Fri. and Sat. nights a live pianist entertains in the lounge beginning around 7:30. Lunch served Mon.–Sat., 11:30 A.M.–3:00 P.M. Dinner served Mon.–Thu., 5:00 P.M.–9:45 P.M.; Fri.–Sat. until 11:00 P.M. **121 Wall St., Bridgeport, 06604; (203) 366-3597.**

Spazzi—$$$

Spazzi is the current trendy Italian eatery in the area, with tile, brick and pillars, small tables rather closely spaced and a few booths. The place is large and can be loud on a busy night. Pasta, homemade daily, takes center stage here. Preparations range from a simple pomodoro sauce over ordinary wheat pasta to black pepper fettucini with oak-grilled hot Italian sausage and goat cheese. There's a small menu of wood oven-baked pizzas and sandwiches and changing specials. Lunch/brunch hours: Mon.–Sun., 11:30 A.M.–3:00 P.M. Dinner served Sun.–Thu., 5:00 P.M.–10:00 P.M.; Fri.–Sat., 4:30 P.M.–11:00 P.M. **1229 Boston Post Rd. (Rte. 1), Fairfield, 06430; (203) 256-1629.**

Stonebridge—$$$

Serving American/Continental cuisine, Stonebridge is located right next to a stone memorial bridge in Milford. The kitchen focuses strongly on seafood, ranging from steamed lobster and king crab to fish and chips. Several of the sandwiches at lunch also feature seafood. At dinner the menu of fish and seafood entrées expands considerably, complemented by steak, chicken and pasta items. At both lunch and dinner there's a small selection of individual pizzas. Stonebridge is light and bright with a white-tablecloth atmosphere. For summertime dining there's an outdoor deck overlooking a natural waterfall. Hours: Sun.–Thu., 11:30 A.M.–last seating at 9:00 P.M.; Fri.–Sat., last seating at 10:00 P.M. The bar, where a light menu is served, is open until the wee hours. **50 Daniels Rd., Milford, 06460; (203) 874-7947.**

Bloodroot—$$ to $$$

This self-described feminist restaurant and bookstore operates out of an innocuous building in a residential neighborhood of Bridgeport. The food is vegetarian, with several vegan options each night. The menu changes daily, but you can expect to find several hearty soups, multigrain breads, salads, casseroles or other substantial entrées and "natural" desserts. You order from a blackboard listing the day's offerings and pay for your meal. The bookstore in back carries many women's studies works, periodicals, poetry, criticism and just plain entertainment. Lunch/brunch hours: Tue. & Thu.–Sun., 11:30 A.M.–2:30 P.M. Dinner hours: Tue. & Thu., 6:00 P.M.–9:00 P.M.; Fri.–Sat., 6:00 P.M.–10:00 P.M. **85 Ferris St., Bridgeport, 06605; (203) 576-9168.**

Services

Local Visitors Information

Coastal Fairfield County Tourism District, 297 West Ave., Norwalk, 06850; (800) 866-7925 or **(203) 854-7825.**

Milford Chamber of Commerce, 5 N. Broad St., Milford, 06460; (203) 878-0681. Hours: Mon.–Fri., 8:30 A.M.–4:30 P.M.

Transportation

If you plan to travel by air, **Sikorsky Memorial Airport in Stratford** at **(203) 576-7498** is serviced by a commuter airline.

Bridgeport is a stop on the Washington-Boston and Washington-Springfield **Amtrak** routes. For more information call **(800) 872-7245. Metro-North** commuter trains serve Fairfield, Bridgeport, Stratford and Milford seven days a week, terminating at New York City in one direction and New Haven in the other. For a schedule call **(800) 638-7646.**

Interstate bus service to Bridgeport is provided by **Peter Pan/Trailways (800-343-9999)** and **Greyhound (800-231-2222).** Local bus service is provided by the **Greater Bridgeport Transit District (203-735-6824)** and the **Milford Transit District (203-783-3258).**

The **Bridgeport and Port Jefferson Steamboat Co.** is a year-round ferry operator providing daily service between Port Jefferson, Long Island (New York) and Bridgeport. The crossing takes about an hour and a half. The fare schedule is complex and subject to change; call for details on pricing and departure times. The dock in Bridgeport is located just off Water St. below State St., one block from the train station and bus terminal. For more information call **(203) 367-3043** (in Connecticut) or **(516) 473-0286** in Long Island.

Greenwich/ Stamford

The two most southwesterly towns in Connecticut are linked by common bonds of history and geography, yet even the casual observer will notice startling differences between them. Stamford is the closest thing to a little Manhattan you'll find in the Constitution State. It's the financial center of southwestern Connecticut by day and the entertainment mecca by night. Clusters of high-rise buildings (among the few to be found in Connecticut outside Hartford) house offices of major corporations, and the Stamford Center for the Arts's two venues, the Palace Theatre and the Forum, feature headline entertainment of all types. Most of the area's nightclubs are here too.

In somewhat marked contrast to Stamford's little big-city atmosphere, much of Greenwich still feels like a village, albeit a very busy and densely populated village. Greenwich Ave., the main thoroughfare, is lined with diminutive two- and three-story buildings that suggest a close tie to the past, and it's not too hard to imagine this crooked street lined with 18th-century market stalls. Whereas Stamford has glittering modern hotels, Greenwich has B&Bs. Stamford's branch of the Whitney Museum has its counterpart in Greenwich's history as an Impressionist art colony. The two towns complement one another so well they make a natural couple.

Atlantic St. in downtown Stamford is the center of the dining and entertainment district. It starts at the Forum at Atlantic St. and Tresser Blvd., stretches past the neoclassical town hall and continues several blocks up Bedford, spilling over onto side streets. In addition to dozens of restaurants, several hotels and the Center for the Arts, you'll find the Stamford branch of New York's Whitney Museum and Stamford Town Center mall all within this one neighborhood. A short drive away the Stamford Museum and Nature Center

is a great combination of farm in the city and art gallery at which to spend some quality family time, and Sterling Farms Golf Course is top-rate. Because of the concentration in Stamford of businesses with a Mon.–Fri. workweek, the little shops that serve the local workforce close on the weekend, and hotels here offer special low rates for weekend stays.

Downtown Greenwich is simply *the* dining and shopping capital of Connecticut with over 150 boutiques and restaurants on Greenwich Ave. between Railroad Ave. and Rte. 1. Strolling this street is an attraction in and of itself. Lovers of art will not want to miss the Bush-Holley House and the Bruce Museum. The former, a historic home and the site of a turn-of-the-century Impressionist art colony, is now a museum open for tours. The latter is a modern gallery with both an art and a natural history focus. Also in Greenwich, Putnam Cottage is a historic site owned by the Daughters of the American Revolution where the area's colonial past comes alive.

Even though Greenwich and Stamford are among the most populous towns in Connecticut, you don't have to forgo great outdoor experiences. For birding, hiking and fishing, look to Greenwich, where several large wooded tracts of land—two National Audubon Society properties, Mianus River Park and Babcock Preserve—showcase the natural beauty of the area. Finally, for a day on the shore, head to Stamford, where town beaches (with some restrictions) are open to the public for saltwater swimming.

History

The early history of Greenwich is surprisingly unclear, and historians today are still trying to work out the details. One thing is sure, however: the proximity of both Greenwich and Stamford to New York has always been important, although this fact has manifested itself in different ways over the years. Native Americans were living in the area when both the Dutch and the English arrived, although their exact identity is not certain. The original En-

338

glish settlement (ca. 1640) was at what's now called Old Greenwich, but the colonists, harassed by the Dutch and the Indians, signed it over to New Netherlands (New York, which was then under Dutch control) in 1642. A year or two later, conflicts between the settlers and the Indians had reached such a height that the Dutch and the English evidently combined to wipe them out, but even that episode is shrouded in mystery. The area came under the jurisdiction of New Haven Colony in 1656, and thence Connecticut Colony when the 1662 charter forced the incorporation of New Haven into Connecticut.

A little more is known about Stamford (then called Rippowam), which was settled by a party from Wethersfield who wanted to leave that town because of some indefinite dissension in the church. Some families arrived in 1641, but three years later some of the same people, evidently dissatisfied with New Haven Colony rule, went to Long Island. Stamford also officially became part of Connecticut in 1662.

As a result of their proximity to New York City, which was under British control for the duration of the Revolutionary War, Greenwich and Stamford saw a lot of activity. If they weren't being pillaged by the British, they were having to sacrifice to raise supplies for Patriot troops.

The most famous local story from that period concerns the derring-do of Gen. Israel Putnam in Feb. 1779. Putnam had been staying at Knapp Tavern (as Putnam Cottage, renamed for him, it is now a museum open to the public) when he was given the news that the British were approaching from the west. With the British within firing range, he rode his horse down a set of stone steps cut into a steep cliff and went east to Stamford for reinforcements. Returning later that day, he and his troops chased the British, who were already retreating, and managed to take 38 prisoners.

When Bridgeport to the east became the terminus for two inland railroads and a rail connection to New York was made just prior to 1850, all the shoreline towns through which the railroad passed, including Greenwich and Stamford, experienced an economic upswing. Nineteenth-century industries that took advantage of the availability of transportation in-

cluded a woolen mill, stone quarries, a felt mill at Glenville and a nuts and bolts factory.

Many prominent New York families as well as successful local families built summer homes in both towns. Two neighborhoods known for their estatelike properties are Belle Haven in Greenwich and Strawberry Hill in Stamford. At the same time, the working-class immigrants who labored at area factories developed their own neighborhoods. That ethnic diversity persists to this day, especially in Stamford. By the end of the 19th century, Greenwich had also become an enclave for New York's Impressionist artists, whose history is told at the Bush-Holley House.

With the trend toward suburbanization in the mid-20th century, Greenwich and Stamford became bedroom communities of New York with residents making a daily commute into the city, made easier by aggressive highway construction programs. Many companies also moved to the area, so that by the mid-1990s half of the ten largest companies in the state and 35% of the top 100 were headquartered in these two towns, including such recognizable names as GTE, Xerox, American Brands, Champion International and Pitney Bowes.

Major Attractions

Bruce Museum

The Bruce Museum, divided between art and natural history, is one of the top museum experiences in Connecticut. It's located in a modern structure with a mutable internal space that can be altered to suit the demands of changing exhibits. On the art side it might be photography, botanical illustration, Connecticut Impressionism—just about anything—and there are usually several exhibits up simultaneously. On the natural history side the exhibits are geared toward children, but adults will probably be surprised to find how much they learn from gorgeous displays on minerals, geology, Native American culture and storytelling and more. In the miniaquarium, you can actually touch and pick up all kinds of living sea creatures. Or, do some nature study outside. A tree trail guide available at the information desk shows the location and gives background information on 21 species of trees planted on the museum grounds. Admission: $3.50 adults, $2.50 seniors and children 5–12, admission is free on Tue. Hours: Tue.–Sat., 10:00 A.M.–5:00 P.M.; Sun., 1:00 P.M.–5:00 P.M. **One Museum Dr., Greenwich, 06830; (203) 869-0376.**

Bush-Holley House

If you are interested in the American Impressionist movement, make time to visit the Bush-Holley House, a stop on the Connecticut Impressionist Art Trail. As a former art colony, it is western Connecticut's equivalent of the Florence Griswold Museum in Old Lyme. Much of the artwork on display in this home setting was created here, allowing visitors the unique experience of comparing the scene of today to what it was 80 or 100 years ago.

The house itself was built in 1732 by a wealthy merchant family from Holland and is interesting for its wealth of ornate woodwork and Connecticut Chippendale furnishings. It became the Holley Inn in 1882, hosting a lively assortment of artists and writers from New York City who reveled in the clear light and open space of the old Connecticut shore. Elmer Livingston McRae, the husband of a later owner, was himself an artist. His studio remains intact in an upstairs room, just as it was left when he died.

At the Bush-Holley House there is something to interest the amateur historian, the aficionado of fine, old furniture and the lover of art. Foremost of these three, however, is the art, hung simply and in abundance on the walls of the house as if for the enjoyment of its long-gone inhabitants. Lectures and other activities go on year-round. Admission: $4 adults, $3 seniors and students, free to children under 12. Hours: Tue.–Fri., noon–4:00 P.M.; Sun., 1:00 P.M.–4:00 P.M.; closed Sat. & the week between Christmas and New Year's. **39 Strickland Rd., Greenwich, 06807; (203) 869-6899.**

Whitney Museum of American Art at Champion

This outpost of the famed New York City museum is located in a large, modern office building that houses the headquarters of the Champion International Corporation. Approximately six shows are mounted in this impressive space per year, many with compelling, contemporary themes. Public programming includes gallery talks on Tue., Thu. & Sat. at 12:30 P.M. Although this is world-class art, thanks to the generosity of the sponsor, admission is free. Hours: Tue.–Sat., 11:00 A.M.–5:00

P.M. Park for free in the Champion garage; enter on Tresser Blvd. **One Champion Plaza (at the corner of Atlantic St. and Tresser Blvd.), Stamford, 06901; (203) 358-7630.**

Festivals and Events

In addition to the listings below, the **Bush-Holley House (203-869-6899),** a historic home/art museum, hosts an annual Art-in-the-Yard event in early June during which artists both amateur and professional come to paint at the site of a former Impressionist art colony. Come to watch, or make a reservation and set up your own easel. Also, the **Stamford Museum and Nature Center** has a series of special farm- and country-related festivals, such as Winterfest in Jan., maple sugaring demonstrations in early Mar., and Spring on the Farm Day in May. For more information call **(203) 322-1646** and see the listing under Children and Families.

Bruce Museum Outdoor Crafts Festival
weekend before Memorial Day

Juried to reflect the Bruce Museum's high standards, this crafts festival is among the most competitive in the state. You'll find both functional and decorative work, with an emphasis on the former. A similar show with a fine arts focus is held on Columbus Day weekend in Oct. The show is open to any style and medium, but there's a leaning toward contemporary work.

There's no additional charge for kids' activities, and show admission also includes museum admission, so it's an incredible bargain. Both festivals take place on wheelchair-accessible museum grounds. Admission: $3. Hours: 11:00 A.M.–5:00 P.M. **One Museum Dr., Greenwich, 06830; (203) 869-0376.**

Sail for the Sound
late June–early July

This three-day (Fri.–Sun.) fund-raiser for the Leukemia Society of America and *Sound-*

Getting There

Greenwich and Stamford are about two hours from Hartford by car under good driving conditions. From Hartford take I-91 south to New Haven and pick up I-95 south, which goes directly to Greenwich and Stamford. For a prettier trip, possibly less traffic and better access to the north side of both towns, take I-91 south to Rte. 15 (Wilbur Cross Pkwy., which becomes the Merritt Pkwy). When driving on local streets, look out for one-way systems in busy areas.

waters, a sailing vessel used for environmental education on Long Island Sound, has two aspects. For the nonsailing public, as many as ten tall ships are on hand at Brewers Yacht Haven (a marina) in Stamford for boarding and short cruises. Tickets are in the neighborhood of $25 per person; call for hours. Also, on Fri. evening there's a black-tie Tall Ships Ball and silent auction at Riverside Yacht Club. For yachting enthusiasts, there's a Yacht Racing Association of Long Island Sound–sanctioned sailing regatta. For more information call **(203) 323-1978.**

World Fest
Summer

There are plans to make this multicultural performing arts festival, whose inaugural year was 1997, an annual event. It will probably take place over four days in mid-Aug., but call to confirm exact dates. In addition to numerous live performances of music, dance and theater, there are arts and crafts exhibits, tall ships on display (but not for boarding), carnival rides and games, children's entertainment and fireworks. Admission: $6 adults, $4 seniors and children. Hours: Thu., 5:00 P.M.–11:00 P.M.; Fri., noon–11:00 P.M.; Sat., 10:00 A.M.–midnight; Sun., 10:00 A.M.–10:00 P.M. The location is **Brewers Yacht Haven at the foot of Washington Blvd. in Stamford.** For more information call **(800) 243-6116.**

Bruce Museum Outdoor Arts Festival
Columbus Day weekend (Oct.)

See the listing for the Bruce Museum Outdoor Crafts Festival above.

The Greenwich Christmas Antiques Show
first weekend in Dec. (Fri.–Sun.)

This annual antiques show featuring primarily museum-quality pieces is the major fund-raiser for the Bush-Holley House, Greenwich's historic house cum art museum. The show takes place at the **Greenwich Civic Center on Harding Rd. in Old Greenwich,** preceded by a Thu. night, $100-per-ticket preview party. Show admission: $10. Hours: Fri., 11:00 A.M.– 7:00 P.M.; Sat., 11:00 A.M.–6:00 P.M.; Sun., 11:00 A.M.–5:00 P.M. For more information call **(203) 869-6899.**

Outdoor Activities

Biking

Mountain Biking

The main trails at **Mianus River Park** in Greenwich are broad gravel and dirt roads that are excellent for mountain biking. Unfortunately, because of past problems with mountain bikers ignoring trail closure signs, accessibility may be limited; obey all postings. The narrow riverside trails should not be biked; erosion is a problem. See the listing under Hiking for directions.

Road Biking

The shoreline parts of Greenwich and Stamford are too congested for biking or privately owned, but there is lovely biking country north of Rte. 1, especially in Greenwich. North of the Merritt Pkwy. it's even better. You should still stay off the main north-south roads because they carry a lot of commuter traffic during rush hours, and there are no shoulders to give

you a buffer from cars, but it's easy to plot a trip on back roads with only short connecting stretches on busy routes. Leave your car at one of the Greenwich town parks (Mianus River and Babcock Preserve) and design an east-west oval ride incorporating Old Mill Rd., John St., Lower and Upper Cross Rds., North and South Stamwich Rds. and June Rd. South. You can try the same approach in Stamford, parking at, say, the Bartlett Arboretum, but you'll find the terrain a bit hillier.

Birding

Audubon Center in Greenwich
The National Audubon Society owns and maintains this 280-acre wildlife sanctuary with a small lake and several marshes at its heart. Over 160 bird species have been known to visit the sanctuary, which has 8 miles of trails with blinds for viewing birds on Mead Lake. The terrain is hilly, so wear hiking boots. Maps are available in the interpretive center, where you'll also find exhibits and rest rooms. The gift shop is a great place to pick up nature items or gifts for the bird lover back home. Every Sat. at 10:00 A.M., June–Aug., & Sun. at 2:00 P.M. the rest of the year (weather permitting) you can join a guided natural history walk here or on a nearby property. The center also organizes outings to other spots in the area where birding is good, and a two-day hawk watch weekend is held here each year in mid-Sept. Picnicking and pets are not allowed. Admission: $3 adults, $1.50 seniors and children. Hours: Tue.–Sun., 9:00 A.M.–5:00 P.M.; closed Mon. & holiday weekends. **613 Riversville Rd., Greenwich, 06831; (203) 869-5272.**

Audubon Fairchild Garden
A short distance from the Audubon Center in Greenwich is another property of the National Audubon Society, wilder but flatter. The trail system takes you through marsh, woodlands and a meadow that comes into its glory in late summer, when it is alive with butterflies. The farther you go from the entrance, the wilder it gets. There is a welcome port-a-potty here, but no water or other facilities. Picnicking and pets are not allowed. Located on **N. Porchuck**

Rd. in Greenwich. For more information call **(203) 869-5272.**

Boating

Boat Launches

You can launch anything up to 30 feet in length into Long Island Sound at West Beach in Stamford for a $25 daily nonresident fee or a $200 nonresident seasonal pass. The cost for residents is $5 and $35, respectively. For more information call the **Stamford Dept. of Parks and Natural Resources** at **(203) 977-4641/4692.**

Charter Brokers

Charter brokers try to match the needs of customers who want a private organized boating experience with boat owners who can offer that service. Most of their business is with large groups, but they welcome small parties too. When you call a broker, you'll be asked some basic questions, such as how many people are in your party and whether you want to go cruising or fishing. Then they make recommendations, and you make the arrangements through them. One piece of advice: call as far in advance as you possibly can—weeks or months, not days. Some charter brokers who operate all along the southwestern shore include **Nautical Holidays (203-637-0270), Norwalk Yacht Charters (203-852-7092), Outdoor Recreation Services (203-336-9117)** and **Fish 'n' Hole** (also fishing specialists; **203-366-0889**). Outdoor Recreation Services also teaches sailing, powerboating and navigation and will custom design curricula.

Cruises

The 80-foot schooner *Soundwaters* sails mid-Apr.–mid-Nov. from several ports along the southwest coast of Connecticut. Two- and three-hour cruises, during which the crew trawls to give passengers a peek at local ocean life, are available to the public. *Soundwaters*'s main function, however, is as an environmental education vessel, so her crew has a lot of experience assisting passen-

gers with special needs. The cost for regularly scheduled cruises is $25–$30 per person. Reservations required. For more information call **(203) 323-1978.**

Marinas

There's a surprising lack of transient berths in Greenwich, but Greenwich Cove is renowned for its beauty as an anchorage. In Cos Cob Harbor at the mouth of the Mianus River, you'll find two marinas with ten transient slips apiece that can handle most boats: seasonal **Greenwich Maritime Center (203-869-8690; VHF 16)** and year-round **Mianus Marine (203-869-2253;** VHF 16). The former sells fuel and has a bit more on the facilities side, and they both do a full range of repair work. Almost all the Cos Cob marinas lie upriver of a bascule bridge with 20 feet vertical clearance. Sailboat owners, note that the bridge is seldom opened at night.

The situation is a bit different in Stamford. **Brewer's Yacht Haven (203-359-4500;** VHF

Small boats moored off Grass Island in Greenwich Harbor.

9) has 50 transient slips, **Harbor Square Marina (203-324-3331)** has 20 and (for boats up to 50 feet) **Stamford Landing (203-965-0065;** VHF 9) has 10. Brewer's does a wide range of repairs and has a full-service restaurant (the Rusty Scupper); the other two offer the pump-out facilities that Brewer's does not. Both Brewer's and Harbor Square sell fuel. For repairs only, try **Harbors End Marine Service (203-965-0888;** VHF 9). All these marinas are open year-round.

For navigational details, charts and complete lists of marine facilities throughout this area, your best source of information is *Embassy's Complete Boating Guide & Chartbook to Long Island Sound.* Contact the publisher at **142 Ferry Rd., Old Saybrook, 06475; (860) 395-0188.**

Fishing

Fishing options are limited in this area but worthwhile. For freshwater fishing, there is a Trout Management Area on the Merriebrook side of the Mianus River in Mianus River Park. Anglers are limited to catch-and-release. For directions, see the listing under Hiking. For saltwater fishing, see the listing for Charter Brokers under Boating, and specify that you want a fishing charter.

Golf

Sterling Farms Golf Course
This 6,082-yard, par 72, 18-hole municipal course was rated one of *Connecticut* magazine's top ten. Nonresidents are allowed weekend play in the afternoon only, but otherwise access is unrestricted. Call for information about tee times. Facilities include a putting green, pro shop, snack bar and restaurant, bar and tennis courts. Lessons and all rentals are available. Season: Mar.–Dec. **1349 Newfield Ave., Stamford, 06905; (203) 461-9090** or **(203) 321-3411.**

Hiking

For information on hiking at the **Audubon Center** and **Audubon Fairchild Garden** in

Greenwich, see the listings under Birding. Trails at the **Bartlett Arboretum** and the **Montgomery Pinetum** are described under Gardens and Arboreta.

Babcock Preserve
The town of Greenwich owns this exceptionally pretty, 297-acre tract of wooded land with a trail network conveniently located on North St. just half a mile north of the Merritt Pkwy. There is a dirt turnoff on the west side of the road and a dirt track flanked by stone pillars leading back into the woods. Pull through the gate and look for the designated parking spots on the left. Hours: dawn–dusk daily, year-round.

Mianus River Park
Trails at this 215-acre park range from broad woods roads through forested high ground to narrow paths along the banks of the Mianus (pronounced my-ANN-is) River, where you have to be careful of rocks and tree roots. In late July and Aug., loosestrife floods the lowlands with swells of purple flowers. In spring and summer bring mosquito repellant so you can hike the lowland sections in comfort. Many loop hikes are possible, and rough maps are posted at some trail junctions. The main entrance is on Cognewaugh Rd. between Hooker and Shannon Lns., where there is parking for many cars. At the Merriebrook Ln. entrance (be careful turning from Westover Rd.; the turn is at a blind curve) there's parking for a few cars at the dirt turnoff on the right-hand side of the road just before the one-lane bridge. If you want to get a map beforehand, contact either the **Greenwich Dept. of Parks and Recreation (101 Field Point Rd. in the town hall; 203-622-7824)** or the **Stamford Dept. of Parks and Natural Resources (888 Washington Blvd., Stamford, 06904; 203-977-4641).**

Horseback Riding

Although most stables in this area give only lessons rather than trail rides, **Windswept Farms (107 June Rd., Stamford; 203-322-4984)** will take any experienced rider out for a jaunt, English or Western saddle, for $38 per person per hour on weekends. Call for reservations.

Ice Skating

There's public skating at **Terry Conners Rink** on Fri. evenings & Thu., Sat. & Sun. afternoons. Nonresident fees are $8 adults, $6 children; resident fees are $4 adults, $2 children. Rental skates are available. Season: July–Mar. The rink is located in **Cove Island Park at the end of Cove Island Rd. in Stamford; (203) 977-4514.**

Swimming

As a guest of a Greenwich resident only, you can swim at that town's beaches on **Little Captain Island** and **Great Captain Island.** They are accessible via ferry during summer, and the experience is unique if you are lucky enough to be treated to it. But even without a resident connection, you can still swim in Long Island Sound. At any time nonresidents may enter any Stamford town beach by non-motorized means (e.g., by bike or on foot) for free. Between Memorial Day and Labor Day nonresidents can enter by car Mon.–Fri. only for a $15 fee; they may not drive in on summer weekends at all. But during the balmy days of Sept., the beaches and Long Island Sound are as beautiful as during the height of the summer (even more so with the crowds reduced), and there are no restrictions on access and no fee collected. There are three Stamford swimming beaches. **Cove Island Park** at the end of Cove Island Rd. and **Cummings Beach** on Shippan Ave. have changing rooms, rest rooms and food concessions in season. Cove Island Park also has paths for roller blading, biking and such, and Cummings has a network of smaller paths for walking. **West Beach** on Shippan Ave. has fewer facilities overall and is the smallest beach of the three. All have picnic facilities. For more information call the **Stamford Dept. of Parks and Natural Resources** at **(203) 977-4641/4692.**

Seeing and Doing

The most current and comprehensive guide to upcoming events, concerts, art shows and more in this area is the *Fairfield County Weekly,* a free periodical available at newsstands, convenience stores and many attractions.

Antiquing

The Antique and Artisan Center

Eighty-five dealers exhibit collector-quality antiques of all periods and styles in this 22,000-square-foot facility. A great deal of it is American furniture, but you'll also find many specialty items. Free parking in the lot. Hours: Mon.–Sat., 10:30 A.M.–5:30 P.M.; Sun., noon–5:00 P.M. **69 Jefferson St. (near Canal St.), Stamford, 06902; (203) 327-6022.**

United House Wrecking

The story goes that all the incredible stuff sold at United House Wrecking comes from old estates that are being demolished. Wherever it comes from, the volume and variety of merchandise are amazing. Not only are there thousands of pieces of furniture, but you'll also find fixtures like entire fireplace surrounds, chandeliers, decorative bits and pieces of façades and massive garden statuary. Hours: Mon.–Sat., 9:30 A.M.–5:30 P.M.; Sun., noon–5:00 P.M. **535 Hope St., Stamford, 06906; (203) 348-5371.**

Art Galleries

Also see the listings for the **Bruce Museum,** the **Bush-Holley House** and the **Whitney Museum of American Art at Champion** under Major Attractions.

Rosenthal Gallery/Sackler Gallery

These two galleries form part of the visual arts component of the Stamford Center for the Arts, described more fully under Performing Arts. The former is located at the Rich Forum and open during box office hours (Mon.–Sat., 10:00 A.M.–6:00 P.M.; Sun., noon–5:00 P.M. except during summer). The latter is located at the Palace and is open on performance days; call **(203) 325-4466** to make an appointment to see it or to find out what is currently hanging in either gallery.

345

Children and Families

Bruce Park Playground

When your kids have had enough of learning for one day, take them across the street from the Bruce Museum to the Bruce Park Playground. Street parking is a bargain at three hours for a quarter. You'll find nearly every playground contraption imaginable, plus picnic tables and rest rooms. Located on **Museum Dr. in Greenwich.**

Stamford Museum and Nature Center

This sprawling complex contains two types of attractions: a historic main building with gallery spaces for art and cultural history exhibits and a series of wheelchair-accessible outdoor farmyard displays geared toward children. There are also 3 miles of trails through woodland, a playground and a picnic area by a pond frequented by ducks and geese. Of special note are the farm tool exhibit in a restored 1750 barn and the Native American peoples display in the main building. If you are interested in historic preservation, make sure to read about the history of the main building, which was once the spectacular home of wealthy New York–based French clothier Henri Bendel.

Special events throughout the year, such as a Jan. Winterfest, maple sugaring in Mar. and cider-making demonstrations in autumn generally focus on aspects of farm life. The setting is ideal for a series of Sat. evening folk concerts offered every summer. Quilting bee demonstrations are given most Mon., 9:30 A.M.–3:30 P.M., & Fri. nights (weather permitting) the public is invited to view the skies through a 22-inch telescope at an observatory on the grounds. Admission: $5 adults, $3 seniors and children 5–13. Hours: Mon.–Sat. & holidays, 9:00 A.M.–5:00 P.M.; Sun., 1:00 P.M.–5:00 P.M.; closed Thanksgiving, Christmas & New Year's Day. At the **junction of Scofieldtown Rd. and High Ridge Rd. (Rte. 137), Stamford, 06903; (203) 322-1646.**

Gardens and Arboreta

Bartlett Arboretum

Bartlett is a small arboretum known mostly for its collection of woody plants. A conifer garden across the street from the main entrance is a high point, and a greenhouse is open daily, year-round, 9:30 A.M.–11:00 A.M. There's an easy trail system, including a swamp boardwalk. Classes and workshops are offered throughout the year, and concerts are given on the grounds on summer Sun. at 4:30 P.M. (bring a blanket). A variety of maps and guides to the arboretum's flora are available in boxes outside the main building. Guided Sun. afternoon tours of the arboretum at 1:00 P.M. are free. Grounds hours: 8:30 A.M.–sunset daily, year-round. **151 Brookdale Rd., Stamford, 06903; (203) 322-6971.**

Montgomery Pinetum/Greenwich Garden Center

Before it became the Montgomery Pinetum, this wooded 102-acre tract was the private

A sheep greets visitors at Stamford Museum and Nature Center.

346

estate of Col. Robert H. Montgomery, who collected specimens of conifers from around the world. Many can still be found here and are now 70 or more years old. There is no detailed guide to the trees, but this is a good place for a pleasant hike right in the center of town, and anyone interested in horticulture will get special enjoyment out of it. A regular schedule of lectures and outings is offered through the Greenwich Garden Center adjacent to the Pinetum, where you can also pick up a trail map and browse an excellent gift shop. The Pinetum is open 8:00 A.M.–sunset daily, Apr. 15–Oct. 15, & Mon.–Fri., 8:00 A.M.–4:00 P.M. the rest of the year. Located on **Bible St. in Cos Cob.** More information on the Pinetum may be obtained from the **Greenwich Parks Dept.** at **(203) 622-7824.** For details on the Greenwich Garden Center call **(203) 869-9242.**

Museums

Putnam Cottage (243 E. Putnam Ave. [Rte. 1], Greenwich; 203-869-9697) is the principal historical museum in this area. Formerly known as Knapp Tavern, it was built in 1690 and first licensed to operate as a tavern in 1734. As a public house it frequently hosted Gen. Israel Putnam, a major Patriot in the Revolutionary War. Nearby is a precipitous ledge down which Putnam rode his horse to escape advancing British troops in 1779. Putnam was riding for reinforcements, with which he returned later in the day to rout the British. Putnam Cottage is now maintained as a museum by a chapter of the Daughters of the American Revolution. Displays include Putnam's uniform and artifacts relating to tavern keeping in the 18th century. The building itself displays the massive fireplaces, wideboard flooring and gun-stock barrel corner posts that are characteristic of late-17th- and early-18th-century Connecticut structures. Although the museum is closed in winter, it briefly reopens for an annual battle reenactment on the last Sun. in Feb., 1:00–3:00 P.M. A small admission fee is charged; free to children under 13. Hours: Wed., Fri. & Sun., 1:00 P.M.–4:00 P.M., Apr.–Dec.

Also see the listings for the Bruce Museum and the Bush-Holley House under Major Attractions, and if you have a specific interest in Stamford history, the **Stamford Historical Society Museum (1508 High Ridge Rd., Stamford; 203-329-1183)** is open Tue.–Sat., noon–4:00 P.M., and worth a stop. Admission: $2 adults, $1 children. The Society also gives tours of the Betsy Barnum House by appointment and has an Antique Quilt Show and Sale over a three-day weekend in late Aug.; call for more information.

Nightlife

Nightclubs come and go, but there are probably more of them in Stamford than any other Connecticut city. Your best approach would be to get a copy of the Fairfield County Weekly, available free at newsstands, convenience stores and restaurants, to review current listings. Two of the more popular and long-lived clubs are the **Art Bar (84 W. Park Place, Stamford, 203-973-0300)** and the **Terrace Club (1938 W. Main St., Stamford; 203-961-9770).** The latter has possibly the biggest dance floor in southwestern Connecticut. The Art Bar is trendier, but the Terrace Club has been around since the 1940s and offers something for everyone with different nights of the week (Wed.–Sun.) devoted to ballroom, country-western and pop/rock dancing and singles dances on occasional Sun. For acoustic music or bookish pursuits such as poetry readings, **Borders Books and Music (1041 High Ridge Rd., Stamford; 203-968-9700)** is always reliable.

Observatories

In addition to the observatory at the **Stamford Museum and Nature Center** (see the listing under Children and Families), the 12-inch reflecting telescope at the Bowman Observatory on the grounds of Julian Curtiss Elementary School is open for free public viewing of the night sky on the second and fourth Tue. of every month (weather permitting) and for special events such as eclipses. Hours: 7:00

P.M.–9:30 P.M. The school is on the **corner of Milbank Ave. and E. Elm St. in Greenwich.** For more information call the Bruce Museum at **(203) 869-0376/6786, ext. 338.**

Performing Arts

Greenwich Symphony Orchestra

Under the leadership of conductor David Gilbert, the GSO performs about ten concerts on five weekends between Oct. and Apr. The GSO's First Chair musicians are also members of the Chamber Players. Dinner and concert ticket packages are available. All performances take place at the **Greenwich High School Auditorium on Hillside Rd.** For schedule and ticket prices call **(203) 869-2664.**

Stamford Center for the Arts

The premier performing arts facility in the area consists of two venues: the Rich Forum, a modern structure seating about 750 people, and the Palace, a magnificent restored vaudeville house dating from the 1920s that seats 1,580. The Forum is frequently host to theatrical events, and the Palace is usually booked with musical acts ranging from folk to classical, dance and a few eclectic acts such as Penn and Teller. Ticket prices vary widely. The **Rich Forum** is at **307 Atlantic St., Stamford, 06901.** The Palace is at **61 Atlantic St.** For more information on both venues call **(203) 325-4466.**

Sterling Farms Theatre

For community theater, head to the Sterling Farms golf/tennis/theater complex. There are two venues, both housed in a 250-year-old barn. The Ethel Kweskin Theatre has a proscenium stage and 156 seats. It's used for large-scale musicals, dramas and comedies. The Dressing Room Theatre is a 100-seat cabaret-style space with tables so you can enjoy your own food and drink (don't forget utensils) while you watch productions of original works. Performances and workshops go on year-round. Ticket prices are $15 adults, $7.50 students at all times and seniors on Sun. **1349 Newfield Ave., Stamford, 06905; (203)**

461-6358. For workshop information call **(203) 329-8207.**

Theatre Works

The only Equity theater in the area performs socially relevant plays (generally new works) in a converted barn on the campus of Sacred Heart Academy, a private school. The company does four productions per season (Sept.–May) and also offers the Purple Cow Children's Theatre for age 3–8 on Sat. mornings and afternoons, May–July. Performances are given Tue.–Sat. nights & Sat. & Sun. afternoons. Evening ticket prices are in the $17–$25 range. **200 Strawberry Hill Ave., Stamford, 06901; (203) 359-4414.**

Shopping

Even when it's crowded, **Greenwich Ave.** is one of the most enjoyable places to shop in the state. It's an old-fashioned, pedestrian-oriented main street. You'll still find the custom ladies' dress shop and the hometown jeweler nestled beside new arrivals like The Gap as well as a mind-boggling array of wonderful restaurants.

Stamford Town Center mall is totally in keeping with the more urban character of Greenwich's neighbor to the east. It's a multistory structure that blends in so well with the other high-rise buildings in the downtown that it's easy to overlook and almost hard to find. You'll find 130 stores with anchors like Saks Fifth Avenue, Macy's and Filene's. Hours are Mon.–Fri., 10:00 A.M.–9:00 P.M.; Sat., 10:00 A.M.–6:00 P.M.; Sun., noon–6:00 P.M. The easiest way to enter the mall if you're driving is directly from its multilevel parking garage. Entrances are located on Atlantic St., Tresser Blvd. and Greyrock Pl. in downtown Stamford. For more information call **(203) 324-0935.**

Sports

Greenwich Polo Club is host to a series of eight high-goal polo matches scheduled on selected Sun. at 3:00 P.M. every June, July and Sept. The gates open at 1:00 P.M. for people to spread out blankets and get settled. Bring a picnic lunch or buy one of the benefit meals offered. There's also general admission grandstand seating. Special events range from informational talks on polo to a tailgate picnic competition, which is open to anyone and usually takes place at the first July match. Cook up the most fantastic spread you can think of; prizes are awarded for Best Theme, Best Food, Best Presentation and more. Admission: $20 per car. The site is **Conyers Farm on North St. in Greenwich**. For more information call (203) 661-1952.

Where to Stay

Inns

Homestead Inn—$$$ to $$$$

Located on the edge of the beautiful Belle Haven residential neighborhood of Greenwich, Homestead Inn enjoys a wonderful setting with expansive lawns and a quietness that doesn't seem possible in this busy area. The rooms in the older building (ca. 1799) are a bit plain, but those in the newer building are quite memorable. They have French doors that let the light stream in (or you can shutter them for privacy), cathedral ceilings, luxuriously large bathrooms, a semiprivate porch for kicking back and taking in a view of the lovely grounds and a refreshing, airy atmosphere. There is a fine restaurant on the main floor of the old building where a Continental breakfast is served in the morning (see Where to Eat section). **420 Field Point Rd., Greenwich, 06830; (203) 869-7500.**

Stanton House Inn—$$$ to $$$$

The Stanton House is a Greenwich historic landmark, a 14,000-square-foot mansion first turned into an inn by Nora Stanton Barney, the granddaughter of suffragist Elizabeth Cady Stanton. It has 24 rooms, many of them quite large and a few with gas or decorative fireplaces. There are also some smaller rooms popular with business travelers and one small suite with a kitchenette and a claw-foot tub in its bathroom. All the rooms have cable TV, and all but two have a private bathroom. The bath-

rooms have a range of modern and old-fashioned fixtures. An expanded Continental breakfast is served at small private tables in the house's original dining room, lit in winter by a gas fireplace. In summer, guests may use an in-ground pool. Although Stanton House is walking distance from the shopping and dining district of Greenwich Ave., the property is still remarkably secluded. **76 Maple Ave., Greenwich, 06830; (203) 869-2110.**

Hotels & Motels

Because business travelers form most of the clientele for hotels in this area, weekend rates are typically lower than weekday rates, and a high level of service is the norm. What's more, to attract weekend visitors, hotels will often offer exceptional package deals. For an extra fee, all the services a business traveler might need are available: assistance with dinner reservations and theater arrangements, laundry and dry cleaning, room service and so forth.

In addition to the hotels listed below, you might also try the **Holiday Inn Select (700 Main St., Stamford, 06901; 203-358-8400)**, the **Stamford Marriott (2 Stamford Forum, Stamford, 06901; 203-357-9555)** and the **Hyatt Regency (1800 E. Putnam Ave., Old Greenwich, 06870; 203-637-1234)**, whose Winfield's Restaurant was the recent winner of the *Connecticut* magazine readers' choice award for best hotel dining in the county. A unique feature of **Greenwich Harbor Inn (500 Steamboat Rd., Greenwich, 06830; 203-661-9800)** is docking privileges (for a fee) for guests arriving by boat. Request a harborside room at this hotel. If all these choices still stretch your budget too much, try the **Susse Chalet Inn and Suites (135 Harvard Ave., Stamford, 06902; 800-258-1989)** or the **Stamford Super 8 (32 Grenhart Rd., Stamford, 06902; 800-800-8000)**. The **Coastal Fairfield County Tourism District (800-866-7925 or 203-854-7825)** can provide you with more listings.

Stamford Suites—$$$$

This all-suites hotel offers three different room layouts, all of which have separate sleeping

349

and living areas, a bathroom with a whirlpool tub and a galley kitchen fully equipped with appliances, utensils and dinnerware. They're rather like one-bedroom apartments at hotel prices. They cater to business travelers on short stays in the city, but the homelike facilities will be welcome to anyone who misses them when on the road. The hotel is walking distance from downtown dining and the Stamford Center for the Arts. **720 Bedford St., Stamford, 06901; (203) 359-7300.**

Sheraton Stamford Hotel—$$$ to $$$$

The Sheraton Stamford is perhaps the best example of how a weekend traveler can get a lot on the Gold Coast for only a little money—the rates drop rather dramatically at the end of the workweek. Standard rooms have either one king or two double beds; there are also one- and two-bedroom suites. There's also a full-service restaurant and an ambiance-laden tavern with a pool table. Exercise facilities include weight-training equipment, an indoor heated pool and a whirlpool. They offer room service and free covered parking as well as a free shuttle to the downtown. It's a bit hard to find; be sure to ask directions. **One First Stamford Pl., Stamford, 06902; (800) 338-9115** or **(203) 967-2222.**

Tara Stamford Hotel—$$$ to $$$$

The Tara Stamford Hotel will give you the impression of a city within a city. They have what's purported to be the largest hotel health club in Stamford, rooftop tennis courts, a heated indoor pool and massage available by appointment. There's an airline ticket office in the lobby and a very nice dining space on the floor of the atrium where you can get three meals a day. Of the 350-plus rooms, inward-facing ones overlook the impressive atrium lobby; outward-facing ones have more natural light but views of the parking areas or surrounding buildings. They cater to business travelers, so every room has a hair dryer, a coffeemaker, an iron and ironing board and a walk-in closet in addition to TV and telephone. They also offer free parking and a free shuttle to downtown. **2701 Summer St., Stamford, 06905; (203) 359-1300.**

Where to Eat

There are more restaurants in the Greenwich/Stamford area than you could shake a stick at. Most restaurants are clustered on and around Greenwich Ave., the traditional, pedestrian-oriented shopping district of Greenwich that makes a pleasant place to walk and window-shop before or after a meal.

Railroad St., at the foot of Greenwich Ave., is indeed where the railroad station is, and because of the commuter presence you'll find a breakfast joint or two, a smoke shop, a newstand and a pub. E. and W. Putnam Aves. (Rte. 1) at the top of Greenwich Ave. carry a lot of through traffic and therefore have less interest to pedestrians, but the restaurants up there are every bit as good as those around the corner. Leave an hour or two for simply walking through this area to peruse menus and moods, selecting whatever seems tempting. After eating, take a constitutional on the quiet residential streets to the east of Greenwich Ave. and count fireflies.

The same approach works in Stamford if you want to eat in town before a show at the Stamford Arts Center, but the choices are not as extensive, and if it's a weekend you're better off choosing in advance and making a reservation to make sure you get a table in time.

In case none of the main listings pique your interest, here are a few more suggestions. The tile and south-of-the-border colors at **Caléxico (379 Greenwich Ave., Greenwich; 203-629-8989)** are right in keeping with its Mexican menu. This is a very casual and inexpensive eatery where the kitchen is open to view, food is served cafeteria-style and you can bring your own alcoholic beverages. For southwestern food, try **Tucson (130 E. Putnam Ave., Greenwich; 203-661-2483)**, where faux ruined walls, cavernous ceilings, a noisy bar and sidewalk tables make a suitably trendy setting for a very young, very tan crowd.

American steak and seafood are the specialty at the **Chart House (3 River Rd., Old Greenwich; 203-661-2128)**, a member of a particularly good chain of high-quality restaurants. The food at **Mediterraneo (366 Greenwich Ave., Greenwich; 203-629-4747)** shows influences from all the countries bordering the Mediterranean Sea, ranging from pizza to lamb kabobs. The interior is ultramodern, with glossy wood floors and a vaguely maritime theme; there's also a seasonal unshaded terrace. **Pasta Vera (48 Greenwich Ave., Greenwich; 203-661-9705)** is a sitdown restaurant specializing in homemade pasta that also has a well-stocked deli counter and food available for take-out. **That-away Café (corner of Greenwich and Railroad Ave., Greenwich, 203-622-0947)** has the best terrace of any restaurant on the street (the sheer size of it provides some small buffer from street noise), where the young suits hang for a drink and a burger or something better.

In the fine dining category, **Amadeus (201 Summer St., Stamford; 203-348-7775)** is widely recognized as perhaps the best Continental restaurant in the area. A visit to **Figaro Bistro de Paris (372 Greenwich Ave., Greenwich; 203-622-0018)** is like a step outside the current time and place for a French meal.

For international cuisine you will not find a superior array of restaurants anywhere else in Connecticut. **El Inca (21 Atlantic St., Stamford; 203-324-9872)** serves Peruvian food with an emphasis on seafood and lunch specials on weekdays. **Kujaku (84 W. Park Pl., Stamford; 203-357-0281)** is considered one of the best Japanese restaurants in Fairfield County, offering a sushi bar, hibachi and private tatami rooms. In its esteemed reputation, **Panda Pavilion (137 W. Putnam Ave. [Rte. 1], Greenwich; 203-869-1111/1209)** is Kujaku's Chinese equivalent, serving Szechuan and Hunan dishes. Finally, **La Maison Indochine (107 Greenwich Ave., Greenwich; 203-869-2689)** is one of only a handful of Vietnamese restaurants in the state.

Restaurant Jean-Louis—$$$$

If you ever wanted to be either Rock Hudson or Doris Day in *Pillow Talk*, dress your very best and make reservations here, because this is exactly the sort of spot where they would have dined. Fittingly, it's located on a side street away from the boisterous young throngs that can descend on the main drag. Chef Jean-

Louis Gerin prepares what his wife Linda calls "nouvelle classique" French fare—traditional in style, but lower in fat, salt and cholesterol. There are only ten tables, so reservations are strongly recommended. Hours: lunch served Fri. only, noon–2:00 P.M. Dinner served Mon.–Fri., 6:00 P.M.–9:00 P.M.; Sat. there are two seatings only, at 6:15 & 9:00 P.M. **61 Lewis St., Greenwich, 06830; (203) 622-8450.**

Bennett's Steak & Fish House—$$$ to $$$$

The name at Bennett's pretty much sums up the menu: its strength is dry-aged beef, and it does six to eight fish and beef specialties nightly. It is actively building its wine inventory, which already contains vintages from all around the world. The atmosphere is white tablecloth but casual, with seating at tables on the main floor of a two-story building with an open atrium and skylights. Private rooms are available on the second level, and there's a small bar. The restaurant is walking distance from the Palace and Rich Forum. Hours: Mon.–Thu., noon–10:00 P.M.; Fri., noon–11:00 P.M.; Sat., 5:00 P.M.–11:00 P.M.; Sun., 5:00 P.M.–9:00 P.M. **24–26 Spring St., Stamford, 06901; (203) 978-7995.**

Da Vinci's—$$$ to $$$$

Considered the best family pizza restaurant in the area before going upscale, Da Vinci's strikes a balance between those two incarnations. Part of the menu is what owner Lisa Vitiello calls old-fashioned Italian comfort food with a 1990s twist, specifically intended to cater to longtime customers. The pizzas are back, but with current toppings and in individual portion sizes. It also offers gourmet sandwiches on focaccia bread, many veal dishes, plus salmon, scampi and more. It has a new look too: warm, with marbleized and sponged walls, al fresco paintings "copied" from Italian masters and terra-cotta–like tile. It's open for lunch & dinner Tue.–Sat. & for dinner only on Sun. Call to confirm hours. **325 Greenwich Ave., Greenwich, 06830; (203) 661-5831.**

La Grange—$$$ to $$$$

The restaurant on the ground floor of the Homestead Inn, showing all the character of its 200 years but enhanced and better illuminated by the modern addition of skylights, offers a fine dining experience. It serves classic French cuisine but with a nod to the locale, so that salade Niçoise and noisette of lamb with potatoes Anna share the menu with Blue Point oysters and Maryland crabcakes. The dining room is romantic, and a former porch has been converted into a glass-enclosed patio. Lunch features a compressed version of the dinner menu. The dessert cart will make your eyes positively pop. Also consider La Grange for a special breakfast. Reservations are required for all meals; moderately dressy. Breakfast hours: Mon.–Fri., 7:00 A.M.–9:30 A.M.; Sat.–Sun. & holidays, 8:00 A.M.–10:30 A.M. Brunch served Sun., 11:30 A.M.–2:30 P.M. Lunch hours: Mon.–Fri., noon–2:30 P.M. Dinner hours: Sun.–Thu, 6:00 P.M.–9:30 P.M.; Fri.–Sat., 6:00 P.M.–10:15 P.M. **420 Field Point Rd., Greenwich, 06830; (203) 869-7500.**

Terra Ristorante Italiano—$$$ to $$$$

With its close-set tables and crowded, noisy atmosphere, the dining experience here feels like attending a huge Italian family reunion. This is a place to bring a group of friends for a celebration, or just to rub elbows with your neighbors. The small menu is Tuscan Italian and American, with pastas and risotto, wood-fired oven pizzas and New American–style entrées. There's a tiny terrace on the side where you can get some air in summer. Reservations essential. Hours: lunch served Mon.–Sat., noon–2:30 P.M.; dinner served from 5:30 P.M., closing between 9:30 & 10:30 P.M. **156 Greenwich Ave., Greenwich, 06830; (203) 629-5222.**

Kathleen's—$$ to $$$$

Phil Costas, chef and owner of Kathleen's, describes his style of cooking as contemporary regional American with French, Italian, southwestern and New Orleans influences, but it's even more international than that, running the gamut from turkey pot pie to roasted Wisconsin duck prepared with Asian flavors to gourmet sandwiches. Patrons with small appetites will welcome the half-portions of pasta available at dinner. In summer Kathleen's is also a genuine sidewalk café, decked out with flowery windowboxes to match the flowery tablecloths. Reservations are recommended all nights of the week. The restaurant is walking distance from the Palace and Rich Forum. Hours: lunch served Mon.–Fri., 11:30 A.M.–3:00 P.M.; dinner served Mon.–Sat. from 5:30 P.M., with the last seating at 9:45 (10:45 on Fri. & Sat.). **25 Bank St., Stamford, 06901; (203) 323-7785.**

Bank Street Brewing Company—$$$

The ornate features of the 1913 Citizens Savings Bank building in which Bank Street Brewing is located have been put to good use: the former marble teller's counter has been converted into a 40-foot bar, and the mezzanine is now the main dining room. It makes 8–10 beers and specializes in English ales, serving them only from tap. (There is one bottled non-alcoholic brew.) The menu ranges from Thai tuna to meatloaf, vegetarian stew served over couscous to fish 'n' chips. The restaurant is right around the corner from the Palace and Rich Forum. Reservations suggested. Hours: lunch served 11:30 A.M.–4:00 P.M. daily; dinner served nightly 5:00 P.M.–11:00 P.M. (until midnight on weekends). **65 Bank St. at Atlantic, Stamford, 06901; (203) 325-2739.**

La Hacienda—$$$

Formerly known as Hacienda Don Emilio, La Hacienda serves both Tex-Mex and excellent Mexican food. It uses a number of regional sauces and offers fresh fish specials every day. Some hard-to-find dishes such as ceviche and Mexican soups are regulars on the menu. Patrons can enjoy before- or after-dinner drinks and cigars in a dedicated sitting area. Lunch served Mon.–Fri., 11:30 A.M.–2:30 P.M.; Sat., noon–4:00 P.M. Dinner served Mon.–Sat., 5:00 P.M.–10:30 P.M. (11:30 P.M. on weekends); Sun., 1:00 P.M.–9:00 P.M. **222 Summer St., Stamford, 06901; (203) 324-0577.**

Meera Indian Cuisine—$$$

Although it doesn't get the publicity of some other Indian restaurants, Meera serves Indian food as fine as any in Connecticut. The menu is large, everything is cooked to your preferred level of spiciness and the food is simply delicious. The decor is a bit on the plain side, but the tables are set nicely and the lighting at dinnertime is warm and low. The restaurant is very convenient to the Stamford Center for the Arts. Hours: lunch served daily 11:45 A.M.–2:30 P.M.; dinner served 5:30 P.M.–10:00 P.M. **227 Summer St., Stamford, 06901; (203) 975-0477.**

Versailles—$$$

For a small taste of France in Greenwich, visit this charming little restaurant and pastry shop. It's more bistro than haute cuisine, and if you like it you can take some with you in the form of their homemade and vacuum-packed terrine, pâté, quiche, salmon and escargots. Everything in the pastry case will also call you by name. French-language newspapers and magazines lie around for perusal. Consider this for breakfast too. Open daily and serving continuously from 7:30 A.M. Lunch is available beginning at 11:00 A.M. & dinner from 5:30 P.M. **315 Greenwich Ave., Greenwich, 06830; (203) 661-6634.**

Centro at the Mill—$$ to $$$

This popular restaurant is set in a renovated felt and gasket mill. The seasonal open-air terrace has a great view of water rushing over the mill dam and planters laden with annual flowers in an explosion of color. The interior is bright and modern, decorated with the colors of Italian tile to match the Northern Italian cuisine. Lunch and dinner menus are virtually the same, with pastas, pizzas, sandwiches and some grilled chicken, fish and steak dishes. Centro has a great ambiance and a location away from the congested center of town. Reservations recommended at lunch and dinner. Hours: lunch served Mon.–Sat., 11:30 A.M.–3:00 P.M.; dinner available Mon.–Sat., 5:30 P.M.–10:00 P.M. (11:00 P.M. on weekends). **328 Pemberwick Rd. just south of Glenville Rd., Greenwich, 06831; (203) 531-5514.**

Fiesta—$$ to $$$

The Stamford area has lots of South American immigrants, and Fiesta is one of many casual restaurants that have sprung up to serve that clientele with authentic fare. They dish up Peruvian food here, which is generally spicy but not particularly hot. The atmosphere is casual, clean and pleasant, with paintings of peasant scenes on the walls and Spanish-language music coming over the sound system. The use of substantive plates and utensils rather than disposable stuff lends Fiesta the air of a Peruvian diner. Try one of the soups, which come steaming hot in huge porcelain bowls. The Lomo Saltado (sort of a stir-fried chicken or beef dish) is also excellent without being too unfamiliar to American palates. The lunchtime crowd is an interesting mix of workers, families and the occasional businessperson. Call for hours; closed Tue. **70 Main St., Stamford, 06901; (203) 348-7300.**

Stationhouse—$$ to $$$

The pubby atmosphere of Stationhouse really distinguishes it from all of the trendy eateries around the corner on Greenwich Ave. It's woody, denlike atmosphere is quite comfortable, with gaslight-type sconces and a bar that stays open late. The food is American, with a number of salads, sandwiches (even a veggieburger), steak, fish and pasta and an à la carte brunch on Sun. Located directly across the street from a movie theater and less than a block from Greenwich train station. Lunch/brunch hours: 11:30 A.M.–3:00 P.M. Dinner served from 5:00 P.M. nightly, ending at 10:30 P.M. Mon.–Wed., 11:00 P.M. Thu.–Sat. & 10:00 P.M. on Sun. **99 Railroad Ave., Greenwich, 06830; (203) 661-1374.**

Bull's Head Diner—$ to $$$

Bull's Head fits into that wonderful category of a diner with a personality. It's a colorful landmark with a clock tower whose arms are made in the shape of a knife and fork. The food is as simple or as hearty as you want it. You can also get it whenever you want it, because they never close. **43 High Ridge Rd. in Bull's Head Shopping Center, Stamford, 06905; (203) 961-1400.**

Love and Serve—$$

You'll think you somehow wandered into the basement café at your college's Student Union when you enter Love and Serve. It's very casual and reminiscent of a cafeteria. Everything served is vegetarian, and many of the dishes

353

are vegan. Prices are very reasonable at both lunch and dinner. Hours: Mon., 11:00 A.M.–6:00 P.M.; Tue.–Sat., 11:00 A.M.–9:00 P.M. **35 Amogerone Crossway, Greenwich, 06830; (203) 861-9822.**

Gourmet Gallery—$ to $$

For breakfast, lunch or deli food, Gourmet Gallery is one of the top spots around. The sandwich offerings are so exhaustive that even the list of sandwich spreads gets its own section of the menu. There is a small salad bar, soups and prepared salads, as well as breakfast items. Hours: Mon.–Fri., 7:00 A.M.–5:00 P.M.; Sat., 8:00 A.M.–4:00 P.M. **100 Greenwich Ave., Greenwich, 06830; (203) 869-9617.**

Coffeehouses, Sweets & Treats

Just walk down Greenwich Ave. at midday or later to find several spots for a quick pick-me-up. Some of the eateries listed in the Where to Eat section, such as Versailles, have dual personalities as both restaurants and bakeries, and you'll find household names like Ben & Jerry's and Baskin-Robbins hawking ice cream. In Stamford, stop in at **Café à la Mode (450 Main St.; 203-973-0900),** a cool refuge on a hot day, for a variety of ice cream concoctions, desserts and beverages. Or, head into the food court of Stamford Town Center Mall across the street for a variety of choices.

Services

Local Visitors Information

Coastal Fairfield County Tourism District, 297 West Ave., Norwalk, 06850; (800) 866-7925 or **(203) 854-7825.** Hours: Mon.–Fri., 10:00 A.M.–5:00 P.M.; Sat.–Sun. (July–Oct. only), 11:00 A.M.–3:00 P.M.

State Welcome Center, located on the Merritt Pkwy. (Rte. 15) northbound between exits 27 and 28 in Greenwich; **(203) 531-1902.** It's open 8:00 A.M.–6:00 P.M. daily, Memorial Day–Labor Day.

Parking

Parking spaces are at a premium in the downtown areas of both Greenwich and Stamford. Parking lots and garages are not always available; come prepared with quarters for meters. In Greenwich, there is diagonal parking up and down Greenwich Ave. Parking just a block or two from the main drag can solve the problem: metered spots on Steamboat Ave. (Greenwich Ave. south of Railroad Ave.) have a 12-hour limit. In downtown Stamford there is a huge parking garage with entrances on Atlantic St., and a lot with an attendant on Broad St. west of Summer St.

Transportation

Interstate bus service to Stamford is provided by two bus lines with toll-free numbers. Call **Peter Pan/Trailways** at **(800) 343-9999** and **Greyhound** at **(800) 231-2222** for schedule and fare information. The greater Stamford region is also served by **CT Transit** at **(203) 327-7433.** The **Greenwich Commuter Connection** runs shuttle buses between the train station and other parts of Greenwich during morning and evening rush hours Mon.–Fri. Buses leave about every half hour, and the one-way fare is currently $1. Call **(800) 982-8420** for information or a route map.

For information on **Amtrak** service to Stamford call **(800) 872-7245. Metro-North** operates a commuter rail line (including weekend service) between New Haven and New York City with local stops in Stamford, Old Greenwich, Riverside, Cos Cob and Greenwich. Call **(800) 638-7646** or **(212) 532-4900** in New York for details.

New Haven

If you were to ask people what they associate with New Haven, the number-one answer, overwhelmingly, would be Yale. Although there is much about New Haven that has nothing to do with this Ivy League school, the university has a hand in much that makes New Haven an enjoyable, enriching place to visit or live. Yale is a commanding architectural force in the city by virtue of its size and the Gothic profile of most of its buildings. The juxtaposition of these buttressed, medieval façades with traditional Yankee Georgian and Federal churches and boxy 20th-century offices gives the downtown a look and feel that is absolutely unique in Connecticut. Because Yale grew up with New Haven, it is inseparable from downtown, and its campus is an aesthetic treat. So integrated are the two that a guided walking tour of the campus (see the Tours section for more information) is perhaps the single best introduction to New Haven. If your time is limited, at least take a walk around the Old Campus, which you can enter from High St. between Chapel and Elm. Originally, this was Yale—all of it. Now it's a quadrangle for first-year students.

New Haven probably has the most active cultural life of any Connecticut city. During the day visit the Yale University Art Gallery, the Yale Center for British Art and the Peabody Museum of Natural History. At night a whole phalanx of theaters—Long Wharf, the Shubert and the Yale Rep, to name a few—join Woolsey Hall, the Palace, Toad's Place and the Coliseum in offering every conceivable type of stage and musical entertainment.

As one of the first settlements in Connecticut, New Haven has a long and fascinating history whose details are revealed at the New Haven Colony Historical Society. From the churches and crypt on the green to the historic Hillhouse Ave. district of mansions, New Haven is filled with pointers to its past that are easily accessible and interpreted for visitors in several guides and tours.

Families with children should board the *Liberty Belle* for a cruise in New Haven Harbor or the schooner *Quinnipiack* for an outing in Long Island Sound with an environmental education aspect. The carousel at Lighthouse Pt. Park will delight small children, and the whole family can enjoy saltwater swimming.

The New Haven area is distinguished by several noteworthy parks. Sleeping Giant, just outside the city in Hamden, is rugged and has a colorful legend behind its name. Within New Haven, East Rock and West Rock Parks, both named for outcroppings of reddish rock that lie at their heart, provide impressive overlooks of the city and surrounding countryside. It was the sight of East and West Rock that caused the Dutch explorer Adriaen Block in the early 1600s to name this area Rodeberg, meaning "red mountain." A tunnel on the Wilbur Cross Pkwy., the extension of the Merritt Pkwy. past New Haven, was blasted right through West Rock. East Rock is the spectacular formation north of New Haven visible on a clear day from the junction of I-95 and I-91.

No discussion of New Haven, however brief, could be complete without a mention of the city's status as the place where hamburgers and pizza were first served to the American public, as well as where the game of Frisbee was invented when some enterprising Yalies discovered that the thin tins in which Mrs. Frisbie's pies (of Bridgeport) were baked had aerodynamic properties. You can still mosey up to the counter at Frank Pepe's for a tomato pie or Louis's Lunch for a beef patty, and as long as you're careful not to hit the pedestrians, the green is still a perfect place to fling a Frisbee.

History

One of Connecticut's first settlements and an independent entity before consolidation of all the Connecticut towns as the Connecticut Colony under the terms of the 1662 charter, home to Yale University since 1716 and one-time cocapitol of the state, New Haven has been central to some of the most significant events in the state's history. Founders Theophilus Eaton, the Reverend John Davenport and a party of others arrived in Boston from England in June 1637. After hearing favorable reports about the land and harbor at Quinnipiac (later New Haven), they settled in the area in Apr. 1638, at first coexisting with the native Quinnipiac Indians. They agreed to "be ordered by those rules which the scripture holds forth to us" only, and called their agreement the Plantation Covenant.

New Haven was laid out geometrically right at the start in nine "squares" that are visible today in the grid pattern of the downtown. The centermost square—the green—is still intact, and nominal references to the others still crop up. One area recently redeveloped goes by the name "The Ninth Square."

Center Church on New Haven green was founded in 1638 and was the only church in the city for over 100 years. In a span of less than two years (1814–1815), all three of the church buildings presently on the green were completed, the middle one being the fourth meetinghouse of the Center Church congregation on the site. The southernmost of the trio (Trinity Church) is the first Gothic Revival church in the country.

One intriguing story from New Haven's early days concerns the three regicides Edward Whalley, John Dixwell and William Goff. These three were among the 59 men who signed the death warrant of Charles I of England, leading to the Protectorate of Oliver and Richard Cromwell that ended 11 years later with the Restoration and reign of Charles II. The new king sought to avenge the death of his father by seeking out and executing all the signers of that warrant. The three men hid successfully in the New World from Charles II's agents, all of them at one time or another abiding in New Haven (see the entry for West Rock Ridge State Park in the Hiking section for some details), where they are memorialized in the names of three thoroughfares: Whalley, Dixwell and Goff.

In 1701 the first university in Connecticut, the Collegiate School, was founded, with classes meeting in a number of towns. Fifteen years later the school found a permanent home in New Haven, and soon thereafter, a new name. Elihu Yale, an Anglican who spent most of his life in England, made some generous donations to the struggling school, and in gratitude it took his name. Although Harvard is 63 years older, Yale awarded the first doctorate degree in the United States.

New Haven saw a great deal of activity during the Revolutionary War. It was strongly Patriot in sympathy, and gunpowder as well as cannon and cannonballs were made here. In 1779 the British burned portions of the city, pillaged and retreated, doing a great deal of damage, but even with superior forces they managed to hold New Haven for only about a day.

New Haven had several suitable mill sites, at one of which Eli Whitney began manufacturing firearms in the final years of the 18th century. Whitney was a graduate of Yale, patent-holder of the cotton gin and the man credited with first using the idea of interchangeable parts to mass-produce something. He built one of the first factory towns for his mill workers, and it was dubbed Whitneyville. Today there is a museum named for him on the site.

Although some of New Haven's rivers could provide water power, none of them could compare to the mighty Connecticut. New Haven had a wonderful port but no good access to inland areas. A plan was contrived to build a canal stretching from New Haven to Northampton, Massachusetts, a distance of more than 80 miles. Digging began in 1825, and three years later the canal was open all the way up to Farmington. What came to be known as the Farmington Canal was completed in 1835. Unfortunately, it was short-lived and not a financial success for its backers. In 1846 much of the Farmington Canal's towpath was used to lay a railroad bed.

As the 1800s progressed, New Haven grew and prospered. It was a center of clock and carriage making as late as the Civil War. In the 1830s it played a role in a landmark lawsuit when the captured *Amistad* slaves (see the listing under Historic Sites for background) were confined briefly in the New Haven jail. The year 1832 saw the founding of what would become the Yale University Art Gallery, when John Trumbull, noted American painter and son of Connecticut's Revolutionary War governor Jonathan Trumbull, made a gift of 100 of his works to the university. The collection is still displayed in the Trumbull Gallery, and Trumbull himself is buried beneath the museum.

New Haven continued as the cocapital of Connecticut with Hartford until just after the Civil War, when the desirability of having one capital finally overcame the historic rivalry between the two cities. New Haven lost out to a more generous offer from Hartford to build a suitable statehouse, and the last legislative session in New Haven adjourned in 1874.

Just after the turn of the century West Haven was a popular destination for fun-seekers

Getting There

New Haven is located about an hour south-southwest of Hartford by car. I-91 makes a beeline between the two cities, merging with I-95 in downtown New Haven. For other transportation options, see the Services section at the end of this chapter.

when Savin Rock was developed as the Coney Island of the Fairfield County shoreline. An area perhaps four times as large as today's Ocean Beach Park in New London was filled with carnival rides and family entertainment, and trolleys and trains brought thousands to the area to enjoy them. The rides have been gone for more than 20 years now, and some of the space is occupied by West Haven's town beaches.

New Haven suffered the ravages of postwar economic contraction twice in this century, just as every other manufacturing city in Connecticut did, but in the 1950s and 1960s New Haven was the recipient of millions of federal dollars for urban renewal. New Haven was supposed to serve as the model for other American cities at a time when many were experiencing a serious decline. It therefore came as a surprise to many that New Haven was not spared the race riots of 1967–1969. Currently a number of companies at a large science park, Yale-New Haven Hospital, Southern New England Telephone and Blue Cross of Connecticut all provide employment to help counteract the diminished manufacturing base of this historic seaport, and Yale University continues to be a stabilizing force.

Major Attractions

East Rock Park

New Haven's largest city park is named for the massive outcropping of traprock on which it lies. With hiking trails, scenic roads, vistas, picnic shelters and grills, playgrounds and other facilities, it is very much a center of summer-

357

time activity. There's a view of New Haven Harbor and Long Island Sound and a 112-foot-tall landmark war memorial called the Soldiers and Sailors Monument at the summit. (The road to the summit is open Apr.–Nov., 8:00 A.M.–sunset daily; Dec.–Mar., Fri.–Sun. only.) The Mill River meanders at the park's base, creating excellent birding habitat. The Pardee Rose Gardens burst into bloom every June and keep going intermittently throughout the summer. The East Rock Ranger Station at Orange and Cold Spring Sts. in the park serves as a nature center (open year-round, Mon.–Fri., 8:30 A.M.–4:30 P.M.) with live animal exhibits, taxidermy and environmental education displays and information about guided walks and other public programs. Admission to the park and nature center is free. The main park entrance is on **East Rock Rd. in New Haven; (203) 946-6086.** The **Pardee Rose Gardens** are located at the intersection of Park Dr. and Farm Rd. in the town of Hamden, which shares the park with New Haven. For more information call **(203) 946-8142.**

New Haven Colony Historical Society

This museum has extensive holdings expressing 350 years of New Haven history through fine art, industrial artifacts, furniture and other functional household items, and thousands of manuscripts, maps, photographs and genealogical records. Highlights of the permanent displays include a gallery devoted to the maritime history of the area and the oft-reproduced Nathaniel Jocelyn portrait of Cinque, the leader of the *Amistad* slaves whose story is told in the Historic Sites section of this chapter. The museum is housed in a 1930s Georgian Revival building designed by J. Frederick Kelly, a noted expert on the restoration of old colonial homes.Hours: Tue.–Fri., 10:00 A.M.–5:00 P.M.; Sat.–Sun., 2:00 P.M.–5:00 P.M. **114 Whitney Ave., New Haven, 06510; (203) 562-4183.**

Peabody Museum of Natural History

The Peabody, affiliated with Yale University, is the only sizable natural history museum in Connecticut. Some strengths of its large collection are a number of reconstructed dinosaur skeletons and extensive exhibits on ancient civilizations, including Connecticut's Native Americans. Hours: Mon.–Sat., 10:00 A.M.–5:00 P.M.; Sun., noon–5:00 P.M.; closed major holidays. On weekdays, $1.50 parking is available in the Audubon Court Garage on Audubon St.; show your museum receipt when leaving. **170 Whitney Ave., New Haven, 06520; (203) 432-5050.**

Yale Center for British Art

Anglophiles and art lovers alike will want to visit this, "the most comprehensive collection of British art outside Great Britain." This is a world-class museum whose holdings include works of art in numerous media from the 16th century onward, all displayed in a statuesque modern building with a central atrium. Inquire about the center's public programming, which includes lectures, films and concerts. Only the prints and drawings and rare books departments as well as the reference library are open to the public in 1998, because the museum is undergoing renovations. The full collection will reopen in Jan. 1999. Admission is free. Hours: Tue.–Sat., 10:00 A.M.–5:00 P.M.; Sun., noon–5:00 P.M.; closed major holidays. **1080 Chapel St., New Haven, 06520; (203) 432-2800.**

Yale University Art Gallery

Directly opposite Chapel St. from the Yale Center for British Art is a modern building directly connected to a Gothic one. The two together form the Yale University Art Gallery, and the juxtaposition of old and new holds true inside as well. You are just as likely to see Roman artifacts as Cubism. The museum is large enough that it would be difficult to take in all the exhibits in one visit. You might want to start with one of the free, hour-long tours, offered Wed. & Sat. at 1:30 P.M., or you can participate in the extensive schedule of lecture programming. Admission is free. Hours: Tue.–Sat., 10:00 A.M.–5:00 P.M.; Sun., 2:00 P.M.–5:00

P.M.; closed major holidays & the month of Aug. **1111 Chapel St., New Haven, 06510; (203) 432-0600.**

Festivals and Events

The monthly newspaper *New Haven Arts*, published by the Arts Council of Greater New Haven, contains an excellent calendar of the month's events. It is distributed free at many restaurants, galleries and performance venues throughout town. Also see the Performing Arts section for more suggestions.

International Festival of Arts and Ideas
last week in June (Wed.–Sun.)

The year 1996 was the first for this instantly successful celebration spotlighting the visual, literary and performing arts in emulation of the Spoleto fest held annually in Charleston, South Carolina. There were over 150 events and almost 400 participating artists, including such diverse luminaries as the Beijing Opera, Ellis and Branford Marsalis, Cirque Baroque and Ladysmith Black Mambazo. The Art on the Edge Festival is the local art component of the International Festival, featuring mostly juried shows in galleries in the Audubon St. area. There are also numerous events for children, including storytelling, puppetry and participatory activities. Most events take place on the green, but many are held in halls, churches, art galleries and at Yale venues. Admission to most shows and performances is free, but you must purchase tickets for a few of the largest. The festival goes on rain or shine. Inquire about off-site parking and shuttles. For more information call **(888) 278-4332.**

Harborfest
Fourth of July weekend (Fri.–Sun.)

This new city festival designed to focus attention on New Haven Harbor combines maritime activities and demonstrations with musical entertainment, activities for kids, food and fireworks to round out the Fourth. It takes place on Long Wharf, which is most easily reached by taking the Long Wharf exit off I-95. Parking is free. Hours: Fri., 5:00 P.M.–11:00 P.M.; Sat.–Sun., 1:00 P.M.–11:00 P.M. For more information call **(203) 946-7821.**

New Haven Jazz Festival
July

What could be a better way to enjoy New Haven on a summer night than a free jazz concert on the green featuring national and international acts like Tito Puente or the Charles Mingus Big Band? It sounds too good to be true, but this summer tradition is for real and has been for almost two decades. Bring a blanket or a lawn chair; seating is not provided. Concerts usually take place on Sat. nights starting around 6:00 P.M. The green is bordered by Chapel, College, Elm and Church Sts. in downtown New Haven. For specific dates and more information call **(203) 946-7821.**

Summertime Street Festival
four days in mid-Aug.

The name says it all. SNET and Elm City Brewing are sponsors of this celebration of summer held in conjunction with the Pilot Pen International Tennis Tournament. The festival starts midweek following the conclusion of the tournament. More than 150,000 people come over four days and nights to enjoy live bands on five stages, dancing, performing arts, a beer garden, street vendors and a finale concert on New Haven green. Sat. is kids' day, featuring special activities, and every evening there are strolling entertainers. The festival takes place on three blocks of Chapel St. between College and Park Sts. Hours: Thu.–Fri., 5:00 P.M.–11:00 P.M.; Sat.–Sun., 1:00 P.M.–11:00 P.M. For dates and more information call **(203) 946-7821.**

North Haven Fair
weekend after Labor Day (Thu.–Sun.)

You can experience the country side of Connecticut without going too far out of the city

359

when you attend North Haven's agricultural fair. Old MacDonald's Farm is an area where kids can get a sense of farm life in days past. It has pig racing, draft animal pulls, a petting zoo, a midway and judging of everything from livestock to apple pies. It also has a big picnic area with tables and benches for resting or eating a meal. Free parking is available on-site and in adjacent lots from which free shuttle buses run. Admission: $6 adults, free to children under 12. Hours: Thu., 5:00 P.M.–11:00 P.M.; Fri., 3:00 P.M.–11:00 P.M.; Sat., 9:00 A.M.–11:00 P.M.; Sun., 10:00 A.M.–8:00 P.M. Held at **North Haven Fairground, Washington Ave. (Rte. 5 near I-91 exit 12) in North Haven; (203) 239-3700.**

If the timing of the North Haven Fair doesn't work for you, perhaps that of the **Orange Country Fair** will. This two-day event is held the third weekend of Sept. at the Orange Fairgrounds on Rte. 152 in Orange. For more information call the town hall at **(203) 891-2122.**

Celebration of American Crafts
mid-Nov.–Christmas

This annual exhibition/sale featuring the work of more than 400 craftspeople from around the country is the main fund-raiser for Creative Arts Workshop, a community visual arts school. More than 10,000 objects are artfully displayed in the school's gallery. You'll find a mix of functional and decorative items, including furniture, pottery, clothing and jewelry in price ranges from $10 to $1,000. Discounted parking is available in the Audubon Court Garage next door to the school. Hours: Mon.–Sat., 11:00 A.M.–5:00 P.M. (until 7:00 P.M. on Thu. in Dec.); Sun., 1:00 P.M.–5:00 P.M.; Christmas Eve, 10:00 A.M.–1:00 P.M. (if applicable). **80 Audubon St., New Haven, 06510; (203) 562-4927.**

UI Fantasy of Lights
Thanksgiving–after New Year's Day

In a twist on the tradition of decorating homes for the Christmas holidays, United Illuminating

(the local electric utility), other sponsors and a host of volunteers annually create a drive-through fantasy world of lighted holiday displays 8–25 feet high in a harborside city park. The displays are quite elaborate, and some even involve animation. Admission is a flat $5 per car. An audiocassette acts as your guide to the displays (you need to provide your own cassette player). Hours: Sun.–Thu., 5:00 P.M.–9:00 P.M.; Fri.–Sat., 5:00 P.M.–10:00 P.M. **Lighthouse Point Park** is at **2 Lighthouse Rd., New Haven, 06515.** For directions call **(203) 777-2000, ext. 603;** for more information try **ext. 262** during business hours.

Outdoor Activities

The South Central Connecticut Regional Water Authority, a local water utility, owns several exceptional bodies of water and the land surrounding them in the New Haven area, including Lake Saltonstall and the Maltby Lakes. Use of them is by permit only. Permits cost $35 per year and provide access for one couple and their children under age 21. Hiking, cross-country skiing, boating and fishing are activities that can be enjoyed on these properties or others along the shore as far east as Madison. Some properties are wheelchair-accessible. Call **(203) 624-6671** for details.

Biking

Biking is allowed on all roads at both **East Rock Park** and **West Rock Ridge State Park,** and both have some stretches of asphalt that are closed to automobile traffic, so you can ride without having to keep an eye out for cars. In East Rock, Trowbridge Dr. and English Dr. are reserved for bicyclists and pedestrians; in West Rock, most of Baldwin Dr. is auto-free. These roads are appropriate for both road bikes and mountain bikes. Be prepared for a climb, since both parks contain high ridges. For directions and more information, see the listings under Major Attractions and Hiking.

360

Birding

There are several good birding spots in New Haven. **East Rock Park** is considered one of the top warbler spots in Connecticut because, like Central Park, it's an oasis in the city. The best time of year for viewing is mid-Apr.–May. The higher park elevations provide a good vantage point for viewing hawks during their fall migration. For more information, see the listing under Major Attractions.

In late Aug.–Thanksgiving there are birders at **Lighthouse Pt. Park** on Long Island Sound every day counting hawks, eagles and falcons. Every fall, 20,000–30,000 of these spectacular birds are seen, rivaling the renowned migration at Hawk Mountain in Pennsylvania. For directions and more information, see the listing under Swimming.

Finally, **West Rock Ridge State Park** lies atop a high ridge that provides optimal conditions for viewing hawks during their fall migration, but there is not always automobile access to the top. For directions and more information, see the listing under Hiking.

Boating

Freshwater

Lake Saltonstall, the largest freshwater body near New Haven, is owned by the South Central Connecticut Regional Water Authority. Boating is allowed by permit only, and only the water authority's own rental rowboats and powerboats with electric motors are allowed on the lake. For more information, see the listing at the start of the Outdoor Activities section.

Saltwater

If you want to get out on saltwater while you're in the New Haven area and you don't have a boat, you can take one of the tours listed under the Cruises section below or try one of the charter brokers listed in the **Greenwich/ Stamford** chapter, some of which operate this far east. If you do have your own boat, the easiest public access to the Sound is at the state boat launch at Lighthouse Pt. Park on Lighthouse Rd. in New Haven.

For navigational details, charts and complete lists of marine facilities throughout this area, your best source of information is *Embassy's Complete Boating Guide & Chartbook to Long Island Sound*. Contact the publisher at **142 Ferry Rd., Old Saybrook, 06475; (860) 395-0188.**

Cruises

Liberty Belle

This 200-passenger, two-level classic wooden motor vessel offers public cruises June 1–Labor Day and private charters Apr.–Oct. Cruises can have a sightseeing focus or a special theme, such as the Oldies Cruise 'n' Dance, the Moonlight Music Dance Party and fireworks viewing during the Fourth of July period. There are evening and afternoon departures as well as a Continental buffet brunch cruise on Sun. Prices range from $10 to $15 for regularly scheduled trips, and charters can be designed to match your interests. Inquire about senior discount days. Parking is free. The *Liberty Belle* departs from Long Wharf Pier located immediately adjacent to I-95 exit 46 (Long Wharf). For more information call **(800) 745-2628.**

Sail the Sound

If you want a really intimate cruise experience, consider chartering *Quiet Passages*, a 45-foot ketch that sails New Haven Harbor May–Oct. She's available for afternoon, evening and all-day excursions beginning at $145 for two people. Passengers are invited to take the helm or help raise the sails. Maximum capacity is six people—just the right size for a family. Reservations required. Reserve several weeks in advance during July and Aug., and at least a week in advance at other times. *Quiet Passages* departs from Oyster Pt. Marina in New Haven near I-95 exit 44. For more information call **(860) 355-9210.**

Schooner, Inc.

Schooner, Inc. sails the 91-foot replica schooner *Quinnipiack* out of New Haven's Long Wharf and several other ports. It offers an R&R sunset cruise as well as evening and afternoon educational "sea adventures," in which it trawls the waters of Long Island Sound with a net, and an onboard biologist interprets the marine life it captures and rereleases. You are invited to bring your own boxed lunch or dinner, as well as beer, wine and other beverages. Reservations are essential. Sea adventures are offered Wed. & Fri., 6:00 P.M.–9:00 P.M., & Sun., 1:00 P.M.–4:00 P.M. The sunset cruise takes place Sun., 5:00 P.M.–8:00 P.M. The cost is $15 for adults and $10 for children under 12. To get to Long Wharf, take I-95 exit 46 and follow the signs. To request a brochure, write to **60 S. Water St., New Haven, 06519** or call **(203) 865-1737.**

Marinas

Oyster Point Marina (203-624-5895; VHF 9) and **Shiner's Cove Marina (203-933-2781;** VHF 16) are the only two year-round marinas with transient slips in this area. Oyster Pt. sells gas, and Shiner's will be able to provide pump-out and repair services. Other possibilities with transient slips and varying degrees of facilities and services are **West Cove Marina (203-933-3000), Waucoma Yacht Club (203-789-9530;** VHF 16) and **Fair Haven Marina (203-777-0523;** VHF 9).

Fishing

Freshwater

The best freshwater fishing areas in the New Haven area are owned by the South Central Connecticut Regional Water Authority. To fish their lakes and streams, you must purchase a special-use permit from the utility in addition to having a state-issued fishing license, but the cost is worth it. **Lake Saltonstall,** the **Maltby Lakes** and **Racebrook** (a stream) are all developed for recreation yet rustic and relatively pristine, offering an outdoor experience that you would not think possible immediately adjacent to a major urban area. Lake Saltonstall is a large body of water in a deep valley surrounded by 1,900 acres of woodland; the Maltby Lakes are three small reservoirs with 2 miles of extremely picturesque shoreline. Lake Saltonstall is considered one of the best largemouth bass fisheries in the state. Rental boats and a wheelchair-accessible fishing dock are

available at Lake Saltonstall. See the listing at the start of the Outdoor Activities section for more information.

Saltwater

There is no established charter fishing industry in New Haven Harbor despite the fact that there are lots of fish here, including blackfish, bluefish and striped bass. You might have luck with one of the charter brokers listed in the **Greenwich/Stamford** chapter. You don't have to go too far to find charter fishing (Milford to the west and Clinton to the east), but if you have a boat, there's no reason not to stay right here. For supplies, maps, advice and tide tables, head for **Master Bait and Tackle (439 Main St. in East Haven; 203-469-6525).** They can equip you for any sort of fishing, fresh- or saltwater—even crabbing. Their hours in season are 5:30 A.M.–8:00 P.M. daily, and only an hour or so less each way in winter.

Hiking

In addition to the options below, see the description of **East Rock Park** under Major Attractions and the listing for the **South Central Connecticut Regional Water Authority** properties at the start of the Outdoor Activities section. Also, several city and other parks are good for strolling rather than hiking. **Lighthouse Pt.,** described under Swimming, has a few footpaths and a lovely beach right on Long Island Sound, but a parking fee is charged in summer. **East Shore Park** on Woodward Ave. nearby has a shoreline trail. Inland and on the west side of town there's **Edgewood Park** bordering Yale Bowl. **Edgerton Park,** described under Gardens and Arboreta, has numerous paths in addition to a conservatory. Finally, if you're staying out West Haven way, don't miss the chance to stroll shoreside at the site of that town's once-famous amusement park at **Savin Rock.** There are several parking lots off Beach St. and Capt. Thomas Blvd. where a $10 nonresident parking fee is collected in summer.

Quinnipiac Trail

The oldest of Connecticut's blue-blazed trails and 23 miles long, the Quinnipiac follows the river of the same name through an undeveloped state park, ascends the hills of Sleeping Giant State Park and then follows traprock ridges all the way to Prospect. It also meets the Regicides Trail, connecting the aforementioned areas with the massive West Rock Ridge State Park. The riverside portion of the trail may not be passable in spring when the river is high. Parking for this portion is on Banton St. in North Haven, or park at Sleeping Giant State Park and pick up the trail there.

Sleeping Giant State Park

The "sleeping giant" for which this park is named is a series of ridges that, when viewed from the south, forms the rough outline of a person sleeping face to the sky. The Sleeping Giant Park Association continues to acquire acreage to expand the park, and it is the association rather than the state that maintains most of the 30-plus miles of trails in Sleeping Giant, although the state does upkeep on the broad gravel Tower Path that leads to a mountaintop lookout built by the Civilian Conservation Corps in the 1930s. There is also a dedicated trail for equestrians that becomes a cross-country ski trail in winter, as well as a nature trail. The blue-blazed trail through the park is the Quinnipiac Trail (see the previous listing), which continues on both sides of the park for a total of 23 miles. Other facilities include picnic tables, a picnic pavilion, fire pits and rest rooms. Maps are available at the entrance. There is a weekend and holiday park use charge of $5 for cars with Connecticut plates and $8 for out-of-state vehicles Apr. 15–Nov. 1. The entrance is on Mt. Carmel Ave. just east of Whitney Ave. in Hamden. Park office: **(203) 789-7498.**

West Rock Ridge
State Park/Regicides Trail

The second of New Haven's pair of prominent, red, traprock ridges (the other is East Rock) forms the spine of this rugged park. It has fewer facilities and ranger patrols than East Rock, but offers something closer to a wilderness experience. A paved road (open to cars in summer only; call for schedule changes) winds up to parking areas at Judges Cave and the

South Overlook. Bicyclists and pedestrians, however, have daily year-round access to this road and Baldwin Dr., which runs north for miles through the park.

The trail system covers nearly the entire perimeter of the park and has numerous connectors that make it possible to tailor the length of your hike to your energy level. The principal one is the Regicides Trail, which follows the crest of the ridge for roughly 6 miles and then meets the Quinnipiac Trail, via which you have access to two other state parks to the east and more ledges to the north. The views from atop these igneous outcroppings are hard to beat. Passage is difficult in places, making excellent footwear essential.

The trail begins at Judges Cave on the road to the South Overlook well inside the park. To get there, take the Baldwin Dr. entrance on Brookside Ave. off Wintergreen Ave. in New Haven and follow the signs. (This road is often closed; be prepared to hike all the way from the entrance, or call the park office at **203-789-7498** to find out when it will be open. If it is closed, park at the West Rock Nature Center across from the entrance.)

Ice Skating

There are several enclosed ice rinks in the New Haven area, making it possible to skate nearly year-round. Each one has a different schedule and fee structure, so call before going. Two facilities that offer skate rentals are the **Edward L. Bennett Ice Skating Rink (One Circle St., West Haven; 203-931-6890)** and the **Hamden Ice Skating Rink (Mix Ave. off Dixwell Ave. behind Hamden High School in Hamden; 203-287-2610).** Rentals are sometimes available at **Veterans Memorial Ice Rink (71 Hudson St., East Haven; 203-468-3367).** A fourth option is the partially enclosed **Ralph Walker Skating Pavilion (Blake Field, 1080 State St., New Haven; 203-946-8007 or 203-946-8029),** whose season is weather-dependent. There are no skate rentals at the present time, but that may change, so inquire.

363

Sleigh and Carriage Rides

There are two places in the New Haven area where, conditions permitting, you can enjoy a sleigh or carriage ride: **Fieldview Farm**, described under Seasonal Favorites, and **Maple View Farm (603 Orange Center Rd., Orange; 203-799-6495).** The folks at the latter can take you for a ride through the woods or on back roads in a reproduction vis-à-vis carriage drawn by a team of Percherons. A hay wagon is also available if you prefer. Minimums apply and reservations are required.

Swimming

Freshwater

The waters of Wharton Brook and Allen Brook, which flow through Wharton Brook State Park, were used for many years to power mills, but since 1948 when Allen Brook was dammed to create a swimming area, they've been used more for pleasure than work. The guarded sandy beach is complemented by bathhouses, a concession stand, picnic tables and shelters and two interconnected loop trails for hiking. Weekdays: $4 for vehicles with Connecticut plates, $5 out-of-state. Weekends: $5 and $8, respectively. Located on Rte. 5 in North Haven. Park office: **(203) 789-7498.**

Saltwater

Lighthouse Pt. Park on New Haven Harbor has a sandy beach for swimming, trails, a picnic grove, a recently restored antique carousel that's delighted children here for over 80 years, a paved boat ramp on the harbor and a bird sanctuary. There is a lighthouse that operated from 1840 to 1877, but you can view it only from the outside. During summer, lifeguards are on duty when available. Carousel hours: Tue.–Fri., 3:00 P.M.–7:00 P.M.; Sat.–Sun., 11:00 A.M.–7:00 P.M., Memorial Day–Labor Day. Open 10:00 A.M.–6:00 P.M. daily, year-round. Fee (in season only): $2 per car weekdays, $3 weekends. The carousel costs $.50 per ride. **2 Lighthouse Rd., New Haven, 06515; (203) 946-8790.**

Seeing and Doing

Art Galleries

The Audubon Arts District is a small New Haven neighborhood where galleries, cafés and boutiques abound. Take a walk down the two blocks of Audubon between Whitney and State Sts., or pick up a copy of *New Haven Arts* and turn to the Exhibits calendar for addresses. Individual galleries are also listed in the *Greater New Haven Guide* available from the **New Haven Convention and Visitors Bureau** at **(800) 332-7829** or **(203) 777-8550.** For information on the Yale University Art Gallery and the Yale Center for British Art, see the listings under Major Attractions.

Creative Arts Workshop

You can see faculty, student and juried shows in this school's gallery Jan.–Oct. Then, mid-Nov.–Christmas, it's the site of the Celebration of American Crafts described under Festivals and Events. The focus of shows is usually on fine art but can also include the decorative arts. In mid-Jan. there is a Sun. open house during which visitors can tour the studios and try out different arts and crafts themselves, such as throwing a pot on a wheel. Call for the date and hours. The school also offers one-day workshops to introduce people to a new medium or cover a special technique. Normal gallery hours: Mon.–Fri., 9:00 A.M.–5:00 P.M.; Sat., 9:00 A.M.–noon. **80 Audubon St., New Haven, 06510; (203) 562-4927.**

Erector Square

Erector Square was the factory in which Eli Whitney and A. C. Gilbert manufactured erector sets and American Flyer toy trains. It now contains approximately 80 leased artist studios and light manufacturing facilities. There is a gallery on-site open Sept.–May, with monthly shows featuring works by contemporary artists from around the country. There are also two international juried shows per year. A shop sells high-quality handmade decorative and functional work. Gallery and store hours: Wed.–Sat., 1:00 P.M.–4:00 P.M. The first Fri. of the month, it's open until 7:30 P.M. for a reception introducing the newest show. **315 Peck St., Bldg. 20, New Haven, 06513; (203) 865-5055.**

John Slade Ely House
The Center for Contemporary Art is housed in this 1905 Elizabethan-style mansion in which seven rooms have been converted into small galleries and a backyard is sometimes pressed into use as a sculpture garden. Work by members of various regional and local arts guilds and schools is complemented by curated shows Sept.–June. Admission is free. Hours: Tue.–Fri., 1:00 P.M.–4:00 P.M.; Sat.–Sun., 2:00 P.M.–5:00 P.M. **51 Trumbull St. between Whitney Ave. and Orange St., New Haven, 06510; (203) 624-8055.**

Children and Families

Some of the biggest attractions for kids in New Haven are not exclusively for kids. The **Shore Line Trolley Museum** (described under Museums) will also fascinate adults. And who could not be thrilled by the reconstructed dinosaurs at the Peabody Museum (see Major Attractions)? At **The Only Game in Town,** a sports-oriented amusement park, there is something to test the skills of both kids and adults, from kiddie bumper boats, a go-cart track and miniature golf courses to indoor batting cages and a lighted driving range. It's open daily, weather permitting, mid-Mar.–Oct. Admission is free; pay as you play. Call for hours. **275 Valley Service Rd., North Haven, 06473; (203) 239-4653.**

Some activities that are strictly kid-oriented include a ride on the restored 1916 carousel at **Lighthouse Pt. Park** (see Swimming) and a trip to the **Eli Whitney Museum (915 Whitney Ave., Hamden, 06517; (203) 777-1833).** Named in honor of the inventor, the museum is a place where kids are encouraged to build things and experiment with their hands. It's housed in a 1910 factory on the site of an armory Whitney built to manufacture the first guns made with interchangeable parts. Also on-site is an 1816 barn that was part of Whitney's factory town and is now used for

dancing , concerts and other special events. Admission: $3 adults, $2 seniors and children 4–18. Hours: Wed.–Fri. & Sun., noon–5:00 P.M.; Sat., 10:00 A.M.–3:00 P.M.

Four times a year kids age 4–8 can attend the **Magic Dragon Children's Concert Series,** in which performers pass out instruments and invite the audience to play along. Tickets are $4 per person; call for dates and times. Concerts are held at **Neighborhood Music School, 100 Audubon St., New Haven, 06510; (203) 624-5189.**

Gardens and Arboreta

Folks with a horticultural bent will appreciate New Haven's **Edgerton Park,** a former estate designed in the style of English landscape gardens. It is walled, adding to its isolation from city noise and eliminating distracting visual elements. Edgerton is ideal for walking, low-speed biking, roller blading and for taking a child in a stroller for a ramble. It's convenient to the Eli Whitney Museum and the Peabody, so it's a good choice if you need to stretch your limbs after a visit to either of those institutions. Inside the park is the Crosby Conservatory, a plant store and a horticultural library. The conservatory and store are open weekdays 10:00 A.M.–5:00 P.M.; Sat.–Sun. 10:00 A.M.–4:00 P.M., year-round. The Sunday in the Park festival held here the second Sun. in Sept. features a petting zoo, a children's playland, hayrides and other family-oriented activities. Inquire about other special events. Hours: dawn–dusk daily, year-round. Enter from Cliff St. or Edgehill Rd. For more information call **(203) 946-8009.**

Historic Sites

Amistad Memorial
This unique, three-sided, bronze public sculpture commemorates an episode (made into a major motion picture in 1997) that is sometimes called the first American civil rights trial. *La Amistad* (meaning "friendship") was a Spanish ship whose crew in 1839 seized about 50 Mende tribespeople from what is now the

365

West African nation of Sierra Leone in order to sell them as slaves in Cuba. The Africans gained control of the vessel and ordered the crew to return them home, but the slave traders managed to pilot the ship north instead. *La Amistad* finally set anchor in Long Island Sound, where the Africans were imprisoned while their fate was decided. A two-year legal battle ensued in which former president John Quincy Adams and future governor Roger Sherman Baldwin argued before the Supreme Court on their behalf. Sympathetic members of the public raised funds to pay the Africans' legal expenses and the cost of their return home when, in 1841, the case was decided in their favor. The sculpture is located in front of New Haven City Hall at 165 Church St., the site of the prison in which the Africans were held in 1839. It is a compelling piece of public art, and a brief version of the *Amistad* story is carved in its base. You can buy a miniature reproduction of the sculpture and get more information about this remarkable story from **The Amistad Committee, 311 Temple St., New Haven, 06511; (203) 387-0370.**

Black Rock Fort and Fort Nathan Hale

The remains of two forts overlooking New Haven Harbor are open to the public at no charge. A brochure is available Memorial Day–Labor Day to provide the background for a self-guided tour. Hours: 10:00 A.M.–6:00 P.M. daily, year-round. Located on **Woodward Ave., New Haven, 06515; (203) 946-8790.**

New Haven Crypt

One of the most fascinating graveyards in Connecticut, belonging to New Haven's oldest congregation, is located beneath the First Church of Christ. The subterranean cemetery, the first in New Haven and originally open-air, was enclosed when the present meeting house (the fourth on the site) was built on top of it in 1814. The oldest stone here dates from 1687. Tours, given Tue., Thu. & Sat., 11:00 A.M.–1:00 P.M., & Sun. at 11:00 A.M. following services, cover both the crypt and the church. First Church, also known as Center Church, is located on New Haven green. Enter on Temple between Elm and Chapel Sts. For more information call **(203) 787-0121.**

Museums

New Haven's major museums—the Peabody, the Yale Center for British Art, the Yale University Art Gallery and the New Haven Colony Historical Society—are described under Major Attractions. In addition to these and the listings below, consider visiting some of the smaller museums in the area. The **Orange Historical Society** maintains a museum of local history and artifacts at the 1830 **Stone-Otis House,** at the corner of Orange Center and Tyler City Rds. in Orange. For more information call **(203) 795-3106.** The **Hamden Historical Society's Jonathan Dickerman House** is located at **105 Mt. Carmel Ave. in Hamden.** For more information call **(203) 248-6030** or **(203) 288-2466.**

Beinecke Rare Book and Manuscript Library

The walls of this unique structure are translucent slabs of Vermont marble that allow a subdued natural light to illuminate the priceless manuscripts and books on display while blocking the solar radiation that would harm them. There is supplemental artificial lighting, but no windows. Some prized items in the Beinecke's collection are a Gutenberg Bible and original Audubon prints. There are four exhibits of rare books and manuscripts annually. The Incunabula collection housed here is made up of volumes printed before 1500, and you can see most of the contents of Yale's library (ca. 1742), which have been gathered and shelved together. The Beinecke is surrounded by a sunken courtyard containing an art installation that includes three sculptures by Isamo Noguchi. Hours: Mon.–Fri., 8:30 A.M.–5:00 P.M.; Sat., 10:00 A.M.–5:00 P.M.; closed Sun., Sat. during Aug. & during Yale recesses. **121 Wall St. (on the campus of Yale University), New Haven, 06520; (203) 432-2977.**

Pardee-Morris House

One of the oldest structures in New Haven is a small museum of 18th-century life run by the New Haven Colony Historical Society. Parts of the Pardee-Morris house date from 1750, others from 1780. The Georgian farmhouse is furnished with period antiques, some original to the property. Allow 45 minutes for a guided tour. It opens the season with a Family Fun Day in late Apr. or early May. Sights include a small Revolutionary War encampment, demonstrations of household skills such as ice cream and butter making and colonial games for kids. Admission to the house and Family Day are free. Hours: Sat.–Sun., 11:00 A.M.–4:00 P.M., approximately late Apr.–Labor Day. **325 Lighthouse Rd., New Haven; (203) 562-4183.**

Shore Line Trolley Museum

For a ride on the oldest continuously operating suburban trolley in the country, visit the Shore Line Trolley Museum. When the Branford Electric Railway opened in 1900, it ran from the green in East Haven to Short Beach in Branford. The stretch of track that's currently in use is only a few blocks shy of what was in service in that year. For a flat fee you can enjoy unlimited rides narrated by a conductor who gives background information on the line. The 3-mile, one-hour trek passes through woods and salt marsh, and on the return portion you stop for a tour of cars in the process of restoration. Back at the main station there's a scale model trolley, displays of fare collection systems, signal systems and electric powering methods and more. Admission: $5 adults, $4 seniors, $2 children 2–11. Open daily Memorial Day–Labor Day; Sun. only during Apr. & Nov.; Sat. & Sun. in May, Sept. & Oct. & from the weekend after Thanksgiving through the weekend before Christmas. Hours: 11:00 A.M.–5:00 P.M. **17 River St., East Haven, 06512; (203) 467-6927.**

Nature Centers

West Rock Nature Center at the foot of West Rock Ridge State Park is a place to see injured animals being rehabilitated. There's a waterfall overlook, trails, a picnic shelter and (during visitors center hours) rest rooms. Admission is free. Nature center hours: Mon.–Fri., 10:00 A.M.–4:00 P.M.; closed holidays. Grounds hours: dawn–dusk daily, year-round. **Wintergreen Ave. at Baldwin Dr., New Haven, 06515; (203) 946-8016.**

Trolley rides are part of the fun at the Shore Line Trolley Museum in East Haven. Photo by Jim Brochin.

Nightlife

Yale University ensures that New Haven has the most active club scene in Connecticut. **BAR (254 Crown St., New Haven; 203-495-1111),** an energetic mix of microbrew beer, loud music, billiards and pizza, is one of several bars in its neighborhood that do a good business with Yale students. For live music, look no further than **Toad's Place (300 York St., New Haven; 203-624-8623),** whose motto is "where the legends play." It books a wide range of rock and blues acts interspersed with occasional oddball stuff. Every night except Mon. there's dancing to DJs at **The Bash (239 College St., New Haven; 203-562-1957).** For a more complete list, pick up a copy of a local paper, the free weekly *New Haven Advocate* or see the *Greater New Haven Guide* available from the **New Haven Convention and Visitors Bureau** at **(800) 332-7829** or **(203) 777-8550.**

Performing Arts

Only Hartford rivals New Haven for the range of performing arts available, and in a competition New Haven would probably win. Yale contributes a lot in this regard. There's the Yale School of Drama's University Theatre, the Yale Repertory Theater, the Yale Cabaret, the Yale Chamber Music Society, the Yale Music School, the Yale Philharmonia, the Yale

Camerata and much more. Call Yale's free events hotline at **(203) 432-9100.** The season for any university-based group will probably coincide with the school year, roughly Oct.–May. Southern Connecticut State University also has an excellent venue in the **John Lyman Center for the Performing Arts (501 Crescent St., New Haven, 06515; 203-392-6154),** offering a broad range of professional and student/faculty entertainment.

Audubon St. is another good place to look for arts entertainment. A number of groups keep performing arts spaces in this area, including the **Educational Center for the Arts (ECA)** and the **Creative Arts Workshop (CAW).** These are schools whose facilities are mostly used by students during the day but are rented out at night for everything from Iranian stand-up comedians to flamenco guitarists. You never know what you'll get. For schedules, call the ECA at **(203) 777-5451** and the CAW at **(203) 562-4927.**

New Haven probably has more active theater groups than any other city in Connecticut. The major groups are listed below, but community theater is also usually well worth seeking out. Listings for all current theatrical shows are found in the free weekly events calendar, *New Haven Arts,* distributed at stores, restaurants and visitors information centers around town. The calendar is published by the **Arts Council of Greater New Haven,** an umbrella organization with ties to virtually all of the performing arts groups in the city. If you don't see what you want here call them at **(203) 772-2788,** and they should be able to help you track it down. If it's major touring musical acts you're looking for call **Veterans Memorial Coliseum (275 S. Orange St.; 203-772-4200)** for a schedule of upcoming shows.

Amarante's Dinner Theatre

The cultural calendar in most cities is heavily weighted toward Fri. and Sat. nights, but Amarante's nicely fills that five-day gap with semiprofessional dinner theater performances on Wed. and Thu. nights and some Sun. afternoons. You begin with a buffet meal in a ballroom setting while strolling musicians and entertainers perform. The show starts two hours later. Weather permitting, you can enjoy cocktails on a deck with a panoramic view of New Haven's harbor and skyline. Amarante's stages three Broadway musicals per season (early June–late Oct.). Tickets cost $38 plus tax for dinner and show. The atmosphere is not formal, but proper attire is required. Wed. & Thu., dinner is at 6:00 P.M. followed by the show at 8:00 P.M.; on Sun. a noon lunch is followed by a show at 2:00 P.M. **62 Cove St., New Haven, 06512; (203) 467-2531.**

Long Wharf Theatre

Long Wharf is New Haven's Equity regional theater, mounting its own productions of established and new works for the stage. It has won numerous awards over the course of more than 30 years, and 20 of its shows have transferred to Broadway or off-Broadway. Long Wharf is actually two venues in one. The main stage is the Newton Schenck Theatre, with a three-quarter stage and 487 seats. Stage II is a black box theater holding 199 seats that can be rearranged according to the requirements of the play. Performances are given Tue.–Fri. at 8:00 P.M., Sat. at 4:00 & 8:30 P.M. & Sun. at 2:00 & 7:00 P.M. Matinees are given some Wed. Free parking. Located **off I-95 exit 46; (203) 787-4282.**

New Haven Symphony Orchestra

The fourth-oldest symphony orchestra in the nation is currently under the leadership of conductor Michael Palmer. It presents several concert series, performing about three times a month Oct.–May. In addition to classics of the orchestral repertoire, the Saturday Night Pops series features accessible works of popular composers as well as seasonal music, and the Sun. afternoon Family Concerts begin with an "instrument petting zoo" in which kids can get up close and personal with orchestral instruments. Guest orchestras and conductors also appear here. Tickets generally run $20–$40 for all but the Family Concerts, which are $12.50 for adults and $7.50 for children. Most concerts take place at Woolsey Hall on the Yale University campus. The box office is at **33 Whitney Ave., New Haven, 06510; (800) 292-6476 or (203) 776-1444.**

Palace Performing Arts Center

The Palace is a 1920s venue currently undergoing renovations where you can find anything from blues to comedy to gospel to rock, depending on the night, and it's located right in the heart of New Haven's dining district. **248 College St., New Haven, 06510; (203) 789-2120.**

Shubert Performing Arts Center

The Shubert has premiered more than 200 shows that went from New Haven to Broadway, earning it the nickname "The Birthplace of the Nation's Greatest Hits." Known as the Shubert Theatre from its opening in 1914 until its rechristening in 1984, its goal is still to present the best in musicals, opera, mime, modern dance, ballet, cabaret jazz and more. The easiest parking is at the Crown Street Garage next door. To order tickets, call **ProTix** at **(800) 955-5566. 247 College St., New Haven, 06510; (860) 624-1825.**

Yale Repertory Theatre

The Yale Rep is located in the former Calvary Baptist Church, a stunning structure in the heart of New Haven built in 1868 and converted for theatrical use in 1970. The Rep stages half a dozen shows per season (Oct.–May) including dramas, comedies, musicals and new works. Most of them are professional, Equity productions, but one is a graduate special project with a cast of Yale School of Drama students working under the guidance of a professional director. Shows are generally at 8:00 P.M. Tue.–Sat. & 7:00 P.M. on Mon., with 2:00 P.M. matinees some Wed. and Sat. Tickets are $25–$30. **Corner of Chapel and York Sts., New Haven, 06520; (203) 432-1234.**

Seasonal Favorites

In an unlikely location on a major highway, **Fieldview Farm (intersection of Rtes. 34 and 121, Orange; 203-795-5415)** is among the oldest farms in Connecticut, having been in the same family for over 350 years. They grind their own flours and make their own yogurt, quiches, dips, sauces and pickles. They offer apples and cider in fall and local produce all summer long. Their location makes it a great place to stop if you want to take home some Connecticut-grown food but don't have time for a ride in the country. Hours: 7:00 A.M.–7:00 P.M. daily except major holidays.

Seasonal produce is even tastier when you've picked it yourself. At **Julie's Orchard and Farm Market (234 Upper State St., North Haven; 203-239-0474)** the pick-your-own opportunities start with blackberries in Aug., continuing with pears, raspberries and over two dozen types of apples from Sept. on and pumpkins before Halloween. They also offer free hayrides around the fields.

Shopping

New Haven doesn't have a large shopping district, but it offers a vibrant atmosphere for what shopping there is. It's fun to hop from storefront to storefront on Chapel St. west of College St., where you'll find the greatest concentration of shops. They're sandwiched in between restaurants and two major art museums (the Yale Center for British Art and the Yale University Art Gallery), so you can alternate activities to keep the day interesting. One block north you'll find **Cutler's Compact Discs (33 Broadway; 203-777-6271)**, one of the largest music stores in Connecticut, if not the largest. Souvenir shopping for a teenager back home? **Yale Co-op (924 Chapel; 800-354-9253 or 203-772-2200)** is the place to get Yale signature items: sweatshirts, baseball caps, jackets, mugs and more. The Co-op is also noted for its huge bookstore, stocked with over 100,000 titles in over 130 categories, including a substantial selection of foreign-language books and many hard-to-find academic works. Hours: Mon.–Sat., 9:45 A.M.–5:30 P.M.; Sun., noon–5:00 P.M.

Sports

Beasts of New Haven

The year 1997 marked the first season for New Haven's AHL hockey team affiliated with the Carolina Hurricanes and the Florida Panthers.

369

They play 40 home games per Oct.–Apr. season at the New Haven Coliseum. Ticket prices are $12–$14 for adults and $10 for kids. For more information call **(203) 777-7878.** Tickets are available through **Ticketmaster** at **(203) 624-0033** or the **Coliseum Box Office** at **(203) 772-4200.**

New Haven Ravens

This Eastern League AA baseball team affiliated with the Colorado Rockies plays an Apr.–Sept. season with over 70 home games at Yale Field. The 6,200-seat stadium is on Rte. 34 in New Haven. Ticket prices run from $15 (luxury box seats) down to $4 (general admission adult) and $2 (children age 6–12 and seniors). The Ravens can be reached at **63 Grove St., New Haven, 06510; (800) 728-3671** or **(203) 782-1666.**

Pilot Pen International Tennis Tournament

This weeklong professional men's singles and doubles tennis tournament in mid-Aug. is an Association of Tennis Professionals (ATP) tour event. The first two days (Sat./Sun.) of the eight-day competition are for qualifiers, followed by six days of tournament play. There are both day and evening sessions. Single-day tickets range from $9 to $57; series ticket pricing is available. It takes place at **Connecticut Tennis Center, Yale University, 45 Yale Ave. in New Haven; (888) 997-4568** or **(203) 776-7331.**

Yale Football

Football fans everywhere owe a debt to former Yale coach Walter Camp, who is credited with codifying the sport as we know it in 1879. Today, Yale's Bulldogs play against other teams in the Ivy League during the Sept.–Nov. season, and in alternate years they host Harvard for the annual Harvard/Yale game. Game time is 12:30 or 1:00 P.M. on select Sat. Tickets are reasonably priced at $13 (premium) and $7 (sideline) for chair-back grandstand seating. Bring your own food and drink for a pregame tailgate party in the parking area. Games are played at Yale Bowl on Derby Ave. in New Haven. For more information call **(203) 432-1456.** If football isn't your thing, Yale has

nearly three dozen varsity sports. You can hear a schedule of upcoming games by calling **(203) 432-9253.**

Tours

For information on tours of **New Haven Harbor** and **Long Island Sound** by boat, see the Cruises section. Tours of **New Haven Crypt** are described under Historic Sites.

Walking Tours

New Haven Colony Historical Society Walking Tour

Using the society's free brochure, you can take a self-guided tour of an area stretching from the green north to the Peabody Museum of Natural History. The route passes significant architecture and landmarks and makes a good introduction to the Yale-dominated section of downtown. Pick up a copy of the brochure at the museum during regular hours: Tue.–Fri., 10:00 A.M.–5:00 P.M.; Sat.–Sun., 2:00 P.M.–5:00 P.M. **114 Whitney Ave., New Haven, 06510; (203) 562-4183.**

New Haven Walking Tour

This free, hour-long tour of the downtown is designed to complement Yale's tour of the university campus. Volunteer guides focus on the architecture and history of the city. The tour is given once a week only, Thu. at noon, Apr.–Oct., but call to confirm. No reservations are needed; just show up a few minutes before departure time at the **Yale Visitors Information Center, 149 Elm St., New Haven, 06520; (203) 432-2300.**

Yale University Walking Tour

For over an hour and at no charge, a student guide escorts you through the beautiful Yale campus, pointing out architectural landmarks and telling colorful stories from the university's past. Tours are given Mon.–Fri. at 10:30 A.M. & 2:00 P.M., & Sat. & Sun. at 1:30 P.M. (closed all major holidays from Thanksgiving to New Year's Day). No reservations are required; just show up ten minutes before tour time at the **Yale Visitors Information Center at 149 Elm St., New Haven, 06520; (203)**

432-2300. The center itself, where you can find a free map of the Yale campus and other information, is open Mon.–Fri., 9:00 A.M.–4:45 P.M., & Sat.–Sun., 10:00 A.M.–4:00 P.M.

Other Tours

New Haven Brewing Company

This hometown brewery founded in 1987 makes 19 boutique beers such as Elm City Connecticut Ale, Elm City Golden Ale and Blackwell Stout. Free tours of the brewery, lasting 45 minutes and followed by a sampling, are given every Sat. at 11:00 A.M. There's also a brewpub and retail store on-site. **458 Grand Ave., New Haven, 06513; (203) 772-2739.**

Shubert Performing Arts Center

Occasionally the Shubert offers free, hour-long tours of backstage areas, including a famous graffiti wall filled with signatures of and artwork by performers going back many years. Call for the next available time. **247 College St., New Haven, 06510; (203) 624-1825.**

Where to Stay

Bed & Breakfasts

Although Three Chimneys is certainly the most elegant B&B in the New Haven area, **Swan Cove (115 Sea St., New Haven, 06519; 203-776-3240)** provides convenient, casual accommodations for boaters coming into Oyster Pt. Marina, and **Bunny's B&B (707 Derby Tpke. [Rte. 34], Orange, 06477; 203-795-9488)** at Fieldview Farm (described under Seasonal Favorites) offers the novelty of waking up to a farm market just outside your door.

Three Chimneys Inn—$$$$

The only B&B in the heart of New Haven is located a few blocks from the green and most of the city's major attractions. It advertises "all the amenities of the 20th century while comfortably setting back the clock," and Three Chimneys really manages to be practical enough for business travelers, romantic enough for couples and accommodating enough for families with all but the smallest

children. Hardwood floors, Oriental rugs, hunting prints, rich fabrics and four-poster beds in most of the ten guest rooms give an overall impression of aristocratic English elegance. King or queen beds are the standard, and three rooms also have pullout sofas. All have private, modern baths, individual climate controls, telephones and TV. Two have gas fireplaces. Elevators inside and outside make all the rooms and the parking lot wheelchair-accessible. A Continental breakfast is served buffet-style in a ground floor café. Parking is in a private, off-street lot. **1201 Chapel St., New Haven, 06511; (203) 789-1201.**

Hotels, Motels & Inns

In addition to the listings below, some other possibilities for overnight accommodations include the downtown **Holiday Inn (30 Whalley Ave. between Dwight and Howe Sts., New Haven, 06511; 203-777-6221)** and the **Long Wharf Susse Chalet Inn and Suites (400 Sargent Dr., New Haven, 06511; 800-258-1989).** The **Holiday Inn/North Haven (201 Washington Ave. North Haven, 06473; 203-239-4225)** is only 15 minutes from downtown by virtue of its location right off I-91. The former **Park Plaza**, a luxury hotel at **155 Temple St.** in the downtown, was being completely refurbished into an **Omni Hotel** and should be open by the time you read this. In addition, a **Courtyard by Marriott** is opening in nearby Orange. For more information on these new hotels or for additional hotel listings call the **New Haven Convention and Visitors Bureau** at **(800) 332-7829** or **(203) 777-8550.**

The Colony—$$$$

This moderately sized downtown hotel has 86 rooms ranging from standard double accommodations to a two-bedroom suite. It's traditionally furnished with dark woods and subdued colors and is convenient to the main Yale campus and to the Yale art galleries. The Colony offers complimentary van service to Tweed/New Haven Airport and the train and bus station. Valet dry cleaning, room service and covered, off-street parking (at extra charge) are all available, and Chuck's Steakhouse is located on the main floor. **1157 Chapel St., New Haven, 06511; (800) 458-8810** (outside Connecticut) or **(203) 776-1234.**

New Haven Hotel—$$$$

The New Haven Hotel probably has the greatest number of amenities of any hotel in the downtown area, including a lap pool, an on-site exercise room and free access to a health and racquet club across the street, as well as the most reasonably priced suites in the city. Furnishings are traditional but updated, colorful and pleasing. It is the most convenient hotel to Yale-New Haven Hospital but also only two blocks from the downtown performing arts district and the Yale campus. You can get three meals a day in Templeton's restaurant on-site, where the upholstered armchairs are a welcome luxury. The lounge makes a good downtown meeting place. Valet parking (at extra charge) and same-day dry cleaning are available. **229 George St., New Haven, 06510; (203) 498-3100.**

Residence Inn—$$$$

This all-suite hotel by Marriott offers the best option for long- or short-term stays in the New Haven area for folks who want some of the conveniences of home. It has several types of suites, ranging from studios to two-bedrooms, all with fully equipped kitchens, many with wood-burning fireplaces (most unusual in a city hotel). Amenities include an outdoor pool, whirlpool, multipurpose sports court, free access to a downtown health and racquet club, valet dry cleaning and a complimentary airport and downtown shuttle. It is also walking distance from Long Wharf with its theater and dock for excursions on Long Island Sound. Inquire about long-term rates, which drop substantially for stays over five nights. **3 Long Wharf Dr., New Haven, 06511; (800) 331-3131** or **(203) 777-5337.**

Where to Eat

Too many choices, too little time will be your refrain in New Haven. Many of the downtown's restaurants are found in one small district on Chapel St. west of the green and College St. between Chapel and Crown Sts., so you can just walk through that neighborhood to pick something you like. In addition, a Little Italy of sorts thrives on Wooster St.

Barkie's—$$$ to $$$$

This new American grill is like an adult version of the hamburger joint where you finished your meal with a mile-high sundae as a kid. Everything is served grilled, including a vegetable sausage so non-meat-eaters can accompany their carnivorous friends at last. Sauces are served on the side so you can douse your dinner as you see fit, and the ice cream is homemade. In reference, or perhaps deference, to the chef's dogs, for whom the restaurant is named, painted canines adorn the counter and bar. Lunch hours: Mon.–Fri., 11:45 A.M.–2:30 P.M. Dinner hours: Mon.–Fri. from 5:00 P.M.; Sat.–Sun., 4:00 P.M.–8:00 P.M. **220 College St. at Crown, New Haven, 06511; (203) 752-1000.**

Chart House—$$$ to $$$$

One of a chain of steak houses in great settings, this Chart House has an oyster bar and a nautical theme by virtue of its location overlooking New Haven Harbor. The cuisine is American with a focus on steaks and seafood; prime rib is a specialty. The clam chowder has been voted best in Boston for four years running. Arrive early for a window table. Reservations recommended. Hours: Mon.–Thu., 5:00 P.M.–last seating at 9:00 P.M.; Fri.–Sat. last seating at 10:00 P.M.; Sun. open at 4:00 P.M. **100 S. Water St., New Haven, 06519; (203) 787-3466.**

Union League Cafe—$$$ to $$$$

Serving country French cuisine, Union League Cafe is one of the more expensive, indulgent and romantic restaurants in New Haven. The 1860 building in which it's housed is a former private club featuring an extraordinary interior with rich woods and a fireplace for a warm glow in winter. Sit windowside to watch the eclectic mix of people walking up and down Chapel St. The food is as hearty and memorable as the atmosphere. Proper attire and reservations recommended. Lunch hours:

Mon.–Fri., noon–2:30 P.M. Dinner hours: Mon.–Thu., 5:30 P.M.–9:00 P.M.; Fri.–Sat., 5:30 P.M.–10:00 P.M. A three-course fixed-price ($21.50) dinner is served 4:00 P.M.–8:30 P.M. on Sun. **1032 Chapel St., New Haven, 06510; (203) 562-4299.**

The Brewery—$$$
The restaurant at New Haven Brewing Company is a fairly new addition to the brewery complex. The whole affair is housed in a former steamship repair facility that makes for an impressive interior. The menu is basically divided between the grill items—steaks and chops—and seafood "off the boat daily." There's also a small separate vegetarian menu, hefty sandwiches available at both lunch and dinner and ten or more of its beers on tap. The humidor is filled with cigars from around the world, and The Brewery advertises the area's largest single malt scotch selection. Live entertainment is offered Thu.–Sat. Hours: Mon.–Thu., 11:30 A.M.–10:00 P.M.; Fri.–Sat., 11:30 A.M.–11:00 P.M.; Sun., 4:00 P.M.–9:00 P.M. **458 Grand Ave., New Haven, 06513; (203) 773-5297.**

Pikas Tapas—$$$
Although you can enjoy this Spanish restaurant when dining alone, it's even better to come with a large group of friends. The vast majority of menu items are tapas: appetizer-size portions of food with a correspondingly small price. Passing tapas around for everyone to sample is tremendous fun, and tables are set with a high stack of plates expressly for that purpose. For those who are proprietary about their food, three tapas gives you about as much food as a standard entrée and cost the same amount of money. There is always a large Platos del Dia (daily specials) menu in addition to the regular one, numerous Spanish vintages on the wine list and a large selection of after-dinner sherries, ports, brandies and dessert wines. **39 High St. (half a block south of Chapel), New Haven, 06511; (203) 865-1933.**

Scoozzi Trattoria and Wine Bar—$$$
Pastas—about 18 kinds—are the highlight of the menu at this Northern Italian restaurant that also serves gourmet pizza, fish and dry-aged beef. Its "flights"—samplers of three or four predetermined wines on a theme—are a unique concept, and the selection changes monthly. It also has a nifty cigar menu describing its offerings in the style of a wine list; on the reverse is the selection of bourbons and scotches. Scoozzi is a little unusual in that the dining room, which overlooks a landscaped sunken courtyard, is below street level. The neon sign you'll see from the street marks the elevator entrance. Hours: lunch served Mon.–Fri., noon–2:30 P.M.; Sat., noon–4:00 P.M. Dinner served Mon.–Thu., 5:00 P.M.–10:00 P.M.; Fri., 5:00 P.M.–11:00 P.M.; Sat., 4:00 P.M.–11:00 P.M.; Sun., 5:00 P.M.–9:00 P.M. **1104 Chapel St. near York, New Haven, 06510; (203) 776-8268.**

Tre Scalini—$$$
One of the more recent additions to New Haven's Wooster St. Italian dining district, Tre Scalini has met with popular acclaim. The large menu features many rustic, flavorful dishes with many options beyond the usual pasta and veal, and the atmosphere is white tablecloth. Lunch served Mon.–Fri., 11:30 A.M.–2:30 P.M. Dinner served nightly 5:00 P.M. (4:00 P.M. on Sun.) until closing. **100 Wooster St. at Franklin, New Haven, 06510; (203) 777-3373.**

Bangkok Garden—$$ to $$$
For Thai food in a white-tablecloth environment, try this restaurant that's won numerous "best of" awards. Hours: 11:30 A.M.–10:00 P.M. daily. The kitchen changes from lunch to dinner at 3:30 P.M. **172 York St., New Haven, 06520; (203) 789-8684.**

Caffé Adulis—$$ to $$$
If you've never tried Ethiopian food, this would be a good place to start. In general, Ethiopian is a spicy cuisine. Many dishes are curries made from a base of *berbere,* a medium-hot pepper paste, and are served with a moist flatbread similar in consistency to crumpets. Both meat-eaters and vegetarians will find adequate variety. In short, a meal at Caffé Adulis will be very delicious and unusual, but it's not for the unadventurous. Afterward, head

373

to the TaftCaffé just down the street (run by the same folks) for coffee and dessert. **254 College St., New Haven, 06510; (203) 777-5081.**

Chavoya's—$$ to $$$

When you crave Mexican food, nothing else will satisfy, and in New Haven the place to get it is Chavoya's. The interior is decorated along a tropical theme, and they have a large and lively lounge with a big-screen TV in which to enjoy the obligatory margarita. Lunch is served Mon.–Fri., 11:30 A.M.–2:30 P.M.; dinner served Mon.–Thu., 4:30 P.M.–10:00 P.M., & Fri.–Sat. until 10:30 P.M. A late-night light menu is served in the lounge until 1:00 A.M. **883 Whalley Ave. near Blake St., New Haven, 06511; (203) 389-4730.**

Frank Pepe's Pizzeria Napoletana/ The Spot—$$ to $$$

When you walk into Pepe's the first thing you see is the coal-fired pizza oven, out of which your meal will come, because pizza is all they do here. The pizzeria has been owned and operated by the same family since 1925. Frank Pepe started the business with "tomato pies," which are just what they sound like: tomato sauce on pizza dough. You still have to order cheese on your pizza or you won't get it. The best-known menu item is the white clam pie. An annex next door called The Spot handles the overflow from Pepe's, but it's the same food despite the fact that they keep different hours. Be prepared for a wait on weekend evenings and come with an appetite, because they don't sell slices. One or the other will be open Mon.–Thu., 4:00 P.M.–10:00 P.M.; Fri.–Sat., 11:30 A.M.–11:30 P.M.; Sun., 2:30 P.M.–10:30 P.M. **157 Wooster St., New Haven, 06511; (203) 865-5762.**

Tandoor—$$ to $$$

The food at this Indian restaurant is excellent, and the atmosphere is absolutely unique: a vintage diner with the lunch counter and booths intact. It's the oddest combination and genuinely fun. There are some great bargains, such as a weekend lunch buffet for $6.95 and a weekday vegetarian lunch special for $3.95. Hours: lunch served 11:30 A.M.–3:00 P.M. daily;

dinner served 5:00 P.M.–10:30 P.M. nightly. **1226 Chapel St., New Haven, 06511; (203) 776-6620.**

Westville Kosher Bakery & Fox's Deli—$$

Whether it's smoked fish, fresh bagels or just good cookies you're after, Westville is the place. It's a bakery and deli in one, with one long display case devoted to lots of prepared foods and another two cases devoted to baked goods. Rather than import bagels from New York City they bake them daily, and the Napoleons are incredible. Because this is a kosher deli, dairy is available from opening until about 11:30 A.M., and meat thereafter until shortly before closing. Eggs and fish are available all day. In addition to prepared food, it also has canned and frozen kosher food items for use in home cooking. Hours: Mon.–Thu., 6:30 A.M.–6:00 P.M.; Fri., 6:30 A.M.–one hour before sunset; Sun., 6:00 A.M.–4:00 P.M.; closed Sat. **1460 Whalley Ave. at Amity, New Haven, 06515; (203) 397-0839** (deli) or **(203) 387-2214** (bakery).

Claire's—$ to $$

Claire's is a self-described "gourmet vegetarian" restaurant. Gourmet might be a stretch, but good is certainly true. This is a casual student hangout where you order at the counter upon entering, pay, have a seat or rummage for silverware out of a basket until your name is called (loudly, to overcome the noise of conversation) and your meal is brought to you. You bus your own table when you are finished. The look is college dining hall. Portions are ample and prices reasonable. The $2.75 mug of soup and miniloaf of bread is one of the best light lunch deals around, and this is one of the few places in Connecticut where a vegetarian can have a real choice. Hours: 8:00 A.M.–10:00 P.M. daily. **1000 Chapel St. at College St., New Haven, 06510; (203) 562-3888.**

Rainbow Gardens Cafe—$ to $$

The menu at Rainbow Gardens is pretty much split between vegetarian and nonvegetarian items, making it a good destination for couples or groups with dissimilar dietary preferences. Like Claire's, it's a casual, self-service place where you order at the counter, your food is brought to you and you bus your own table, but the atmosphere is more put together. Fare is generally light, with lots of sandwiches, salads and pasta-based entrées. What meat they have is generally in the form of chicken. There is no actual garden here (in fact, the cafe is below street level), but the decor strives to give an outdoorsy impression. Breakfast is available all day on weekends, and desserts tend toward the humongous—one of their brownies could feed four! Hours: Mon.–Thu., 9:00 A.M.–8:00 P.M.; Fri.–Sat., 9:00 A.M.–9:00 P.M.; Sun., 10:00 A.M.–7:00 P.M. **1022 Chapel St., New Haven, 06516; (203) 777-2390.**

Louis' Lunch—$

This luncheonette claims to be where America was introduced to the hamburger. Four generations of the same family have run it since Louis Lassen came up with the idea of grinding up beef and shaping it into a patty back in 1900. Burgers are broiled vertically, a method that keeps the fat content low, so even if you're on a restricted diet, you might be able to give Louis' a try. And talk about purists! They eschew all the condiments—ketchup, mayo, pickles, even mustard. They feel that they work too hard to bring you a fresh burger to have the flavor masked by all sorts of unnecessary add-ons. You *can* get onion, tomato and cheese and real fountain sodas to wash it down. At night the menu expands to include hot dogs, steak sandwiches, potato salad and baked beans. Hours: Mon.–Wed., 11:00 A.M.–4:00 P.M.; Thu.–Sat., 11:00 A.M.–2:00 A.M.; closed Sun. & during Aug. **261–263 Crown St., New Haven, 06511; (203) 562-5507.**

Coffeehouses, Sweets & Treats

With the possible exception of Greenwich, there are more coffeehouses in New Haven than anywhere else in Connecticut. Walk anywhere near the Yale campus, down Audubon St. or down Chapel St., and you shouldn't have to go more than a block before encountering one. **Atticus Bookstore Cafe (1082 Chapel St.; 203-776-4040)** is another in the blos-

soming horde of coffee shop/bookstore combinations. **Elm City Roasters (59 Elm St.; 203-776-2555)** roasts its own about twice a week. **Perry's Coffee House (896 Whalley Ave.; 203-397-2811)** in the Westville section of town offers lots of coffee-based beverages from around the world, as well as teas, juices, sodas and a slew of other things to drink. It also serves breakfast and lunch, baked goods and other sweets. **TaftCaffé (263 College St.; 203-776-4200)** serves all kinds of comforting beverages, including herbal teas, cider, cocos, juice "tonics" and smoothies. It has a computer terminal and allows customers to go online at no charge, which entitles them to bill themselves as a "cybercafe." Finally, chain coffeehouse **Willoughby's Coffee & Tea** has three locations in New Haven: at **1006 Chapel St. (203-789-8400), 258 Church St. (203-777-7400)** and **276 York St. (203-773-1700).**

Services

Local Visitors Information

Long Wharf Visitors Information Center, 355 Long Wharf Dr. (take I-95 exit 46 and follow the signs), **New Haven, 06511; (800) 332-7829** or **(203) 777-8550.** Hours: Mon.–Fri., 10:00 A.M.–7:00 P.M.; Sat.–Sun., 10:00 A.M.–5:00 P.M., Memorial Day–Labor Day only.

New Haven Convention and Visitors Bureau, One Long Wharf Drive, New Haven, 06511; (800) 332-7829 or **(203) 777-8550.** Hours: Mon.–Fri., 8:30 A.M.–5:00 P.M., year-round.

SNET Access is an automated current events hotline sponsored by Southern New England Telephone. Dial **(203) 498-5050** and then punch in the code 1315 to access current information on theater, music and other activities in New Haven. The **Small Business Council of the Greater New Haven Chamber of Commerce** publishes a great guide to the area's restaurants. To request a copy, contact them at **195 Church St., New Haven, 06510;**

375

(203) 787-6735. Or stop by during office hours: Mon.–Fri., 8:00 A.M.–5:00 P.M.

Yale Visitors Information Center, 149 Elm St., New Haven, 06520; (203) 432-2300. Hours: Mon.–Fri., 9:00 A.M.–4:45 P.M.; Sat.–Sun., 10:00 A.M.–4:00 P.M. It has information on Yale facilities and events as well as general information about the city of New Haven and is located right on the green in downtown.

Transportation

Tweed-New Haven Airport (203-946-8283) and **Sikorsky Memorial Airport** in Stratford **(203-576-7498)** are serviced by commuter airlines. All of the airports in the greater New York area are also possibilities. For limousine (van) service to and from Laguardia and White Plains call **Connecticut Limousine** at **(800) 472-5466.**

New Haven is a stop on two **Amtrak** routes that connect it with Boston, Springfield (Massachusetts), New York and Washington, D.C. Call **(800) 872-7245** for schedules and fares. Commuter rail service to New York is available through **Metro-North** at **(800) 638-7646.** For local rail service to the east as far as New London call **Shore Line East** at **(800) 255-7433.**

Interstate bus service to New Haven is available through **Greyhound** at **(800) 231-2222** and **Peter Pan/Trailways** at **(800) 343-9999.** Bus service within the city and surrounding areas is provided by **CT Transit** at **(203) 624-0151** or **(203) 785-8930 (TDD).** For information about service for the elderly and handicapped, call the **Greater New Haven Transit District** at **(203) 288-6282.** The **Yale Shuttle** runs Mon.–Fri. during the day only but is an inexpensive way to get to all the Yale museums. Call **(203) 432-9790** for a schedule and more information.

376

Norwalk

Norwalk has been recently developing into southwestern Connecticut's version of Mystic. Since the mid-1980s the neighborhood known as SoNo (a contraction of South Norwalk) has been experiencing a renaissance in response to redevelopment centered around the area's biggest attraction, the Maritime Aquarium. Restaurants, shops and nightspots are now clustered on and around Washington St., a local history museum has just opened and the waterfront is being remade into a state heritage park and greenway that will link SoNo with Mathews Park and Norwalk's spectacular Victorian estate museum, the Lockwood-Mathews Mansion. All of this activity—a fitting prelude to Norwalk's 350th anniversary in 2001—means more for visitors to see and do, much of it centered around the city's rich maritime past and present.

Norwalk is still home to the leading oyster producer on the East Coast, Tallmadge Bros., who farm 22,000 watery acres (yes, oysters are farmed). Conditions in Norwalk Harbor are nearly ideal for the bivalves, and folks have been harvesting them here for thousands of years. Only Louisiana and (occasionally) Washington lead Connecticut in oyster production, but Connecticut's Blue Point Eastern oysters are considered the tastiest and have the highest dollar value of any state's output. You can sample them at the Oyster Festival, a huge, multifaceted outdoor celebration held here every Sept.

Norwalk and the towns that surround it offer visitors the best access for the broadest range of activities on Long Island Sound of any coastal town in southwestern Connecticut. Most people visit the beaches at Sherwood Island State Park in Westport. Others take a sailing or windsurfing lesson. Several schools operate locally, and if you already know how to pilot watercraft, there are many places to rent a boat too. Another water-oriented activity is the ferry trip to Sheffield Island, one of the Norwalk Islands, where you can tour a historic lighthouse.

The shore isn't the only thing here, however. Weston has a rural, mountainous feel and is home to Devil's Den, the largest nature preserve in southwestern Connecticut and a great hiking destination. In contrast, Westport is cosmopolitan and openly considers itself a suburb of New York City. Dining, summer stock theater and shopping in its very posh downtown are what draw people to the town best known for famous residents such as Paul Newman and Martha Stewart.

Wilton is notable as the site of the only national park in Connecticut. Weir Farm was the home and workplace of Impressionist painter J. Alden Weir and is the only U.S.

A tour group views the opulence of the partially restored Lockwood-Mathews Mansion Museum, Norwalk. Photo by Stuart Smith/Coastal Fairfield Convention and Visitors Bureau.

national park with American painting as the focus of its preservation efforts. Combine a visit to Weir Farm with a stop at the Silvermine Guild of Artists, a combination school, gallery and shop in New Canaan. Art is also the theme of the SoNo Arts Celebration held every Aug. Quirky and highly energized yet very family-friendly, it's one of the best events of any kind in the state.

History

Settled in 1651 as a Connecticut Colony town by families from the Hartford area, Norwalk was the "mother town" of this region—the one from which most of the towns surrounding it were taken over time. Families moved inland to areas now in Weston, Wilton and New Canaan from about 1700 on.

This stretch of the coast saw a lot of activity during the Revolutionary War. It is said that Nathan Hale departed from Norwalk when he set out for Long Island on his ill-fated spying mission in 1776. In Apr. 1777 British Gen. Tryon landed troops at Compo Hill in Westport and began the march that would culminate in

the attack on Danbury and the Battle of Ridgefield. There was a skirmish in that part of Westport (then Fairfield) a few days later when the British were retreating. The Battle of Norwalk, during which the town was burned, occurred in July 1779. A wide variety of industries were locally important. The streets of the lyrically named Silvermine district that overlaps Norwalk, Wilton and New Canaan are quiet and residential today, but early residents had the mistaken notion that there was valuable ore in the surrounding hills. The real source of riches turned out to be the many mills that were built on Silvermine River, turning out boots, shoes, wooden knobs and dowels, stone and earthenware articles, ships, wagons, sleighs, candles and hats. In fact, Norwalk was second only to Danbury in hat production.

What is now the downtown shopping district of Westport was lined with wharves and warehouses 200 years ago. The same was true of South Norwalk, which had long been known as Old Well because boats replenished their water supply there. Shipping experienced a boom in the 1840s when the railroad came through. Around that time Norwalk and Bridgeport were in competition to become the county seat. Although Norwalk was a major economic center, it had actually lost population to western migration at a time when Bridgeport was growing. By the late 1800s the character of the area was changing. Westport was becoming a resort, and small fishing villages such as Rowayton were starting to draw summer people. Meanwhile, all of Norwalk's heretofore independent neighborhoods (including South Norwalk, which had been a city since 1871) were consolidated as the city of Norwalk in 1913.

Today the greater Norwalk area has as broad an economic base as ever. Companies headquartered locally include business information providers Dun & Bradstreet, the accounting firm of Deloitte and Touche, the merchandiser Caldor and computer mail-order retailers Micro Warehouse and Mac Warehouse. And in refreshing counterpoint, there are the oyster boats, symbol of the city's hope to manage its growth, respect its resources and tie together the past, present and future.

Major Attractions

Lockwood-Mathews Mansion Museum

This extraordinary edifice was one of the first great seaside summer estates, built by the ultrawealthy LeGrand Lockwood in the late 19th century. A Norwalk native (and its first millionaire), Lockwood returned to his hometown to build a summer palace after making a fortune in a brokerage firm and railroads. His fortunes reversed during his lifetime, so the mansion quickly changed hands and did not long receive the upkeep it required. Only a few of the mansion's 50 rooms have been restored, and at a cost of $50,000–$100,000 per room, it's not hard to see why. The sheer Victorian excess of ornamentation is awesome. The mansion is especially noted for its exquisite frescoes and marble and wood inlay. The house itself is not the only attraction. There are also changing historical exhibits, and the mansion permanently houses an exceptional collection of music boxes. Admission: $5 adults, $3 seniors and students, children under 12 free. Open Feb.–mid-Dec. Hours: Tue.–Fri., 11:00 A.M.–3:00 P.M.; Sun., 1:00 P.M.–4:00 P.M. Closed major holidays. Hour-long tours are given on the hour, with the last tour starting one hour before closing time. **295 West Ave., Norwalk, 06850; (203) 838-1434.**

Maritime Aquarium/ IMAX Theater

Formerly known as the Maritime Center, the Maritime Aquarium was recently rated by a major magazine as one of ten great aquariums to visit in the country. Its emphasis is all aspects of life (including human life) in and around Long Island Sound. As you move through the displays you learn about wildlife from successively lower depths, starting with salt marsh and culminating with a shark exhibit, so it seems as if the Sound is being revealed to you layer by layer. There are also touch tanks, periscopes, exhibits on boat building and deep-sea diving and much more.

Getting There

Norwalk is one and a half to two hours southwest of Hartford by car, depending on traffic conditions. There are two equally good routes you can take. The first is I-91 south to either Rte. 15 (Merritt Pkwy.) south or I-95 south. The other speedy option is I-84 west to Rte. 8 south to either Rte. 15 (Merritt Pkwy.) south or I-95 south. The Merritt Pkwy. crosses the northern part of town and I-95 the southern part; both experience heavy congestion during rush hour.

Seal feedings (several times a day) are something to stick around for. If you want to experience the Sound firsthand, take a boat study cruise where you'll get to collect specimens and view them up close. Even in winter (weather permitting) boats go out for viewing harbor seals.

The IMAX theater is the only one in Connecticut and, with its eight-story-wide, six-story-high screen and 70mm projection system, must be experienced to be believed. Each screening is an incredible journey someplace spectacular. Aquarium admission: $7.75 adults, $6.50 seniors and children age 2–12. There is a separate fee schedule for the IMAX

Seal feeding time is popular with onlookers at the Maritime Aquarium, Norwalk.

theater and for the boat study cruises; combination aquarium/theater tickets are available. Reservations are recommended for the cruises. Hours: 10:00 A.M.–5:00 P.M. daily (until 6:00 P.M. July 1–Labor Day); closed Thanksgiving and Christmas. **10 N. Water St., Norwalk, 06854; (203) 852-0700.**

Sheffield Island Lighthouse

In years past, several lighthouses were built on the Norwalk Islands, a chain of 13 outcroppings at the mouth of the Norwalk River. The current one dates from 1868. It was in operation until 1902, when it was abandoned in favor of a more suitable location. It's open to the public for tours and accessible via a small ferry boat that visitors can pick up a few steps from Washington St. The crossing takes 40 minutes, during which the captain treats passengers to fascinating stories about the history of the island chain.

At the island there is a brief, informal tour of the lighthouse. On the clearest days you can see the silhouette of the World Trade Center's twin towers in New York City on the horizon without even climbing to the observation deck. If you opt to spend a bit of time on the island, you can swim or hike the perimeter and explore a bit. The latter two activities are best at low tide, so you might want to check a tide table to plan your visit. The ferry operates late June–Labor Day with two to four round-trips per day, and also runs on weekends and holidays in spring and during Sept., weather permitting. Cost: $9 adults, $8 seniors, $7 children 12 and under. The dock is near the intersection of Washington and Water Sts. in South Norwalk, but this area is scheduled to be redeveloped into a state heritage park, so call **(203) 838-9444** to confirm all details. If you have your own boat, you can also moor off Sheffield Island, row ashore (they can lend you a dinghy) and visit for a small fee.

Sherwood Island State Park

The only developed shoreline state park in Fairfield County and the oldest Connecticut state park is a wonderful spot to swim, fish or scuba dive in Long Island Sound. In addition to the 1.5-mile beach (guarded in summer), there are picnic groves, open space for field sports, a small nature center (open summer only, Wed.–Sun., 10:00 A.M.–4:30 P.M.), a small history center with park artifacts (open summer weekends, 10:00 A.M.–5:00 P.M.), a nature trail with a written guide and interpretive programs. From surface streets you can reach the park via the Sherwood Connector road off Rte. 1. Pets are not permitted Apr. 15–Sept. 30. Admission (May–Sept.; charged weekends only prior to Memorial Day and after Labor Day): $5 weekdays and $7 weekends for vehicles with Connecticut plates, $8 weekdays and $12 weekends for out-of-state vehicles. Hours: 8:00 A.M.–sunset daily, year-round. Located off **I-95 exit 18 in Westport; (203) 226-6983.**

Weir Farm

The only U.S. national park in Connecticut is devoted to the land and studios of J. Alden Weir, a noted painter of the late 1800s and early 1900s best remembered for his Impressionist work. Weir traded a $560 painting by another artist for 153 acres of farmland in what was then rural Connecticut back in 1882. He and a group of friends who congregated at Weir Farm in an informal art colony painted many scenes from its landscape over the course of 40 years. A map entitled "Weir Farm Historic Painting Sites Trail" shows reproductions of a dozen of these works, guiding visitors to the vantage points from which most of them were painted.

The studios can be toured only at designated times since there are artists in residence. Currently these hour-long tours are given Wed.–Sat. at 10:00 A.M., but call to confirm. Walking tours of the property (but not the studios) take place Sat. & Sun. at 2:00 P.M. There is also a 20-minute video introduction to Weir Farm, a laser disc on which you can view Weir's works (no original canvases are on display) and other interpretive information. Trails in the park connect with those of the Weir-

380

Leary-White Preserve; a map is available in the visitors center. Visitors center hours: 8:30 A.M.–5:00 P.M. daily, Apr.–Nov. During the remainder of the year, the center is open Mon.–Fri. only, and there are no weekend tours or walks. **735 Nod Hill Rd., Wilton, 06897; (203) 834-1896.**

Festivals and Events

Norwalk Harborsplash

weekend between Mother's Day and Memorial Day

With a focus on the preservation and enjoyment of Norwalk's waterfront, Harborsplash combines activities on the water with performing and visual arts for both children and adults. Rowing and kayaking races, harbor tours, rides on sailboats and educational vessels from the Maritime Aquarium and a full schedule of entertainment are some highlights. The festival takes place throughout the SoNo district around Washington and N. Main Sts., as well as at other locations. There is no gate admission charge, but some activities involve a fee. Hours: 11:00 A.M.–4:00 P.M. both days. For more information call the **Coastal Fairfield County Tourism District** at **(800) 866-7925** or **(203) 854-7825.**

Afternoon of Jazz Festival
last Sun. in June

The lawn in front of the Gallaher estate in Norwalk's beautiful Cranbury Park is the perfect setting for a summer afternoon of traditional and contemporary jazz by major performers. Pack a picnic and bring a blanket or lawn chair. Tickets are in the $30 range if purchased by mid-May and higher thereafter. Hours: noon–8:00 P.M. For more information call the **Jackie Robinson Foundation** at **(212) 290-8600.** Tickets are available through **Ticketmaster** at **(203) 624-0033.** The park entrance is on Grumman Ave.

Round Hill Highland Scottish Games
Sat. closest to Fourth of July

You don't have to be Scottish to enjoy this day of traditional tests of strength and skill, as well as piping, dancing, singing, storytelling and food. While the official participants engage in the hammer throw or the sheaf toss, spectators can sign up to compete in a tug-of-war, footraces and other games. The location is **Cranbury Park on Grumman Ave. in Norwalk.** Admission: $10 adults, $5 seniors and children 5–12. Hours: 9:00 A.M.–6:00 P.M. For more information call **(203) 324-1094.**

The Great Race
mid-July

The exact date and time of this annual series of small craft races down the Saugatuck River depends on the tides. There are competitions for canoes, kayaks and racing shells, as well as homemade watercraft that can get pretty strange, such as the one built entirely of milk cartons that participated one year. Land-based activities (the race often coincides with the town's Outdoor Art Show) keep it interesting for spectators. Located in **downtown Westport where the Boston Post Rd. crosses the river.** For more information call **(203) 454-6564.**

World Music Festival
third weekend in July (Sat.–Mon.)

Music, foods and arts and crafts from around the world are all part of this festival held at the outdoor Levitt Pavilion behind the public library on Jessup St. in Westport. Sun. is the main day for international music. There's always a big-name artist on Mon. evening, a Norwalk Symphony family concert on Sat. evening and a black-tie dinner gala. Sun. hours: noon–9:00 P.M. Ticket prices vary by event, with discounts for students and seniors and a special three-day rate of $75. Call **(203) 226-7600** for a schedule, prices and details on the rain policy.

381

SoNo Arts Celebration
first full weekend in Aug.

This lively street festival is held on and around Washington St. in South Norwalk's waterfront district. The celebration began over 20 years ago when a group of local artists with lofts in the area decided to have a sidewalk show. Their exhibition quickly grew to its current size: 150 artist vendors, continual live music beginning Sat. morning on four stages and 80,000 visitors over three days. Fri. night is typically limited to indoor events such as gallery openings and screenings. Two signature events are a half-mile human-powered moving sculpture race, held around noon on Sat., and a Mardi Gras–like puppet parade, which takes place around 3:00 P.M. on Sun. The festival is hugely popular, so get there early for a parking space nearby, or take a free shuttle bus from designated remote parking lots. Hours: Fri., 6:00 P.M.–10:00 P.M.; Sat., 10:00 A.M.–midnight; Sun., 11:00 A.M.–6:00 P.M. Check local newspapers for a schedule or call **(203) 866-7916.**

382

Some of the characters you'll encounter at the SoNo Arts Celebration Puppet Parade, South Norwalk. Photo by Tim Holmstrum/SoNo Arts Celebration.

Oyster Festival
weekend after Labor Day

Norwalk's biggest event celebrates oystering's important role in the city's history. Many activities, such as tall ships open for touring and boat excursions in the harbor, are water-related, but there are also upward of 225 juried artists and crafters, music, oyster shucking and oyster slurping contests, an area dedicated to kids' games and loads of refreshments. Admission: $7 adults, $5 seniors, $3 children 6–12. There may be an additional charge for some activities. Hours: Fri., 5:00 P.M.–11:00 P.M.; Sat., 10:00 A.M.–11:00 P.M.; Sun., 10:00 A.M.–9:00 P.M. The location is **Veterans Memorial Park in East Norwalk.** Follow signs to designated parking lots and take the free shuttle buses provided. For more information call **(203) 838-9444.**

Norwalk International in Water Boat Show
third week in Sept. (Thu.–Sun.)

One of the largest boat shows in Connecticut takes place at Norwalk Cove Marina on Calf Pasture Beach Rd. in East Norwalk in the earliest days of autumn. The main draw is exhibitors showing off their newest watercraft models, but there are also boating and fishing seminars, some games and rides for children, prize giveaways, small sailboat rides and food vendors. Hours: 10:00 A.M.–6:00 P.M. each day. Admission: $7 adults, $3 children 6–12. For more information call **(212) 922-1212.**

Outdoor Activities

Biking

Unlike most of the densely populated shore towns, Norwalk has one excellent spot for mountain biking: **Cranbury Park,** the city's largest open space. There are 8 miles of pretty trails through woodland and meadow, plus a huge lawn on which to relax or picnic and easy parking. The entrance is on Grumman Ave.;

call **(203) 854-7806** for more information. Another town park with blazed trails for biking is **Wilton Town Forest** in Wilton. There are entrances and parking lots on Branch Brook Rd. and at the intersection of Boas Ln. and Patrick Ln.

If some quiet roads and picturesque scenery are all you're after, Noroton Pt. in the Rowayton section of Norwalk is a neighborhood of small and well-kept beach houses on a hilly promontory. The streets are narrow and winding, and the houses are as much fun to look at as the Sound. The two main roads leading into the area are Rowayton Ave. and Bluff Ave. The streets along the east side of Norwalk Harbor are also engaging and quiet, since most of them dead-end at the water, and they're just minutes from the SoNo district with its restaurants and other diversions. Just over the town line in Westport, the upper part of Seymour Pt. is another neighborhood of beach houses. The lower part of the point, however, is private. The Compo district of Westport in and around Longshore Park is also very pleasant, as is the Greens Farms part of Westport (Beachside Ave. especially is a neighborhood of impressive waterfront estates) and the Tokoneke section of Darien. If you want to ride a distance, head to any residential area north of the Merritt Pkwy. and keep to the side roads. You can also give **Sound Cyclists** a call at **(203) 840-1757**. This local bicycling club organizes group rides, and they invite nonmembers to join in.

Boating and Windsurfing

Boat Launches and Marinas

The only state boat launch in the area is just above the mouth of the Saugatuck River in Westport. To access it from Rte. 136 (Bridge St. at the Saugatuck River) go approximately one-quarter mile east, turn on Underhill Pkwy. and follow signs to the ramp under the I-95 bridge. A fee is charged in summer.

In Darien, **The Boatworks (203-866-9295;** VHF 68) is the marina most strongly oriented toward transient boaters. There's

more available in Norwalk Harbor, where **Norwalk Cove Marina (203-838-5899;** VHF 9) is the largest facility. They have 100 transient berths, sell gas, do all repairs, can handle any size boat and offer pump-out service and a pool. **Norwest Marine, Inc. (203-853-2822;** VHF 68) has 20 transient berths, sells gas and does most repairs. Seasonal **Norwalk Visitor's Dock (203-849-8823;** VHF 9) at Veteran's Park has 20 transient berths, pump-out service and fresh water, and it's only a five-minute walk from Washington St. in South Norwalk. In Westport, **Cedar Point Yacht Club (203-226-7411;** VHF 78) has a few transient berths, and **Coastwise Marina (203-226-0735;** VHF 16) has transient moorings and a launch service; both sell gas. For navigational details, charts and complete lists of marine facilities throughout this area, your best source of information is *Embassy's Complete Boating Guide & Chartbook to Long Island Sound.* Contact the publisher at **142 Ferry Rd., Old Saybrook, 06475; (860) 395-0188.**

Cruises

For information on Maritime Center outings and sightseeing excursions to the Sheffield Island Lighthouse, see the listings under Major Attractions. In addition, the 80-foot schooner *Soundwaters* occasionally sails out of Norwalk. For more information, see the listing in the **Greenwich/Stamford** chapter.

Lessons, Rentals and Tours

Norwalk is somewhat of a center for instruction in sailing and boating. **Longshore Sailing School (260 S. Compo Rd. in Longshore Club Park, Westport, 06880; 203-226-4646)** teaches both adults and youths boating, small craft and catamaran sailing, kayaking and windsurfing. They also have a combination tennis/sailing instruction program and rent rowboats, canoes, sea kayaks and small sailboats during summer. **Norwalk Sailing School (P.O. Box 157, Georgetown, 06829; 203-852-1857)** offers private sailing instruction for adults, group classes for youths, windsurfing lessons, rental of boats and windsurfers and regular windsurfing races on midweek evenings. **Sound Sailing Center (160 Water St., Norwalk, 06854; 203-838-1110)** gives group and private sailing lessons at many levels, offers evening seminars and racing during summer and rents boats ranging from 18-foot centerboard sailboats to catamarans to 44-foot offshore yachts. For instruction in canoeing and kayaking as well as organized freshwater and saltwater trips, call **White Creek Expeditions (99 Mayanos Rd., New Canaan, 06840; 203-966-0040). Women's Sailing Adventures (39A Woodside Ave., Westport, 06880; 800-328-8053 or 203-227-7413)** is a sailing school for women doing both local instruction and extended outings to various domestic and international destinations.

Other rental options include **Overton's Boat Livery (80 Seaview Ave., Norwalk; 203-838-2031),** where you can get 16-foot dories for fishing and sightseeing spring through fall, and **Outdoor Sports Center (80 Danbury Rd. [Rte. 7], Wilton; 203-762-8324),** offering canoes and kayaks.

Charter brokers are a popular way to go if you are looking for a trip on a fully crewed boat, and catered meals are often included. See the **Greenwich/Stamford** chapter for an explanation of what charter brokers are and what they have to offer, as well as the names and numbers of several that operate in this area. Also try **D&P Charters (203-866-9671)** for scuba, cruising and fishing expeditions. The **Small Boat Shop (144 Water St., Norwalk; 203-854-5223)** leads guided kayak tours of Norwalk Harbor and the Norwalk Islands weekends and holidays mid-May–Oct., conditions permitting. Experience is not required, but reservations are.

Fishing

Most area tackle shops carry supplies for both freshwater and saltwater fishing. A few places to try include **The Bait Shop, (99 Rowayton Ave., Norwalk; 203-853-3811), Compleat Angler (1089 Post Rd., Darien; 203-655-9400)** and **Fisherman's World (Seaview Ave., East Norwalk; 203-866-1075).**

Freshwater

During the summer in coastal Connecticut towns, everyone's attention turns to Long Island Sound, but if it's trout you want there is some freshwater access. The **Norwalk River** is easily accessible along intermittent stretches of Rte. 7 wherever there's a pullout and no postings against trespassing. Despite the highway, the atmosphere can be surprisingly tranquil if you select the right spot. The **Saugatuck River** is also stocked. The best place to access it is right below Saugatuck Dam in Devils Glen Park, a really pretty spot on Valley Forge Rd. with a series of pools and cascades. A brief stretch of the river alongside Ford Rd. in Westport is restricted to fly fishing.

Alpine **Saugatuck Reservoir** and three other large bodies of water in southeast Connecticut are private water supplies open for fishing to members of the public who obtain a special permit from the owner, **Bridgeport Hydraulic Co. (BHC).** Some town halls and tackle shops (BHC can provide a list) and all BHC offices carry the permit ($20 per season or $5 per day, free to seniors and the handicapped). For more information call **(203) 336-7788.**

Saltwater

Here as elsewhere in southwestern Connecticut, charter vessels and charter brokers provide most of the access to open water for fishing. Two local charter operators are *Miss Nora* (203-866-9671) and *My Bonnie* (203-866-6313), both out of Norwalk. Both can take small groups throughout western Long Island Sound for whatever is running between Apr. and Nov. See the **Greenwich/Stamford** chapter for an explanation of charter brokers and the services they offer. If you prefer to fish from shore, two good spots are **Sherwood Island State Park** and the pier at **Calf Pasture Beach.** Admission is charged at both spots in summer.

Hiking

For information on hiking at **New Canaan Nature Center** and **Woodcock Nature Cen-**

384

ter, see the listings under Nature Centers. They are among the most accessible hiking spots in the area; the listings below are for somewhat more remote and rugged trail systems. The **Saugatuck Valley Trails** are exceptional for hiking and are described in the **Danbury** chapter, although they overlap several towns in this area. Another hiking option is **Wilton Town Forest,** described under Biking. Finally, for instruction in rock climbing and organized hiking trips, contact **White Creek Expeditions (99 Mayanos Rd., New Canaan, 06840; 203-966-0040).**

Devil's Den Preserve

At more than 1,600 acres, Nature Conservancy–owned Devil's Den is the largest nature preserve in southwestern Connecticut. Its 20 miles of trails cross woodland and wetland, climbing to some high ridges yielding good vistas and passing several sites of historical significance, such as old sawmills and charcoal pits. There are often guided walks, lectures and classes at the preserve; call for a schedule. Pets and picnicking are not permitted. The trails of Devil's Den connect with those of the Saugatuck Valley Trails listed in the **Danbury** chapter. Hours: dawn–dusk daily, year-round. Enter at 33 Pent Rd. in Weston. For more information call **(203) 226-4991** on weekdays, 9:00 A.M.–5:00 P.M.

Weir-Leary-White Preserve

The trails in this Nature Conservancy–owned tract of land in Wilton connect with those on the Weir Farm National Historic Site property. The best way to get a map is to pick one up at the Weir Farm visitors center (for hours and directions, see the listing under Major Attractions), or just look for the dirt pullout on the west side of Nod Hill Rd. between Pelham Ln. and Granite Dr. in Wilton. A map is posted at this entrance, and a map box a little farther on should be stocked. The terrain is gently rolling for the most part, with the red trail crossing some steep hillsides. There are meadows in various stages of succession as well as woodland and swamp, making for a nice variety. The complexity of the trail system makes it possible to hike virtually any distance.

Horseback Riding

Stonyside Farms (corner of Kensett Ave. and Kensett Dr., Wilton; 203-762-7984) offers trail rides (English saddle) through Norwalk's huge Cranbury Park for $25 per person per hour. The best availability is on weekdays, although weekends are possible. Reservations required.

Ice Skating

A few hours a week are set aside for public skating at **Darien Ice Rink (54 Old King's Hwy., Darien; 203-655-8251),** which is open year-round. Admission is $5, and skate rentals are $2. Call for a schedule.

Seeing and Doing

The most current and comprehensive guide to upcoming events, concerts and art shows in this area is the *Fairfield County Weekly,* a free periodical available at newsstands, convenience stores and many attractions.

Antiquing

Although the antiques stores in this area are somewhat scattered rather than congregated in a small district, they are well worth seeking out. You can find high-quality estate items if you know what you're looking for. Riverside Dr. in Westport and Rte. 7 through Wilton are two of the best stretches to try. Be sure to stop at **Cannondale Village,** a tiny hamlet/railroad station where the buildings have been turned into retail shops and a restaurant. Hours are Tue.–Sun., 11:00 A.M.–5:00 P.M. Located on **Cannon Rd. off Rte. 7 in Wilton; (203) 762-2233.**

Art and Art Galleries

Silvermine Guild Arts Center (1037 Silvermine Rd., New Canaan, 06840; 203-966-5617) is a combination art school, gallery and shop where you can see a wide range of work in different media. Part of Silvermine's attraction is its beautiful setting in a woodsy residential neighborhood. Combine a visit with lunch at nearby Silvermine Tavern for a really nice outing. Admission: $2 donation. Hours: Tue.–Sat., 11:00 A.M.–5:00 P.M.; Sun., noon–5:00 P.M. There are short gaps between shows, so call before going.

Norwalk's City Hall at **125 East Ave.** is the home of an important collection of Works Progress Administration (WPA) murals painted at the height of the Depression. Six artists painted the 26 canvases that were specifically created for the public spaces of this government building. Some depict local people engaged in everyday activities, whereas other series are devoted to Mark Twain, the Wilton/Danbury area and the voyages of Marco Polo. They can be viewed Mon.–Fri., 9:00 A.M.–5:00 P.M., using a self-guided tour brochure. For more information call **(203) 866-0202.**

Children and Families

Although it sounds odd, a major area attraction for kids is a dairy and grocery store. Small children delight as much in **Stew Leonard's** as they do in amusement parks. At every turn there's a talking cow or a robotic chicken singing a silly song. If you've got to do some stocking up anyway, you might as well have fun. Hours: 7:00 A.M.–11:00 P.M. daily; closed Christmas Day & early on other major holidays. **100 Westport Ave. (Rte. 1), Norwalk, 06851; (203) 847-7213.**

Museums and Historic Sites

For information on touring the **Lockwood-Mathews Mansion Museum** or **Weir Farm**, see the listings under Major Attractions. Most area towns also have museums focusing on local history. The newest is the **Norwalk Museum,** located in that city's beautiful 1912 Old City Hall. Its unique format features an interior courtyard with stylized turn-of-the-century storefronts in whose windows items from the museum's collections are displayed. Strengths

include American needlework, clocks, silver and maritime artifacts. Admission by donation. Hours are tentatively Tue.–Sat., 10:00 A.M.–5:00 P.M., & Sun., 1:00 P.M.–5:00 P.M. Call to confirm. **Corner of N. Main and Marshall Sts., Norwalk, 06854; (203) 866-0202.**

A large complex of buildings is maintained by the **New Canaan Historical Society (13 Oenoke Ridge, New Canaan; 203-966-1776).** They include an 18th-century homestead with period furnishings, a one-room schoolhouse, a tool museum and more. To catch all of them open at once, visit Wed., Thu. or Sun., 2:00 P.M.–4:00 P.M. (also Tue. & Fri. in July & Aug.). Admission: $3.

Mill Hill Historic Park (Wall St. and East Ave., Norwalk; 203-846-0525) comprises three historic buildings in a park setting in downtown Norwalk. The trio is made up of an 1826 little red schoolhouse, a 1740 lawyer's office and an 1835 home. Artifacts on display date from the early years of the town through 1850. Bring your kids to the children's festival in early Oct. for a day of weaving, food preservation, dressing up in colonial costumes and more. Enter from Wall St. Admission by donation. Hours: Sun., 1:00 P.M.–4:00 P.M., May–Oct.

The **Westport Historical Society's Wheeler House (25 Avery Pl., Westport; 203-222-1424)** is a historic home with three beautiful period rooms and an octagonal stone barn with a Westport chronology. Call ahead if you want to tour the barn so they can arrange for adequate staff. You can also purchase a map for a self-guided driving tour of the town's significant architectural and historic sites. Admission by donation. Hours: Tue.–Sat., 10:00 A.M.–3:00 P.M.

The **Wilton Heritage Museum (249 Danbury Rd. [Rte. 7], Wilton; 203-762-7257)** is a 1757 house with five period rooms and changing exhibits. Admission: $2 adults, $1 seniors. Hours: Tue.–Thu., 10:00 A.M.–4:00 P.M. Last but not least, the **Bates-Scofield Homestead (45 Old King's Hwy. North, Darien; 203-655-9233)** is an 18th-century home opened to the public by the Darien Historical Society. Hours: Thu. & Sun., 2:00 P.M.–4:00 P.M.

The **SoNo Switchtower Railroad Museum** is a new attraction scheduled to open by the time this book appears. A local chapter of the National Historic Railway Society is restoring one of the last remaining intact switch towers in the country. The tower's machinery controlled the flow of train traffic through South Norwalk for many years. It's located at the corner of Washington and N. Main Sts. in South Norwalk. Tentative hours are Sat. & Sun., 10:00 A.M.–5:00 P.M., May–mid-Oct. For updated information call the **Coastal Fairfield County Tourism District** at **(800) 866-7925** or **(203) 854-7825.**

Nature Centers

The **New Canaan Nature Center (144 Oenoke Ridge, New Canaan; 203-966-9577)** has perhaps the biggest area nature center. Inside the main building are a number of hands-on natural science exhibits for kids. There's also a network of woodland walking trails and a greenhouse, as well as a cider house and maple sugar shed open seasonally. Call for a schedule of public programs. Admission by donation. Building hours: Tue.–Sat., 9:00 A.M.–4:00 P.M. Also open during the school year on Sun., noon–4:00 P.M.; closed holidays. Grounds hours: dawn–dusk daily, year-round.

The live and mounted animal exhibits and programs at **Woodcock Nature Center (56 Deer Run Rd., Wilton; 203-762-7280)** emphasize local ecology. There are also 2 miles of easy trails and boardwalks through woodland and wetland, plus a self-guided nature trail with informative plaques. Call for a schedule of organized hikes and other child- and family-oriented activities. The building is open weekdays only during summer, Tue.–Sun. the rest of the year. Hours are 9:30 A.M.–5:00 P.M. Tue.–Sat. & noon–4:00 P.M. on Sun. Closed major holidays and for inclement weather. Trails open dawn–dusk daily, year-round.

The **Nature Center for Environmental Activities (10 Woodside Ln., Westport; 203-227-7253)** is a 62-acre wildlife sanctuary with 2 miles of easy wood-chip trails and a butterfly and bird garden. It also has a small museum building with natural science exhibits, but call before going because it can be closed to the public for special programming. Admission: $1 adults, $.50 children 12 and under. Building hours: Mon.–Sat., 9:00 A.M.–5:00 P.M.; Sun., 1:00 P.M.–4:00 P.M. Hands-on exhibits are open weekends only. Grounds hours: 7:30 A.M.–dusk daily.

Nightlife

In addition to having some great family attractions, the SoNo district also offers numerous dining options, theaters and several clubs with live music. **Shenanigans (80 Washington St.; 203-853-0142)** is your basic small music club offering a wide range of acts, including rock 'n' roll and reggae bands. Across the street, you'll find SoNo's nod to two of the newest trends at **The Loft Martini and Cigar Bar (97 Washington St.; 203-838-6555),** where you can also catch live music on Wed., Thu. & Sun.—nights when stages are dark at a lot of other places. **Tra-peze (18 S. Main St.; 203-853-2123),** just around the corner, is a bar/restaurant with a trendy interior, live music several nights a week and good food. The **Crown SoNo Regent Theater (66 N. Main St.; 203-899-7979)** multiplex shows first-run movies; **SoNo Cinema (15 Washington St.; 203-866-9202)** is the place to go for foreign films, documentaries, art flicks and out-of-the-ordinary stuff.

If you're partial to folk music (although that's not all they offer) check out some of the local coffeehouses. They often feature exceptional talent in very casual but unbeatably intimate settings. Most coffeehouses take the summer off, so call for a schedule and to check performance times and prices. The **Assorted Friends Coffee House (203-972-6246)** is located at the **United Methodist Church of New Canaan** at **165 South Ave.** on the second Fri. of each month, and the **Good Folk Coffee House (203-866-4450)** is held the fourth Sat. of each month at the **United Methodist Church** at the **corner of Rowayton and Pennoyer Aves. in Rowayton.**

Performing Arts

This area has quite a rich cultural calendar, especially as regards theater. Westport is the local theater capital, with two summer stock venues that have been going for more than 50 years: **Westport Playhouse (25 Powers Ct., Westport; 203-227-4177)** and **White Barn Theatre (452 Newtown Ave., Westport; 203-227-3768)**. The former has a season running June–Sept. with performances Mon.–Sat. at 8:30 P.M. & matinees on Wed. at 2:00 P.M. & Sat. at 5:00 P.M. Tickets range from $10 to $33. The latter presents a new show every weekend in Aug. only, with performances Sat. & Sun. at 8:00 P.M. Tickets are $30. Both theaters are in rustic converted barns. During the rest of the year, community theater is available at **Wilton Playshop (Lover's Ln., Wilton; 203-762-7629)** and **New Canaan's Powerhouse Theater (679 South Ave. in Waveny Park, New Canaan; 203-966-7371)**. Call for details.

One of the great pleasures of summer is an outdoor concert in a pretty setting. Locally, **Levitt Pavilion** fills that role. It's an outdoor stage on a hill above the Saugatuck River in downtown Westport. Every summer 60 free nights of entertainment and half a dozen ticketed events take place there, including the World Music Festival described under Festivals and Events. You'll find children's performers; big band, reggae, rock, pop, jazz, blues and classical music; theater; dance and more on the schedule. Bring a blanket or folding chair for seating on the open lawn. The stage is located behind the public library on Jesup Rd., walking distance from all the dining and shopping in town. For a schedule and ticket prices call **(203) 226-7600.**

Fans of chamber music will want to check out the four concerts comprising the **Silvermine Chamber Music Series** every summer at the **Silvermine Guild (1037 Silvermine Rd., New Canaan; 203-966-5618)**. They occur about every third Fri. at 8:00 P.M., starting in late June. Tickets are $20 adults, $15 seniors and students.

Norwalk Concert Hall (125 East Ave., Norwalk; 203-854-7900) hosts a wide range of shows, including regular performances by the **Norwalk Symphony (203-866-2455)**. It gave four classical concerts, two pops concerts and two family concerts per Oct.–May season. Tickets are $15–$35, with discounts for students and seniors. Kids age 6 and under go free at family concerts. Last but not least, the **Westport Arts Center (17 Morningside Dr. South, Westport; 203-222-7070 or 203-226-1806)** is a former school that's been converted into a community arts resource. It's a place to catch visual arts, theater, dance, music and children's performers, in addition to workshops for all ages.

Scenic Drives

All of the towns in this area have numerous lovely neighborhoods that are pleasant to drive through on a nice day. Near the shore, some of the most enjoyable, both from a visual and a driving standpoint, are Compo and Hillspoint Rds. through the Compo section of Westport, and Beachside Ave. through the Greens Farms district. The Beach House on Hillspoint Rd. is the perfect place to stop for lunch. Traffic is always a consideration near the shore. If you want to get away from it, head for the wooded northern reaches of Wilton, New Canaan and especially Weston, where the drive on Valley Forge Rd. down the west shore of Saugatuck Reservoir is unbeatable. There's a small park at the southern end of the reservoir that's good for taking a break.

Sports

The **Ox Ridge Charity Horse Show,** a benefit hunter/jumper event held the second week in June, is among the top horse shows in the country and one of the largest in the Northeast. It's almost a week long, starting on a Tue. and going through the following Sun.'s $35,000 grand prix main event. Hours expand as the week goes on, but in general there's something going on from early in the morning until late afternoon each day. Admission varies by day, ranging from $5 per car Tue.–Fri. to $7 per adult, $5 per child on Sun. The Ox Ridge Hunt

Club also hosts several other shows June–Sept. **512 Middlesex Rd., Darien, 06820; (203) 655-2559.**

Where to Stay

Bed & Breakfasts

The Cotswold Inn—$$$$

The Cotswold Inn is an elegant B&B, a place where the word "distinctive" really fits and you go when you want to splurge on something really special. Once you pull down the driveway you'll feel like you're nestled away in some quaint manor in England, but you're still within walking distance from downtown Westport. There are only four rooms in this old colonial home, each with a queen bed, full bath, TV and telephone. The Wheller Suite also has a twin sleigh bed in an area adjoining the main bedroom and a fireplace. Guests have access to the health club equipment at the town YMCA. A Continental breakfast is included. **76 Myrtle Ave., Westport, 06880; (203) 226-3766.**

Hotels, Motels & Inns

Accommodations in this area tend to be pricey. For somewhat more moderate rates, depending on the night, also try the **Westport Inn (1595 Boston Post Rd. East, Westport, 06880; 800-446-8997** or **203-259-5236)** and the **Norwalk Inn (99 East Ave., Norwalk, 06851; 800-537-8483** or **203-838-5531).** The **Coastal Fairfield County Tourism District** at **(800) 866-7925** or **(203) 854-7825** would be happy to make other suggestions if you need them.

Courtyard by Marriott—$$$$

Somewhat moderate weekend rates at this business traveler–oriented hotel make a stay here within reason for the leisure traveler. Standard rooms have one king or two double beds, and there are some king suites as well. Features include a pool, a laundry facility, valet dry cleaning on weekdays, an exercise room, a breakfast buffet and hospitality food Mon.–Thu. **474 Main Ave., Norwalk, 06851; (800) 647-7578** or **(203) 849-9111.**

The Inn at Longshore—$$$$

One of the principal perks that comes with a stay at this inn uniquely located inside a Westport town park is access to the golf course that surrounds it. Inn guests can reserve tee times as if they were town residents. This former estate and private club also has tennis courts, an outdoor pool, a playground and an abundance of lawns and paved paths for walking. Two rooms have unobstructed water views. Of the rest, third-floor rooms are preferable. Rooms are spacious with a pleasant mixed English and New England country decor. There's also a handful of one-bedroom suites. Continental breakfast is included, and there's a good on-site restaurant. Because this is a tourist-oriented inn, you'll find lower rates here on weeknights. **260 Compo Rd. South, Westport, 06880; (203) 226-3316.**

The Inn at National Hall—$$$$

A multi-million-dollar restoration of an 1873 Italianate brick building that was once the town hall has yielded a truly luxurious inn. It took a team of artists to create the extraordinary trompe l'oeil paintings and stenciling that are at the heart of the inn's rich Euro-flavored decor. There are 15 rooms and suites in all, some with special features like lofts, staircases, balconies or direct views of the Saugatuck River, on which the inn lies just across a bridge from the main shopping district of Westport. They all sport canopied four-poster beds, yards of sumptuous fabrics for bed curtains and draperies, luxurious baths, refrigerators, entertainment systems, robes, slippers and more. Continental breakfast is included, and the restaurant on the main floor is rated four stars by *The New York Times*. Room service, valet dry cleaning and business services are available; transportation and massages can be arranged. Guests have access to Westport's huge YMCA for health club facilities. **2 Boston Post Rd. (Rte. 1), Westport, 06880; (800) 628-4255** or **(203) 221-1351.**

389

Sheraton Four Points Hotel—$$$$

The second of the two major business class hotels opposite the Merritt 7 office park was recently renovated when this was converted from a Day's Inn, so it's in excellent condition. Weekend rates here are lower than midweek rates. There's an on-site restaurant, room service, fitness equipment and valet dry cleaning. **426 Main Ave., Norwalk, 06851; (888) 806-4786 or (203) 849-9828.**

The Roger Sherman Inn—$$$ to $$$$

The Roger Sherman Inn is among the best of the moderately priced inns in the area. It's situated in a sprawling old house with a large lawn and a French/Continental restaurant on the main floor that make the inn very popular for functions. The rooms vary quite a bit, so it's best to inquire for details, but they all have a private bath, TV and telephone. Continental breakfast is included, and laundry and dry cleaning services are available on weekdays. **195 Oenoke Ridge Rd., New Canaan, 06840; (203) 966-4541.**

Where to Eat

The Roger Sherman Inn—$$$$

The light, airy dining rooms and elegant, cheerful decor make this an out-of-the-ordinary spot for breakfast, lunch or dinner. The setting is a colonial-era home with broad lawns for strolling and porches for relaxing. The kitchen's specialty is Continental and French cuisine. Sat. night dinner is fixed price at $45. Open for breakfast Mon.–Fri., 7:00 A.M.–10:00 A.M.; Sat.–Sun., 8:00 A.M.–10:00 A.M. Lunch served noon–2:00 P.M. daily (Sun. brunch starts at 11:30 A.M.). Dinner served nightly from 6:00 P.M. **195 Oenoke Ridge, New Canaan, 06840; (203) 966-4541.**

The Beach House—$$$ to $$$$

The food at this restaurant would be right at home in a much more formal setting, but The Beach House is on the cute and informal side, right on the beach, breezy, light-filled and window-lined, sporting views of a picturesque cove. Seafood, often with a Creole or Asian touch, is the specialty, but there are also salads, pastas and many other choices. Open Wed.–Sun., serving lunch & Sun. brunch noon–3:00 P.M. & dinner from 6:00 P.M. **233 Hillspoint Rd., Westport, 06880; (203) 226-7005.**

Côte d'Azur—$$$ to $$$$

As you might surmise from its name, the cuisine at this restaurant is French, specifically Provençal. It has a pleasing gold and sea foam color scheme that gets you in the mood for the food. Open Tue.–Sat., it seats for lunch noon–2:30 P.M. & for dinner 6:00 P.M.–9:00 P.M. weeknights, 10:00 or 11:00 P.M. on weekends. **86 Washington St., South Norwalk, 06854; (203) 855-8900.**

Da Pietros—$$$ to $$$$

Serving dinner only, Da Pietros specializes in Northern Italian and Southern French cuisine. The restaurant's storefront setting, a short walk from downtown Westport, makes the elegant and welcoming interior a pleasant surprise. It's quite small and intimate, with only about ten tables, so reservations are essential. Hours: Mon.–Sat., 5:00 P.M.–10:00 P.M. **36 Riverside Ave., Westport, 06880; (203) 454-1213.**

Meson Galicia—$$$ to $$$$

One of a tiny handful of restaurants in Connecticut serving authentic Spanish food, Meson Galicia represents something unique yet not too foreign for most American palates. It's decorated with pine furniture and a tile floor to look somewhat like a hacienda dining room, but numerous windows and plain overhead lighting keep it bright. The lunch offerings are basically the same as at dinner, so Meson Galicia is a good choice for a substantive midday meal, although you could also eat light. Open for lunch Tue.–Fri., noon–2:30 P.M., & for dinner Tue.–Sun. from 6:00 P.M. **10 Wall St., Norwalk, 06850; (203) 866-8800.**

Restaurant at National Hall—$$$ to $$$$

Located on the first floor of the opulent Inn at National Hall, this restaurant enjoys a waterfront patio on the Saugatuck River for al fresco dining in good weather. The kitchen's Continental cuisine is rated four stars by *The New York Times*. Many of the dishes have an international (usually Asian) influence, and the menu changes seasonally. Lunch includes some items from the dinner menu plus several lighter but equally upscale options, and a champagne jazz brunch is served on Sun. Inquire about the Sun. night cabaret dinner program. Lunch served Mon.–Sat., 11:30 A.M.–2:00 P.M. Sun. brunch: noon–3:00 P.M. Dinner served from 6:00 P.M. nightly. **2 Boston Post Rd. West (Rte. 1), Westport, 06880; (800) 628-4255 or (203) 221-1351.**

Amberjack's—$$$
Located in a former bank building with an open floor plan and soaring ceiling, Amberjack's feels contemporary and traditional, polished yet moderately casual at the same time. The menu—American with a seafood focus—could be described the same way. You can people-watch from the bar at the front or enjoy a breeze coming off the harbor on the side terrace. Open daily for lunch, noon–3:00 P.M., & for dinner from 5:30 P.M. **99 Washington St., South Norwalk, 06854; (203) 853-4332.**

Barcelona—$$$
Barcelona serves a menu of cold and hot tapas, appetizers and entrées with a wide-ranging Mediterranean flavor in a casual, lively wine bar setting. The wine list is fairly large, and there are regular wine specials by both the bottle and the glass as well as some specialty beers in the bottle and on tap. It's a somewhat loud place with a bar up one side (cigars available) and tables up the other, perfect for hanging out with a bunch of friends. There's also a patio for summer use. The range of food choices and portion sizes should accommodate any group of mixed appetites. Hours: lunch served Mon.–Fri., noon–2:30 P.M.; dinner served from 5:00 P.M. nightly. **63 N. Main St., South Norwalk, 06854; (203) 899-0088.**

Bluewater Cafe—$$$
Perhaps the best moderately priced, casual restaurant in downtown New Canaan, Blue-

water Cafe serves a mix of Italian and American dishes. With only about ten small tables, it's quite intimate yet not claustrophobic. The aqua-and-white color scheme and nautical paintings create a relaxing atmosphere, and the windowside tables for two are rather romantic. Hours: open daily 11:30 A.M.–2:30 P.M. for lunch & from 5:30 P.M. on for dinner. **15 Elm St., New Canaan, 06840; (203) 972-1799.**

The Brewhouse—$$$
The Brewhouse is the restaurant at the site of the New England Brewing Co., a local microbrewery. A history of the company and the microbrewery renaissance is told on the menu between the beer and wine lists and makes for interesting reading. The wide-ranging menu is hard to pin down, but features a lot of seafood as well as traditional German dishes such as Wiener schnitzel and sauerbraten. The beautiful, atriumlike dining room is filled with brewmaking machines and utensils, and the walls are adorned with a collection of beer memorabilia billed as "one of the finest in the United States." There is also a brick terrace for outdoor dining. Hours: Mon.–Thu., 11:30 A.M.–10:00 P.M.; Fri.–Sat. until 11:00 P.M.; Sun. until 9:00. **13 Marshall St., South Norwalk, 06854; (203) 853-9110.** Self-guided or guided tours of the New England Brewing Co. can be taken Wed. & Sun. at 11:00 A.M. & 4:00 P.M. & Sat. at 11:00 A.M.

The Lime—$$$
The closest thing to a Greenwich Village bistro in this part of the world falls halfway between health-food restaurant and ethnic grill. It's one of the few restaurants to offer vegetarians a moderate number of choices, yet meat-eaters will find plenty to satisfy. At lunch there's lighter fare such as sandwiches and meal salads, and home-style desserts are always on hand. Lunch hours: Mon.–Sat., 11:00 A.M.–4:00 P.M. Dinner served Mon.–Sat., 5:00 P.M.–10:00 P.M.; Sun., 4:00 P.M.–9:00 P.M. **168 Main Ave., Norwalk, 06851; (203) 846-9240.**

Pasta Nostra—$$$
From the name of this restaurant and the pasta machines displayed in the window, it's

391

pretty clear what to expect on the menu. Fresh, homemade pastas are the specialty. The interior is unpretentious, almost cafeteria-like, which only seems to underscore that the emphasis is on the food. Open Wed., 6:00 P.M.– 9:30 P.M.; Thu.–Sat., 5:30 P.M.–10:30 P.M. **116 Washington St., South Norwalk, 06854; (203) 854-9700.**

Silvermine Tavern—$$$

Combine a streamside setting, a lovely deck, a building with a history and good food and you get Silvermine Tavern. The sprawling colonial structure has a rich Yankee ambiance. The menu features a lot of traditional favorites such as pot roast, many grilled dishes and pasta. The Sun. champagne buffet spread is a local institution, and Thu. is roast beef buffet night. Preparation is straightforward but very tasty, and you won't regret leaving room for dessert. While you're waiting for your meal, ask your server to bring you a copy of the two-page "History of Silvermine Tavern," which will help bring the building and grounds to life. Inquire about the monthly wine events, which combine dinner with a tasting of about a dozen wines for one fixed price. Lunch hours: Mon. & Wed.–Sat., noon–3:00 P.M. Sun. brunch: 11:00 A.M.–2:30 P.M. Dinner served Mon., Wed. & Thu., 6:00 P.M.–9:00 P.M.; Fri.–Sat., 6:00 P.M.– 10:00 P.M.; Sun., 3:30 P.M.–9:00 P.M. **194 Perry Ave. at Silvermine Ave., Norwalk, 06850; (203) 847-4558.**

SoNo Seaport—$$$

The only real waterside eatery in South Norwalk serves up your basic fast seafood along with steamed lobster, broiled fish and steaks. On a cool, pleasant day, the outdoor deck is a nice place to relax with your order from the oyster bar and watch boats cruise up and down the Norwalk River. A fish market is next door so you can pick up something for tomorrow's dinner on your way home. Hours: 11:00 A.M.–10:00 P.M. daily. **100 Water St., South Norwalk, 06854; (203) 854-9483.**

Donovan's—$ to $$

Donovan's is an excellent choice for anyone looking for inexpensive eats and a relaxed

place to kick back with the newspaper and a beer in SoNo. The atmosphere is that of a well-worn neighborhood bar, but the place and the food are very family-oriented. The pressed-tin ceiling, pictures of boxers practically papering the walls, scuffed wooden floor and simple wooden tables and booths give it an old-time flavor that's very comfortable. It serves a basic menu of sandwiches, burgers, salads and homemade desserts complemented by daily specials, and the New England clam chowder is among the best around. Hours: Sun.–Thu., 11:30 A.M.–1:00 A.M.; Fri.–Sat., 11:30 A.M.–2:00 A.M. Located at **Washington and Water Sts., South Norwalk, 06854; (203) 838-3430.**

Reid's Country Cupboard—$ to $$

If you like coffee shops, you'll feel right at home in this neighborhood breakfast and lunch spot. It serves all the standard breakfast items, sandwiches, salads and a few daily specials in a comfortable hometown diner atmosphere. The restaurant is located at the end of a short alley off Elm St. next to Bluewater Cafe. Hours: Mon.–Sat., 7:00 A.M.–3:00 P.M.; Sun., 7:30 A.M.–2:00 P.M. **17 Elm St., New Canaan; (203) 966-6163.**

Services

Local Visitors Information

Coastal Fairfield County Tourism District, 297 West Ave., Norwalk, 06851; (800) 866-7925 or **(203) 854-7825.** Hours: Mon.–Fri., 10:00 A.M.–5:00 P.M.; Sat.–Sun. (July–Oct. only), 11:00 A.M.–3:00 P.M. Request the Connecticut Yankee Weekend Getaways discount coupon book for substantial savings at local attractions and hotels.

State Welcome Center, located in the McDonald's restaurant in the rest area on I-95 between exits 11 and 13 northbound in Darien; **(203) 655-8289.** It's open 8:00 A.M.– 6:00 P.M. daily in spring & summer, 9:00 A.M.– 5:00 P.M. daily in fall & winter.

Transportation

The South Norwalk train station and several smaller stations in surrounding communities are served by **Metro-North** commuter trains connecting them with New York and New Haven. South Norwalk is also the start of the Metro-North line running up to Danbury. In neighboring Bridgeport or Stamford, you can also change to Amtrak trains. Call **800-638-7646** for Metro-North schedule and fare information, **(800) 872-7245** for **Amtrak**. Bus transportation within Norwalk and surrounding towns is provided by the **Norwalk Transit District** at **(203) 853-3338**. Some limited service is also provided by **CT Transit** at **(203) 327-7433**.

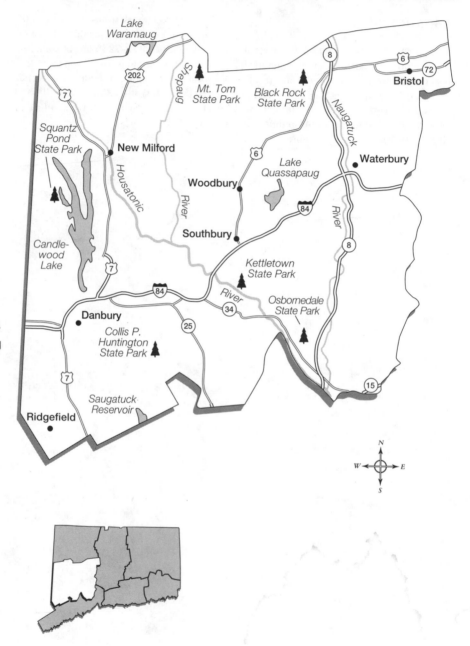

Housatonic and Naugatuck River Valleys

Housatonic and Naugatuck River Valleys

Danbury

Danbury, the population and economic center of upper Fairfield County, is perhaps best known (recreationally at least) as the home of Richter Park, a municipal golf course that has been rated among the top 25 public courses in the country. It's got a beautiful ridge-top setting on a road lined with New England's characteristic old stone walls. If golf isn't your thing, try Candlewood Lake on the northern edge of the city. This is the largest freshwater body in the state, with opportunities for boating, fishing and swimming.

The suburban and rural towns around Danbury provide more open spaces for outdoor activities. Saugatuck Reservoir in Redding, which is open for fishing by special permit, is so pristine and undeveloped you'll think you're in Vermont and not an hour and a half from New York City. Nearby Huntington State Park is one of the best mountain biking spots in Connecticut. Over in Newtown you can hike the forested hills alongside the Housatonic River at Paugussett State Forest, and the list could go on and on.

The last place you'd expect to find a major theater is in quiet New Fairfield, north of Danbury. Yet Gateway's Candlewood Playhouse offers stage productions that equal many Broadway shows. If you're going to a show, you'll probably want dinner, and few parts of Connecticut offer more culinary variety than Danbury. One benefit of the city's extremely diverse population is a concentration of ethnic restaurants. In addition to great American, French and Italian food, you can find Portuguese, Ecuadorian, Thai, Peruvian, Vietnamese, Middle Eastern and more.

Finally, Ridgefield to the south is a very beautiful and vibrant little town that would make an excellent destination in itself. The compact nature of the town means that you can park your car and get around on foot all day without having to repeatedly find a parking space. The Aldrich Museum of Contemporary Art here is world-class, and the Keeler Tavern is among the most engaging historical museums in the state.

History

The Indians are said to have called what is now Danbury by the name "Paquiag," meaning cleared land, suggesting that this area has been the location of permanent settlements for a long time. Colonists arrived on the scene in the 1680s as the growth in population of the original coastal and Connecticut River Valley communities forced a new generation to look for land elsewhere. Most of the original settlers came from Norwalk, and over the next 30 years the whole area surrounding Danbury was settled.

During the Revolutionary War, supplies for Patriot troops were warehoused at Danbury. The British, frustrated by their inability to end the war quickly and eager for any kind of victory, were aware of the stockpiled goods and attacked on Apr. 26, 1777. Their 2,000 troops vastly outnumbered the local militia, and little could be done to stop them from burning the town. The loss of valuable material, including tents and medicine, was a real blow.

Danbury's own Paul Revere was Sybil Ludington, who at the young age of 16 rode through neighboring Putnam County, New York, warning residents that the British were burning Danbury. (She is remembered in a bronze sculpture in front of the library at Main and West Sts.) Patriots began gathering to drive the enemy off, and seeing this, British Gen. Tryon ordered a retreat. Militia members led by Brig. Gen. David Wooster followed hot on their heels.

The British evacuated Danbury on a route through Ridgefield, where Patriots under the command of Gens. Gold Selleck Silliman and then-loyal Benedict Arnold were waiting. With the British trapped between two prongs of American troops, a fight was forced. The Battle of Ridgefield was the only inland battle Connecticut experienced during the war. Wooster was killed in the fight, and a British cannonball fired that day is still lodged in the side of the Keeler Tavern Museum on Main St.

Nearby Redding was the site of what is called Connecticut's Valley Forge. Because of its proximity to New York, which was in British hands for virtually the duration of the war,

southwestern Connecticut was constantly in danger of attack. To protect the area, Maj. Gen. Israel Putnam and the right wing of the Continental army encamped in Redding at what is now Putnam Memorial State Park during the winter of 1778–1779. The winter was severe, food and clothing were in short supply and mutiny was in the air, but Putnam managed to control the troops and they pulled through, breaking camp the following Mar. The encampment was the first historic site in Connecticut to be preserved as a state park.

Danbury's onetime moniker, Hat City, leaves little doubt what industry fired its transformation from quiet backwater to urban center. The first recorded hat factory in the country was established here in 1780 by Zadoc Benedict. Its output: three hats a day. By 1910, 6,000 people were employed in several dozen hat factories that sometimes turned out 10,000 hats a day—more than any other American city. "We Crown Them All" became the city's unofficial motto.

Although hatting brought jobs and income to Danbury, it had its dark side. Exposure to the mercury used in the manufacturing process caused workers to develop a severe neurological disorder called "Hatter's Shake" (believed to be the origin of the phrase "mad as a hatter"), and vast quantities of the industry's noxious waste products were dumped into Danbury's Still River, contaminating it (a problem that's been largely reversed). The demand for hats declined slowly from 1910 on, but in the post–World War II years, the drop-off was precipitous. A generation later, the last hat factory closed. The greater Danbury area actually made the transition to a more diversified economy pretty well, a process that began during the Depression when the need for a broader employment base was recognized. Currently companies as recognizable as Duracell, Union Carbide and Ethan Allen are headquartered in the area.

With competition from nearby Danbury Fair Mall, retail stores in the downtown have a hard time making a go of it, so in recent years there has been a concerted effort to develop a dining and entertainment district. There are several good restaurants, taverns, nightspots

and coffeehouses in the area, many of them clustered on Ives St. a block away from Main. A major ice skating rink is slated for construction, and the old Palace Theater may be restored and reopened.

Major Attractions

Aldrich Museum of Contemporary Art

The Aldrich is the cultural center of Ridgefield. In addition to the changing exhibits and permanent outdoor sculpture garden, there is a series of jazz concerts on Fri. nights in summer, as well as a lecture series and poetry and short-story readings. Art Daze is a series of three-afternoon (Tue.–Thu., 1:00 P.M.–5:00 P.M.) classes for children age 6 and up, from late July to late Aug. Each week focuses on a theme or medium. Talks on current shows are also offered on Sun. at 2:00 P.M. Admission is $3 for adults, $2 for seniors and students. Hours: Tue.–Sun., 1:00 P.M.–5:00 P.M. **258 Main St., Ridgefield, 06877; (203) 438-4519.**

Candlewood Lake

The story of Candlewood Lake is a fascinating one. Three-quarters of a century ago, there was no lake here. In its place was the Rocky River Valley, filled with small farms, marshes and a gorge at its northern end where the Rocky River had eaten away the bedrock on its northward descent to the Housatonic River. In the mid-1920s the Connecticut Light and Power Co. developed plans to dam the Rocky River, flooding the valley for the purpose of generating electricity. In 1928 Candlewood Lake was born—along with stories about the lost communities under its waters. The valley was logged before flooding commenced, and standing buildings were razed or burned. Everything wooden was removed to prevent it from floating to the top later on. A cemetery also lies under Candlewood, although the bodies were removed to another resting place before flooding. Today Candlewood Lake offers visitors a variety of recreational opportunities: boating, waterskiing, scuba diving and swimming. See the listings below for more information.

Richter Park

The golf course at Richter Park, the most renowned public course in Connecticut and consistently rated one of the top such courses in the United States for the last decade, often overshadows all the other great facilities and activities at this green heart of Danbury: hiking trails, cross-country skiing, tennis courts, an arts center and a great restaurant. Like so many public spaces, Richter Park was once a private estate. In 1968 Irene Myers Richter gave her home and 85-acre property to the city of Danbury as

a memorial to her late husband Stanley L. Richter. The 18-hole golf course opened in 1972. See the listing under Golf for more.

The popular Musicals at Richter theater series takes place at Richter House, right next door to the restaurant/pro shop. Several clay-surface tennis courts are open to the public on a first-come, first-served basis at no charge. For hiking there are two woodland tracks through mountainous terrain on the grounds of Richter and adjacent Farrington Park; a trail map is available at the clubhouse. In winter, staff cut cross-country ski tracks of varying levels of difficulty with a snowmobile. Finally, the restaurant on the green serves really excellent food in a gracious atmosphere. The grounds of Richter Park are open dawn–dusk year-round. **100 Aunt Hack Rd., Danbury, 06811; (203) 792-2550.**

Squantz Pond State Park

Originally a natural lake, Squantz Pond is now an arm of artificial Candlewood Lake, from which it is separated only by a narrow causeway. Squantz Pond offers swimming, fishing, a boat launch and a designated scuba diving area. Canoes and paddleboats are available to rent, scores of picnic tables are located amid trees along the shore and hiking trails follow the west side of the lake and climb into the hills of adjacent Pootatuck State Forest. The pond is named for Chief Squantz, a Pootatuck Indian sachem from whose sons the surrounding land was acquired by colonists in the 1720s. An entrance fee is charged daily Memorial Day–Labor Day and on weekends until Columbus Day or so. It ranges from $5 to $7 for cars with Connecticut plates to $8–$12 for out-of-state cars. Hours: 8:00 A.M.–sunset, year-round. Located on **Short Woods Rd. just off Rte. 39 in New Fairfield; (203) 797-4165.**

Festivals and Events

Biker Rallies
Sun. during warm weather

If it's Sun. morning, don't be surprised or alarmed by all the motorcyclists congregating outside Marcus Dairy, a diner/dairy bar by Danbury Fair Mall. A minirally is held here every Sun. as long as the weather is reasonable, and there are also four major rallies during the season. There are vendors selling all sorts of merchandise, but the real reason to go is to turn an envious eye on all the beautiful bikes parked up and down the road. **Marcus Dairy** is at **5 Sugar Hollow Rd. off I-84 exit 3 in Danbury; (203) 748-9427.**

Patriot's Weekend
first weekend in May

This renowned military encampment and battle reenactment is a celebration to honor veterans of all wars. It takes place at the site of an actual Revolutionary War encampment known as Connecticut's Valley Forge, in 1778–1779. The event is presented by Sheldon's Horse, the 2nd Continental Light Dragoons, the first commissioned cavalry regiment in the United States, now a nonprofit educational organization. This curious name reflects the 18th-century use of the word "horse" to mean a mounted unit.

Patriot's Weekend is noted for its authenticity. Artillery, infantry and cavalry units from around New England and the mid-Atlantic states are invited to participate. Military demonstrations go on throughout the event, and each day is capped with a "real" battle reenactment in which there is not a predetermined outcome. Admission is by donation. Hours: Sat., 11:00 A.M.–4:00 P.M. (battle starts around 3:00); Sun., 11:00 A.M.–3:00 P.M. (battle starts around 1:30). **Putnam Park is located at the junction of Rtes. 58 and 107 in Redding.** For more information call **(860) 675-8461.**

Arts and Crafts Shows
early May and mid-Aug.

The **Ridgefield Guild of Artists,** a nonprofit group promoting the arts in west-central Connecticut, sponsors two crafts shows a year in beautiful Ballard Park in the center of Ridgefield. They both draw upward of 125 exhibitors, both local and not, showing their handmade work. No kits, imports or machine-manufactured goods are allowed. Dates are usually the Sun.

Getting There

Getting to Danbury from Hartford is easy. It's about a 60-mile drive, for which you should leave an hour and a quarter. Hop on I-84 westbound and keep going to exits 8–3. Exits 6 and 5 will get you closest to downtown, and exit 3 will take you directly to Danbury Fair Mall on the west side of town.

before Mother's Day and the third Sun. in Aug. Admission is free. **Ballard Park is on Rte. 35 in the heart of Ridgefield.** For more information call the Guild Thu.–Sun. between 1:00 P.M. and 5:00 P.M. at **(203) 438-8863.**

WRKI I-95 FM/STP Mini Grand Prix™
late May/early June

The streets of downtown Danbury become a racecourse for miniature Indy-style cars in this annual fund-raiser for the Arthritis Foundation. About two dozen drivers with corporate sponsors come from around the country to participate. Short heats throughout the morning determine starting position for the race, which begins around 3:00 P.M. from the intersection of Main and White Sts. A festival with kiddie rides, food and sponsor tents is a center of activity throughout the day after 10:00 A.M. The night before the race there is an informal "prix-race" party in which prizes are given to the participants for best-designed car, fastest tire change and best pit crew uniform. The party is open to the public; call for ticket prices. For more information contact the **Arthritis Foundation Connecticut Chapter Development Dept.** at **(800) 541-8350.**

CityCenter Danbury Summertime Festival of the Arts
early June–mid-Sept.

With the recent expansion of this festival to a four-night-per-week format, there's some sort of free outdoor entertainment going on in downtown Danbury most summer evenings. The acts cover a broad spectrum ranging from children's entertainers to jazz, barbershop, top 40, acoustic guitar and theater. Performances take place Wed.–Sat. at 6:30 P.M. at **Danbury green on Ives St. Park** in the municipal lot (there is a charge) directly opposite. For more information call **CityCenter Danbury** at **(203) 792-1711.**

Monroe Strawberry Festival
Father's Day weekend

More than a quarter-century ago the **Monroe Congregational Church** decided to have a small fund-raiser at which members of the congregation would bake and sell strawberry pies, shortcakes and breads. Over time it blossomed into a major event, but it never lost its country fair flavor. The berries—2 tons a year—are still picked by hand at a nearby farm, and pies and biscuits for the shortcake are all baked at the church. A juried craft show, entertainment and old-fashioned games for children round out the activities. Admission is free. Hours: Sat., 10:00 A.M.–5:00 P.M.; Sun., 11:00 A.M.–5:00 P.M. The festival takes place on **Monroe green on Rte. 111 at Church St.** For more information prior to the event call **(203) 261-0037.** On the day of the festival call the church directly at **(203) 268-9327.**

Danbury Ethnic Cultural Festival
last weekend in June

About 20 ethnic clubs and organizations representing the cultural diversity of the region participate in this annual celebration that began almost two decades ago. The focus is on family fun, with music, singing, dancing, storytelling, games and foods from around the world. The festival takes place at **Rogers Park Jr. High School in Rogers Park at Main and South Sts. in Danbury.** Admission is free. Hours: Fri., 5:00 P.M.–11:00 P.M.; Sat., 10:00–midnight; Sun., 10:00 A.M.–10:00 P.M.

Gasball Festival
last Sat. in Aug.

Named for the landmark Yankee Gas storage ball that dominates the intersection of Patriot Dr. and Pahquioque Ave., the Gasball Festival is an alternative music and arts celebration with a sense of humor. From noon to midnight the Danbury green on Ives St. is the scene of live original music, crafts and food vendors and offbeat site-specific sculpture. Admission is free. Park in the municipal lot off Patriot Dr. For more information call **Gallery 13** at **(203) 790-6754** or **CityCenter Danbury** at **(203) 792-1711.**

A Taste of Greater Danbury
first Sun. after Labor Day

Come sample the culinary expertise of 30–40 local restaurants in this gastronomic gala at Danbury green on Ives St. Also, there are two entertainment stages: one with music for adults and another with magic, storytelling, face painting and more for children. Admission is free; a voucher system is used for food purchases. Hours: 11:00 A.M.–7:00 P.M. For more information call **CityCenter Danbury** at **(203) 792-1711.**

Brookfield Craft Center Holiday Exhibit & Sale
mid-Nov.–Dec. 30

The most renowned crafts center in western Connecticut expands its year-round shop to more than three times its normal size during this event and features the work of more than 250 artisans from across the country as well as students. Everything from clothing and jewelry to pottery, basketry, weaving, glassware and more are displayed in a converted mill by a waterfall on the Still River. See the listing under Crafts Centers for more information about the center. Holiday Exhibit hours: Mon.–Sat., 10:00 A.M.–5:00 P.M. (until 8:00 P.M. on Fri.); Sun., noon–5:00 P.M.; closed Thanksgiving Day & Christmas. Located on **Rte. 25 just east of Rte. 7, Brookfield, 06804; (203) 775-4526.**

First Night
New Year's Eve

Danbury is one of several Connecticut cities to stage First Night, a family-oriented performing arts celebration to ring in the new year. Performances begin as early as 3:00 P.M. (children's programming is concentrated in the afternoon and early evening hours) and continue until midnight. All sorts of entertainment—theater, singing, music, dance—go on at a large number of downtown locations, topped off with a countdown to midnight at Danbury green on Ives St. Admission is by purchase of a button on sale at several locations in town. Buy it in advance, because the price goes up as New Year's Eve gets closer. An information center is always open the evening of the event, where you can pick up a schedule and make a last-minute button purchase. For more information call **CityCenter Danbury** at **(203) 792-1711.**

Outdoor Activities

Mountain Workshop is an outdoor adventures tour organizer that just can't be pigeonholed. Although they are located in Ridgefield, their trips feature destinations across western Connecticut and in neighboring New York state, and their activities run the gamut from sea kayaking to rock climbing to caving. Most trips are geared for intermediate or beginner skill levels. For a complete schedule of the season's trips, contact them at **P.O. Box 625, Ridgefield, 06877; (203) 438-3640.**

Biking
Mountain Biking

Collis P. Huntington State Park, shared by Redding, Bethel and Newtown, is extensively crisscrossed with excellent mountain bike trails. There are said to be 25 miles worth, making it one of the best places in the state to ride. The entrance, marked by a wolf and bear sculpture, is on Sunset Hill Rd. off Rte. 58 in Redding. For more information call **(203) 797-4165.**

Road Biking

Like many parts of Connecticut, the Danbury region is a mix of congested urban areas and quiet residential or rural districts. Having a nice ride is mostly a matter of staying away from the busiest streets. The entire town of Redding is appropriate for touring. Ditto Newtown, with the exception of Rtes. 25, 6 and 34 and Church Hill Rd. In Bethel and Ridgefield, you should avoid Rtes. 302 and 7 and use caution in the villages, but otherwise go wherever the road takes you.

Boating

See the **New Milford** chapter for information on **Lake Lillinonah** and the **Woodbury** chapter for information on **Lake Zoar. Squantz Pond** is described under Major Attractions.

Candlewood Lake

At over 5,000 acres, Candlewood Lake is the largest freshwater body in Connecticut and very popular with boaters and water-skiers. It's an especially interesting lake to boat on because of a long, north-south orientation, an irregular shoreline and the presence of islands at the northern end. Although motorboat wakes are a problem, the northern end of Candlewood is quiet enough for canoeing, especially if you stay near shore and explore all the little nooks and crannies. One launch is located on Rte. 39 about midway up the west side of the lake just south of the causeway that separates Candlewood from Squantz Pond. A second launch is at the southern end of the lake on Forty Acres Mountain Rd. in Danbury. A launch fee is charged in summer at both locations. For rental craft, try **Echo Bay Marina (227 Candlewood Lake Rd., Brookfield, 06804; 203-775-7077), Gerard's Marina (120 Old Town Park Rd., New Milford, 06776; 860-354-3929)** and **Pocono Marina (16 Forty Acre Mountain Rd., Brookfield, 06804; 203-790-1919),** all of which are on the opposite side of the lake in towns covered in the **New Milford** chapter. For boater services on the west side of the lake, head for **Chatterton Marina** at **5 Shore Dr., New Fairfield; (203) 746-9138.** One seasonal motel **(Candlewood Inn, 506 Candlewood**

Lake Rd., Brookfield, 06804; 203-775-4517) offers guests dockage.

Pierrepont Lake
This secluded, 45-acre lake in Seth Low Pierrepont State Park is a picturesque spot for launching a canoe or other car-top boat. Portaging is kept to a minimum since you can park at waterside, and if you are in the mood for a hike after your paddle, the park's moderately sized trail system is only steps away. The entrance is not especially well marked. Look for the dirt pullout on the east side of Barlow Mountain Rd. in Ridgefield just north of the sharp turn it takes at North St.

Fishing

Bridgeport Hydraulic Co. Reservoirs
Four of the prettiest bodies of water in southwestern Connecticut, including alpine Saugatuck Reservoir shared by Weston and Redding, are private water supplies open for fishing to members of the public who obtain a special permit from the owner, **Bridgeport Hydraulic Co. (BHC).** Some town halls, some tackle shops (BHC can provide a list) and all BHC offices carry permits. For more information contact BHC at **(203) 336-7788.**

Candlewood Lake
Fairly deep, Candlewood Lake is a drowned valley created when the Rocky River was dammed for power generation purposes. Trout, largemouth bass, yellow perch and catfish are all found here. Fishing is best from a boat; the shoreline is almost entirely privately owned. There is minimal shore access at the causeway midway up the west side that separates the lake from Squantz Pond. All the caveats given for Lake Lillinonah in the **New Milford** chapter also apply at Candlewood, especially as regards bass tournaments, but there are no consumption advisories in effect.

Squantz Pond
Trout, largemouth bass and walleye are all for the taking in Squantz Pond, where there's a boat launch and excellent shore access in the state forest land on the western side. A parking fee is charged in summer. For directions

and more information, see the listing under Major Attractions.

Other Lakes
Two shallow lakes with good largemouth bass populations are **Mamanasco Lake** in Ridgefield and **Pierrepont Lake** in Seth Low Pierrepont State Park. Internal combustion engines are prohibited at the former, and only nonmotorized boats are allowed at the latter. Mamanasco is best fished from a boat because of private ownership of the shore, but Pierrepont Lake is surrounded by state park land that provides good access for shore fishing.

Golf

Richter Park
Rated one of the top 25 public golf courses in the country by *Golf Digest* and lauded by *Connecticut* magazine for its grooming and the "bristling efficiency" with which it is run, Richter Park is definitely a golf course worthy of being a destination. Some stats: 18 holes, par 72, 6,307 yards. The main problem is getting a tee time, which can only be done in person. Play is restricted to residents until 2:00 P.M. on weekends and 10:00 A.M. on weekdays. Danbury residents may sign up for weekday tee times at 7:00 A.M. and nonresidents at 8:00 A.M. Weekend tee times for residents and nonresident season pass holders are determined by a Thu. 6:00 A.M. lottery. On weekends, nonresidents can sign up for afternoon tee times beginning at 11:00 A.M. Be prepared for hefty fees. It offers a full range of rentals plus a putting green, lessons, showers and tennis courts. After your game, enjoy a meal at the excellent full-service restaurant on-site. **100 Aunt Hack Rd., Danbury, 06811; (203) 792-2551.** For more information on the park as a whole, see the listing under Major Attractions.

Whitney Farms Golf Course
Considered one of the best golf courses in Connecticut, Whitney Farms tends to get crowded and slow (in an effort to speed up play, use of motorized carts is mandatory and the cost is included into the greens fee), but getting a tee time should be easier than at Richter. Regard-

less of your residency, call at 8:00 A.M. Thu. for weekend tee times, one week ahead for weekday tee times. Whitney Farms is an 18-hole, par 72, 6,262-yard course known for challenging water hazards on nearly every hole. Facilities include practice areas for driving, chipping and putting, lockers, showers, lessons and a full-service restaurant, but they do not rent clubs. **175 Shelton Rd. (Rte. 110), Monroe, 06468; (203) 268-0707.**

Hiking

Between Danbury and the Merritt Pkwy. far to the south, numerous preserves and zoning regulations discourage a high population density. There is stunning beauty to be found here and a couple of wonderful guides to help you find it. The *Newtown Trails Book* is a collection of trail maps done in the style of the *Connecticut Walk Book*. The maps show the route of trails in the town on land owned by the state, the local land trust (the oldest in Connecticut) and private parties. The book is available for $15 from the **Cyrenius H. Booth Library, 25 Main St., Newtown, 06470; (203) 426-4533.**

The *Book of Trails* serves the same purpose for trails in Redding, including the land trust portions of the Saugatuck Valley Trails described below and Devil's Den Preserve in neighboring Weston. It's available for $10 from the office of the **Redding town clerk** at **P.O. Box 1028, Redding, 06875; (203) 938-2377.**

In addition to the listings below, also see those for **Richter Park** and **Squantz Pond State Park** under Major Attractions, plus **Collis P. Huntington State Park** under Biking. For information on other open spaces that overlap towns in this area, see the **Norwalk** chapter.

Bear Mountain Reservation
The trails at Bear Mountain traverse hemlock and deciduous forest and open fields buzzing with wildlife and eventually descend to the western shore of Candlewood Lake. A map is posted at the entrance. Follow the signs for Bear Mtn. Reservation/JFK Hiking Trails from the intersection of Bear Mountain Rd. and Rte. 37 in Danbury. For more information call the **Danbury Parks and Recreation Dept.** at **(203) 797-4632.**

Paugussett State Forest
Divided into two portions generally referred to as the upper and lower or north and south sections, heavily wooded Paugussett State Forest lies on the banks of the Housatonic River. There are overlooks of the river at occasional points on the trails. At Paugussett North, look for a landmark oak tree at the crest of a hill on the blue-blazed Lillinonah Trail. Its trunk somehow grew to form a donut, with a hole right through the middle. A small box tacked to the tree usually contains a logbook where hikers are invited to share thoughts and poems. At Paugussett South, the blue-blazed Zoar Trail makes a 6.5-mile loop, but some connectors make it possible to follow a shorter route. Both trails are mapped in the *Connecticut Walk Book* and the *Newtown Trails Book*. The entrance to Paugussett North is on Hanover Rd. in Newtown. Look for a dirt pullout just south of the state boat launch opposite Pond Brook Rd. Paugussett South can be accessed from Great Quarter Rd. and Stone Bridge Rd. off Rte. 34 in Newtown.

Saugatuck Valley Trails
The Bridgeport Hydraulic Co. (BHC), The Nature Conservancy, Redding Land Trust and Aspectuck Land Trust together maintain a 40-mile system of interconnected trails to the west and northwest of Saugatuck Reservoir that are collectively known as the Saugatuck Valley Trails. A great variety of terrain is packed into a small area here. Saugatuck Falls Natural Area alone contains a swift-running river, a waterfall, hemlock forest on rolling mountains and fields that are purposely mowed to halt forest succession.

You can pick up the trails from many points along Rte. 53, which hugs the western shoreline of the reservoir, but you must have a BHC trail map with you (the map serves as your permit) when on any BHC portion of the system. To get a free copy by mail call **BHC** at **(203) 336-7788.** This map is indispensable regardless of which portion of the trail system you hike on, since it shows all the trails and also pinpoints parking areas.

The best access point for Saugatuck Falls is at the turnout opposite John Read Middle

School on Rte. 53 several miles south of the Rte. 53/Rte. 302 intersection in Bethel; traveling south, the school will be on your left and the turnout on your right.

Seth Low Pierrepont State Park

This small but lovely state park is extremely convenient to the center of Ridgefield. The start of the trail follows the shore of Pierrepont Lake, a good spot for canoeing and fishing, then passes through marsh and forest, with a couple of hilltop overlooks. Follow the white blazes from the entrance to a kiosk where a map of the trail system is posted. The entrance is on Barlow Mountain Rd. just north of the sharp turn it takes at North St. For more information call **(203) 797-4165.**

Tarrywile Park

Tarrywile Park is exceptional for its proximity to downtown Danbury. Seven miles of trails meander through woodland, fields and along ponds. A map is posted at the upper parking lot. The mansion on the property is a community center offering story hours for children, orienteering classes and other programs throughout the year; call for a schedule. The grounds are open dawn–dusk daily, but rest rooms are only available during mansion hours, Mon.–Fri., 8:30 A.M.–4:30 P.M. Located on **Southern Blvd., Danbury, 06810; (203) 744-3130.**

Williams Park

Williams Park is a 200-acre tract with 5 miles of trails through mixed woodland, wetland and meadow, including the highest point in Brookfield, from which there are good views. The park is tucked away off Rte. 25 just west of Rte. 133 in Brookfield. The entrance is opposite the public library. For a map or more information call the **Brookfield Parks and Recreation Dept.** at **(203) 775-7321.**

Horseback Riding

Meadowbrook Farms can take parties of up to six people (minimum age: 6) horseback riding on a wooded trail system in a pretty, rural section of Newtown. A fee of $20 per person per hour includes equipment (they ride Western) and a guide. The season starts in spring

and lasts as late as the weather permits. Reservations required. **34 Meadowbrook Rd., Newtown, 06470; (203) 270-0906.**

Ice Skating

Public skating hours are held regularly at **Ridgefield Skating Center (111 Prospect Ridge Rd., Ridgefield; 203-438-5277),** which is open from late autumn through Mar. There are no skate rentals. Call for a schedule.

In the Air

Western Connecticut has some lovely scenery, such as Candlewood Lake and the Housatonic River Valley, that lends itself to being viewed from the air, and fall foliage is even more beautiful when seen massed below. **Curtiss Air (203-798-7565)** and **ProntoAire (203-748-0890)** are two operators offering scenic rides in four-seater aircraft year-round out of Danbury's municipal airport. Fares can be as low as $30 for a short trip in the local area to a few hundred dollars for flights down to the Statue of Liberty, the Hudson River Valley or Long Island Sound.

Hot-air ballooning is another option. **Balloon Hollow, Inc. (203-426-4250)** gives early morning and late afternoon rides lasting one to one and a half hours for about $175 per person.

Skiing and Snowmobiling

There are no commercial skiing areas in this region, but there is lots of good free cross-country terrain if you've got your own equipment. Try **Richter Park** (described under Major Attractions), where skiing is allowed on the golf course when snow cover is sufficient to prevent damage to the greens. **Tarrywile Park, Williams Park** and **Bear Mountain Reservation** (all described under Hiking) have a mix of open fields and woodland trails with both gentle and steep grades. **Collis P. Huntington State Park** (described under Biking) has numerous broad wooded roads and more of a wilderness atmosphere.

404

When snow cover is at least 6 inches, several of the trails through **Squantz Pond State Park** (described under Major Attractions) and neighboring **Pootatuck State Forest** are designated for snowmobile use. A straight section of trail here leads to two loops above the pond following the contours of three small peaks. Sign in at the logbook and follow the blazes.

Swimming

The primary public beach in the area is at **Squantz Pond State Park,** described under Major Attractions. Because it's a state park, there are no residency requirements, and in addition to the beach, the park offers many other recreational opportunities.

A second option extremely convenient to downtown Danbury and I-84 exit 6 is the town beach on **Candlewood Lake.** It's open and guarded 9:00 A.M.–dusk daily, Memorial Day–Labor Day, but it is restricted to town residents only on weekends and holidays. The resident admission fee is $7 for an adult season pass; resident children are free. Nonresidents must pay $6 per adult, $3 per child. There are rest rooms, changing rooms and a concession stand, but no facilities for activities other than swimming. The beach is located on Hayestown Rd. in Danbury at the very southern tip of the lake. For more information call **Danbury Parks and Recreation Dept.** at **(203) 797-4632.**

There is also a beach on **Great Hollow Lake** at Wolfe Park in Monroe, one of the most well rounded municipal recreation facilities around. In addition to the beach and a pool there are playgrounds, playing fields, hiking trails, tennis and basketball courts and several picnic areas. Nonresidents will pay a premium for the privilege, however; call for parking and beach access rates. The entrance is at Cross Hill and Cutler's Farm Rds. For more information call the **Monroe Parks and Recreation Dept.** at **(203) 452-5416.**

Seeing and Doing

Antiquing

Recently, a former fire hose factory in the Sandy Hook part of Newtown was "recycled" into a multidealer antiques store and offices. The **Rocky Glen Mill** showroom occupies about 7,000 square feet on one floor, where about 35 dealers are represented. You'll find everything from furniture to small decorative items, crystal and china, artwork, textiles and even the occasional garden ornament. There is also a small café at the rear where you can get bagels, croissants, sandwiches and specialty coffees. Hours: 10:00 A.M.–5:00 P.M. daily. Café hours: Mon.–Fri., 8:30 A.M.–4:00 P.M.; Sat.–Sun., 10:00 A.M.–4:00 P.M. **75 Glen Rd., Sandy Hook, 06482; (203) 426-4469.**

Art Galleries

Art is a theme in Ridgefield, where you'll find the Aldrich Museum of Contemporary Art (described under Major Attractions) and the Weir Farm (shared with the neighboring town of Wilton and described in the **Norwalk** chapter). For an art-filled day trip combine a visit to these two institutions with stops at a couple of commercial galleries. **Branchville Soho Gallery (14 West Branchville Rd. at the railroad station, Ridgefield; 203-544-8636)** features both regional and international talent producing work ranging from abstract art to photorealism. Hours: Thu.–Sat., 1:00 P.M.–4:00 P.M. (Sat. until 5:00); closed Jan., Feb., July & Aug.

The utilitarian but well-lit gallery of the **Ridgefield Guild of Artists (Halpin Ln., Ridgefield; 203-438-8863)** showcases the work of mostly local artists. The Guild also offers classes and hangs a juried show once a year. To get to Halpin Ln., come down Prospect Ridge from Prospect St. to avoid problems with a one-way system.

Children and Families

If you'd like to involve your child in a program designed to increase environmental awareness or foster an interest in science, history or the arts, contact **The Discovery Center (P.O. Box 926, Ridgefield, 06877; 203-438-1063)** and **New Pond Farm Education Center (101 Marchant Rd. at Umpawaug Rd., West Redding, 06896; 203-938-2117).** The former has no actual *center*—its programs take place at sites throughout the area—but

New Pond Farm does feature hiking trails and a working farm. Most activities are organized in advance; call for a schedule and ask about New Pond Farm's annual May Fair, Native American Celebration and Apple Harvest.

A seasonal activity with an arts twist is the weekend theater series of fairy tale interpretations and other children's programming offered by community theater **Musicals at Richter** on selected summer Sat. Admission is only $5. See the Performing Arts section for more.

At first glance, **Mother Earth Gallery (806 Federal Rd., Brookfield, 06804; 203-775-6272)** appears to be just a nice shop selling gems, crystals, fossils and other natural wonders. But behind a plain door at the rear is a room designed to look like a mine in which small children get a chance to prospect for gems in sandpits. For the sake of atmosphere, the room is unlit and kids are outfitted with helmets and headlamps. At $10 per child for 5–10 minutes of mining it's not cheap, but miners get to keep everything they find.

The robotic animals at **Stew Leonard's (99 Federal Rd., Brookfield, 06804; 203-790-8030)** always delight young children. See the **Norwalk** chapter for the scoop on this offbeat grocery store cum amusement park with two locations. And finally, negotiations are ongoing for the construction of a major children's museum in a stunning 1896 structure known as Hearthstone castle in Danbury. Call **Tarrywile Park** at **(203) 744-3130** for more information.

Crafts Centers

Founded in 1954, the **Brookfield Craft Center** offers its students the opportunity to learn fun, useful and expressive skills and is very much at the nexus of artisanship in the Danbury area. The school and gallery are housed in a 1790s gristmill and a few outlying buildings perched above a small waterfall on the Still River. Some of the finest student work is on display and for sale in the center's gallery, open daily. Even if you're not spending a lot of time in the area, don't discount the possibility of taking a class—some are only one day in length, and the instructors are top-notch. Gallery hours: Mon.–Sat., 9:00 A.M.–

5:00 P.M.; Sun., noon–5:00 P.M. Located on **Rte. 25 just east of Rte. 7, Brookfield, 06804; (203) 775-4526.** Parking is a little farther down the road on the opposite side.

Equestrian Events

The public is invited to view the **2nd Company Governor's Horse Guard** as it does equestrian drills Wed. at 7:00 P.M., mid-Apr.–Oct., & Sun. at 8:00 A.M. the rest of the year. See the listing for the 1st Company Governor's Horse Guard in the **Farmington** chapter for a description of their maneuvers. It's free, and it takes place on the grounds of Fairfield Hills Hospital in Newtown. From Mile Hill Rd. through the Fairfield Hills complex, follow the signs that say "To GHG." For more information call **(203) 426-9046.**

Museums and Historic Sites

In addition to the listings below, also consider a visit to the **Scott-Fanton Museum (43 Main St., Danbury, 06810; 203-743-5200),** a pair of 18th-century buildings with a hodgepodge of contents. The most interesting displays are the Dodd Hat Shop, which honors the critical role the hat industry played in the development of Danbury, and the Revolutionary War exhibits. The museum is open Wed.–Sun., 2:00 P.M.–5:00 P.M., with admission by donation.

Affiliated with Scott-Fanton is the **Charles Ives Birthplace,** a restored 1780s home at **5 Mountainville Rd.** where Danbury's musical native son was born. Ives was a prolific composer of the early 20th century known for a sometimes dissonant, experimental style that gave expression to small-town American life. Tours are by appointment; call the Scott-Fanton Museum for details.

The **Brookfield Historical Society Museum (corner of Rtes. 133 and 25 in Brookfield Center; 203-740-8140)** maintains a gallery for its exhibits of local artifacts, and another local history museum is the **Matthew Curtiss House (44 Main St., Newtown; 203-426-5937),** one of a number of historic homes to grace Newtown's main street. Highlights of this 1750 saltbox include a gargantuan fireplace and period furniture and utensils. Call for hours at both sites.

Military buffs will not want to miss the **Military Museum of Southern New England (125 Park Ave., Danbury, 06810; 203-790-9277),** where one of the strengths is a special collection of U.S. World War II tank destroyer units. The displays incorporate vehicles, weapons, clothing and documentation. Hours are Tue.–Sat., 10:00 A.M.–5:00 P.M.; Sun., noon–5:00 P.M., and admission is $4 for adults, $2 for seniors, active duty military and children 6–18.

Danbury Railway Museum
Danbury's beautifully restored 1903 train station became the site of a new museum in 1996. The exhibits rotate, so you can come back every few months and see something different. One focus of the displays is the New York, New Haven and Hartford line that once ran through here before being absorbed into the Pennsylvania Central around 1969 and subsequently into Metro-North, the commuter rail line whose new Danbury station is about three blocks away. The museum recently acquired several cutaways of passenger cars, and every year around the Christmas holiday, exhibit space is given over to a model train display that is a big attraction for children as well as collectors. Out in the railyard there are several cars and a locomotive to explore. The museum charters Metro-North trains for special excursions to the Hudson Valley for sightseeing and New York City for a day of shopping in early Dec. Also in Dec. kids can take a short ride with Santa. Admission: $2 adults, $1 children 3–15. Hours: Tue.–Sun., 10:00 A.M.–4:00 P.M., Apr.–Dec.; open Thu.–Sun. only Jan.–Mar. **120 White St. (at Patriot Dr.), Danbury, 06810; (203) 778-8337.**

Keeler Tavern Museum
For 130 years one of Ridgefield's original houses was the site of an inn and tavern kept by the Keeler family. Built on one of the first subdivisions of land in Ridgefield when the town was settled in 1708, the house grew and was altered many times over the years; an intriguing series of drawings in the dining room shows how the building might have appeared

at different stages. There are many artifacts here, but one particular must-see is the intact cannonball fired during the Battle of Ridgefield in 1777, which still lies imbedded in a structural post of the house. A large formal garden out back, walled and paved in brick, provides a nice spot to relax after the tour. The museum is the site of many special programs, concerts and dinners throughout the year, including a series of Christmas luncheons in early Dec.; call for details. Open Wed., Sat. & Sun., 1:00 P.M.–4:00 P.M., & by appointment; last tour starts 3:20 P.M.; closed Jan. **132 Main St., Ridgefield, 06877; (203) 438-5485.**

Putnam Memorial State Park
During the severe winter of 1778–1779, Patriot troops led by Maj. Gen. Israel Putnam were stationed here in readiness for a possible sequel to the 1777 British raid on Danbury. No fighting ever occurred, but the site came to be known as Connecticut's Valley Forge for the awful conditions the soldiers endured. The park features several monuments commemorating the events of those years, trails, a small museum exhibiting Revolutionary War artifacts (open Sat., Sun. & holidays, 10:00 A.M.–5:00 P.M., Apr. 15–Oct. 15) and a lovely picnic area by a small lake. The park is split in two by Rte. 58. The entrance to the western side where the monuments are is off Rte. 107 just south of Rte. 58. The entrance to the east side with the picnic area is on Rte. 58 just north of Rte. 107. Two massive stone pillars in which the words "Putnam Park" are carved mark the spot, which otherwise looks like a private estate. Park hours: 8:00 A.M.–sunset daily, year-round. Phone: **(203) 797-4165.**

Nightlife

Downtown Danbury after dark seems pretty quiet, but actually the town has one of the most active entertainment districts in the state. It seems hidden because most of it is centered around Ives St. one block away from the main drag. **Tuxedo Junction (2 Ives St.; 203-748-2561)** is a rock 'n' roll/dance club that can handle moderately big bands. Three major restaurants—Ciao, Two Steps and

Mimi's—are all located here as well. Half a block away you'll find **Seattle Espresso (262 Main St.; 203-748-6618)**, which encourages you to stay a while by providing comfy chairs, games and lots of battered reading material. It also has once-a-month receptions for the artists whose work graces the walls. If you love smoky, dim neighborhood bars, give **Hat City Ale House (253 Main St.; 203-790-4287)** a try. Microbrew beers, cigars and high-backed booths where you could get lost in the dark are their specialty. And keep an eye on the **Palace Theater** at **173 Main St.** A former movie house, it will hopefully reopen in the near future as a performing arts complex.

When Danbury Fair Mall opened in the mid-1980s, it gave rise to a second shopping district west of the downtown, and that's where you'll find **Boston Billiards (20 Backus Ave., Danbury; 203-798-7665)**. This upscale billiards hall gives the impression of a private club. On a Fri. or Sat. night the wait for tables can stretch into hours (it's first-come, first-served), so come early or on a slower night. If you arrive late, kick back and enjoy a long, tall one at the bar overlooking the playing floor and a wall-sized TV monitor on which you can watch the evening's sports offerings. The slender but adequate menu consists of appetizers and a couple of dishes that could make a meal.

Neighboring Bethel has a few hot spots. **Bethel Cinema (269 Greenwood Ave.; 203-778-2100)** is one of the best movie houses in Connecticut for foreign and art films. It also shows first-run movies of merit, and it has an adjoining restaurant so you can make a night of it all in one place. Just down the street you'll find **Dr. Java's (114 Greenwood Ave.; 203-791-8121)**, a small, casual coffeehouse offering poetry readings on Wed. and jazz, folk and blues by small bands and solo performers on Sat. Light food and desserts are available.

For a small-town moviegoing experience at an unbeatable price, check out **Edmond Town Hall Theater (45 Main St., Newtown; 203-426-2475)**. It's an auditorium locally famous for its first- and second-run $2 movies. Snacks are available, but it's traditional to visit the quaint red Newtown General Store next door

for ice cream or simple eats beforehand. Also be sure to check out the village's landmark flagpole a half-block away, popular with photographers due to its massive size.

Finally, one exceptional entertainment option is located in neighboring New York state, such a short hop over the border (and so worth the trip) that it must be included. The **Towne Crier Cafe (62 Rte. 22, Pawling, New York 12564; 914-855-1300)** offers unparalleled entertainment from the sort of artists it's just plain hard to find playing live in these parts: blues and Cajun bands, acoustic singer/songwriters, fusion guitarists, traditional folk acts and a regular line of groups from Britain. They also have an annual New Year's Eve party with a whole roster of musical and comedy acts. Dinner is served a couple of hours before performance time, and the food is as good as the entertainment. Performances are on Fri., Sat. & Sun. nights only, with an open mike night on Wed. & microbrew nights on Wed. & Thu. Shows begin at 8:00 or 9:00 P.M. Dinner is served Wed.–Sun., and lunch/brunch is available on weekends. Call for directions.

Performing Arts

Community theater groups are very active in this part of Connecticut and perfectly capable of delivering inspiring performances. Runs are typically short, and performances are given anywhere from two to four nights per week with occasional matinees. Tickets are a bargain at $10–$15. Most local theaters take a break during the winter, but call each one individually to check on what's coming up. The **Country Players of Brookfield** perform at **Brookfield Playhouse, Rt. 25** (enter through the public library driveway roughly across from Long Meadow Rd.), **Brookfield, 06804; (203) 775-0023**. You can reach the **Town Players of Newtown** at **(203) 270-9144**. Their stage is at the **Little Theatre, Orchard Hill Rd., Newtown, 06470**. A renovated barn is the venue for 30-plus-year-old **Ridgefield Workshop for the Performing Arts (37 Halpin Ln., Ridgefield, 06877; 203-431-9850)**, which also offers acting classes in summer and fall. As part of its regular season, it does an annual murder mystery dinner around Halloween and a special Christmas program.

Danbury Music Center

The primary mission of this umbrella organization for the Danbury Symphony Orchestra, Danbury Community Orchestra and Danbury Concert Chorus is to give local musicians a chance to perform and for others to enjoy their music. It has a full season of over 20 performances Sept.–May, including annual productions of *The Nutcracker*, Handel's *Messiah* and a young people's concert. Some concerts take place at a small venue in the Center, but the bigger shows are held in the Danbury High School auditorium or local churches. With the exception of *The Nutcracker*, all concerts are free. **256 Main St., Danbury, 06810; (203) 748-1716.**

Danbury Theatre Company

Formerly known as Danbury Actors Repertory Theatre, or D'ART, this professional, non-Equity company stages shows that run the gamut of theatrical productions but makes a special attempt to present challenging contemporary drama. The setting is the intimate second floor of Danbury's St. James Episcopal Church, where conventional auditorium seating accommodates about 150 people. The company produces about five shows annually in a season that runs Sept.–June. Performances are at 8:00 P.M. on Fri. & Sat., 7:30 P.M. on Sun. Ticket prices are $13–$15. **25 West St., Danbury, 06810.** To make reservations or for more information call **(203) 790-1161.**

Gateway's Candlewood Playhouse

The in-house company of Candlewood Playhouse has presented its own productions of Broadway-quality theater and major musicals for over 30 years, presenting about one show per month May–Dec. The house seats 600 with ticket prices in the $19–$30 range and discounts for matinees. Evening performances are Tue.–Thu. at 8:00 P.M., Fri. at 8:30 P.M., Sat. at 5:00 P.M. & 9:00 P.M. & Sun. at 7:00 P.M. Matinees are given at 2:00 P.M. on Sun., Wed. & occasionally Thu. A restaurant on the premises serves a preshow dinner buffet; dinner and show packages are available. **25 Rt. 39 (just east of Rt. 37), New Fairfield, 06812; (203) 746-4441.**

Ives Center

The season for this concert venue, located in a 39-acre, parklike setting on the grounds of Western Connecticut State University, runs from the end of June through Labor Day, during which about seven ticketed and four free events are presented. Two of the most popular events in recent years have been the Jazz Festival and the Fourth of July Pops and Fireworks concert. The stage is a huge, open-sided gazebo by a pond with a sloping field in front that can accommodate an audience of 5,500 people. Reserved chair seating is available, or you may bring a blanket or lawn chair, a cooler and a picnic. The Ives Center is off University Blvd. off Mill Plain Rd. in Danbury. For reservations or more information call **(203) 837-9226.** Tickets are also available through **Ticketmaster** at **(203) 744-8100.**

Musicals at Richter

This community theater stages three musicals each summer in an outdoor setting next door to Richter Golf Course. The audience is encouraged to bring lawn chairs, blankets, picnic dinners and coolers, although food is for sale and rental chairs are available. Its season runs June–Aug. Performances take place Thu.–Sun. at 8:30 P.M. with no Sun. performance the last week of each show. Tickets are in the $10–$15 range. It even offers a golf cart shuttle service to and from the parking lot if you're loaded down with too much stuff. **Richter House** is at **100 Aunt Hack Rd., Danbury, 06811.** Park in the Cafe on the Green lot. For more information or ticket sales call **(203) 748-6873.**

Spinning Wheel Inn & Dinner Theatre

With a unique twist on conventional dinner theater, Spinning Wheel does four-act shows with a break between each act, during which you're served one course of a four-course meal (soup, salad, entrée of your choice and dessert). Because of their unique format, all their shows are original works written for Spinning Wheel. The food can match the theme of the show, so inquire for details on the menu. They only do two or three shows per year. One, with a Christmas theme involving caroling, comedy and drama, is always staged between

409

Thanksgiving and New Year's. The other two are in spring and late fall into winter. Ticket prices ($35–$55) include the show, the meal, taxes and gratuity. **Rte. 58, Redding Ridge, 06876; (203) 938-3823** or **(203) 938-2511.**

Scenic Drives

The best routes for scenic drives are much the same as those recommended for bicycle touring above. All the back roads of Newtown, Redding, Ridgefield and Monroe are mostly pretty wooded lanes with the occasional farm, park or lake for variety. In a car the loop around Candlewood Lake also becomes practical. From the center of Danbury head north on Rte. 37, then east on Rte. 39. After a short while you'll start to have glimpses of the lake through the trees as you skim the shore. You'll go right past the entrance to Squantz Pond State Park, an ideal spot to stop for a picnic or a hike. Continuing up Rte. 39 you'll cut away from Candlewood Lake but you'll have views of Squantz Pond for a short distance. Then it's just a peaceful wooded road all the way to and through Sherman center, at which point you'll head east on Rte. 37. On the next stretch of road, you'll find a beautiful old farm at the crest of a hill with great northwestern views. Berries are available here in season. Continue on to Rte. 7 and go south. A couple of miles down look for Candlewood Lake Rd. North on your right. At this point you'll start to head down the quiet east side of the lake. Follow this street to Sullivan Rd., go right and pick up Candlewood Lake Rd. South. You'll have a long stretch of great lake views most of the way to Federal Rd. in Brookfield.

Seasonal Favorites

Late Feb. and Mar. is the time for maple sugaring. The process of turning maple sap into syrup and sugar can be seen at **McLaughlin Vineyard,** described under Wineries. While you're there, do some wine tasting.

In autumn **Blue Jay Orchard (125 Plumtrees Rd., Bethel, 06801; 203-748-0119)** is the essence of New England: hayrides, apples, pumpkins in the field, a petting zoo, made-on-the-premises pies, honey and much more. Plan to spend several hours.

Shopping

Shopping in this area is best enjoyed as part of a scenic drive in which the travel between pockets of unique shops is as enjoyable as the shopping itself. There's a small cluster of neat stores near the **Brookfield Craft Center (Rte. 25 just east of Rte. 7, Brookfield, 06804 ; 203-775-4526),** which is one of the best places around to get beautiful, functional, maybe even one-of-a-kind handmade items. Before or after you shop you must wander the small but exquisite grounds. See the listing under Crafts Centers for details.

Ridgefield is probably the single best shopping destination around. It's extremely picturesque, chock-full of antiques stores and other little shops and the scale of the town is small enough that you can probably see everything in an afternoon. There's a slew of excellent restaurants here as well, making it a good place to park the car for the day and hoof it. Don't miss **Hay Day Market (21 Governor St.; 203-431-4400),** a specialty grocer with deli foods, extensive cheese and produce sections, gifts and flowers, plus a wine and liquor shop next door.

If it's large-scale shopping you're after, **Danbury Fair Mall (off I-84 exit 3; 203-743-3247)** is the place to go. A cut above the average mall, it is very attractive, airy and bright, and it has good-quality anchor stores. If traveling with kids, make sure to treat them to a ride on the magnificent carousel at the rear of the food court.

Wineries

DiGrazia Vineyard

This family-run and self-proclaimed "boutique" winery, which began as the avocation of medical doctor Paul DiGrazia, is a good place to pick up a memorable bottle of wine with a truly northeastern flavor. In addition to an array of conventional wines, several of the winery's 20 or so offerings are made from characteristically New England ingredients such as apples and sugar pumpkins. Wine lovers who are sensitive to sulfites will be interested in DiGrazia's sulfite-free vintages; many others are low in sulfites. You can have a tasting, browse the shop and tour the fermentation tanks and the bottling operation in 30–45 minutes. **131 Tower Rd., Brookfield, 06804; (203) 775-1616.**

McLaughlin Vineyard

The tasting room at this 20-acre winery is rather plain and unadorned, but the view from the terrace outside is quite soothing: rows of trained grapevines marching over gentle hills and a broad lawn lined with large shade trees. McLaughlin specializes in dry table wines meant to be paired with food. It produces both whites and reds from seyval blanc, chardonnay, merlot and other grapes, about 60% of which are estate-grown. Tours take 45 minutes to one hour and are given at 2:00 P.M. every day, June–Christmas, Sat. & Sun. at 2:00 P.M. in other months & by appointment. Tasting room hours: 11:00 A.M.–5:00 P.M. daily, year-round.

Several times a summer, the lawn at the vineyard is pressed into use for a series of evening jazz concerts that pull a good crowd. The music begins at 6:30 P.M. and ends by 9:00 P.M. to make it possible for families to attend. Admission to concerts is $12 per car. **Alberts Hill Rd., Newtown, 06470; (203) 426-1533.**

Where to Stay

Bed & Breakfasts

Far View Manor—$$$$

From the front door of this spacious, hilltop B&B you can see miles and miles—hence the name. Since Far View has only one guest room, you can be assured of total privacy during your stay. Half of the house—a large bedroom with king bed, an enormous great room with a remarkable stone fireplace and a private bath with tub—is dedicated to guests. A Continental breakfast is included. **803 N. Salem Rd., Ridgefield, 06877; (203) 438-4753.**

Hotels, Motels & Inns

The listings below represent an across-the-board sample of what's available in this area. Other choices include **The Elms Inn (500 Main St., Ridgefield, 06877; 203-438-2541),** conveniently located just half a block from Ridgefield's shops and restaurants; **Ridgefield Motor Inn (296 Ethan Allen Highway [Rte. 7], Ridgefield, 06877; 203-438-3781),** offering moderately low-priced accommodations that are clean and in good condition and an Indian restaurant next door and the **Berkshire and Stony Hill Best Westerns,** located respectively at **11 and 46 Stony Hill Rd. [Rte. 6], Bethel, 06801; 800-528-1234.** Run by the same family, both of these establishments are moderately priced and easily reached from I-84. If you're traveling on a tight budget, the **Days Inn (78 Federal Rd., Danbury, 06810; 203-743-6701)** is the least expensive of all the chain hotels in the area, yet the rooms are still quite satisfactory. For additional suggestions, contact the **Housatonic Valley Tourism District** at **(800) 841-4488** or **(203) 743-0546.**

Danbury Hilton & Towers—$$$$

The most luxurious hotel in the Danbury area caters to business travelers, so inquire about lower weekend rates. Standard rooms are quite nice, but there are also concierge floors on which rooms come with bathrobes, fax machines, Continental breakfast, hospitality food in a private lounge and other extras. A café, restaurant, lounge and exercise facilities are all on-site, and the hotel offers room service. Located off I-84 at exit 2. **18 Old Ridgebury Rd., Danbury, 06810; (800) 445-8667** or **(203) 794-0600.**

Ethan Allen Inn—$$$$

This large hotel serves as a conference center for the Ethan Allen headquarters right next door, so it's got Ethan Allen furnishings, many different room arrangements including suites and lots of facilities, such as a sauna and exercise room, outdoor pool, racquetball court and a full-service restaurant. Valet dry cleaning and an in-house laundry are available.

411

Children 18 and under stay free. **Mill Plain Rd. (off I-84 exit 4), Danbury, 06810; (800) 742-1776** or **(203) 744-1776.**

Mary Hawley Inn—$$$$

This old Newtown institution, formerly called the Hawley Manor Inn, underwent a makeover in 1997 and now has three spacious, neutrally decorated inn rooms with large baths to offer travelers. See Where to Eat for information on the restaurant, which is just steps away. **19 Main St., Newtown, 06470; (203) 270-1876.**

West Lane Inn—$$$$

This stately 1849 home is close enough to the busy main drag of Ridgefield to be convenient, yet far enough removed from it to be quiet. It retains its Victorian character inside and out. All 20 rooms have queen four-poster beds, traditional furnishings, a private bath with tub, TV, telephone and voice mail. Laundry service is available, and a Continental breakfast is served on the veranda or in a formal dining room. Some rooms have working fireplaces for winter ambiance. **22 West Ln., Ridgefield, 06877; (203) 438-7323.**

Stonehenge—$$$ to $$$$

Set well back from the main road, Stonehenge is like a small resort property. A small number of rooms are divided between the main house and a couple of outlying cottages. Those in the main house are spacious, elegant and in perfect condition, with traditional furnishings, four-poster beds and private, attached bathrooms. The cottage rooms are smaller and more budget-friendly. A Continental breakfast is included. Located on **Stonehenge Rd. off Rte. 7, a mile or two south of Rte. 35, Ridgefield, 06877; (203) 438-6511.**

Twin Tree Inn—$$$

If this were a hotel instead of a motel and it had a brand name on it, you'd be paying twice the price. It doesn't even charge extra for cribs and roll-away beds. Everything here, inside and out, is very well kept up, and the rooms have the feel of a much higher priced establishment. The rooms in the rear are slightly larger and quieter and only a few dollars more than those in front, and they have a small outdoor seating area. The price also

includes a Continental breakfast. **1030 Federal Rd. (Rte. 7), Brookfield, 06804; (203) 775-0220.**

Camping

Mountain Lakes Camp—$

This county of Westchester, New York–owned tract of land overlapping Ridgefield, Connecticut, offers year-round camping. It has tent sites, cabins for 4–20 people (the largest have bathrooms), lean-to sites and a cottage with a kitchen, living room and wood stove. Activities include hiking, biking, rowboat and canoe rental and swimming, as well as ice skating and cross-country skiing in winter. Located on **Mountain Lakes Rd. off Hawley Rd., North Salem, NY; (914) 242-6309.**

Webb Mountain—$

Monroe is the only town in Connecticut to provide camping with no residency or group requirements. A small number of sites with a great deal of privacy are available Memorial Day to the end of Oct. Each one has a picnic table and fire pit and accommodates up to five people for $5 per night. Pit toilets are provided, and there's access to a blue-blazed trail for hiking. You must obtain the permit in person at Monroe town hall at 7 Fan Hill Rd. during the following hours: Mon.–Thu., 9:30 A.M.–4:30 P.M. The office is usually closed for lunch at midday, around 1:00–2:00 P.M. Call **(203) 452-5400** if you need directions.

Where to Eat

Danbury's ethnic diversity shows itself in the variety of foods available at area restaurants. **Bangkok (Nutmeg Square, Newtown Rd., Danbury, 06810; 203-791-0640)** is actually one of the best Thai restaurants in Connecticut despite its shopping mall location; **Sangeet (296 Rte. 7, Ridgefield; 203-894-1080)** serves Indian cuisine. At **Panda West (93 Mill Plain Rd., Danbury; 203-730-8888)** you can get excellent Chinese in a semiformal atmosphere, and **Sushi Yoshi (132 Federal Rd., Brookfield; 203-775-1985)** serves excellent Japanese food.

You can get wonderful Italian food throughout Connecticut, and this area is no exception. This list wouldn't be complete without mention of **Boccaccio's (4 Cotton Tail Rd., New Fairfield; 203-746-9900)**, where the wall murals suggest Italian scenes; **Mona Lisa (43 S. Main St., Newtown; 203-426-6685)**, where a glassed-in sunroom at the front of the dining room makes a cheery setting even after the sun has set; intimate **Nicola's (20 White St., Danbury; 203-778-2710)** in the Ives St. section of downtown Danbury; **George's Pizza Restaurant (One Dodgingtown Rd. [Rte. 302], Newtown; 203-426-2715)**, a tavern-like, family-run place serving much more than pizza, and **Mimi's (75 Main St., Danbury; 203-730-0200)**, a jumping downtown spot with a crowded, smoky bar in stark contrast to a quiet dining room where everything is served "family-style" in portions for two or more. Large portions of Italian and Greek specialties, low prices, a kid's menu and a hometown restaurant atmosphere make **Country Pizza (418 Main St., Monroe; 203-261-0223)** very suitable for family dining. With an equally informal setting, **1st & Last Cafe (2 Pembroke Rd. [Rte. 37], Danbury; 203-790-8662)** is well known for brick-oven pizza.

For good, solid American food, moderate prices and a family-friendly atmosphere, try **Olde Newtown Tavern (160 S. Main St. [Rte. 25], Newtown, 06470; 203-270-6300).** **Plain Jane's (208 Greenwood Ave., Bethel, 06801; 203-797-1515)** is tucked into a tiny strip mall but is worth a search if you're in the mood for pastas, salads and light chicken and fish dishes. And the newly refurbished **Mary Hawley Inn (19 Main St., Newtown, 06470; 203-270-1876)** has both a casual taproom and a dressy restaurant popular with an older crowd that serves traditional New England fare.

You can never know about too many breakfast and lunch places. **Sandy Hook Diner (98 Church Hill Rd., Sandy Hook; 203-270-2998)** serves breakfast and lunch only, also starting at 6:00 A.M., with some interesting specials on weekends. It's especially convenient if you're in town to visit the Rocky Glen Mill antiques showroom. **Leo's (271 S. Main St., Newtown; 203-426-6881)** serves some of the most elaborate breakfast dishes around, as well as some of the most unusual sandwiches at lunch. See the listing in the **Woodbury** chapter for details. Also try **My Place (Queen St. shopping center, corner of Queen St. and Church Hill Rd., Newtown; 203-270-7061)**, a hometown eatery that does breakfast, lunch and dinner every day of the week starting at 6:00 A.M.

The Inn at Ridgefield—$$$$

The Inn at Ridgefield, serving Continental cuisine, is one of the most formal dining options in the area. Dinner can be ordered à la carte or fixed price ($38 per person) for four courses. A pianist entertains on Fri. & Sat. nights. In summer you can enjoy outdoor dining on a side terrace. Lunch served Mon.–Sat., noon–2:00 P.M. Sun. brunch, noon–3:00 P.M. Dinner hours: Mon.–Thu., 6:00 P.M.–9:30 P.M.; Fri.–Sat. until 10:30 P.M.; Sun., 3:00 P.M.–8:00 P.M. **20 West Ln. (Rte. 35), Ridgefield, 06877; (203) 438-8282.**

Ondine—$$$$

Perhaps the most elegant, formal dining experience in Danbury, Ondine offers a fixed-price ($42) menu that features classic health-conscious French dishes and contemporary preparations. Dinner consists of five courses: appetizer, salad, soup, entrée and dessert, with a relatively large number of choices in each category. The wine list emphasizes French and American vintages. Rather than having a breakfast orientation, the Sun. brunch ($25) is like a lighter version of dinner. A jacket is required for gentlemen, but some are kept on hand if you are unprepared. Reservations recommended. Hours: Tue.–Sat., 5:30 P.M.–9:30 P.M.; Sun. brunch served noon–2:00 P.M. & dinner served 4:00 P.M.–8:00 P.M. **69 Pembroke Rd. (Rte. 37), Danbury, 06811; (203) 746-4900.**

Dolce Vita—$$$ to $$$$

All too easy to miss if you drive past too quickly, this is a lovely, intimate, white-tablecloth restaurant serving Northern Italian food. The interior is divided into several small dining rooms that make it feel very private. Dress nicely. Hours: Tue.–Sun., noon–10:00 P.M.

413

(11:00 P.M. on weekends). **52½ Pembroke Rd., New Fairfield, 06812; (203) 746-0037.**

The Elms Inn—$$$ to $$$$

This Ridgefield institution is building a solid reputation under new management. It's located in a sprawling old home whose central hall is painted with a modern folk art mural depicting the Battle of Ridgefield. An elegant, not-too-formal dining room is to one side; a woody, cool and dark tavern to the other. Both are warmed by firelight in winter. There's also a deck for summer dining. Lunch is served off an upscale tavern menu. At dinner a small menu of New American–style dishes is enhanced by an array of innovative side dishes. Hours: Wed.–Sun., 11:30 A.M. until 9:00 or 10:00 P.M. **500 Main St., Ridgefield, 06877; (203) 438-2541.**

Stonehenge—$$$ to $$$$

The high quality of the food and the atmosphere at Stonehenge (as well as the expense) make this restaurant a place to spend a special night out. It's one of the few restaurants where you can expect perfection from appetizer to dessert. The French menu features premium ingredients and a style of presentation that elicits as many ooh's and aah's as the taste. In addition to dinner, there is a $26 fixed-price Sun. brunch. Hours: Tue.–Fri., 6:00 P.M.–9:00 P.M.; Sun. brunch served 11:30 A.M.–2:30 P.M. & dinner 4:00 P.M.–8:00 P.M. Located on **Stonehenge Rd. off Rte. 7, a mile or two south of Rte. 35, Ridgefield, 06877; (203) 438-6511.**

Cafe on the Green—$$ to $$$$

This sleeper is actually one of the best all-around restaurants in Danbury. It's located at Richter Park next to the golf course, but this is no clubhouse. The large dining room is elegant and romantic after dark, the waiters are clad in tuxedos and there's outdoor seating in summer. Yet, because of the golfer crowd, it opens early with a full breakfast menu, and it serves both light fare and a dinner menu (Northern Italian and American with some tableside preparation) at lunch. Proper attire is neat casual during the day and dressy in the evening. Reservations recommended. Hours: 6:00 A.M.–10:00 P.M. (Fri.–Sat. until 11:00) daily. Call to confirm winter hours. **100 Aunt Hack Rd., Danbury, 06811; (203) 791-0369.**

Bentley's—$$$

Don't show up at this excellent Italian eatery without a reservation on a Fri. or Sat. night. Bentley's is small and popular. And once you've tried the food, you'll know why. Although the tables are so close that you feel like jumping in on your neighbors' conversations, if you're in an outgoing mood, you'll definitely enjoy the dining experience at Bentley's. Lunch served Tue.–Fri., 11:30 A.M.–2:30 P.M. Dinner hours: Sun.–Wed., 5:00 P.M.–9:00 P.M., & Thu.–Sat. until 10:00 P.M. **One Division St., Danbury, 06810; (203) 778-3637.**

Caputo's East Ridge Café—$$$

From the moment you bite into the grilled sweet peppers and bread that appear automatically on your table as an appetizer, you'll know Caputo's is going to deliver excellent Italian food. It also offers burgers and pizza at lunch, a few American entrées at dinner, an extensive wine and microbrew beer list and a fairly inexpensive à la carte brunch on both Sat. and Sun. Several small alcove tables for two offer a bit more privacy than the main dining room, and an outdoor brick patio is open for dining in summer. Reservations suggested. Hours: 11:30 A.M.–11:00 P.M. daily; brunch served Sat.–Sun. until 3:00 P.M. **5 Grove St. at Prospect, Ridgefield, 06877; (203) 894-1940.**

Christopher's—$$$

Christopher's delivers a real New England dining experience in an 1822 vintage colonial home with multiple small dining rooms, fireplaces and broad plank floors. The varied American menu features steaks, prime rib, pasta and more. A table in front of the fireplace in the east room in winter is one of the most romantic you'll find in town. Reservations recommended. Hours: Mon.–Thu., 4:00 P.M.–10:00 P.M.; Fri.–Sat. until 10:30 P.M.; Sun., 3:30 P.M.–9:00 P.M. **Rte. 7 (just north of Rte. 25), Brookfield, 06804; (203) 775-4409.**

Biscotti—$$ to $$$

Biscotti serves what the native Italian chef calls provincial Italian cooking. The specialty is handmade pasta. Both the menu (which in-

414

cludes numerous vegetarian choices) and the wine list are quite extensive. At lunch, light fare, such as omelettes and sandwiches, is offered. Biscotti's decor looks like the interior of an Italian country house at harvest time, with faux grapevine garlands strung from the rafters and rustic wooden tables and chairs. It's a bit hard to find. Your best bet is to locate the landmark Hay Day Market. Enter the parking lot across the street from the rear of the market, and you'll see Biscotti in front of you. Lunch hours: Tue.–Sat., 11:30 A.M.–3:00 P.M. Sun. brunch served 9:00 A.M.–3:00 P.M. Dinner hours: Tue.–Thu., 5:30 P.M.–9:30 P.M.; Fri.–Sat. until 10:00 P.M.; Sun. until 9:00 P.M. **3 Big Shop Ln., Ridgefield, 06877; (203) 431-3637.**

Ciao Cafe & Wine Bar—$$ to $$$

Ciao serves up a mix of Italian dishes ranging from light and calorie-conscious to rich and decadent. The black-and-white color scheme creates a modern and clean-lined atmosphere, although the bar to one side is pubby and often quieter than some of the others downtown. The "wine bar" portion of the name refers to the selection of almost 50 wines by the glass. Hours: Sun.–Thu., 11:30 A.M.–10:00 P.M.; Fri.–Sat. until 11:00 P.M. **2-B Ives St., Danbury, 06810; (203) 791-0404.**

Emerald City Café—$$ to $$$

The restaurant at Bethel Cinema is not simply an adjunct to the theater. You should give it consideration regardless of whether you'll be seeing a movie after your meal, but this is the most convenient way to combine dinner and a show. With a word from you, the staff will make sure you get to your movie on time. The menu cannot be pigeonholed. You'll find Italian, American, Asian and Middle Eastern dishes, and the kitchen seems to do them all creditably well. Hours: lunch served Tue.–Fri., 11:30 A.M.–2:30 P.M.; Sun. brunch served 10:00 A.M.–2:30 P.M.; dinner served Tue.–Sun. from 5:00 P.M. **269 Greenwood Ave., Bethel, 06801; (203) 778-4100.**

Sesame Seed—$$ to $$$

"Eclectic" aptly describes Sesame Seed, a perennial Danbury favorite. Tag sale furnishings (the second floor is a lot less cluttered and a little more conventional), an old house setting and a menu that caters equally to vegetarians and meat-eaters make it stand out from the crowd. The food shows a grab bag of influences including American, Italian and Middle Eastern, but most dishes have some kind of twist that makes them a tad unusual. Reservations essential on weekends. Lunch served Mon.–Sat., 11:30 A.M.–3:00 P.M. Dinner served Mon.–Sat. from 5:00 P.M., closing at 9:30 P.M. weekdays & 10:30 P.M. on Fri. & Sat. **68 W. Wooster St., Danbury, 06810; (203) 743-9850.**

Two Steps Downtown Grille—$$ to $$$

One of the main places to hang out with friends in downtown Danbury, Two Steps Downtown Grille draws a lively crowd of people who enjoy circulating between the central bar and tables on two levels. Get a table or a booth upstairs if you want a little more peace and quiet. The interior is a neat-looking stripped-down former firehouse with all sorts of humorous paraphernalia suspended from the ceiling. The menu is American/southwestern with a Caribbean influence, running the gamut from fresh seafood to chili to sandwiches and lots of finger food. It also does a bargain all-you-can-eat American Sun. brunch. If you like the food, inquire about the occasional Wed. night cooking classes. Hours: Mon.–Thu., 11:30 A.M.–10:00 P.M.; Fri.–Sat., 11:30 A.M.–midnight; Sun. 10:00 A.M.–10:00 P.M., with brunch served until 2:00 P.M. **5 Ives St., Danbury, 06810; (203) 794-0032.**

Gail's Station House—$ to $$$

At Gail's, the pancakes are homemade, and the buckwheat cakes are the best you can get outside of homemade. Gail's does all sorts of wonderful flavors, all accompanied with real maple syrup. Lunch is mostly soups and sandwiches, dinner is an eclectic mix of dishes that changes weekly and there are always a few veggie options. The mismatched chairs, wildflowers in San Pellegrino bottles and fiddle music on the PA system give the impression of an Old West train station pressed into new service. A bakery features breads, muffins and a lot of bar cookies, and don't forget to ask about the hats.

Hours: Mon.–Sat., 7:00 A.M.–3:00 P.M. & (Wed.–Sat. only) 5:30 P.M.–9:30 P.M.; Sun., 8:00 A.M.–8:00 P.M. Breakfast served Mon.–Sat. until 3:00 P.M. & Sun. until closing. **378 Main St., Ridgefield, 06877; (203) 438-9775.**

Los Andes Restaurant—$$

This family-run restaurant specializes in Ecuadorean food, which is distinctly different from Mexican. You may come across dishes based on unfamiliar ingredients, such as tripe soup, but the menu is in both Spanish and English, so you always know what you're getting. Do try the irresistible fried yellow corn, which tastes like exotic popcorn, and beware the hot pepper condiment. Hours: Mon.–Thu., 11:00 A.M.–10:00 P.M.; Fri.–Sun. until 11:00 P.M. **281 Main St., Danbury, 06810; (203) 790-5439.**

Station House—$ to $$

This friendly little eatery at West Redding railroad station is a wonderful place to hang out with the newspaper or a group of friends, especially on a weekend morning. It does a wide range of breakfast items, including fabulous huge skillet concoctions. Dinner is simple eats like burgers and hot dogs. Breakfast and lunch hours: weekdays except Tue., 7:30 A.M.–3:00 P.M.; Sat.–Sun., 8:00 A.M.–3:00 P.M. Also open for dinner Wed.–Mon., 5:30 P.M.–9:30 P.M. **3 Side Cut Rd., Redding, 06896; (203) 938-8933.**

Coffeehouses, Sweets & Treats

If you've ever wanted to taste things like cheesecake with a graham cracker crust converted into ice cream form, **Dr. Mike's** is your place. This locally famous ice cream maker specializing in "boutique" flavors has two retail locations: **158 Greenwood Ave. in Bethel (203-792-4388)** and at the **intersection of Rtes. 25 and 59 in Monroe (203-452-0499).** Down Ridgefield way, make it a point to leave room for dessert at **Ridgefield Coffee Company (419 Main St. [Rte. 35], Ridgefield, 06877; 203-438-9380).** Sidewalk tables on the town's main drag are as close as you'll come to a French café in Connecticut, and

it also serves light food with a European flair. Also check out the listings for Seattle Espresso and Dr. Java's given under Nightlife.

Services

Local Visitors Information

CityCenter Danbury, 190 Main St. at West St., Danbury 06810; (203) 792-1711. Hours: Mon.–Fri., 8:00 A.M.–5:00 P.M. Request the "What's Up Downtown" guide.

Housatonic Valley Tourism District, P.O. Box 406, 46 Main St., Danbury, 06810; (800) 841-4488 or **(203) 743-0546.** Tell them your interests and they can send you literature from the Pastimes series, flyers that cover all the area attractions based around certain themes, such as military heritage or activities for children.

State Welcome Center, located off I-84 eastbound between exits 2 and 3; **(203) 797-4155.** This free rest area has shaded picnic tables and grills, rest rooms, vending machines and a visitors center. Visitors information is available 8:00 A.M.–6:00 P.M. daily in spring & summer, 9:00 A.M.–5:00 P.M. in fall & winter. All other facilities are open continuously.

Transportation

Danbury is served by two interstate bus lines which both have toll-free numbers for schedule and fare information. You can reach **Bonanza Bus Lines** at **(800) 556-3815** and **Peter Pan/Trailways** at **(800) 343-9999.** For regional bus service north to New Milford and south to Ridgefield, call the **Housatonic Area Transit District** at **(203) 744-4070.**

Daily **Metro-North** commuter rail service connects Redding, Bethel and Danbury with South Norwalk and thence New York and New Haven. For fare and schedule information call **(800) 638-7646.**

New Milford

Halfway up the Connecticut/New York border is a cluster of small towns that form a boundary between the busy Danbury area and a broad expanse of very small communities stretching north to the Massachusetts state line. New Milford, the largest town of the five covered in this chapter, has a classic New England green lined with shops, churches, a library, a post office and a few offices. Washington is a picturesque hilltop academy town whose commercial district is actually found in the hamlet of Washington Depot. Bridgewater, Roxbury and Sherman are primarily residential towns with an abundance of quiet roads and beautiful scenery.

The area is richly endowed with bodies of water that provide ample opportunities for outdoor recreation. Lake Waramaug and Mt. Tom State Parks, both of which are shared by Washington and several other towns, offer swimming and car-top boating, the northern part of Lake Lillinonah is accessible from Bridgewater, where you can launch a motorboat at a state ramp and the Shepaug River running through Washington and Roxbury is a stream suitable for canoeing and fishing. Steep Rock Reservation along that river's banks is among the best local spots for hiking.

Events, such as the Bridgewater Country Fair and New Milford Days or classes at the Institute for American Indian Studies or the Silo Cooking School, are often what bring people here, but on nearly any day of the week you'll be able to engage in shopping in New Preston or a visit to Hopkins Vineyard to select a souvenir bottle of local wine.

Topping off your day with a good meal won't be a problem. The options reflect the broad mix of people who live here, from working folks on a budget to celebrities who favor Roxbury as a location for their country homes. Most are squarely in the middle, but there are also exclusive establishments like Washington's May-

flower Hotel and family restaurants offering inexpensive home-style cooking. The same is true of accommodations, where you can blow a hefty chunk of salary in a weekend or pay a very reasonable price.

History

Although there was activity up and down the Housatonic River in the 17th century, New Milford history really begins in earnest with Chief Waramaug of the Pootatuck Indians deeding the Weantinock (sometimes spelled Weantinogue) Valley to settlers in 1703. Families moved in slowly for the first five years, many of them coming from Milford, hence the name New Milford. When New Milford became a town in 1712, the settlers numbered only about 70.

There is a local legend that, if true, would have happened very early in the area's history. It is said that Chief Waramaug's daughter Lillinonah was betrothed to a white man who, before their marriage, had to make a long journey to visit his family. Lillinonah waited for his return, but a year later he had not reappeared, and sick from despair, she contrived to kill herself. Paddling a canoe out into a gorge above some deadly rapids on the Housatonic River, she threw away the paddle and awaited her fate. As the currents carried her toward certain death, she heard her lover calling from above. He had returned just in time to view Lillinonah's demise. He leaped into the river, and the two met eternity together. Whether the story is true or not, the rapids did exist—until they were submerged by the creation of Lake Lillinonah in the 1930s. The gorge is just a mile or two below the village of New Milford. A small, undeveloped state park overlooks it and is officially called Lover's Leap.

Getting back to matters of fact, from the early 1740s until 1761 shoemaker Roger Sherman was a resident in New Milford before moving to New Haven. In 1755 he was a local representative to the General Assembly. Sherman is the only man to sign all four founding documents of the United States: the Articles of Association of 1774, the Declaration of Independence of 1776, the Articles of Confederation of 1777 and the Constitution in 1783. The neighboring town of Sherman is named for him.

Iron mining and smelting were important industries throughout northwestern Connecticut in the 18th and 19th centuries, and this area was no exception. A deposit of siderite, a mineral rich in iron ore, was discovered in Roxbury and mined beginning in 1750. It was smelted on the spot, and some of the iron undoubtedly found its way to a plow foundry established in New Milford in 1800. Despite almost 125 years of continuous activity, the mining and smelting operation was rarely lucrative. The blast furnace was restored in the

mid-1980s, and other buildings may be restored as funds become available. You can see them along the hiking trails at Mine Hill Preserve.

The Housatonic Railroad that ran from Massachusetts to Bridgeport came through New Milford in 1840, so when the first tobacco crop was planted here in 1848 there was a ready means of getting it to market. Over the next 75 years, buttons, pottery and silver wares were made locally and shipped out by rail. Tobacco cultivation eventually died out, although the remains of some of the tobacco barns that came to dot the countryside can still be found here and there. The railroad still exists as a freight line, and the passenger depot is the home of the local chamber of commerce.

In the 1920s interest was expressed in damming the Rocky River in New Milford for power generation. The Rocky River Power Co. was born—and so was Candlewood Lake. (See the **Danbury** chapter for recreational opportunities on the lake.) The 1930s brought more water projects in the form of the downriver dams that created Lake Lillinonah, and the local landscape came to be much as it is today.

In 1977 evidence of Indian habitation was uncovered along the banks of the Shepaug River in Washington and carbon-dated to an age of approximately 10,200 years, making it the oldest such site known in Connecticut. Not coincidentally, the Institute for American Indian Studies is also located in Washington and is an essential stop for anyone interested in learning more about Connecticut's indigenous population.

Festivals and Events

Roxbury Pickin' and Fiddlin' Contest
Sat. of the second full weekend in July

This extraordinary family event for music lovers is not a concert but a competition, so come prepared to hear musicians of all ability levels play traditional bluegrass and country tunes on acoustic stringed instruments. The location is a large mowed field. Wear shoes that cover your feet to avoid being cut by stubble, and bring a blanket or lawn chair. Basic foods are on sale, but lots of folks bring elaborate picnic spreads. Rain date: Sun. Free parking. Admission: $8 adults, children 12 and under free. Hours: 5:00 P.M. until late. The field is **opposite the intersection of Rtes. 67 and 199 in Roxbury.**

New Milford Days
last weekend in July (Fri.–Sat.)

This juried craft show on the town green features up to 200 exhibitors. Performances by musical guests and children's entertainers go on all day, interspersed with the occasional contest. Food options range from festival fare to real meals from area restaurants, and there's a tented seating area so you can actually take a break while you eat. Admission is free. Hours: 10:00 A.M.–10:00 P.M. both days. For more information call **(860) 354-6080.**

Bridgewater Country Fair
third full weekend in Aug. (Fri.–Sun.)

One of the state's larger fairs, Bridgewater draws about 60,000 people annually. Popular fair events include the Pet Parade in which area children show off their animal companions, the antique tractor pull and the lumberjack contest, which draws competitors from as far away as Canada. In addition, you'll find all the agricultural exhibits, rides, food and entertainment that make country fairs great family fun. Admission: $5 adults, $4 seniors on Sat. & Sun., children under 12 free. Hours: Fri., 4:00 P.M.–11:00 P.M.; Sat., 8:00 A.M.–11:00 P.M.; Sun., 8:00 A.M.–6:00 P.M. Midway rides usually start up around 10:00 A.M. Held at **Bridgewater Fairgrounds on Rte. 133 in Bridgewater.** Arrive early to park near the fairgrounds; later in the day you'll have to follow signs to remote lots and use the free shuttle buses. For more information call **(860) 354-4730.**

Getting There

New Milford is two hours west and a little south of Hartford by car. Although the easiest route is I-84 west to Rte. 7 and north to New Milford, a much prettier (but longer) back way is Rte. 44 to Rte. 202. This drive will take you through the beautiful Farmington River Valley and historic Litchfield and pass just a stone's throw from Lake Waramaug before bringing you straight to New Milford green.

The Inn on Lake Waramaug's Special Events
year-round

The Inn on Lake Waramaug's calendar of five special events throughout the year is a tough one to characterize. They range from the silly to the sublime. For the Huckleberry Finn Raft Race, held Labor Day weekend, contestants must fashion a floating vessel for under $25 and race a short distance on the lake. On the other end of the spectrum, the handbell choir from Center Congregational Church of Torrington gives a Christmas concert. There's also a Fourth of July Festival of the Flares, the Live Turkey "Inn-vitational" and an early July Frog Jump Jamboree. Food and drink are always available, and all events take place on the grounds of The Inn on Lake Waramaug at **107 North Shore Rd., New Preston, 06777; (860) 868-0563.**

Outdoor Activities

It's easy to plan outdoor recreational activities in the New Milford area by yourself, but if you want the convenience of a guided outing or just want to meet some new people while exploring the outdoors, call **Small World Adventures.** This small business organizes daylong hiking, caving and rock-climbing trips in the area, as well as weekends in Maine for sea kayaking and more. The cost for day trips is usually in the $25–$60 range. Reservations are required but can be made on short notice. For more information call **(860) 350-6752.**

Biking

Mountain Biking

There are few off-road places in this area where mountain biking is encouraged but plenty of back roads to bump around on. River Rd. off Boardman Rd. in New Milford becomes dirt and follows the east bank of the Housatonic River for a couple of miles into Gaylordsville before turning into asphalt again. (Keep straight to the general store at Rte. 7 if you need refreshment.) Backtrack to return to your car. In the middle of River Rd. there's one very evident dirt road that cuts away to the east and makes a nice detour.

Also consider riding in the Bridgewater neighborhood described under Road Biking. On a mountain bike you can negotiate the abandoned street labeled on maps as Lover's Leap Rd. This leads to a striking promontory above the Housatonic River, trails through tiny, undeveloped Lover's Leap State Park and a lovely abandoned bridge over the river by Lower Grove St. in New Milford.

Road Biking

The loop around **Lake Waramaug** is one of the prettiest rides in the area, and it's flat. For parking your best bet is the lot at Lake Waramaug State Park at the northwest tip of the lake. Although you will have to pay a fee in season, don't try to park at any of the town beach areas or on private land, or you'll return to find a ticket.

If you are in shape for climbing hills, another exceptionally beautiful spot is Northrup St. and its side roads in Bridgewater. You can park at the boat launch on Rte. 133 at the Housatonic River bridge or at Clatter Valley Park on Clatter Valley Rd. Northrup and Christian Sts. are flat and bucolic, but if you descend toward the Housatonic River just remember that you'll have to climb back out. The ride along the river on Lillinonah Lake Rd. is worth it, though.

Boating

Lake Lillinonah

Lake Lillinonah is really the Housatonic River where it has spread out behind Shepaug Dam. The shores are largely undeveloped (the southwestern shore is state forest land) except for a house here and there. This is a popular spot for motorboaters and jet skiers. The 45 m.p.h. speed limit shouldn't crimp your style too much. One public boat launch is located on the Bridgewater side of the lake where Rte. 133 crosses it. Another is located on Hanover Rd. in Newtown (fee charged on weekends), which is most easily reached via Obtuse Rock Rd. off Rte. 133 in Brookfield. The launch area is on the left several miles down. For canoe and kayak rentals, sales, instruction and guided outings, contact **Black Duck Boat Works (143 West St., New Milford; 860-350-5170).**

Mt. Tom State Park

Mt. Tom Pond is 615 acres of beautiful canoeing territory easily accessible from a main road. Because motors are prohibited, you won't have to worry about a wake, and there is the added benefit of a seasonal swimming area, concessions, bathhouses and rest rooms. See the listing under Swimming for details.

Shepaug River

This Class II river is fed by a small watershed, and water flow from upriver reservoirs is tightly controlled, making it a reliable canoeing and kayaking waterway only Feb.–Apr. For a quick gauge of whether the water level is high enough to make it down the river without having to portage, check its height off tiny Titus Rd. in the center of Washington Depot. If there are absolutely no rocks visible, you're okay. Put in at one of two places. There's an access point on Valley Rd. off Rte. 341 just north of Rte. 202 in Woodville. From here down to its confluence with the Bantam River the Shepaug is fast-moving and twisty, suitable only for small canoes and kayaks. The other good put-in spot is on the Bantam River where Stoddard Rd. crosses it in Litchfield. There is a broken dam a short distance down, but it can be safely run in high water if you are an experienced boater and portaged easily in low water. From the point where the Shepaug and the Bantam join, the river is easy yet exciting. You can make a short trip of it by taking out in Washington Depot or continue to Hodge Park in Roxbury, which is nothing more than an unlabeled riverside strip of ground where the Shepaug briefly flows right along the northwest side of Rte. 67 west of the town center. There is no practical take-out spot below Hodge Park, and there is a dangerous gorge, so make sure to get out early enough. The whole distance takes about four hours to travel.

Fishing

Lake Lillinonah
Despite some factors that make fishing difficult, Lake Lillinonah is popular. It's such a good sportfishing area for largemouth and smallmouth bass that the boat launches can be quite crowded in spring and early summer with tournament participants. Yellow and white perch and sunfish are also numerous. As for the difficulties, there's a fair amount of pressure from other people fishing; there's a high level of boat and waterski activity (come early or late in the day when traffic is at an ebb), and regular drawdowns for hydroelectric power generation can affect currents. Be aware that there are consumption advisories on all species here except yellow perch and sunfish. There's good access at two state boat launches, one on the Bridgewater side of the Rte. 133 bridge, the other on Hanover Rd. in Newtown. Next to the Newtown launch is a swath of state forest land with a waterside trail you can follow to some good shore fishing spots. There's also good ice fishing for northern pike and white perch on the Shepaug arm of the lake in winters when it is frozen, although the consumption advisories still apply. You can access this area from Berry Rd. in Bridgewater. Take it to the dead end, park and fish.

Mt. Tom Pond
Mt. Tom Pond in Mt. Tom State Park is stocked with brown, brook and rainbow trout. You can fish adjacent to the beach area or from a canoe or rowboat. See the listing under Swimming for directions and details.

Shepaug River
There is basically only one spot to access the Shepaug, and on summer weekends it's usually nabbed early, but on weekdays you might have the place all to yourself. The access area is known as Hodge Park in Roxbury. You won't find it on a map, though, nor is there a sign. When you drive east on Rte. 67 from Bridgewater toward Roxbury, the river briefly flows parallel to the road on the left-hand side. You'll see a pullout and a gentle decline to the river's edge. Trout are stocked just upriver of this point.

Hiking

Candlewood Lake Nature Trail
Brought to you by Connecticut Light and Power, this easy three-quarter-mile interpretive trail hugs the eastern shore of Candlewood Lake at a spot known as Dike Pt. in New Milford. Picnic tables with grills and great views across the water make this a nice stopping place for lunch, and there's access for launching car-top boats. Open dawn–dusk, Memorial Day–Labor Day. The entrance is on Old Town Park Rd. seven-tenths of a mile from Sullivan Rd. in New Milford.

Housatonic Range Trail
One of Connecticut's blue-blazed trails cuts across the mountainous Housatonic Highlands, a geological plateau formation on the very western edge of the state. In recent years there's been some encroachment on the trail, but some portions remain untouched. You'll find an access point at the corner of Rte. 37 and Candlewood Mtn. Rd. in New Milford. Park on the only open corner; the trail enters the woods immediately. A pipeline cut briefly interrupts the trail, but other than that it's hemlock and deciduous forest for 1.5 miles to the summit of Candlewood Mountain. A half-mile side loop named Kelly's Slide near the summit is steep but enjoyable. Follow the blazes carefully; there are a couple of tricky spots.

Mine Hill Preserve
Less than five minutes down the trail from the parking lot at Mine Hill Preserve you'll come upon the eerie remains of the awesome, hulking

mass of Roxbury Furnace, lurking incongruously in the midst of a mature hemlock and hardwood forest. Farther along the 3.5-mile trail is the preserve's namesake mine, which can be seen but not entered. (The mine shafts are highly unstable, so for public safety grates block the way.) Ore from this mine fed the furnace and sustained a whole town that existed at the foot of Mine Hill Rd. in the third quarter of the 19th century. Now the shafts are home only to bats and other wild creatures. The Roxbury Land Trust, owner of the preserve, is trying to document and preserve the site and is also involved in a bat count. The Trust asks that you do not remove even the smallest souvenir from the site or attempt to enter the mine, which will disturb the bats. A trail map is posted near the trailhead, and you can get a copy for a small charge at the **land trust's office (7 South St., Roxbury; 860-350-4148),** the **Minor Memorial Library (23 South St., Roxbury; 860-350-2181)** and the **town clerk's office in town hall (29 North St. [Rte. 67], Roxbury; 860-354-3328).**

Mt. Tom State Park

The trail system at Mt. Tom is not extensive—there's essentially just one short loop—but it leads to a stone observation tower at the summit of Mt. Tom (1,291 feet) that yields a rewarding view of the surrounding countryside. The distance is not great, and the elevation gain is only about 400 feet from the parking lot to the summit, so this is a good choice for families with small children or weekend hikers who don't want to risk blisters. If you packed a swimsuit, you can work up a (modest) sweat on the trail and then go for a swim in Mt. Tom Pond to cool off. See the listing under Swimming for more information.

Pratt Center

This community nature center has about 5 miles of trails around and up Mt. Tom (a different Mt. Tom than the one where the state park is located). The grounds are open dawn–dusk, and a map is posted on a bulletin board near the entrance. For information on nature programs see the entry under Children and Families. **163 Paper Mill Rd., New Milford, 06776; (860) 355-3137.**

Steep Rock Reservation/ Hidden Valley

Just minutes from the center of Washington Depot are two lovely wooded preserves. True to its name, some of the trails in Steep Rock are quite steep, but in both sections you can also walk trails along the Shepaug River with little elevation change. There's also an old roadbed in Steep Rock that climbs gently and takes you over the top of an abandoned railroad tunnel. To get to Steep Rock, take River Rd. in Washington Depot and drive until you cross a bridge over the Shepaug River and come to the parking lot. To reach Hidden Valley, take Rte. 47 north from the center of Washington Depot and look for a parking area on your right a short distance up the road. If you find a footbridge leading to a trail, you're in the right place. On summer weekends Steep Rock is severely overcrowded; save this for a weekday hike. Rough maps are posted at Hidden Valley but not at Steep Rock. Detailed maps are available from the **Steep Rock Association** office for a modest fee; **(860) 868-9131.**

Sunny Valley Preserve

This Nature Conservancy–owned preserve consists of 1,850 acres of woodland and active farmland in several parcels across Bridgewater and New Milford. Some trails take you along the edges of fields (take care not to disturb livestock or crops). Other trails wind through deep woods, descending to the Housatonic River. A good starting point is at the trail blazes at the parking pullouts on Iron Ore Hill Rd. in Bridgewater. Trail maps may be obtained at the **preserve office** at **8 Sunny Valley Ln., New Milford, 06776; (860) 355-3716.** Grounds hours: dawn–dusk daily, year-round. Guided hikes or other interpretive programs are occasionally offered, including an annual farm day on the Sat. of Columbus Day weekend when you can see animals and farm equipment, take a hayride or buy a pumpkin.

Horseback Riding

If you have your own horse, a ring with half a dozen jumps is available at the entrance to **Steep Rock Reservation.** Shows are held here twice a year to benefit Steep Rock Association. You can also ride anywhere in Steep Rock or **Hidden Valley,** which are described under the Hiking section.

H.O.R.S.E. of CT

A unique animal rescue operation that attempts to rehabilitate and adopt out its charges also offers trail rides by appointment on 46 acres of private and state forest land. Tack and helmets are provided. Families are welcome to drop in to give kids a chance to pet and feed the horses, although it's best to call first. Locals, take note: for $25 a month you "sponsor" a horse and your child can learn the basics of equine care. **43 Wilbur Rd., Washington, 06777; (860) 868-1960.**

Ice Skating

Canterbury School

This excellent private school rink is open for public skating for $3 per person every weekday morning late Oct.–mid-Mar. except when New Milford public schools are closed. They also have family skating hours on certain Sun. afternoons. Call for exact hours or just show up weekdays around 9:00 A.M. Rental skates are not available, but they can sharpen yours. To get to the rink from the green in town, go up Aspectuck Ave. to Elkington Farm Rd., turn right and park in the lot a few feet down on the right. The rink is across the road. For more information call the rink's shop at **(860) 350-1432.**

Gunnery Rink

Washington's private prep school rink is open for public skating on Sun. from Thanksgiving (possibly earlier) through the first week of Mar. Currently the hours are 4:30 P.M.–7:30 p.m. at a cost of $5 per person. There are no skate rentals. Finding the rink is a little tough. Going southeast on Rte. 47 through Washington, crest the hill, pass the church and take the very next left. You have to drive back a ways past some playing fields to get to the rink. For more information call the Gunnery switchboard at **(860) 868-7334.**

Swimming

There is a guarded sandy beach, concessions, a bathhouse and rest rooms on Mt. Tom Pond in Mt. Tom State Park. An entrance fee is charged Memorial Day–Labor Day: $4 for vehicles with in-state plates and $6 for vehicles with out-of-state plates on weekdays; $5 and $8, respectively, on weekends. Hours: 8:00 A.M.–dusk daily, year-round. Located on **Rte. 202 approximately midway between New Preston and Bantam.** Park office: **(860) 868-2592.**

Seeing and Doing

Art Galleries

Washington Art Association is a vital community art center with a good gallery space showing and selling the work of artists from around the country, much of it local or regional. Its annual Clothesline Art Sale, held Fourth of July weekend every year, draws big crowds. Get there early if you are shopping seriously because stuff gets snapped up fast. It also sponsors special events, lectures and film programs throughout the year. Hours: Mon., Tue. & Thu.–Sat., 10:00 A.M.–5:00 P.M.; Sun., 2:00 P.M.–5:00 P.M. To find the gallery, look for the large, ornate town hall in the center of Washington Depot. A narrow plaza runs alongside it. The gallery is a large building with a brick facade at the very end. Phone: **(860) 868-2878.**

Children and Families

Family programs focusing on natural science are offered weekly at the **Pratt Center,** which also has hiking trails, community gardens and barnyard animals in residence during the summer. Programs take place year-round and include activities such as campfires, storytelling, night and day hikes and wildlife observation. Call for a schedule. **163 Paper Mill Rd., New Milford, 06776; (860) 355-3137.**

423

Museums and Historic Sites

Institute for American Indian Studies

The IAIS began in 1975 as the American Indian Archaeological Institute. Focused at first on collecting and interpreting archaeological evidence of Native American culture in northwestern Connecticut, it has over the years become more of a full-service museum, adding exhibits and programs and opening its doors to the public more and more. There is a large permanent indoor exhibit of Indian artifacts and lore, an outdoor exhibit of bark- and reed-covered dwellings typical of Connecticut's Indians, special events in areas such as ethnobotany, music and storytelling and more. Admission: $4 adults, $2 children 6–16. Hours: weekdays & Sat., 10:00 A.M.–5:00 P.M.; Sun., noon–5:00 P.M.; closed Mon. & Tue., Jan.–Mar. **Curtis Rd. off Rte. 199, Washington, 06793; (860) 868-0518.**

New Milford Historical Society Museum

Portraits, photos, fine furniture and many other artifacts document New Milford's families and industries in a trio of buildings at the top of New Milford's green. Attached to the Colonial Revival main gallery is the Knapp House (ca. 1800), set up with a period dining room and parlor interpreted to the late 1800s, a kitchen set up as it might have been when the house was built and collections of toys and household implements. Also on the property is the former Elijah Boardman store, which now houses a collection of 20th-century paintings of New Milford subjects. Hours: Thu., Fri. & Sun., 1:00 P.M.–4:00 P.M., from Memorial Day until the last weekend in Oct., & by appointment & for special events. Admission: $3 adults, $1.50 seniors and students. **6 Aspetuck Ave., New Milford, 06776; (860) 354-3069.**

The Historical Society also maintains two other properties: the **Hill and Plain Schoolhouse** (on Sullivan Rd. near Candlewood Lake Rd. South), a one-room school restored to the early 1900s with period books and maps, and

Brown's Forge (Brown's Forge Rd.), where most of New Milford's iron tools and horseshoes were made from 1870 into the 20th century. The equipment is still extant but never fired up. Hours for both are Sun., 1:00 p.m.–5:00 P.M., July & Aug. only.

Other Museums and Sites

The **David Northrop Jr. House (10 Rte. 37 in Sherman; 860-354-6598)** is an early 1800s Federal farmhouse in the process of being restored by the Sherman Historical Society. It has had a varied and interesting life as a family home, a saloon (there's a small ballroom on the second floor), a boardinghouse and Sherman's post office for 20 years. There is a small gallery exhibiting artifacts, occasional special programs, a garden, a short boardwalk trail out back and a gift shop. Admission is free. Hours: Sat.–Sun., 1:00 P.M.–4:00 P.M., May–Oct., & by appointment.

The exhibits at **Washington's Gunn Memorial Historical Museum (at the intersection of Wykeham Rd. and Rte. 47 in Washington; 860-868-7756)** attempt to illuminate the lives of local people through the objects they left behind. There are period room exhibits containing antiques from area families and changing exhibits of items from the museum's extensive collection of artifacts. Take a detour into the library next door to see the murals of H. Siddons Mowbray. Hours: Thu.–Sun., noon–4:00 P.M.; closed major holidays. Admission is free.

The **Merwinsville Hotel** and railroad ticket office **(One Brown's Forge Rd. in Gaylordsville; 860-350-4443)** is also under restoration. Although much work remains to be done, it's an architecturally interesting building, and a few small exhibits have been installed. Hours: Sun., 2:00 P.M.–4:00 P.M., July–Sept. Admission is free.

Last but not least, the planned **Museum of Contemporary Impressionism (29 Church St., New Milford)** will display works from 1950 and later, the core of the collection made up of works by the late Bernard Lennon, a local Impressionist painter. Call the **Chamber of Commerce** at **(860) 354-6080** for more information.

Nightlife

Nightlife in the small towns in this area is limited to local bands playing at restaurants, coffeehouses and pubs such as **Bank St. Coffee House (56 Bank St., New Milford; 860-350-8920)** for jazz, blues, folk or classical on Fri. & Sat. starting around 8:30 P.M. Check local newspapers for listings.

Performing Arts

Community theaters are very active in this part of the world. **Theatreworks New Milford (5 Brookside Ave., New Milford; 860-350-6863),** located in a former church, offers five to six productions annually. Its selections, which can include musicals, dramas and comedies, often have an off-Broadway flavor. Tickets: $12, $10 seniors and students.

Also located in a former church (seating is in pews!), the **Sherman Players (860-354-3622)** stage about five popular works per year in a season running Apr.–Thanksgiving. Tickets: $12 adults, $10 seniors and students. There is a ramp for wheelchair access. The playhouse is in the center of Sherman. Enter through the driveway at the IGA sign on Rte. 39 just north of Rte. 37.

A third option is **Stage II Theater and Opera Company (61 Bank St., New Milford; 860-354-8601),** which is affiliated with New Milford's School of Performing Arts. It presents comedy, drama, classics and opera in a small, black-box theater, and they occasionally bring in guest artists. Its season runs Sept.–May. Ticket for most shows are $15 adults, $12 seniors and students.

Scenic Drives

This area is one in which many of the principal roads are largely free of traffic and quite picturesque, especially in Washington and Roxbury. Rte. 67 from New Milford to Roxbury, continuing on Rte. 317 to Woodbury is not a designated scenic drive, but it's one of the prettiest routes in Connecticut. At the Woodbury end you'll find the state's premier antiquing district and a wide variety of restaurants. Rtes. 47, 109 and 199 are also very beautiful, and the lattermost takes you past the Institute for American Indian Studies.

The circle of roads around Lake Waramaug in New Preston is another possibility. They take you past a state park and several lovely resort hotels. At the state park, stop for a paddleboat ride. Alternatively, the tasting room at Hopkins Vineyard makes a nice detour. Many restaurants ring the lake.

Seasonal Favorites

I always know it's autumn when the pumpkins appear at the corner of Rtes. 202 and 109 in New Milford. Park Lane Cider Mill is a small place that sells cider pressed on-site, pumpkins and apples by the pound, peck and bushel. It's open Oct.–Dec., generally 10:00 A.M.–5:00 P.M. daily.

Shopping

There is no main shopping district in this area. Instead, each town or hamlet has a few unique places to check out. **Tiny New Preston** on Rte. 45 near Rte. 202 is an enclave of specialty shops and antique stores in a picturesque setting. The hand-thrown flowerpots of Guy Wolff, whose work has been featured in national magazines, are displayed in his nearby shop on Rte. 202 just north of Rte. 341 in Washington. Call **(860) 868-2858** for hours. **Washington Depot** at the intersection of Rtes. 47 and 109 also has a clutch of enjoyable stores.

Book lovers will be thrilled to find **Reid & Wright Antiquarian Books (860-868-7706)** situated in a rebuilt barn on Rte. 202 between Marble Dale and New Preston. In addition to two floors of books, antiquarian and not, there are maps, framed prints and more.

The Silo (44 Upland Rd., New Milford; 860-355-0300) is a combination specialty food and cookware store, art gallery and cooking school run by occasional New York Pops conductor Skitch Henderson and his wife Ruth, who are also noted cookbook authors. Situated in a barn on a back road several miles outside town, the store is a beautiful place to shop for the chef in your life. And if you love to cook you might enjoy a stop at the retail store of New Milford's own **Egg & I Farm (355 Chestnutland Rd. in New Milford; 888-265-7675)**, "New England's premier pork producer," named after the classic black-and-white comedy movie spoofing city folks who move to the country.

In New Milford proper there is a small but growing assortment of one-of-a-kind stores on Bank St. and Church St., and in the hamlet of Gaylordsville on Rte. 7 you'll find antiques at the **Bittersweet Shop (860-354-1727)**, an almost unimaginable selection of baskets and other household items at **The Basket Shop (860-354-6202)** and decorative items at **The American Heritage Shop (860-350-4988)**. Down Rte. 7 in the other direction you'll find **The Elephant's Trunk** outdoor flea market, one of the largest in the state. It takes place Sun., 6:30 A.M.–3:00 P.M., rain or shine, mid-Mar.–Dec. (weather permitting). Admission is $1. For more information call **(860) 355-1448.**

Wineries

Hopkins Vineyard offers one of the best overall winery experiences in Connecticut, with a beautiful setting in a picturesque red barn overlooking Lake Waramaug, a good restaurant (Hopkins Inn) just a few steps away and a bright, airy and well-maintained tasting room. The vineyard is on the site of a former family dairy farm that was converted to grape production in 1979. The land has been in the same family for over 100 years. The fields, with rows of vinifera and hybrid grapes, are right outside the door to the tasting room. High-season (May–Dec.) hours are Mon.–Fri.,

10:00 A.M.–5:00 P.M.; Sat., 10:00 A.M.–6:00 P.M.; Sun., 11:00 A.M.–6:00 P.M. Off-season (Jan.–Apr.) hours are Fri.–Sun., 10:00 A.M.–5:00 P.M. Tours are given Sat. & Sun. at 2:00 P.M. **22 Hopkins Rd., New Preston, 06777; (860) 868-7954.** Follow the "Wine Trail" signs at intersections around Lake Waramaug, and you'll have no trouble finding the winery.

Where to Stay

Bed & Breakfasts

Barton House—$$$

This new B&B is conveniently located walking distance from New Milford's green in an attractive and traditional 19th-century colonial with a truly expansive backyard and nice outdoor spaces for eating or relaxing. There are two comfortable rooms, both with private bath, plus several appealing common areas to enjoy. **34 East St. (Rte. 202), New Milford, 06776; (860) 354-3535.**

Behind-the-Columns B&B—$$$

Tucked away on a quiet side road, this B&B is located on a beautiful property with rolling lawns, lovely gardens and a small pond and picnic area. Accommodations are in a converted outbuilding detached from the main house, and breakfast is served in the room or on the front deck, so there is a large degree of privacy. The comfortable room features a queen bed and spotless bath with shower. The anteroom has a built-in twin bed for a third person or a child. **157 Calhoun St., Washington Depot, 06794; (860) 868-1698.**

The Quid—$$$

The Quid's proprietor, Susan Rush, runs this small, exceedingly private B&B on land that's been in her family for several generations. Her home is a converted tobacco barn with exposed beams, cathedral ceilings and beautiful wideboard floors. A ground-floor room with a king bed, a daybed and a private shower is spacious and opens directly onto a wooden deck overlooking a wooded hillside, a pond and distant fields. A smaller upstairs room furnished with twin beds is also quite pleasant and comes with a large bath. A third room with a single bed could accommodate a child or extra person. A full breakfast is included. The Quid is a little hard to find; get explicit directions. **245 Second Hill Rd., New Milford, 06776; (860) 354-6143.**

River Bend—$$$

True to its name, this one-room B&B is indeed situated a stone's throw from a bend in the Shepaug River in one of the Litchfield Hills' loveliest towns. The guest room, with a private entrance and bath, is located in an ell attached to the main house. A queen feather bed with a down comforter, a romantic floral motif, ample space to stretch out, friendly hosts and a full breakfast served in the room all promise to make River Bend a very positive stopover. **168 Baker Rd. (Rte. 67), Roxbury, 06783; (860) 354-1214.**

Hotels, Motels & Inns

Most accommodations in this area are pricey, but there are inexpensive inn rooms as well as a modern apartment to be had at **Hopkins Inn (22 Hopkins Rd., New Preston, 06777; 860-868-7295),** which also has a good restaurant and is next door to the vineyard of the same name.

The Boulders Inn—$$$$

For an inn that combines scenic beauty, fine dining and a refined but distinctly country atmosphere, you could hardly do better. The 1895 Victorian main house was built as a private home, and visitors today easily might imagine that they are the houseguests of some fabulously wealthy host. If you want to swim or tan, a private beach on Lake Waramaug is only steps away. Alternatively, explore the woods on the inn's own hiking trail. If you want almost total privacy, guest houses with romantic fireplaces tucked away at the edge of the woods will make you feel like you're miles from anywhere. Plumbing does vary from room to room,

so be sure to specify a bathtub if that is important to you. Ask about the Modified American Plan rates, which include both breakfast and dinner. Located on **Rte. 45 (East Shore Rd.), New Preston, 06777; (800) 552-6853 or (860) 868-0541.**

The Inn on Lake Waramaug—$$$$

This inn and restaurant offering all-inclusive pricing is a good choice if you plan to park the car and spend your vacation close to your accommodations. Rates include afternoon tea, a four-course dinner and a full breakfast, although in the off-season the arrangement can be more flexible to allow you to sample other area restaurants. (Note: A 15% service charge is added to the room rate at checkout.) Rooms in the main building, which is a 1790 colonial and has been an inn since 1880, have the feeling of a sprawling farmhouse. Two detached guest houses have rooms decorated in a more modern style with wall-to-wall carpeting and fireplaces; artificial logs are provided. All beds are queen; some rooms in the newer buildings also have a twin. The Inn has a small private beach where you can swim or launch one of the canoes provided. **107 North Shore Rd., New Preston, 06777; (800) 525-3466 or (860) 868-0563.**

The Mayflower Inn—$$$$

Once the private Ridge School, The Mayflower Inn is one of fewer than 30 American *Relais & Chateaux* lodging establishments. Membership in this exclusive European organization certifies that the hotel offers the highest standards of accommodation, and there are only about 450 members worldwide. It wasn't always this way: the Mayflower has had many owners and varying amounts of attention or neglect over the years. But in 1992 it was "brought back to life," as the owners describe the transformation, and today the Mayflower is about luxury, fresh flowers, pampering and service. There are 25 sumptuous rooms all with private baths in three buildings. An on-site fitness club is open early and late. Located on **Rte. 47 about half a mile east of Washington, 06793; (860) 868-9466.**

427

Homestead Inn—$$$

This comfortable little inn about half a block from New Milford's green has rooms in two buildings: a mid-1800s Victorian house, formerly a private residence, and a newer, one-story structure that used to be a restaurant. A recent redecoration was very successful. Beautiful wall finishings complement antique and reproduction furniture for an overall look that is quaint and old-fashioned but well kept. All rooms have private, attached baths, and most rooms have a sink outside the bathroom. Air conditioning, TVs and telephones are also available, and an expanded Continental breakfast buffet comes with the room. **5 Elm St., New Milford, 06776; (860) 354-4080.**

Camping

There is a lovely state park campground ($) on Lake Waramaug. See the **Kent** chapter for details.

Where to Eat

Although all the towns in the New Milford area are small, thanks to their location on the edge of busy, populous Fairfield County, there is a larger number of good restaurants here than you might otherwise expect. In addition to the listings below, you might also try **Arizona Grill and Cafe (38 Bee Brook Rd. [Rte. 47], Washington Depot; 860-868-2239)**, specializing in southwestern cuisine; **Panda Empire (254 Danbury Rd. [Rte. 7], New Milford, 06776; 860-350-8888)**, a Chinese restaurant serving excellent food in a white-tablecloth atmosphere; **G. W. Tavern (20 Bee Brook Rd. [Rte. 47], Washington Depot; 860-868-6633)**, serving what they call "creative American comfort food"; **North Country Steakhouse (329 Kent Rd. [Rte. 7 immediately south of Rte. 37], New Milford; 860-355-5141)**, where you can get a good steak in a quiet, tavernlike colonial home with a massive fireplace and **Rudy's (122 Litchfield Rd. [Rt. 202], New Milford; 860-354-7727)**, a local institution that has gone by the simple moniker "a Swiss place" for many years and is popular with an older crowd.

For more casual and inexpensive eats, try **Country Pizza (One Sawmill Rd., Sherman, 06784; 860-355-5105)**, serving pizza and family-style Italian food in an old farmhouse; **Marble Dale Pub (Rte. 202, Marble Dale, 06777; 860-868-1496)**, a great place to grab a beer, some pub food or a full meal with friends after a day on the trail or the river; **The Dining Car (40–46 Railroad St., New Milford, 06776; 860-350-5090)**, a casual family restaurant where you can get sandwiches, American and Italian food at reasonable prices; **The Boathouse Café (107 North Shore Rd., New Preston, 06777; 860-868-6255/0563)**, a seasonal dog-and-burger-type grill on the shore of Lake Waramaug where you can park your canoe while you eat; **Grand Patisserie (27 Main St., New Milford, 06776; 860-354-4525)**, a bakery that also offers light breakfast and lunch fare and **Fabled Foods (59 Bank St., New Milford, 06776; 860-354-1144)**, a full-service restaurant and upscale deli and bakery featuring "artisan breads."

Adrienne—$$$ to $$$$

The 1996 winner of *Connecticut* magazine's readers' poll award for best new restaurant in Litchfield County is located in a white colonial on Rte. 7 just north of New Milford. Traditional decor and soft lighting complement the period wideboard floors and fireplaces in three small dining rooms. The menu, which changes seasonally, showcases hearty but refined American dishes with regional and international influences. Hours: Tue.–Sat., 5:30 P.M. until closing. **218 Kent Rd. (Rt. 7), New Milford, 06776; (860) 354-6001.**

The Boulders Inn—$$$ to $$$$

The dining rooms at The Boulders Inn are a complement to this establishment's equally fine accommodations. Not only is the food, which draws from many ethnic traditions, excellent, but the setting is superb (see Where to Stay for details). The dining rooms are richly furnished, and an open terrace with a view out over Lake Waramaug is available in summer. This is fine dining at its best, and you should dress accordingly. Hours: Thu., 6:00 P.M.–8:00 P.M.; Fri.–Sat., 6:00 P.M.–9:00 P.M.; Sun., 5:00 P.M.–8:00 P.M. Located on **Rte. 45 (east side of lake), New Preston, 06777; (860) 868-0541.**

The Inn on Lake Waramaug—$$$ to $$$$

This combination inn and restaurant serves a menu of New American dishes that changes seasonally and has been noted by *Wine Spectator* magazine for its wine selection. The food is complex and hearty—definitely something for a special evening. The main dining room is popular for functions but still intimate. There's also a seasonal canopied deck for summer dining. A full breakfast is served some mornings, but call ahead for availability. Dinner is served Mon.–Sat., 6:00 P.M.–9:00 P.M., & on Sun., 5:00 P.M.–8:30 P.M. Sun. brunch is served 11:00 A.M.–2:00 P.M. Located on **North Shore Rd., New Preston, 06777; (860) 868-0563.**

The Mayflower Inn—$$$ to $$$$

The Mayflower Inn is an opulent lodging and dining establishment also described under Where to Stay. The menu, which changes daily, advertises that the kitchen uses "organically raised meats, grains and produce from local New England farms when possible." Overall it is Continental/American in flavor, but it can show regional and international influences depending on how the available ingredients might best be showcased. Its house-smoked salmon is a specialty. It offers a wide selection of wines by the glass and has received a *Wine Spectator* award. The Mayflower Inn also serves breakfast and lunch daily and makes a lovely setting for any meal you wish to make a bit out of the ordinary. Proper attire is dressy casual or better. Open for breakfast 7:30 A.M.–10:00 A.M., for lunch noon–2:00 P.M. & for dinner 6:00 P.M.–roughly 9:00 P.M. daily. The bar is open midday from 11:30 A.M. until midnight in summer. Located on **Rte. 47 about half a mile east of Washington town center, Washington, 06793; (860) 868-9466.**

The Bistro—$$$

The atrium dining room and exposed brick interior here is as clean and stylish as the restaurant's New American menu with Asian influences. Everything has a twist on the ordinary. The lunch menu is small, with some lighter fare but still somewhat challenging flavor combinations. Offerings change weekly, but certain dishes reappear, and most nights there are a few Thai selections thanks to a Thai chef. The Tap Room is a comfortable, contemporary bar on the second floor. Lunch served Mon.–Sat., 11:00 A.M.–3:00 P.M.; Sun., noon–4:00 P.M. Dinner hours: 5:00 P.M.–10:00 P.M. daily. The full menu is available Wed.–Sat. only; a Tap Room menu is available other nights. **31 Bank St., New Milford, 06776; (860) 355-3266.**

Carmela's—$$$

Carmela's is the local place to go for excellent Italian food and a softly lit, romantic atmosphere. It has an extensive selection of pastas, a large repertoire of steak, chicken, seafood and veal dishes and a wide array of gourmet pizzas. The high-quality yet accessible menu makes this a great place for couples and family groups. In summer their patio overlooking the green is the closest thing in these parts to an urban sidewalk café. Hours: Tue.–Thu., 11:30 A.M.–10:00 P.M.; Fri.–Sat. until 11:00 P.M.; Sun., 12:30 P.M.–8:30 P.M. Located on **Main St. near Bridge St. (on the green) in New Milford, 06776; (860) 355-5000.**

Darwoods—$$$

Not as trendy in its decor as some other restaurants in New Milford but every bit as good in terms of food, Darwoods is an especially apt choice if you want a quiet place for conversation since there is no bar to generate noise. It's a white-tablecloth restaurant whose look is softened by lace curtains half shielding the view to the street. It serves American cuisine with some Italian touches. Hours: open daily for lunch 11:30 A.M.–2:30 P.M.; dinner served Tue.–Sun. from 5:00 P.M. **51 Bank St., New Milford; (860) 355-5440.**

Le Bon Coin—$$$

Seemingly stranded on a rather lonely but beautiful stretch of road, this French restaurant has received consistently high marks for its food over the years and offers something a

429

Housatonic and Naugatuck River Valleys

little different from the ordinary. Try a Chateaubriand for two or Mediterranean compositions of fish or chicken. The menu advertises that the chef will prepare vegetarian and low-cholesterol plates on request. Seating is cozy and uncrowded, mostly at intimate tables for four. Food is served at a leisurely pace, so come here when you have time to devote to a meal. Luncheon hours: Mon. & Thu.–Sat., noon–2:00 P.M. Dinner hours: Mon. & Wed.–Fri., 6:00 P.M.–9:00 P.M.; Sat., 6:00 P.M.–10:00 P.M.; Sun., 5:00 P.M.–9:00 P.M. Located on **Rte. 202 about five minutes east of Rte. 45, New Preston, 06777; (860) 868-7763.**

American Pie Company—$$ to $$$
A bakery in addition to a restaurant, this place offers both quantity and quality at a reasonable price. The atmosphere is very friendly, informal and family-oriented. The fairly extensive menu is American fare ranging from sandwiches and steaks to pasta, with several daily specials and standard breakfast items. Perhaps the best thing is the chicken pot pie, which will feed two ordinary appetites easily. Hours: Mon. (breakfast & lunch only) 9:00 A.M.–2:00 P.M.; Tue.–Thu., 8:30 A.M.–8:00 P.M.; Fri.–Sat., 8:00 A.M.–9:00 P.M.; Sun., 8:00 A.M.–8:00 P.M. Hours are later in summer, and the bakery is open at 6:00 A.M. Mon.–Fri. **29 Rte. 37, Sherman Center, 06784; (860) 350-0662.**

Doc's—$$ to $$$
Doc's serves Italian-inspired cuisine featuring handmade pastas, specialty pizzas and satisfying salads. There is one small dining room separated from the kitchen by a counter and a picnic table outside where they will seat you if you ask. Its location at the foot of Lake Waramaug and its casual atmosphere makes it a good choice for anyone spending the day hiking or biking around the area and yet looking for a memorable meal. Hours: Wed.–Sun., 5:00 P.M. until closing. There may also be lunch in summer Thu.–Sun. starting at noon; call to confirm. Located at the **intersection of Rte. 45 and Flirtation Ave., New Preston, 06777; (860) 868-9415.**

Hopkins Inn—$$ to $$$
Austrian and Swiss specialties served by staff in traditional Austrian dress are what you'll find at Hopkins Inn, which is especially popular with an older crowd. A beautiful shaded stone terrace affords lovely views of Lake Waramaug. Go for the view and stay for the Toblerone sundae. A selection of The Hopkins Inn salad dressings are available for purchase if you want to take some home. Reservations are required for lunch and dinner. The restaurant is closed Jan. 2–late Mar., and lunch is served May–Oct. only. Breakfast is available daily, 8:30 A.M.–9:30 A.M. Lunch hours are Tue.–Sat., noon–2:00 P.M. Dinner is served Tue.–Thu., 6:00 P.M.–9:00 P.M.; Fri., 6:00 P.M.–10:00 P.M.; Sat., 5:30 P.M.–10:00 P.M.; Sun., 12:30 P.M.–8:30 P.M. A midafternoon menu of light items is served Tue.–Sat. until 3:30 P.M. during summer months. **22 Hopkins Rd., New Preston, 06777; (860) 868-7295.**

Oliva—$$ to $$$
Tucked up above the road in an unusual building at the northern end of New Preston's cluster of antique shops and galleries, Oliva has a pleasant terrace and an interior combining traditional coziness and clean-lined modernity. The fare is Northern Italian. Lunch served Thu.–Sun., noon–2:30 P.M.; dinner served Wed.–Sun. from 5:00 P.M. **18 East Shore Rd., New Preston, 06777; (860) 868-1787.**

The Pantry—$ to $$$
This combination restaurant, deli and bakery is an excellent place to have an informal but memorable meal or to stock up on provisions or picnic fixings; it has an extraordinary cheese case. The menu changes daily; on any given day it has several hearty soups or stews; fruit, cheese, smoked fish and pâté plates; varied entrées; sandwiches; several vegetarian options; deli salads and health foods. Breads, pies and other desserts are made fresh in the bakery. Hours: Tue.–Sat., 10:00 A.M.–6:00 P.M.; Continental breakfast served until 11:00 A.M.; eat-in service until 5:00 P.M.; take-out only for the last hour. Located **behind the Hickory Stick Bookshop at the junction of Rtes. 47 and 109 in Washington Depot; (860) 868-0258.**

Black Bear Coffee Roasters—$$

Located on a fairly unpopulated stretch of road between New Milford and New Preston, Black Bear is worth a drive. Few places can beat its sunny, airy interior first thing in the morning. The exceedingly small number of tables hints that it is geared for the pastry-and-coffee crowd, but it is fully capable of a more complicated and satisfying breakfast or lunch. As you might surmise from the name, it offers coffees (roasted on the premises) by the pound or the cup and also stocks an array of coffee-time paraphernalia, housewares and gifts. Hours: Mon. & Wed.–Fri., 8:00 A.M.–5:00 P.M.; Sat.–Sun., 9:00 A.M.–5:00 P.M. **239 Rte. 202, New Preston, 06777; (860) 868-1446.**

Coffeehouses, Sweets & Treats

Bank St. Coffee House—$ to $$

New Milford's only coffeehouse serves soups, sandwiches, bagels, desserts and coffee by the cup or the pound. It also features musical entertainment on Fri. & Sat. starting around 8:30 P.M. Hours: Mon.–Thu., 7:00 A.M.–6:00 P.M. (Wed.–Thu. until 9:30 P.M. in summer); Fri.–Sat., 7:00 A.M.–11:30 P.M.; Sun., 8:00 A.M.–4:00 P.M. **56 Bank St., New Milford, 06776; (860) 350-8920.**

Bridgewater Village Store—$

Locally made chocolates, specialty breads and coffees, deli items, groceries and some seating for eating in are all available at this quaint store attached to the local post office. Hours: Mon.–Fri., 6:00 A.M.–6:00 P.M.; Sat., 7:00 A.M.–6:00 P.M.; Sun., 7:00 A.M.–3:00 P.M. (5:00 P.M. in summer). **27 Main St. South (Rte. 133 at Hat Shop Hill Rd.), Bridgewater, 06752; (860) 354-2863.**

Sugar 'n Spice—$

The menu at Sugar 'n Spice can be summed up in two words: ice cream. This is where to come when you want to beat the heat with something cool and creamy. It might not open early enough for serious ice cream fans, but it stays open late. Hours are noon–9:00 P.M. daily in season. Located on **River Rd. about one block off Rte. 47, Washington Depot, 06794; (860) 868-3030.**

Services

Local Visitors Information

Housatonic Valley Tourism District, P.O. Box 406, 46 Main St., Danbury, 06810; (800) 841-4488 or **(203) 743-0546.**

Litchfield Hills Travel Council, P.O. Box 968, Litchfield, 06759; (860) 567-4506.

Visitors Information Center, in the former train station at **11 Railroad St. (corner of Bridge St./Rte. 202) in New Milford.** Open from the first weekend in May until the last weekend in Dec. Hours: Fri., 2:00 P.M.–5:00 P.M.; Sat., 10:00 A.M.–4:00 P.M.; Sun., 10:00 A.M.–2:00 P.M. For more information call the **New Milford Chamber of Commerce** at **(860) 354-6080.**

Transportation

Bus service between Washington and the northwestern region of the state is provided by the **Northwestern Connecticut Transit District.** For fare and schedule information call **(860) 489-2535.** For information on bus service south toward Danbury and Redding call the **Housatonic Area Transit District** at **(203) 744-4070.**

Waterbury

Cradled in the narrow Naugatuck River Valley, Waterbury's landscape resembles San Francisco's in character. Steep hills climb precipitously to the east and west, yielding long views from their summits. It is just such a hill that I-84 crests as it enters the city from the west. When you come into Waterbury from that direction, your eye will be drawn immediately to a tall, red brick clock tower on the left—the largest in New England—that completely dwarfs everything else within view. The tower crowns Union Station, a once-bustling railroad terminal that still sees commuter train activity but has mostly been converted into offices for Waterbury's daily newspaper, the *Republican-American*. A little farther on, the twin spires and dome of St. Anne's French-Canadian church, a monumental neo-Gothic cathedral on your right, reach heavenward. These two spectacular edifices are clues to Waterbury's past as a major industrial center and the destination of thousands of immigrants, principally from Europe's Catholic countries, who sought financial security in mill jobs around the turn of the 20th century.

Waterbury, and indeed all the towns in the Naugatuck River Valley, typified the northern manufacturing city. Mills up and down the valley turned out clocks, buttons, rubber shoes, woolens, wire, cotton goods and more. In Waterbury itself, brass products reigned supreme—so much so that Waterbury came to be known as Brass City. This industry is gone, but its memory lives on in numerous references such as the new Brass Mill Center Mall.

The prosperity that brass built is still reflected in Waterbury's architecture. In the Hillside district northwest of the downtown, mill owners built grand Queen Anne, Greek Revival, Stick Style, Georgian Revival and English Tudor homes that are best enjoyed on a walking tour of the area. Waterbury's wealthy not only lived in style, they also died that way. Riverside Cemetery, by Rte. 8 and the Naugatuck River, contains many impressive monuments, including a life-sized elk marking the grave of

the founder of the fraternal organization commonly known as the Elks.

Waterbury's green on W. Main St. between Bank and Church Sts. is classically beautiful, lined with memorials, public sculptures and landmark buildings. Nearby, the comparatively petite St. John's Episcopal Church has windows designed by Louis Comfort Tiffany. Also on the green is one of Connecticut's best museums, the Mattatuck, a combination fine art gallery, cultural center and industrial history museum that uniquely balances the artistic and workaday aspects of Waterbury life.

If the Mattatuck Museum is partly the story of what once was made in Connecticut, then Howland-Hughes is the story of what still is. For many years Howland-Hughes was Waterbury's elegant downtown department store. Except for a brief period of time around 1902 when a fire closed the store for reconstruction, it has been in continuous operation since 1890. But by the mid-1990s it could not compete with the surge of suburban malls, and it became Howland-Hughes—The Connecticut Store, stocking only goods made in Connecticut. Not only is it the best place in the state to shop for souvenirs—everything on the shelves will be an authentic reminder of your visit—but its vintage mahogany counters and electrified gas fixtures will take you back in time.

Just outside Waterbury there are more great attractions. Bristol, to the north, has two excellent museums (the American Clock and Watch Museum and the New England Carousel Museum) and the oldest continuously operating amusement park in the country, Lake Compounce. For outdoor activities, look to the recreation areas at Thomaston Dam and Northfield Brook Lake, where developed facilities provide exceptional opportunities for hiking, swimming, picnicking and motor biking.

History

Mattatuck was the Native American place-name for the area now called Waterbury. First surveyed by colonists in 1657 and first settled by families from Farmington in the mid-1670s,

432

the town was only moderately well situated for agriculture, and in its early days growth was slow. The original Waterbury plantation was a large area stretching up and down the valley and including parts of what are now a half-dozen surrounding towns. Throughout the colonial and Revolutionary War period population remained low, with many Waterbury natives migrating to the western frontier or elsewhere looking for better farmland. It was not until the advent of the Industrial Revolution that Waterbury really expanded, at first modestly and then explosively. From humble beginnings as a center of clock and button manufacturing in the early 1800s, Waterbury became the country's foremost producer of brass products.

Industry made not only Waterbury but a whole string of towns up and down the valley. The names Thomaston and Terryville are derived from the names of two men who virtually founded the local clock-making industry: Seth Thomas and Eli Terry. The term "Naugahyde" derives from Naugatuck, where it was made. The various industries that thrived in the valley dovetailed with one another nicely, creating a symbiotic relationship. Rolling mills supplied sheet metal to makers of brass products; brass was in turn fashioned into buckles fitted to rubber galoshes, gears for clocks and parts for pin-tumbler locks.

When the railroad came through in the mid-1800s, one of the principal obstacles to selling manufactured goods—poor roads—was removed. New markets led to the boom period of industrial growth in the valley, and by 1900 Waterbury's population had increased 20-fold over its numbers a century earlier.

The brass factories required thousands of employees. Waterbury's Big Three brass manufacturers, Anaconda American, Chase Brass and Scovill Manufacturing, actively recruited workers from Europe, and thousands poured in. The growth in population led to the incorporation of many new towns in the valley, most of them taken from the original Waterbury plantation of the 1600s.

In the immigrant neighborhoods one nationality succeeded another. The Irish were first, comprising (with their U.S.–born chil-

433

dren) almost 44% of Waterbury's population by 1876. The next wave was French-Canadian, then Italian, Russian and Lithuanian. Waterbury is still one of the most racially diverse cities in Connecticut, and new groups continue to replace the old, with Puerto Ricans among the more recent arrivals.

A 1902 fire that destroyed virtually all the downtown came at a time when Waterbury was booming. The structures that replaced what had burned were designed by notable architects and architectural firms such as Cass Gilbert and McKim, Mead and White. Gilbert went on to design the U.S. Supreme Court building in Washington, D.C.

Enthusiastic riders cool off on the new Thunder River white-water attraction at Lake Compounce. Photo by Wendy J. Riling.

Brass reigned supreme until the middle of the 20th century, but the falloff in demand after the close of World War II combined with the development of plastics and other factors that led to a general decline of American manufacturing after 1950, especially in the Northeast, sent the industry into a tailspin. A mere 20 years later the brass mills were history.

Since the demise of brass, the valley's employment base has become more diversified. A great deal of manufacturing still goes on, and much of it still has to do with metals. Many of today's companies are headed by individuals who worked in the brass mills and spun off the technology developed there for other purposes. Some even started their enterprises with loans from their former employers. Although there is no one industry that dominates the landscape and the life of the city the way the brass mills once did, Waterbury remains a center of business activity and Connecticut's foremost melting pot.

Major Attractions

Lake Compounce

First opened in 1846, this oldest continuously operating amusement park in the country recently went through a major renovation with upgrades and the addition of new rides. Nestled between wooded hills, beautiful Lake Compounce provides a constant backdrop to the activity. Among the recent additions are a steel boomerang roller coaster (the only one in New England), a revolving gondola/Ferris wheel ride (one of only three in the country) and a white-water raft ride. You'll also find old-fashioned classics such as a wooden roller coaster and a 100-foot Ferris wheel. For folks who aren't into thrill rides, there's a small beach, a miniature golf course, a chairlift to the top of Southington Mountain for a panoramic view of the countryside from the 750-foot summit, a refurbished 1911 trolley running lakeside, the original narrow-gauge train that once belonged to William Gillette of Gillette Castle fame (see the **Old Saybrook/ Old Lyme** chapter) and a museum documenting the history of the lake and the land. Season: Memorial Day–Labor Day with extended hours a possibility; call for specifics. Hours: open at 11:00 A.M., closing at 10:00 P.M. on Mon., Wed. & Thu., 11:00 P.M. Fri.–Sun.; closed Tue. Flat-rate, ride-all-day tickets are $18.95 adults, $13.95 seniors and anyone under 48 inches in height. General admission tickets including beach access but no rides are only $3.95, and per-ride tickets are available if you only want to go on a few. Kids under 3 and parking are free. **822 Lake Ave. (off Rte. 229), Bristol, 06010; (860) 583-3631.**

Mattatuck Museum

One of the best museums in Connecticut, the Mattatuck is housed in the most modern building to line Waterbury's town green (an interesting contrast to the classical splendor of nearby Immaculate Conception Catholic Church). It specifically documents the long, busy history of Waterbury, but because the town's story— that of a community vastly transformed by both the coming and going of industry—is one repeated time and again throughout the state and the country, the Mattatuck is universal in its pertinence.

There is a reconstruction of an early settler's house and a sizable display on the brass industry. Two contrasting vignettes—

one showing a typical Victorian-era industrialist's sitting room, the other a typical worker's kitchen from the same period—are an example of the thoughtful presentation that makes the Mattatuck so effective.

The second floor houses one of the best art galleries around, with constantly changing exhibits that display works from the museum's permanent collection of paintings, sculpture, prints and drawings by contemporary artists, Connecticut Impressionists and others. A café is on-site as well. Evening programming and tours round out the Mattatuck's contribution to local cultural life (see Nightlife and Tours for details). Admission to the museum is free. Hours: Tue.–Sat., 10:00 A.M.–5:00 P.M.; Sun., noon–5:00 P.M.; closed Mon., as well as Sun. in July & Aug. Museum store hours: Tue.–Sat., 10:00 A.M.–4:00 P.M. Café hours: Tue.–Sat., 11:00 A.M.–3:00 P.M. **144 W. Main St., Waterbury, 06702; (203) 753-0381.**

U.S. Army Corps of Engineers Recreation Areas

Because of the general propensity of the Naugatuck River to flood, several decades ago the U.S. Army Corps of Engineers was called in for an ambitious flood-control project involving several dams in the region. These dams control the flow of water on the Naugatuck itself as well as on feeder waterways. As a side benefit, they created prime recreational facilities for biking, hiking, picnicking, fishing and other outdoor activities, the two principal ones being **Thomaston Dam** and **Northfield Brook.**

Drive along the crest of Thomaston Dam or park and gaze at the lovely Naugatuck Valley stretching away to your north. A marker on the upstream face of the dam indicates the high-water point (87.2 feet) in June 1984, when floodwaters would have inundated downstream communities had the dam not been in place.

Part of the recreation area is frequently used as a remote-control aircraft field, and a network of dirt roads designed for trail bike use in summer and snowmobile use in winter gives adherents of these sports some designated turf without the hazards of multiple-use trails.

Getting There

Waterbury is located about 40 minutes southwest of Hartford on I-84. For information on train and bus service, see the Services section at the end of this chapter.

Northfield Brook offers swimming in a small pond, fishing in the pond and the stream that feeds it and a loop trail of moderate length. Ruins of several 19th-century mill-pond dams lie on Northfield Brook.

Hours at both areas are 8:00 A.M.–sunset daily, year-round, and admission is free. The top of Thomaston Dam is open year-round, weather permitting. It's located on Rte. 222 in Thomaston 2 miles north of the center of town. At Northfield Brook the main road and parking area are gated mid-Oct.–mid-Apr., but you can walk, bike or ski in. **Northfield Brook is on Rte. 254 in Thomaston.** For more information call **(203) 758-1723.**

Festivals and Events

American Tour de Sol
mid-May

This annual road race featuring alternative energy vehicles starts from Waterbury in some years. About 50 electric, solar-assisted and hybrid vehicles ranging from cars to mopeds—some made by major manufacturers, some made by students and enthusiasts—take part. Spectators can view the vehicles and talk to the engineers who designed them in Library Park at Grand and Meadow Sts. in Waterbury for three days leading up to the race. The cars are also on display at each of the nightly stopover points on the weeklong tour. The starting point is in front of City Hall on Grand St.

Unlike conventional road races, this competition is not just about speed. Since the race's organizer, the **Northeast Sustainable Energy Association (NSEA),** is dedicated to finding viable alternatives to fossil-fueled transportation, the scoring system emphasizes practicality by rewarding efficiency and driving range within certain speed parameters. The city of departure varies from year to year, but Waterbury is working hard to host it every other year. For more information contact NSEA at **(413) 774-6051**.

Balloons Over Bristol
Memorial Day weekend (Fri.–Sun.)

Organized by the Bristol Jaycees on the first weekend of summer, this is one of the largest hot-air balloon rallies in the Northeast. Bring your camera for the balloon launchings at 6:00 A.M. and 6:00 P.M., conditions permitting. For a fee you can even be part of one. Launched rides (where you float free for up to an hour) run $175 per person, and quick rides (where you go up and come back down while attached to the ground via a tether) are in the $10 range. Call to make a reservation for a launched ride. Tethered rides are usually first-come, first-served.

A large craft fair, live music, carnival rides and food vendors go on throughout each day. The world's largest maze is a regular highlight. Most activities start up around 10:00 A.M. or noon. Call for a schedule of special events, or check out *The Hartford Courant*'s special pull-out section on the festival, published during the prior week. Admission to the event is free; pay as you go. Hours: Fri., 5:00 P.M.–9:00 P.M.; Sat.–Sun., 6:00 A.M.–8:00 P.M. The festival takes place at **Bristol Eastern High School on Rte. 229 about half a mile from Rte. 6.** For more information call **(860) 584-5790**.

Wolcott Country Fair
third full weekend in Aug. (Fri.–Sun.)

Although the Naugatuck Valley is associated with industry, the Wolcott Country Fair still preserves the area's original agricultural heritage and provides a wonderful forum for family fun. See wool go from sheep to yarn, visit the home show and commercial crafts tents and root for a favorite in the popular wood-chopping contest. Children's games (no pre-registration required) are held Sat. & Sun. around midday. Ride bracelets allow children

to go on all the rides Sat. & Sun. afternoon for one low price. Entertainment can range from country and western bands to an Elvis impersonator. If the noise and excitement get to you, you can always head over to the incubator to watch chicks hatch. A fireworks display ends the fair on Sun. evening. On-site parking costs $1, or park in a free remote lot and take a shuttle bus. Admission: $5 adults, $3 seniors, children under 13 free. Hours: Fri., 1:00 P.M.–11:00 P.M.; Sat., 10:00 A.M.–11:00 P.M.; Sun., 10:00 A.M.–10:00 P.M. **Wolcott Fairground** is at the **corner of Woodtick and Todd Rds. in Wolcott**; follow signs from Rtes. 322 or 69. For more information call **(860) 879-5466**.

Terryville Country Fair
second weekend after Labor Day (Fri.–Sun.)

Just as the air starts to carry the first scents of autumn, Terryville Country Fair comes around. Popular events include the English horse show Sat. morning, the Western horse show Sun. morning, children's games on Sat. afternoon, bingo all three nights, a kielbasa dinner on Fri. and a chicken barbeque on the weekend. The skies are lit up with fireworks on Fri. and Sat. nights. Admission: $5 adults, $3 seniors, children 12 and under free. Hours: Fri., 5:00 P.M.–10:00 P.M.; Sat., 8:00 A.M.–10:00 P.M.; Sun., 8:00 A.M.–6:00 P.M. **Terryville Fairground** is **on Scott Rd. off Rte. 6 in Terryville**. For more information call **(860) 283-9300**.

Mum Festival
Sept./Oct.

Many years ago Bristol was the Mum Capital of the World. Bristol Nurseries used to cultivate these colorful flowering plants by the thousands, and despite the demise of that industry the town continues its two-week-long traditional celebration featuring a beauty pageant, a parade with floats made largely from mums, a carnival and food festival and other activities. The festival starts on the fourth Fri. of Sept. Schedules are distributed free at local

436

businesses and published in the *Bristol Press* a week in advance. All events are free. For more information call **(860) 584-4718.**

Pumpkin Festival
next to last Sun. in Sept.

This juried art festival with over 150 exhibitors also features seasonally themed activities such as pumpkin decorating and the crowning of a Pumpkin King and Queen. Located in **French Memorial Park at the junction of Rtes. 67 and 8 in Seymour.** Admission is free. Hours: 9:00 A.M.–5:00 P.M. Rain date: the following Sun.

Witch's Dungeon Horror Museum
late Oct.

The longest-running Halloween exhibit in the United States was begun by a makeup and prop specialist for TV and film who used his connections in those industries to get mask casts of famous movie monsters of the 1930s and 1940s such as Frankenstein and the Phantom of the Opera. He's re-created 13 scenes from classic horror films accompanied by authentic soundtracks. The museum is authorized by Universal Studios, the company that made many of the films. Vincent Price even did a voice track and donated the suit he wore in *House of Wax.* The museum is open the last three weekends (Fri.–Sun.) of Oct., 7:00 P.M.–10:00 P.M. Admission: $.99 adults, $.50 children. **90 Battle St., Bristol, 06010; (860) 583-8306.**

Outdoor Activities

The **South Central Connecticut Regional Water Authority** owns two beautiful watershed properties, **Lake Bethany** in Bethany and **Lake Chamberlain** in Woodbridge, that are open for recreational use by permit only for a small charge. These are exceptional areas worth the effort and expense of getting the permit. There are paved walking paths and hik-ing trails at both, plus lake fishing, wheelchair lakeside access and equestrian trails at Lake Chamberlain. Permits cost $35 per year and provide access for one couple and their children under age 21. Information on access is provided when you obtain the permit. For more information call **(203) 624-6671** during normal business hours.

Biking

On summer weekends, the 58-mile network of trails at Thomaston Dam resounds with the noise of motorbikes. On weekdays, however, these dirt and paved trails, which wind through woodland and open terrain with some tricky mounds to negotiate, are often deserted and make a superb mountain biking course. Trying to coexist on the trails is *not* recommended, for the safety of everyone concerned. Even if you don't think others are around, pay strict attention to the one-way system in effect here. The Recreation Area is on Rte. 222 a few miles north of the Thomaston town center. To get to the trails, drive over the dam and continue to the blacktopped turnaround where you can go no farther. Trails are open to motorbike and mountain bike use May 1–Oct. 14. (Note: All-terrain vehicles are prohibited.) In order to motorbike, you must obtain an inexpensive registration from the **Dept. of Motor Vehicles; (860) 842-8222** (in Connecticut) or **(800) 842-8222** (out-of-state). Park hours: 8:00 A.M.–sunset or 8:00 P.M., whichever comes first. For more information on **Thomaston Dam** call **(860) 283-5540.**

Fishing

U.S. Army Corps of Engineers Recreation Areas
The lakes at **Northfield Brook, Black Rock** and **Hancock Lake** are all stocked with trout, and warm-water species such as bass occur naturally. The entrance to Black Rock is on Rte. 109 about a mile west of Rte. 6. This is *not* the same as Black Rock State Park. The reservoir here is not developed for anything other than fishing, so it should be nice and quiet, and there's plenty of shore access.

437

Gone fishin' at Osbornedale State Park. Photo courtesy Connecticut Department of Environmental Protection.

Hancock Lake is located on Waterbury Rd. off Rte. 262 in Plymouth.

Other Lakes and Ponds

Shore fishing is allowed at **Black Rock Pond** in Black Rock State Park anywhere but in the swimming area and at **Pickett's Pond** in Osbornedale State Park. Trout and panfish are found in both spots. For more information, see the listings under Swimming and Hiking.

Hiking

Black Rock State Park

Several miles of trails and two possible loops in this state park are crossed by the blue-blazed Mattatuck Trail. One hike takes you past the landmark "Black Rock"—named for the color imbued by graphite—and a lookout from an elevation of 800 feet. You may catch occasional glimpses of Black Rock Pond, where there is a beach. Just across Rte. 6 from the park, the Mattatuck Trail passes through a cave. A parking fee is charged in summer. For directions and more information, see the listing under Swimming.

Mattatuck Trail

The Mattatuck is one of the blue-blazed trails described in the *Connecticut Walk Book*. Of its three parts, the longest is the continuous

stretch from Wolcott to Litchfield that takes hikers past Buttermilk Falls on Hancock Brook in Plymouth. The waterfall happens to be near an easy access point. Park in the dirt pullout at the intersection of Lane Hill Rd. and S. Main St. in Plymouth and hike up Lane Hill. Turn at the blue blaze on the right, and you'll come to Buttermilk Falls in under two minutes. A second easy access point is Black Rock State Park on Rte. 6/202 in Watertown, but a vehicle parking fee is required in summer. A third option is the U.S. Army Corps of Engineers Recreation Area at Hancock Lake, located on Waterbury Rd. off Rte. 262 in Plymouth. The pullout off S. Main St. at the top of the lake is closest to the trail, although it's open only seasonally.

Naugatuck State Forest

Old logging roads good for hiking crisscross a parcel of the Naugatuck State Forest shared by the towns of Naugatuck, Oxford and Beacon Falls. For access, follow Cold Spring Rd. in Beacon Falls north about half a mile past the spot where the pavement ends. Follow signs to High Rock Grove, a big ledge visible from Rte. 8 that yields a nice view of the Naugatuck River Valley, or to cool, shady Spruce Brook Ravine. Hours: 8:00 A.M.–sunset daily, year-round. Forest office: **(203) 264-5169.**

Osbornedale State Park

Osbornedale's 400 acres offer a mix of woodland and open field that is increasingly rare in Connecticut and especially good for birding. The terrain is moderately hilly. A trail map is posted by Pickett's Pond right at the entrance, where large numbers of geese congregate. At least one trail leads down to the Osborne Homestead Museum and Kellogg Environmental Center 2 miles away. Hours: 8:00 A.M.–sunset daily, year-round. Enter from Chatfield St. opposite Derby High School in Derby. Park office: **(203) 735-4311.**

Other Trails

Ansonia Nature and Recreation Center (10 Deerfield Ln., Ansonia; 203-736-9360) makes a nice contrast to some of Connecticut's wilder places. The trails are manageable for small kids, guided hikes are scheduled frequently and there's a playground and picnic tables. The same is true at **H. C. Barnes Memorial Nature Center (175 Shrub Rd., Bristol; 860-589-6082)**, where there's also a free nature center with animal exhibits. At **Northfield Brook Recreation Area**, described under Major Attractions, a 1.7-mile loop trail circumnavigates the park, taking you up a steep hillside above the picnic areas and then along Northfield Brook for your return trip.

Horseback Riding

B&R Riding Stables (Roaring Brook Rd., Prospect; 203-758-5031) and **Hillside Equestrian Meadows (1260 Woodtick Rd., Wolcott; 203-879-6863)** offer guided rides on wooded trails by reservation only. At B&R the rate of $20 per hour includes helmets, and there is a small picnic area for patrons to enjoy. They can accommodate kids age 10 and above. At Hillside the cost is $30 for a one-and-a-half-hour ride. They take children as young as 6, but you have to bring your own head protection.

Skiing and Snowmobiling

There are no commercial cross-country ski areas at which to rent equipment or find groomed trails, but if you own skis, cut your own trails at some local parks. The mixed woodland and open fields of **Osbornedale State Park**, described under Hiking, offer some impressive views of the surrounding countryside and a gentle landscape that beginner and intermediate skiers will appreciate. **Ansonia Nature and Recreation Center** at **10 Deerfield Lane in Ansonia** is hillier and more for experienced skiers. For more information call **(203) 736-9360.**

Snowmobilers can enjoy two designated snowmobile trail networks in the area whenever the snow cover is at least 6 inches. At **Naugatuck State Forest** a system of loops on 11 miles of old logging roads makes it possible to design a trip of almost any length without much doubling back. For directions, see the listing under Hiking. The other option is **Thomaston Dam**, where an incredible 58 miles of trails reserved for motorbikes in summer are the exclusive domain of snowmobilers in winter (Oct. 14–May 1). For more information, see the listing under Biking.

Sleigh and Carriage Rides

Wood Acres (68 Griffin Rd., Terryville; 860-583-8670) offers year-round, horse-drawn rides in carriages and sleighs that can accommodate four to six people as well as larger vehicles for bigger groups. They take you down country roads through 25 acres of woods. Prices start at $75 for a 45-minute trip. Light refreshments are provided, and groups can enjoy an hour of postride warm-up time in a hayloft "lounge" with a wood stove.

Swimming

The sandy beach on **Black Rock Pond in Black Rock State Park** is the best place around to take a dip. Lifeguards are on duty daily, 10:00 A.M.–6:00 P.M., Memorial Day–Labor Day, but the beach is open 8:00 A.M.–dusk if you feel comfortable swimming without supervision. There's a full range of facilities here including bathhouses, rest rooms, concessions and picnic tables, as well as hiking trail access. Memorial Day–Labor Day, a parking fee of $5 weekends and holidays and $4 weekdays is charged for in-state vehicles. For out-of-state vehicles, the fees are $8 and $5. Located on **Rte. 6/202 half a mile south of Rte. 109 in Watertown; (860) 677-1819.**

Families looking for a shallow pond where small children can swim might be interested in the tiny beach at **Northfield Brook**, described under Major Attractions. Access is free, but it's unguarded.

Seeing and Doing

Museums

For information on the area's major historical institution, the Mattatuck Museum, see the listing under Major Attractions. In addition,

439

virtually every town in the Naugatuck River Valley has a local history museum. Town clerks can usually provide a phone number if you want to tour them. Plus, Terryville's history as an important lock manufacturing town is documented at the **Lock Museum of America (230 Main St., Terryville; 860-589-6359),** which houses an impressive collection of locks, keys, doorknobs, knockers, striker plates and more.

American Clock & Watch Museum

The well-informed guides have lots of interesting stories to tell about the museum's collection of more than 3,000 timepieces, which are beautifully exhibited in the shell of an 1801 colonial house, and a video presentation fills you in on the history of the clock-making industry, which was vital to Connecticut's economy in the mid-1800s. Outside, the lovely Sundial Garden is named for the world's first timepiece. For hard-to-find books on horological topics, be sure to visit their excellent gift shop. The museum is in Bristol's historic Federal Hill residential district where the city's wealthy built their mansions, and a walking-tour guide is available at the cashier for $1. Admission: $3.50 adults, $3 seniors, $1.50 children 8–15. Hours: 10:00 A.M.–5:00 P.M. daily, Apr.–Nov. **100 Maple St., Bristol, 06010; (860) 583-6070.**

New England Carousel Museum

The collection of antique carousel pieces at this museum includes examples of the historic styles of horses and chariots and has information about the creating and restoring processes. One display is a functional shop where carvers are sometimes at work. A Braille script is available for the visually impaired. Admission: $4 adults, $3.50 seniors, $2.50 children 4–14. Hours: Mon.–Sat., 10:00 A.M.–5:00 P.M.; Sun., noon–5:00 P.M.; closed major holidays & Mon.–Wed., Dec.–Mar. **95 Riverside Ave. (Rte. 72), Bristol, 06010; (860) 585-5411.**

Osborne Homestead Museum

Frances Eliza Osborne was a talented businesswoman prominent in Derby in the early 1900s, serving as president, vice president or treasurer of several metal products and textile manufacturers and having a partnership in many more. Where money was concerned, she seemed to have the golden touch: she inherited a fortune, made a fortune and married a fortune. Osborne left her house, 400 acres of land and an endowment to the state, but only on the condition that her housekeeper have lifetime use of it all.

The mid-1800s farmhouse, which was overhauled during the Colonial Revival movement, holds Osborne's rare collections of silver, dinnerware, porcelain, first edition Currier & Ives prints and many cows, a reference to the dairy farm she and her husband Waldo Stewart Kellogg ran so famously. There are also a formal garden, a rose garden and a shade rockery. Guided tours, offered year-round, take about half an hour. Admission: $1. Tour hours: Tue. & Thu., 10:00 A.M.–2:00 P.M.; Sat.–Sun., 10:00 A.M.–4:00 P.M. **500 Hawthorne Ave., Derby, 06418; (203) 734-2513.**

Nature Centers

The **Kellogg Environmental Center (500 Hawthorne Ave., Derby; 203-734-2513)** on the grounds of the Osborne Homestead Museum contains displays on Connecticut's habitats, wetland birds, hawk migration and more. There is a good gift shop stocked with a large selection of nature books and insect-collecting paraphernalia such as nets, lenses and bug boxes. It also offers many programs such as bird walks and nature photography workshops. Admission is free except for special events, and hiking on neighboring Osbornedale State Park is also free. Nature center hours: 8:30 A.M.–4:00 P.M., weekdays only during winter; Tue.–Sat. during summer & early autumn.

For more expanded weekend hours, look to the **H. C. Barnes Memorial Nature Center (175 Shrub Rd., Bristol; 860-589-6082)** where there are several miles of trails in addition to live animal exhibits and taxidermy. It offers a lecture, walk or other program on a nature topic every Sun., 1:30 P.M.–3:00 P.M. Programs cost $2 per person or $10 per family. Nature center admission is $2 age 10 and up, $1 age 5–9. Nature center hours: Wed.– Fri., 2:00 P.M.–5:00 P.M.; Sat., 10:00 A.M.–5:00 P.M.; Sun., noon–4:00 P.M. Ground hours: dawn– dusk daily.

Nightlife

Waterbury is not known for clubs or nightspots, but there are a couple of unique things that go on after hours. The **Mattatuck Museum (144 W. Main St., Waterbury; 203- 753-0381)** runs a poetry slam (a competitive form of the art) the third Fri. of every month, 7:30 P.M.–10:00 P.M., and a dance slam (again, a competition, *not* slam dancing) the second Fri. of each month during the same hours. Every Wed. during open drawing studio (6:00 P.M.–8:00 P.M.), a model poses for as many people as show up to sketch. They provide ea- sels; you bring supplies. There are special events too; call for a schedule. The cost for most programs is a $5 donation.

The **Actors Colony (179 Roosevelt Dr., Seymour; 203-734-2551)**, normally a cater- ing facility, offers dancing to the sounds of an 18-piece big band on the first Sun. of each month, 6:00 P.M.–10:00 P.M. The $15 per per- son price includes a buffet dinner.

Performing Arts

The largest dramatic productions in the area are staged by **Seven Angels Theater (on Plank Rd. in Hamilton Park in Waterbury; 203-757-4676)**, an Equity company who home venue is the Hamilton Pavilion. It pre- sents ten shows a year including musicals, drama, cabaret and a lot of new work. Evening performances are given Thu.–Sun. at 8:00 P.M. Matinee times are Thu., Sat. & Sun. at 2:00 P.M., year-round. Inquire about dinner/show packages. Other local community and semi- professional theaters include **Clockwork Rep- ertory Theatre (133 Main St., Oakville; 860-274-7247)** and **The Strand Theater (203-888-0083)**.

Thomaston Opera House (158 Main St., Thomaston; 860-283-6250) is an impres- sive structure set in a block of stately brick buildings on Thomaston's main street. Built in 1884 the 525-seat playhouse has a notable interior, much of which has been restored through ongoing volunteer efforts. It's a local cultural center offering everything from com- munity theater, performances by touring com- panies, occasional children's shows and concerts and more.

Look to the **Waterbury Symphony Or- chestra** and conductor Leif Bjaland for a rich balance of classical, pops and family musical programming. They give occasional Sat. night and Sun. afternoon performances in addition to one popular outdoor summer concert at The Hollow in nearby Woodbury. Their normal venue is the 800-seat Fine Arts Center audito- rium at **Naugatuck Valley Community Tech- nical College** at **750 Chase Pkwy. in Waterbury.** Tickets are in the $15–$35 range. For more information call **(203) 574-4283.**

Scenic Drives

The narrow valley in which Waterbury lies is best appreciated from a high vantage point. Climb Congress or Avon Sts. to the west of downtown in late afternoon for a commanding view of the city's church spires and towers bathed in golden light. Or take a slow ramble south to north down Oronoke Rd. in the south- western part of town for a stunning western prospect of undulating hills. For rural vistas, you'll have to get away from the city. The drive up Rte. 222 from Thomaston Dam through Harwinton is especially pretty, and the view from the dam is spectacular. Finally, towns like Woodbridge, Bethany and Prospect are surprisingly rural and worthy of exploration, given their position between Waterbury and New Haven.

Shopping

Brass Mill Center Mall
Autumn 1997 saw the completion of a major new mall for Waterbury. It's a genuinely nice shopping experience with many merchants you won't see at competing malls. Hours are Mon.–Sat., 10:00 A.M.–9:30 P.M.; Sun., 11:00

A.M.–6:00 P.M. It's located off **I-84 exits 22 and 23 or from Hamilton Ave. in Waterbury.** For more information call **(203) 755-5003.**

Howland-Hughes— The Connecticut Store

For authentic made-in-Connecticut souvenirs, there's no better place to go than Howland-Hughes; 150 Connecticut manufacturers, production craftspeople, authors and artists are represented at this classic former department store, whose beautiful vintage fixtures are still intact. Whenever possible the displays also give background information on the makers of the products. A new feature called the Living Factory is basically a showcase of local manufacturing technology, complete with machinery and working craftspeople. Another highlight is a 1963 lunch counter, called the Connecticut Café, down in the basement along with Connecticut Booksellers, an antiquarian bookstore with a general focus on American literature. Hours: Tue.–Sat., 9:30 A.M.–5:00 P.M.; closed Sun. & Mon. except during the holiday season, when the store is also open on Mon., 9:30 A.M.–5:00 P.M., Thu. until 8:30 P.M. & on the two Sun. prior to Christmas, 11:00 A.M.–4:00 P.M. **120–140 Bank St. (near Grand), Waterbury, 06702; (800) 474-6728** or **(203) 753-4121.**

Tours

Mattatuck Museum Tours

The Mattatuck Museum offers a wide range of tour options including walking tours of historic districts, half-day tours of the museum's collections and bus field trips lasting from a half day to two days. The latter focus on the architecture and culture of New England villages from the 18th to the 20th centuries. Reservations required; call **(203) 753-0381** a minimum of one week in advance and inquire about rates.

Naugatuck Railroad Co.

The Naugatuck Railroad operates excursion trains between Waterville station in Waterbury and Thomaston Dam on a line formerly operated by the Boston & Maine Railroad. The route goes through Mattatuck State Forest with several river crossings and a stop at Thomaston Dam for a view down the narrow, wooded, picturesque valley. The round-trip takes one hour and 20 minutes. The train runs on weekends, early May–Oct., plus holidays and during the Christmas season; call for departure times. Fare: $8 adults, $6 children 12 and under. The station is at **176 Chase River Rd. near Huntington Ave. in Waterbury; (203) 575-1931.**

Walking Tours

Waterbury has some eminently walkable neighborhoods and parks. Pick up a free copy of "Legacy and Promise," a 48-page walking tour guide to all nine towns represented by the Waterbury Region Convention and Visitors Bureau. This brochure leads you on a trek around the green and past the historic buildings of surrounding areas, such as the Victorian homes of the Hillside neighborhood north of downtown and the broad mix of architectural styles in the Overlook neighborhood to the west of Fulton Park.

Where to Stay

Bed & Breakfasts

The House on the Hill—$$$$

This 1888 Victorian in Waterbury's Hillside neighborhood, noted for its rich collection of homes built by wealthy industrialists 100–150 years ago, features four suites with period decor and private baths. Each suite has some unique quality: one is located in a turret of the house, another has a private porch, a third has a kitchen and the fourth has two bedrooms with a shared bath. They all have a TV, telephone and a tea kettle. A full breakfast is included. Overflow B&B guests can also be accommodated in nearby Seventy Hillside, which is principally used for conferences and weddings. **92 Woodlawn Ter., Waterbury, 06710; (203) 757-9901.**

Chimney Crest Manor—$$$ to $$$$

This 1930s Tudor mansion in Bristol's historic Federal Hill district was built by a prominent clock maker and spring manufacturer. It survived a period of neglect and has been largely returned to a state in keeping with its manorial character. There are six guest rooms, four of them suites. Two offer enough space for families with two or more children, Children ages 7 and up are accommodated. There are several common rooms, including a palatial parlor and a sunroom, in which to curl up with a good book or a cup of tea. A full breakfast can be enjoyed outside in warm weather. **5 Founders Dr.** (a tiny gated private road off Woodland St. between Belridge Rd. and Bradley St.), **Bristol, 06010; (860) 582-4219.**

The Graham House—$$$
Located in an 1840s farmhouse that was once the homestead of a dairy farm, The Graham House is the closest B&B to the Taft School and the only one in Watertown. There are three rooms (one with private bath, two with a shared bath) furnished with double beds and country decorations replete with quilts, dolls and rustic handcrafts. A full breakfast is included. **1002 Middlebury Rd., Watertown, 06795; (860) 274-2647.**

Hotels, Motels & Inns

Like everything in this value-conscious town, rates for accommodations are exceedingly reasonable. Many hotels in Waterbury cater to business travelers and drop their rates on weekends to boost occupancy. The listings below represent just a few of the better hotels. For more options call the **Waterbury Region Convention and Visitors Bureau** at **(203) 597-9527.**

Radisson—$$$ to $$$$
The closest hotel to Lake Compounce amusement park has standard hotel rooms with one king or two double beds and a few suites. Located outside the downtown area, the hotel has an on-site restaurant that serves three meals a day and provides room service. It also has an indoor pool, an exercise room and a sauna. **42 Century Dr. (off Rte. 229), Bristol, 06010; (800) 333-3333 or (860) 589-7766.**

Sheraton Four Points Hotel—$$$ to $$$$
The largest full-service hotel in the Waterbury area is actually outside the center of the city near the Cheshire town line, just off I-84. Rooms are arranged around a four-story atrium lobby where two restaurants and a bar are located. Recreational facilities include an indoor pool, a sauna, a whirlpool, an exercise room and racquetball courts. **3580 E. Main St., Waterbury, 06705; (800) 325-3535 or (203) 573-1000.**

Courtyard by Marriott—$$$
Recently renovated, this small hotel in Waterbury's downtown area features pleasant rooms with brand-new furnishings. Some rooms have a Jacuzzi, and suites come with a stocked kitchenette, a fully private bedroom and a pullout couch. Facilities include a small workout area, an indoor pool and spa, a sauna and a restaurant serving breakfast and dinner. Located within walking distance from the Mattatuck Museum and several restaurants. **63 Grand St., Waterbury, 06706; (203) 596-1000.**

Quality Inn—$$$
The Quality Inn offers two classes of accommodation: standard rooms with two double or one queen or king bed and Jacuzzi rooms with an in-room whirlpool bath. It has an outdoor pool, an informal restaurant on-site serving three meals a day and a location convenient to I-84. **88 Union St., Waterbury, 06706; (800) 221-2222 or (203) 575-1500.**

Camping

Black Rock State Park—$
There are 96 wooded sites at this state park featuring a developed beach on Black Rock Pond, hiking trails, ball fields and horseshoe pits (shoes not provided). Each site has a picnic table and fire pit, and there are picnic groves by the pond. Facilities include flush toilets, hot showers and a dump station for RVs. As a plus, rangers lead public programs

443

for both adults and children at a small nature center. Located on **Rte. 6/202 in Watertown.** Campground office: **(860) 283-8088.** Park office: **(860) 677-1819.**

Where to Eat

When it comes to dining, few places match Waterbury for value. The city's culinary strength is in its Italian restaurants, reflecting the fact that Italians make up a larger percentage of Waterbury's population than any other ethnic group. Because the city is historically oriented toward value-conscious, hard-working people, prices are exceedingly reasonable.

Carmen Anthony's—$$$ to $$$$
In a recent *Connecticut* magazine readers' poll, Carmen Anthony's took the prize for best steak in New Haven County. This combination steak house and Italian restaurant encourages loyalty by inviting repeat customers to keep a stock of their favorite wine in a wine locker called the "library." There's plenty of room to stretch out at spacious booths and large tables, plus a separate, low-key bar. Open for lunch Mon.–Fri., 11:00 A.M.–2:00 P.M. Dinner served Mon.–Fri., 5:00 P.M.–10:00 P.M.; Sat., 5:00 P.M.–11:00 P.M.; Sun., 4:00 P.M.–9:00 P.M. **496 Chase Ave., Waterbury, 06704; (203) 757-3040.**

Diorio—$$$ to $$$$
Diorio is interesting for its food and its history. Several years ago the whole downtown block in which it lies was going to be torn down for redevelopment, but the façades were saved, along with the 1927 Diorio barroom, with its high-backed mahogany banker's booths, tin ceiling and mirror etched with Waterbury scenes behind the marble and brass bar. The full menu is served in the barroom as well as in a new dining room. The cuisine is Northern Italian with Asian and other influences and features wild game and many steak and chop selections. Open for lunch Mon–Fri., 11:30 A.M.–2:30 P.M., & for dinner Mon.–Sat., 5:30 P.M.–10:00 P.M. **231 Bank St., Waterbury, 06702; (203) 754-5111.**

Bacco's—$$$
Bacco's has a solid hold on its status as the best pizza restaurant in town, but it also serves a full menu of pasta, grinders, veal and chicken prepared three or four ways, steaks and seafood. There's a casual pizza room if you're just getting a pie and a regular dining room where the full menu is served. Dining room hours: Tue.–Fri., 11:30 A.M.–10:00 P.M.; Sat., 4:00 P.M.–11:00 P.M.; Sun., noon–8:00 P.M. Pizza room open Tue.–Sun. from 11:30 A.M., closing Tue.–Thu. at 10:30 P.M., Fri.–Sat. at 11:30 P.M., Sun. at 9:30 P.M. **1230 Thomaston Ave., Waterbury, 06704; (203) 755-0635.**

Cafe 4 Fifty 7—$$$
With a menu firmly focused on fish and seafood, Cafe 4 Fifty 7 offers some welcome contrast to the overwhelming majority of Waterbury's Italian restaurants (although you can still get Italian here). The atmosphere is casual, and it's within walking distance of the downtown hotels. Hours: lunch served Mon.–Fri., 11:30 A.M.–2:30 P.M.; dinner served Mon.–Thu., 5:30 P.M.–9:00 P.M., & Fri.–Sat. until 10:00 P.M. **457 W. Main St., Waterbury, 06702; (203) 574-4507.**

Drescher's Restaurant—$$$
Waterbury's oldest restaurant, built in 1868, this casual place with dark wood and big old booths serves German, Continental and Italian food. It has a jazz duo on Sat. evenings, and it's within walking distance from downtown hotels. Hours: open for lunch at 11:30 A.M., closing Mon.–Wed. at 9:00 P.M., Thu.–Sat. at 10:00 P.M. **25 Leavenworth St., Waterbury, 06702; (203) 573-1743.**

The Hills Tavern—$$$
The restaurant at Western Hills Golf Course is worth a stop even if you're not playing a round. It serves American fare such as steaks, prime rib and sandwiches, plus a $10.95 Sun. brunch in an informal publike atmosphere. Prices are reasonable, portions humongous. Reservations suggested on weekends. Hours: noon–9:00 P.M. daily (sometimes closed for lunch Mon.–Wed., so call before going); Sun. brunch served 11:00 A.M.–2:00 P.M. Located on **Park Rd., Waterbury, 06706; (203) 755-1331.**

Bellissimo Restaurant and Tavern— $$ to $$$$

Yet one more addition to the plethora of Waterbury's great Italian restaurants, Bellissimo also serves regional American fare and is known for having the best Sun. brunch in town. Rather than the conventional eggs and pancakes breakfast fare, its brunch features frittata, pastas, veal, an all-you-can-eat shrimp selection, pizza, a salad bar with antipasta ingredients, a full dessert menu and more for $16.95 (adults) and $7.95 (children 4–10). A light pub menu is available in the tavern, and it operates a deli and pizzeria next door called The Cookery, which is also an espresso bar, with dessert and coffee available all the time and entertainment nightly. Hours: Mon.–Sat., 11:30 A.M.–10:00 P.M.; Sun. brunch served 10:30 A.M.–2:00 P.M. & dinner served 4:00 P.M.–8:00 P.M. Tavern open 11:00 A.M.–midnight. **625 Chase Ave. at Cooke, Waterbury, 06704; (203) 754-3898.**

The Grotto—$$ to $$$

After almost six decades in Waterbury, The Grotto is a local family dining institution. The specialty is homemade pastas and sauces, which you can eat in the dining room or buy ready-to-cook at home. (Half of the business is a store that sells gift baskets and other items.) The dining room is made to look like an indoor sidewalk café, complete with a cement floor, street lamps, stop signs and murals of Waterbury. Dining room hours: Tue.–Thu., 11:00 A.M.–7:30 P.M.; Fri.–Sat. until 8:00 P.M. The store opens at 9:00 A.M. **634 Watertown Ave., Waterbury, 06708; (203) 754-0295.**

Brownie's—$$

At this little downtown luncheonette, you can get anything from the menu at any hour, and it's open from Fri. morning through Sun. lunch. Hours: Mon.–Thu., 6:00 A.M.–4:30 P.M.; then open continuously from Fri. at 6:00 A.M. to Sun. at 12:30 P.M. **354 W. Main St., Waterbury, 06702; (203) 574-5012.**

Exhibition Café—$$

The restaurant at the Mattatuck Museum serves gourmet sandwiches, seasonal soups and salads, plus luscious desserts, the best chocolate chip cookies in town and other treats. Although the only full meal it serves is lunch, it's also open in the morning for coffee and baked goods. Lunch hours: Tue.–Sat., 11:00 A.M.–2:00 P.M. **144 W. Main St., Waterbury, 06702; (203) 753-2452.**

Frankie's—$ to $$

If you're driving down Watertown Ave. and you see a large parking lot mobbed with people, you've probably found Frankie's. This roadside joint serves classic fast food—burgers, onion rings, fried clams. In typical 1950s fast-food style, you order from the window and then eat in your car. Hours: 11:00 A.M.–10:00 P.M. daily. **700 Watertown Ave., Waterbury, 06708; (203) 753-2426.**

Services

Local Visitors Information

Waterbury Region Convention and Visitors Bureau, 21 Church St., Waterbury, 06702; (203) 597-9527. Hours: Mon.–Fri., 8:30 A.M.–5:00 P.M., year-round.

Transportation

Metro-North commuter trains serve Waterbury, Naugatuck, Beacon Falls, Seymour, Ansonia, Derby and Shelton seven days a week, connecting through Bridgeport and terminating at New York City in one direction and New Haven in the other. For a schedule call **(800) 638-7646** or **(212) 532-4900.**

Waterbury is served by two interstate bus lines that both have toll-free numbers for schedule and fare information. You can reach **Bonanza Bus Lines** at **(800) 556-3815** and **Peter Pan/Trailways** at **(800) 343-9999.** For regional bus service within the Naugatuck Valley region call **Northeast Transportation Company** at **(203) 753-2538** and the **Valley Transit District** at **(203) 735-6824.** The **Greater Waterbury Transit District** at **(203) 757-0535** can provide information about service for the elderly and disabled.

Woodbury

Woodbury equals antiques. That simple equation probably explains 90% of the tourism in the area. Collectors flock here, drawn in equal parts by the heaviest concentration of high-quality antiques dealers in Connecticut (many specializing in 18th- and 19th-century American furniture) and a beautiful semirural setting that makes shopping a real pleasure.

The area also boasts a couple of attractions that make it easy to combine the rather adult pursuit of antiquing with family entertainment. Middlebury is the location of a small but action-packed amusement park by the name of Quassy (short for Quassapaug, the lake on whose shore it lies), and Woodbury Ski & Racquet is the most well rounded commercial recreational facility in the state, offering tennis, skateboarding, in-line skating and mountain biking in summer and skiing and snowboarding in winter. It's also the site of several summer music festivals, including a big Reggae Fest every year.

If you're in the mood for a scenic drive, amble down Rte. 188 for a look at the picture-perfect Middlebury town green. Middlebury is an academy town, one of many in Connecticut whose Etonesque appearance can be traced to the presence of a private school. The Westover School was designed by Theodate Pope, an innovative architect of the early 1900s whose story is told in the **Farmington** chapter.

The area also lays claim to two exceptional historic home museums (the Glebe House and the Bellamy-Ferriday House), both of which also have fine gardens, a pair of state parks (Kettletown and Southford Falls) that seem far more remote than they are and great dining in every price range. Adding up all its good qualities, it becomes evident that Woodbury is actually a great deal more than just antiques.

History

The Pomperaug Valley in which Woodbury lies is a geological oddity. A tiny glacial rift valley, formed when the African and North American continents were still attached but beginning to separate, this valley is an almost exact duplicate of the Central Valley in miniature, right down to the traprock ridge that forms its spine. The flat lay of the land and fertile, relatively rock-free soil made this area one of the first to be settled in the Western Uplands.

The first English families came from Stratford on the Connecticut shore in 1673 and purchased land from the native Pootatuck Indians. Woodbury was at the start a frontier town, so several houses were fortified against Indian attack. After about a generation, other towns such as Middlebury, Southbury and Bethlehem were incorporated from Woodbury.

Woodbury is perhaps most notable for its role in the development of religious tolerance in the United States. Because religious differences with the Church of England were a motivating force behind the Puritan immigration to the New World, there was a great deal of popular resistance to the establishment of that church in New England. This was all the more true just before, during and after the Revolutionary War, since the church was identified with Tories and the British enemy.

In 1783 there were only 14 Episcopal clergymen in the state. In Mar. of that year they gathered at the Glebe House in Woodbury to elect a bishop—the first in the New World—from among their ranks, choosing Reverend Samuel Seabury. That is why the Glebe House is called "the home of American Episcopacy." Today it is an excellent historic home museum.

In the early 20th century Southbury was the site of a community of Russian emigrés, most of whom had fled Russia after the 1917 revolution. It all began when Ilya Tolstoy, son of famed novelist Leo Tolstoy, drove through the area in the early 1920s and was struck by its resemblance to the landscape of his childhood. He purchased some land, others followed and soon there was a tiny summer and weekend community thriving here. The neighborhood still exists, although few (if any) of the original families remain.

Throughout its existence Woodbury and the surrounding towns were principally agricultural, making the transition to suburbia with little in the way of an industrial stage in between. The physical beauty of the landscape has been largely preserved and has much to do with the appeal of the area today.

Major Attractions

Antiquing

Woodbury is the antiques capital of the state, and in recent years, Southbury has been added to its roster of dealers, so it is possible for a really dedicated shopper to spend several days making the circuit of stores here. Of the two towns, Woodbury is *the* place for major acquisitions and dealers with international contacts. Woodbury's dealers have banded together into an association that publishes a small directory and map to its members' locations to make things easy for customers. Many dealers also do appraisals, repairs and restorations. If you are looking for a dealer with a particular specialty, contact the **Woodbury Antique Dealers Association** at **P.O. Box 496, Woodbury, 06798**; they'll send you a copy of the directory. Many of the single-dealer showrooms are large and set in beautiful surroundings, making the Woodbury antiquing experience something special. In Southbury you'll also find dealers whose inventory is mostly collectibles or a little bit of everything. Try **New to You (203-264-2577; in Bennett Square at the intersection of Poverty Rd. and S. Main St.), Upstairs/Downstairs Antiques (203-262-8839; on Bullet Hill Rd.)** or the new multidealer space at **Heritage Village (203-262-8900; in the Bazaar building on Heritage Rd.).**

Quassy Amusement Park

Quassy is a small park with about two dozen carnival rides, many of them designed for small children. The great thing is that there is no exorbitant admission fee. Instead, you pay per ride or get a day pass for a reasonable $10.95. Swimming is available at a small sandy beach on Lake Quassapaug, there are

free magic shows and a petting zoo, games and concessions and a picnic grove. Season: early June–early Sept. and on selected days in spring and autumn. Call for hours, and inquire about Bargain Days, 25-cent Nights and special events.

As the year inches toward Christmas, Quassy reopens, transformed into a Holiday Village filled with Christmas displays and decorated with half a million lights. Santa Claus has been known to put in regular personal appearances. During this period, there is a flat admission charge of $12.95 for adults, $10.95 for seniors and $7.95 for children 5–12. Admission includes all rides and entertainment. Located on **Rte. 64 just west of Rte. 188 in Middlebury, 06762; (800) 367-7275** or **(203) 758-2913**. For hours and information during the Christmas season call **(888) 817-2682**.

Other Attractions

Catnip Acres Herb Nursery

Known for its nice demonstration gardens (come before midsummer to see them at their best) and a great gift shop with all sorts of herbal items, the nursery also offers weekday and weekend workshops in the culinary, decorative and medicinal use of herbs and luncheons held the first Sat. of each month. Hours: Mon.–Sat., 10:00 A.M.–5:00 P.M.; Sun., 11:00 A.M.–5:00 P.M.; closed Jan. 15–Mar. 1. **67 Christian St., Oxford; (203) 888-5649.**

Festivals and Events

Bethlehem Fair
second weekend in Sept. (Fri.–Sun.)

Bethlehem's country fair is a nice treat for the kids since it usually falls on the weekend after they return to school. They'll get a kick out of watching the turtle race, the pedal tractor pull and the largest frog contest, or they can make scarecrows. There's a midway, of course, opening early in the day, and all the farm animals and agricultural exhibits you'd expect at a country fair. Admission: $5 adults, $3 seniors (Sat. & Sun.), children under 12 free when accompanied by an adult. Hours: Fri., 5:00 P.M.–9:00 P.M.; Sat., 8:00 A.M.–9:00 P.M.; Sun., 8:00 A.M.–5:30 P.M. The fairgrounds are located on **Rte. 61 north of Rte. 132 in Bethlehem.** For more information call **(203) 266-5350.**

Bethlehem Christmas Festivities
day after Thanksgiving to Christmas

The day after Thanksgiving, this little town of Bethlehem starts to get a lot of attention. One of the attractions is the annual pilgrimage many make to this tiny community to have their Christmas greeting cards postmarked with the name of the town that figures so prominently in the nativity story. In addition, the Bethlehem post office continues a tradition of making a large selection of commemorative holiday rubber stamps available to the public in its lobby. The ritual begins a day or two after Thanksgiving, during normal post office counter hours. The Bethlehem post office is on **Rte. 132 about one-quarter mile east of Rte. 61, Bethlehem, 06751; (203) 266-7910.**

There is also a Christmas Festival held the first Fri. and Sat. in Dec. The town center is filled with vendors selling Christmas crafts and other gifts, including the town's own collectible pewter tree ornaments. Carolers and bell choirs provide musical entertainment, and horse-drawn hayrides are a favorite with kids. No admission is charged, but there is a fee for hayrides. Hours: Fri., 5:00 P.M.–10:00 P.M.; Sat., 10:00 A.M.–5:00 P.M. Free parking is available in the **Bethlehem Fairgrounds on Rte. 61 north of Rte. 132**, and free shuttles take you to the event. For more information call **(203) 266-5557.**

Outdoor Activities

Although **Woodbury Ski & Racquet** is best known as a ski area, this all-around outdoor recreation facility also offers in-line skating, tennis, skateboarding and mountain biking on several miles of cross-country ski trails in summer. In fact, this was one of the first skateboard and in-line parks on the East Coast. It also has major music festivals the third Sun. of every month, May–Aug. The Reggae Fest is always in June; alternative music and world music are also regular concert themes. If you want to stay on-site, rustic camping is even available for $20 per night with shower, toilets and other facilities in the lodge. Located on **Rte. 47, 4 miles northwest of Rte. 6, Woodbury, 06798; (203) 263-2203.**

Biking

Mountain Biking

At **Hop Brook Lake,** described under Swimming, several miles of trails ringing a 21-acre artificial lake provide some good biking terrain, with the added benefit of rest rooms and other facilities. Some trails are designated for hiking, so check a map when you arrive. In general, those to the east of the access road are multiple use.

The **Larkin State Park Trail** is an abandoned rail bed offering 8–10 miles of linear biking through some spectacular scenery, but you must be willing to control your speed and dismount for equestrians. See the listing under Horseback Riding for more information.

Road Biking

The western part of Southbury along the Housatonic River is very quiet and suitable for biking. River Rd., which winds right alongside the river, is the best stretch. You can leave your car at the tiny parking area in front of the George C. Waldo Preserve (there is no sign—just look for a dirt pullout on the river side) on Purchase Brook Rd. nearby. Not far away, Russian Village Rd. goes through a unique neighborhood that was a Russian enclave during the years following the Russian Revolution. Stop at the onion-domed chapel to read the brief history of Churaevka, as the community was known. **Kettletown State Park** (described under Hiking) and the neighborhood around it is also a good destination, but on summer weekends you'll have to pay a parking fee to leave your car there.

Birding

Nine miles of trails on old carriage roads wind through **Bent of the River Audubon Center,** a 554-acre bird sanctuary with diverse habitats including woodland, old meadows and riparian areas. More than 100 bird species migrate through or nest in the area. Call the resident caretaker at **(203) 264-5098** to make an appointment for a visit and to get directions.

Getting There

Woodbury is about an hour west-southwest of Hartford. By car, the easiest approach is on I-84. Exit 15 puts you on Rte. 6, the main thoroughfare through town. For other transportation options, see the information under the Services section at the end of this chapter.

Boating

The waters of the Housatonic River above Stevenson Dam, known as **Lake Zoar,** are excellent for motorboating any day of the week and for canoeing on weekdays when it's quieter. You can launch a car-top boat from the beach at Kettletown State Park (see the listing under Hiking). Any type of boat can be launched from the boat ramp at the end of Scout Rd. in Southbury. A fee is charged on summer weekends at both locations.

Fishing

Lakes and Ponds

Hop Brook Lake, described under Swimming, is part of a developed recreation area. Because of its size, the facilities and the easy access, it would make an especially good place to go fishing with your child. Brook, rainbow and brown trout are stocked here. Largemouth bass and other warm-water species, such as crappie, bluegill and yellow perch, are also found. You can fish from a canoe or rowboat or from anywhere on the shore except the beach. The brook that feeds the lake is also easily accessible.

See the **New Milford** chapter for detailed information (including important consumption advisories) on **Lake Lillinonah,** which also borders Southbury. If you want to avoid crowds at the upriver boat launches, you can access Lillinonah from an undeveloped tract of state land in Southbury called the George C. Waldo State Park Scenic Preserve. The only entrance to the preserve is at an unlabeled dirt pullout on Purchase Brook Rd. south of Little York Rd. in Southbury.

Lake Zoar, a drowned portion of the Housatonic Valley, is defined by Stevenson Dam at the southern end and Shepaug Dam at the northern end. It's very similar to Lake Lillinonah, which is described in detail in the **New Milford** chapter, and all the caveats given there (especially about the bass tournaments) apply here. It's okay to eat white perch, yellow perch and sunfish, but you should release all other species. Shore fishing access to Lake Zoar's east side is from the boat launch described under the Boating section; from Kettletown State Park, described under Hiking, and from beautiful River Rd. in Southbury, where you can pull off anywhere that's not posted against fishing. Access to the west shore is from the south section of Paugusett State Forest, where you'll have to hike a distance to get to the water. Enter the forest from Great Quarter Rd. or Stone Bridge Rd., both of which are off Rte. 34 in Newtown.

Rivers and Streams

The **Pomperaug River** is one of the more heavily stocked trout streams in the area. Anglers frequent access points at the bridges over the river on Jacks Bridge Rd. and West Side Rd. in Woodbury, where they can walk up and down the banks.

The second principal trout stream in the area, the **Weekeepeemee River,** is accessible at the junction of Rtes. 132 and 47 in Woodbury, along the lower stretches of Rte. 132 and streamside portions of Peter Rd., Weekeepeemee Rd. and Chohees Trail.

Hiking

About half a dozen loops of various distances are possible in wooded, mountainous **Kettletown State Park.** The network is described in detail in the *Connecticut Walk Book* as the Pomperaug Trail. On some paths there are overlooks of Lake Zoar or evidence of old charcoal pits. There's also a short nature trail; a guide is available at the campground office. A small swimming area on the lake provides the means for a refreshing dip after your hike, and there are full picnic facilites. The weekend parking fee is $5 for in-state vehicles and $8 for out-of-state vehicles, Memorial Day–Labor Day. Park hours: 8:00 A.M.–sunset daily, year-round. Located on **Georges Hill Rd. in Southbury.** Park office: **(203) 264-5169.**

The falls at **Southford Falls State Park** are located below a dam on Eightmile Brook where a match factory once existed. Follow the stream and you'll come to a covered bridge and a boardwalk through a lush, natural garden of ferns and riparian plants. The path eventually leads to a lookout tower on a short side trail. Follow the red blazes to make a loop that takes about an hour and a half to hike. Hours: 8:00 A.M.–sunset daily, year-round. Located on **Route 188 just south of Rte. 67 in Oxford.** Park office: **(203) 264-5169.**

For other options, see the entries for **Hop Brook Lake** under Swimming and **Flanders Nature Center** under Nature Centers.

Horseback Riding

Take your pick of English or Western saddles for a trail ride through 300 acres of woodland at **High Lonesome Rose-Hurst Stable (119 Southford Rd., Middlebury; 203-758-9094).** It can accommodate kids over age 5, and helmets are provided. Rates are $20 per hour.

If you are looking for a place to ride your own horse, the **Larkin State Park Trail,** also known as the Larkin Bridle Path, is intended for equestrian use. It's part of an abandoned railroad line that once connected Waterbury and eastern New York state. Eight to ten miles of the rail bed are now state-owned and minimally maintained. Other uses are not restricted, so you may encounter hikers and bikers. The best access is from Rte. 63 between Hop Brook Dam and Porter Rd. in Middlebury, where there are some roadside pullouts for parking and a marker at the trailhead.

Ice Skating

The pond at **Southford Falls State Park** is maintained for skating, and signs are posted when the ice is not safe. Located on **Rte. 188**

south of Rte. 67 in Oxford. Park office: (203) 264-5169.

In the Air

Airline pilot Thad Burr runs **Gone Ballooning,** whose name is not only a takeoff on "Gone Fishing" but also an acronym for "Gondolas Over New England." He flies year-round, and his basket accommodates up to four passengers. Burr charges $190 for the first person, $90 for every person thereafter. Flights last about an hour and 15 minutes. **5 Larky Rd., Oxford, 06478; (203) 888-1322.**

Skiing & Snowboarding

Whatever you want to do in the snow, **Woodbury Ski & Racquet** is the place to go locally. The elevation is very modest, but it was one of the first ski areas to cater to snowboarders, and it tries very hard to accommodate an incredible range of activities. It offers 12 miles of cross-country trails, 18 downhill trails, 1 chair lift, 3 surface lifts and night skiing. For snowboarders, it has launch ramps, half pipes, slide rails and other challenges in a snowboard park. In addition, it allows snowshoeing, sled-dogging, tubing and sledding. Hours are 9:00 A.M.–10:00 P.M. daily in three sessions, $20 for days and evenings, $15 for nights. You can get rental equipment, new and used gear and instruction in the ski shop. Located on **Rte. 47, 4 miles from Rte. 6, Woodbury, 06798; (203) 263-2203.**

Swimming

Hop Brook Lake is a U.S. Army Corps of Engineers recreation area offering unguarded swimming on a 21-acre pond. Other activities include canoeing, hiking and biking, fishing and picnicking. Interpretive walks and talks are given on summer weekends; call for a schedule or pick one up at the information booth. There is a fee for swimming ($1 per adult age 12 and up, with a maximum of $3 per car), but everything else is free. Hours: 8:00 A.M.–dusk, mid-Apr.–mid-Oct. The grounds are open for use during off-season months, but the entrance is gated. Located on **Rte. 63 opposite Rte. 188 in Middlebury.** Park office: **(203) 729-8840.**

There's also a small beach at **Kettletown State Park** on Lake Zoar, a much more substantive body of water than Hop Brook Lake. You can also fish and picnic nearby or launch a car-top boat. A parking fee applies on summer weekends. For more information, see the listing under Hiking.

Seeing and Doing

Art Galleries

Many of the dealers listed in the directory available from the Woodbury Antique Dealers Association also carry fine arts, and the guide gives a brief explanation of each dealer's specialty. Woodbury galleries tend to showcase representational art, often by local or regional artists, mostly in the form of oils, watercolors and sculpture. Some suggestions to start with are the **Randall Tuttle Fine Art Gallery (742 Main St. South, Woodbury; 203-263-2207/2458),** with changing shows from late spring through Dec.; **Beaux Arts Gallery (Barclay Square, corner of Rtes. 6 and 64, Woodbury, 203-263-3939)** and **The Fine Line Gallery (682 Main St. South, Woodbury, 203-266-0110).** At **Linda Nelson Stocks Art and Antiques (35 Main St. North, Woodbury; 203-263-5460),** you'll find the store namesake's original offset lithographs and oils of 19th-century American scenes and porcelain collector folk art villages. Ask around when you visit these galleries and you'll quickly find your way to the others.

Museums

In addition to the listings below, the historical societies of Bethlehem, Woodbury, Southbury and Middlebury maintain museums documenting their respective towns and occasionally showing the work of local artists or other

451

special exhibits. In Bethlehem the museum is located at the intersection of Rtes. 61 and 132 opposite the Bellamy-Ferriday House. One special display is a collection of pewter Bethlehem Christmas town medallions from years past. Hours are Wed., Sat. & Sun., 1:00 P.M.–4:00 P.M. For more information call **(203) 266-5188.**

Middlebury's collection of local artifacts is housed in a two-room schoolhouse (ca. 1890) open by appointment only. For more information call the Middlebury public library, where the museum maintains a small exhibit room, at **(203) 758-2634.**

The **Old Town Hall Museum of Country Living** is located on Rte. 172 in the heart of South Britain, the onetime political and economic center of Southbury. It mounts changing exhibits about events and people relevant to Southbury history and maintains a genealogical library in the former South Britain library a few doors south. The museum is open Wed., 1:00 P.M.–4:00 P.M., year-round; the library's hours are Wed., 10:00 A.M.–noon. Both can also be visited by appointment. For more information call **(203) 262-0632** during open hours; at other times leave a message at **(203) 264-8825.**

Woodbury's **Hurd House** incorporates what is believed to be the oldest building in Litchfield County and is filled with antique household items and furniture. A barn on the property holds a display of old farm implements and items excavated from the grounds. The museum is open Sun., July–Sept., 2:00 P.M.–4:00 P.M., & Thanksgiving morning. The historical society also maintains a schoolhouse open by appointment. Located at **25 Hollow Rd. in Woodbury; (203) 266-0305** during open hours.

Bellamy-Ferriday House & Garden

Originally the home of Bethlehem's first minister, Reverend Joseph Bellamy, and later the summer residence of the wealthy Ferriday family of New York, this property passed into the hands of the Antiquarian and Landmarks Society shortly after the last Ferriday (Caroline) passed away in 1990. There is a strong connection between Reverend Bellamy and Caroline Ferriday despite the fact that they were unrelated: Ferriday was fascinated by Bellamy and over the years collected much of his work and many of his possessions, bringing them home, so to speak. The house is furnished as it might have been in the early 1900s when the Ferridays first acquired the property. Guides give insight into many aspects of the house and Caroline Ferriday's possessions. The formal garden (ca. 1920) behind the house is worth the $5 ($1 for children) admission price all by itself. Gardening lectures and workshops are also held on the grounds throughout the year, and plants are often for sale. Hours: Wed., Sat. & Sun., 11:00 A.M.–4:00 P.M., May–Oct. **9 Main St. North (Rte. 61 just north of Rte. 132), Bethlehem, 06751; (203) 266-7596.**

The Glebe House and Gertrude Jekyll Garden

The Glebe House is noted for being the site where the first Episcopal bishop in the New World was elected in 1783, and having on its grounds the only garden planned by renowned British garden designer Gertrude Jekyll extant in the United States. The former is notable as a benchmark occurrence in the wane of Congregational power that occurred in the 18th century and the growing separation of church and state; the latter because of the deceased Jekyll's undying influence on English and American gardeners. The guides who lead tours are versed in all sorts of interesting tidbits concerning the tools and customs of daily life in Revolutionary War times. Admission: $4 adults, $1 children under 12. Hours: Wed.–Sun., 1:00 P.M.–4:00 P.M., Apr.–Nov., & by appointment. Located on **Hollow Rd. between Rte. 317 and Rte. 6 in Woodbury, 06798; (203) 263-2855.**

Nature Centers

Flanders Nature Center covers 1,300 acres and incorporates the Van Vleck Farm and Whittemore sanctuaries. Demonstrations for children and adults throughout the year include maple sugaring in Mar. (see Seasonal Favorites), bird and frog walks, stargazing and other seasonally appropriate activities. An organic farm on-site provides the opportunity to view or participate in sheep shearing, wool spinning, butter churning and other fundamental chores familiar to our ancestors. In Dec. Flanders offers pick-your-own, cut-your-own Christmas trees from a tree farm. Access to the trails is free, as are many of the programs. Office hours are Mon.–Fri., 9:00 A.M.–5:00 P.M.; the sanctuaries are open dawn–dusk daily. The main office is located at the **intersection of Church Hill and Flanders Rds., Woodbury, 06798; (203) 263-3711.** The Van Vleck Farm trailheads are located about a quarter-mile down Church Hill Rd. Whittemore Sanctuary is off Rte. 64 near the Woodbury/Middlebury town line.

Scenic Drives

You'd be hard-pressed to find an unattractive road in this area. Parts of Rte. 6, which serves as Woodbury's main street, are commercially developed, as is a narrow strip of roads around I-84, but there's never any major congestion. Rte. 6 from Woodbury to Watertown is exceptionally pretty, as is Rte. 132 through Bethlehem and Rte. 188 in Oxford.

Seasonal Favorites

On weekends during Mar. and the latter half of Feb. you can see maple sap tapped at **Flanders Nature Center** and boiled down into syrup. Free demonstrations are given Sat. & Sun., 3:00 P.M.–5:00 P.M., and maple syrup and candies are offered for sale. The season is variable, so call to confirm days and hours before going. The sugarhouse is on **Cowles Rd. a short distance off Flanders Rd. in Woodbury; (203) 263-3711.**

Shopping

What more logical location for a year-round Christmas store than a town called Bethlehem? Now entering its third decade, **The Christmas Shop (18 East St. [Rte. 132 just east of Rte. 61], Bethlehem; 203-266-**

The first Episcopal bishop in the New World was elected at the 18th-century Glebe House in Woodbury. Photo courtesy Litchfield Hills Travel Council.

7048) is an institution, drawing Christmas addicts and pragmatic, off-season bargain hunters even during the summer months. In addition to an astonishing array of ornaments, nutcrackers and snow-covered tabletop villages, the shop also stocks a selection of Americana and crossover gifts that are appropriate for holidays other than Christmas. Hours: Tue.–Sat., 10:00 A.M.–6:00 P.M., & Sun., noon–5:00 P.M.

Bethlehem is also the location of the Abbey of Regina Laudis, a contemplative Benedictine monastery and 350-acre working farm. About 40 nuns here support themselves in part through items they make and sell through the **Little Art Shop (273 Flanders Rd., Bethlehem; 203-266-7637)** on the premises. Their work includes decorative wrought iron, cheese made from milk from their dairy herd, handwoven blankets and scarves, pottery, candles and their own CD of Gregorian chants. The public is invited to attend services; call the shop for a schedule of masses and vespers. Shop hours: Thu.–Tue., approximately 10:00 A.M.–noon & 1:30 P.M.–4:00 P.M. (Sun. until 3:30).

If bargain hunting is your thrill, head for the **Woodbury Golf Driving Range (Rte. 6 just south of Rte. 64)** on Sat. morning for a popular flea market. Admission is free. Hours:

8:00 A.M.–1:30 P.M. For more information call **(203) 263-2841.**

Where to Stay

Bed & Breakfasts

The Dutch Moccasin—$$$ to $$$$

The Dutch Moccasin is a rambling structure that bears all the hallmarks of a colonial-era home: wideboard floors, a "beehive" oven at the rear of the fireplace, chestnut timbers and more. Each room is highly individual. Some rooms have more of a youth hostel feel; others sport unfinished stenciled wood in the style of a rustic ski lodge. Baths may be private or shared. A full breakfast is included. Call for directions. **51 Still Hill Rd., Bethlehem, 06751; (203) 266-7364.**

Merryvale—$$$ to $$$$

What Woodbury lacks in quantity of lodging establishments it makes up for in quality at Merryvale. When proprietors Pat and Gary Nurnberger acquired this 200-year-old colonial home, they completely refurbished the five individually decorated guest rooms, each with unique features and great views. Wooden floors, luxurious bed linens and private baths are found throughout. The decor is flowery, light and bright. The third-floor bedroom lies alone above the rest up a set of garret stairs, mysteriously and romantically remote from the rest of the house. A full breakfast is included. **1204 Main St. South (Rte. 6), Woodbury, 06798; (203) 263-3067.**

Butterbrooke—$$$

One of the oldest houses in Oxford is home to this B&B, whose upper floor has been converted into one guest suite consisting of a small bedroom with a double bed, a large sitting room with a wood-burning stone fireplace and a private bath with a three-quarter tub and shower. Out back there's a quarter-acre pond for skating in winter or angling for sunfish and bass in summer. A full breakfast is included in the rate, and in summer a dinner incorporating vegetables from gardens on the property is possible at an additional charge. **78 Barry Rd., Oxford, 06478; (203) 888-2000.**

Tucker Hill Inn—$$$

This 20th-century center-hall colonial has a long history of accommodating guests, having been a tearoom and an inn over the years and a B&B for the last dozen. There are four guest rooms with traditional furnishings. Two rooms have private baths and two share a bath. Bed sizes vary, and some rooms have air-conditioning. Even though the house is only a few seconds off a major road, woods creep right up to the back of the property, and the house is sheltered by gigantic trees, so you feel like you're in the country. A full breakfast is included. **96 Tucker Hill Rd., Middlebury, 06762; (203) 758-8334.**

Hotels, Motels & Inns

Heritage Inn—$$$$

Heritage Inn is a resort located next to Heritage Village, a large retirement community. The decor, room size and overall feel is in the same class as a Hilton or Sheraton. As a guest you have the use of heated indoor and outdoor pools, racquetball courts, a workout room, outdoor tennis courts, a sauna, a game room with pool tables and more. For an additional fee you can tee off at Heritage Village's 9-hole and 18-hole golf courses. The Pomperaug River runs right outside, and rooms that face this pretty little stream are a little more expensive. Heritage Village's shops and restaurants are just steps away. Heritage Inn is priced the same as other hotels in the same quality category that don't offer a fraction of the facilities you'll get here, so if you make use of all of them, it's a very good value. Families traveling in winter will probably appreciate all the activities available for kids. Inquire about package deals. Located at **Heritage Village, Heritage Rd., Southbury, 06488; (203) 264-8200.**

Southbury Hilton—$$$ to $$$$

Formerly a Radisson, but a Hilton since the summer of 1996, this is a large, easily accessible hotel right off I-84. You'll find more businesspeople than families staying here, and the price reflects that, but it is close to the Quassy Amusement Park and antiquing in Woodbury and Southbury. Except for two honeymoon suites with Jacuzzi baths, there is basically one class of room, and some are wheelchair-accessible. A restaurant and a lounge are on-site, and room service is available. An indoor pool, Jacuzzi, exercise room and sauna comprise the health facilities. **1284 Strongtown Rd. (at I-84 exit 16), Southbury, 06488; (203) 598-7600.**

Curtis House—$$ to $$$

The Curtis House is billed as the oldest inn in Connecticut, having been in operation since 1754. The rooms and furnishings are old-fashioned and reasonably priced. Each room has a different layout and bath arrangement (some private, some shared). There's also a restaurant on the main floor. **506 Main St. South (Rte. 6), Woodbury, 06798; (203) 263-2101.**

Camping

For rustic sites, also see the listing for **Woodbury Ski & Racquet** at the start of the Outdoor Activities section.

Kettletown State Park—$

There are 72 sites at Kettletown, an inexplicably underused campground on Lake Zoar. Those on the "infields" of the campground loops (and some of the others too) are quite open but grassy and attractive. Most of the other sites are at least bordered by trees, and a few back up against the lake. On weekends the lakeside sites may be a bit noisy because motorboats are allowed on the lake. Your camp fee also entitles you to use of the sandy beach on Lake Zoar. Facilities include hot showers, flush toilets and a dump station. Ranger-led nature walks are offered on summer Sat. and Sun. Camp office: **(203) 264-5678.** Park office: **(203) 264-5169.** There is also a youth group camping area here available free to nonprofits; call the **Western District Headquarters** at **(860) 485-0226** for permit information.

Where to Eat

In addition to the listings below, consider some of these options (note that Main St. South is Rte. 6): **Constantine's (1143 Main St. South, Woodbury, 06798; 203-263-2166),** known for its large portions of Italian and Greek specialties at reasonable prices, is a favorite with Woodbury locals; **Curtis House (506 Main St. South, Woodbury, 06798; 203-263-2101),** located in the oldest inn in the state, serves traditional Yankee dishes such as roasts, pot pies and simply prepared seafood and has been recognized for its value; **Miguels (757 Main St. South, Woodbury, 06798; 203-263-0002),** the only place for miles to get Tex-Mex and southwestern dishes; **Sandwich Construction Co. (670 Main St. South in Middle Quarter Mall, Woodbury, 06798; 203-263-4444),** which has found award-winning ways of filling the space between two slices of bread and also serves breakfast items and **New Morning Natural Foods (Middle Quarter Mall, Woodbury, 06798; 203-263-4868),** whose selection of take-out vegetarian deli food by the pound or piece is unbeatable in this neck of the woods.

455

Carol Peck's Good News Café—$$$ to $$$$

Noted restauranteur Carol Peck's popular local eatery serves "New American food with a healthful twist." Meats are free-range and antibiotic-free; the kitchen uses seasonal, frequently organic vegetables and everything is made on the premises. The excellent hearty soups and fresh whole-grain bread make a perfect light lunch. Seating is in two dining rooms, one that is casual with small tables, a long bar and changing artwork decorating the shelves and walls, and the other only slightly more formal. A jazz quintet entertains on Sat. night. Except Tue. when the restaurant is closed, it serves continuously from 11:30 A.M. (noon on Sun.). Last seating is at 10:30 P.M. on Fri.–Sat. & 10:00 P.M. other nights. **694 Main St. South (Rte. 6 just south of Rte. 64), Woodbury, 06798; (203) 266-4663.**

The Olive Tree—$$$ to $$$$

Recently recognized in a *Connecticut* magazine readers' poll for best Continental food and best prime rib in Litchfield County, The Olive Tree also has one of the largest menus around. Seafood commands the largest chunk of it, plus there are six to ten offerings each of beef, veal, chicken and pasta, making for a substantial list of choices. It offers lighter lunch fare such as sandwiches, meal salads and soups in addition to several entrées. Lunch hours: Tue.–Sat., 11:00 A.M.–2:30 P.M. Dinner hours: Tue.–Thu., 4:30 P.M.–9:00 P.M.; Fri.–Sat., 5:00 P.M.–10:00 P.M.; Sun., noon–8:00 P.M. **Barclay Square (corner of Rtes. 6 and 64), Woodbury, 06798; (203) 263-4555.**

John's Café—$$$

This intimate little eatery on Woodbury's main street has the sort of American food that draws upon many cuisines yet often showcases regional and local foods. You'll find chicken served with the international mix of basmati rice and portabella mushrooms, pasta "fazool" and fish 'n' chips served in the genuine English style with malt vinegar. These are complemented by pizzas, grilled steak and lamb, pastas and specials. At lunch there are gussied-up sandwiches and burgers and a handful of entrées. The wine list is mainly Californian, with helpful suggested food pairings. Lunch served Tue.–Fri., 11:30 A.M.–2:30 P.M.; Sat.–Sun., noon–2:30 P.M. Dinner hours: Tue.–Sat., 5:30 P.M.–9:00 P.M.; Sun. until 8:00 P.M. **693 Main St. South (Rte. 6 just south of Rte. 64), Woodbury, 06798; (203) 263-0188.**

Timbers on the Green—$$$

With its soaring beamed ceiling, chaletlike interior and tables set with white linens, Timbers is a pleasing combination of elegant and rustic. Lunch is served buffet-style ($10.50) but is not your ordinary all-you-can-eat spread. There is a wide choice of very good quality American foods. Dinner is off a menu with a focus on classics like prime rib, Caesar salad, grilled salmon and chicken marsala, supplemented by daily specials. Reservations are required for Sun. brunch and recommended for weekend evenings. Lunch hours: Mon.–Sat., noon–2:00 P.M. Dinner hours: Mon.–Fri., 5:30 P.M.–10:00 P.M.; Sat., 6:00 P.M.–10:00 P.M.; Sun. 5:30 P.M.–9:00 P.M. Sun. brunch: 11:00 A.M.–2:30 P.M. Located in **Heritage Village in the Inn building, Heritage Village Rd., Southbury, 06488; (203) 264-8325.**

Charcoal Chef—$$ to $$$

Charcoal Chef is an informal, family-oriented restaurant whose specialty is charcoal-broiled steaks, burgers, seafood and chicken. It's popular with locals, as evidenced by the packed parking lot on weekend nights. The fast service, however, keeps the crowd moving. Hours: Mon.–Thu., 8:30 A.M.–8:00 P.M.; Fri.–Sat., 8:30 A.M.–9:30 P.M.; Sun., noon–8:00 P.M. **670 Main St. North (Rte. 6), Woodbury, 06798; (203) 263-2538.**

Junipers—$$ to $$$

The teal and plum decor at Junipers gives a first impression of understated elegance; it's only when you start really examining your surroundings that you realize the restaurant shares the same warehouselike interior as the rest of the shopping center building in which it's found. When you look at the menu, you're also liable to do a double take. Lunch here has to be the best bargain in town. The portions are what you would expect at dinner, but hardly anything goes for more than $7. There are several pastas, pot roast and many chicken and fish dishes. On Sun. there is a fixed-price lunch (soup or salad through dessert and coffee) served all afternoon for only $11.95. Lunch hours: Mon.–Sat., noon–2:30 P.M.; Sun., noon–4:00 P.M. Dinner hours: Mon.–Thu., 5:00 P.M.–9:00 P.M.; Fri.–Sat., 5:00 P.M.–10:00 P.M.; Sun., 5:00 P.M.–9:00 P.M. Located in the **Heritage Village Bazaar, 450 Heritage Rd., Southbury, 06488; (203) 264-8416.**

Leo's—$$ to $$$

A small and popular chain of three restaurants in western Connecticut, Leo's is perhaps best known for its large and delicious breakfasts and creative sandwiches. The Southbury location is the only one of the three to serve dinner, Thu.–Sun. only. Leo's is also notable for being one of the few restaurants in this part of the country where you can find knishes, blintzes, challah French toast and lox, and the breakfast menu is available at all times. It's hard to beat Leo's for everyday dining. Unfortunately, it's never open late. Hours: Mon.–Wed., 8:00 A.M.–2:30 P.M.; Thu.–Sat., 8:00 A.M.–8:30 P.M.; Sun., 8:00 A.M.–8:00 P.M. Located in **Bennett Square (corner of Main St. South and Poverty Rd.), Southbury, 06488; (203) 264-9190.** There's another Leo's at **900 Straits Tpke., Middlebury, 06762; (203) 598-0166.** Call for hours.

The Natural Merchant—$$

This natural foods store/cum restaurant is the best place around to get eat-in vegetarian food. It serves lunch and Sun. brunch on a pergola-covered outdoor seating area in summer, and there's a pleasant, rustic indoor dining room available year-round. Also check out the bulk nuts and fruits, which make great healthful snack foods for the road. Hours: Mon.–Sat., 11:00 A.M.–3:00 P.M.; Sun. brunch, 10:00 A.M.–3:00 P.M.; the store keeps longer hours. **142 Main St. North (Rte. 6), Southbury, 06488; (203) 264-9954.**

Coffeehouses, Sweets & Treats

For a coffee-and-pastry breakfast or a light lunch, stop in at **Playhouse Corner** in Southbury, a small complex of shops on the southwest corner of South Main St. and Rte. 6. One specialty at **The Bakery (203-264-1606;** open daily from 6:00 A.M. to somewhere between 4:00 P.M. & 6:00 P.M.) is cinnamon nut Russians, a rich breakfast roll that is a local favorite and sells out early in the day. At **The**

European Shoppe (203-262-1500, open Mon.–Fri., approximately 6:30 A.M.–4:00 P.M.; Sat., 7:30 A.M.–1:00 P.M.; Sun., 8:00 A.M.–1:00 P.M.) you'll be able to savor a cup of Green Mountain (a Vermont roaster) coffee along with a bagel or the sandwich special of the day. For ice cream straight from the source, visit **Rich Farm Ice Cream Shop (203-881-1040)** on Rte. 67 near Christian St. in Oxford. The milk for its ice cream comes from the cows at this family farm, and the shop is little more than a stand next to the cornfields. When the weather's warm, it's open Sun.–Thu., noon–9:00 P.M.; Fri.–Sat. until 10:00 P.M.

Services

Local Visitors Information

Litchfield Hills Travel Council, P.O. Box 968, Litchfield, 06759; (860) 567-4506.

Waterbury Region Convention and Visitors Bureau, 21 Church St., Waterbury, 06702; (203) 597-9527. Hours: Mon.–Fri., 8:30 A.M.–5:00 P.M., year-round.

Transportation

Southbury is served by two interstate bus lines that both have toll-free numbers for schedule and fare information. You can reach **Bonanza Bus Lines** at **(800) 556-3815** and **Peter Pan/Trailways** at **(800) 343-9999.** For regional bus service into the Naugatuck Valley region call the **Greater Waterbury Transit District** at **(203) 757-0535.**

457

Index

458

The Connecticut Guide

Index

464

Index

465

The Connecticut Guide

467

469

Photo by Krag Lehmann.

About the Author

An avid outdoorswoman, Amy Ziffer's interest in the natural and human history of New England and love of travel throughout the region are deeply rooted. Many of her earliest memories are of the beauty of her home state of Connecticut as she experienced it in her hometown of Norwalk.

She has lived in Texas, New York, Massachusetts, Florida and California, as well as overseas. Although each of these places had something to offer, none of them drew her heart more than the memory of the seemingly immeasurable expanse of Long Island Sound at Calf Pasture Beach and the mysterious woodland of Cranbury Park.

After earning a bachelor of music degree from the Berklee College of Music in Boston, she worked as an audio engineer in the entertainment industry, was a staff editor for Home & Studio Recording and *Fine Gardening* magazines and worked as a freelance writer.

Amy now lives in Sherman, Connecticut, a small town in the state's mountainous northwest. She studies landscape design and is slowly building a library of books on Connecticut and New England history.